STRUGGLE FOR EMPIRE

A volume in the series
Conjunctions of Religion and Power in the Medieval Past
Edited by Barbara H. Rosenwein

A full list of titles in the series appears at the end of the book.

STRUGGLE FOR EMPIRE

KINGSHIP AND CONFLICT
UNDER LOUIS THE GERMAN,
817–876

ERIC J. GOLDBERG

Cornell University Press
Ithaca and London

Publication of this book is aided by a grant from the Book Subvention Program of the Medieval Academy of America.

First published 2006 by Cornell University Press
First printing, Cornell Paperbacks, 2009

Printed in the United States of America

Library of Congress Cataloging-in-Publication Data

Goldberg, Eric Joseph, 1969–
    Struggle for empire : kingship and conflict under Louis the German, 817-876 / Eric J. Goldberg.
        p. cm. — (Conjunctions of religion and power in the medieval past)
    Includes bibliographical references and index.
    ISBN–13: 978-0-8014-3890-5 (cloth : alk. paper)
    ISBN–13: 978-0-8014-7529-0 (pbk. : alk. paper)
    1. Ludwig, King of the East Franks, 805–876. 2. Germany—Kings and rulers—Biography. 3. Germany—History—To 843. 4. Germany—History—843–918. 5. Franks—History—814–843. 6. Franks—History—843–987. I. Title. II. Conjunctions of religion & power in the medieval past.
    DD134.3.G65 2006
    943'.014'092—dc22

                                2005018413

Cloth printing   10 9 8 7 6 5 4 3 2 1
Paperback printing   10 9 8 7 6 5 4 3 2 1

To Meg

dilectae coniugi nostrae

The hearts of kings are greedy and never satisfied.

Regino of Prüm

CONTENTS

ACKNOWLEDGMENTS

Carolingian kings did not rule alone. They depended on innumerable people—bishops, abbots, counts, noblemen and women, vassals, servants, and especially their wives and children—to help them transform their
ideas and ambitions into concrete actions. In a similar way, I have frequently
turned to many people for help and support while researching and writing
this book. I wish to thank them here.

During my years of training as a medieval historian, I benefited from the
generous assistance and encouragement of many scholars. At the University
of Pennsylvania, Edward Peters first sparked my interest in medieval history
in his evening seminars in Van Pelt Library, and he urged me to pursue my
study of Charlemagne's family in graduate school. At the University of Virginia, Thomas Noble proved himself to be an ideal adviser, an inspiring
mentor, and a warm human being. He helped train me in the arcane skills of
Carolingian history, and he guided my early research on Louis the German's reign. The Deutscher Akademischer Austauschdienst awarded me a
fellowship to support my research in Germany in 1995–96, and during that
time Rudolf Schieffer kindly allowed me to work in the wonderful setting of
the Monumenta Germaniae Historica in Munich. The following year, the
German Historical Institute granted me a fellowship so I could continue my
research and writing while teaching in southern California. While I was living there, Patrick Geary generously encouraged my work, and I also greatly
benefited from my friendship and discussions with three gifted young Carolingian historians: Warren Brown, Jason Glenn, and Hans Hummer.

As I began to write the present book, many other people and institutions
offered me support. In 1999–2000, the Institute for Research in the Hu-

manities at the University of Wisconsin, Madison, gave me a Friedrich Solmsen Postdoctoral Fellowship and an office on Observatory Hill where I wrote the first chapters. Since the autumn of 2000, my colleagues in the history department at Williams College have inspired me with their devotion to teaching and scholarship, while my students at Williams have never ceased to impress me with their intelligence, curiosity, work ethic, and willingness to listen to me excitedly ramble on about early medieval politics. In 2003–4, Williams College granted me a generous leave so that I could finish this project, and during that time I benefited from the support of the National Endowment for the Humanities and the American Council of Learned Societies. Moreover, in 2002 the Medieval Academy of America awarded me its Book Subvention Prize to help cover the costs of publishing this monograph. I also owe debts of gratitude to two German historians who also were working on Louis the German as I finished this book: Wilfried Hartmann, who kindly invited me to participate in a conference on Louis the German at Lorsch in October 2002, and Boris Bigott, who shared with me his excellent scholarship on the east Frankish Church.

I especially thank the people who generously offered to read, critique, and comment on various stages of my book manuscript: John Ackerman, Hans Hummer, Simon MacLean, Rosamond McKitterick, Janet Nelson, the late Timothy Reuter, Barbara Rosenwein, Jonathan Shepard, Margaret Willard, and Herwig Wolfram. Their detailed suggestions have made this a far better book than I could have written by myself. Of course, all the mistakes and shortcomings in it remain my own.

If there is one thing the Carolingians teach us, it is the importance of family in our lives. I thank my father and mother, Roger and Jane; my sister, Eve; my stepmother, Gerda; my late grandfather, Sherwood; and the extended Goldberg and Jacobs families. Words cannot fully express my profound gratitude for their support, interest, and love over the years as I worked on this book.

Finally, I thank my wife, Meg, without whose unflagging encouragement, patience, and love I could not have finished this project. She put up with my unending conversations about Carolingian politics and sources, encouraged me in moments of self-doubt, and gave insightful comments on every page of this book. At the same time, Meg established her own distinguished career as a scholar and historian and gave us two wonderful daughters, Abigail and Claire. This book is dedicated to Meg as a token of my deepest appreciation, admiration, respect, and love. I will never forget.

NOTE ON TERMS AND NAMES

Frankish Europe in the age of the Carolingian kings looks alien to us. The Franks had their own world, full of kingdoms, provinces, and peoples, and they never could have predicted the existence of modern European nations. To avoid misleading anachronism, I have discarded modern national terminology to describe ninth-century peoples and places and instead employ the language of the sources. For example, I translate *Francia* simply as "Francia" (rather than "France"), *Boemani* as "Bohemians" (rather than "Czechs"), and *Carantani* as "Carantanians" (rather than "Carinthians"). I have encountered a specific difficulty with the classical term *Germania* and the related words *Germani* and *Germanicus*, which historians often misleadingly translate as "Germany," "Germans," and "German." Like the Romans before them, Carolingian authors used *Germania* to refer to the diverse regions along and beyond the Rhine inhabited by numerous Germanic and, by the ninth century, Slavic peoples. They did not use *Germania* to denote a coherent polity or ethnic group in the same way that we do today when we use "Germany" and "Germans." To convey this distinction, I have left *Germania* untranslated.

To describe Bavaria's eastern frontier provinces of Upper Pannonia, Lower Pannonia, Carantania, and Carniola, I employ "Eastland," which is a translation of the contemporary Latin phrase used to describe that frontier zone, *plaga orientalis*. In two cases I have used geographic or ethnic terms that do not appear in the sources. First, for the sake of convenience, I use the term "Franconia" to describe the eastern half of the Frankish kingdom of Austrasia. That province stretched from the middle Rhine around Mainz and Worms to the borders of Thuringia east of Würzburg. Although the term "Franconia" did not appear in the sources until the eleventh century, it effectively conveys the emerging geopolitical identity of that strategic region in ninth-century politics. Moreover, to describe the various groups of Scandinavian pirates who increasingly raided the Continent and England during the ninth century, I employ the well-known term "Vikings," even though Carolingian chroniclers did not use that term, instead calling them "Northmen."

Throughout this book, I have anglicized names when such names are available. Thus I render Hludowig as Louis, Karol as Charles, Hemma as Emma, and so on. Like most royal dynasties, the Carolingians gave the same few names to male members of their family generation after generation. To help distinguish among the various Louises, Charleses, Pippins, and Carlomans, I have used their traditional modern cognomens (e.g., Charles "Martel," "Charlemagne," Louis "the Pious," Louis "the German," Charles "the Bald,") or referred to them by a combination of Roman numerals and the region in which they ruled (e.g., Pippin II of Aquitaine, Louis II of Italy). The one traditional cognomen I have rejected is that of Louis the German's youngest son, Charles "the Fat": there is no historical evidence that Charles was unusually corpulent, and, in our weight-obsessed modern culture, it unfortunately suggests that he was a slothful, "do-nothing" prince. I therefore simply refer to him as Charles III.

Following the convention of modern historical scholarship, I refer to noble families by the "leading names" that male members often had: the Carolingians (after the name Karol), the Konradiner (after Conrad), the Liudolfings (after Liudolf), and so on. However, these family names are modern scholarly inventions and do not imply some kind of primitive "clan" solidarity among members of the same kin group. Early medieval aristocratic families were full of strife and competition as individual members struggled to secure their wealth, power, status, and access to royal patronage, often in competition with their relatives.

To distinguish between the names of saints and the churches dedicated to those saints, I hyphenate and abbreviate the latter. I therefore call the seventh-century Irish missionary Saint Gall, but I refer to the Alemannian monastery dedicated to him as St.-Gall. The parenthetical dates following personal names refer to reigns or years in office, not life spans.

There are many good English translations of Carolingian sources. Nevertheless, unless otherwise noted, I have translated these sources anew to convey the nuances of the Latin (and, in a few cases, the Frankish and Old Saxon). But translation is, of course, a form of interpretation. Like writers today, Carolingian authors frequently used the same word to convey different meanings, and I therefore have often been forced to translate the same

Latin word differently according to the context. For example, depending on context, the word *regnum* could signify a "kingdom," "realm," or "province," whereas *dux* could mean "duke," "leader," "commander," or "client ruler." To convey such nuances, I have provided the Latin word or phrase parenthetically to clarify my translations.

ABBREVIATIONS

AA   *Annales Alamannici*, in *Untersuchungen zur frühalemannischen Annalistik: Die Murbacher Annalen, mit Edition*, ed. Walter Lendi (Freiburg, 1971).

AAM   *Annales Altahenses maiores*, ed. Wilhelm von Giesebrecht, MGH *SS* 20 (Hanover, 1868), 772–824.

AB   *Annales de Saint-Bertin*, ed. Félix Grat, Jeanne Vielliard, and Suzanne Clémencet (Paris, 1964).

Adelerius of Fleury, *Miracula*   Adelerius of Fleury, *Miracula sancti Benedicti*, ed. Oswald Holder-Egger, in MGH *SS* 15 (Hanover, 1887), 474–97.

Ado, *Chronicon*   Ado of Vienne, *Chronicon*, ed. Georg Heinrich Pertz, in MGH *SS* 2 (Hanover, 1829), 315–23.

Adonis Continuatio   *Adonis Continuatio prima*, ed. Georg Heinrich Pertz, in MGH *SS* 2 (Hanover, 1829), 324–25.

AF   *Annales Fuldenses sive annales regni Francorum orientalis*, ed. Friedrich Kurze, MGH *SRG* 7 (Hanover, 1891).

AF(B)   *Annales Fuldenses, Bavarian Continuation* (as in *AF*).

AF(M)   *Annales Fuldenses, Mainz Continuation* (as in *AF*).

Agnellus, *Liber pontificalis*   Agnellus of Ravenna, *Liber pontificalis ecclesiae Ravennatis*, ed. Oswald Holder-Egger, in MGH *SRL* (Hanover, 1878), 265–391.

AH   *Annales Hildesheimenses*, ed. Georg Waitz, MGH *SRG* (Hanover, 1878).

AI   *Annales ex annalibus Iuvavensibus antiquis excerpti*, ed. Harry Bresslau, in MGH *SS* 30.2 (Hanover, 1934), 727–47.

AMP   *Annales Mettenses Priores*, ed. Bernhard von Simson, MGH *SRG* (Hanover, 1905).

Andrew of Bergamo, *Historia*   Andrew of Bergamo, *Historia*, ed. Georg Waitz, in MGH *SRL* (Hanover, 1878), 220–30.

Annalista Saxo   *Annalista Saxo*, ed. Georg Waitz, in MGH *SS* 6 (Hanover, 1844), 542–777.

ARF   *Annales regni Francorum*, ed. Friedrich Kurze, MGH *SRG* 6 (Hanover, 1895).

Astronomer, *VH*   Astronomus, *Vita Hludowici imperatoris*, ed. and trans. Ernst Tremp, MGH *SRG* 64 (Hanover, 1995).

Auctarium Garstense   *Auctarium Garstense*, ed. Wilhelm Wattenbach, in MGH *SS* 9 (Hanover, 1851), 561–69.

AV   *Annales Vedastini*, ed. B. von Simson, MGH *SRG* (Hanover, 1909).

AX   *Annales Xantenses*, ed. B. von Simson, MGH *SRG* (Hanover, 1909).

CCCM   *Corpus Christianorum: Continuatio Mediaevalis* (Turnhout, 1966–2004).

Constantine, *De administrando*   Constantine Porphyrogenitus, *De administrando imperio*, ed. and trans. Gy. Moravcsik and R. J. H. Jenkins (Washington, DC, 1967).

Conversio   *Die "Conversio Bagoariorum et Carantanorum" und der Brief des Erzbischofs Theotmar von Salzburg*, ed. Fritz Lošek, MGH Studien und Texte 15 (Hanover, 1997).

Corvey   *Die alten Mönchslisten und die Traditionen von Corvey*, vol. 1, ed. Klemens Honselmann (Paderborn, 1982).

DArnulf   *Die Urkunden Arnolfs*, ed. Paul Kehr, in MGH *Diplomata regum Germaniae ex stirpe Karolinorum*, vol. 3 (Berlin, 1940).

DCIII   *Die Urkunden Karls III*, ed. Paul Kehr, in MGH *Diplomata regum Germaniae ex stirpe Karolinorum*, vol. 2 (Berlin, 1936–37).

DCarloman   *Die Urkunden Karlmanns*, ed. Paul Kehr, in MGH *Diplomata regum Germaniae ex stirpe Karolinorum*, vol. 1 (Berlin, 1934).

DCB   *Receuil des Actes de Charles II le Chauve, roi de France*, ed. Georges Tessier, 3 vols. (Paris, 1943–55).

DCharlemagne   *Die Urkunden Karls des Grossen*, ed. Engelbert Mühlbacher, in MGH *Diplomata Karolinorum*, vol. 1 (Berlin, 1956).

DLG   *Die Urkunden Ludwigs des Deutschen*, ed. Paul Kehr, in MGH *Diplomata regum Germaniae ex stirpe Karolinorum*, vol. 1 (Berlin, 1934).

DLoI   *Die Urkunden Lothars I*, ed. Theodor Schieffer, in MGH *Diplomata Karolinorum*, vol. 3 (Berlin, 1966).

DLoII   *Die Urkunden Lothars II*, ed. Theodor Schieffer, in MGH *Diplomata Karolinorum*, vol. 3 (Berlin, 1966).

DLY   *Die Urkunden Ludwigs des Jüngeren*, ed. Paul Kehr, in MGH *Diplomata regum Germaniae ex stirpe Karolinorum*, vol. 1 (Berlin, 1934).

Einhard, *VK*   Einhard, *Vita Karoli Magni*, ed. Georg Pertz, MGH *SRG* (Hanover, 1911).

Ermanrich, *Vita Hariolfi*   Ermanrich of Ellwangen, *Vita Hariolfi*, ed. Viktor Burr, *Ellwangen 764–1964*, vol. 1 (Ellwangen, 1964), 9–49.

Ermanrich, *Vita Sualonis*   Ermanrich of Ellwangen, *Vita Sualonis*, ed. Andreas Bauch, in *Quellen zur Geschichte der Diözese Eichstätt*, vol. 1: *Biographien der Gründungszeit* (Regensburg, 1984).

Ermold, *In Honorem*   Ermoldus Nigellus, *In Honorem Hludowici Pii*, ed. and trans. Edmond Faral, in *Ermold le Noir: Poème sur Louis le Pieux et Épîtres au roi Pépin* (Paris, 1932).

Flodoard, *Historia*   Flodoard, *Historia Remensis Ecclesiae*, ed. Martina Stratmann, MGH *SS* 36 (Hanover, 1998).

Freising   *Die Traditionen des Hochstifts Freising*, vol. 1: *744–926*, ed. Theodor Bitterauf, Quellen und Erörterungen zur bayerischen und deutschen Geschichte, n. s. 4 (Munich, 1905).

Fulda   *Codex Diplomaticus Fuldensis*, ed. Ernst Friedrich Johann Dronke (Kassel, 1850).

Grimalt Codex   Grimalt Codex, Stiftsbibliothek St. Gallen 397.

Heliand   *Heliand*, ed. Otto Behaghel, *Heliand und Genesis*, 10th ed. (Tübingen, 1996).

Hincmar, *De ordine palatii*   Hincmar, *De ordine palatii*, ed. Thomas Gross and Rudolf Schieffer, MGH *Fontes* 3 (Hanover, 1980).

Lampert, *Annales*   Lampert of Hersfeld, *Annales*, ed. Oswald Holder-Egger, in *Lamperti Monachi Hersfeldensis Opera*, MGH *SRG* 38 (Hanover, 1894).

Lorsch   *Codex Laureshamensis*, vols. 1–3, ed. Karl Glöckner (Darmstadt, 1929–36).

Lorsch Rotulus   Lorsch Rotulus, Stadt- und Universitätsbibliothek Frankfurt, MS Barth. 179.

Ludwig Psalter   Ludwig Psalter, Berlin, Staatsbibliothek Theol. lat. fol. 58.

MGH   Monumenta Germaniae Historica

Capitularia   *Capitularia*, Legum Sectio II, *Capitularia Regum Francorum*, 2 vols. (Hanover, 1883–97).

Concilia   *Concilia*, Legum Sectio III, 3 vols. (Hanover, 1893–1984).

Epistolae   *Epistolae*, 8 vols. (Hanover, 1887–1939).

Fontes   *Fontes Iuris Germanici Antiqui in usum scholarum separatim editi*, 13 vols. (Hanover, 1909–86).

Formulae   *Formulae Merowingici et Karolini Aevi*, Legum Sectio V, ed. Karl Zeumer (Hanover, 1886).

Necrologia 6   *Necrologia Germaniae*, suppl. 6, ed. Paul Piper (Berlin, 1884).

Poetae Latini   *Poetae Latini Aevi Carolini*, 4 vols. (Hanover, 1881–99).

SRG   *Scriptores rerum Germanicarum in usum scholarum separatim editi* (Hanover, 1871–1987).

SRL   *Scriptores rerum Langobardicarum et Italicarum, saec. 6–9* (Hanover, 1878).

SS   *Scriptores*, 30 vols. (Hanover, 1824–1924).

Nithard   Nithard, *Historiarum libri IV,* ed. Ernest Müller, MGH *SRG* (Hanover, 1907).

Notker, *Continuatio*   Notker the Stammerer, *Breviarium regum Francorum, continuatio,* ed. Georg Heinrich Pertz, in MGH *SS* 2 (Hanover, 1829), 329–30.

Notker, *GK*   Notker the Stammerer, *Gesta Karoli magni imperatoris,* ed. Hans F. Haefele, MGH *SRG*, n. s. 12 (Berlin, 1959).

Otfrid, *Liber evangeliorum*   Otfrid von Weissenburg, *Evangelienbuch,* ed. and trans. Gisela Vollmann-Profe (Stuttgart, 1987).

Passau   *Die Traditionen des Hochstifts Passau,* ed. Max Heuwieser, Quellen und Erörterungen zur bayerischen Geschichte, n. s. 6 (Munich, 1930).

PL   *Patrologiae Cursus Completus, Series Latina,* ed. J.-P. Migne, 221 vols. (Paris, 1841–66).

Radbert, *Epitaphium Arsenii*   Radbert, *Epitaphium Arsenii*, ed. Ernst Dümmler, in *Abhandlungen der Königlichen Akademie der Wissenschaften zu Berlin, Phil.-Historische Abhandlungen* 2 (1900): 1–98.

Ratpert, *Casus sancti Galli*   Ratpert, *Casus sancti Galli*, ed. and trans. Hannes Steiner, MGH *SRG* 75 (Hanover, 2002).

Regensburg   *Die Traditionen des Hochstifts Regensburg und des Klosters S. Emmeram*, ed. Josef Widemann, Quellen und Erörterungen zur bayerischen Geschichte, n. s. 8 (Munich, 1943).

Regino, *Chronicon*   Regino of Prüm, *Chronicon*, ed. Friedrich Kurze, MGH *SRG* 50 (Hanover, 1890).

Rimbert, *Vita Anskarii*   Rimbert, *Vita Anskarii*, ed. Georg Waitz, MGH *SRG* 55 (Hanover, 1884).

St.-Gall   *Urkundenbuch der Abtei Sanct Gallen*, 2 vols., ed. Hermann Wartmann (Zurich, 1863–66).

Thegan, *GH*   Thegan, *Gesta Hludowici imperatoris*, ed. and trans. Ernst Tremp, MGH *SRG* 64 (Hanover, 1995).

VC   *Vita Constantini*, in *Zwischen Rom und Byzanz: Leben und Wirken der Slavenapostel Kyrillos und Methodios nach den Pannonischen Legenden und der Klemensvita. Bericht von der Taufe Russlands nach der Laurentiuschronik*, trans. Josef Bujnoch, Slavische Geschichtsschreiber 1 (Graz, 1958).

Visio Karoli   *Visio Karoli Magni*, ed. Patrick J. Geary, "Germanic Tradition and Royal Ideology in the Ninth Century: The *Visio Karoli Magni*," reprinted in Patrick J. Geary, *Living with the Dead in the Middle Ages* (Ithaca, 1994), 74–76.

VM   *Vita Methodii*, in *Zwischen Rom und Byzanz: Leben und Wirken der Slavenapostel Kyrillos und Methodios nach den Pannonischen Legenden und der Klemensvita. Bericht von der Taufe Russlands nach der Laurentiuschronik*, trans. Josef Bujnoch, Slavische Geschichtsschreiber 1 (Graz, 1958).

Waltharius   *Waltharius*, ed. and trans. Denis M. Kratz, in *"Waltharius" and "Ruodlieb"* (New York, 1984), 2–71.

Widukind   Widukind, *Rerum gestarum Saxonicarum libri III*, ed. Paul Hirsch, Max Büdinger, Wilhelm Wattenbach, Albert Bauer, and Reinhold Rau, in *Quellen zur Geschichte der sächsischen Kaiserzeit* (Darmstadt, 1977).

Wissembourg   *Traditiones Wizenburgenses: Die Urkunden des Klosters Weissenburg, 661–864*, ed. Karl Glöckner and Anton Doll (Darmstadt, 1979).

WUB 1 *Wirtembergisches Urkundenbuch*, ed. Königliches Staatsarchiv in Stuttgart (Stuttgart, 1849).

Zürich *Urkundenbuch der Stadt und Landschaft Zürich*, vol. 1, ed. Jakob Escher and Paul Schweizer (Zurich, 1888).

SECONDARY WORKS

AK *Archiv für Kulturgeschichte*

APAW *Abhandlungen der preussischen Akademie der Wissenschaften: Philosophisch-historische Klasse*

BM Johann Friedrich Böhmer and Engelbert Mühlbacher, *Regesta Imperii*, vol. 1: *Die Regesten des Kaiserreichs unter den Karolingern, 751–918*, 2nd ed. (Innsbruck, 1908).

Böhmer and Will, *RGME* 1 Johann Friedrich Böhmer and Cornelius Will, *Regesten zur Geschichte der Mainzer Erzbischöfe*, vol. 1 (Innsbruck, 1887).

CH, ed. Godman and Collins *Charlemagne's Heir: New Perspectives on the Reign of Louis the Pious*, ed. Peter Godman and Roger Collins (Oxford, 1990).

DA *Deutsches Archiv für Erforschung des Mittelalters*

DLB 148 *Dictionary of Literary Biography*, vol. 148: *German Writers and Works of the Early Middle Ages: 800–1170*, ed. Will Hasty and James Hardin (Detroit, 1995).

Dümmler, *GOR* 1–3 Ernst Dümmler, *Geschichte des ostfränkischen Reichs*, 3 vols., 2nd ed. (Leipzig, 1887–88).

EME *Early Medieval Europe*

FDG *Forschungen zur Deutschen Geschichte*

FS *Frühmittelalterliche Studien*

HZ *Historische Zeitschrift*

JEH *Journal of Ecclesiastical History*

JML *Journal of Medieval Latin*

JVNS *Jahrbuch des Vereins für niederdeutsche Sprachforschung*

LDZ, ed. Hartmann *Ludwig der Deutsche und seine Zeit*, ed. Wilfried Hartmann (Darmstadt, 2004).

Leyser, *Communications* 1 Karl J. Leyser, *Communications and Power in Medieval Europe*, vol. 1: *The Carolingian and Ottonian Centuries*, ed. Timothy Reuter (London, 1994).

LMA   *Lexikon des Mittelalters* (Munich, 1977–98).

MGSL   *Mitteilungen der Gesellschaft für Salzburger Landeskunde*

MIÖG   *Mitteilungen des Instituts für österreichische Geschichtsforschung*

MJGK   *Mainfränkisches Jahrbuch für Geschichte und Kunst*

MÖIG   *Mitteilungen des österreichischen Instituts für Geschichtsforschung*

NA   *Neues Archiv*

NCMH 2   *New Cambridge Medieval History*, vol. 2: *C. 700–c. 900*, ed. Rosamond McKitterick (Cambridge, 1995).

NCMH 3   *New Cambridge Medieval History*, vol. 3: *C. 900–c. 1024*, ed. Timothy Reuter (Cambridge, 1999).

NDB   *Neue Deutsche Biographie* (Berlin, 1953–2002).

RV   *Rheinische Vierteljahrsblätter*

SA   *Südostdeutsches Archiv*

SBAW   *Sitzungsberichte der bayerischen Akademie der Wissenschaften: Philosophisch-Historische Klasse*

SKAW   *Sitzungsberichte der kaiserlichen Akademie der Wissenschaften: Philosophisch-Historische Klasse*

SMGB   *Studien und Mitteilungen zur Geschichte des Benediktinerordens*

SMRH   *Studies in Medieval and Renaissance History*

SS Spoleto   *Settimane di Studio di Centro Italiano di Studi sull'alto Medioevo*

TRHS   *Transactions of the Royal Historical Society*

Wattenbach, Levison, and Löwe, DGM 6   Wilhelm Wattenbach, Wilhelm Levison, and Heinz Löwe, *Deutschlands Geschichtsquellen im Mittelalter*, vol. 6 (Weimar, 1990).

ZDA   *Zeitschrift für deutsches Alterthum*

ZGO   *Zeitschrift für die Geschichte des Oberrheins*

ZSP   *Zeitschrift für slavische Philologie*

ZWL   *Zeitschrift für württembergische Landesgeschichte*

STRUGGLE FOR EMPIRE

INTRODUCTION

In the mid-880s at the monastery of St.-Gall, a monk named Notker wrote the *Deeds of Charlemagne* for Charlemagne's great-grandson, the Frankish emperor Charles III. Although Notker ostensibly wrote his work to recount Charlemagne's virtues and accomplishments, he betrayed his mounting fears for the future of the Carolingian royal dynasty. Charles III had recently reunited his great-grandfather's empire, but he lacked a legitimate male heir. In the hope of inspiring Charles III to save his family from extinction, Notker told a story of how the elderly Charlemagne had predicted the greatness of Charles III's father, Louis the German (826–76). According to Notker, Charlemagne's son, Louis the Pious, had brought the six-year-old Louis the German to court after instructing him how to behave modestly and politely in the emperor's presence. Notker recounted:

When the inquisitive emperor on the first or second day spied [Louis the German] standing among the other attendants, he asked his son, "Whose little boy is that?" [Louis the Pious] responded, "He is mine and also yours, if you deign to have him." The emperor commanded, "Bring him to me." When this was done, the emperor kissed the little boy and sent him back to his former place. But from that moment [Louis the German] was conscious of his dignity and scorned to stand second to anyone save the emperor himself. He therefore mustered his courage, stood as tall as he could, and moved to take a place next to his father as his equal.

When Louis the Pious asked his son why he dared to do this, Louis the German replied, "When I was your inferior, I stood behind you among my fellow soldiers, as was fitting. But now I am your equal and fellow soldier, and I therefore rightly stand on equal footing with you." Charlemagne heard his grandson's bold response and predicted: "If that little boy survives, he will one day be great."[1]

As is often the case with medieval chroniclers, one cannot simply accept Notker's anecdote about the young Louis the German as historical "fact." Notker wrote a decade after Louis the German's death, making it unlikely that he had any detailed information about Louis's childhood three-quarters of a century earlier. On a deeper level, however, Notker's anecdote about Louis the German's determination to stand second to Charlemagne captures the central political dynamic of ninth-century Europe. After Charlemagne's death in 814, his descendants contended with one another over the fate of the Frankish empire and the question of who would be the next Charlemagne. In this book I explore the struggle for Charlemagne's empire through the fifty-year reign of Louis the German, one of the longest-ruling Carolingian kings. Throughout his political career, Louis the German emulated his famous grandfather and sought to reunite as much of the empire as possible. But in his story about Louis's visit to Charlemagne's palace, Notker discreetly omitted the central challenge to Louis's lifelong ambitions for power: the fact that he had several brothers. They were a major obstacle to Louis's political aspirations, because, according to Frankish custom, all royal sons had a claim to a kingdom. As a result, Louis the German's reign is the story of an early medieval ruler's struggle for power and empire in a political system defined by dynastic fragmentation and multiple kingdoms. How to reconcile the ideal of imperial unity with the realities of partible inheritance and royal competition: this was to be the central dilemma of Louis the German's reign and the politics of ninth-century Carolingian Europe.

STRUGGLE FOR EMPIRE

Louis's lifelong struggle for the Frankish empire was the outgrowth of the rise of the Carolingian dynasty over the previous hundred years. During the early eighth century, the Carolingians had emerged as the most power-

---

[1] Notker, *GK* 2.10, pp. 65–66.

ful Frankish family in Europe.[2] The Carolingians were Frankish aristocrats like the other leading families, but they rose to prominence over their peers by using their "harder fists and sharper elbows."[3] In 751 the Carolingian ruler Pippin III deposed the last Frankish king from the ancient Merovingian dynasty and seized the throne, thereby initiating more than two centuries of Carolingian kingship. During the previous centuries, the Merovingian kings had divided their territories among all their sons, giving them one or more of the three traditional Frankish kingdoms in Gaul: Neustria, Austrasia, and Burgundy.[4] As a result of this fragmented political system, competition for territories, economic resources, and prestige among rival kings drove Frankish politics. However, by a series of dynastic accidents and political designs, the early Carolingians managed to unite the Frankish kingdoms under a single ruler for four consecutive generations. It was during this unprecedented period of concentrated royal power that the Carolingian rulers Charles Martel (714–41), Pippin III (741–68), and Charlemagne (768–814) transformed the Frankish kingdom into a European empire. After unifying Neustria, Austrasia, and Burgundy, these three Carolingians conquered the surrounding rival principalities and kingdoms: Aquitaine, Lombard Italy, Alemannia, Bavaria, Thuringia, Saxony, and Frisia. Pope Leo III officially recognized the dominant power of the Carolingian dynasty when he crowned Charlemagne emperor on Christmas day in 800. Thus the Carolingians revived the Roman ideal of a united Christian empire in western Europe after a three-century hiatus.

There were, however, daunting obstacles to sustaining a united Frankish Europe. The Carolingian empire consisted of a sprawling conglomeration of provinces and peoples only loosely bound together through loyalty to the king, a rudimentary system of government, and the Catholic Church. Communications were slow, royal assemblies were periodic, and the king could be in only one part of the kingdom at a time. Carolingian kingship therefore tended to be "supervisory" in nature, since rulers had to govern the vast empire with the cooperation of the great aristocratic families, who held power on a local level. Moreover, it was only a matter of time before a Carolingian king died and left multiple male heirs, all demanding kingdoms of

---

[2] For the early Carolingians, see Rosamond McKitterick, *The Frankish Kingdoms under the Carolingians, 751–987* (London, 1983), 16–76; Roger Collins, *Charlemagne* (Toronto, 1998), 23–37; Paul Fouracre, "Frankish Gaul to 814," in *NCMH* 2:85–109; idem, *The Age of Charles Martel* (Harlow, 2000).

[3] McKitterick, *Frankish Kingdoms*, 38.

[4] For the Merovingians, see Ian Wood, *The Merovingian Kingdoms, 450–751* (London, 1994).

their own according to custom. This happened in 840, when Charlemagne's heir, Louis the Pious (814–40), died and left behind three adult sons: Louis the German and his two brothers, Lothar I (817–55) and Charles the Bald (838–77).[5] From that moment on, Europe returned to the time-honored tradition of multiple Frankish kings competing against one another for territories, wealth, and status.

The unprecedented successes of the Carolingians during the eighth century had dramatically altered the stakes of dynastic politics, however. The ninth-century Carolingians now ruled an expanded empire, so the territory over which they fought was considerably larger than the Frankish kingdoms under the Merovingians. And the monarchy had more resources at its disposal than ever before. The Carolingians had increased the royal lands by uniting their own family estates with properties confiscated from the Merovingians and other rival dynasties, and they had tightened their control of the distribution of "public" offices—counties, bishoprics, monasteries, and benefices—throughout the empire.[6] At the same time, the Carolingians benefited from a slowly growing European economy of more active local markets and royal mints, efficient estate management, and increasing long-distance trade.[7] As a result, more wealth, territory, and power were up for grabs in the ninth century than during any other era of Frankish history.

In this way, a fractious and bitter dynastic struggle for the Carolingian empire animated ninth-century politics. Yet historians traditionally have approached this period through two alternate models: the decline of empires and the birth of nations.[8] Until recently, scholars of medieval Europe tended to view the ninth century as a dismal footnote to Charlemagne's reign, a sentiment that Geoffrey Barraclough summed up when he described the period as the "Decline and Fall of the Carolingian Empire."[9]

[5] For the reign of Louis the Pious, see *CH*, ed. Godman and Collins; Egon Boshof, *Ludwig der Fromme* (Darmstadt, 1996).

[6] For Carolingian government, see François Louis Ganshof, *Frankish Institutions under Charlemagne*, trans. Bryce Lyon and Mary Lyon (Providence, 1968); Karl Ferdinand Werner, "Missus-marchio-comes: Entre l'administration centrale et l'administration locale de l'empire carolingien," in *Histoire comparée de l'administration (IVe–XVIIIe siècle)*, ed. Werner Paravicini and Karl Ferdinand Werner, Beihefte der Francia 9 (Munich, 1980), 191–239; McKitterick, *Frankish Kingdoms*, 77–105; Janet L. Nelson, "Kingship and Royal Government," in *NCMH* 2:383–430.

[7] For the Carolingian economy and trade, see Adriaan Verhulst, "Economic Organization," in *NCMH* 2:481–509; idem, *The Carolingian Economy* (Cambridge, 2002); Mark Blackburn, "Money and Coinage," in *NCMH* 2:538–59; Michael McCormick, *Origins of the European Economy: Communications and Commerce, AD 300–900* (Cambridge, 2001).

[8] Simon MacLean, *Kingship and Politics in the Late Ninth Century: Charles the Fat and the End of the Carolingian Empire* (Cambridge, 2003), 1–11.

[9] Geoffrey Barraclough, *The Crucible of Europe: The Ninth and Tenth Centuries in European History* (Berkeley, 1976), chap. 3.

During this era, it was believed, the nations of France and Germany emerged from the decaying corpse of Charlemagne's empire.[10] This teleological view of the ninth century arose from the knowledge that Louis the German's son Charles III (876–88) died without a legitimate heir in 888. As a result, the Carolingians lost their monopoly on Frankish kingship and their empire fragmented into a series of successor kingdoms, including a west Frankish–"French" kingdom and an east Frankish–"German" kingdom. Because modern historians approached the ninth century with the events of 888 in mind, they posited an inevitable story of Carolingian imperial decline and French and German national birth. In the nineteenth and early twentieth century nationalist historians used this "birth of nations" narrative to legitimize the recent creation of France and Germany by tracing the roots of those nations back to the distant Carolingian past. In this way, scholars presented the ninth century as the great turning point between Carolingian imperial history and French and German national history.

Much of the early scholarship on Louis the German was made to fit into the framework of these "decline-of-empires" and "birth-of-nations" narratives. One historiographical school presented Louis as an uncreative, lackluster, weak ruler who embodied the alleged decline of Charlemagne's family.[11] Johannes Fried, for example, asserted that Louis "failed" to create a strong regime, resulting in an "astonishing weakness" of royal power after his death. Summing up this view, Fried wrote: "Louis was in fact resting on his predecessors' laurels; he was not an innovator. His government was, as it were, backward-looking."[12] Other scholars, however, have interpreted Louis as an important "founding father" of Germany. This interpretation arose from the fact that Louis inherited the territories east of the Rhine when he and his two brothers divided the Carolingian empire among them in the Treaty of Verdun of 843. Because Louis united for the first time the

[10] For two collections of essays that embody this earlier trend in the historiography, see Theodor Mayer, ed., *Der Vertrag von Verdun, 843* (Leipzig, 1943); Hellmut Kämpf, ed., *Die Entstehung des deutschen Reichs* (Darmstadt, 1976). For a detailed discussion and critique of the "birth of nations" narrative for the early Middle Ages, see Carlrichard Brühl, *Deutschland-Frankreich: Die Geburt zweier Völker* (Cologne, 1990). Brühl convincingly argues that it is anachronistic to speak of France and Germany before the eleventh century. In the ninth and tenth centuries, Continental rulers continued to think of themselves as Frankish kings ruling Frankish kingdoms.

[11] Wilfried Hartmann, *Ludwig der Deutsche* (Darmstadt, 2002), 15, discusses this interpretation.

[12] Johannes Fried, "The Frankish Kingdoms, 817–911: The East and Middle Kingdoms," in *NCMH* 2:155. See further: Johannes Fried, *Der Weg in die Geschichte: Die Ursprünge Deutschlands bis 1024* (Berlin, 1994), 417; Kathy Lynne Roper Pearson, *Conflicting Loyalties in Early Medieval Bavaria: A View of Socio-Political Interaction, 680–900* (Aldershot, 1999), 128–29, 138, 140.

lands that later became the medieval German kingdom, historians since the 1730s have dubbed him Ludwig der Deutsche, Louis the German.[13] Indeed, much of the scholarship on Louis's reign has been shaped, either consciously or unconsciously, by the larger question of the origins of Germany. Paul Kehr, the editor of Louis's diplomas during the 1930s, described Louis as "the first German king" and the founder of a "German *Reich*," and he suggested that Louis's reign shed important light on Germany's rightful national borders in the wake of World War I.[14] Wilfried Hartmann framed his important study of Louis's reign with the overarching question, "What significance did Louis the German actually have for the foundation of the later German kingdom?"[15] In this way, historians have often approached Louis's reign, and indeed the entire ninth century, with preconceived notions about what the historical narrative should be: imperial decline and national birth.

Louis, however, was neither an incompetent ruler nor the intentional founder of an east Frankish–"German" kingdom. Instead, he was a traditional Carolingian king. Growing up in the early ninth century, Louis viewed his world through the dual lenses of the Frankish kingdoms and Charlemagne's empire. Throughout his reign, Louis aspired to reunite as much of the Carolingian empire as possible under his own rule. In this sense Fried was correct: Louis was backward looking, but he also looked to the future—the future reunification of the empire, with himself seated on Charlemagne's throne. To be sure, Louis's kingship laid the foundations for an east Frankish kingdom that, in the eleventh century, was transformed into the medieval kingdom of Germany. However, it was never Louis's intention to create an enduring kingdom beyond the Rhine. Instead, he consistently struggled to expand his borders westward into the traditional heartlands of Frankish royal power. At the same time, Louis planned for his three sons to divide his kingdom among themselves after his death, which indicates he did not see his eastern kingdom as lasting. To the modern Western mind accustomed to nation-states with rigid borders, the temporary and fluid nature of ninth-century kingdoms is difficult to understand. But Louis and his contemporaries thought in the dynamic terms of kingship, dynasties, and

[13] Louis's cognomen "the German" has its roots in ninth-century sources, since the *Annals of St.-Bertin* consistently described him as "rex Germaniae" and "rex Germanorum." Pope Nicholas I and the anonymous *Vision of Charlemagne* also referred to Louis as "rex German(ic)us." However, these authors used this terminology in the sense of the antique province of Germania east of the Rhine. They did not mean that Louis ruled a united "German" or "Germanic" people. For the historiography on Louis's reign and the history of his modern cognomen, see Brühl, *Deutschland-Frankreich*, 137–41; Hartmann, *Ludwig der Deutsche*, 1–17.

[14] Paul Kehr, "Die Kanzlei Ludwigs des Deutschen," *APAW* (1932): 1.

[15] Hartmann, *Ludwig der Deutsche*, 5–6, 256–58, at 256.

power, not static polities. In his lifelong pursuit of power, Louis ruled with considerable political skill in the tradition of his predecessors. While I retain Louis's modern nationalistic cognomen for the sake of convenience, I do so only to distinguish him from the other Carolingian Louises, not to characterize his kingship.

KINGSHIP AND CONFLICT

The struggle for the Carolingian empire was a source of both political opportunity and instability for Charlemagne's descendants. To retain power in the face of dynastic competition, ninth-century Carolingian kings constantly sought to expand their borders over the heartlands of the Frankish kingdom. By ruling ever-larger territories, kings could increase their economic resources, reward their followers with lands and offices, and thereby cement political allegiances to the throne. Yet the push for empire, a necessary fact of political survival, inevitably triggered discord and conflict. As Louis the German and his brothers, nephews, and sons sought to expand their power and become the next Charlemagne, their actions led to counteractions by rival kings. As a result, dynastic conflict was at the heart of ninth-century Carolingian politics.

The last two generations of scholars have emphasized this centrality of political conflict to early medieval kingship. As Karl Leyser demonstrated in his 1979 book on the tenth-century Ottonian emperors, rule and conflict went hand in hand in early medieval societies.[16] This fundamental insight has led historians to reject the traditional division of the Carolingian era into an eighth-century "rise" and a ninth-century "decline." Instead, scholars now stress the political continuities across the eighth and ninth centuries, extending even into the tenth.[17] This emphasis yields two important conclusions: that the ninth-century Carolingians were not impotent, "do-nothing" kings, and that supposedly "strong" and "great" eighth-century Carolingians such as Charles Martel and Charlemagne were in fact often quite vulnerable. Janet Nelson expressed it best when she described Charle-

---

[16] Karl J. Leyser, *Rule and Conflict in an Early Medieval Society: Ottonian Saxony* (London, 1979).

[17] For recent scholarship that emphasizes the political continuities throughout the Carolingian period, see Fouracre, *Age of Charles Martel*, esp. 12–32; Stuart Airlie, "*Semper fideles?* Loyauté envers les Carolingiens comme constituant de l'identité aristocratique," in *La Royauté et les élites dans l'Europe carolingienne*, ed. Régine Le Jan (Lille, 1998), 129–43; MacLean, *Kingship and Politics*.

magne's reign as "one goddamned crisis after another."[18] Nelson's wonderfully blasphemous description of Charlemagne's rule could be applied to every Carolingian king. Throughout the Carolingian period, political conflict among competing Carolingian kings and rival aristocratic factions drove politics. In this sense, the Carolingian seizure of the throne in 751 did not represent an end but rather a beginning, for it launched the Carolingians' two-century struggle to maintain royal power in the face of frequent opposition.[19] It is a testament to the skill, resourcefulness, and determination of the Carolingians, in the eighth as well as ninth century, that their dynasty held on to power for so long.

This emphasis on the political continuities throughout the Carolingian period has led to an important reevaluation of ninth-century kingship. Until recently, the standard study of the ninth-century Carolingians was the second edition of Ernst Dümmler's three-volume positivist masterpiece, *Die Geschichte des ostfränkischen Reichs* (1887–88), the first two volumes of which dealt with the reigns of Louis the German and his contemporaries.[20] However, since the 1990s, historians such as Janet Nelson, Egon Boshof, and Simon MacLean have reevaluated the reigns of Charlemagne's descendants, including Louis the Pious, Charles the Bald, and Charles III.[21] Louis the German also has received renewed interest. In 2002 Wilfried Hartmann published an insightful survey of Louis's reign in light of recent scholarship, and that same year Boris Bigott published an important study of Louis's relations with the east Frankish Church.[22] In addition, Wilfried Hartmann organized an international conference on Louis the German in 2002, the proceedings of which were published as a collection on the politics and culture of the east Frankish kingdom.[23] Rather than seeing the ninth century as an

---

[18] Janet L. Nelson, "Making a Difference in Eighth-Century Politics: The Daughters of Desiderius," in *After Rome's Fall: Narrators and Sources of Early Medieval History*, ed. Alexander Callander Murray (Toronto, 1998), 172.

[19] Airlie, *"Semper fideles?"* 137.

[20] Dümmler, *GOR* 1–2.

[21] Important recent studies of ninth-century Carolingian politics include *CH*, ed. Godman and Collins; Margaret T. Gibson and Janet L. Nelson, eds., *Charles the Bald: Court and Kingdom*, 2nd rev. ed. (Aldershot, 1990); Janet L. Nelson, *Charles the Bald* (London, 1992); *NCMH* 2, chaps. 4–6, 12–16; Boshof, *Ludwig der Fromme*; MacLean, *Kingship and Politics*.

[22] Hartmann, *Ludwig der Deutsche*; Boris Bigott, *Ludwig der Deutsche und die Reichskirche im Ostfränkischen Reich (826–876)* (Husum, 2002).

[23] *LDZ*, ed. Hartmann. See further: Dieter Geuenich, "Ludwig der Deutsche und die Entstehung des ostfränkischen Reichs," in *Theodisca: Beiträge zur althochdeutschen und altniederdeutschen Sprache und Literatur in der Kultur des frühen Mittelalters*, ed. Wolfgang Haubrichs, Ernst Hellgart, Reiner Hildebrandt, Stephan Müller, and Klaus Ridder (Berlin, 2000), 313–29; Stuart Airlie, "True Teachers and Pious Kings: Salzburg, Louis the German, and Christian Order," in *Belief and Culture in the Middle Ages: Studies Presented to*

inevitable story of decline and decay, this scholarship demonstrates that, until Charles III's illness and death in 887–88, Charlemagne's descendants were effective rulers who succeeded at consolidating their power, overcoming political crises, and continuing the vibrant intellectual and cultural life that characterized the Carolingian Renaissance.

A fundamental theme of this scholarship is the independent power of the Frankish nobility.[24] By the seventh century, a hereditary nobility dominated landholding, political office, and the Church throughout western Europe. The power of the nobles was autonomous, rooted in their families' lineage, landed wealth, social prestige, and private armies of vassals. While these nobles maintained their regional identities (as Neustrians, Austrasians, Aquitanians, Bavarians, and so forth), the creation of a Frankish empire and the frequent intermarriage among noble families meant that most ninth-century noblemen also considered themselves Franks. (In this sense, Frankishness was similar to Roman identity half a millennium earlier.) Throughout the Carolingian empire, this hybrid Frankish nobility shared a common culture based on Catholic Christianity, participation in royal government, military service, an ethos of dignity, and conspicuous consumption. In 1939 the influential German historian Gerd Tellenbach called attention to the most powerful Frankish families that held lands throughout the empire, a group he aptly called the "imperial aristocracy" [Reichsaristokratie].[25] The Carolingians themselves had emerged out of this aristocracy, and it was only with the help of other leading families that they usurped the Frankish throne in 751. The Carolingians constantly needed to cultivate the support of the most powerful nobles to rule their empire, which amounted to a vast network of interrelated aristocratic families. Rather than engaging in a zero-

---

Henry Mayr-Harting, ed. Richard Gameson and Henrietta Leyser (Oxford, 2001), 89–105. The scholarship of Roman Deutinger unfortunately was brought to my attention too late to be incorporated into this book: "Königsherrschaft im Ostfränkischen Reich. Ein pragmatische Verfassungsgeschichte der späten Karolingerzeit," Habilitationsschrift, Munich, 2004.

[24] For the Frankish nobility in the late Merovingian and Carolingian periods, see Karl J. Leyser, "The German Aristocracy from the Ninth Century to the Early Twelfth Century," *Past and Present* 41 (1968): 25–53; Karl Ferdinand Werner, "Important Noble Families in the Kingdom of Charlemagne—A Prosopographical Study of the Relationship between King and Nobility in the Early Middle Ages," in *The Medieval Nobility: Studies on the Ruling Classes of France and Germany from the Sixth to the Twelfth Century*, ed. and trans. Timothy Reuter (Amsterdam, 1978), 137–202; Stuart Airlie, "The Aristocracy," in *NCMH* 2:431–50; Régine Le Jan, *Famille et pouvoir dans le mond Franc, VIIIe–Xe siècles* (Paris, 1995); Paul Fouracre, "The Origins of the Nobility in Francia," in *Nobles and Nobility in Medieval Europe*, ed. Anne J. Duggan (Woodbridge, 2000), 17–24.

[25] Gerd Tellenbach, *Königtum und Stämme in der Werdezeit des Deutschen Reiches* (Weimar, 1939), 41–69.

sum power struggle between royal and aristocratic interests, kings ruled by co-opting and further empowering already powerful regional elites.[26] As Karl Ferdinand Werner summed up, "the complete dependence of the king on the nobility is . . . what needs to be stressed."[27]

The ubiquitous regional power of the aristocracy means that Carolingian kingship must be studied within the larger framework of the Frankish nobility. To understand the dynamic relationship between kings and nobles, one must keep in mind Frankish inheritance custom.[28] Like the Carolingians, Frankish nobles practiced partible inheritance, meaning that all sons (and often daughters as well) had a claim to a share of their parents' wealth and family lands. The dividing of family resources generation after generation was a constant source of instability for the Frankish nobility, because a nobleman's wealth and status could change suddenly, depending on the vagaries of inheritance and dynastic survival. To counter the unpredictability of inheritance, ambitious Frankish nobles competed for royal favor, what Tellenbach aptly labeled *Königsnähe*—"nearness to the king." It was through royal patronage and *Königsnähe* that a noble could win the coveted "honors"—benefices, countships, military commands, court offices, bishoprics, and monasteries—that enabled him to make the quantum leap from mere nobleman to "magnate," a man whose wealth and power made him terrifyingly great (*magnus*). The great noble families considered these public offices to be their birthright, but they still depended on the favor, or at least the acquiescence, of the Carolingians to hold on to them. This right to distribute and revoke honors and offices was one of the most important sources of the Carolingians' royal power.

The dependence of the nobles on royal patronage was also a central cause of political instability and conflict. There never were enough honors to go around, and some nobles were inevitably left out in the cold. Throughout the history of the Carolingian monarchy, magnates who felt the king unjustly withheld their "rightful" honors frequently formed conspiracies and rebelled. As a result, aristocratic conflict and the competition for *honores*, wealth, and status constantly shaped and reshaped Carolingian politics. This political volatility intensified in the 830s because of Louis the Pious's multiple heirs. For the rest of the ninth century, the courts of Louis the German and his brothers, sons, and nephews became rival centers of power and patronage, resulting in what Matthew Innes has aptly called the "zenith

[26] This is the central argument of Matthew Innes's important book, *State and Society in the Early Middle Ages: The Middle Rhine Valley, 400–1000* (Cambridge, 2000), esp. 4–12, 251–63.

[27] Werner, "Important Noble Families," 176.

[28] Leyser, "German Aristocracy," 36–39.

of Carolingian politics."[29] The ninth-century struggle for the Carolingian empire was stoked from below, since the nobles' insatiable desire for *honores* exerted pressure on Charlemagne's descendants to expand their territories at their relatives' expense in order to increase the resources needed to reward their supporters. The nobles' ongoing quest for royal patronage meant that they seldom formed lasting political solidarities, either as extended family "clans" or as rigid political factions.[30] Like the Carolingians themselves, Frankish magnates tended to act as individuals driven by self-interest and the interests of their immediate relatives (especially their sons). The result was a political system of overlapping royal and aristocratic interests characterized by volatility, fluidity, and competition.

The centrality of kingship, the nobility, and conflict to Carolingian politics highlights several themes that run through this study of Louis the German's reign. The first is the importance of dynastic history. It is a testament to the success of the Carolingians that, by the late eighth century, the Frankish nobility had come to accept Carolingian kingship as an established fact. Instead of attempting to topple the Carolingian monarchy outright, rebellious nobles rallied around rival Carolingian kings and expectant heirs and encouraged strife among them. (In this way, aristocratic rebellions, although often directed against individual Carolingian rulers, paradoxically confirmed the royal authority of their dynasty.) Thus, while political conflict and fluid aristocratic factions propelled Carolingian kingship, the ever-changing structure of the Carolingian family dictated the shape of politics at any given moment. Time and again, the political conflicts of the ninth century arose out of specific dynastic events within the Carolingian family: births, deaths, comings of age, and especially contests over inheritance. In short, Carolingian dynastic history dictated the parameters of Frankish political history.

Second, the importance of kingship and conflict underscores the political significance of warfare. In recent years, historians have begun to take seriously the overwhelming pervasiveness of violence and warfare in the early Middle Ages.[31] The Franks were a soldier aristocracy, and they prided

[29] Innes, *State and Society*, 210–22.

[30] For critiques of the Frankish cognatic clan model, see Leyser, "German Aristocracy," 25–53; Constance Bouchard, "Family Structure and Family Consciousness among the Aristocracy in the Ninth to Eleventh Centuries," *Francia* 14 (1986): 639–58. Nelson, *Charles the Bald*, 174–80, and MacLean, *Kingship and Politics*, 162–63, stress the fluidity of Frankish political factions.

[31] For recent approaches to these topics, see Timothy Reuter, "Plunder and Tribute in the Carolingian Empire," *TRHS*, 5th ser. (1985): 75–94; Karl Leyser, "Early Medieval Warfare," reprinted in Leyser, *Communications* 1:29–50; Guy Halsall, ed., *Violence and Society in the Early Medieval West* (Woodbridge, 1998); idem, *Warfare and Society in the Bar-*

themselves on their military prowess, the possession of valuable armor and weapons, and skill at horseback riding and hunting. Indeed, it was during the ninth century that the martial secular ethos of "knighthood" first emerged among the Frankish nobles.[32] However, historians often have divorced warfare from the study of the reigns of individual kings. This is problematic, for early medieval rulers spent much of their time, energy, and resources planning for and executing military campaigns. As in the case of most kings, Louis went to war almost every year, either leading his armies in person or sending them out under the command of his sons and generals. On more than a few occasions, the outcome of a single battle changed the trajectory of his career. The extremely high stakes of ninth-century Carolingian politics—aristocratic support, territories, kingdoms, and political survival—meant that kings were willing to go, indeed had to go, to the battlefield to defend their power and expand their borders. To wage war effectively, Louis devoted considerable attention and resources to military logistics: raising armies, appointing generals, planning invasion routes, arranging for supplies, laying siege to fortified centers, forming alliances, and negotiating treaties. Any study of ninth-century politics must therefore take seriously the centrality of warfare, armies, and military organization to Carolingian kingship.

Warfare took on a heightened significance for Louis's reign because of his kingdom's volatile eastern borders with the Slavs.[33] Louis ruled over the longest "open" frontier in medieval Europe, stretching some six hundred miles from Hamburg on the lower Elbe to Lake Balaton in what is today Hungary. Throughout his reign, Louis struggled to subject neighboring Slavic "barbarians" to Frankish overlordship and make them pay tribute, a policy that demanded frequent and difficult military campaigns in the east against rebel peoples. This warfare along the Slavic frontiers was inter-

---

barian West, 450–900 (London, 2003); Bernard S. Bachrach, *Early Carolingian Warfare: Prelude to Empire* (Philadelphia, 2001).

[32] Karl J. Leyser, "Early Medieval Canon Law and the Beginnings of Knighthood," reprinted in Leyser, *Communications* 1:51–71; Janet L. Nelson, "Ninth-Century Knighthood: The Evidence of Nithard," reprinted in *The Frankish World, 750–900*, by Janet L. Nelson (London, 1996), 75–87; Eric J. Goldberg, "'More Devoted to the Equipment of Battle Than the Splendor of Banquets': Frontier Kingship, Martial Ritual, and Early Knighthood at the Court of Louis the German," *Viator* 30 (1999): 41–78; Dominique Barthélemey, "La chevalerie carolingienne: Prélude au XIe siècle," in Le Jan, *Royauté*, 159–75; Régine Le Jan, "Frankish Giving of Arms and Rituals of Power: Continuity and Change in the Carolingian Period," in *Rituals of Power from Late Antiquity to the Early Middle Ages*, ed. Frans Theuws and Janet L. Nelson (Leiden, 2000), 281–309.

[33] I explore this topic in Goldberg, "Ludwig der Deutsche und Mähren: Eine Studie zu karolingischen Grenzkriegen im Osten," in *LDZ*, ed. Hartmann, 67–94.

twined with the politics of Louis's kingdom, since ambitious Slavic rulers skillfully allied with the enemies and rivals of the Frankish king. Throughout his reign, Louis was forced to juggle as best he could his imperialist ambitions in the west and his wars against the Slavs in the east. In this sense, Louis was representative of many early medieval kings. Because of the geopolitical fluidity of kingdoms and empires, royal politics and frontier warfare were inextricably linked.

Finally, the focus on kingship and conflict highlights a central methodological argument of this book: the importance of political chronology and narrative history. The last two generations of early medieval historians have tended to move away from the closely chronological approach to politics that German historians such as Dümmler pioneered in the nineteenth century. Since the work of Karl Leyser, many historians have turned to anthropology to gain insights into broad aspects of early medieval political culture such as kinship, ritual, violence, memory, and emotions.[34] Work of this kind emphasizes the force of early medieval cultural norms such as monastic piety, aristocratic dignity, and friendship in shaping the political behavior of kings and nobles. This anthropologically minded scholarship has greatly expanded our understanding of early medieval politics by highlighting the noninstitutionalized and socially constructed nature of power, and this book draws extensively on its accomplishments. Yet by focusing on the "unwritten rules" of early medieval politics, scholars have sometimes obscured the highly reactive and improvisational nature of kingship. Rulers such as Louis the German lived in "real time" and had to respond to each political crisis—or, more often than not, to multiple interrelated crises—as they arose. As a result, kings faced conflict and crisis as self-conscious political actors who used creativity and improvisation to defend their power.[35] Thus, to understand the political behavior of Louis the German or any other early medieval king, we must pay close attention to chronology and context. The Carolingians on the whole were resourceful and inventive rulers, and close attention to political chronology enables us to see how and why.

[34] For several collections of essays that capture this historiographical trend and the diversity of its views, see Reuter, *Medieval Nobility;* Wendy Davies and Paul Fouracre, eds., *The Settlement of Disputes in Early Medieval Europe* (Cambridge, 1986); Gerd Althoff, *Spielregeln der Politik im Mittelalter* (Darmstadt, 1997); Halsall, *Violence and Society;* Barbara H. Rosenwein, ed., *Anger's Past: The Social Uses of an Emotion in the Middle Ages* (Ithaca, 1998); Theuws and Nelson, *Rituals of Power;* Gerd Althoff, Johannes Fried, and Patrick J. Geary, eds., *Medieval Concepts of the Past: Ritual, Memory, Historiography* (Cambridge, 2002).

[35] This point is eloquently made in Simon MacLean, "The Carolingian Response to the Revolt of Boso, 879–887," *EME* 10 (2001): 21–48, at 46.

The study of Carolingian kingship requires the historian to use a wide range of surviving historical evidence. Although historians often bemoan the dearth and fragmentary nature of early medieval sources, the fact that Louis the German lived during the heyday of the educational and cultural reforms known as the Carolingian Renaissance means that there exist an unusual number of histories, letter collections, works of literature, and other written and visual materials from which to piece together his long reign.[36] The relative richness of the surviving historical evidence means that chronicles—the traditional backbone of political history—can be checked against one another for accuracy and augmented with other, nonnarrative sources that have sometimes been neglected in studies of kingship. This abundance of sources is important because chroniclers often wrote with political and ideological agendas and therefore distorted, fabricated, or omitted information.[37] Although much information about Louis's long reign has been lost, much too has been preserved in a wide range of surviving sources.

Historians have traditionally based their studies of Louis's reign on the so-called *Annals of Fulda*, the chief ninth-century east Frankish chronicle.[38] The *Annals of Fulda* provide an independent account of Carolingian history from the 830s to 888 (with a Bavarian continuation that goes up to 901), and they focus on the political and ecclesiastical events in the kingdom of Louis and his descendants. Yet this reliance on the *Annals of Fulda* is problematic. Between 838 and 863, this historical work seems to have been written (or at least supervised) by Rudolf (d. 865), a Fulda monk and scholar who had little

---

[36] The best survey of ninth-century east Frankish sources is Wattenbach, Levison, and Löwe, *DGM* 6. For the rise of literacy and writing under the Carolingians, see Rosamond McKitterick, *The Carolingians and the Written Word* (Cambridge, 1989).

[37] For the propagandistic nature of Carolingian historical writing, see Rosamond McKitterick, "Political Ideology in Carolingian Historiography," in *The Uses of the Past in the Early Middle Ages*, ed. Yitzhak Hen and Matthew Innes (Cambridge, 2000), 162–74.

[38] Concerning the *AF*, see Wattenbach, Levison, and Löwe, *DGM* 6:671–87; *The Annals of Fulda*, trans. Timothy Reuter (Manchester, 1992), 1–14; Richard Corradini, *Die Wiener Handschrift Cvp 430: Ein Beitrag zur Historiographie in Fulda im frühen 9. Jahrhundert* (Frankfurt, 2000); Rosamond McKitterick, *History and Memory in the Carolingian World* (Cambridge, 2003), 33–35; MacLean, *Kingship and Politics*, 24–27. For examples of overviews of Louis's reign largely based on the *AF*, see Pierre Riché, *The Carolingians: A Family Who Forged Europe*, trans. Michael Idomir Allen (Philadelphia, 1983), 185–89; Fried, "The East and Middle Kingdoms," 145–55; Hartmann, *Ludwig der Deutsche*, 18–79, 104–22.

direct contact with Louis's court.[39] As a result, between the 830s and the mid-860s, the reports of Louis's activities in the *Annals of Fulda* are often vague, fragmentary, and superficial, and they frequently omit important events in Louis's reign.[40] After Rudolf's death, the *Annals of Fulda* were continued at Mainz by an author (or authors) in the circle of Archbishop Liutbert (863–89), who became Louis's archchaplain in 870.[41] Only beginning in 869 do the *Annals of Fulda* recount royal politics in more detail, presumably because of Liutbert of Mainz's new position at court. Thus, the *Annals of Fulda* became more closely connected with Louis's palace during only the last eight years of his life, and even then they were not an "official" record of Louis's reign written by a member of his immediate entourage. As a result, the *Annals of Fulda* do not provide anything close to the detail found in other Carolingian chronicles such as the *Royal Frankish Annals* or the *Annals of St.-Bertin*. By privileging the *Annals of Fulda*, historians have often achieved only a one-dimensional understanding of Louis's reign, an understanding that confirms his reputation as a ruler of little originality or interest.

Fortunately, a number of other ninth-century chronicles and histories can be used to augment the *Annals of Fulda*. For the reign of Louis the German's father, Louis the Pious, there are the *Royal Frankish Annals*, which cover the years through 829.[42] There were also two important biographies written about Louis the Pious: the *Deeds of Emperor Louis*, written by Thegan, the assistant bishop of Trier, in 837; and the *Life of Emperor Louis*, com-

---

[39] For Rudolf's authorship, see Wattenbach, Levison, and Löwe, *DGM* 6:678–81; J. M. Michael Wallace-Hadrill, *The Frankish Church* (Oxford, 1983), 330; *Annals of Fulda*, trans. Reuter, 3–7; Hartmann, *Ludwig der Deutsche*, 6–7. Rudolf seems to have written the annals at the monastery of Fulda until 847, at which point he apparently accompanied his former abbot and teacher, Raban, to Mainz when Raban became archbishop. Thereafter, the *Annals of Fulda* were written at Mainz until after Louis's death. Nevertheless, for the sake of convenience, I follow convention and refer to this chronicle as the *Annals of Fulda*.

[40] To give just a few specific examples: the *Annals of Fulda* do not report the rebellions of Prefect Ratpot and Carloman during the 850s, the marriages of Louis's three sons, his 865 Frankfurt succession decree, and his conflict with the Byzantine missionaries Constantine and Methodius. Moreover, the Fulda annals offer little detail about Louis's diplomacy with fellow Carolingians and the Slavs, and they also shed little light on the ceremony and ideology of his court. This led Reuter, in *Annals of Fulda*, 7, to suggest that Rudolf's "original" version was "more like a bundle of loose notes and jottings" than a coherent historical work.

[41] Wattenbach, Levison, and Löwe, *DGM* 6:681–83; *Annals of Fulda*, trans. Reuter, 7. Scholars rightly reject the earlier argument that Rudolf's pupil, Meginhard, continued the *Annals of Fulda* during the years 864–87: *AF*, vii–viii.

[42] Concerning the "revised" version of the *ARF*, see Collins, *Charlemagne*, 4–6; idem, "The 'Reviser' Revisited: Another Look at the Alternative Version of the *Annales Regni Francorum*," in Murray, *After Rome's Fall*, 191–213.

posed soon after Louis the Pious's death in 840 by an anonymous author, commonly known as the Astronomer because of his interest in astrological phenomena.[43] Two major histories also come from the west Frankish court of Louis the German's younger half-brother, Charles the Bald: the *Four Books of Histories* by Charlemagne's illegitimate grandson, Nithard, which describe in vivid detail the civil wars during the 830s and early 840s; and the *Annals of St.-Bertin*, which cover the years 830–82 and were written by Bishop Prudentius of Troyes (843–61) and, after his death, by Archbishop Hincmar of Reims (845–82).[44] In addition, there are several valuable eastern annals, each written from its own regional perspective and not directly associated with any Carolingian court: the so-called *Annals of Xanten*, the *Annals of St.-Vaast*, the *Annals of Hildesheim*, and a number of now fragmentary annals from Salzburg.[45] Also written at Salzburg in 870 is the *Conversion of the Bavarians and the Carantanians*, a historical work of great importance for Louis's relations with the Slavs.[46] Moreover, several historical works written soon after Louis's death contain reliable information about his reign: Ratpert's *Misfortunes of St.-Gall*, written about 884; Notker of St.-Gall's *Deeds of Charlemagne*, composed for Charles III about 885; and Regino of Prüm's *Chronicle*, composed at Trier for Bishop Adalbero of Augsburg (the guardian of Louis the German's great-grandson, King Louis the Child) about 906.[47] All these works were written to advance the specific political agendas of

[43] See Ernst Tremp's introduction to Thegan, *GH;* and Astronomer, *VH*, 1–11, 53–98. See further Tremp, *Studien zu den "Gesta Hludowici imperatoris" des Trierer Chorbischofs Thegan*, in MGH *Schriften* 32 (Hanover, 1988).

[44] Concerning Nithard and his *Four Books of Histories*, see Bernard Scholz, trans., *Carolingian Chronicles* (Ann Arbor, 1970), 21–30; Karl Leyser, "Three Historians," in Leyser, *Communications* 1:19–26; Janet L. Nelson, "Public *Histories* and Private History in the Work of Nithard," reprinted in *Politics and Ritual in Early Medieval Europe*, by Janet L. Nelson (London, 1986), 195–237. For the *AB*, see Janet L. Nelson, "The *Annals of St.-Bertin*," in Gibson and Nelson, *Charles the Bald*, 23–40; *The Annals of St.-Bertin*, trans. Janet L. Nelson (Manchester, 1991), 1–16.

[45] The *Annals of Xanten* were written in the lower Rhine region, probably at Ghent and then Cologne, and provide an independent account from 812 through 873. The *Annals of St.-Vaast* provide information about the last years of Louis's reign. They were written at the monastery of St.-Vaast, Arras, and record the years between 873 and 900.

[46] Concerning the *Conversio*, see the introduction of Fritz Lošek in his edition of the *Conversio*, 5–8. See further, *Conversio Bagoariorum et Carantanorum: Das Weissbuch der Salzburger Kirche über die erfolgreiche Mission in Karantanien und Pannonien*, ed. and trans. Herwig Wolfram (Vienna, 1979); Herwig Wolfram, *Salzburg, Bayern, Österreich: Die "Conversio Bagoariorum et Carantanorum" und die Quellen ihrer Zeit* (Vienna, 1995).

[47] On Notker's *GK*, see especially MacLean, *Kingship and Politics*, 199–229. In addition, in 881 Notker composed a short history of the Carolingian dynasty covering the years 840–81, a work that focuses on Louis the German and his sons: Notker, *Continuatio*. For Ratpert's history of St.-Gall, see the introduction of Hannes Steiner, *Casus sancti Galli*, 1–80.

their authors, and they therefore are full of biases, inaccuracies, lacunae, and selective presentations of historical events. Nevertheless, they are essential for checking the accuracy of, and filling the numerous silences in, the *Annals of Fulda*.

To supplement the information provided by chroniclers, the historian must turn to a number of other kinds of sources. Diplomas and charters are one critical body of documents.[48] Carolingian kings issued diplomas recording grants of lands, rights, and other privileges to churchmen (usually bishops and abbots) as well as to their lay supporters. Approximately 170 genuine diplomas issued by Louis survive for the years 830–76, averaging about four diplomas per year.[49] In addition to royal diplomas, there is an unusually rich cache of charter collections from east Frankish monasteries and bishoprics such as St.-Emmeram (Regensburg), Freising, Passau, St.-Gall, Lorsch, Fulda, and Corvey.[50] Like chronicles, diplomas and charters do not provide straightforward historical information. Royal diplomas by design were meant to magnify the king's power and emphasize his God-given authority, while charters were intended to defend the rights of ecclesiastical institutions over lands. Moreover, diplomas and charters tend to obscure the political context surrounding a given transaction, since they were couched in the formulaic language of pious donations for the benefit of one's soul.

Nevertheless, if used carefully, diplomas and charters provide an underexploited repository of information for the study of kingship, politics, and warfare. Because wealth and power in Frankish Europe were based on land, important political events such as military campaigns, royal assemblies, and

---

[48] For the sake of convenience, I distinguish between *diplomas* formally issued by kings and drawn up by court scribes, and nonroyal *charters*. For *charters*, I follow the definition of Wendy Davies, Paul Fouracre, and Warren Brown: any document (except diplomas) "record[ing] the transfer or confirmation of property rights or privileges or other transactions" (Davies and Fouracre, *Settlement of Disputes*, 270; Warren Brown, *Unjust Seizure: Conflict, Interest, and Authority in an Early Medieval Society* [Ithaca, 2001], 17n39).

[49] This is comparable to the surviving diplomas of Charlemagne and Lothar I (both about four per year), although Louis the Pious and Charles the Bald had much higher annual averages (approximately 18 and 12, respectively). A significant number of Louis's diplomas have not survived. We have very few from lay recipients, nor do we have any from the important eastern bishoprics of Augsburg, Cologne, Constance, Freising, Hamburg, Mainz, Trier, and Worms. For Louis's diplomas and chancery, see Kehr, "Kanzlei Ludwigs des Deutschen," 1–32; idem, "Die Schreiber und Diktatoren der Diplome Ludwigs des Deutschen," *NA* 50 (1935): 1–105; Kehr's introduction to *DLG*, xiii–xxxiii; Hartmann, *Ludwig der Deutsche*, 9–10, 125; Bigott, *Ludwig der Deutsche*, 251–64; Nicholas Brousseau, "Die Urkunden Ludwigs des Deutschen und Karls des Kahlen—ein Vergleich," in *LDZ*, ed. Hartmann, 95–119.

[50] Concerning these east Frankish cartularies, see McKitterick, *Carolingians and the Written Word*, 77–134; Patrick Geary, *Phantoms of Remembrance: Memory and Oblivion at the End of the First Millennium* (Princeton, 1994), 87–100.

aristocratic rebellions were often accompanied by donations and exchanges of lands among the king, nobles, and the Church. Since diplomas and charters often contain detailed information about the transaction in question (the donors, recipients, lands, witnesses, and date and location of the transaction), they enable the historian to uncover politics on a local level that is usually obscured by the king-centered reports of the chroniclers. A central methodological argument of this book is that diplomas and charters can be used to compensate for the often vague reports of the chroniclers and to shed new light on kingship, royal ideology, warfare, and local politics.

Another important body of nonnarrative evidence comprises legal decrees by the king and the Church. Unlike his predecessors, Louis does not seem to have recorded his royal decrees in written Latin documents known as capitularies (so called because they were organized into *capitula*, or chapter headings), presumably because of the lower levels of Latin literacy among his Germanic-speaking lay subjects.[51] Nevertheless, Louis issued joint capitularies with his brothers and nephews during their numerous meetings, and many of these survive. Moreover, following Carolingian tradition, east Frankish Church synods issued canons addressing matters not only of ecclesiastical reform but also of government and secular politics. It often is difficult to ascertain the extent to which these decrees were actually carried out, and in some cases it seems that they were not. Nevertheless, these legal texts illuminate the specific concerns of the king and magnates at precise moments in time.

Although Louis must have sent numerous letters to kings, popes, bishops, abbots, and counts, very few survive. Fortunately, several important east Frankish letter collections still exist, including two from leading east Frankish intellectuals: Einhard (d. 840), the lay abbot of Seligenstadt and Charlemagne's famous biographer; and Raban, the abbot of Fulda (822–41) and later archbishop of Mainz (847–56). Other letters relevant to Louis's reign are scattered throughout the ninth-century evidence, including collections from Popes Nicholas (858–67), Hadrian II (867–72), and John VIII (872–82). In addition to letters, there are numerous surviving works of Latin literature, hagiography, theology, and poetry by east Frankish churchmen, as well as a significant corpus of vernacular literature in Frankish and Old Saxon. For Louis's conflict with the Slavic kingdom of Moravia, moreover, the *Lives* of Saints Constantine (Cyril) and Methodius, written in Old Church Slavonic, are of chief importance.[52] Like chronicles, almost all sur-

[51] McKitterick, *Carolingians and the Written Word*, 21–22; Janet L. Nelson, "Literacy in Carolingian Government," reprinted in Nelson, *Frankish World*, 9–12.

[52] Josef Bujnoch, trans., *Zwischen Rom und Byzanz: Leben und Wirken der Slavenapostel Kyrillos und Methodios nach den Pannonischen Legenden und der Klemensvita: Bericht von der*

viving literary sources were political in one way or another, since writing and the production of manuscripts were based in centers of aristocratic wealth and power: bishoprics, monasteries, convents, and royal courts. Any author, poet, or scribe therefore had a vested interest in contemporary politics, and these political loyalties and concerns often found expression in their literary works. By situating literary sources within a precise political chronology, therefore, historians can uncover competing ideologies at rival centers of power.

One final body of evidence consists of liturgical manuscripts—that is, religious books containing prayers, benedictions, and other texts related to the celebration of the Mass. Several liturgical manuscripts from Louis's court survive, including two that belonged to his archchaplains, Baturich of Regensburg (817–48) and Grimald of St.-Gall (841–72). In 826/7, Baturich of Regensburg commissioned a collection of prayers and blessings for Louis's court, while Grimald of St.-Gall possessed a manuscript known as the Grimalt Codex, which he and his scribes filled with miscellaneous texts related to service in the palace.[53] In addition, there are a number of other religious manuscripts associated with Louis's court, including Louis's own private book of prayer, the Ludwig Psalter, his copy of Wandalbert of Prüm's *Martyrology*, and a scroll containing litanies for Louis's court known as the Lorsch Rotulus.[54] These liturgical and religious manuscripts provide a wealth of information about the culture, ceremonies, symbolism, and ideology of Louis's palace not reported in other sources. They enable a richer understanding of how Louis and his ecclesiastical supporters employed liturgy and the visual arts to legitimate his struggles for power.

Taufe Russlands nach der Laurentiuschronik, Slavische Geschichtsschreiber 1 (Graz, 1959). English translation and commentary in *The "Vita" of Constantine and the "Vita" of Methodius*, trans. Marvin Kantor and Richard S. White, Michigan Slavic Materials 13 (Ann Arbor, 1976). Francis Dvornik, *Byzantine Missions among the Slavs: Saints Constantine-Cyril and Methodius* (New Brunswick, NJ, 1970), offers an extended commentary on the historical value of these two Old Church Slavonic *vitae*.

[53] Baturich of Regensburg's pontifical: Munich, Clm 14510, fols. 1–75; Grimalt Codex: St. Gall 397. Concerning these two liturgical manuscripts, see Bernhard Bischoff, "Bücher am Hofe Ludwigs des Deutschen," in *Mittelalterliche Studien*, by B. Bischoff (Stuttgart, 1981), 3:187, 201–10.

[54] Ludwig Psalter: Berlin, Staatsbibliothek Theol. lat. fol. 58; Wandalbert of Prüm, *Martyrology:* Biblioteca Apostolica Vaticana, Reg. lat. 438; Lorsch Rotulus: Stadt- und Universitätsbibliothek Frankfurt MS Barth. 179. Concerning the Lorsch Rotulus, see Astrid Krüger, "*Sancte Nazari ora pro nobis*—Ludwig der Deutsche und der Lorscher Rotulus," in *LDZ*, ed. Hartmann, 184–202.

PART I
WINNING A KINGDOM

CHAPTER ONE
THE YOUNG KING, CA. 810-829

On January 28, 814, the sixty-five-year-old Charlemagne died at the royal palace in Aachen. With his passing, the Franks mourned the death of their most successful ruler since the foundation of the Frankish kingdom three centuries earlier. Charlemagne had built on the successes of his father, Pippin III, and by conquering the Lombard kingdom, Bavaria, and Saxony he transformed the Frankish kingdom into an empire. By his death, the Frankish empire encompassed a staggering array of peoples and provinces that stretched from the Pyrenees Mountains to the Elbe River and from the North Sea to central Italy. Although Charlemagne first and foremost remained a king of the Franks, his imperial coronation in 800 by Pope Leo III recognized his preeminence in western Europe, revived the Roman imperial title after a three-century hiatus, and asserted the Frankish king's parity with the eastern Byzantine emperor in Constantinople.

In 813, Charlemagne had designated his only surviving son, Louis the Pious, heir to the empire. When Charlemagne died the following year, Louis the Pious, now thirty-six, succeeded his father as emperor of Frankish Europe. Louis the Pious was a gifted ruler whose first fifteen years on the throne in many ways represented the political and cultural high point of the Carolingian empire.[1] It was during these halcyon days of the Carolingian

[1] For positive evaluations of Louis the Pious's early reign, see François Louis Ganshof, "Louis the Pious Reconsidered," reprinted in *The Carolingians and the Frankish Monarchy*, by F. L. Ganshof (London, 1971), 261–72; Thomas F. X. Noble, "The Monastic Ideal as a Model for Empire: The Case of Louis the Pious," *Revue Bénédictine* 86 (1976): 235–50; idem, "Louis the Pious and His Piety Reconsidered," *Revue Belge* 58 (1980): 297–

monarchy that Louis the German grew up at his father's court. From his years of training in the imperial entourage, Louis matured into an educated, cultured, and ambitious prince. Yet Louis's political aspirations clashed with the realities of dynastic politics. In 817, Louis the Pious appointed Louis the German's eldest brother, Lothar I (817–55), as co-emperor and heir to the bulk of the empire. In contrast, Louis the Pious made Louis the German the subordinate king of the peripheral region of Bavaria. Louis's ambitions for power and his rivalry with Lothar soon became the central preoccupation of his career.[2]

BIRTH AND INHERITANCE PLANS

Through his mother as well as his father, Louis the German inherited the bluest kind of Frankish blood. He was born during the last years of Charlemagne's reign to Louis the Pious and his first wife, Ermengard. Ermengard was a Frankish noblewoman from the Rupertiner (Robertian) family and a member of the highest echelons of the Frankish aristocracy.[3] Ermengard's father was Count Ingram of Hesbaye (the region west of Aachen), and other distinguished members of her family included the influential bishop and reformer Chrodegang of Metz (742–66), Cancor (d. 711), who founded the important Rhineland monastery of Lorsch, and Count Robert of Worms (d. 822). Ermengard presumably gave birth to Louis in Aquitaine, the region of Gaul south of the Loire River where Louis the Pious ruled before Charlemagne's death. The landscape of Aquitaine was full of towns, churches, estates, vineyards, and noble families with deep roots in the Roman past. The

316; Karl Ferdinand Werner, "*Hludovicus Augustus:* Gouverner l'empire chrétien—Idées et réalités," in *CH,* ed. Godman and Collins, 3–123; Josef Semmler, "*Renovatio Regni Francorum:* Die Herrschaft Ludwigs des Frommen im Frankenreich 814–829/830," in *CH,* ed. Godman and Collins, 125–45; Boshof, *Ludwig der Fromme,* 91–181.

[2] For the early career of Louis the German, see Dümmler, *GOR* 1:1–70; Gustav Eiten, *Das Unterkönigtum im Reiche der Merovinger und Karolinger* (Heidelberg, 1907), 114–32; Hartmann, *Ludwig der Deutsche,* 24–34. Brigitte Kasten, *Königssöhne und Königsherrschaft: Untersuchungen zur Teilhabe am Reich in der Merowinger- und Karolingerzeit,* MGH *Schriften* 44 (Hanover, 1997), 165–95, offers a valuable analysis of Louis the Pious's relations with his sons.

[3] For Ermengard and the Rupertiner-Robertians, see Thegan, *GH,* chap. 4, p. 178; Astronomer, *VH,* chap. 8, pp. 306–9; Riché, *Carolingians,* 138 and table 4; Silvia Konecny, "Die Frauen des karolingischen Königshauses" (Ph.D. diss., University of Vienna, 1976), 89, 99; Matthew Innes, "Kings, Monks and Patrons: Political Identities and the Abbey of Lorsch," in Le Jan, *La Royauté,* 304–9; Innes, *State and Society,* 51–59.

Louis the German's father. A portrait of Emperor Louis the Pious, armed with the cross of Christ and the shield of faith. From a copy of Raban's *In Praise of the Holy Cross* (ca. 840). © Bibliotheca Apostolica Vaticana (Vatican), Reg. lat. 124, fol. 4v.

future "German" Louis therefore spent his first years in the most Romanized province north of the Alps.

As was the case for all medieval rulers, the structure of the royal family set the trajectory for Louis's life. At the time of his birth, Louis's parents had two sons who already were young men: Lothar I, born in 795, and Pippin, born about 797.[4] Louis the Pious recognized his third son as throne-worthy alongside his two brothers, since Louis the Pious gave him his own royal name. The Franks pronounced Louis as *Hlu-do-vig* (precursor of the modern Ludwig), a warlike name that literally meant "famous battle" in Frankish.[5] Louis was the name of the renowned Frankish king Clovis (an archaic spelling of Louis) who had converted to Catholicism and founded the Frankish kingdom in the decades around 500. Clovis's descendants—the Merovingians—had ruled the Frankish kingdom until the Carolingian coup d'état in 751. Charlemagne had revived this venerable royal name by giving it to Louis the Pious, presumably to foster fictitious Carolingian claims that they were related to the Merovingians and therefore not usurpers. Louis the Pious continued this revival of Merovingian names by bestowing his own name on Louis the German. (Lothar likewise was an old Merovingian name.) By selecting the ancient royal name of Louis for his third son, Louis the Pious indicated that he would inherit a kingdom alongside his two brothers should he survive to adulthood.

The fact that no contemporary chronicler recorded the date of Louis's birth is not surprising. At that time, Charlemagne was still emperor, and Louis the German's birth therefore was not particularly important. In his *Deeds of Charlemagne*, Notker told the story of how the elderly Charlemagne had predicted his young grandson's future greatness, and he went on to report that Louis, who died in 876, lived "until his seventieth year."[6] Notker therefore indicated that Louis must have been born in 805 or 806.[7] Yet one must be cautious about accepting Notker's seemingly straightforward account. Since Notker was writing in the mid-880s, it is unlikely that he had

[4] Louis the German also had two sisters, Rotrud and Hildegard, whose birthdates are unknown. Here and elsewhere, I have consulted Karl Ferdinand Werner's important article on Charlemagne's descendants: "Die Nachkommen Karls des Grossen bis um das Jahr 1000 (1–8 Generation)," in *Karl der Grosse*, vol. 4: *Das Nachleben*, ed. Wolfgang Braunfels and Percy Ernst Schramm (Düsseldorf, 1967), 403–84.

[5] Ermold, *In Honorem*, bk. 1, ll. 82–84, p. 10, translated *Hluto* as "praeclarum," *Wicgch* as "Mars."

[6] Notker, *GK* 2.10, pp. 65–66. Notker closely modeled this anecdote on the elderly Jacob's blessing of Joseph's sons in Genesis 48.

[7] Historians generally have followed Notker and dated Louis's birth to 805 or 806: Dümmler, *GOR* 1:17 and n. 2; BM 1338b; Werner, "Die Nachkommen," table; Bigott, *Ludwig der Deutsche*, 54.

Winning a Kingdom

reliable information about Louis's birth and childhood. Indeed, Notker probably invented the story about Louis the German's visit to Charlemagne's court to flatter Louis the German's son, Charles III, for whom he wrote. Because Notker knew Charlemagne had died in 814 and Louis in 876, he apparently asserted that Louis had lived "until his seventieth year" to corroborate his fictitious tale.

More reliable information about the date of Louis's birth comes from three independent sources.[8] At various dates between August 814 and June 824, the Astronomer, Archbishop Adalram of Salzburg, and Ermold the Black all described Louis as a boy, or *puer*—a term the Franks used to designate a noble boy until he reached the age of fifteen.[9] If Louis was not yet fifteen between August 814 and June 824, then he must have been born at some point between June 809 and August 814. Within this five-year window, the date of 810 is most likely. In August 825, Louis the Pious sent Louis the German to Bavaria to begin ruling in person, and it is probable that he did so because his namesake had recently come of age.[10] If this is correct, then Louis would have been born before the end of August in the year 810 (half a decade later than Notker claimed), making his brothers Lothar and Pippin about fifteen and thirteen years his senior, respectively. To the young Louis, therefore, his brothers probably seemed like distant, and perhaps intimidating, grown men.

As for all princes, the issue of inheritance had a profound impact on Louis the German's reign. Louis lived during an era of experimentation in royal inheritance practices, which created both opportunities as well as conflicts for ninth-century Carolingians. The Franks had a patrimonial concept of kingship, meaning that they divided the kingdom among their royal sons like a piece of family property. According to Frankish custom that went back to Clovis, all royal sons had a claim to a portion of their father's kingdom.[11]

---

[8] Here my arguments echo those of Hartmann, *Ludwig der Deutsche*, 24–28.

[9] Astronomer, *VH*, chap. 24, p. 356, referred to Louis as "puerilibus adhuc consistentem in annis" in 814. Adalram of Salzburg (821–36) gave the young king of Bavaria a codex in which he described him as "summe puer . . . Hludowice," perhaps on the occasion of his visit to the imperial court in 823; Percy Ernst Schramm and Florentine Mütherich, *Denkmale der deutschen Könige und Kaiser* (Munich, 1981), 1:126, 238, no. 33; BM 774. In describing the 824 Breton campaign, Ermold described Louis the German as "Hludowice puer"; Ermold, *In Honorem*, bk. 4, l. 2011, p. 152. For Carolingian age terminology, see Paul Edward Dutton, "Beyond the Topos of Senescence: The Political Problems of Aged Carolingian Rulers," in *Aging and the Aged in Medieval Europe*, ed. Michael M. Sheehan (Toronto, 1990), 84–85.

[10] *ARF*, s.a. 825, p. 168.

[11] For Frankish royal inheritance practices and their evolution under the Carolingians, see Franz-Reiner Erkens, "*Divisio legitima* und *unitas imperii*: Teilungspraxis und Einheitsstreben bei der Thronfolge im Frankenreich," *DA* 52 (1996): 423–85.

Although in theory there was a single kingdom of the Franks (*regnum Francorum*), it in fact consisted of three geographically and historically distinct kingdoms: Neustria, in northern Gaul west of the Carbonnière Forest; Austrasia, the region of Gaul east of the Carbonnière Forest, extending as far as the middle Rhine; and Burgundy, in southeastern Gaul along the Saône and Rhône rivers. These three kingdoms, collectively known as the kingdom of the Franks or as Francia, made up the heartland of Frankish kingship and government, since it was here that royal estates, palaces, cities, and other sources of royal income were most plentiful. Because of the Frankish custom of partible inheritance, Frankish politics usually centered around the struggles of male members of the royal family to secure one or more of the three kingdoms that made up the *regnum Francorum*.

Through political maneuvering and the chances of dynastic survival, the early Carolingians managed to unite the *regnum Francorum* four generations in a row, creating an unusually long period of centralized royal power. This period of political unification coincided with the creation of the Carolingian empire through the conquests of the surrounding kingdoms and principalities. This doubling of the territories under Frankish rule gave the Carolingians an opportunity to experiment with royal inheritance practices based on their evolving concepts of royal power. One can see this in Charlemagne's inheritance plans. In spite of his imperial coronation, Charlemagne saw himself first and foremost as a king of the Franks whose empire arose out of his accumulation of numerous kingdoms and peoples. His cumbersome imperial title reflected this multi-ethnic, but ultimately Frankish, concept of empire: "Charles, the most serene augustus crowned by God, the great and pacific emperor governing the Roman empire, and by the mercy of God king of the Franks and Lombards." Charlemagne emphasized the importance of kingship over the *regnum Francorum* in his division plan of 806, known as the Division of the Kingdoms.[12] At that time, Charlemagne had three sons: Charles the Younger, Pippin, and (the youngest) Louis the Pious. In an inheritance scheme that reflected his desire to keep the *regnum Francorum* intact, Charlemagne bequeathed to Charles the Younger all of Neustria, Austrasia, and Burgundy, as well as the territories east of the Rhine. In contrast, he left his younger two sons kingdoms of roughly equal size but consisting of newly acquired territories that were geographically peripheral to Francia. Charlemagne did not pass on his imperial title, but he instead granted all of his sons the title of king. In this way, Charlemagne

[12] *Divisio regnorum*, in MGH *Capitularia* 1:126–30. Concerning the 806 division, see Peter Classen, "Karl der Grosse und die Thronfolge im Frankenreich," in *Festschrift für Hermann Heimpel* (Göttingen, 1972), 3:109–34.

sought to preserve for the next generation a united *regnum Francorum* under the rule of a traditional king of the Franks.

In spite of these plans, Charlemagne's 806 division never came to pass. Pippin died in 810 and Charles the Younger in 811, unexpectedly leaving Louis the Pious as Charlemagne's lone heir. Thus in 813 the elderly Charlemagne summoned Louis the Pious to Aachen, crowned him emperor, and named him heir to the united empire—with the exception of the Lombard kingdom in Italy, which Charlemagne granted to Pippin's illegitimate son, Bernard. The early deaths of Pippin and Charles call attention to an ever-present source of uncertainty and instability in Frankish politics: the possibility of a royal son's premature death. The average life expectancy of a Carolingian man who survived infancy was only about forty years, and at any age he might die suddenly from illness or injury.[13] A prudent Carolingian king therefore could not be satisfied with only one son. History taught that he needed two or three to ensure that at least one would survive him.

In contrast to Charlemagne, Louis the Pious had a heightened sense of the importance of his imperial title and a united Christian empire.[14] Louis the Pious seems to have been influenced by his circle of ecclesiastical advisers, who argued that the empire was an institution created by God for the defense of the Church and propagation of the Faith. Indeed, the fact that his elder two brothers had unexpectedly died seems to have convinced Louis the Pious that God had selected him to preserve a united Christian empire.[15] The new emperor therefore believed that he should not divide the empire like a patrimonial estate but rather preserve it for future generations according to God's will. Louis the Pious moved to ensure this "unity of the empire" in his famous 817 inheritance decree, the *Ordinatio imperii* (Ordering of the empire), a document that was to have a lasting impact on Louis the German's career and on ninth-century politics.[16] At the 817 Aachen assembly, the nobles urged Louis the Pious to proclaim a succession decree for his three sons that followed the tradition of partible inheritance. However, heeding the advice of his inner circle of ecclesiastical advisers, the emperor bequeathed the imperial title and the bulk of the empire to his eldest son, Lothar. Before the assembled nobles, Louis the Pious crowned Lothar

---

[13] Dutton, "Beyond the Topos," 91–94.

[14] Ganshof, "Louis the Pious Reconsidered," 263–64; Egon Boshof, "Einheitsidee und Teilungsprinzip in der Regierungszeit Ludwigs des Frommen," in *CH*, ed. Godman and Collins, 176–77.

[15] Louis the Pious expressed this belief in the prologue to the *Ordinatio imperii*, in MGH *Capitularia* 1:270–71.

[16] Ibid., 270–73; François Louis Ganshof, "Some Observations on the *Ordinatio imperii* of 817," in Ganshof, *Carolingians*, 273–88; Boshof, "Einheitsidee und Teilungsprinzip," 176–82; Kasten, *Königssöhne*, 168–82.

Louis the German's older brother and rival. A majestic portrait of Emperor Lothar I (ca. 842). This portrait shows Lothar sitting upon a throne, wearing magnificent regal attire and a crown covered with gold and gems, and carrying a ceremonial staff and sword. From the Lothar Psalter, London, British Library Add. MS 37768, fol. 4r. By permission of the British Library.

co-emperor and named him heir to Francia (Neustria, Austrasia, and Burgundy), Frisia, Saxony, Thuringia, Alemannia, Alsace, and Italy. The emperor set aside much smaller peripheral kingdoms for his younger two sons. Pippin, who had been king of Aquitaine since 814, became heir to Aquitaine, Gascony, the march of Toulouse, and several adjacent counties in Septimania and Burgundy.[17] Louis the Pious named the young Louis the German king of Bavaria, including the adjacent Nordgau and frontiers over the Avars, Carantanians, Bohemians, and other Slavs.[18] Although Pippin and Louis were to rule Aquitaine and Bavaria as kings, the *Ordinatio imperii* spelled out in detail their subordination to their eldest brother, the emperor.[19]

From the point of view of royal ideology, the *Ordinatio imperii* represented the high point of Carolingian imperial kingship. Through it, Louis the Pious endeavored to transform Frankish patrimonial kingship into a Christian emperorship that united all the peoples of western Europe into a holy Christian empire. From the practical viewpoint of dynastic politics, however, Louis the Pious's plan to bequeath a united empire to Lothar was fraught with political tensions and latent conflict. Writing with the benefit of retrospection, Thegan asserted that the *Ordinatio imperii* made Pippin of Aquitaine and Louis the German "indignant." By this term, Thegan indicated that the emperor's younger sons saw the planned uneven division as an affront to their aristocratic sense of dignity (*dignitas*) because it ignored their rightful claims as royal heirs.[20] Louis the Pious knew he was riding roughshod over the time-honored Frankish tradition of partible inheritance, but he was confident that he was carrying out God's will. The question of how to reconcile the ideal of imperial unity with the fractious reality of dynastic politics and partible inheritance was to be the central dilemma of Louis the German's long career.

The party immediately threatened by the *Ordinatio imperii* was Louis the German's cousin, Bernard, who had ruled Lombardy as king since 810. The 817 decree disinherited Bernard outright, since it named Lothar the ruler of Italy.[21] Bernard wasted no time mustering a response. Later that same year,

---

[17] *Ordinatio imperii*, chap. 1, in MGH *Capitularia* 1:271.
[18] Ibid., chap. 2, p. 271.
[19] Ibid., chaps. 4–8, 10, 13–16, pp. 271–73.
[20] Thegan, *GH*, chap. 21, p. 210. On the role of *dignitas* in early medieval politics, see Gerd Althoff, "Königsherrschaft und Konfliktbewältigung im 10. und 11. Jahrhundert," reprinted in Althoff, *Spielregeln*, 21–56. Karl Heinrich Krüger, "Herrschaftsnachfolge als Vater-Sohn-Konflikt," *FS* 36 (2002): 225–40, places the conflict between Louis the Pious and his sons within a broader context.
[21] *Ordinatio imperii*, chap. 17, in MGH *Capitularia* 1:273.

Bernard organized a conspiracy with many distinguished Frankish magnates, both lay nobles and bishops, to defend his regime south of the Alps.[22] Louis the Pious quickly overcame his nephew's rebellion, and he ordered Bernard to be blinded to remove any chance of his reclaiming the throne. But the emperor's henchmen bungled the procedure, causing Bernard to suffer in agony for several days before dying of his wounds. Such were the high stakes of rebellion in the Carolingian empire. Nevertheless, Bernard's conspiracy was an ominous foreshadowing of things to come. He had organized a serious rebellion within only several months of the *Ordinatio imperii;* Pippin of Aquitaine and Louis the German had much more time to plot how to undermine the 817 division plan.

THE MAKING OF A CAROLINGIAN PRINCE

While his brothers went off to rule Italy and Aquitaine in 817, the young Louis remained in the imperial entourage until he came of age.[23] Louis the German grew up during the highpoint of the Carolingian Renaissance, the educational, ecclesiastical, and cultural reforms aimed at reviving Latin letters and Christian learning throughout the empire.[24] Spending his early years at his father's court, Louis had access to the best education available to a layman in centuries. According to Regino, Louis was "sufficiently instructed not only in the secular disciplines, but in the ecclesiastical disciplines as well."[25] In the early Middle Ages, the "ecclesiastical disciplines" focused on the seven liberal arts: Latin grammar, rhetoric, and logic (together known as the *trivium*) as well as geometry, mathematics, astronomy, and music (the *quadrivium*). Louis seems to have been trilingual. His mother tongue was Frankish (a Germanic dialect), and he spoke early Romance, which he pre-

---

[22] *ARF,* s.a. 817, 818, pp. 147–48; Thomas F. X. Noble, "The Revolt of King Bernard of Italy in 817: Its Causes and Consequences," *Studi Medievali* 15 (1974): 315–26.

[23] Astronomer, *VH,* chap. 24, p. 356. Louis the Pious may have sent his son on a brief tour of Bavaria in 817–18 to introduce him to the magnates of his future kingdom; Astronomer, *VH,* chap. 29, p. 380. For the role of the court in the education and acculturation of young noblemen, see Matthew Innes, " 'A Place of Discipline': Carolingian Courts and Aristocratic Youth," in *Court Culture in the Early Middle Ages,* ed. Catharine Cubitt (Turnhout, 2003), 59–76.

[24] For the Carolingian Renaissance in general, see Rosamond McKitterick, ed., *Carolingian Culture: Emulation and Innovation* (Cambridge, 1994); John J. Contreni, "The Carolingian Renaissance: Education and Literary Culture," in *NCMH* 2: 709–57.

[25] Regino, *Chronicon,* s.a. 876, p. 110.

sumably learned as a young boy in Aquitaine.[26] Louis was also fluent in Latin—so much so that he composed Latin verse and dreamed in Latin, two signs of true linguistic fluency.[27] The young Louis had a tutor (*pedagogus*) from Bavaria named Egilolf, who presumably oversaw his education in the ecclesiastical disciplines.[28] Louis the Pious apparently selected Egilolf as his son's tutor because he had ties to an influential Bavarian family from the region around Freising, the Huosi, as well as to the powerful prefect of Bavaria, Audulf (799–818).[29] In this way Egilolf could prepare the young Bavarian king to rule his future kingdom with the support of the regional nobility.

The evidence suggests that Louis the German was not inclined toward speculative thinking or abstract philosophy. Instead, his intellectual interests focused on the Bible. "He possessed singular wisdom," Notker wrote, "that he always increased by turning his sharp mind to the constant study of the Scriptures."[30] Abbot Raban of Fulda (822–41), the most prolific biblical commentator of the ninth century, was pleased when he personally witnessed the young prince's Christian piety and learning, and he urged Louis to continue his study of the Scriptures to prepare himself to be king.[31] Louis's formal education probably focused on the books in Louis the Pious's court library, which contained numerous bibles, works of theology by the Church Fathers and Carolingian scholars, and classical texts such as Seneca's *Moral Letters* and Pliny's *Natural History*.[32] The few surviving books Louis is known to have possessed as a youth confirm the impression of his interest in the Scriptures and theology. He had a copy of Saint Ambrose's *On the Holy Spirit*, and he also possessed a beautiful Psalter, known today as the Ludwig Psalter, that would have served as his private book of prayer.[33]

Another surviving manuscript that belonged to the young Louis was a

[26] Louis demonstrated his fluency in both tongues at Strasbourg in 842 and Koblenz in 860: Nithard 3.5, pp. 35–37; *Conventus apud Confluentes*, in MGH *Capitularia* 2:157–58.

[27] For a surviving poem composed by Louis, see *Ad Baldonem*, in MGH *Poetae Latini* 2:643–44. Late in life, Louis dreamed that his father spoke to him *Latino eloquio: AF*, s.a. 874, p. 82. There is no evidence that Louis the German, unlike his father and grandfather, learned Greek: cf. Einhard, *VK*, chap. 25, p. 30; Thegan, *GH*, chap. 19, p. 200.

[28] *Freising* 397a.

[29] Concerning Egilolf and Audulf, see *DCharlemagne* 206; *Freising* 397a–c; Hermann Schreibmüller, "Audulf: Der frühest bezeugte Graf im Taubergau," *MJGK* 3 (1951): 53–69; Michael Mitterauer, *Karolingische Markgrafen im Südosten: Fränkische Reichsaristokratie und bayerischer Stammesadel im österreichischen Raum* (Vienna, 1963), 57–61, 134.

[30] Notker, *GK* 2.11, p. 68. Here Louis followed in the intellectual footsteps of his father: Thegan, *GH*, chap. 19, p. 200.

[31] Raban, *Epistolae*, nos. 18, 37, in MGH *Epistolae* 5:422, 474.

[32] Bernhard Bischoff, "The Court Library of Louis the Pious," in *Manuscripts and Libraries in the Age of Charlemagne*, by B. Bischoff, trans. Michael M. Gorman (Cambridge, 1994), 76–92.

[33] Schramm and Mütherich, *Denkmale*, 127, 239–40, nos. 34–35.

Louis the German's prayer book. This beautiful Psalter illuminated in the Franco-Saxon style was made for Louis the German at the monastery of St.-Omer in northern Francia in the second quarter of the ninth century. The illustration shows the dedication pages, with the beginning of the first psalm, "Beatus vir . . ." (Blessed is the man . . .).

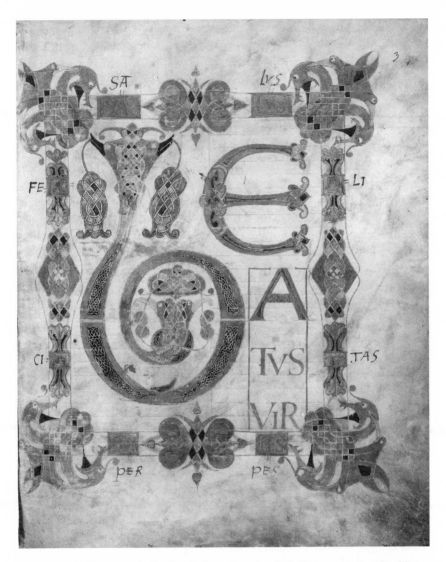

Written in gold letters in the borders is the acclamation "Hludowico regi vita salus felicitas perpes" (Everlasting life, health, and happiness to King Louis). The gold letters have become blurred from oxidation, and a later hand has written the acclamation in black letters. Staatsbibliothek zu Berlin—Preussischer Kulturbesitz, MS theol. lat. fol. 58, fols. 2v–3r.

copy of the *Sermon on the Creed against the Jews, Pagans, and Arians*, mistakenly ascribed to Saint Augustine. Adalram of Salzburg gave this theological treatise to the boy Louis, perhaps on the occasion of his visit to Louis the Pious's court in 823.[34] Although there were no pagans or Arians to speak of in the Carolingian empire, it is possible that Adalram selected the *Sermon on the Creed* to prepare the young Bavarian king for encounters with the numerous Jewish merchants who plied their trade along the Danube River.[35] The Carolingians guaranteed freedom of worship for the Jewish minority in Europe, and Louis the Pious made further decrees protecting Jews.[36] Yet, like many of his contemporaries, Louis the German probably felt uneasy about the Jews' rejection of Christ, since their disbelief forced Christians to question the truth of their own faith. What made the Jews especially problematic for Christians was their shared belief in the Old Testament, and, unlike the Christians, the Jews could study it in the original Hebrew instead of relying on Saint Jerome's Latin translation. To refine his understanding of the Old Testament, Raban of Fulda consulted the ancient works of the Jewish historian Josephus, and he also discussed the Scriptures with a Jewish scholar. Yet, in a letter to Louis, Raban felt it necessary to distance himself from the Jewish faith. He explained in his commentary on the book of Kings: "I inserted in many places the writing of the Jewish historian Josephus and also the opinions of a certain Jew who these days excels in the learning of the Law—not so that I might entice the unwilling reader into accepting the tradition of that people, but rather to leave these matters to the reader's judgment and examination."[37] Like Raban, Louis probably viewed the Jews with a combination of toleration, fascination, and mistrust.

Louis may have been interested in vernacular Frankish poetry as well as Latin literature. His copy of the *Sermon on the Creed* contains a unique vernacular poem known as the *Muspilli* (Judgment).[38] This fragmentary 103–line poem is found on the empty pages and lower margins of Louis's manu-

---

[34] BM 774.

[35] The early tenth-century "Inquisition on the Raffelstetten Tolls" largely equated merchants with Jews: "mercatores, id est Iudei et ceteri mercatores"; *Inquisitio de theloneis Raffelstettensis*, chap. 9, in MGH *Capitularia* 2:252. See further Herwig Wolfram, *Grenzen und Räume: Geschichte Österreichs vor seiner Entstehung* (Vienna, 1995), 324.

[36] Wallace-Hadrill, *Frankish Church*, 393–403.

[37] Raban, *Epistolae*, no. 18, in MGH *Epistolae* 5:423.

[38] On the *Muspilli*, see Wolfgang Haubrichs, *Geschichte der deutschen Literatur von den Anfängen bis zum Beginn der Neuzeit*, vol. 1: *Von den Anfängen zum hohen Mittelalter*, pt. 1: *Die Anfänge: Versuche volksspachiger Schriftlichkeit im frühen Mittelalter (c. 700–1050/60)* (Frankfurt, 1988), 385–89; Cyril Edwards, "German Vernacular Literature: A Survey," in McKitterick, *Carolingian Culture*, 148–50. For the rise of vernacular literary production during Louis's reign, see Dieter Geuenich, "Die volkssprachliche Überlieferung der Karolingerzeit aus der Sicht des Historikers," *DA* 39 (1983): 104–30.

script, and it combines vernacular heroic poetry with biblical and apocryphal accounts of the apocalypse and final judgment. It commences with a dramatic battle between armies of angels and demons for the soul of the deceased:

For as soon as the soul sets out on that road,
And leaves its body lying there,
Then an army comes from the starry heavens,
And another from the blackness of hell. There they clash together.
The soul must worry until the judgment arrives
About which army will take him away.
For if Satan's army triumphs,
It will then lead the soul to where it will suffer
In fire and gloom. That is the most ghastly fate.[39]

After this frightening vision of the soul's judgment, the *Muspilli* goes on to warn the reader to repent, abandon evil ways, and (echoing Carolingian legislation) avoid perverting justice in public courts by accepting bribes. The *Muspilli* was written into Louis's manuscript "in an unpracticed hand of the later ninth century, probably from court," suggesting that Louis may have copied it himself.[40] It is therefore possible that the *Muspilli* gives us a direct window into Louis's mind as a Frankish prince: his vernacular mother tongue, predilection for heroic poetry and military imagery, concern for the morality of government and the exercise of power, and preoccupation with the salvation of his soul.

This education based on Scripture and theology instilled Louis with a deep Christian piety. The young prince probably was influenced by his father's close adviser, Abbot Benedict of Aniane, a vigorous monastic leader under whose guidance Louis the Pious sought to enforce Benedictine monasticism throughout the empire.[41] Abbot Raban urged Louis the German to shun the "effeminacy of pleasures" and emulate the great figures of the Bible to earn the "distinction of manhood."[42] But this highly ascetic brand of Catholicism had the potential to create deep psychological tensions within the hearts of Frankish noblemen, since the demands of secular politics—wealth, sex (to produce heirs), ambition, and warfare—conflicted with

[39] *Muspilli*, ll. 1–10, in *Althochdeutsches Lesebuch*, ed. Wilhelm Braune, 16th ed. (Tübingen, 1979), 86.
[40] Bischoff, "Bücher am Hofe Ludwigs des Deutschen," 188.
[41] Mayke De Jong, "Carolingian Monasticism: The Power of Prayer," in *NCMH* 2:630–34.
[42] Raban, *Epistolae*, no. 34, in MGH *Epistolae* 5:468–69.

the monastic ideals of poverty, chastity, humility, obedience, and the renunciation of violence.[43] Moreover, the Church taught that legions of horrifying demons haunted this world and sought to win souls for eternal hellfire—or at least for long, agonizing stays in purgatory. Not even a great Church reformer such as Charlemagne was safe. The *Vision of Wetti*, written in the mid-820s at Reichenau, reported that a savage beast gnawed on Charlemagne's genitals in purgatory to punish him for his numerous concubines and illegitimate children.[44] Lying in bed at night, Louis worried about his soul and the souls of his relatives. On one occasion he had a horrifying dream of his father suffering in purgatory, an experience that disturbed him profoundly.[45] In response to these deep spiritual concerns, Louis, like many laymen and laywomen, embraced a highly monastic style of piety centered on prayer, fasting, penance, and devotion to relics and saints. Notker even went so far as to compare Louis to his monastic heroes, Saints Ambrose and Martin:

> With the exception of those things without which the worldly state cannot exist, that is marriage and the use of arms, in all things he proved himself very similar to or (if it is permissible to say so) even greater than Ambrose. He was Catholic by faith, exceptionally devoted to God, and an untiring friend, protector, and defender of the servants of Christ. . . . He was more devoted than all other men to prayer, fasts, and divine services. Following the example of Saint Martin, no matter what he was doing, he seemed to be praying as if in the presence of the Lord. He abstained from meat and gourmet foods on certain days, and during the time of litanies he was accustomed to walk barefoot to church behind the cross.[46]

Louis's Christian culture and learning shaped his understanding of politics. Everywhere the young prince turned, he was surrounded by courtly imagery and literature that glorified the Franks and the Carolingian kings in highly Christian, Roman, and imperial terms. The palace complex at Aachen, where Louis presumably spent much of his childhood, was a monument to Charlemagne's achievements, and it was adorned with classical columns, statues, and other treasures that his grandfather had carted off

---

[43] Janet L. Nelson, "Monks, Secular Men and Masculinity, c. 900," in *Masculinity in Medieval Europe*, ed. D. M. Hadley (London, 1999), 121–42; and, more generally, Julia M. H. Smith, "Religion and Lay Society," in *NCMH* 2:654–78.

[44] Heito, *Visio Wettini*, chap. 11, in MGH *Poetae Latini* 2:271.

[45] *AF*, s.a. 874, p. 82. Concerning this event, see chap. 9.

[46] Notker, *GK* 2.10–11, pp. 66, 68–69.

from Italy. While attending Mass in the Aachen church, the young Louis would have frequently gazed on his grandfather's sarcophagus and its grandiose inscription: "Under this tomb lies the body of Charles, the great and orthodox emperor, who gloriously expanded the kingdom of the Franks and reigned with great success for forty-seven years."[47] Louis the Pious's new large palace at Ingelheim was decorated with hundreds of columns and frescos that showed the great heroes of pagan antiquity such as Cyrus, Hannibal, and Alexander the Great succeeded by an even greater line of Christian rulers: Constantine the Great, Theodosius, Charles Martel, Pippin III, and Charlemagne.[48]

As a youth, Louis presumably also would have read (or at least heard discussions about) the numerous works of Carolingian historical writing that circulated at his father's palace. This court-centered royal historiography presented a triumphalist view of Frankish and Carolingian history that portrayed the Franks as God's new Chosen People and the Carolingians as the heirs of the Old Testament kings and Roman emperors.[49] The *Earlier Annals of Metz*, for example, which were written in approximately 806 with close connections to Charlemagne's court, gave a dramatic triumphal account of the rise of the Carolingians from Pippin II (d. 714) to Charlemagne that freely mixed the language of Frankish kingship and Roman emperorship.[50] Another work of Carolingian history that Louis may have read was Einhard's *Life of Charlemagne*, a copy of which circulated at Louis the Pious's court by 828.[51] Einhard painted a very Frankish picture of the great emperor (he consistently referred to Charlemagne as *rex* rather than *imperator*), and he stressed that Charlemagne's greatness came not from his imperial coronation but rather from his numerous conquests, which had doubled the size of the *regnum Francorum*.[52] This court art, architecture, and literature would have instilled in the young Louis the German a profound belief in God's favor for the Frankish people and his dynasty, a deep admiration for Charlemagne, and a sense that the symbols and language of the late Roman empire were the natural trappings of Frankish kingship.

As a youth Louis also received his training in what Regino called the

---

[47] Einhard, *VK*, chap. 31, pp. 35–36.

[48] Ermold, *In Honorem*, bk. 4, pp. 156–64.

[49] McKitterick, "Political Ideology," 162–74.

[50] Paul Fouracre and Richard A. Gerberding, trans., *Late Merovingian France: History and Historiography, 640–720* (Manchester, 1996), 340–49; Yitzhak Hen, "The Annals of Metz and the Merovingian Past," in Hen and Innes, *Uses of the Past*, 175–90.

[51] For debates about the dating of the *Life of Charlemagne*, see Paul Edward Dutton, ed. and trans., *Charlemagne's Courtier: The Complete Einhard* (Peterborough, 1998), xviii–xxiv.

[52] Einhard, *VK*, preface, chap. 15, pp. 1, 17–18.

"secular disciplines": horseback riding, wielding weapons, and military leadership. For a model of vigorous manhood, Louis need look no farther than his own father, who was known for his "strong chest, broad shoulders, and arms so powerful that no one could equal him in shooting a bow or in throwing a spear."[53] One can get a sense of Louis's military training from an abridgement of the late Roman military manual of Vegetius, *On the Military Sciences*, which Raban composed during the mid-ninth century.[54] In this abridgement of Vegetius, Raban outlined a rigorous daily regimen for the young noblemen at court. Raban stressed that the goal of a nobleman's military training was to become a skilled soldier on horseback (*eques*). A young nobleman began by practicing on a wooden horse, at first climbing up unarmed and then carrying his shield, sword, and spear.[55] Ultimately, he was expected to leap on his horse from all directions while fully armed with his sword unsheathed. This tough secular ideal of manhood was aggressively drilled into young boys. Raban wrote:

> Today boys and adolescents are raised in the households of princes so that they learn to endure harsh and adverse conditions and suffer hunger, cold, and the heat of the sun. For if a boy progresses beyond this age without such training and discipline, his body quickly becomes lazy. Thus the well-known popular saying: "By puberty one can become a mounted soldier, but rarely if ever at an older age." This is because a person maintains the discipline learned at an early age, since it seems natural while growing up amid the other enjoyments and pleasures of those years. It is better that a trained adolescent never reach the age of fighting than live beyond it without such training.[56]

The political culture of Louis's world was therefore chivalric in the original sense of the word. "Chivalry" arose out of the Latin term for a warhorse, *caballus*, and a Frankish nobleman like Louis was "horsy" in that he spent much of his life riding, talking about, caring for, and smelling of horses.

In addition to riding, Raban enumerated other skills a young nobleman was expected to learn: fighting with a shield, sword, and spear, archery, and swimming.[57] Boys armed with heavy wicker shields and clubs were to train

[53] Thegan, *GH*, chap. 19, p. 200.

[54] Raban, *De procinctu Romanae miliciae*, ed. Ernst Dümmler, *ZDA* 15 (1872): 443–51. Raban composed this work for Louis the German's nephew, Lothar II.

[55] Ibid., chap. 12, p. 448. On the role of horses in the Frankish world, see Bernard Bachrach, "*Caballus et Caballarius* in Medieval Warfare," in *The Study of Chivalry*, ed. Howell Chickering and Thomas H. Seiler (Kalamazoo, 1988), 173–211.

[56] Raban, *De procinctu Romanae miliciae*, chap. 3, p. 444.

[57] Ibid., chaps. 6–9, pp. 446–47.

ETSYRIAM SOBAL· ETCONVERTIT
IOAB· ETPERCUSSIT EDOM INVAL
LESALINARUM·XII MILIA·

An aristocratic society obsessed with armor, weapons, and horses. This illumination from the Golden Psalter of St.-Gall (late ninth century) shows the military exploits of King David's general Joab, as mentioned in the title of Psalm 59: "et convertit Ioab et percussit Edom[aeam] in valle Salinarum XII milia" (and when Joab returned and killed twelve thousand Edomites in the Valley of Salt). The artist has rendered Joab as a Frankish lord (shown with a beard, flowing red cloak, and spear couched forward) surrounded by his retinue of vassals and standard-bearer holding aloft a dragon banner. Stiftsbibliothek St. Gallen, Codex 22, p. 140.

by attacking wooden posts while leaping forward, backward, and side to side.[58] The favorite pastime of Frankish noblemen, hunting, brought together in a thrilling and dangerous way the skills required for riding and fighting.[59] Through hunting a nobleman learned to wield his weapons with deadly effect while riding hard over rough terrain, often in pursuit of dangerous animals. "Hunters of stags, boars, and bears . . . are especially suited to warfare," Raban noted, "because they have greater toughness, physical strength, and rigorous training."[60] Louis the Pious made frequent hunting trips to the Ardennes Forest, the Vosges Mountains, and the region around Frankfurt, and as a youth, Louis the German probably accompanied his father on many of these excursions.[61] Through hunting he would have become accustomed to danger, violence, and the sight of gore at an early age.

The most demanding aspect of Louis's military training would have been learning how to organize and command large armies effectively. Military historians of earlier generations painted a picture of Carolingian warfare as the dawn of the "feudal knight," while more recently some have presented Carolingian campaigns as "primitive war" involving small-scale "heroic" raids in search of easy plunder.[62] In reality Carolingian warfare was far more complex than these models suggest. Carolingian armies often combined infantry and mounted soldiers, and the key to their success was organization and tactical flexibility. Thus Raban emphasized the importance of marching in tight formation, reconnaissance, surprise attacks, laying siege to fortified centers, and overcoming defensive ditches and barricades.[63] A copy of Vegetius's *On the Military Sciences* later circulated at Louis the German's court, and it is possible that he turned to this late Roman military manual for models of strategy, organization, and logistics.[64]

[58] Ibid., chap. 6, p. 446.

[59] Einhard, *VK*, chap. 22, p. 27; Pierre Riché, *Daily Life in the World of Charlemagne*, trans. Jo Ann McNamara (Philadelphia, 1988), 75–76; Jörg Jarnut, "Die frühmittelalterliche Jagd unter rechts- und sozialgeschichtlichen Aspekten," *SS Spoleto* 31 (1985): 765–808.

[60] Raban, *De procinctu Romanae miliciae*, chap. 4, p. 445.

[61] Thegan, *GH*, chap. 19, p. 204.

[62] For critiques of the feudal knight model, see Bernard S. Bachrach, "Charles Martel, Mounted Shock Combat, the Stirrup, and Feudalism," *SMRH* 7 (1970): 49–75; idem, "Medieval Military Historiography," in *Companion to Historiography*, ed. Michael Bentley (London, 1997), 203–20; Fouracre, *Charles Martel*, 145–50. For the plundering raids model, see Reuter, "Plunder and Tribute," 75–91. Bachrach, *Early Carolingian Warfare*, and Halsall, *Warfare and Society*, esp. 71–110, offer two important recent studies of Carolingian warfare.

[63] Raban, *De procinctu Romanae miliciae*, chap. 5, p. 445.

[64] Bischoff, "Bücher am Hofe Ludwigs des Deutschen," 211.

The need to master the art of military leadership was particularly pressing for Louis, since as the future king of Bavaria he was to assume responsibility for the empire's volatile southeastern border with the Slavs. Charlemagne's conquest of the Avar empire to the east of Bavaria precipitated a century of turmoil among the Slavs in central eastern Europe, forcing him and his successors to intervene repeatedly in the Bavarian frontier provinces of Upper and Lower Pannonia.[65] Louis the German witnessed the complexities of frontier warfare in the east during his father's prolonged conflict with Liudewit, the rebel Slavic ruler of Lower Pannonia.[66] In the years 819–23, Liudewit led a serious uprising against Frankish overlordship and attempted to create an independent Slavic kingdom that encompassed Lower Pannonia, Carantania, Carniola, and Dalmatia. Only after repeated campaigns did Louis the Pious overcome Liudewit and restore a semblance of order to the Bavarian marches. Liudewit's bold attempt to create an independent Slavic kingdom must have impressed on the young Louis the necessity of good military leadership and planning for maintaining control of his future kingdom's frontiers.

Louis the German got his first taste of frontier warfare in a campaign against the Bretons when, in 824, the Breton ruler Wihomarc broke his treaty with the Franks and rebelled.[67] That autumn, Louis the Pious gathered Frankish troops and divided them into three armies. The emperor led one himself, assigned his son Pippin of Aquitaine and Count Hugh of Tours to joint command of the second, and placed Louis the German (technically still a *puer*) and Count Matfrid of Orléans in charge of the third. When the Frankish armies invaded, the Bretons prudently retreated into the mountains and forests and refused to meet the Franks in open battle. For over a month the Frankish armies laid waste to the region with fire and sword, eventually forcing the Bretons to surrender, pledge loyalty, and hand over hostages. In this way the 824 Breton campaign gave Louis firsthand experience in the classic strategies of Carolingian frontier warfare: invasion with multiple armies, harrying of the countryside to destroy the rebels' food supply, and the taking of hostages to guarantee future loyalty. This expedi-

---

[65] For Charlemagne's conquest of the Avars, see Wolfram, *Grenzen und Räume*, 233–41; Walter Pohl, *Die Awarenkriege Karls des Grossen 788–803* (Vienna, 1988). P. M. Barford, *The Early Slavs* (Ithaca, 2001), offers the best survey of early Slavic history in English.

[66] *ARF*, s.a. 818–23, pp. 149–53, 155–56, 158, 161; Wolfram, *Grenzen und Räume*, 242–47; Charles R. Bowlus, *Franks, Moravians, and Magyars: The Struggle for the Middle Danube, 788–907* (Philadelphia, 1995), 60–71.

[67] *ARF*, s.a. 824, p. 165; Ermold, *In Honorem*, bk. 4, pp. 152–54; Julia M. H. Smith, *Province and Empire* (Cambridge, 1992), 64–67.

tion was an appropriate initiation to warfare for Louis, since he would spend much of his adult life carrying out similar campaigns against the Slavs in the east.

Louis the German came of age around the year 825. At that time Louis the Pious presumably bestowed on his son the badge of secular manhood—the swordbelt—during a formal ceremony.[68] By all reports, Louis had become a talented and capable prince: handsome, intelligent, prudent, eloquent, and pious.[69] Although these were stock Carolingian royal virtues, there is no reason to think that contemporaries were inventing them out of thin air. Authors may have exaggerated Louis's personal qualities, but they could not falsify them altogether, since they wrote for audiences who knew Louis and his family. Above all, contemporaries placed unusual emphasis on Louis's qualities as a soldier: his physical strength, toughness, valor, and devotion to the military life. Nithard, who was a cousin and admirer of Louis, described him as "of medium physique, very handsome, skilled in every exercise, daring, generous, prudent, and eloquent."[70] Notker, who had reliable information about Louis through his abbot, Grimald, similarly portrayed him as possessing a good physique, eyes shining like stars, a deep booming voice, and extraordinary physical strength.[71] Notker mentioned that Louis's sons were tall and blond, suggesting that Louis himself had a large stature and fair hair.[72] Notker admired Louis's charm and sense of humor, but he juxtaposed these good-natured qualities with his ability to command obedience with a glance of his piercing eyes.[73] In imitation of Charlemagne, Louis reportedly preferred simple Frankish woolen clothing and iron armor to luxurious fashions, and he berated soldiers he caught wearing jewelry or precious attire.[74] Regino depicted Louis as a model Carolingian, and he likewise called attention to his devotion to the military life:

[68] On the Frankish ritual of belt giving, see Leyser, "Early Medieval Canon Law," 51–71; Le Jan, "Frankish Giving of Arms," 281–309.

[69] For an assessment of Louis's personality that emphasizes his piety, see Wilfried Hartmann, "Ludwig der Deutsche—Portrait eines wenig bekannten Königs," in *LDZ*, ed. Hartmann, 1–26.

[70] Nithard, 3.6, p. 37. Note that Nithard also was describing Louis's younger half brother, Charles the Bald.

[71] Notker, *GK* 2.11, 2.18, pp. 67–68, 88–89. For Grimald's royal service during the 840s–860s: Ratpert, *Casus sancti Galli*, chaps. 8–9, pp. 190–218; Ermanrich, *Epistola ad Grimaldum*, in MGH *Epistolae* 5:536–37, 539; Kehr, "Kanzlei," 8–13; Josef Fleckenstein, *Die Hofkapelle der deutschen Könige*, vol. 1: *Grundlegung: Die Karolingische Hofkapelle* (Stuttgart, 1959), 170–76. Notker personally saw Louis on at least one occasion when Louis visited St.-Gall, probably in 857: Notker, *GK* 1.34, p. 47; Ernst Tremp, "Ludwig der Deutsche und das Kloster St. Gallen," in *LDZ*, ed. Hartmann, 142–45.

[72] Notker, *GK*, 1.34, p. 47.

[73] Ibid., 2.11, 2.18, pp. 69–70.

[74] Ibid., 2.17, pp. 87–88.

He was a most Christian prince, Catholic by faith, and adequately instructed not only in secular disciplines, but in ecclesiastical disciplines as well. He was the most zealous administrator in matters of religion, peace, and justice. He was very cunning by nature, extremely prudent in counsel, and guided by sober discretion in the giving and revoking of public offices. He was unusually successful in battles and more devoted to the equipment of battle than the splendor of banquets. For him the instruments of war were the greatest treasure, and he loved the hardness of iron more than the glitter of gold.[75]

According to Regino, even in old age Louis still possessed unusual toughness (*duricia*) and warlike spirit (*animositas*) that commanded the respect of the nobles.[76]

Of all Regino's comments, the most striking is his description of Louis as "extremely cunning by nature" [ingenio callidissimus]. *Callidus* could mean "shrewd," "skilled," or "astute," but it also carried with it strong overtones of cunning, slyness, and craftiness. Although cunning became more commonly cited as a royal virtue in the tenth century, it was unusual to come across this characteristic in the canon of Carolingian attributes because of its negative connotations.[77] Of course, all Carolingian rulers out of necessity had to possess a good amount of political cunning to survive, but this personality trait seems to have been especially pronounced in Louis. The imperial librarian, Gerward, likewise emphasized Louis's ability to plot cunningly and lay traps for his adversaries, while the *Annals of Fulda* stressed his cleverness and trickery in diplomacy and warfare.[78] Indeed, political cunning and with it an insatiable desire for power were to be the defining characteristics of Louis's career. Even Regino, who admired Louis, had to admit that he could be shockingly ruthless: "forgetting brotherhood and alliances of blood, forgetting pact[s] . . . made through mutual agreement, indeed forgetting oaths by which he had bound himself with solemn promises before God."[79] As another chronicler put it, Louis was determined to "keep a firm grip on supreme royal power" against all rivals.[80]

Louis's cunning, Realpolitik, and desire for power must be seen within the context of the aristocratic ethos of dignity. *Dignitas* was at the heart of

---

[75] Regino, *Chronicon*, s.a. 876, p. 110.
[76] Ibid., s.a. 870, pp. 100–101.
[77] Heinrich Fichtenau, *Living in the Tenth Century*, trans. Patrick J. Geary (Chicago, 1991), 168–69, 406–9.
[78] *AX*, s.a. 834, p. 9; *AF*, s.a. 848, 863, pp. 37, 56–57.
[79] Regino, *Chronicon*, s.a. 866, p. 90.
[80] *Adonis Continuatio*, 324–25.

Carolingian political culture. As Regino emphasized, dignity was a social measurement of a man's nobility, courage, wisdom, and ultimately power.[81] Dignity dictated who sat at the head of the banquet hall, wore the most splendid clothes, had the largest retinue of vassals, gave the most magnificent gifts, and had the greatest political influence. For a nobleman to suffer an insult without avenging it was to lose face, respect, and status, and competition over *dignitas* therefore was a constant source of political discord and turmoil in the kingdom. The Carolingians shared in this aristocratic ethos of dignity, and it therefore is not surprising that Thegan identified Louis's sense of *dignitas* as the root cause of his outrage over the *Ordinatio imperii*.[82] Because Charlemagne had achieved the greatest extent of Carolingian power, he naturally became the yardstick against which Louis and other ninth-century Carolingians measured themselves. In this way, Louis's sense of dignity was intertwined with his emulation of his famous grandfather. As Notker summed up, Louis "was conscious of his dignity, and he scorned to stand second to anyone but Emperor [Charlemagne]."[83]

Louis's political cunning did not necessarily contradict his deep Christian piety. Although people today usually see these qualities as antithetical, to the Carolingian mind they could be two sides of the same coin. The Franks believed in a sacred continuum of power that originated with God in heaven and descended down to the king on earth. For this reason, ninth-century people tended to see a ruler's terrestrial power as the reflection of his moral qualities and favor with God. This was the central message of the Old Testament: that throughout history, God rewarded the righteous and destroyed the wicked. As a result, Louis would have seen the accumulation of power as the inevitable corollary to his sincere piety. Louis especially would have imbibed this mindset through reading and rereading the psalms in the Ludwig Psalter. Because medieval people believed that King David had written the psalms, that Old Testament book offered a prince such as Louis the fundamental framework for understanding his special relationship with God. The second psalm, for example, placed these words on David's—and therefore on Louis's—lips:

I am established king by the Lord upon His holy mountain of Zion, and I
    speak His decree.
The Lord said to me, "You are my son. Today I have begotten you.
Ask Me, and I will make all the peoples your inheritance and the ends of the
    earth your possession.

81 Regino, *Chronicon*, s.a. 888, p. 129.
82 Thegan, *GH*, chap. 21, p. 210.
83 Notker, *GK* 2.10, p. 66.

You will smash the other kings with a rod of iron and break them like a potter's
   vessel."
So now understand, O kings, and judges of the earth be warned:
Serve the Lord in fear and praise Him with trembling.
Follow His teachings and the paths of justice so that the Lord does not become
   angry,
For His wrath is quickly kindled. Blessed are those who seek refuge in Him.

Behind Louis's lifelong pursuit of power seems to have been his belief in
God's shaping of his destiny, just as God had shaped the destiny of King
David.

FROM PRINCE TO KING

   Louis the Pious dispatched his namesake to Bavaria in 825, and he arrived in his kingdom the following year.[84] As king of Bavaria, Louis ruled a
rich and well-organized province with a distinctive history and strong independent political identity.[85] The region had been a Roman frontier
province, and the remnants of classical civilization were visible across the
countryside: Roman roads, villas and estates, pockets of Romance-speaking
populations, and fortresses along the old Danube frontier such as Regensburg, Passau, and Lorch. The Lech River marked Bavaria's western boundary with Alemannia, and to the south the Alps separated Bavaria from Italy.
North of the Danube was the region known as the Nordgau, with the two
important royal estates of Lauterhofen and Ingolstadt. To the east of
Bavaria were the eastern marches of Upper Pannonia, Lower Pannonia,
Carantania, and Carniola—collectively known as the Eastland (*plaga orientalis*)—inhabited by a mixed population of Slavs, Avars, Bavarians, and
Franks. Bavaria's political stability depended on control of this volatile fron-
tier region.

   [84] The *ARF*, s.a. 825, p. 168, state that Louis the Pious sent Louis the German to
Bavaria in August 825, although the Bavarian king was still at Aachen in late January 826;
BM 824. Louis the German's diplomas calculated the beginning of his reign as falling between March 27 and May 27, 826: Dümmler, *GOR* 1:25 and nn. 3, 5, 6; Eiten, *Unterkönigtum*, 117–18; Bigott, *Ludwig der Deutsche*, 54. In early June 826, Hitto of Freising's
chancery began dating its charters "in the year when King Louis, the son and namesake
of Emperor Louis, came to Bavaria"; *Freising* 532–36.
   [85] On early medieval Bavaria, see esp. Kurt Reindel, "Grundlegung: Das Zeitalter der
Agilolfinger (bis 788)," in *Handbuch der bayerischen Geschichte*, 2nd ed., ed. Max Spindler
(Munich, 1981), 99–245; Wolfram, *Grenzen und Räume*, 71–138.

During the seventh and early eighth centuries, a Frankish dynasty known as the Agilolfings had ruled Bavaria as independent dukes. Under the Agilolfings Bavaria had become a prosperous and powerful polity, and they created a strong ducal regime with the help of the Church. They established five Bavarian bishoprics (Freising, Passau, Regensburg, Salzburg, and Säben), founded numerous monasteries (including Kremsmünster, Niederalteich, Mondsee, Innichen, and Mattsee), held ecclesiastical reform synods, and sent out missionaries to convert the Slavs of neighboring Carantania. Because the Agilolfings were serious rivals, Charlemagne resolved to eliminate them. In 788, through the use of largely trumped-up charges of infidelity, Charlemagne deposed the last Agilolfing duke, Tassilo III, and imprisoned him and his son.[86] Bavaria had become part of the Carolingian empire.

Louis arrived in Bavaria during a period of mounting crisis in the southeast. The defeat of the Slavic rebel Liudewit in 823 had not ended the instability in the region, and a new rival of the Franks soon emerged—the Bulgars.[87] The Bulgars were a warlike Turkic-speaking people from the Asiatic steppes north of the Black Sea, and they had migrated into the fertile lower Danube plain in the later seventh century. Ruled by a monarch known as the khan, the Bulgars created an empire on the doorsteps of Byzantium. The ambitious Khan Ormurtag (ca. 815–31) established a thirty-year peace treaty with Constantinople, streamlined the administration of the Bulgar empire, and built a vast royal capital at Pliska with massive walls, paved streets, sewers, and a fortified palace. Ormurtag also expanded his borders up the Danube, probably as far as Belgrade, thereby threatening Frankish control of Lower Pannonia.[88] To secure his conquests, in 824 Ormurtag sent ambassadors to Louis the Pious requesting a peace treaty that would establish clear borders between their two empires.

Louis the Pious rejected Ormurtag's overtures, however, and the Bulgar khan responded swiftly.[89] In 827, Ormurtag sent a fleet up the Drava River, the waterway that separated Upper from Lower Pannonia. The Bulgar force was victorious: it attacked local Slavic populations with fire and sword, expelled the Slavic dukes who ruled as clients of the Franks, and replaced them

---

[86] Collins, *Charlemagne*, 81–88; Stuart Airlie, "Narratives of Triumph and Rituals of Submission: Charlemagne's Mastering of Bavaria," *TRHS*, 6th ser., 9 (1999): 93–119.

[87] Concerning the Bulgars, see Jonathan Shepard, "Slavs and Bulgars," in *NCMH* 2:229–37; Tsvetelin Stepanov, "The Bulgar Title ΚΑΝΑΣΥΒΙΓΙ: Reconstructing the Notions of Divine Kingship in Bulgaria, AD 822–836," *EME* 10 (2001): 1–19; Barford, *Early Slavs*, 75–76, 91–94.

[88] Wolfram, *Salzburg*, 312–13.

[89] *ARF*, s.a. 824–26, pp. 164–70.

with Bulgar governors.[90] At that time, the two Frankish magnates in charge of the southeastern frontiers were Counts Baldric and Gerold (II), whom the *Royal Frankish Annals* described as "guards of the Avar border" and "prefects of the Pannonian frontier."[91] Balderic was the Frankish duke of Friuli, while Gerold was the new prefect of the Bavarian Eastland.[92] At the Aachen assembly in February 828, Louis the Pious blamed the loss of Lower Pannonia on Balderic of Friuli's "cowardice."[93] Louis the Pious therefore revoked Balderic's honors and divided the march of Friuli into four separate counties: Carantania, Carniola, Istria, and a now greatly reduced Friuli.[94]

Although the emperor justified Balderic's downfall on his cowardice, evidence suggests that Louis the German and Prefect Gerold played a role in bringing it about. Both Louis and Gerold were present at the Aachen assembly at which Balderic was stripped of his power, and without question they were the chief beneficiaries of his overthrow.[95] The province of Carantania at this time passed into the control of the Bavarian king and his eastern prefect, something that could not have happened without the dissection of the Friulian march. Louis secured his control of that region by replacing its indigenous Slavic client rulers (*duces*) with Frankish-Bavarian counts.[96] Louis could justify the annexation of Carantania on the basis of the *Ordinatio imperii*, which explicitly included Carantania as part of his Bavarian kingdom.[97] But as the ruler of Italy, Lothar had controlled Friuli (including Carantania) since 817. Balderic's downfall in 828 and the resulting Bavarian annexation of Carantania therefore represented Louis's first aggressive move against his eldest brother. With the removal of the powerful Friulian duke, Louis the German took command of the counteroffensive against the Bulgars. In 828, Louis led a campaign against the Bulgars and succeeded in driving them out of Lower Pannonia, soon ending Ormurtag's attempts to annex that region.[98] The young king of Bavaria could boast his first independent military success.

In the midst of these events, Louis also asserted his control over another

---

90 *ARF*, s.a. 827, p. 173.

91 *ARF*, s.a. 826, pp. 169–70. On Balderic and Gerold, see Philippe Depreux, *Prosopographie de l'entourage de Louis le Pieux (781–840)* (Sigmaringen, 1997), 119, 210–11.

92 *ARF*, s.a. 819, 820, pp. 151, 153.

93 *ARF*, s.a. 828, p. 174.

94 Wolfram, *Grenzen und Räume*, 247; idem, *Salzburg*, 308–10.

95 BM 850.

96 *Conversio*, chap. 10, p. 121; Wolfram, *Salzburg*, 306–10.

97 *Ordinatio imperii*, chap. 2, in MGH *Capitularia* 1:271.

98 The Bulgars attacked Lower Pannonia again in 829 but apparently could not recapture the region; *AF*, s.a. 828–29, pp. 25–26. Raban ordered his monks at Fulda to chant one thousand Masses for the success of Louis's 828 Bulgar campaign; *Epistolarum Fuldensium fragmenta*, in MGH *Epistolae* 5:518.

of Bavaria's strategic frontier regions—the Brenner Pass, the Alpine route that connected southern Bavaria with northern Italy. On December 31, 827, at the Alpine monastery of Innichen (southeast of the Brenner Pass), a nobleman named Quartinus made a major grant of properties to Innichen.[99] Present at the transaction were Louis's two Bavarian supporters, Bishop Hitto of Freising (who also was abbot of Innichen) and Count William.[100] Quartinus's grant to Innichen included a number of strategic estates along the Brenner route: the fortress (*castellum*) at Vipiteno, a large cluster of estates near Vipiteno, an estate near Bolzano, and another near Innsbruck. Quartinus's grant again illustrates Louis's emerging rivalry with Lothar. Balderic's downfall and the transfer of Carantania to the kingdom of Bavaria were sure to anger Lothar, and Louis therefore needed to defend the Alpine passes against a possible attack from Italy. Quartinus's grant to Hitto of Freising accomplished just that, and the bishops of Freising would guarantee Louis's control of the Brenner Pass for the remainder of his reign. As early as 828, Louis and his Bavarian supporters were preparing for open conflict with his eldest brother.

Louis's efforts to win Carantania and the Brenner Pass highlight his vulnerability to Lothar in the late 820s. Lothar, who was some fifteen years older than Louis, had a tremendous head start on his political career. In 821 Louis the Pious had reconfirmed the *Ordinatio imperii*, thus guaranteeing Lothar's status as co-emperor and heir to the bulk of the empire. Later in 821, Louis the Pious arranged a marriage between Lothar and Ermengard, the daughter of the powerful Count Hugh of Tours.[101] Within a few years, Lothar had a male heir, whom he named after his father (and who would become the future Emperor Louis II of Italy, 840–75). In Italy Lothar had established a strong regime: he enforced justice and decreed laws, and on Easter Day in 823 in Rome, Pope Paschal re-crowned him emperor and augustus.[102] Moreover, since the early 820s, Lothar issued his own diplomas for his Italian supporters with a title that heralded his status as co-emperor:

---

[99] *Freising* 550a. Reflecting the importance of this grant, Quartinus confirmed it twice in the following months: on January 17, 828, at the fortress of Vipiteno in the presence of Bishops Hitto of Freising and Arpeo of Säben and Count William; and again on July 4, 828, at nearby Bressanone in the presence of Arpeo and William; *Freising* 550b–c. Concerning this grant, see Bowlus, *Franks, Moravians, and Magyars*, 95–98, although our interpretations differ.

[100] Several months earlier, Bishop Hitto and Count William had held an assembly at Linz with some Slavic nobles at the command of Louis's eastern prefect, Gerold; *Freising* 548.

[101] *ARF*, s.a. 821, pp. 155–56; Astronomer, *VH*, chap. 34, pp. 402–5; Konecny, "Frauen," 94–95.

[102] *ARF*, s.a. 823, pp. 160–61.

"Lothar Augustus, son of the unconquered lord Emperor Louis."[103] Louis's other brother Pippin likewise had a considerable lead: he had ruled Aquitaine since 814 and married in 822, and his first son (the future Pippin II of Aquitaine) was born soon thereafter.[104]

Louis quickly began to establish his own independent regime in Bavaria. He resided mainly at Regensburg, a city that possessed all the benefits of a civilized urban capital with deep Roman roots.[105] Regensburg was a large second-century Roman fortress defended by high stone walls, each with a central fortified gate. The entire fortress had a rectangular perimeter of 1,770 by 1,475 feet and encompassed an area of about sixty acres. By the eighth century, Regensburg had become the capital of the Agilolfing dukes, and in 739 the city formally became a bishopric. Charlemagne confirmed Regensburg's standing as the political capital of Bavaria by residing there during his annexation of Bavaria and the wars with the Avars. Within Regensburg's walls were a royal palace and a cathedral dedicated to Saint Peter, while outside were the royal monastery of St.-Emmeram and a port on the Danube. A rich nexus of royal estates supplied the city with food. As a former Roman fortress, Regensburg was situated on the network of Roman roads leading to Upper Pannonia, Alemannia, and the Brenner Pass.

At Regensburg, Louis surrounded himself with the ceremony and symbolism of a traditional Carolingian king. In 826 or early 827, the chancery of Baturich of Regensburg compiled a pontifical (a Mass book for a bishop) for ceremonies at the court of the new Bavarian king. Baturich had close ties to Louis: he was bishop of Louis's Bavarian capital, and in 833 Louis appointed Baturich his archchaplain. Baturich's pontifical contains royal acclamations (*laudes regiae*) that were to be chanted for Louis during the celebration of the Mass and other ceremonial occasions at court.[106] Royal acclamations were a liturgical prayer for a Carolingian ruler that situated his kingship

---

[103] Lothar's first surviving diploma dates December 18, 822; *DLoI* 1. For Lothar's imperial ideology, see Elina Screen, "The Importance of Being Emperor: Lothar I and the Frankish Civil War, 840–843," *EME* 12 (2003): 25–51.

[104] Pippin of Aquitaine married the daughter of Count Theodbert of Madrie in 822; Astronomer, *VH*, chap. 35, pp. 410–11. On Pippin of Aquitaine's career, see Roger Collins, "Pippin I and the Kingdom of Aquitaine," in *CH*, ed. Godman and Collins, 363–89.

[105] On early medieval Regensburg, see Peter Schmid, *Regensburg: Stadt der Könige und Herzöge im Mittelalter* (Kallmünz, 1977); Carlrichard Brühl, *Palatium und Civitas: Studien zur Profantopographie spätantiker Civitates vom 3. bis zum 13. Jahrhundert*, vol. 2: *Belgica I, beide Germanien und Raetia II* (Cologne, 1990), 219–55.

[106] Munich, Clm 14510, fols. 39v–41r. On royal acclamations, see Ernst Kantorowicz, *Laudes Regiae: A Study in Liturgical Acclamations and Medieval Ruler Worship* (Berkeley, 1946). The royal acclamations date the compilation of Baturich's pontifical to 826 or early 827, since they mention Pope Eugene II (824–27) but not Louis's wife, Emma, whom Louis married in 827.

within the sacred hierarchy of heavenly and terrestrial power. They had a triumphant, militaristic tone to them, and they culminated with the refrain "Christ conquers! Christ rules! Christ commands!" On Christian feast days two singers and the entire choir recited the royal acclamations responsively. The acclamations in Baturich's pontifical, each line of which was to be chanted three times, read in part:

Hear us Christ: grant life to our lord Eugene [824–27], by God's decree the
    highest pontiff and universal pope!
Savior of the world: You must help him!
Hear us Christ: grant life and victory to our lord Augustus Louis [the Pious],
    the great and pacific emperor crowned by God!
Saint Mary: You must help him!
Hear us Christ: grant life to his most excellent sons the kings!
Saint Peter: You must help them!
Hear us Christ: grant life and victory to our lord King Louis [the German]!
Saint Paul: You must help him!
Hear us Christ: grant life and victory to the army of the Franks!
Saint Andrew: You must help them!
Hear us Christ: grant life to our lord Baturich, the bishop chosen by God!
Saint Emmeram: You must help him!

Although these acclamations for Louis were highly formulaic, they reflected the political ideology of his court. By describing all of Louis the Pious's sons as kings (*reges*) and naming only Louis the Pious as emperor, they flagrantly ignored the *Ordinatio imperii* and Lothar's status of co-emperor. From the outset, therefore, the ceremonies of Louis's court suggested his rejection of the 817 succession plan.

Baturich's pontifical also contains two coronation blessings (*ordines*) that presumably were used during a formal crowning of Louis as king of Bavaria.[107] Since the elevation of Pippin III to the throne in 751, coronations and ceremonial crown-wearings had become important royal rituals for

[107] Munich, Clm 14510, fols. 72v–74r; *Ordines coronationis Franciae: Texts and Ordines for the Coronation of Frankish and French Kings and Queens in the Middle Ages*, ed. Richard A. Jackson (Philadelphia, 1995), 1:66–68. The fact that no chronicler reported a coronation for Louis has led scholars to doubt that he was crowned, contributing to the false impression that the east Frankish kingdom was a ceremonial backwater during the ninth century; Dümmler, *GOR* 1:26; Eiten, *Unterkönigtum*, 118; Percy Ernst Schramm, "Salbung und Krönung bei den Ostfranken bis zur Thronbesteigung König Heinrichs I," in *Kaiser, Könige und Päpste: Gesammelte Aufsätze zur Geschichte des Mittelalters* (Stuttgart, 1968), 2:287–302; Timothy Reuter, *Germany in the Early Middle Ages* (London, 1991), 120; Kasten, *Königssöhne*, 196.

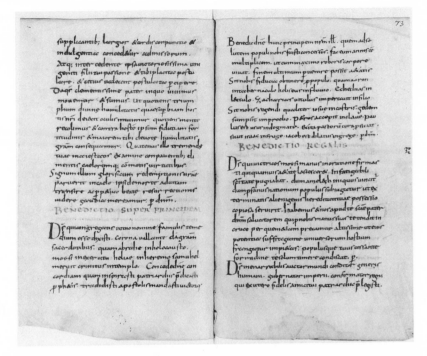

Coronation blessings (*ordines*). These blessings, titled "Benedictio super principem" (Blessing for the prince) and "Benedictio regalis" (Royal blessing), are found in a liturgical manuscript that was made in 826 or 827 for Bishop Baturich of Regensburg. These *ordines* may have been used for a coronation ceremony when Louis the German arrived at Regensburg in 826 to take up the kingship over Bavaria. Bayerische Staatsbibliothek, Clm 14510, fols. 72v—73r.

sanctifying the power of the Carolingian kings and setting them apart from the rest of the nobility.[108] The texts in Baturich's pontifical were based on the oldest surviving Carolingian coronation blessings that date to Charlemagne's reign, thus placing Louis's kingship within the tradition of his predecessors.[109] One blessing read:

> Ineffable God . . . , through the intercession of all the saints, richly reward the distinguished King [Louis] here with his army. Set him on the throne of the kingdom with steadfast security. Watch over him through the intervention of all the saints like Moses in the reeds, Joshua and Gideon in the world, and long-haired Samuel in the temple. . . . May You be his breastplate against the troops of his enemies, helmet in

[108] Carlrichard Brühl, "Fränkischer Krönungsbrauch und das Problem der 'Festkrönungen,'" *HZ* 194 (1962): 265–326; Janet L. Nelson, "The Lord's Anointed and the People's Choice: Carolingian Royal Ritual," in Nelson, *Frankish World*, 99–131.

[109] *Ordines coronationis Franciae*, ed. Jackson, 51–65.

times of danger, patience in times of prosperity, and eternal shield for protection. Stand before him so that the peoples keep faith with him and that the magnates and great men might be at peace. Let him love charity, abstain from avarice, speak justice, and uphold the truth. May his people prevail, united with the blessing of eternity, so that they might always remain the victors rejoicing in peace throughout the years. In the [name of the] Lord.

It is significant that the blessings emphasized the participation of magnates, great men, and army, without whose support Louis's royal claims were vain. A Freising charter from the 820s suggests which Bavarian magnates would have been present at Louis's court during his coronation. It lists "all the crowning men" [omnes coronatores viri], including Bishops Adalram of Salzburg, Hitto of Freising, Baturich of Regensburg, Reginher of Passau, and Agnus of Eichstätt, five abbots, twelve counts, and two judges.[110] Here one sees why nobles took royal rituals such as coronations seriously: their right to come to the palace and take part in such ceremonial events confirmed their social status and participation in government. The king was the apex of the noble hierarchy of which they were all a part. Crown-wearings, royal acclamations, and other court rituals such as feasting and hunting therefore served as important moments of consensus between a ruler and the nobility.

The most important milestone in Louis's early career was his marriage. This event was bound up with the politics of his father's court. In 818, Louis the German's mother, Ermengard, had died, and the following year Louis the Pious took a noblewoman named Judith as his second wife.[111] Judith's father was a member of the Frankish Welfs from Bavaria, and her mother was a noblewoman from a powerful Franco-Saxon family known as the Ecbertiner. The new empress was beautiful, intelligent, cultured, and ambitious, and through her influence at court her relatives rose to positions of power. In 823, an event occurred that was to have a profound impact on ninth-century politics: Judith gave birth to a boy. This event was highly problematic, since the *Ordinatio imperii* made no provision for a fourth son.

[110] *Freising* 463.

[111] On the Welfs and Empress Judith, see Josef Fleckenstein, "Über die Herkunft der Welfen und ihre Anfänge in Süddeutschland," in *Studien und Vorarbeiten zur Geschichte des grossfränkischen und frühdeutschen Adels*, ed. Gerd Tellenbach, Forschungen zur oberrheinischen Landesgeschichte 6 (Freiburg, 1957), 71–136; Konecny, "Frauen," 89–102, 137; Michael Borgolte, *Die Grafen Alemanniens in merowingischer und karolingischer Zeit: Eine Prosopographie* (Sigmaringen, 1986), 288–89; Elizabeth Ward, "Caesar's Wife: The Career of Empress Judith, 819–829," in *CH*, ed. Godman and Collins, 205–27; Nelson, *Charles the Bald*, 75–104, 177–79; Depreux, *Prosopographie*, 279–86; Bernd Schneidmüller, *Die Welfen: Herrschaft und Erinnerung (819–1252)* (Stuttgart, 2000), 46–50.

Nevertheless, by giving his new son the eminently royal name Charles (the future Charles the Bald, 838–77), Louis the Pious signaled that he would also inherit a kingdom. Louis the Pious's decision to recognize Charles as throne worthy was a dangerous gamble, since his three sons by his first marriage were sure to oppose sharing their already contested inheritance with a fourth brother. At the same time, Louis the Pious dangerously undermined the rhetoric of his own regime, which was based on the 817 ideal of the "unity of the empire." Louis the Pious was trying to have it both ways: to preserve a united Christian empire while at the same time providing kingdoms for all four sons. Because he foresaw the tensions this additional division would create, Louis the Pious had Lothar stand as Charles's godfather—a ploy that would have little success. The future careers of Louis the Pious's four sons would be closely entwined, sometimes as allies but more often as bitter rivals.

In 827, Louis the Pious arranged Louis the German's marriage to Judith's own sister, Emma.[112] Through this marriage, Louis the German became his father's brother-in-law, a highly unusual arrangement that reflected the influence of Judith and the Welfs at court. The main chronicles of Louis the Pious's reign—the *Royal Frankish Annals* and the biographies by Thegan and the Astronomer—remained silent about the marriage, which suggests that some contemporaries felt uncomfortable about this peculiar union. Only the *Annals of Xanten*, written by the court librarian, Gerward, offered a terse report: "King Louis accepted the sister of Empress Judith as his wife." It is difficult to fathom Louis's attitude toward his bride. He may have been suspicious of his stepmother's influence at court, but he also may have seen his marriage into this powerful family as giving him political leverage against Lothar. Moreover, within the context of the approaching Bulgar campaign of 828, Louis may have needed the marriage to secure the support of the Bavarian nobles, since Emma hailed "from a most noble lineage of Bavarians."[113] The Bavarian nobles did take notice: the chancery of Bishop Hitto of Freising, a member of the prominent Bavarian Huosi family, began dating its charters "in the year that Emperor Louis's son, King Louis, returned to Bavaria with his wife."[114]

---

[112] The *AX*, s.a. 827, p. 7, date Louis's marriage to 827. However, the Freising charters date Louis's return to Bavaria *cum coniuge* as falling between January 11 and March 29, 828; *Freising* 554–57, 559–60, 571–75, 579, 581a. It therefore seems that Louis married Emma in 827 but did not return with her to Bavaria until early 828. On this issue, see further: Hartmann, *Ludwig der Deutsche*, 64 and n. 186; Bigott, *Ludwig der Deutsche*, 55.

[113] Thegan, *GH*, chap. 26, p. 214 (in reference to Emma's sister, Judith).

[114] *Freising* 554–56, 557a, 559, 560. Louis's marriage to Emma does seem to have coincided with an expansion of his powers, since another Freising charter described 827 as the year when "King Louis, the son of Emperor Louis, took power over the Bavarians"; *Freis-*

Most important, Louis's marriage to Emma gave him a chance to produce a legitimate male heir and thereby establish his kingship on equal footing with his elder brothers. In a political system based on a royal dynasty, an heir was essential for a king's power, since otherwise his reign literally was a dead end. The then approximately seventeen-year-old Louis wasted no time: the very next year Emma gave birth to their first daughter, Hildegard.[115] Emma's ability to bear children was crucial for her political survival, since otherwise Louis probably would have tried to divorce her in his quest for an heir. Indeed, Notker and Regino listed fertility alongside nobility and intelligence as Emma's most praiseworthy qualities.[116] Louis and Emma's union was to be the longest Carolingian marriage on record: Emma would die only months before Louis in 876, after forty-nine years as husband and wife.

Louis's decision in 828 to name his first daughter Hildegard highlights his continued territorial ambitions and determination to undermine the *Ordinatio imperii*. Hildegard had been the name of Louis's grandmother, Charlemagne's wife, who was a member of the powerful Udalriching family of Alemannia and a descendant of the last Alemannian duke, Godfrey.[117] By giving his daughter this illustrious name, Louis hinted at his territorial ambitions in neighboring Alemannia, which the *Ordinatio imperii* allotted to Lothar.[118] With the Danube River and Roman roads all leading westward from Bavaria through Alemannia, that region was a crucial transit zone—a region through which the king was forced to travel between royal heartlands—to reach Francia.[119] If Louis wanted to expand his kingdom westward, he first needed to control that region. Indeed, Louis's marriage to Emma strengthened his claims to Alemannia, since the Welfs had ties to that region as well as to Bavaria.[120] Having secured his control of Bavaria's frontiers in Lower Pannonia, Carantania, and the Brenner Pass, Louis was preparing to challenge Lothar's inheritance claims in the heart of the empire.

---

ing 585a. In early 829, we hear for the first time of a formal judicial court being held in Bavaria at Louis's command; *Freising* 578.

[115] For Louis and Emma's children, see Werner, "Die Nachkommen," 451–52 and table.

[116] Notker, *Continuatio*, 329; Regino, *Chronicon*, s.a. 876, pp. 110–11.

[117] Einhard, *VK*, chap. 18, p. 22; Thegan, *GH*, chap. 2, p. 176.

[118] It is also significant that Louis's grandmother Hildegard had been the great aunt of his eastern prefect, Gerold II. Thus, by choosing the name Hildegard for his daughter, Louis emphasized both his ambition to rule Alemannia as well as his blood relationship with his chief Bavarian generalissimo.

[119] Ursula Schmitt, *Villa Regalis Ulm und Kloster Reichenau: Untersuchungen zur Pfalzfunktion des Reichsklostergutes in Alemannien (9.–12. Jahrhundert)* Veröffentlichungen des Max-Planck-Instituts für Geschichte 42 (Göttingen, 1974), 23–31.

[120] Borgolte, *Grafen*, 288–89.

CHAPTER TWO
FATHER AND SONS, 830-838

In 829, the scholar Walahfrid Strabo composed a poem titled "On the Statue of Theoderich" for the imperial court.[1] In that work, Walahfrid betrayed his unease with the growing tensions in the royal family over the issue of inheritance. He described Lothar as the "great hope of our holy kingdom," although he expressed his wish that the young Charles the Bald might also receive a realm. Pippin ominously had fallen from his father's favor: Walahfrid noted the Aquitanian king's conspicuous absence from the palace and hoped that he "might not lose his honors." Walahfrid also worried about the nineteen-year-old king of Bavaria. He praised Louis's character, valor, and military victories, but he voiced concern about the Bavarian king's dissatisfaction with his small kingdom: "Though your portion be small, yet glory will keep you company. Grieve not: what you lack in wealth, you reap through harmony."

Walahfrid's hopes for Carolingian harmony were soon dashed. During the 830s, the aging Louis the Pious faced repeated rebellions from his adult sons, causing the most serious constitutional crisis in the history of the Carolingian monarchy.[2] On one level, the rebellions of the 830s are not surprising, since throughout the Middle Ages elderly kings often faced restless

---

[1] Michael W. Herren, "The 'De imagine Tetrici' of Walahfrid Strabo: Edition and Translation," *JML* 1 (1991): 118–39.

[2] Boshof, *Ludwig der Fromme*, 171–212, offers a good overview of the politics of this period. See further: Dümmler, *GOR* 1:39–138; Nelson, *Charles the Bald*, 86–104; Bigott, *Ludwig der Deutsche*, 53–77.

sons who chafed to rule in their own right.[3] But the rebellions of the early 830s were unusually dramatic. They twice resulted in the emperor's temporary overthrow, something that had not happened before to a Carolingian ruler. These turmoils were ultimately of Louis the Pious's own making, since they were driven by his sons' desperation to work out the irreconcilable contradictions in the *Ordinatio imperii*, the birth of Charles the Bald, and the emperor's inability to arrive at a lasting plan for the division of the empire. Throughout this period, Louis the German pursued a consistent strategy of seeking to expand his territories into Francia, thereby putting him on a crash course with Lothar. By the late 830s, Louis the German managed to undermine the *Ordinatio imperii* and establish a claim to an expanded kingdom.

The rebellions of the 830s were particularly volatile because they intersected with the ever-present struggles for power and *dignitas* within the Frankish nobility. To back up their competing inheritance claims, the emperor's sons needed the political and military support of Frankish magnates—bishops, abbots, counts, and other powerful noblemen—who commanded large private armies of vassals.[4] Historians have sometimes assumed that the ninth-century nobles were divided into rigid political "parties," one being an "Imperial Unity Party" loyal to Lothar and the *Ordinatio imperii*, and another supporting the traditional divisibility of the empire among all royal sons.[5] In reality, aristocratic factions remained extremely fluid, with nobles frequently changing sides according to self-interest and the exigencies of the moment.[6] Although a united empire might benefit the most powerful lay and ecclesiastical magnates because it enabled them to accrue and maintain far-flung offices and estates, Louis the Pious's younger sons could win the magnates' support if they promised them power and *Königsnähe* within their future kingdoms. Indeed, the magnates sought to exploit the tensions in the royal family for their own advantage as a means to secure patronage. In this way the nobles stoked the Carolingian fraternal rivalry and rebellions from below, transforming a dynastic conflict over inheritance into an empirewide political crisis. The result was a general period of political instability and volatility that both highlighted and exposed the inherent weaknesses in the Carolingians' dependence on the Frankish nobility.

[3] Janet L. Nelson, "Last Years of Louis the Pious," in *CH*, ed. Godman and Collins, 147–59.

[4] Halsall, *Warfare and Society*, 71–110, stresses the significance of private retinues of vassals for Carolingian warfare.

[5] For example, see Boshof, *Ludwig der Fromme*, 129–34, 173–77; Bigott, *Ludwig der Deutsche*, 60–77, 116–18.

[6] Erkens, "*Divisio legitima* und *unitas imperii*," 423–85; MacLean, *Kingship and Politics*, 162–63.

Louis the Pious's regime had been remarkably stable during the 820s. During this period, the emperor began to spend noticeably more time in the Rhineland and at the palace of Frankfurt, which he rebuilt in 822.[7] This decision to spend less time in the traditional western regions of Frankish power reflects the fact that Louis the Pious was building his support among the east Frankish and Saxon nobles, whom the Astronomer called the Germani.[8] Empress Judith and her family, the Welfs and Ecbertiner, were members of this group, since they hailed from Bavaria, Alemannia, and Saxony. As Louis the Pious and his sons struggled over the inheritance of the empire, these eastern nobles increasingly played a pivotal role in Carolingian politics.

The event that precipitated the first rebellion was Louis the Pious's attempt to create a kingdom for Charles the Bald in 829. With the support of his new chamberlain, Bernard of Septimania, Louis the Pious decreed that Charles would inherit a kingdom consisting of Alemannia, Chur, Alsace, and part of Burgundy.[9] The inclusion of Alemannia in Charles's kingdom reflected Judith's influence, since the Welfs held lands in that region. Writing in 837, Thegan reported that Lothar, Pippin, and Louis the German were all "indignant" about the 829 division. Lothar was the most outspoken in his opposition to the new division, since it took away from the lands earmarked for him in the *Ordinatio imperii*. This in turn angered Louis the Pious, who dismissed Lothar to Italy and removed his name as co-emperor from his diplomas.

Lothar's dismissal provided the opportunity for a group of Frankish nobles, who resented the dominance of Bernard of Septimania and the Welfs at court, to rebel.[10] According to the *Annals of St.-Bertin* (which seem to offer the most reliable account of the 830 rebellion), early that year Louis the Pious called for an unpopular campaign against the Bretons at Bernard's

[7] Nelson, *Charles the Bald*, 76.

[8] Astronomer, *VH*, chaps. 24, 45, pp. 356–57, 460–661.

[9] Thegan, *GH*, chap. 35, p. 220; *AX*, s.a. 829, p. 7; Nithard, 1.3, p. 3. For the events of the years 828–29, see François Louis Ganshof, "Am Vorabend der ersten Krise der Regierung Ludwigs des Frommen: Die Jahre 828 und 829," *FS* 6 (1972): 39–54. For Bernard and his rise to power, see Collins, "Pippin I," 380–86; Depreux, *Prosopographie*, 137–39.

[10] Two leaders of the rebellion were the former counts of Tours and Orléans, Hugh and Matfrid, who had fallen from favor in the wake of Bernard's meteoric rise at court: Depreux, *Prosopographie*, 262–64, 329–31.

urging.[11] Sensing widespread opposition, the magnates who opposed Bernard and the Welfs formed a conspiracy against the emperor and won over a significant part of the army at Paris. (Louis the Pious had ridden ahead of the army to the Breton border.) To legitimate their uprising, the rebels needed the sanction of a Carolingian leader, and they therefore sent messengers to Lothar and Pippin, urging them to join the rebellion. By the time Pippin arrived at the rebel camp, the goal of the conspiracy had become radical: "to depose [the emperor], destroy their stepmother [Judith], and kill Bernard." When Louis the Pious confronted the rebels at Compiègne, Pippin took his father into custody and had Judith and her brothers imprisoned in monasteries. According to later sources, Pippin and the rebels justified their actions by accusing Judith and Bernard of being lovers and deluding the emperor through witchcraft, thereby presenting the uprising as a "loyal palace revolution."[12] When Lothar arrived from Italy, he quickly asserted control of the rebellion and took steps to put the *Ordinatio imperii* into effect. He reinstated himself as co-emperor, took over custody of his father and Charles the Bald, and condemned several of his father's supporters to imprisonment or blinding.

During the 830 rebellion, Louis the German steered an independent course from the one pursued by his brothers. At the 829 Worms assembly he had been on good terms with his father, and on that occasion the emperor made a grant for the Alemannian monastery of Reichenau at the request of "our beloved son Louis, king of the Bavarians."[13] But the young Louis could not have been happy about the concession of Alemannia to Charles, since it seriously impeded his ability to expand his kingdom westward into Francia. Indeed, Louis's intervening before his father on the behalf of Abbot Erlebald of Reichenau reveals that he had already begun to court supporters in Alemannia. Louis further indicated his Alemannian ambitions by naming his first son Carloman, born around 830. Carloman had also been the name

---

[11] Of all the major sources for the rebellion of 830, only the *AB*, s.a. 830, pp. 1–3, were written soon after the events transpired: *Annals of St.-Bertin*, trans. Nelson, p. 6. The authors of the other major sources wrote several years or decades after the fact: Thegan, *GH*, chap. 36, pp. 220–22; Astronomer, *VH*, chap. 44, p. 48 and n. 644; Nithard, 1.3, p. 4; Radbert, *Epitaphium Arsenii*, bk. 2, pp. 71–73. For attempts to reconstruct these events, see Dümmler, *GOR* 1:55–64; Boshof, *Ludwig der Fromme*, 182–91. But for the difficulty of using the later sources to do so, see Elizabeth Ward, "Agobard of Lyons and Paschasius Radbertus as Critics of the Empress Judith," in *Women in the Church*, ed. W. J. Sheils and Diana Woods (Oxford, 1990), 15–25.

[12] Astronomer, *VH*, chap. 44, pp. 454–57; Radbert, *Epitaphium Arsenii*, bk. 2, p. 72; Boshof, *Ludwig der Fromme*, 182–83. Dümmler, *GOR* 1:56 and n. 2, misunderstood Radbert's opaque Latin and stated that it was Louis the German, rather than Pippin, who leveled the charges of adultery and witchcraft against Bernard and Judith.

[13] BM 869.

of Charles Martel's eldest son, who had ruled over Austrasia and Alemannia in 741–48, and was remembered for his subjugation of Alemannia to Frankish rule in the bloody battle of Cannstadt in 746.[14] The name Louis selected for his first son thus carried strong connotations of Alemannian kingship and emphasized his aspirations to rule that region.

It is not clear if Louis joined up with the rebels in 830.[15] If he did, he apparently remained at their camp only briefly, since he knew Lothar would use the uprising as an opportunity to reassert his imperial status. While being held in custody by Lothar, Louis the Pious secretly sent messengers to Louis and Pippin, offering to increase their inheritances if they helped him regain the throne. Not surprisingly, his younger sons jumped at the offer. At the Nijmegen assembly in early October, Louis the Pious skillfully managed to regain the nobles' support and thereby reassert his power, especially through the backing of the eastern nobles.[16] Writing six years later, Thegan stressed the prominent role Louis the German played in coming to his father's aid during the 830 rebellion and at the Nijmegen assembly.[17] At the time, however, Louis's support of his father was not so straightforward. Although the Nijmegen assembly began in early October, Louis was still at Regensburg on October 6.[18] Thus Louis did not arrive at Nijmegen until after his father had regained the throne, probably after the middle of the month. Louis presumably had delayed coming to his father's aid until he was sure which way the political winds were blowing.

Louis the Pious nevertheless rewarded Louis and Pippin for their support, however hesitant it may have been. In February 831, the emperor held an assembly at Aachen at which he sentenced the rebels to imprisonment or exile and cleared Judith and Bernard of wrongdoing (although he prudently declined to reinstate Bernard as chamberlain). At this assembly, he drew up a new division of the empire, known simply as the Division of the Kingdom, in which he abandoned the *Ordinatio imperii* and its ideal of imperial unity

[14] Fouracre, *Age of Charles Martel*, 169.

[15] The *AB*, Thegan, Astronomer, and Nithard all do not mention Louis the German at the rebel camp. The only author explicitly to claim that Louis joined the rebels is Radbert, *Epitaphium Arsenii*, bk. 2, p. 72. However, the reliability of Radbert's report is questionable, since he does not seem to have finished it until 856 or later: David Ganz, "The *Epitaphium Arsenii* and Opposition to Louis the Pious," in *CH*, ed. Godman and Collins, 537–50, at 539–40. Cf. Dümmler, *GOR* 1:56 and n. 2.

[16] Astronomer, *VH*, chap. 45, pp. 460–65; *AB*, s.a. 830, pp. 2–3. In the following months, Louis the Pious rewarded many members of the *Germani* for their support, including Bishops Bernold of Strasbourg and Victor of Chur and Abbots Raban of Fulda and Tatto of Kempten: BM 883, 889–94.

[17] Thegan, *GH*, chaps. 36–37, pp. 222–24.

[18] *DLG* 2.

under Lothar.[19] Louis the Pious now revoked Lothar's imperial title and all his territories except Italy and divided the empire among his younger three sons.[20] In drawing up the new inheritance plan, the emperor followed two general guidelines: that Louis, Pippin, and Charles keep the kingdoms they already had (Bavaria, Aquitaine, and Alemannia) and that each get part of highly coveted Francia. Pippin received Aquitaine and most of Neustria, while Charles was assigned Alemannia, Burgundy, Provence, Gothia, and "middle Francia" between Trier and Reims.[21] Louis's portion spanned from Bavaria to the English Channel, encompassing Bavaria, Thuringia, Saxony, Austrasia, Frisia, and the northern portion of Neustria. Louis the Pious had learned his lesson, however, so he inserted a novel "filial loyalty clause" that left open the possibility of revising his sons' inheritances according to their behavior.[22] For the time being, Louis the Pious limited his older sons to their previous kingdoms while he kept the young Charles the Bald with him at court.

Louis the German's immediate reward was expanded power in Bavaria. In the course of the 830 rebellion, he began issuing royal diplomas in his own name, which apparently was one of the secret concessions his father made to him while still in Lothar's custody.[23] The right to issue diplomas indicates a considerable expansion of Louis's powers. Diplomas typically recorded a king's grant or confirmation of any of a host of beneficial arrangements for his supporters: royal lands, rights, protection, and the like. Louis's ability to issue diplomas therefore suggests that he had taken control of the royal lands and public offices (counties, benefices, bishoprics, monasteries, and other important posts) in Bavaria and could distribute them to his supporters as he saw fit.

Diplomas also gave Louis a powerful medium for making statements about his royal authority. In his diplomas Louis adopted the lofty title "king of the Bavarians by the gift of Divine Grace" (*divina largiente gratia rex Baioariorum*). Through this title, Louis not only stressed the divine sanction of his royal power but also hinted at his own imperial ambitions and emula-

[19] *Regni divisio*, in MGH *Capitularia* 2:20–24. On this division, see Dümmler, *GOR* 1:62–64; Heinz Zatschek, "Die Reichsteilungen unter Kaiser Ludwig dem Frommen," *MIÖG* 49 (1935): 186–224, here at 191–94; Kasten, *Königssöhne*, 191–92.

[20] Nithard, 1.4, p. 4.

[21] *Regni divisio*, chap. 14, in MGH *Capitularia* 2:24.

[22] Ibid., chap. 13, p. 23.

[23] *DLG* 2. Louis issued this diploma on October 6, 830, at Regensburg. At this time, Louis also made grants to the monastery of Herrieden in southeastern Franconia, which suggests that his father had granted him that monastery as an additional concession: *DLG* 3, 5.

tion of his grandfather, since Charlemagne in 813 had introduced the *divina largiente gratia* formula in his diplomacy with the Byzantine emperor.[24] Louis authenticated his diplomas with an elegant royal seal that provides the first surviving visual image of him, albeit an idealized one.[25] Louis's seal depicted him with a beard in profile and surrounded by the symbols of royal authority: an ornate crown, the Roman military cloak, and a shield and spear. Like his royal title, Louis's seal suggested his emulation of his imperial predecessors, since it was modeled on the imperial metal bulls of Charlemagne and Louis the Pious (which in turn emulated the iconography of Roman imperial coins). Louis's chancery dated his diplomas according to his and his father's—but not Lothar's—regnal years, again highlighting his rejection of Lothar's imperial status. In short, Louis's new diplomas asserted the divine sanction of his kingship, his rejection of Lothar's imperial claims, and his own quasi-imperial political ambitions.

Whatever optimism Louis the German had for the 831 division was soon shattered. At the Ingelheim assembly in May 831, Louis the Pious summoned Lothar and the exiled rebels, pardoned them, and returned them to favor, thereby making clear that he had no intention of upholding the new Division of the Kingdom and its filial loyalty clause.[26] The Franks valued clemency as a royal virtue, but Louis the Pious employed it dangerously, since by pardoning the rebels he further undermined the nobles' confidence in his ability to make a lasting succession plan. Indeed, the Astronomer identified excessive *clementia* as Louis the Pious's single greatest fault.[27] Pippin was the first to show his outrage by refusing to attend the 831 Thionville assembly.[28] This in turn angered the emperor, who announced an upcoming assembly in early 832 at Orléans to deal with his rebel Aquitanian son.

[24] Herwig Wolfram, "Lateinische Herrschertitel im neunten und zehnten Jahrhundert," in *Intitulatio II: Lateinische Herrscher- und Fürstentitel im neunten und zehnten Jahrhundert*, ed. Herwig Wolfram, *MIÖG* Ergänzungsband 24 (Vienna, 1973), 22, 65, 105. In his 813 correspondence with Constantinople, Charlemagne had used the title "divina largiente gratia imperator et augustus idemque rex Francorum et Langobardorum." No other ruler used the *divina largiente gratia* formula before Louis the German adopted it in 830.

[25] Percy Ernst Schramm, *Die deutschen Kaiser und Könige in Bildern ihrer Zeit, 751–1190* (Munich, 1983), 322 (no. 49); Genevra Kornbluth, *Engraved Gems of the Carolingian Empire* (University Park, PA, 1995), 23–24 and fig. 40. None of Louis the German's seal matrices survives, although the designs are evident from the wax seals attached to his diplomas.

[26] *AB*, s.a. 831, p. 4; Astronomer, *VH*, chap. 46, pp. 466–67.

[27] Astronomer, *VH*, prologue, chap. 45, pp. 284, 464.

[28] *AB*, s.a. 831, 832, p. 5; *AX*, s.a. 831, pp. 7–8; Astronomer, *VH*, chaps. 46–47, pp. 468–69.

The earliest surviving image of Louis the German. This is Louis's first seal, which he used as king of Bavaria between 830 and 833 (and then occasionally until 861). The seal shows Louis in profile wearing a crown and military cloak. Next to him are the martial emblems of a spear and shield. The inscription reads: "† Hludowicus rex." From a diploma dated August 18, 831. Munich, Bayerisches Hauptstaatsarchiv, Regensburg/St.-Emmeram Urk. 2. Photograph courtesy of the Lichtbildarchiv, Marburg.

Louis the German likewise refused to accept his father's pardoning of Lothar, and in late March 832 he also rebelled. His objective was to annex Alemannia, win over the nobles of that region, and then seize as much of Francia as possible.[29] In effect, Louis was seeking to take possession of the territories earmarked for him in the 831 division, and the crucial eastern transit zone of Alemannia (previously given to Charles) as well. Louis's 832 rebellion was a considerable gamble, and he mustered a broad-based army. The *Annals of St.-Bertin* reported that he invaded Alemannia "with all the Bavarians he could rally to him: freemen, slaves, and Slavs." Louis's con-

[29] *AB*, s.a. 832, pp. 4–5. See further: Astronomer, *VH*, chap. 47, pp. 468–69; Thegan, *GH*, chap. 39, pp. 224–27; *AX*, s.a. 832, p. 8; *AF*, s.a. 832, p. 26; Dümmler, *GOR* 1:65–72; BM 899a–c.

Winning a Kingdom

scription of slaves and Slavs was highly unusual, indicating his desperation to rally as large an army as possible.[30]

To raise such a broad-based army, Louis needed to secure the support of the Bavarian magnates, who were responsible for mustering local troops. Louis assembled them on the eve of his uprising at the palace of Altötting in southeastern Bavaria, where he celebrated Easter. Three days later, on March 27, the king made a grant to Adalram of Salzburg, presumably to win the support of the powerful Bavarian archbishop.[31] Louis heightened the ideological significance of this grant by making it on the feast day of Salzburg's patron saint, Rupert, who had been a Frankish missionary bishop to Bavaria in the early eighth century. By honoring Saint Rupert, Louis sought to exploit the religious patriotism of the Bavarian elite and make his kingdom's patron saint the special protector of the upcoming rebellion. At the same time, Louis called attention to his own illustrious lineage, since he was related to Saint Rupert through his mother, the Rupertiner Ermengard.[32] Louis also formed a *coniuratio* with the nobles against his father.[33] A *coniuratio* was a sworn association—often confirmed at a banquet—whose members pledged mutual support toward a given objective. It was unusual for Carolingian kings to form sworn associations with the nobles, since such unions implied a familiar camaraderie among all involved, which tended to lessen the majesty that the Carolingians worked so hard to create. That Louis was willing to form such an association highlights his desperation to win as much aristocratic support for his 832 rebellion as possible. There would have been plenty of opportunities for banquets and drinking, and thus opportunities to confirm the oaths, among Louis and his supporters at Altötting during their observance of Easter and the feast of Saint Rupert.

Archbishop Adalram was not the only magnate present at Altötting. The diploma recording Louis's grant to Salzburg reports that Counts Ernest and Werner also participated in the transaction. Ernest and Werner were not

[30] One of the slaves in Louis's army may have been an unfree priest named Hunroc, whom Louis manumitted soon after the rebellion: *DLG* 10.

[31] *DLG* 7.

[32] On Saint Rupert and the Rupertiner, see Michael Gockel, *Karolingische Königshöfe am Mittelrhein* (Göttingen, 1970), 298–301; Innes, *State and Society*, 55, 175–76, 264 (fig. 10).

[33] *AAM*, s.a. 832, p. 784, reported that Louis formed a *coniuratio* with the eastern nobles when he reached the middle Rhine, but it is likely that he had already done this with the Bavarians before he left his kingdom. On *coniurationes*, see Karl Brunner, *Oppositionelle Gruppen im Karolingerreich* (Vienna, 1979), 17–20; Gerd Althoff, *Verwandte, Freunde und Getreue: Zum politischen Stellenwert der Gruppenbindungen im früheren Mittelalter* (Darmstadt, 1990), 119–33.

members of the old Bavarian nobility but rather east Frankish nobles who rose to power in Louis's service at this time.[34] The *Annals of Fulda* referred to Ernest as "first among the king's friends" and "greatest among all of Louis's great men" and to Werner as "one of the leading men of the Franks."[35] Louis promoted Ernest and Werner to strategic frontier commands in Bavaria's eastern marches, where lands were plentiful and lordships were there for the making. Ernest became commander over the Bohemian marches, while Werner received a county in Upper Pannonia.[36] Ernest and Werner, who were related to each other through marriage, both hailed from families on the middle Rhine, and Ernest's sister was married to the powerful Franconian count, Gebhard of the Lahngau.[37] Ernest and Werner also had ties to Alemannia, since their names appeared together in several entries from the 830s in the confraternity books of St.-Gall and Reichenau.[38] ("Confraternity books" or *libri memoriales* were monastic books listing the names of a monastery's patrons, for whom the monks prayed.) It is likely that Louis promoted Ernest and Werner because their connections helped underpin his claims to an expanded eastern kingdom. Ernest and Werner had hitched their wagon to the young Louis's star. They would dominate the politics of his court for the next three decades.

With the support of the Bavarian nobles, Louis launched his rebellion in early April 832. Louis set out with his troops for Alemannia, where he won over the nobles of that region. After annexing Alemannia, Louis and his growing army set out for the middle Rhine. His destination was significant: the middle Rhine around Mainz, Worms, and Frankfurt was the wealthy royal heartland of eastern Austrasia, where Louis the Pious had built up his support in the 820s. Whichever king controlled that region could dominate all the lands along and east of the Rhine. Louis encamped at Lampertheim across the Rhine from Worms, where he won over additional eastern nobles

[34] Mitterauer, *Karolingische Markgrafen*, 125–37, 153–59; Gockel, *Karolingische Königshöfe*, 302–5; Innes, *State and Society*, 203–4. Ernest and Werner do not seem to have held offices under Louis the Pious, although Werner was a descendant of the former eastern prefect under Charlemagne, Werner I: Depreux, *Prosopographie*; Bowlus, *Franks, Moravians, and Magyars*, 98–103.

[35] *AF*, s.a. 849, 861, 865, pp. 38, 55, 63.

[36] Ernest appeared at Louis's court as early as 829, but he was not explicitly referred to as a count until 837: *DLG* 1, 7; *Regensburg* 29. His command over the Bohemian marches is implied by the *AF*, s.a. 849, p. 38. For the debated location of Werner's county, see Wolfram, *Salzburg*, 318 and n. 645, 328.

[37] Concerning Count Gebhard, see Donald C. Jackman, *The Konradiner: A Study in Genealogical Methodology*, Veröffentlichungen des Max-Planck-Instituts für Europäische Rechtsgeschichte, Sonderhefte 47 (Frankfurt, 1990), 87–89.

[38] *Confraternitates Sangallenses*, col. 23 (ll. 22–29); and *Confraternitates Augienses*, cols. 386 (ll. 34–40), 411 (ll. 19–20); MGH *Necrologia* 6:15, 262–63, 273.

for his *coniuratio*. Once again, Louis presumably exploited his Rupertiner connections, since his mother's family hailed from the middle Rhine and included the powerful Rhineland count, Rupert.[39] One magnate who joined Louis's rebellion was Ratpot, another east Frankish nobleman with lands on the middle Rhine. In return for his support, Louis appointed Ratpot the new prefect of the Bavarian Eastland as the successor of the recently deceased Gerold II.[40] But when Louis the Pious rallied a large army at Mainz on April 18, the majority of the east Franks and Saxons lost confidence in the younger Louis's rebellion and threw their support behind the emperor.[41] Louis the Pious and his army then crossed the Rhine, forcing his son and his remaining supporters to retreat to Bavaria.

A reconciliation between Louis the German and his father took place in May 832 at Augsburg, just beyond the borders of Bavaria. The emperor compelled his son to appear outside the city on the plain known as the Lechfeld, where Charlemagne had forced Duke Tassilo III of Bavaria to submit to him in 787.[42] Louis the Pious now reenacted that dramatic event, with his rebellious son playing the role of Tassilo. The implication was clear: either submit or be deposed like the last Agilolfing duke. Louis the German wisely chose the former course and swore never to rebel again.[43] A revealing additional piece of information about the meeting comes from the twelfth-century *Life of Saint Reginswind*, which has been shown to contain reliable information about the events of 832, despite its late composition.[44] According to that source, Louis's chief lay supporter, Ernest, "mighty in arms and renowned," accompanied him to Augsburg. During the meeting, Louis the Pious reportedly treated Ernest with honor and gave him a benefice at Lauffen on the Neckar River in southern Franconia. This report is significant because it underscores Ernest's political connections and ambi-

---

[39] Innes, *State and Society*, 126, 200–201.

[40] Immediately after Louis's rebellion, his father granted several estates on the middle Rhine that he had revoked from Ratpot, implying that Ratpot had supported his son: BM 904. Concerning Ratpot, see Mitterauer, *Karolingische Markgrafen*, 91–103; Bowlus, *Franks, Moravians, and Magyars*, 98–113; Wolfram, *Salzburg*, 310–11. Another magnate Louis now won over was the recently disgraced Matfrid, who had returned to his family's lands on the middle Rhine: *AB*, s.a. 832, pp. 4–5; Innes, *State and Society*, 198 and n. 108.

[41] Abbot Tatto of Kempten, whose Alemannian monastery was located near the Bavarian border, had appeared at Louis the Pious's court on March 28, and it is possible that he warned the emperor of his son's plot: BM 899. Tatto seems to have acted as an envoy between the Bavarian and imperial courts on several occasions.

[42] *ARF*, s.a. 787, p. 78. On this event, see Airlie, "Narratives of Triumph," 111–12.

[43] *AB*, s.a. 832, p. 5; Thegan, *GH*, chap. 39, pp. 226–27.

[44] *Ex vita Reginswindis*, chaps. 1–5, in MGH SS 15:359–60; Hansmartin Schwarzmaier, "Die Reginswindis-Tradition von Lauffen: Königliche Politik und adelige Herrschaft am mittleren Neckar," *ZGO* 131 (1983): 163–98.

tions outside Bavaria. Louis the German wanted to exploit Ernest's ties to the east Rhenish territories, but Ernest expected lands in those regions in return for his support. The emperor recognized this aristocratic pressure his son faced and made the grant to placate, and perhaps win over, his son's chief supporter.

Louis the Pious spent the next few months securing the support of the eastern nobles. He made grants to Count Gebhard of Lahngau (Ernest's brother-in-law) and Abbot Teutgar of Herrieden, to the latter of whom he gave lands on the middle Rhine that he had confiscated from his son's supporter, Ratpot.[45] Louis the Pious then set off with an eastern army to confront the rebellious Pippin in Aquitaine.[46] At this point, the emperor decided to punish Louis and Pippin for their rebellions.[47] Louis the Pious revoked Pippin's kingdom and sent Pippin with his wife and children in custody to Trier. He then decreed another new division of the empire between Lothar and Charles. The emperor gave Aquitaine to Charles and had the nobles of that region swear loyalty to him. His next step was to divide the rest of the empire between Lothar and Charles—with the exception of Louis's kingdom of Bavaria. However, because of the tumultuous subsequent events, this new division never took effect. The daring Pippin escaped from imprisonment, fled back to Aquitaine, and rallied his supporters once again in rebellion. An unusually bitter winter set in that made travel all but impossible, and in December the emperor was forced to retreat from Aquitaine "in a manner far less honorable than was fitting."

THE FIELD OF LIES

Despite their mutual rivalry and mistrust, Lothar, Pippin, and Louis had become united in their opposition to their father's creation of a kingdom for Charles. In early 833, the three brothers formed another conspiracy and set

[45] BM 901–4.

[46] Adrevald of Fleury recounted with disgust the havoc these "peoples from beyond the Rhine" [Transrenani] wrought in Francia, yet he acknowledged that the emperor was compelled to rely on them because he distrusted the west Franks: *Ex miraculis S. Benedicti*, chap. 27, in MGH SS 15:491. In Aquitaine Louis the Pious stripped Bernard of his frontier command and bestowed the Spanish march on Berengar of Toulouse: Brunner, *Oppositionelle Gruppen*, 80; Depreux, *Prosopographie*, 131–32.

[47] Astronomer, *VH*, chap. 47, pp. 468–73; Thegan, *GH*, chap. 41, pp. 226–29; *AF*, s.a. 832, p. 26.

out from their respective kingdoms to converge forces against their father.[48] Louis the Pious responded swiftly and rallied an army at Worms, where he distributed grants to his eastern supporters.[49] Meanwhile, Lothar, Pippin, and Louis gathered their forces into a large army in Alsace, south of Worms.[50] Lothar's trump card was that he had brought with him Pope Gregory IV (828–44), thereby attempting to give the new rebellion a heightened level of legitimacy.[51] Pope Gregory IV supported the *Ordinatio imperii* and its ideal of imperial unity under Lothar, however; his presence therefore was a potential threat to Pippin of Aquitaine and Louis the German as well as to Louis the Pious.

Louis the Pious and his sons came to a standoff on the Rotfeld near Colmar in Alsace, a place that soon became known as the Field of Lies because of the ensuing betrayal of the emperor by his sons and magnates. At a tense meeting with the pope, Louis the Pious and his bishops accused Gregory IV of inspiring discord in the empire. In response the pope asserted that he desired only the unity of the Church and that he had come to aid in restoring peace and harmony between father and sons. After these negotiations failed, the Frankish nobles once again found themselves in the difficult position of having to choose between two generations of Carolingians. The Astronomer reported how the sons eventually won the upper hand: "partly led away by bribes, partly enticed by promises, partly terrified by threats," the nobles gradually deserted the emperor and went over to the three sons.[52] Finally, on June 30, Louis the Pious surrendered, and Lothar took him and the ten-year-old Charles the Bald into custody. Louis the German had his stepmother/sister-in-law, Judith, guarded in his own tent before she too was imprisoned.

Before departing the Field of Lies, the three brothers made a new three-way division of the empire.[53] Although no exact record of the 833 division survives, the evidence indicates it was a compromise between the 817 *Ordi-*

---

[48] Once again, the *AB* offer the only detailed contemporary report of the rebellion: *AB*, s.a. 833, pp. 8–10. Mayke De Jong, "Power and Humility in Carolingian Society: The Public Penance of Louis the Pious," *EME* 1 (1992): 29–52; and Boshof, *Ludwig der Fromme*, 192–210, offer good treatments of the 833 rebellion.

[49] BM 920–24.

[50] Before the rebellion, the younger Louis had been at Regensburg and Osterhofen in Bavaria in the company of the bishops of Regensburg and Passau: *DLG* 8, 9, 11.

[51] On Gregory IV's role in the events of 833, see Boshof, *Ludwig der Fromme*, 192–95; Johannes Fried, "Ludwig der Fromme, das Papstum und die fränkische Kirche," in *CH*, ed. Godman and Collins, 266–70.

[52] Astronomer, *VH*, chap. 48, pp. 476–78.

[53] Ibid., chap. 48, p. 478; *AX*, s.a. 833–34, pp. 8–9. On the 833 division, see Dümmler, *GOR* 1:81–83; BM 925d; Zatschek, "Reichsteilungen," 198–216.

natio imperii and the 831 Division of the Kingdom. Following the 817 plan, Lothar alone bore the imperial title, and he compelled his brothers and all the nobles to swear fidelity to him. Lothar's territories included the bulk of Francia: Austrasia west of the Rhine, most of Neustria, Burgundy, Frisia, Provence, as well as Italy. As one chronicler summed up, "the *regnum Francorum* was given over to Emperor Lothar."[54] Nevertheless, Pippin and Louis pressured Lothar into recognizing their possession of enlarged kingdoms that corresponded somewhat to the 831 division. Pippin once again took possession of Aquitaine and, in addition, the countship of Anjou in Neustria.[55] Louis compelled Lothar to recognize his rule over all the eastern territories of the empire: Austrasia east of the Rhine (that is, Franconia), Saxony, Thuringia, Alsace, Alemannia, as well as Bavaria.[56] In this way, the 833 division slightly modified the kingdom set aside for Louis in 831. Louis was forced to give up his claims to the wealthy region of western Austrasia as well as Frisia, which went to Lothar. But as compensation he received the territory to which he had long aspired: Alemannia and, in addition, neighboring Alsace. The territories Louis received in 833 made sense geographically and politically; they comprised Louis's longtime Bavarian kingdom, the strategic transit zone of Alemannia, a piece of the Frankish heartland in the form of eastern Austrasia, and the contiguous territories of Alsace, Saxony, and Thuringia. A full decade before the Treaty of Verdun, the blueprint for Louis's future kingdom had taken shape.

Lothar, however, soon made clear that he still hoped to enforce the *Ordinatio imperii*. In the words of Nithard, Louis and Pippin "saw that Lothar wanted to claim the whole empire for himself and make them his inferiors, and they resented this."[57] When Lothar held an assembly at Compiègne in October 833, Louis refused to attend, thereby proclaiming his opposition to his eldest brother. Lothar's supporters feared that Louis the Pious might still regain the throne as he had in 830, and Lothar therefore orchestrated a dramatic abdication ceremony at Soissons, during which he and the bishops forced his father to resign his imperial title. With little choice in the matter, Louis the Pious confessed that he had ruled badly, placed his sword on the

---

[54] *AH*, s.a. 833, p. 16.

[55] Eiten, *Unterkönigtum*, 99–100. This kingdom was significantly smaller than the regions designated for Pippin in 831, revealing his recent political weakness. Dümmler, *GOR* 1:82 and n. 2, and 101, incorrectly stated that Pippin received all of Neustria.

[56] The clearest description of Louis's expanded eastern kingdom in 833 comes from the *AB*, s.a. 838, p. 24. Zatschek, "Reichsteilungen," 201, mistakenly claimed that Louis's kingdom in 833 extended as far as St.-Quentin in the Vermandois.

[57] Nithard, 1.4, p. 6.

altar, and exchanged his royal attire for the garb of a penitent. It seemed that Lothar had finally fulfilled his long-held imperial aspirations.

At this moment, Louis the German used the mounting sympathy for his father to rally opposition to Lothar. "With Emperor Louis languishing in custody," Gerward wrote, "his son Louis cunningly began to plot against his brother Lothar . . . and set traps for him."[58] Between October 833 and February 834, Louis the German assembled his father's eastern supporters at Frankfurt, where he made grants to the three most powerful abbots east of the Rhine: Gozbert of St.-Gall, Adalung of Lorsch, and Raban of Fulda.[59] Others loyal to the two Louises also appeared at Frankfurt: Bishop Baturich of Regensburg; Louis the Pious's half brothers, Bishop Drogo of Metz and Abbot Hugh of St.-Quentin; Abbot Grimald of Wissembourg; and Count Gebhard of Lahngau.[60] Louis sent several embassies to Lothar demanding that their father be treated more humanely, and when those failed he held an adversarial face-to-face meeting with Lothar in December at Mainz.[61] When Lothar again refused to lighten the conditions of their father's custody, Louis "began to plot with his men how he might deliver his father from imprisonment."

While rallying his father's supporters at Frankfurt, Louis reorganized his court administration to assert his expanded eastern kingship.[62] As king of Bavaria, Louis had only a diminutive administration, headed by Abbot Gozbald of Niederaltaich, who served as both archchaplain and chancellor.[63] After the Field of Lies, Louis expanded his administration along the lines of the imperial court by separating the two offices. As archchaplain, Louis appointed Baturich of Regensburg, his longtime Bavarian supporter.[64] As his high chancellor, Louis designated Abbot Grimald of Wis-

[58] *AX*, s.a. 834, p. 9. See further Astronomer, *VH*, chap. 49, pp. 480–85.

[59] *DLG* 13–15. Louis's gift to Fulda included estates that he had confiscated from Count Poppo of Grabfeld, the leader of the east Frankish Babenberg family and presumably Lothar's supporter: BM 989; Kehr's introduction to *DLG* 15.

[60] Astronomer, *VH*, chap. 49, p. 484; Thegan, *GH*, chap. 47, p. 240; *DLG* 13.

[61] Thegan, *GH*, chaps. 45–47, pp. 238–40; *AB*, s.a. 833, pp. 10–11.

[62] Kehr, "Kanzlei Ludwigs," 6–7; Fleckenstein, *Hofkapelle* 1:167–69.

[63] Concerning Gozbald, see *DLG* 2; Fleckenstein, *Hofkapelle* 1:166–68. On the basis of an entry in Reichenau's confraternity book, Gerd Althoff suggests that Gozbald was related to the Hattonians: Gerd Althoff, "Über die von Erzbischof Liutbert auf die Reichenau übersandten Namen," *FS* 14 (1980): 239–40.

[64] Baturich is not explicitly described as Louis's *summus capellanus* until 844: *DLG* 35. However, Louis seems to have granted Baturich the position in 833, when he appears as *ambasciator* in Louis's first diploma as "rex in orientali Francia": *DLG* 13. An *ambiascator* was a person who communicated the king's command for the court scribes to draw up a diploma recording a transaction, and he therefore usually was involved in some way with the transaction.

sembourg.[65] Grimald was the scion of an Austrasian family from the region around Trier. Grimald's uncle, Hetti (814–47), and his brother, Thietgaud (847–63), were consecutive archbishops of Trier, and his relative, Waldo (786–806/14), had been abbot of Reichenau, where Grimald had been a student and teacher. Grimald had spent time at Charlemagne's court and served as Louis the Pious's chancellor during the 820s. In return for his services, Louis the Pious had granted Grimald extensive properties in Alemannia and made him abbot of Wissembourg in Alsace.[66] Thus, by appointing Grimald his high chancellor, Louis asserted that his palace, not Lothar's, was the seat of true political continuity with his father's and grandfather's regimes.[67] Moreover, Grimald's far-flung political connections, lands, and offices gave Louis badly needed political footholds in Alemannia, Alsace, and Austrasia.

Louis also expressed his expanded kingship through a new diploma format.[68] He now abandoned his title "king of the Bavarians by the gift of Divine Grace" and proclaimed that he was simply "king by the favor of Divine Grace" (divina favente gratia rex). The new royal title indicated Louis's claims to unlimited, "absolute" kingship, since it did not restrict his rule to a single people or province.[69] Louis also introduced a new royal seal that visually equated him with his grandfather and father. At the center of the new seal was a beautiful antique oval gem depicting the Roman emperor Hadrian, and the inscription around it read, "O Christ, protect King Louis!"[70] Louis had closely modeled his new Hadrian seal on the seals of Charlemagne and Louis the Pious, which had similar antique gems with

[65] DLG 17; Dieter Geuenich, "Beobachtungen zu Grimald von St. Gallen, Erzkapellan und Oberkanzler Ludwigs des Deutschen," in Litterae Medii Aevi: Festschrift für Johanne Autenrieth, ed. Michael Borgolte and Herrad Spilling (Sigmaringen, 1988), 55–61; Depreux, Prosopographie, 221–22.

[66] DLG 17.

[67] A point stressed by Ermanrich of Ellwangen: Epistola ad Grimaldum abbatem, in MGH Epistolae 5:536.

[68] DLG 13; Zatschek, "Reichsteilungen," 204. Suggesting his weaker position in the west, Pippin continued to call himself "king of the Aquitanians" and to date his diplomas according to his and his father's reigns: Eiten, Unterkönigtum, 112–13; Zatschek, "Reichsteilungen," 204–5; Collins, "Pippin I," 386–89.

[69] Louis modeled his royal title on the "absolute" imperial titles of Louis the Pious and Lothar: divina ordinante providentia imperator augustus. See Wolfram, "Lateinische Herrschertitel," 104–5, 110–12; Brühl, Deutschland-Frankreich, 158–59.

[70] Schramm, Die deutschen Kaiser, 64, 322 (no. 50). Schramm speculated that Louis may have plundered this gem from his father's imperial treasury at the Field of Lies. On the Carolingian use of Roman gems for royal seals in general, see Kornbluth, Engraved Gems, 22–24; Ildar H. Garipzanov, "The Image of Authority in Carolingian Coinage: The Image of a Ruler and Roman Imperial Tradition," EME 8 (1999): 213–14.

bearded emperors and the same "O Christ, protect...!" inscription.[71] Louis's fondness for this seal is seen in the fact that he used it for the rest of his reign and had it carefully remounted in 867 after it cracked.[72] Louis's new diplomas also dropped his father's name from the dating clause and instead read, "in the first year of the reign of lord King Louis in east Francia." In the ninth century, the term "east Francia" (*orientalis Francia*) indicated the region inhabited by the east Franks (*orientales Franci*), usually meaning the province of Franconia stretching eastward from the middle Rhine to the region around Würzburg.[73] But Louis's court used the term *orientalis Francia* in a more general sense, indicating all the eastern territories under Frankish lordship—not only Franconia, but also Bavaria, Saxony, Alemannia, Thuringia, and the Slavic marches. By using *orientalis Francia* rather than the classical equivalent, *Germania*, Louis emphasized the Frankish nature of his kingship. At the same time, the term *orientalis Francia* hinted at Louis's ambitions to rule the heartlands of the Frankish kingdom, since Carolingian chroniclers sometimes equated the east Franks with the Franks of Austrasia.[74] Louis's novel claim to rule "in east Francia" therefore was a statement of fact as well as intention, suggesting his ambitions to rule a kingdom that encompassed all Austrasia as well as the territories east of the Rhine.

In early 834, Louis the German led a well-executed offensive against Lothar that reveals his growing skill in diplomacy and warfare.[75] Louis commanded a large eastern army of Bavarians, Saxons, Alemans, and Austrasians, while Pippin, whom Louis had won over to his plan, led an army of Aquitanians and Neustrians. Louis and his army moved with such speed that he seems to have taken Lothar by surprise, forcing him to retreat from Aachen to Paris. Louis had been at Frankfurt on February 5, and by February 28 he had almost reached Paris by way of Aachen and Soissons.[76] This was a journey of some four hundred miles, an impressive feat in a three-week period.[77] Such a rapid campaign with a large army was a considerable

---

[71] Schramm, *Die deutschen Kaiser*, 45, 157, 160.

[72] Kehr's introduction to *DLG*, p. xxxiii.

[73] Karl Bosl, *Franken um 800: Strukturanalyse einer fränkischen Königsprovinz*, 2nd ed. (Munich, 1969), 10–12; Brühl, *Deutschland-Frankreich*, 102–11. The *ARF*, s.a. 820, 823, pp. 153, 160; and Einhard, *VK*, chaps. 15, 18, pp. 18, 22, use the terms *orientalis Francia* and *orientales Franci* to indicate Franconia and its inhabitants.

[74] *AMP*, s.a. 688, p. 1; *ARF*, s.a. 787 (both versions), pp. 78–79.

[75] *AB*, s.a. 834, pp. 11–12; Astronomer, *VH*, chaps. 50–51, pp. 484–90.

[76] *AX*, s.a. 834, p. 9.

[77] For mounted rates of travel, see Bernard S. Bachrach, "Animals and Warfare in Early Medieval Europe," *SS Spoleto* 30 (1985): 717–19 and nn. 46, 50.

Louis the German's second seal. Louis introduced this seal after the Field of Lies in 833 to articulate his claims to an expanded kingdom "in east Francia." The seal matrix contained an elegant antique gem depicting the bust of the Roman emperor Hadrian. The inscription reads "† Xpe protege Hludoicum regem" (O Christ: protect King Louis!). Louis the German modeled this seal on those of Charlemagne and Louis the Pious, which likewise used antique gems with bearded Roman emperors and the "Xpe protege" inscription. Louis's Hadrian seal became a cherished piece of east Frankish regalia. He used it for the remainder of his reign, and he had the gem remounted in 867 when it cracked. His son and his great-grandson, Louis the Younger and Louis the Child, respectively, likewise used this seal. From a diploma dated May 18, 875. Staatsarchiv Bamberg, Bamberger Urk. 2. Photograph courtesy of the Lichtbildarchiv, Marburg.

accomplishment in terms of military organization and logistics, suggesting Louis's growing abilities as a general. When Lothar learned of Louis's rapid approach, he fled with his men to Burgundy, leaving behind his father and Charles the Bald. The bishops who were present reinvested Louis the Pious with the royal robes, crown, and arms on Sunday, March 1, at the royal monastery of St.-Denis. However, Louis the Pious apparently did not fully trust Pippin and Louis, since he stalled for some time before meeting them face-to-face.[78] As with most diplomatic ceremonies and political rituals, only after private negotiation could there be a public gesture of accord. Thus, two weeks later on March 15, Louis the Pious "joyfully" received Pippin, Louis, and their followers at Quierzy and thanked them for their help.[79]

Louis the German emerged from the 833–34 rebellion with a heightened reputation for his skillful rescue of his father. Although the emperor dismissed Pippin back to Aquitaine, he kept Louis with him to celebrate Easter at Aachen and to go hunting in the Ardennes.[80] Revealing the younger Louis's favor, the emperor noted in a diploma for Abbot Tatto of Kempten that he made the grant "at the request and suggestion of our dear son the most glorious King Louis."[81] Once again, Louis's intervention on the behalf of a powerful Alemannian abbot suggests his growing influence in that region. Moreover, the fact that Louis the Pious dropped his son's former title, king of the Bavarians, indicates that he now recognized his son's claims to an expanded eastern kingdom. At this time, Louis the German sent to Rome his Bavarian supporter, Bishop Hitto of Freising.[82] On May 23, Hitto delivered a (now lost) letter from Louis the German to Pope Gregory IV, presumably informing him of Louis the Pious's reinstatement as emperor. In August 834, the two Louises set out against Lothar with a large army, which included "all the people who lived beyond the Rhine." After Pippin brought reinforcements, Lothar had no choice but to submit at Chouzy, swearing that he

[78] This explains the chronological confusion in the sources noted by Dümmler, *GOR* 1:95 and n. 2.

[79] *AB*, s.a. 834, p. 12.

[80] Nithard, 1.5, p. 8; Thegan, *GH*, chap. 48, pp. 240–42; Astronomer, *VH*, chap. 52, p. 492. Also present were Judith and Charles the Bald, who were reunited with the emperor.

[81] BM 929; Dümmler, *GOR* 1:99n1.

[82] Hitto returned from this mission with the relics of Saints Alexander and Justin for his church of Weihenstephan at Freising: *Translatio sanctorum Alexandri papae et Iustini presbyteri*, chap. 1, in MGH SS 15.1: 286–88; *Freising* 629. Lothar was still in Burgundy, giving Hitto a window of opportunity to make this journey via the Brenner Pass, which he controlled on Louis the German's behalf. In Burgundy, Lothar and his supporters continued to resist the emperor and waged a bloody vendetta against the family of Bernard: Thegan, *GH*, chap. 52, p. 244.

would never rebel again.[83] The emperor banished Lothar and his supporters to Italy, ordering them never to come to Francia without his permission.

Despite Louis the German's favor with his father, for the time being Louis the Pious reasserted his rule east of the Rhine.[84] The emperor resumed appointing bishops and abbots in Germania, and he made grants to magnates in all the eastern territories save Bavaria: Bishop Hunberg of Würzburg; Abbots Warin of Corvey, Marcward of Prüm, Raban of Fulda, and Tatto of Kempten; Abbess Tetta of Herford; the Alsatian convent of Hohenburg; and Count Adalbert of Metz.[85] Moreover, Louis the Pious took back control of the strategic Rhenish cities of Mainz and Worms, at the latter holding an assembly in 836, and he sent troops against the northern Slavs to secure his northeastern borders.[86] Thus, while the emperor in theory recognized Louis the German's claims to an expanded inheritance, for the time being he was determined to maintain a firm grip on the reins of power in the east.

Throughout the remainder of the 830s, Louis the German worked hard to remain in his father's good graces. He regularly attended his father's assemblies (Lothar did not), and in his diplomas he often praised his father as "our lord and father Louis the most outstanding emperor."[87] When Emma gave birth to their second son around 835, Louis named the boy *Hludowig*—known to historians as Louis the Younger (876–82)—in honor of the emperor. As a sign of Louis the German's continued favor, at the 836 Thionville assembly his father allowed him to grant his supporter, Count Werner, rich royal lands on the middle Rhine, an indication that the emperor still recognized his son's claims to an expanded eastern kingdom.[88] Throughout the 830s, Louis continued to claim to rule "in east Francia" in his diplomas, even though his father had in practice limited his rule to Bavaria. Louis the German seems to have enjoyed popularity among the eastern nobles, some of whom supported his claims to an expanded kingdom. Abbot Gozbert of St.-Gall, for example, dated his monastery's charters to the dual reigns of "Emperor Louis and the younger Louis, king of the Alemans."[89] The clearest expression of Louis the German's popularity was Thegan's *Deeds of Emperor Louis*, written in 837, in which Thegan ex-

[83] Thegan, *GH*, chaps. 54–55, pp. 248–50; *AX*, s.a. 834, p. 9.

[84] Nelson, "Last Years," 147–59; Bigott, *Ludwig der Deutsche*, 76–77.

[85] BM 927, 929, 932, 935, 941, 948, 952, 954, 964, 971, 977, 977a, 978. For Louis the Pious's eastern ecclesiastical appointments during these years, see Bigott, *Ludwig der Deutsche*, 64–69.

[86] BM 963a; *AB*, s.a. 838, pp. 25–26.

[87] BM 941 (835), 962 (836), 963 (836), 970 (837), 970 (838), 977 (838); *DLG* 15, 17, 22, 23.

[88] *DLG* 19; Innes, *State and Society*, 202–4.

[89] *St.-Gall* 344, 358.

tolled the younger Louis as his father's beloved namesake, favorite son, and stalwart defender.[90] Thegan concluded his biography with the image of the younger Louis as his father's most worthy son, "just as from the beginning of the world the younger brother often exceeds the older in merit," as in the cases of Abel, Isaac, Jacob, David, and Louis the Pious himself.[91] In contrast, Thegan showed considerable hostility toward Lothar and ambivalence toward Pippin. Thegan circulated his biography around the imperial court, and it apparently reflected the high favor the younger Louis enjoyed there at the time.

Yet others urged a reconciliation with Lothar. Soon after the 833–34 rebellion, Raban composed a long letter for the emperor about the "honoring of parents and the obedience of their sons," in which he enumerated scriptural citations demonstrating the sinfulness of rebellious children.[92] But Raban concluded by urging Louis the Pious to pardon Lothar once again and thereby imitate the father of the biblical Prodigal Son. As Louis the Pious grew old and approached death, the eastern magnates increasingly found themselves in the difficult position of having to decide between supporting Lothar or Louis the German.

CONSOLIDATION IN BAVARIA

Throughout these tumultuous events, Louis continued to consolidate his power in his political base, Bavaria. Louis knew that he would have to fight Lothar for a share of Francia when their father died, and he could do that only with the support of the Bavarian nobles and firm control of Bavaria's troublesome eastern frontiers. During the 830s, Louis frequently resided at the Bavarian capital of Regensburg, and he also visited the cluster of royal estates to the southeast, including Altötting, Ranshofen, and Osterhofen.[93] Once he received the authority to issue diplomas, Louis began to make grants to the leading Bavarian bishops and abbots to shore up their support.[94] Louis the Pious's grants to the Bavarian Church had slowed considerably during the 820s, suggesting that the region's bishops and abbots had

---

[90] Thegan, *GH*, chaps. 36, 37, 39, 40, 45–48, 54, 55, pp. 222, 224–26, 238–42, 248, 250.

[91] Ibid., chap. 57, p. 252 (referring to chap. 3, p. 178).

[92] Raban, *Epistolae*, no. 15, in MGH *Epistolae* 5:403–15.

[93] Regensburg: *DLG* 2, 6, 8, 10–12, 20; Altötting: *DLG* 3, 7, 21–24; Ranshofen: *DLG* 1, 4, 5; Osterhofen: *DLG* 9, 18.

[94] *DLG* 2–9, 11, 18, 20–23, 25; Bigott, *Ludwig der Deutsche*, 22–30.

been languishing from a lack of *Königsnähe* for some time.[95] But with Louis the German now residing full time in the region, the Bavarian churchmen found a new source of royal patronage. An important moment in Louis's consolidation over the Bavarian Church occurred in 836, when Archbishop Adalram of Salzburg died and was succeeded by Liupram (836–59). Liupram had been a faithful supporter (*fidelis*) and benefice holder of Louis's since the early 830s, and his promotion to archbishop presumably took place through Louis's influence.[96] Over the next two decades, the king would richly reward Archbishop Liupram for his political support.[97]

In Bavaria Louis not only rewarded his supporters but punished his opponents. Lothar had briefly been king of Bavaria between 814 and 817, and he still had connections to the nobles of that region.[98] After helping his father recover the throne in 831, Louis returned to Bavaria, where he granted properties at Pfettrach (east of Freising) to the monastery of Herrieden.[99] Louis's diploma explained that these properties "formerly had been the personal property of a certain man named Rato. He forfeited them because of his treachery, and they came into the jurisdiction of our power according to the law." Rato apparently was a supporter of Lothar's, since the next year he appeared at Lothar's court in Italy looking for another grant of land.[100] Moreover, in November 834, Louis the Pious decreed that royal legates travel throughout the empire to correct usurpations of Church lands, banditry, and lawlessness that had taken place during Lothar's rebellions.[101] In response, Louis the German sent his count of the palace, Timo, on a judicial circuit of Bavaria.[102] In a poem addressed to Louis known as the "Song of Count Timo," a Freising churchman recounted in gory detail how Timo had punished criminals in the Bavarian king's name: "Upon arrival [at Freising], the count orders bandits hung, eyes put out for violent acts, and noses disgracefully mutilated with ugly wounds for crimes. This one loses a foot, the other a hand."[103]

During the 830s, Louis also supervised a major administrative reorgani-

[95] BM 588, 598, 606, 607, 625, 707, 740, 778, 850, 853.

[96] *DLG* 7. Cf. Bigott, *Ludwig der Deutsche*, 73–74, who assumes that Louis allowed his father to maintain the "imperial prerogative" to appoint bishops within Bavaria.

[97] *DLG* 21, 22, 23, 25, 46, 60.

[98] For Lothar's brief tenure in Bavaria, see Depreux, *Prosopographie*, 298–300.

[99] *DLG* 5.

[100] *DLoI* 10.

[101] Astronomer, *VH*, chap. 53, pp. 498–500.

[102] Concerning Timo, see *Freising* 603; *Regensburg* 29; Mitterauer, *Karolingische Markgrafen*, 169–75; Brunner, *Oppositionelle Gruppen*, 121–22.

[103] *Carmen de Timone comite*, ll. 65–68, in MGH *Poetae Latini* 2:120–24; Brown, *Unjust Seizure*, 1–5.

zation of Bavaria's eastern frontiers.[104] Louis promoted two of his Frankish supporters to powerful frontier commands: Ernest, who held properties on the Danube near Linz, apparently became commander of the Bohemian marches; and Ratpot became the powerful prefect of the Eastland. Although previous eastern prefects had had their seat at the old Roman fortress at Lorch, Louis moved Ratpot's seat farther east to Tulln, where he gave Ratpot rich benefices and properties.[105] Ratpot's headquarters at Tulln was strategically located for communications and the movement of troops in the region, since it had a port on the Danube and was located at the intersection of several major Roman roads. Under his command were a number of subordinate frontier counts. One was the Frankish nobleman, Werner, whose county lay in Upper Pannonia. Members of a powerful Bavarian family known as the Wilhelminer also rose to power in the Eastland under Louis, including Counts William of the Traungau, Rihheri of Szombathely, and Pabo of Carantania. Thus by the late 830s, the defense of Bavaria's eastern frontiers was in the hands of a group of Franks and Bavarians closely allied to the king.

As in all frontier regions, landholding underpinned Frankish power. Since Charlemagne's conquest of the Avar empire, the Bavarian bishoprics and monasteries had accumulated extensive estates in the southeast to support their ongoing missionary work and church building among the Slavs.[106] At the same time, ecclesiastical landholding provided the foundation for the Franks' military presence in the marches, since armies could be effective only if there were estates from which to provision them.[107] Many of the land grants Louis made to Bavarian churchmen during the 830s were located in the southeast.[108] These estates were concentrated along the middle

[104] Mitterauer, *Karolingische Markgrafen*, 85–159; Bowlus, *Franks, Moravians, and Magyars*, 90–113; Wolfram, *Grenzen und Räume*, 248–50; idem, *Salzburg*, 298–316.

[105] Ratpot's *comitatus* bordered on the county of Szombathely to the southeast (*DLG* 38). Ratpot possessed half of the royal fisc as well as properties at Tulln (*DLG* 96; *Regensburg* 29) and properties at Pitten on the Roman road south of Vienna (*Freising* 898b–c).

[106] This is vividly portrayed in the *Conversio*, written at Salzburg in 870. For the missionary work of the Bavarian Church in the southeast, see Wilhelm Störmer, "Zum Problem der Slawenmission des Bistums Freising im 9. Jahrhundert," *MGSL* 126 (1986): 207–20; Heinrich Koller, "König Ludwig der Deutsche und die Slawenmission," in *Historia docet: Sborník prací k poctě šedesátých narozenin prof. PhDr. Ivana Hlaváčka*, ed. Miloslav Polívka and Michal Svatoš (Prague, 1992), 167–92; Egon Boshof, "Das ostfränkische Reich und die Slavenmission im 9. Jahrhundert: Die Rolle Passaus," in *Mönchtum-Kirche-Herrschaft 750–1000*, ed. Dieter R. Bauer, Rudolf Hiestand, Brigitte Kasten, and Sönke Lorenz (Sigmaringen, 1998), 51–76; Bigott, *Ludwig der Deutsche*, 167–77.

[107] Bowlus, *Franks, Moravians, and Magyars*, esp. 25–32.

[108] *DLG* 2 (in the Wachau north of the Danube), 3 (at Melk, Pielach, and Grünz), 8 (the *antiquitus castrum* of Herilungoburg), 9 (near Schönabrunn south of Carnuntum), 18 (at St.-Andrä east of Tulln), 25 (at the confluence of the Ybbs and Danube adjacent to the

Danube in Upper Pannonia between Linz and Carnuntum (Petronelle) in what is today northern Austria. Louis's counts, including Ernest, Ratpot, Werner, and William, likewise held lands along the Danube, and they often granted and exchanged these frontier estates with Bavarian monasteries. One example is the grants made by the powerful Wilhelminer count of the Traungau, William. In 833, William bequeathed his lands near Linz to St.-Emmeram, and Prefect Ratpot stood as first witness to his grant.[109] The following year, William gave St.-Emmeram lands west of Tulln in return for benefices on the Danube between Passau and Linz.[110] These lands along the Danube were ideal for supplying troop movements by land or river, since they were situated along the old Roman road on the south shore of the Danube. Thus, through landholding and exchanges of strategic estates, Louis and the Bavarian bishops, abbots, and counts became jointly responsible for the Christianization and military defense of Bavaria's frontiers.

While shoring up his control of the Bavarian Eastland, Louis once again clashed with Lothar over the Brenner Pass. When Lothar returned to Italy in 834, he and his supporters began seizing lands claimed by the papacy.[111] This angered Louis the Pious, who in 837 announced a major campaign to Italy.[112] The emperor justified this journey as a pilgrimage to Rome, but he also intended to bring Lothar to heel. He planned to bring a large army that included his sons Louis and Pippin, and he commanded that supplies and quarters be prepared for him along the entire route to Rome. As the favored son, Louis the German readily complied. During Lent in early 837, he was at the Bavarian palace of Altötting making preparations for the Italian campaign with his two chief supporters, Archbishop Liupram of Salzburg and Prefect Ratpot, to whom he made several grants.[113] On April 8, Abbot Tatto of Kempten, a frequent messenger between the imperial and Bavarian courts, also appeared at Altötting. Presumably in response to his father's demand for supplies for the imperial army, Louis granted Kempten the privi-

---

Roman road). In 831 Louis had also granted Salzburg an estate near Gurk, the county seat of Carantania: *DLG* 4.

[109] *Regensburg* 26 (at Schönering, Kematen, and Puchham).

[110] Ibid., 27 (at Perschling).

[111] *AB*, s.a. 836, p. 19.

[112] *AB*, s.a. 837, p. 21; Thegan, *GH, continuatio*, p. 256; Astronomer, *VH*, chap. 55, pp. 508–10.

[113] *DLG* 21–23. The king issued these diplomas on February 23 and 24. I interpret the "vir inluster Hruotbaldus comes" in *DLG* 21 to be a misspelling of Ratpot's name, since otherwise there is no mention of a Hruotbald among Louis the German's supporters, and because the honorific title *vir inluster* seems especially appropriate to Ratpot's rank as prefect of the Eastland. It is possible that the royal scribe misspelled Ratpot's name because he confused it with the name of Salzburg's patron saint, Rupert (Hruotbertus), whom he mentioned in *DLG* 22 and 23.

lege of taking six carts of salt annually from the salt springs at Reichenhall without having to pay royal taxes or tariffs.[114]

It seems that Louis the German gathered his army at Regensburg on the eve of his departure for Italy. A St.-Emmeram charter dated 837 (the month and day are not recorded) reports that Prefect Ratpot bequeathed all his properties at Tulln to the monastery of St.-Emmeram during an assembly at Regensburg.[115] Ratpot's properties at Tulln were extensive, since the St.-Emmeram charter valued them at 2,400 *denarii*—roughly 170 head of cattle. Ratpot's donation to St.-Emmeram was a gesture of solidarity with the king: Louis's archchaplain, Baturich of Regensburg, was abbot of St.-Emmeram, and Ratpot made his grant "in the presence of the king, his great men, and all those serving him." The charter lists twenty-four of Louis's chief lay supporters as witnesses. In the place of honor as first witness was Ernest, and he was followed by Counts Werner, Timo, William, Rihheri, Pabo, and many others. The presence of so many high-ranking counts at Regensburg points to the conclusion that Ratpot made the grant on the eve of the invasion of Italy, when Louis was mustering his army at his Bavarian capital.[116] Ratpot's grant therefore suggests the political solidarity of Louis's Bavarian magnates, their determination to support their king in his ongoing rivalry with Lothar, and their patriotic devotion to St.-Emmeram, the patron saint of Louis's royal capital.

Although in disfavor, Lothar was far from inactive. When he learned of his father's invasion, he ordered his supporters to seize the Alpine passes and barricade them with strong fortifications.[117] As a result, Louis the Pious was forced to call off his campaign soon after he set out in June 837.[118] It seems that Lothar's barricading of the Brenner Pass likewise forced Louis the German to call off his invasion. On September 23, Louis issued a diploma for Liupram of Salzburg at a location called Ohoberg, which may have been

[114] *DLG* 24.

[115] *Regensburg* 29. Although there is no report of it, it seems that Louis had converted Ratpot's benefices at Tulln into personal property, on the condition that he bequeath them to the monastery of St.-Emmeram. According to the terms of the grant, Ratpot would give his property at Tulln to St.-Emmeram upon his death if he had no heirs. If he had a male heir, however, the son could buy back his father's land for 200 *solidi*.

[116] If it is correct that Ratpot made his grant to St.-Emmeram during the mustering of Louis's Bavarian army for the Italian campaign, then it seems that the army departed before August 28, 837. On that day at Regensburg, Bishop Baturich exchanged lands with a certain Ucciand, and there is no overlap between the witnesses to Ratpot's grant and Baturich's exchange with Ucciand: *Regensburg* 28.

[117] *AB*, s.a. 837, p. 22: "Hlotharius autem clusas in Alpibus muris firmissimis arceri praecepit."

[118] The emperor justified calling off the campaign because of a Viking attack on Frisia: BM 965c.

Obernberg in the Stubai Alps.[119] Obernberg was located north of Vipiteno, where Bishop Hitto of Freising held the strategic fortress guarding the Brenner route to Italy. Lothar's supporters apparently had seized Freising's estates along the Brenner route to block Louis the German's invasion, and we later hear that Bishop Odalschalk of Trent had usurped Freising's lands at Bolzano "at the prompting of evil men."[120] As a result, Louis seems to have halted his army's march to Italy and returned to Bavaria.

Although the 837 Italian campaign was a failure, it benefited Louis by securing his position as the emperor's favorite son. It was precisely at this time that Thegan wrote his *Deeds of Emperor Louis*, which painted a favorable picture of the emperor's namesake. Louis attended his father's Aachen assembly in late 837, at which the elderly emperor announced yet another new division of the empire. He granted the fourteen-year-old Charles the Bald Neustria, Frisia, part of Burgundy, and a number of adjacent counties.[121] In the opinion of one contemporary, Louis the Pious gave Charles the "best part of the *regnum Francorum*."[122] Unlike Louis's previous attempts at division, this one did not simply outline a possible future kingdom for Charles. Instead, Louis the Pious immediately installed Charles as king and had the magnates of those regions swear loyalty to him. But the 837 division also reflected Louis the German's continued favor. He was the only brother present when his father decreed Charles's new kingdom, and he gave his assent to it.[123] More important, the new division did not infringe on the eastern kingdom that Louis had claimed since 833, since Charles's new kingdom consisted chiefly of territories west of the Meuse River (plus Frisia on the North Sea). Indeed, because Charles's kingdom mostly did not extend beyond the Meuse, the new division implied a significant increase of Louis's eastern kingdom, which would now include all of Austrasia. The 837 division therefore was a statement of Louis's continued favor—and Lothar's disfavor—with their father.

Louis's favor with his father only ran so deep, however, and at this point he overstepped the emperor's recent show of support. In early March 838, Louis sent his father a letter requesting that he be granted the same powers

[119] *DLG* 25; Theodor Sickel, "Beiträge zur Diplomatik, I: Die Urkunden Ludwig's des Deutschen bis zum Jahre 859," *SKAW* 36.3 (1861): 354n1. Kehr rejected Sickel's identification of Ohoberg as Obernberg, without an explanation or alternate interpretation.

[120] Only months before Lothar's death in 855, Louis and Bishop Anno of Freising reclaimed Freising's lands at Bolzano with the cooperation of Emperor Louis II of Italy: *DLG* 72.

[121] BM 970a; Nelson, *Charles the Bald*, 94–95.

[122] *AF*, s.a. 838, p. 28.

[123] *AB*, s.a. 837, pp. 22–23.

as Charles: that he now become king of the eastern magnates and rule independently in the east.[124] Louis also asked his father to pardon his absence from court, since he had arranged to meet with Lothar in March in the Alps at Trent. Louis apparently had demanded this Alpine summit with Lothar to regain control of the Brenner Pass, which his brother had seized the previous year.[125] However, when the emperor learned of this meeting, he feared another rebellion, since he still distrusted Lothar.[126] The emperor immediately sent messengers throughout the empire to muster his army in case another coup was under way, and he demanded that Louis come to Aachen and give an account of his actions. In April Louis came to the palace in the company of his supporters, undoubtedly many of the magnates who had witnessed Ratpot's grant to St.-Emmeram the previous year. "After discussing everything in depth," the *Annals of St.-Bertin* reported, "he affirmed with an oath, along with those in whom he had most confidence, that he had not contemplated anything against the fidelity and honor he owed his father in that meeting."[127] Satisfied for the moment, the emperor dismissed Louis and commanded him to attend the upcoming assembly at Nijmegen in May.

Louis now returned to Bavaria to respond to a new rebellion in Lower Pannonia. At this time, a Slavic prince named Ratimar governed Lower Pannonia as a client ruler of the Franks. In 838, Ratimar rebelled against Louis the German by harboring a Slavic outlaw named Pribina, whose ad-

---

[124] The content of Louis's letter to his father is recorded in *Formulae Augienses*, no. 7, in MGH *Formulae*, pp. 367–68. Concerning this *formula*, the Latin of which is extremely opaque, see Dümmler, *GOR* 1:73–74; Konrad Beyerle, "Von der Gründung bis zum Ende des freiherrlichen Klosters (724–1427)," in *Die Kultur der Abtei Reichenau*, ed. Konrad Beyerle (Munich, 1925), 99–100, 210n50; Karl Schmid, "Königtum, Adel und Klöster zwischen Bodensee und Schwarzwald," in Tellenbach, *Studien und Vorarbeiten*, 287–88; Bigott, *Ludwig der Deutsche*, 70–71.

[125] On the basis of the later reports of Nithard, 1.6, p. 9, and the Astronomer, *VH*, chap. 59, p. 524, historians have traditionally interpreted the 838 meeting as a sign of the brothers' anger about Charles's new kingdom: BM 971d; Dümmler, *GOR* 1:125; Nelson, *Charles the Bald*, 95–96; Boshof, *Ludwig der Fromme*, 235. However, the contemporary *AB*, s.a. 838, p. 23, and *AF*, s.a. 838, p. 28, do not indicate that anger over the new division was the motive for the brothers' meeting. Because the 837 division set Louis up to become heir to all Austrasia, it is unlikely that he opposed the new inheritance decree. Since Nithard and the Astronomer (both writing in the early 840s) knew of Lothar's later hostilities toward Charles, it seems that they projected this animosity back on the 838 Trent meeting. From a strategic perspective, it is unlikely that Lothar and Louis would have launched a rebellion from Trent, which was far removed from the center of power in Francia.

[126] Here the elderly emperor's thinking may have been influenced by Louis the German's enemies, Archbishop Otgar of Mainz and the Hattonian brothers, Counts Adalbert, Hatto, and Banzleib, who were at court at this time: BM 972, 973, 977a, 980, 984c.

[127] *AB*, s.a. 838, pp. 23–24.

venturous career illustrates the rough-and-tumble political volatility of the Franco–Slavic frontiers.[128] According to the *Conversion of the Bavarians and Carantanians*, Pribina originally ruled the large Slavic fortress of Nitra east of Vienna.[129] However, the Slavic ruler of neighboring Moravia, Moimir, exiled Pribina from Nitra around 833, presumably because of his close political ties to the Franks. (Pribina seems to have been married to a member of the Bavarian Wilhelminer family, and around 827 Adalram of Salzburg had consecrated a church Pribina built at Nitra.)[130] Pribina fled with his followers to Prefect Ratpot, who in turn presented him to Louis the German.[131] Louis now saw an opportunity to hire a group of foreign "barbarian" mercenaries, a common Carolingian practice.[132] Louis ordered that Pribina be baptized in Salzburg's church of Traismauer on the Danube and then serve with his followers in Ratpot's army. After a few years, however, a dispute broke out between Ratpot and Pribina, forcing Pribina and his followers into exile, first among the Bulgars and then at the court of Ratimar of Lower Pannonia.

Because Lower Pannonia was part of Ratpot's prefecture, Ratimar's harboring of Pribina was tantamount to rebellion. In 838, Louis therefore sent Ratpot at the head of a large Bavarian army to crush Ratimar.[133] Ratimar fled the region, while Pribina and his followers took refuge with the Bavarian count of Carniola, Salacho, who brokered a reconciliation between Ratpot and Pribina. Louis now devised a plan to solve the ongoing instability in Lower Pannonia by making Pribina himself the new client ruler of that region.[134] Louis conceded the large region between the Raab, Drava, and Danube rivers to Pribina, where he was to rule as Louis's faithful *dux*.[135]

[128] Concerning Pribina, see Agnes Sós, *Die slawische Bevölkerung Westungarns im 9. Jahrhundert*, Münchener Beiträge zur Vor- und Frühgeschichte 22 (Munich, 1973), 28; Peter Štih, "Pribina: Slawischer Fürst oder fränkischer Graf?" in *Ethnogenese und Überlieferung: Angewandte Methoden der Frühmittelalterforschung*, ed. Karl Brunner and Brigitte Merta (Vienna, 1994), 209–22; Wolfram, *Salzburg*, 311–16.

[129] For the early medieval fortress at Nitra, see Bohuslav Chropovský, "The Situation of Nitra in the Light of Archaeological Finds," *Historica* 8 (1964): 5–33.

[130] *Conversio*, chap. 11, p. 122 and n. 130; Wolfram, *Salzburg*, 323. This report apparently was a later marginal notation that was subsequently incorporated into the text.

[131] *Conversio*, chap. 10, pp. 120–22.

[132] Halsall, *Warfare and Society*, 111–16.

[133] *Conversio*, chaps. 10–11, p. 122; *AI*, s.a. 838, p. 740; *Auctarium Garstense*, s.a. 838, p. 564; Wolfram, *Salzburg*, 311–14.

[134] Here Louis was employing a proven Carolingian strategy of installing "barbarian" rulers to defend a contested frontier region. For this Carolingian practice with regard to the Vikings, see Simon Coupland, "From Poachers to Gamekeepers: Scandinavian Warlords and Carolingian Kings," *EME* 7 (1998): 85–114.

[135] Previously, Lower Pannonia had been the region south of the Drava. Now Louis rotated the border between *Pannonia superior* and *Pannonia inferior* ninety degrees, making the Raab River the boundary in accord with the border between the dioceses of Salzburg

Louis and Ratpot chose Zalavár on the southwestern tip of Lake Balaton as Pribina's ducal seat. As had become common among ninth-century Slavic rulers, Pribina built a large fortress as his seat of power. Zalavár was particularly well situated for a frontier fortress: the site had been settled since the Roman period, and it was surrounded by impenetrable forests and swamps along the Zala River. Pribina constructed an extremely well fortified castle (*castrum munitissimum*) that became known as Moosburg, the Swamp Fortress.[136] The report in the *Conversion of the Bavarians and Carantanians* makes explicit the intimate connection between Pribina's fortress and his lordship over land and men: "The king gave Pribina as a benefice the region of Lower Pannonia around the Zala River. He then settled there, built a fortress in a certain forest and swamp on the Zala River, gathered the surrounding peoples, and greatly thrived in that land."[137] For over two decades, Pribina ruled Lower Pannonia from his fortress at Moosburg, serving as a bulwark against the Bulgars to the southeast and the Moravians to the north. With Lower Pannonia now secure, Louis could turn his attention westward to the looming conflict with Lothar.

During the 830s, Louis the German had taken significant steps toward undermining the *Ordinatio imperii* and Lothar's claims to the empire. Louis had secured his control of Bavaria and its marches and gathered around him a group of loyal Bavarian and Frankish magnates committed to the expansion of his kingdom westward. By positioning himself as the emperor's loyal son, Louis the German had won his father's recognition for his expanded inheritance, which included some or all of Austrasia. But Louis the German's position remained precarious, since it depended on the continued favor of his elderly father. With the future of the empire at stake, the temporary favor of an aging emperor would prove insufficient to secure his son's political future.

---

and Passau. Although the *Conversio* does not specify when Louis granted this benefice to Pribina, it must have occurred between Ratpot's campaign against Ratimar in 838 and the point at which Louis converted Pribina's benefice into allodial lands in 847: *DLG* 46. Within this time frame, it is probable that Louis the German established Pribina in Lower Pannonia soon after the 838 campaign. With Louis the Pious's death and renewed conflict with Lothar on the horizon, Louis the German undoubtedly was eager to secure his eastern borders.

136 Regino, *Chronicon*, s.a. 880, p. 117.
137 *Conversio*, chap. 11, p. 122.

CHAPTER THREE
THE FIGHT FOR SURVIVAL, 838-843

I n 838, the approximately twenty-eight-year-old Louis unexpectedly fell from his father's favor, precipitating the first
major crisis of his reign. For the next five years he was
forced to take up arms against his father and Lothar to defend his claims to an expanded eastern kingdom with a foothold in Austrasia. The result was the great Carolingian civil war in which, for the first time
since the battle of Tertry in 687, Franks killed fellow Franks in major military engagements.[1] During the civil war, Louis managed to defend his inheritance claims through a combination of patronage, negotiation, threats,
and, when all else failed, armed conflict on the battlefield. Louis emerged
from these years of crisis with an expanded kingdom "in east Francia" and
growing recognition of his abilities as king and military leader.[2]

The Carolingian civil war was not simply a conflict among Louis the
Pious's sons, however. The Frankish magnates played a decisive role, since
the competing kings needed their support to fill the ranks of their armies.
This was a period of great political fluidity among the Frankish elite, with
nobles continuing to switch sides in their desperation to secure their political futures after Louis the Pious's death. The eastern magnates were especially prominent in this contest, because it was along and east of the Rhine
that Lothar and Louis clashed most violently for territories and aristocratic

---

[1] For the battle of Tertry, see Fouracre, *Age of Charles Martel*, 40, 48.

[2] On the politics of these years, see Dümmler, *GOR* 1:126–238; Brunner, *Oppositionelle
Gruppen*, 117–19; Nelson, "Last Years," 147–59; idem, "Public *Histories*," 195–238; idem,
Charles the Bald, 92–137; Boshof, *Ludwig der Fromme*, 232–51; Hartmann, *Ludwig der
Deutsche*, 35–44; Bigott, *Ludwig der Deutsche*, 77–95.

support. As always, the flashpoint of politics remained land and *honores*. Throughout the seventh and eighth centuries, Franks from Austrasia had colonized beyond the Rhine, winning lands, lordships, churches, and brides throughout Germania.[3] As a result, the most powerful Austrasian families tended to have estates, offices, and political connections on both sides of the Rhine. But Louis's determination to claim an expanded kingdom threatened to cut in half the *honores* of the most powerful eastern magnates, since the rules of Carolingian succession stipulated that a nobleman could swear loyalty to, and hold offices and benefices from, only one king. In this way the civil war among Louis the Pious's sons became a crisis for the entire Frankish elite.

FATHER AGAINST SON

When Louis the German arrived at the Nijmegen assembly in June 838, he still enjoyed his father's favor. On June 14, Louis the Pious confirmed a land exchange between Abbot Tatto of Kempten and Louis the German's Bavarian supporter, Count Waning.[4] Louis the Pious's diploma records that he made the confirmation at the request of "our beloved son and namesake, the glorious King Louis," indicating that the emperor still recognized his son's claim to an expanded eastern kingdom. But soon thereafter, Louis unexpectedly fell from his father's graces. The author of the *Annals of St.-Bertin*, who was a supporter of Louis the Pious, was surprised at this turn of events: "There was a great argument, quite different from what should have happened. Louis lost whatever he had usurped from his father's possession on this side of and beyond the Rhine. His father resumed possession of Alsace, Saxony, Thuringia, Austrasia, and Alemannia."[5]

What had precipitated Louis's sudden fall from favor? The answer lies in the unresolved issue of royal succession. Charles the Bald's fifteenth birthday fell during the 838 Nijmegen assembly on June 13. Charles's coming of age would have been a matter of public celebration, and it undoubtedly sparked continued discussions about Charles's future kingdom. Nithard, who probably was at court around this time, described the backroom negotiations around this burning issue:

---

[3] Wood, *Merovingian Kingdoms*, 160–64; Fouracre, *Age of Charles Martel*, 99–118.

[4] BM 978. Waning had witnessed Ratpot's grant to St.-Emmeram in 837, and his name appeared in the entries in the St.-Gall and Reichenau confraternity books alongside Louis's other *fideles*, including Ernest, Ratpot, and Werner.

[5] *AB*, s.a. 838, p. 24; *AF*, s.a. 838, p. 29.

Old age had beset [Louis the Pious], who was threatened with infirmity from his various troubles. The queen mother and leading nobles, who were working on Charles's behalf according to his father's wishes, feared that his brothers' hatred would seek to destroy Charles if [Louis the Pious] died without settling his affairs. They therefore thought it wise that the father win over one of his sons as [Charles's] supporter so at least these two united sons could overcome a rival faction if the other brothers were unwilling to be at peace after [Louis the Pious's] death.[6]

Louis the German had long been his father's loyal supporter, and he hoped to be tapped as his half brother's guardian. Indeed, Louis the Pious's recent 837 division suggested this would be the case, since it implied that Charles would receive Neustria, Louis Austrasia, and leave only Italy and Aquitaine for Lothar and Pippin.

A group of eastern magnates thwarted Louis the German's plans, however. The leaders of these eastern magnates were Archbishop Otgar of Mainz and Count Adalbert of Metz, who, in the menacing words of Nithard, "each bore so much hatred for Louis that he wanted him dead."[7] Otgar of Mainz was archbishop of the largest archdiocese in the Carolingian empire. Although the city of Mainz was located on the western bank of the Rhine, its massive archdiocese covered much of the territories beyond the Rhine. Adalbert was the head of a powerful Frankish family known as the Hattonians, who had risen to great power under Louis the Pious.[8] Adalbert of Metz and his two brothers, Counts Hatto and Banzleib, held property, benefices, and counties throughout the empire: in Toulouse, Le Mans, Metz, the Wormsgau, Nassau, Alemannia, and Saxony.[9] By the late 830s, the Hattonians were extremely influential at Louis the Pious's court. Adalbert was the imperial doorkeeper, and his brother Hatto had become Charles the Bald's guardian.[10]

Otgar of Mainz, Adalbert of Metz, and Adalbert's brothers vigorously opposed Louis the German's creation of an eastern kingdom, since it threatened to sever them from their political power east of the Rhine. For them,

---

[6] Nithard, 1.6, p. 10. See further Astronomer, *VH*, chap. 54, pp. 504–7 and n. 827.

[7] Nithard, 2.7, p. 21. The *AF*, s.a. 841, p. 32, referred to Adalbert as the "instigator of the disputes" against Louis.

[8] On the Hattonians, see Dümmler, *GOR* 1:128 and nn. 3, 4; Brunner, *Oppositionelle Gruppen*, 114, 118; Schmid, "Königtum, Adel und Klöster," 282–91; Eric J. Goldberg, "Popular Revolt, Dynastic Politics, and Aristocratic Factionalism in the Early Middle Ages: The Saxon *Stellinga* Reconsidered," *Speculum* 70 (1995): 485–96; Depreux, *Prosopographie*, 69–72.

[9] BM 799, 907, 932, 972, 973, 999.

[10] BM 999; Nelson, *Charles the Bald*, 97.

an *Ordinatio imperii*–type division that favored Lothar was far more acceptable: if Louis were once again limited to Bavaria and Lothar received a kingdom that spanned from Francia to the Elbe River, then they could continue
to hold their offices and benefices on both sides of the Rhine. To accomplish
this, however, they needed to undermine Louis's position as the favored son
and to rehabilitate Lothar. Here a convergence of political developments favored their scheme. In the summer of 837, an epidemic in Italy had carried
off many of Lothar's longtime supporters, creating a window of opportunity
for Otgar and Adalbert to position themselves as Lothar's political backers
at court.[11] Moreover, to tarnish Louis the German's image as the loyal son,
Otgar and Adalbert may have been behind the false rumor that Louis's 838
Trent meeting with Lothar was treasonous.[12]

At the 838 Nijmegen assembly, Otgar, Adalbert, and their supporters
convinced the elderly emperor to select Lothar rather than Louis as
Charles's guardian.[13] A Fulda charter drawn up at the Nijmegen assembly
on June 14 reports which eastern nobles were present: Otgar of Mainz,
Adalbert of Metz, his brother Hatto, as well as Bishop Drogo of Metz, four
Saxon bishops, Abbot Raban of Fulda, and Counts Gebhard of the Lahngau
and Poppo of Grabfeld.[14] Indeed, this Fulda charter may record the immediate cause of the "great argument" that served as the pretext for Louis the
German's fall from favor. With the participation of Louis, Charles, and the
assembled nobles, the emperor settled a dispute over a property east of
Frankfurt between Raban of Fulda and a certain Gozbaldus. Raban was a
stalwart supporter of Louis the Pious and Lothar, while Gozbaldus seems to
have been Louis the German's *fidelis* and former chaplain, Abbot Gozbald of
Niederalteich.[15] The emperor and his nobles decided the case in favor of
Raban of Fulda, which may have sparked the sudden quarrel between father
and son that ended in Louis the German's disgrace. With Otgar and Adalbert's support, the emperor moved forward with a new succession plan. In
September 838, he publicly invested Charles with weapons and crowned

[11] BM 967b.

[12] Otgar, Adalbert, Hatto, and Banzleib were frequently at Louis the Pious's court
during the first half of 838, and the emperor rewarded Adalbert and Banzleib with grants
immediately after he learned about the meeting at Trent: BM 972, 973, 977a, 980, 984c.

[13] Nithard 1.6, pp. 10–11; Astronomer, *VH*, chaps. 54, 59, pp. 504–7, 528. The Astronomer, whose chronology is confused at this point, incorrectly dated these events to
835. Nelson, *Charles the Bald*, 97–99, suggests a date of 838–39.

[14] *Fulda* 513.

[15] Gozbald possessed a church at Kleinochsenfurt near the contested estate (Bigott,
Ludwig der Deutsche, 40 and n. 159), and Louis the German later appointed Gozbald
bishop of Würzburg, likewise located nearby. The Fulda charter referred to Gozbald's
"fratres," perhaps a reference to his monks at Niederalteich.

him king of Neustria, and he announced that he would divide the empire (save Bavaria and Aquitaine) between Lothar and Charles the following summer.

This fall from favor precipitated the first great crisis of Louis the German's reign. Indeed, there is a glaring lacuna in his diplomas between September 837 and December 840—a period of over three years—suggesting that his court chancery ceased to function during this period of turmoil. Louis asserted that his disgrace was the result of the "jealousy of his father's counselors," and he reverted to the strategy he had employed in his previous rebellions: rallying his Bavarian supporters, marching to the middle Rhine, and attempting to win over the eastern nobles.[16] In late November 838 Louis arrived at Frankfurt with his army. Louis's seizure of Frankfurt was ideological as well as practical. Frankfurt was the main royal palace complex east of the Rhine, and in late 838 it was stocked with food and supplies because his father had planned to winter there.[17] As he had done in 832, Louis won over as many Alemans, Austrasians, and Thuringians as he could and formed a sworn association (*coniuratio*) with them.[18] In an effort to prevent his father from crossing the Rhine, Louis ordered the construction and garrisoning of fortresses (*castella*) along the east bank and at Frankfurt.[19] But throughout history, the Rhine has facilitated more than hindered traffic across it. In early January, Louis the Pious managed to cross the river with a force of almost three thousand and rallied the Saxons to him, "partly through the threats and partly through the persuasions of Count Adalbert."[20] Taken by surprise, the Alemans, Austrasians, and Thuringians deserted Louis the German, forcing him and his supporters to retreat to Bavaria.

The emperor spent the next several months reasserting his rule east of the Rhine. Louis the Pious made an impressive string of grants to his eastern supporters, including a gift of lands in Alemannia to Adalbert of Metz.[21] The emperor also distributed important eastern monasteries and countships to his faithful men (*fideles*). He revoked the possession of Wissembourg

---

[16] *AF*, s.a. 838, p. 29; Astronomer, *VH*, chaps. 60–61, pp. 530–32.

[17] *AB*, s.a. 838, p. 26. Regino, *Chronicon*, s.a. 876, p. 111, called Frankfurt the "chief seat of the eastern kingdom."

[18] *AB*, s.a. 839, p. 27; *AH*, s.a. 838, p. 17.

[19] *AB*, s.a. 838, 839, pp. 26–27; *AF*, s.a. 841, p. 31.

[20] *AF*, s.a. 839, p. 29. Adalbert's brother, Margrave Banzleib of Saxony, presumably played a role.

[21] *St.-Gall* 357; *Fulda* 523, 524; BM 977 (Tetta of Herford), 978 (Tatto of Kempten), 985 (Adalbert of Metz), 987 (Raban of Fulda), 989 (Raban of Fulda), 990 (Tatto of Kempten), 991 (Walahfrid of Reichenau), 994 (Walahfrid of Reichenau), 996 (Raban of Fulda and Poppo of Grabfeld), 998 (Tatto of Kempten), 999 (Adalbert of Metz), 1004 (Raban of Fulda), 1006 (Poppo of Grabfeld), 1007 (Humbert of Würzburg).

from Louis's high chancellor Grimald and gave it to Otgar of Mainz; he made Walahfrid the new abbot of Reichenau; and he promoted Judith's brother, Conrad, to a number of Alemannian counties.[22] In 839–40 the emperor also made four grants to Raban of Fulda, and in one of those diplomas he dismissed his namesake's earlier rule in east Francia as an exercise of "illegitimate power" [indebita potestas].[23] Louis the German finally submitted to his father at Bodman in Alemannia around Easter in a meeting described by the Astronomer:

> Although against his will, his son came before him there as a suppliant. After being rebuked by his father he confessed that he had acted wickedly and asserted that he would mend his ways in the future. Giving way to his accustomed tender kindness, the emperor pardoned his son and rebuked him. At first the emperor gave him a tongue lashing that made him feel small, as was fitting. But he later comforted his son with gentler words and allowed him to return to his [Bavarian] kingdom.[24]

Perhaps the elderly emperor's willingness to pardon his son arose out of his love as a grandfather. It seems that a very pregnant Queen Emma accompanied Louis the German to the Bodman meeting and there gave birth to their third son, whom they named Charles (the future Charles III, 876–87), in honor of Charlemagne.[25] As it turned out, the Bodman meeting was the last time Louis would see his father in this world.

At an assembly in June 839 at Worms, Louis the Pious reconciled himself with Lothar and proclaimed a new division of the empire between his eldest and youngest sons.[26] An unexpected recent event had greatly altered the succession question. On December 13, 838, Pippin of Aquitaine had died suddenly, leaving behind two sons, the sixteen-year-old Pippin II of Aquitaine and the nine-year-old Charles of Aquitaine. Louis the Pious had no intention of recognizing the inheritance claims of his grandsons, and he

[22] Dümmler, *GOR* 1:129 and nn. 1, 6; BM 991, 994; Borgolte, *Grafen*, 165–70; Bigott, *Ludwig der Deutsche*, 70–71. Louis the Pious also sent several armies against the Danes and Elbe Slavs: BM 982c, 995b.

[23] BM 987, 989, 996, 1004; *Fulda* 524; *DLG* 15.

[24] The Astronomer is the only source for this meeting. Nevertheless, the scholarly skepticism about whether this meeting actually took place seems unwarranted: Astronomer, *VH*, chap. 62, pp. 532–34 and n. 928; BM 989b.

[25] The *AA*, s.a. 839, p. 178, seem to indicate that Charles III was born in Alemannia. The most likely context for Emma's visit to that region in 839 is her husband's meeting with his father at Bodman.

[26] For the 839 division, see Dümmler, *GOR* 1:132; Nelson, *Charles the Bald*, 99–101.

now divided the empire (save Bavaria) into an eastern and western kingdom divided by the Meuse River. Lothar received the eastern half: Austrasia, Alsace, Alemannia, Chur, Thuringia, Saxony, and Frisia.[27] Before departing for Italy, Lothar swore numerous oaths promising to defend Charles's kingdom after their father's death. This division undoubtedly pleased Otgar of Mainz, Adalbert of Metz, and their eastern supporters, since it would enable them to maintain their offices, benefices, and power on both sides of the Rhine after Louis the Pious died.

The 839 division was a serious blow to Louis the German because it undermined his already tenuous claim to the eastern territories. Even more threatening was the fact that Louis the Pious had revoked the properties of his *fideles* outside Bavaria.[28] If Louis the German could not defend his followers' lands, they would soon desert him and go over to Lothar. To make matters worse, in the 839 division Louis the Pious had significantly reduced the size of Louis the German's Bavarian kingdom by giving Lothar the Nordgau, the region north of Regensburg with the royal manors of Lauterhofen and Ingolstadt that had been considered part of Bavaria since 817. The emperor sent an embassy to his namesake, threatening to invade Bavaria unless Louis the German swore never to leave his kingdom without his father's express permission. Louis agreed, but on the condition that his father restore his supporters' lands. Louis the Pious tentatively gave his consent and then set out against Pippin II of Aquitaine, who was in rebellion because of his disinheritance. The emperor left the defense of Germania in the hands of his eastern supporters, including Counts Hatto of Nassau, Poppo of Grabfeld, and Gebhard of Lahngau.[29]

In January 840, Louis the German once again "claimed the part of the kingdom beyond the Rhine on the grounds that it was due to him by right."[30] As usual, the magnates of Bavaria remained the backbone of Louis's support, and they rallied the local troops on the behalf of their king. A Freising charter sheds light on how the emerging civil war impacted local communities. On December 10, 839, at Daglfing (south of Freising), the Bavarian count Ratolt, who had witnessed Ratpot's grant to St.-Emmeram

---

[27] *AB*, s.a. 839, pp. 31–32. To bind Lothar more closely to Charles, Louis the Pious and Judith orchestrated two marriages between the imperial family and Lothar's supporters. Charles's full sister, Gisele, married Count Eberhard of Friuli, while Judith's brother, the Alemannian count Conrad, married Lothar's sister-in-law, Adelaide.

[28] *AB*, s.a. 839, pp. 32–33.

[29] Einhard, *Epistolae*, no. 41, in MGH *Epistolae* 5:130–31; Goldberg, "Popular Revolt," 486–87.

[30] *AF*, s.a. 840, p. 30. Louis the Pious received a report of his son's rebellion in early February at Poitiers, which suggests that Louis the German arrived on the middle Rhine some time in January: *AB*, s.a. 840, p. 36.

two years earlier, made a generous gift of lands and serfs to Freising.[31] Ra-tolt made his grant in the courtyard of his manor "while manfully girded with his sword," during what appears to have been a local muster of the army on the eve of Louis's departure for the middle Rhine. Present in Ra-told's courtyard were Bishop Erchanbert of Freising, Ratolt's retinue of vassals and relatives, and the locals of the district. Ratolt gave the land to Freising for the redemption of his soul, perhaps because he feared for his own safety during the march west. But his donation was also a communal act, performed with the participation of his vassals, relatives, and "all the local men." Ratolt's grant was a statement of local solidarity between a count and the soldiers of his county on the eve of a risky campaign.

Louis again made Frankfurt the headquarters of his uprising, and he won over many east Franks, Saxons, and Thuringians to his cause "through cautious deliberation."[32] Once again, the nobles hedged their bets: if Louis's rebellion succeeded, he would reward them. If it failed, they could claim that he had forced them to swear loyalty against their will.[33] The emperor was furious when he learned of his son's new uprising, and he sent ahead Bishop Drogo of Metz and Count Adalbert of Metz to guard the west bank of the Rhine. After Easter, in spite of increasingly poor health, the emperor once again managed to cross the Rhine with an army and put his son to flight. With his father in hot pursuit, Louis had no choice but to retreat through Thuringia into the land of the Slavs. This was a humiliating blow to Louis's prestige as a leader: he was forced to bribe the Slavs to give him safe passage, and he returned to Bavaria "with great difficulty."[34]

Louis the Pious's health continued to decline, and an eclipse on May 5 was an omen that his end was near. The ailing emperor returned westward by ship until his condition forced him to anchor at an island in the Rhine near Ingelheim, where he was confined to bed in a tent.[35] Sensing his approaching death, the emperor now divided the Carolingian regalia—the crowns, weapons, vessels, books, and garments—among his sons.[36] This was

[31] *Freising* 634. For Ratolt, see Mitterauer, *Karolingische Markgrafen,* 218–20, 226.

[32] Nithard, 1.8, p. 12; Astronomer, *VH,* chap. 62, p. 540; *AF,* s.a. 840, p. 30.

[33] Ado, *Chronicon,* 231, claimed that Louis forced the *primi Germaniae* to swear perfidious oaths to him.

[34] *AF,* s.a. 840, pp. 30–31; *AB,* s.a. 840, p. 36; Nithard, 1.8, p. 12; Astronomer, *VH,* chap. 62, p. 542.

[35] As the emperor returned to Frankfurt, he once again made grants to his eastern supporters, including Raban of Fulda and Hunbert of Würzburg: BM 1004–7. Count Poppo of Grabfeld also was in Louis the Pious's entourage.

[36] Astronomer, *VH,* chap. 63, p. 548. On Louis the Pious's death and burial, see Janet L. Nelson, "Carolingian Royal Funerals," in Theuws and Nelson, *Rituals of Power,* 155–60.

an important symbolic act: he was expressing through the physical emblems of kingship whom he wanted to inherit his empire. Reflecting his enduring anger toward Louis the German, he divided the regalia between only Lothar and Charles, thereby symbolically disinheriting his namesake. Yet Drogo of Metz and others at Louis the Pious's bedside were deeply worried about Louis the German's rebellion, since he showed no signs of abandoning his claims to an expanded eastern kingdom. They therefore urged the dying emperor to make peace with him. The Astronomer reported:

> At first the emperor spoke only of his heart's bitterness. After thinking for a short time, he tried to enumerate with his remaining strength how many times and how much he had been troubled by his son, and by doing so how his son had sinned against nature and God's commandment. "But because he is unable to come before me now to make amends," he said, "for my part I will make amends with him. With God and you as witnesses, I forgive him all the sins he committed against me. But it will be your duty to remind him that, even though I pardoned his deeds repeatedly, he caused his father's hair to grow thin from sadness and despised the commandments and warnings of God, the common Father of us all."[37]

Louis the Pious died soon thereafter, on June 20, after an imperial reign of twenty-seven years, and Drogo had him buried with honor in the basilica of St.-Arnulf at Metz. The Astronomer noted that on his deathbed Louis the Pious called out "Huz! Huz!"—Frankish for "Away! Away!"—to ward off a demon he saw coming for his soul.[38] For everyone at his bedside, that demon was civil war.

BATTLES AND VICTORIES

When news of the emperor's death reached Bavaria, Louis knew his long-anticipated showdown with Lothar had arrived. For the third time in as many years, he hurried to the middle Rhine where he rallied a "strong force of east Franks to defend the part of the kingdom east of the Rhine."[39] Fortune now unexpectedly smiled on Louis. At this time his nemesis, Count

[37] Astronomer, *VH*, chap. 63, p. 550.
[38] Ibid., chap. 64, p. 552.
[39] *AF*, s.a. 840, p. 31.

Adalbert of Metz, fell seriously ill for almost a year, depriving Lothar of his chief lay supporter in the east.[40] On August 8, 840, perhaps in response to his illness, Adalbert, the self-styled "humble servant of Christ," gave a rich grant of properties at Walluf (northeast of Mainz) and Koblenz to Fulda "for my immeasurable sins and crimes."[41] But Adalbert's pious donation was also an act of defiance against Louis: he was granting properties west of the Rhine to Fulda in central Germania, thereby asserting the territorial cohesion of Lothar's kingdom that embraced both sides of the Rhine.

Louis moved quickly to secure the eastern territories. He now crossed the Rhine and took possession of Worms, which would have been stocked with food and supplies for the assembly his late father had planned to hold there. Louis left a garrison at Worms and then went to meet a group of Saxons he had recently won over.[42] Meanwhile, Lothar sent out messengers claiming the empire for himself and promising rewards to his supporters and death to those who resisted.[43] Exploiting the malleability of political rituals, Lothar justified his claim to the entire empire on the grounds that his dying father had sent him the imperial scepter and crown.[44] In August Lothar held an assembly at Ingelheim with his supporters, including many prominent eastern bishops and abbots: Otgar of Mainz, Drogo of Metz, Hetti of Trier, Samuel of Worms, Ratold of Strasbourg, Badurad of Paderborn, and Raban of Fulda.[45] Lothar decided to attack Louis first, and he put his brother's garrison at Worms to flight after a short skirmish.[46] Lothar and his army then crossed the Rhine at Mainz and headed for Frankfurt. But at that moment Louis returned from Saxony with a large army and unexpectedly met up with Lothar. After a tense exchange of messengers, the two brothers agreed to an armistice for the night. The following morning Louis prepared his troops for battle.

A popular perception of medieval warfare is that large, "pitched" battles

---

[40] Nithard, 2.7, p. 21.

[41] *Fulda* 529. Adalbert made the grant at Walluf. His scribe dated the charter "in the days of Emperor Louis on August 8," even though Louis the Pious had been dead for almost two months. The reason for this unusual dating clause apparently was that Lothar had not yet arrived from Italy.

[42] Nithard, 2.1, p. 14. The translation by Bernard Walter Scholz, in *Carolingian Chronicles: "Royal Frankish Annals" and Nithard's "Histories"* (Ann Arbor, 1972), 142, is misleading.

[43] Lothar was at Strasbourg on July 24–25, where he made grants to Abbots Silvanus of Pfäfers and Sigimar of Murbach: *DLoI* 44, 45.

[44] *AF*, s.a. 840, p. 31; *AX*, s.a. 840, p. 11.

[45] MGH *Concilia* 2.2, ed. Albert Werminghoff (Hanover, 1908), 792–93; Bigott, *Ludwig der Deutsche*, 77–79.

[46] Following this victory, Lothar granted an estate to Drogo's monastery of St.-Arnulf, the resting place of his father, for the salvation of his father's soul: *DLoI* 46.

on an open field were the norm, with generals seeking "decisive" victories over their opponents. In reality, military commanders usually sought to avoid decisive battles because of their high stakes and extreme unpredictability, unless the odds were overwhelmingly in their favor. Otherwise, they preferred sieges, surprise attacks, and especially negotiated settlements.[47] Nevertheless, in the summer of 840, Louis was willing to risk it all in open battle against Lothar, a sign of his desperation to defend his claims to an expanded eastern kingdom. Luckily for him, Lothar backed down at the last minute: "When Louis opposed him manfully," Nithard recounted, "Lothar despaired of defeating him without battle. Thinking he could more easily overcome Charles, he called off the battle on the condition that they would meet again at the same place on November 11."[48] Although one must allow for Nithard's bias in favor of Louis, Lothar's decision to avoid battle must have seemed shameful. Louis had gambled and won, boosting his reputation as a brave and "manly" leader. In the midst of a civil war in which the loyalty of the nobles was up for grabs, such ideological victories were critical, since a ruler's reputation for bravery and military skill could convince the vacillating nobles that he was the king to back.

Louis used this armistice to strengthen his support in the east. He won over the east Franks, Alemans, Saxons, and Thuringians through the usual combination of patronage and intimidation ("some by force, some by threats, some by granting honors, and some through other special terms"), and he once again placed garrisons in his forts along the Rhine.[49] In Alemannia Louis seized control of the three most important monasteries, St.-Gall, Kempten, and Reichenau, and drove out their abbots, who opposed him.[50] Winning over bishoprics and monasteries was essential for gaining control of a contested region such as Alemannia. Bishops and abbots were powerful local leaders who controlled large amounts of land, wealth, and prestige, and they therefore could raise large private armies on a king's behalf. During the winter of 840–41, Louis also drove out Lothar's supporter, Abbot Raban of Fulda, and asserted his control of that important Franconian monastery.[51] Around this time, Louis further strengthened his support in Franconia and

[47] Bachrach, *"Caballus et Caballarius,"* 184; Reuter, *Germany,* 129; Nelson, *Charles the Bald,* 141.

[48] Nithard, 2.1, p. 14; *AX,* s.a. 840, p. 11.

[49] *AF,* s.a. 840, 841, p. 31; *AB,* s.a. 841, pp. 36–37.

[50] At St.-Gall and Reichenau, Louis appointed loyal monks named Engilbert and Ruadhelm, respectively, while he gave Kempten to his supporter, Erchanbert of Freising: Dümmler, *GOR* 1:144–45; Bigott, *Ludwig der Deutsche,* 81–84.

[51] A Fulda charter dated February 22, 841, omits Raban's name and is dated "in the first year of the reign of the younger Louis, king in east Francia": *Fulda* 531. The common opinion is that Raban retired as abbot in late 841 after the battle of Fontenoy (June 25,

the Rhineland by appointing Ratleig, a nobleman from Cologne and the abbot of Seligenstadt on the Main, to be his new high chancellor.[52]

When Lothar failed to show for the scheduled November 11 meeting, Louis made his second trip to Saxony to win over the Saxon nobles, who were divided in their support between him and Lothar.[53] Louis's sojourn in Saxony demonstrates the range of strategies a ruler could use to win control of a contested region: distributing patronage to powerful local families, seizing control of ecclesiastical institutions and economic resources, and punishing opponents. Louis held court at Paderborn, the first Carolingian assembly in Saxony in twenty-five years. At this time, Louis's opponent, Bishop Badurad of Paderborn, seems to have been in the west with Lothar, and Louis therefore held this assembly at his enemy's expense. While at Paderborn, Louis drove another of Lothar's supporters, Bishop Goswin of Osnabrück, into exile, and he installed a loyal Hersfeld monk named Hemmo at the vacant bishopric of Halberstadt.[54]

Louis also secured the support of the powerful abbot of Corvey, Warin (826–56). Abbot Warin was the head of an influential Franco-Saxon family, the Ecbertiner.[55] Louis had a claim to Warin's loyalty through his wife, Queen Emma, who was related to the Ecbertiner through her mother.[56] Warin had been raised at Louis the Pious's court, and he had become a skilled soldier before he decided to embrace the monastic life.[57] After becoming abbot of Corvey in 826, Warin had been a leading supporter of Louis the Pious, and in return the emperor made numerous land grants to Corvey.[58] Warin's family was very powerful in Saxony: his brother, Count Cobbo, held a county near Osnabrück, while his sister, Addila, later became abbess of Herford, Corvey's sister monastery. Louis now issued four diplo-

---

841), but this charter suggests that Louis had removed Raban by February 841. Cf. Dümmler, *GOR* 1:176; Bigott, *Ludwig der Deutsche*, 41, 90–92.

[52] Louis appointed Ratleig between September 837 and December 840: Kehr, "Kanzlei," 8; Fleckenstein, *Hofkapelle* 1:171; Bigott, *Ludwig der Deutsche*, 165–66.

[53] Nithard, 4.2, p. 41. For Louis's visit to Saxony in 840, see Goldberg, "Popular Revolt," 487–92; Bigott, *Ludwig der Deutsche*, 85–87.

[54] BM 1365k; Dümmler, *GOR* 1:145 and n. 3, 185–86 and n. 3; Bigott, *Ludwig der Deutsche*, 44, 74.

[55] Sabine Krüger, *Studien zur sächsischen Grafschaftsverfassung im 9. Jahrhundert* (Göttingen, 1950), 71–79; Goldberg, "Popular Revolt," 487–92. Corvey was partly responsible for the defense of the Saxon frontiers against the Slavs and Danes: Karl Leyser, "Henry I and the Beginning of the Saxon Empire," reprinted in Karl Leyser, *Medieval Germany and Its Neighbours, 900–1250* (London, 1982), 16–19.

[56] Fleckenstein, "Über die Herkunft der Welfen," 115n244; Goldberg, "Popular Revolt," 489–90.

[57] *Translatio sancti Pusinnae*, in MGH SS 2:681–82; Widukind, 3.2, p. 130.

[58] BM 830, 922–24, 927, 935.

mas for Corvey, confirming the monastery's lands and rights and granting Corvey several additional estates.[59] One of these estates was Empelde (north of Corvey), which Louis had confiscated from Adalbert's brother, Banzleib, the margrave of Saxony. Significantly, however, Louis did not confirm Corvey's earlier exemption from military service, since he now required Warin's support in the war against Lothar.[60] Louis also permitted Warin's brother, Cobbo, to divert the tithes from the bishopric of Osnabrück (whose bishop Louis had driven into exile) to his siblings' monasteries of Corvey and Herford. In return for this generosity, the Ecbertiner joined the ranks of Louis's most trusted supporters.[61]

The Paderborn assembly also provided a forum for Louis to justify his claims to Saxony before the assembled Saxon nobles. Indeed, the Corvey diplomas provide our first insight into Louis's royal ideology since his father's death. In one diploma, Louis defended the legitimacy of his rule in Saxony on three grounds: as the defender of the Church, as a divinely chosen king, and as his father's rightful heir.[62] In these diplomas, Louis repeatedly praised his late father as most excellent, most Christian, most serene, most pious, and most noble. The implication was that Louis did not hold his father responsible for his disinheritance in 838 but rather that he blamed the "jealousy of his [father's] counselors"—especially Otgar of Mainz and Adalbert of Metz.[63] To Louis's mind, therefore, his long-standing claim to an eastern kingdom that encompassed Saxony remained legitimate and unbroken.

After an indecisive campaign against Charles in the west, in early 841 Lothar returned to confront Louis in the east. The soldier-historian Nithard, a prominent participant in this civil war, highlighted the tremendous influence of Otgar of Mainz and Adalbert of Metz in Lothar's councils of war. He wrote:

> Lothar devoted his whole mind to considering how he could overcome
> Louis by trickery or force or, preferably, do away with him altogether.
> In this matter he brought together Bishop Otgar of Mainz and Count
> Adalbert of Metz, who each bore so much hatred for Louis that he

---

[59] *DLG* 26–29. These are Louis's first surviving diplomas in three years, suggesting that his recent victory over Lothar coincided with a general turn around of his fortunes.

[60] Bigott, *Ludwig der Deutsche*, 87 and n. 180 (correcting Goldberg, "Popular Revolt," 491).

[61] Nithard, 4.3, p. 44; *Translatio sancti Germani*, chap. 15, in MGH *SS* 15:13; *DLG* 61, 73, 93, 95, 128, 132.

[62] *DLG* 26.

[63] The *AF*, s.a. 838, p. 29, blamed Louis the German's fall from favor on the *invidia consiliantium* of his father.

wanted him dead. Like a reinforcement in the fratricide, Adalbert now had recovered from the sickness that had put him out of action for almost an entire year. At that time Adalbert was so skilled in counsel that no one dared to question a thing he said. At his instigation Lothar gathered an infinite multitude and set out for the Rhine.[64]

In April Lothar managed secretly to transport his forces across the Rhine near Worms. "As usual, Lothar sent ahead men to try to win over the vacillating people with gifts and threats. The people who were with Louis began to fear that they could not resist such a large army. Some of them defected to Lothar, while others abandoned Louis and turned in flight."[65] In the midst of this turmoil, some of Louis's followers betrayed and almost captured him.[66] However, Louis and his supporters once again managed to escape and return to Bavaria. Lothar judged that his brother was finished, and he therefore left behind Adalbert to receive oaths from the eastern nobles and prevent Louis from leaving Bavaria. Reflecting his promotion to generalissimo of the east, Nithard gave Adalbert the new title "commander [dux] of the Austrasians."[67]

At this moment Louis received an urgent message from Charles the Bald pleading for help against Lothar.[68] It is likely that Louis had been angling for an alliance with his half brother against Lothar ever since his disinheritance in 838, especially when it became clear that Lothar intended to seize the entire empire for himself. In the summer of 841 this alliance became a reality. In May, only weeks after retreating to Bavaria, Louis and his supporters set off westward to come to Charles's aid.

Defending the Roman road through Alemannia was *dux* Adalbert at the head of a large eastern army. Louis now faced considerable odds against him, since his army, still made up mostly of Bavarians, was probably exhausted and significantly smaller than Adalbert's pan-Austrasian force. In this moment of crisis, however, Louis managed to pull off a stunning military victory of the first order. Instead of facing Adalbert in open battle near the Bavarian–Alemannian border, Louis turned north, crossed the Danube, and entered the geographically distinct region known as the Ries. Some fifteen million years ago, an asteroid had smashed into the earth in the Ries,

---

[64] Nithard, 2.7, pp. 20–21.

[65] During the first half of 841, Lothar made grants to Chur, Prüm, and Fulda: *DLoI* 55–57, 60, 61.

[66] Nithard, 2.7, p. 21; *AF,* s.a. 841, pp. 31–32; *AB,* s.a. 841, p. 37; *AX,* s.a. 840, p. 11.

[67] Nithard, 2.7, 2.9, pp. 21, 23.

[68] *AF,* s.a. 841, p. 32; Nithard, 2.9, p. 23.

creating a massive crater fifteen miles wide that divides the Swabian Alb and Frankish Jura mountain ranges. As a result, the Ries contains a dense network of rivers and streams that flow from the surrounding mountains into the Wörnitz River, a tributary of the Danube. By drawing Adalbert into the Ries (a region through which Louis otherwise seldom traveled), Louis apparently sought to break up Adalbert's larger army, forcing it to make numerous river crossings that would make it vulnerable to a surprise attack.[69] Then on Friday, May 13, after Adalbert's army had crossed the Wörnitz River, Louis sprung his trap: "he suddenly engaged a great battle with them," "hurling himself on the troops Lothar had stationed against him."[70] Taken by surprise, Adalbert's army turned in flight, and a bloody rout ensued. Louis's forces slaughtered most of their opponents (*maxima eorum pars*), leaving a huge number of dead (*innumerabilis multitudo hominum*) on the field. The mighty Adalbert himself died in the carnage, sending shock waves throughout the empire.[71]

Louis's victory in the Ries was a tremendous, albeit horrifically bloody, success: he had broken out of Bavaria, destroyed Lothar's eastern army, and eliminated Adalbert. Moreover, Louis's soldiers undoubtedly stripped the corpses of their valuable and highly prized Frankish swords and armor. Thus, although relatively few in number, Louis's Bavarian army henceforth would be unusually well equipped, down to the rank-and-file soldiers. The battle of the Ries greatly boosted Louis's growing reputation as a gifted general. Nithard reported that word of Louis's victory spread quickly throughout the empire, and that Charles and his soldiers were overjoyed when they heard the news.[72] The Ries was also an ideological victory, since Louis could claim that it demonstrated God's favor for his inheritance claims against Lothar. Two apparent survivors of Adalbert's eastern army were Raban and his brother, Count Guntram. Only seven days after Louis's victory, Raban and Guntram had retreated to their family estate at Rohrbach, west of Worms. At Rohrbach, Count Guntram made a last-ditch attempt to prevent Louis from seizing his lands: he granted all his lands on both sides of the Rhine to Fulda, thereby placing them beyond Louis's reach since, in theory

---

[69] River crossings were one of the best opportunities for surprise attacks, since an army became divided and disorganized while moving its forces across: Vegetius, *Epitome of Military Science*, trans. N. P. Milner, 2nd ed. (Liverpool, 1996), 3.7, p. 79.

[70] For the numerous reports of the battle in the Ries, see Ratpert, *Casus sancti Galli*, chap. 7, p. 188; *AF*, s.a. 841, p. 32; *AB*, s.a. 841, p. 37; Grimalt Codex, 27; *AI*, s.a. 841, p. 740; *Auctarium Garstense*, s.a. 841, p. 564. The *AI* specify that Louis attacked Adalbert's army *ultra ripam Werinza*.

[71] Chroniclers far and wide noted Adalbert's death: BM 1369d.

[72] Nithard, 2.9, p. 23.

at least, a king would not confiscate a monastery's lands.[73] Raban then gave some of these lands back to Guntram as a precarial grant.[74] But whereas the lands Guntram gave Fulda were on both sides of the Rhine, those he received back in precarial arrangement were all west of the Rhine. After Louis's overwhelming victory in the Ries, Guntram and Raban apparently foresaw the inevitability of Louis's kingdom east of the Rhine.

The Ries, however, did not end the civil war. Louis and his army now faced the daunting journey west to join forces with Charles, who at this time was some 250 miles away at Châlons-sur-Marne in central Francia. When they arrived at Charles's camp three weeks later, they were exhausted and suffering from an acute lack of horses, many of which apparently had died in the Ries and during the subsequent forced march west.[75] Charles greeted Louis with joy, since he was in a tense standoff with Lothar and expecting to fight a battle any day.[76] The half brothers immediately struck an alliance of "brotherly love" that they confirmed with a banquet. Although Louis and Charles still hoped for a negotiated settlement with Lothar, they now realized that a pitched battle was "the only way to cut through the competing loyalties and, quite literally, reduce the number of Carolingian competitors."[77] Louis and Charles were especially concerned about the morale of their soldiers, many of whom still were reluctant to kill fellow Franks. During the ensuing days, Louis, Charles, and the bishops in their army attempted to convince their followers that they had God and justice on their side in the conflict with Lothar.[78] They even offered Lothar all the treasure they had with them—save their arms and horses—if he would agree to an equitable division of the empire. However, Lothar had formed an alliance with Pippin II of Aquitaine, who was on his way with reinforcements. After the brothers spent several more days engaging in dead-end negotiations and cat-and-mouse pursuit, on Friday, June 24, Pippin arrived at Lothar's camp near Fontenoy in northwestern Burgundy.[79] Lothar immediately threw

---

[73] *Fulda* 534, 535. (Both should be dated May 20, 841.) On this grant, see Innes, *State and Society*, 64–68, 208–9, although Innes does not mention its connection with Louis's victory in the Ries.

[74] A precarial grant was a lease of land, usually from a bishopric or monastery, for a specified period, often the lifetime of the recipient. The recipient paid an annual rent to the Church for the land, and the Church could revoke the property at any time, thereby making the recipient's possession of it "precarious." Fouracre, *Age of Charles Martel*, 137–45.

[75] Nithard, 2.10, pp. 24–25.

[76] *AB*, s.a. 841, pp. 35–36; Nithard, 2.9, pp. 23–24.

[77] Nelson, *Charles the Bald*, 116.

[78] Nithard, 2.9, p. 24; Janet L. Nelson, "Violence in the Carolingian World and the Ritualization of Ninth-Century Warfare," in Halsall, *Violence and Society*, 90–107.

[79] Nithard, 2.10, pp. 24–27; *AB*, s.a. 841, p. 38.

down the gauntlet and reasserted his claim to the entire empire. Realizing that their brother had no intention of negotiating further, Louis and Charles responded with an ultimatum: by the next morning Lothar either agree to a division or meet them on the battlefield and let God settle the dispute. Confident of Pippin II's Aquitanian reinforcements, Lothar chose battle.

The bloody battle of Fontenoy took place on Saturday, June 25, 841.[80] At dawn Louis and Charles stationed a third of their troops on the crest of a hill overlooking Fontenoy, and they placed the rest of their army at the hill's base. Lothar and Pippin arranged their battle lines opposite them. Surprise attack was impossible, since both armies undoubtedly had scouts patrolling throughout the night. According to the terms of the truce, the kings waited until 8:00 a.m. and then gave the signal to attack. The battle raged in three separate engagements along a small stream known as the Burgundians' Brook. As the more experienced general, Louis led his battle-hardened Bavarian troops against Lothar's vanguard. Lothar displayed considerable personal bravery, but after a desperate battle he was forced to withdraw when his troops fled. Agnellus of Ravenna recounted:

> The armies became confused in each other like a spider's shining web. Weapons rang and bright shields flashed. Many were terrified, fled, and fell by the sword with pounding hearts and great screams. Dressed in full armor, Lothar waded into the middle of the host amid fleeing enemies and hacking swords. . . . Fighting bravely alone, he threw down numerous bodies with his sharp spear. Alone he vanquished, but all his men turned in flight. Sitting on his shaggy steed and adorned with purple ornaments, he drove his horse forward with his heels and crushed his enemies with his blows. Thus he fought alone like ten men so that the empire would not be divided among so many kings, each on his own throne.[81]

Meanwhile nearby, Charles overcame Pippin II's large Aquitanian force, while Charles's supporter, Count Adalhard, fought Lothar's third contingent to a draw. In the end, Lothar's third contingent also fled, giving the field to Louis and Charles.

[80] For the battle of Fontenoy, see Dümmler, *GOR* 1:154–59; Nelson, *Charles the Bald*, 117–21.

[81] Agnellus, *Liber pontificalis*, chaps. 173–74, pp. 389–90. (Agnellus apparently based his report on firsthand accounts of those who accompanied Archbishop George of Ravenna to Fontenoy.) Agnellus called Louis "Baioariorum rex," implying that his army still consisted mostly of Bavarians. Engelbert, *Versus de pugna quae fuit acta Fontaneto*, in MGH *Poetae Latini* 2:138–39, likewise emphasized Lothar's personal bravery at Fontenoy.

The battle of Fontenoy confirmed why generals usually avoided "decisive" battles. Although Louis and Charles emerged as the victors, the cost in human life on both sides was horrific. It is difficult to give an estimation of the number of dead, but by all accounts it was shockingly high. "There was such slaughter on both sides," the *Annals of Fulda* reported with dismay, "that the present age cannot remember such carnage among the Frankish people."[82] Agnellus of Ravenna stated that 40,000 died in Lothar's and Pippin II of Aquitaine's army alone, a number that probably is exaggerated but nevertheless conveys the magnitude of the loss of life.[83] Andrew of Bergamo reported that "many thousands" died at Fontenoy, with the death toll particularly heavy among Pippin II's Aquitanians.[84] The majority of the dead probably came from the lesser nobles and freemen, who made up the rank-and-file of Carolingian armies. These common soldiers faced far greater danger in battle, since they generally lacked the expensive iron armor that gave significant protection to kings and nobles. (In this regard, Louis's Bavarian soldiers would have had a critical advantage at Fontenoy from the arms and armor captured in the Ries.) But in spite of this monstrous loss of life, in the end the battle of Fontenoy was not decisive: no Carolingian died, and the majority of the magnates survived. The civil war would drag on.

Nevertheless, the battle was an important ideological victory for Louis and Charles. Lothar's retreat from the battlefield was seen as cowardly, damaging his reputation as emperor.[85] Moreover, Louis and Charles claimed that their victory proved God's support for their inheritance claims. Louis and Charles restrained their soldiers from slaughtering their fleeing foes, thereby demonstrating their desire to avoid further bloodshed. The next day they celebrated Mass on the battlefield, comforted the wounded, and buried the dead—friends and enemies alike. They also sent out messengers offering pardon to any of Lothar's supporters who came over to their side. An assembly of their bishops proclaimed that Louis, Charles, and their soldiers were not at fault for the carnage, since "they had fought for justice and fairness alone, as had been made manifest through a judgment of God."[86]

Just as important, Louis and Charles won a "huge quantity of booty" at

[82] *AF*, s.a. 841, p. 32. Regino, *Chronicon*, s.a. 841, p. 75, with exaggeration presented Fontenoy as the beginning of the end of Frankish military might: "In that battle the strength of the Franks was so diminished and their renowned valor so weakened that afterward they could not extend their borders nor even defend them."

[83] Agnellus, *Liber pontificalis*, chap. 174, p. 390.

[84] Andrew of Bergamo, *Historia* 7, in MGH *SRL*, 226.

[85] *AB*, s.a. 841, p. 38.

[86] Nithard, 3.1, pp. 28–29. The *AF*, s.a. 841, p. 32; and Ratpert, *Casus sancti Galli*, chap. 7, p. 188, similarly interpreted Louis and Charles's victory as the manifestation of divine will.

Fontenoy.[87] As usual, the dead would have been stripped, putting what literally must have been mountains of valuable arms, armor, and other equipment in the hands of Louis and Charles's soldiers. One significant windfall was the capture of Archbishop George of Ravenna, who had joined Lothar's army in the hope of winning independence for his archbishopric from Rome.[88] George reportedly brought with him three hundred horses laden with golden crowns, vessels, chalices, and gems to bribe Lothar and his advisers. In this way the vast treasures of the former Byzantine city of Ravenna fell into Louis's and Charles's hands. (After the battle, Louis and Charles wanted to send George into exile, but Empress Judith, who was at Fontenoy in Charles's entourage, convinced her son and brother-in-law to pardon the archbishop and send him back to Ravenna.) With these vast treasures, Louis and Charles could generously reward their followers and entice more nobles to abandon Lothar. Moreover, Lothar's royal treasury was captured at Fontenoy as well, which had important symbolic implications for Louis.[89] Although Louis the Pious had not given him any of the Carolingian regalia, the capture of Lothar's treasury meant that Louis could now claim a share. This in turn suggested that Fontenoy was a "judgment of God" in favor of Louis's and Charles's kingship.

In late June 841, Louis set out from Fontenoy with "high hopes" to consolidate his victories in the east.[90] He arranged to meet Charles in Burgundy on September 1, since Lothar was still at large and had not relinquished his imperial claims. In mid-August Louis made his first reported visit to the royal manor at Salz in eastern Franconia, where he put to rest the rumor spread by Lothar's partisans that he had been injured and Charles killed at Fontenoy. He now won over considerable numbers of Austrasians, Thuringians, Alemans, and Saxons, "partly through terror tactics and partly through grants of favor."[91] One supporter Louis rewarded was his former chaplain, Abbot Gozbald of Niederalteich, to whom he made a rich grant of lands at Ingolstadt "in return for his most devoted service to our Majesty."

[87] Nithard, 3.1, p. 28.

[88] Agnellus, *Liber pontificalis*, chaps. 173–74, pp. 389–91; Agnellus of Ravenna, *The Book of the Pontiffs of the Church of Ravenna*, trans. Deborah Mauskopf Deliyannis (Washington, DC, 2004), 17–19.

[89] Adelerius of Fleury, *Miracula*, chap. 41, pp. 498–99.

[90] Nithard, 3.2, pp. 29–30. Charles set out to confront Pippin II, who maintained his claim to Aquitaine.

[91] *AF*, s.a. 841, p. 32; *AB*, s.a. 841, p. 39. (Nelson, in her translation of *Annals of St.-Bertin*, p. 51, accidentally makes Lothar the subject of this sentence.) Lothar was at Aachen in late July and at Mainz in late August, where he made grants to Raban: *DLoI* 60, 61.

The following year Louis appointed Gozbald the new bishop of Würzburg, transforming him into one of the most powerful magnates in Franconia.[92]

Yet even in defeat, Lothar refused to give up. In August 841, he again attempted to cross the Rhine, "intending to drive Louis into foreign lands."[93] But the balance of power had tipped decidedly in Louis's favor, and he quickly forced Lothar to retreat.[94] To prevent Louis from reuniting forces with Charles, Lothar stationed Otgar of Mainz on the west bank of the Rhine. However, in early 842 Charles drove off Otgar's forces, enabling Louis to reach the opposite shore of the Rhine with a large army.[95] The two brothers met at Strasbourg in Alsace and renewed their alliance of "brotherly love."[96]

To confirm this alliance, Louis, Charles, and their followers swore the famous Strasbourg Oaths on February 14, 842. The reason the Strasbourg Oaths are famous is not completely historical. In his *Four Books of Histories*, Nithard reported that Louis, Charles, and their supporters swore the oaths in the vernacular tongues—the *lingua Romana* (early Romance) and the *lingua Teudisca* (Frankish).[97] Nithard then inserted the vernacular texts of these oaths into his Latin narrative, thus providing the earliest surviving example of Romance and one of the earliest passages in Frankish. Because Louis and Charles were in the midst of a war that resulted in the creation of an eastern and western kingdom, nationalist historians interpreted the oaths as symptoms of an incipient German and French national consciousness. But the Strasbourg Oaths must be viewed in the context of ninth-century Carolingian politics, not modern European nationalism. As we have seen, Louis had formed sworn associations (*coniurationes*) with his supporters on several occasions during his struggles, and the previous year he had formed an alliance of "brotherly love" with Charles that likewise would have included the

---

[92] *DLG* 30, 41.

[93] *AF*, s.a. 841, pp. 32–33; *AB*, s.a. 841, p. 39; Nithard, 3.3, p. 31.

[94] Nevertheless, Lothar set out westward against Charles "with a good number of Saxons, Austrasians, and Alemans," indicating that he still had significant support among the eastern nobility: Nithard, 3.3, p. 32. While departing from Louis's kingdom, Lothar celebrated the marriage of his daughter at Worms: *AF*, s.a. 841, pp. 32–33. Although the identity of Lothar's son-in-law is unknown, this marriage probably was connected to Lothar's attempts to bolster his waning support in the east.

[95] *AF*, s.a. 843, p. 33. For the subsequent campaign against Lothar and his supporters, see Nithard, 3.4–3.7, pp. 35–39; *AB*, s.a. 842, pp. 40–41.

[96] The *AB*, s.a. 842, p. 40, referred to the Strasbourg Oaths as an alliance of *fraternitas* and *amicitia*.

[97] Nithard, 3.5, pp. 35–37. Concerning the Strasbourg Oaths, see Dümmler, *GOR* 1:171–72; Nelson, *Charles the Bald*, 122–23; McKitterick, "Introduction: Sources and Interpretation," in *NCMH* 2:11–12.

swearing of oaths. On those occasions, the oaths were probably performed in the vernacular so that everyone involved could understand them. On one level, therefore, the Strasbourg Oaths were nothing new—except that for the first time we have a detailed report of them.

What does make the Strasbourg Oaths unusual is that they reveal a significant level of discontent among Louis's and Charles's followers, who criticized their kings for not capitalizing on their hard-won victory at Fontenoy and thus for allowing the civil war with Lothar to drag on.[98] By 842, the nobles were exhausted and deeply worried about a prolonged conflict. As Nithard summed up, "having tasted danger, all the leading men did not want another battle."[99] Concerned about the growing unrest among their troops, Louis and Charles swore the Strasbourg Oaths to reassure their followers that they remained committed to the fraternal alliance through which they hoped to bring the civil war to an end. Louis admitted this much in his speech, in Romance, to Charles's followers: "Since we know that you doubt the stability of our faith and the firmness of our brotherhood, we have commanded this oath to be sworn between us in your sight." After reviewing Lothar's crimes against them, each king swore an oath, Louis in Romance and Charles in Frankish, so that each other's army could understand him. Louis swore: "For the love of God and the common salvation of the Christian people and ourselves, from this day forward, as far as God grants me knowledge and power, I will treat my brother with regard to aid and everything else as a man should rightly treat his brother, as long as he does the same to me. Furthermore, I will not enter into any dealings with Lothar that might with my consent harm my brother Charles." Their followers then swore their own oath of loyalty to the kings, Louis's men in Frankish and Charles's in Romance. These oaths made the nobles responsible for maintaining Louis and Charles's alliance, since they pledged to withdraw their support if either Louis or Charles broke the agreement.[100]

After the swearing of the Strasbourg Oaths, Louis and Charles consolidated their control over the Rhineland, the region that lay at the heart of the conflict between Lothar and Louis. The brothers received the surrender of the strategic west Rhenish cities of Speyer, Worms, and Mainz that had remained bastions of Lothar's supporters. At Worms, Louis and Charles halted for several days and continued to win over eastern nobles. Meanwhile, Louis's and Charles's troops reportedly caused considerable destruction in the Rhineland, a common occurrence when large armies were forced

[98] Nithard, 3.2, p. 29.
[99] Ibid., 4.6, p. 48.
[100] A point also stressed by the *AB*, s.a. 842, p. 40.

to requisition supplies from the surrounding countryside (a situation that naturally shaded into pillaging and theft).[101] At Worms, Louis's Saxon supporter, Count Bardo, a close ally of Abbot Warin of Corvey, brought the news that the Saxons who previously had supported Lothar now pledged to serve Louis.[102] Bishop Drogo of Metz also came over to Louis and Charles's camp, a defection that was a serious blow to Lothar.[103] At this moment Louis received a large reinforcement of Bavarians and Alemans, led by his twelve-year-old eldest son, Carloman. The appearance of Carloman in the sources for the first time is significant: with his eldest son approaching manhood, Louis was ready to introduce Carloman to his followers and have him play a role in politics and warfare.

Louis, Charles, and Carloman now led their forces northward down the Rhine to confront the remnants of Lothar's army, which included Otgar of Mainz and Count Hatto. When they arrived at Koblenz, Louis and Charles heard Mass in the church of St.-Castor, once again using Christian ritual to underscore the justice of their conflict with Lothar. They then donned their armor, boarded their ships, crossed the Moselle, and put Lothar's forces to flight. Lothar retreated to Aachen, where he gave out large bribes from the imperial treasury in a desperate attempt to retain his dwindling supporters.

Louis and Charles were determined to capitalize on this most recent victory. In late March they pushed on to Aachen and forced Lothar to flee to Burgundy with his few remaining followers.[104] As at Fontenoy, Louis and Charles called an assembly of churchmen to legitimate their actions. But Louis and Charles now went a step further, urging the bishops formally to transfer the royal power from Lothar to them. After reviewing Lothar's crimes and condemning his abilities as a ruler, the bishops decreed that God had sanctioned Lothar's overthrow. They reportedly addressed Louis and Charles with the following words: "By divine authority we admonish, ask, and command you to receive the kingdom and rule it according to God's will." By now a rumor had reached them that Lothar had fled to Italy, so Louis and Charles agreed to divide the entire empire north of the Alps between themselves.[105] Each king selected twelve of his men to come up with

[101] The *AX*, s.a. 842, pp. 12–13.

[102] Nithard, 3.7, p. 38. Count Bardo frequently appeared as a witness and donor in Corvey charters: *Corvey* 127, 139, 140, 163, 172, 190, 257, 272, 283. He later died fighting the Slavs on a campaign led by Louis: *AF*, s.a. 856, p. 47.

[103] *DCB* 9.

[104] Nithard, 4.1, pp. 40–41.

[105] *AF*, s.a. 842, p. 33. Nelson, *Charles the Bald*, 124, argues that this division was not made in earnest but rather as an attempt to put pressure on Lothar to negotiate. Yet the rumor of Lothar's retreat to Italy points to the conclusion that Louis and Charles in fact were serious about the division.

the boundaries of the new division. The role of the magnates in making this division (and all subsequent divisions) highlights how the ties of leading families to various provinces shaped conflicts over royal succession. Nithard, who was one of these men, stressed that their chief concern was not only that the wealth and size of the two kingdoms be equal but also that the kingdoms coincide with the ties of noble families (*affinitas*) to specific regions. This had been the central preoccupation of the eastern magnates: that the division among Louis the Pious's sons not separate them from their estates and offices on both sides of the Rhine. Only a division that took aristocratic *affinitas* into account could be acceptable.

Although no precise record of the March 842 division project survives, the general outlines are clear: Louis received an expanded Austrasian kingdom that included the Carolingian capital at Aachen, while Charles got an expanded western kingdom that encompassed Neustria.[106] In effect, this renewed the outlines of the 837 division between Louis and Charles that had never materialized because of Louis's disgrace the following year. A diploma of Louis's dated March 26 suggests that he now saw his reign as beginning a new phase.[107] Louis adopted the new title "king by the grace of God" (*gratia Dei rex*), which echoed the royal titles used by Pippin III and Charlemagne (*gratia Dei rex Francorum*). Louis also ceased dating his diplomas according to his rule "in east Francia" and simply calculated his reign from the time of his father's death, thereby underscoring the direct political continuity between the two regimes. It is significant that Louis made this grant on Palm Sunday, the festival that commemorated Christ's arrival in Jerusalem. Just as Christ had triumphantly entered the Jewish capital on that day, so Louis, Christ's representative, had taken control of the Carolingian capital. Louis then traveled to the important city of Cologne on the lower Rhine, where he celebrated Easter and consolidated his rule further.[108] There he received the submission of the citizens of Cologne, their archbishop-elect, Liutbert, and the neighboring Saxon nobles. For the moment, Louis had vastly increased his kingdom to include Austrasia and all the territories beyond the Rhine. The 842 division turned out to be short lived, however, and Louis soon reverted to his previous "in east Francia" diploma format. Neverthe-

---

[106] It is likely that the Meuse served as the border between the two kingdoms, as in the divisions of 837, 839, and 870. Nithard mentioned that Louis received Frisia, although he left several lines blank, suggesting that the twenty-four noblemen never fully worked out the details: Nithard, 4.1, pp. 41–42.

[107] *DLG* 31. Louis gave Abbot Adalung of Inden the estate of Gressenich (both near Aachen). Concerning this diploma, see Bigott, *Ludwig der Deutsche*, 88–89, although Bigott interprets the unusual wording as the product of the disorganization of Louis's court.

[108] Nithard, 4.2, p. 41; Bigott, *Ludwig der Deutsche*, 90.

less, the 842 division highlights Louis's desire to rule all Austrasia from Aachen like a traditional Carolingian king. As it turned out, he would have to wait another twenty-eight years until he sat again on Charlemagne's throne.

Louis and Charles's plans for a new division of the empire were thwarted by Lothar, who had not fled to Italy but was rallying fresh forces in Burgundy. Louis and Charles united their armies once again and marched against him.[109] Realizing that he was beaten, Lothar had no choice but to acknowledge that he had acted unjustly, and he requested a three-way division of the empire. Although Louis and Charles had hoped to divide the empire between them, their supporters' desire for peace forced them to accept Lothar's offer. After numerous diplomatic exchanges and meetings, the three brothers announced a truce until October 1, when they would meet at Metz, where their father was buried, to work out the three-way division.

As soon as the truce was struck, Louis set out for Saxony to deal with a serious popular revolt that had erupted during the civil war. This popular revolt, known as the Saxon Stellinga uprising, illuminates the oppressive social and economic conditions on which the Frankish monarchy, Church, and nobility rested.[110] According to Frankish law, there were only two social classes—free and unfree. In reality, however, Frankish society was far more complex and hierarchic. The vast majority of the population—perhaps as great as 80 percent—consisted of agricultural laborers or "peasants" living in small villages: free farmers, various kinds of serfs (semi-free farmers who were bound to the land they worked), and, at the bottom of the social hierarchy, outright slaves.[111] The nobility made up the upper stratum of society (probably some 5–15 percent of the total population), although this group likewise broke down into many different substrata: kings, great magnates, middle-level nobles, vassals of the great men, local notables, as well as well-to-do freemen. The nobles' dominance arose chiefly from the wealth they derived from agricultural estates, which, to generalize greatly, typically consisted of the lord's manor and farm, surrounded by a number of smaller homes and farms held by dependent serfs.[112] Serfs were semi-free in that they were bound to the land (that is, they could not freely pack up and move), and they owed the lord dues as well as services, usually plowing, sow-

[109] BM 1371b–f.
[110] Many chroniclers noted the Stellinga uprising: Nithard, 4.2, p. 42; *AF*, s.a. 842, pp. 33–34; *AB*, s.a. 841, pp. 38–39; *AX*, s.a. 841, 842, pp. 12–13. For the discussion that follows, see Goldberg, "Popular Revolt," 467–501.
[111] For the complexity of landholding, status, and village life in Carolingian rural society, see Chris Wickham, "Rural Society in Carolingian Europe," in *NCMH* 2:510–37.
[112] Verhulst, *Carolingian Economy*, 31–60.

ing, and harvesting the lord's fields (the demesne) a certain number of days per week. This so-called classic manorial system (which in reality had tremendous regional variation) originated in the Frankish heartlands west of the Rhine. However, in the course of the Frankish expansion during the sixth through eighth centuries, the Franks exported this manorial strategy to the surrounding provinces of western Europe via the estates of the king, nobility, and Church.

Before Charlemagne's conquest of the region, Saxony had four distinct social groups: the nobles (*edhilingui* in the Old Saxon tongue), free (*frilingi*), semi-free (*lazzi*), and slaves. It seems that Saxon society was somewhat less hierarchic and oppressive than that in Francia. Although the *edhilingui* were the most wealthy and powerful group, the *frilingi* and *lazzi* had a say in local assemblies, and they apparently owed only dues, but not services, to their *edhilingui* landlords. However, Charlemagne's conquest worsened the condition of the *frilingi* and *lazzi*, since the Saxon peasants on estates confiscated by the king, Church, and Frankish nobles now were compelled to render services as well as dues to the lord. For example, the benefice at Empelde that Louis the German confiscated from Adalbert's brother, Banzleib, in 840 consisted of a "lord's demesne farm with the houses and other buildings along with twenty servile tenements belonging to it."[113] Another factor that worsened the social and economic conditions of the Saxon *frilingi* and *lazzi* was Christianity. Charlemagne equated conquest with conversion, and he demanded that all Saxons renounce polytheism and accept baptism under penalty of death. While the Saxon nobles embraced Christianity quite willingly, the *frilingi* and *lazzi* associated the new religion with Frankish oppression. Moreover, the newly erected Church compelled all Saxons to pay the tithe—one-tenth of their annual income—to support the local bishop and parish priests. As a sign of their resentment of Frankish domination, the Saxon peasants clung to their ancestral polytheistic beliefs throughout the ninth century.

Despite what must have been widespread resentment of noble lords among the agricultural laborers, large-scale popular revolts were unusual in early medieval Europe. This is because a mob of angry, half-starved peasants wielding pitchforks was no match for a small, disciplined troop of heavily armed nobles on horseback. Peasant resistance to aristocratic domination therefore usually took less spectacular forms, such as refusal to render dues and services, appeals to the king and his representatives, or flight. However, the political chaos caused by the Carolingian civil war and the infighting among the Saxon nobles gave the *frilingi* and *lazzi* a rare opportu-

---

[113] *DLG* 29.

The king's view of the proper social order. A picture of a barefoot peasant with a wide-brimmed hat and sickle harvesting wheat under the hot August sun. The caption reads "Augustum mensem Leo fervidus igne perurit" (The burning sign of Leo consumes the month of August with fire). This image comes from Louis the German's copy of Wandalbert of Prüm's *Martyrology*, made at Reichenau in the third quarter of the ninth century. It suggests the general attitude of the king and nobles about the proper role of agricultural laborers in Frankish society. © Bibliotheca Apostolica Vaticana (Vatican), Reg. lat. 438, fol. 18r.

nity to unite against them and revolt in 841. "That year throughout all Saxony," Gerward wrote, "the serfs rose up violently against their lords. They called themselves Stellinga"—a militant name that meant "comrades in arms" in Old Saxon—"and committed much madness. The serfs violently persecuted and humiliated the nobles of that land."[114] As part of their rebellion, the Saxon peasants openly renounced Christianity and reverted to polytheism. As a sign of his desperation after Fontenoy, Lothar even appealed to the Stellinga, promising them their traditional rights and customs in return for support against Louis. Lothar's appeal ultimately backfired, because the nobles saw it as an unholy alliance against themselves and the Church. For the moment, however, Louis feared the Stellinga would unite with the neighboring polytheistic Danes and Slavs and drive the Franks and Christianity out of Saxony altogether.

In this way, the Stellinga uprising illustrates one of the main reasons why the nobles wanted an end to the civil war as quickly as possible. Such prolonged warfare and social upheaval threatened to open the floodgates to peasant resistance and thereby undermine the very foundations of Frankish aristocratic power. Thus, as soon as Louis struck the armistice with Lothar in the late summer of 842, he headed east to make an example out of the Stellinga:

> Louis traveled throughout Saxony, where by force and terror he crushed all those still opposing him. He captured all the leaders of that unholy scheme, men who had abandoned the Christian faith and resisted him and his faithful men with such determination. He punished 140 of them with beheading, hung fourteen on the gallows, maimed innumerable others by amputating their limbs, and left no one able to oppose him further.[115]

While Louis's actions seem horrific today, contemporary chroniclers (who of course came from the nobility) praised him for acting "bravely" and "nobly" and subjecting the Saxon peasants to "their proper natural state."[116] When the bold Saxon peasants rebelled once again several months later, the now united Saxon nobility easily slaughtered them in a great bloodbath. In the words of Nithard, "the rebels were crushed by the very legitimate authority without which they had dared to rise up."[117]

[114] *AX*, s.a. 841, p. 12.
[115] *AB*, s.a. 842, pp. 42–43.
[116] *AX*, s.a. 842, p. 13; *AF*, s.a. 842, pp. 33–34; Nithard, 4.4, p. 45.
[117] Nithard, 4.6, pp. 48–49.

In early October 842, the three brothers each sent forty nobles to Metz to come up with a division of the empire. As always, distrust and scheming pervaded relations among Louis the Pious's sons, making negotiations slow going.[118] It soon became clear that they could not agree to a division because they lacked detailed information about the location and extent of all the royal resources. The kings therefore resolved that their 120 representatives would travel throughout the empire and compile a written survey (*descriptio*) of all the bishoprics, monasteries, royal palaces, manors, estates, benefices, and markets.[119] Only a detailed written survey would enable the brothers to calculate the royal resources of the various regions and arrive at a "really fair division of the kingdom" [aequissima regni divisio]. Unfortunately this written survey does not survive, but its mere existence emphasizes that the inheritance struggle among Louis the Pious's heirs was to a significant extent a contest for the economic and material foundations of the Frankish monarchy. This desire to control the rich royal heartlands of Francia would remain at the core of Carolingian dynastic politics for the remainder of the ninth century.

In August 843, more than three years after their father's death, Lothar, Louis, and Charles met at Verdun in central Francia, where they agreed to a three-way division of the empire based on the *descriptio* compiled over the previous nine months.[120] For generations, historians viewed the resulting Treaty of Verdun as the "birth certificate" of France and Germany.[121] Like the Strasbourg Oaths, however, the 843 division must be viewed in its ninth-century context. First, extreme distrust still dominated relations among Louis the Pious's heirs and their followers. Thousands, if not tens of thousands, had died during the civil war, and nobles on every side had unresolved grievances and scores to settle. Everyone must have viewed the 843 division as a temporary respite in the hostilities, and it would therefore be more accurate to speak of the Truce of Verdun. Realpolitik would continue,

---

[118] Ibid., 4.4–4.5, pp. 45–47.

[119] *AB*, s.a. 842, p. 43; *AF*, s.a. 842, p. 33; Nithard, 4.5, p. 47.

[120] On the Treaty of Verdun, see esp. Dümmler, *GOR* 1:200–215; François Louis Ganshof, "On the Genesis and Significance of the Treaty of Verdun (843)," in Ganshof, *Carolingians*, 289–302; Nelson, *Charles the Bald*, 132–36.

[121] For example, see Georg Waitz, *Ueber die Gründung des deutschen Reichs durch den Vertrag von Verdun* (Kiel, 1843); Mayer, *Vertrag von Verdun*.

and the 843 truce would be broken as soon as the opportunity presented itself. Moreover, Lothar and Louis already had multiple sons, meaning that the empire would have to be divided once again within a generation. Everyone at Verdun would have been shocked to learn that the 843 division cast such a long shadow on the political map of Europe.

As with previous divisions of the empire, this one was probably codified by the brothers in an official written document, although it does not survive. Nevertheless, chroniclers give a general picture of the borders of the resulting three kingdoms. Linguistic or "national" identities played no role whatsoever. The brothers' chief concern was an equal division of royal resources, balanced by a consideration for the ties of noble families to specific regions. The general outlines were clear from the outset, since each brother began with his longtime kingdom: Italy for Lothar, Bavaria for Louis, and Aquitaine for Charles. The real issue was where to draw the boundaries in central Francia. As the eldest brother, Lothar claimed the imperial title and the Carolingian capital at Aachen. As a result, Lothar received a long and narrow middle kingdom that included Frisia, western Austrasia, Alsace, eastern Burgundy, Provence, and Italy. Charles received everything to the west: Neustria, Aquitaine, and Septimania.

In light of his disinheritance in 838, Louis won the most at Verdun. He received all the lands east of the Rhine: Bavaria, Alemannia, Chur-Rhaetia, eastern Austrasia (that is, Franconia), Thuringia, and Saxony. In addition, Louis compelled Lothar to concede to him the important Austrasian cities and districts of Mainz, Worms, and Speyer on the west banks of the Rhine.[122] This final concession was a significant victory for Louis, since the middle Rhine was extremely wealthy in terms of episcopal cities, counties, palaces, ports, markets, and royal estates.[123] The Rhineland also was rich in royal vineyards, and Regino specified that Louis wanted that region "because of its abundance of wine."[124] Louis's chief Frankish supporters, Ernest, Ratpot, and Werner, all held lands on the middle Rhine, and his kingdom therefore coincided with the political connections and *affinitas* of his magnates. Another reason Louis demanded the Rhineland was ecclesiastical organization. The huge archdiocese of Mainz extended along and east of the Rhine, encompassing the eastern bishoprics of Worms, Speyer, Strasbourg, Constance, Augsburg, Eichstätt, Würzburg, Paderborn, Halberstadt, and Hildesheim. Thus, by compelling Lothar to concede the west bank of the middle Rhine, Louis strengthened the ecclesiastical foundations

---

[122] *AB*, s.a. 843, p. 44. Note that Louis surrendered Alsace (which he had claimed in 833–38) to Lothar.

[123] Gockel, *Karolingische Königshöfe*; Innes, *State and Society*.

[124] Regino, *Chronicon*, s.a. 842, p. 75.

of his eastern kingdom through two archdioceses: Mainz and Salzburg.[125] Although territorially vast and diverse, Louis's eastern territories also made sense in terms of communications. The Rhine, Danube, and Main rivers enabled him to travel rapidly and move cargo easily via ship, and the Roman roads along the Rhine and Danube made possible efficient travel and transportation on land. Thus, although Louis for the moment had failed to win all of Austrasia, he could be reasonably pleased with the 843 division.

The technical terms of the Treaty of Verdun were like those of early Carolingian divisions. Although the Treaty of Verdun created three independent kingdoms, in theory a united *regnum Francorum* endured. At Verdun the brothers swore mutual oaths of brotherly love and peace, and they agreed to meet regularly to discuss the welfare of the kingdom and the Church. As in previous Carolingian divisions, bishoprics and monasteries were allowed to keep their lands throughout the empire, irrespective of political boundaries, and nobles similarly continued to hold personal properties wherever they were found. However, to avoid conflicting political loyalties, nobles and freemen were to commend themselves to only one of the three brothers and hold benefices and offices only from him.

Although Louis had defended his claims to an expanded eastern kingdom at Verdun, the backbone of his political support remained the nobles of Bavaria. Thus, before coming to Verdun, Louis had spent the winter of 842–43 in Bavaria with his followers.[126] The enduring prominence of the Bavarian magnates in Louis's counsels is illustrated by a Freising charter, dated August 10, 843, drawn up "at Dugny near the city of Verdun where the settlement was reached among the three brothers, Lothar, Louis, and Charles, and the division of their kingdom was made."[127] This Freising charter recorded an important transaction between Louis's Bavarian supporter, Bishop Erchanbert of Freising, and a certain Paldricus, who apparently was the former margrave of Friuli, Balderic.[128] For the massive sum of 250 pounds of silver (5,000 *denarii*, equivalent to some 350 head of cattle), Erchanbert of Freising purchased all of Balderic's lands in Bavaria, presumably

---

[125] However, there were discrepancies between the borders of kingdoms and archdioceses: Mainz's see of Strasbourg fell within Lothar's middle kingdom, while the Saxon sees of Münster, Minden, Osnabrück, and Bremen belonged to the archdiocese of Cologne, a city in Lothar's middle kingdom. Moreover, the bishopric of Chur in Louis's kingdom was part of the archdiocese of Milan: Dümmler, *GOR* 1:209–11.

[126] Nithard, 4.6, p. 48.

[127] *Freising* 661. It is only from this charter that the specific date of the Treaty of Verdun is known.

[128] Wilhelm Störmer, *Früher Adel: Studien zur politischen Führungsschicht im fränkisch-deutschen Reich vom 8. bis 11. Jahrhundert* (Stuttgart, 1975), 2:275–76; Roper Pearson, *Conflicting Loyalties*, 204–8.

because Balderic had selected Lothar as his lord and therefore was adapting his landholding to the post-843 political map. The Freising charter contains an unusually long witness list of 99 names. The very first witness was Louis's Bavarian count of the palace, Fritilo, indicating that Erchanbert's purchase of Balderic's lands took place with the king's knowledge and approval. Following Fritilo are the names of 5 Bavarian counts, 71 men without title, 7 Frisian royal vassals, and 15 of Balderic's own vassals. There is considerable overlap between the names in the 843 Verdun witness list and the witnesses of Ratpot's grant to St.-Emmeram in 837: of the 24 names that appear in Ratpot's grant, almost half appear on the Verdun witness list.[129]

The Freising charter therefore highlights the continued prominence of Louis's longtime Bavarian supporters through the Treaty of Verdun. During the civil war, the Bavarian bishops, abbots, counts, and nobles were the ones who had consistently supported Louis and risked life and limb for him in the Ries and at Fontenoy. Not surprisingly, these nobles figured prominently in Louis's entourage at Verdun. Although Louis had received an expanded kingdom in 843, it would take him over a decade to transform his Bavarian kingship into one that embraced all his eastern territories.

[129] Cf. *Regensburg* 29.

PART II

KING IN EAST FRANCIA

CHAPTER FOUR
FRONTIER WARS, 844–852

Although Louis had won much at Verdun, the approximately thirty-four-year-old king faced daunting challenges in consolidating his power beyond the Rhine. His territories were politically fragmented, and many of them were poorly governed, unstable, and in the hands of regional magnates whose loyalty was questionable. But the greatest immediate threat Louis faced was the Slavs. At Verdun Louis inherited the longest open frontier in Carolingian Europe, stretching almost six hundred miles from Hamburg in the north to Lake Balaton in the southeast. Beyond these eastern borders lived numerous Slavic peoples under the rule of kings, princes, and warlords. The Slavic frontiers presented Louis with opportunities as well as serious challenges for his nascent eastern regime.

Throughout his reign, Louis struggled to enforce the traditional Carolingian policy of tributary lordship over the Slavs. By and large, the Carolingians were not interested in territorial expansion into Slavic eastern Europe. This decision was practical in that their empire already was too big to be ruled easily, and the center of Carolingian wealth was in the Frankish heartlands west of the Rhine. As a result, the Carolingians sought to rule the Slavs indirectly through loyal Slavic princes who rendered annual tribute. Charlemagne had first established tributary lordship over client Slavic rulers, and Louis the Pious had continued that policy.[1] In this way, the Car-

---

[1] For Louis the Pious's relations with the Slavs and Danes, see *ARF*, s.a. 815, 822, 823, 826–29, pp. 142, 159, 160, 168–78; *AB*, s.a. 831, 836, pp. 4, 19–20; Raimund Ernst, "Karolingische Nordostpolitik zur Zeit Ludwigs des Frommen," in *Östliches Europa:*

olingians attempted to defend their eastern borders through a buffer zone of loyal Slavic rulers and to secure a valuable source of income. This policy also had important ideological dimensions. Einhard identified the subjugation of the Slavs as one of the keys to Charlemagne's greatness, while the anonymous *Vision of Charlemagne*, written in the circles around Louis the German's court, likewise drew an explicit connection between Carolingian power and the subjugation of neighboring "barbarians."[2] Tributary overlordship also carried with it strong overtones of imperial power, since the Franks equated an emperor and augustus with a ruler over many peoples.[3] Thus, by upholding his predecessors' policy toward the Slavs, Louis the German asserted his quasi-imperial might and parity with his father and grandfather.

Louis, however, faced considerable challenges in reestablishing Frankish dominion in Slavic eastern Europe. In the chaos of the civil war, ambitious Slavic rulers had thrown off the yoke of Frankish overlordship, seeking to establish themselves as independent kings. Although Frankish authors dismissed the Slavs as uncivilized barbarians, Slavic rulers often were far-sighted, cunning, and wealthy princes who pursued complex strategies of diplomacy and intrigue against the Frankish kings. Moreover, by the ninth century, Slavic rulers increasingly defended themselves through networks of sophisticated fortresses, which made Frankish military campaigns against them difficult, expensive, and dangerous. Heightening the danger of this frontier warfare was the fact that Louis's magnates often fought among themselves when on campaign, thereby exposing his armies to devastating Slavic surprise attacks. The fact that Louis pursued this policy of tributary overlordship in spite of these considerable obstacles highlights the threat posed by independent Slavic rulers. If Louis failed to subject the neighboring Slavs to his power, they threatened to undermine his rule by allying with his enemies and rivals within Frankish Europe. Louis had no choice but to wage war against the Slavs, since the internal stability of his kingdom depended on bringing neighboring Slavic rulers to heel.[4]

Spiegel der Geschichte. Festschrift für Manfred Hellmann zum 65. Geburtstag, ed. Carsten Goehrke, Erwin Oberländer, and Dieter Wojtecki (Wiesbaden, 1977), 81–107.

[2] Einhard, *VK*, chap. 15, p. 18; *Visio Karoli*, 76.

[3] Notker, *GK* 1.26, p. 35.

[4] For Frankish frontier warfare, see Reuter, "Plunder and Tribute," 75–94; idem, "The End of Carolingian Military Expansion," in *CH*, ed. Godman and Collins, 391–405. However, Reuter overestimated the significance of plunder and thus underestimated the economic costs of frontier warfare. For a corrective that highlights the importance of tributary overlordship, military organization, and siege warfare, see Goldberg, "Ludwig der Deutsche und Mähren," 67–94. For Carolingian and Ottonian frontier politics in

THE SLAVS, MILITARY ORGANIZATION, AND FRONTIER WARFARE

By the ninth century, the Slavs had emerged as serious rivals to the Franks for the control of central eastern Europe. Although Carolingian authors described the Slavs as treacherous barbarians, there is considerable evidence of the complexity and sophistication of ninth-century Slavic economic, political, and military organization.[5] The ninth-century Slavic world was becoming wealthier as the scope of its trade expanded.[6] Franks, Slavs, Jews, and Turks gathered in eastern European markets to trade valuable goods, such as slaves, precious metals, furs, horses, livestock, textiles, salt, and wax.[7] This trade chiefly benefited the Slavic elite, who attained a high level of cultural sophistication rivaling that of the Franks. Slavic nobles wore luxurious clothing and jewelry, carried finely made weapons, hosted lavish banquets, rode on horseback, hunted with falcons, and traveled with retinues of soldiers.[8] As a result of this trade, ninth-century Slavic rulers had

---

general, see Julia M. H. Smith, *"Fines imperii*: The Marches," in *NCMH* 2:169–89; Gerd Althoff, "Saxony and the Elbe Slavs in the Tenth Century," in *NCMH* 3:278–80.

[5] Peter G. Heather, "Frankish Imperialism and Slavic Society," in *The Origins of Central Europe*, ed. Przemyslaw Urbańczyk (Warsaw, 1997), 171–90, stresses the role that Frankish diplomacy and warfare played in accelerating the formation of Slavic kingship and kingdoms, calling the process a Frankenstein Effect. For Frankish stereotypes of the Slavs, see Dümmler, *GOR* 1:223n3.

[6] M. M. Postan and Edward Miller, eds., *The Cambridge Economic History of Europe*, 2nd ed. (Cambridge, 1987), 2:474–502; McCormick, *Origins*, 548–64.

[7] Carolingian sources mentioned this active long-distance trade in Scandinavian-Slavic eastern Europe: *Capitulare missorum in Theodonis villa datum secundum, generale*, chap. 7, in MGH *Capitularia* 1:123; Rimbert, *Vita Anskarii*, chap. 24, pp. 52–53; *AF*, s.a. 873, pp. 78–79; *Inquisitio de theloneis Raffelstettensis*, in MGH *Capitularia* 2:249–52. An important source for tenth-century trade among the Slavs is the travel account of the Jewish merchant Ibrahim ibn Yaqub: Georg Jacob, trans., *Arabische Berichte von Gesandten an germanische Fürstenhöfe aus dem 9. und 10. Jahrhundert* (Berlin, 1927), 11–18; Barford, *Early Slavs*, 254–55.

[8] *AF*, s.a. 864, 870, 871, pp. 62, 70, 75. Archeological finds from ninth-century Moravia provide a glimpse at the stunning material wealth of the Moravian elite: Josef Poulík, "The Latest Archaeological Discoveries from the Period of the Great Moravian Empire," *Historica* 1 (1959): 5–70; idem, "Mikulčice: Capital of the Lords of Great Moravia," in *Recent Archaeological Excavations in Europe*, ed. Rupert Bruce-Mitford (London, 1975), 1–31; Susan Beeby, David Buckton, and Zdeněk Klanica, *Great Moravia: The Archaeology of Ninth Century Czechoslovakia* (London, 1982); Ján Dekan, *Moravia Magna: The Great Moravian Empire: Its Art and Times* (Bratislava, 1980); Barford, *Early Slavs*, 110–11.

increasing wealth at their disposal through taxes and tribute. They could translate this wealth into political power by staging more extravagant courts, buying alliances, paying mercenaries, and winning larger groups of followers.

Another sign of the power and wealth of ninth-century Slavic rulers was their construction of large fortresses. Archaeologists have shown that Slavic rulers consolidated their power over land, people, and trade by building so-phisticated strongholds that were defended by ramparts, palisades, stone walls, towers, and fortified gates.[9] One well-excavated ninth-century Slavic fortress was located at Gars-Thunau, not far from the Frankish–Slavic bor-der in what is today Lower Austria.[10] Situated on a high promontory above the Kamp River, this fortress encompassed about fifty acres, making it only slightly smaller than Louis's Bavarian capital of Regensburg. High granite-faced walls crowned with a wooden palisade defended Gars-Thunau, and two-story towers flanked its large gates. The proliferation of such Slavic fortresses posed a serious military challenge to Louis. At the first sign of an invading Frankish army, the Slavs typically moved their forces, livestock, and wealth to safety behind their walls. This meant that Louis could not launch small-scale raids to plunder booty from his eastern neighbors. In-stead, he needed large, well-supplied armies that could lay siege to, and cap-ture, rebel Slavic fortresses. In addition, the Carolingians were forced to build their own frontier forts to defend their eastern borders against the Slavs.[11] As one archeologist summed up the situation along the Franco–Slavic borders, "the struggle for power and lordship was a struggle for fortresses."[12]

The prolonged civil war caused a dramatic breakdown of Frankish lord-ship over the Slavs. Neighboring "barbarian" rulers had good intelligence about Frankish politics, and they skillfully took advantage of political con-flicts within the Carolingian family. When Louis the German rebelled against his father in 838, a general uprising erupted along the Elbe that in-

[9] For the proliferation of large fortresses in ninth-century Slavic Europe, see Miroslav Štěpánek, "Die Entwicklung der Burgwälle in Böhmen vom 8. bis 12. Jahrhun-dert," in Siedlung und Verfassung Böhmens in der Frühzeit (Wiesbaden, 1967), 49–69; Joachim Herrmann, "Herausbildung und Dynamik der germanisch-slawischen Sied-lungsgrenze im Mitteleuropa," in Die Bayern und ihre Nachbarn, vol. 1, ed. Herwig Wol-fram and Andreas Schwarcz (Vienna, 1985), 269–80; Čeněk Staňa, "Mährische Burgwälle im 9. Jahrhundert," in Die Bayern und ihre Nachbarn, vol. 2, ed. Herwig Friesinger and Falko Daim (Vienna, 1985), 158–208; Martin Gojda, The Ancient Slavs: Settlement and Soci-ety (Edinburgh, 1991), 16–57; Barford, Early Slavs, 104–12, 131–33.
[10] Herwig Friesinger, Die Slawen in Niederösterreich (St. Pölten, 1976), 24–26; Wol-fram, Grenzen und Räume, 311–12.
[11] For Carolingian frontier forts, see ARF, s.a. 806, 808–11, pp. 121, 125–26, 129–32, 135.
[12] Herrmann, "Herausbildung und Dynamik," 278.

King in East Francia

cluded the Danes, Obodrites, Wilzes, Linones, Sorbs, and Colodices.[13] In 840, Louis the German had been forced to bribe the Slavs to allow him to return through their lands to Bavaria, an unprecedented occurrence that must have undermined his reputation among the Slavic peoples. Moreover, when the Stellinga rebelled in 841–42, Louis feared that they might unite with the neighboring Elbe Slavs and Danes and create a "pagan coalition" that would drive the Franks from Saxony.[14] Here one sees clearly why Louis was so determined to reestablish Frankish overlordship in the east: if left unchecked, Slavic rebellions could spark a general uprising that would threaten the internal stability of his kingdom.

After Verdun, Louis waged campaigns almost every year against rebel Slavic peoples, either in person or under the command of his magnates and sons. To support this ongoing frontier warfare, Louis developed a complex military infrastructure throughout his kingdom and appointed powerful frontier prefects to defend his eastern borders.[15] Although Louis at first selected these prefects from among his chief supporters (such as Ernest and Ratpot), in the 850s he promoted his eldest two sons to frontier commands: Carloman in the Bavarian Eastland and Louis the Younger in eastern Saxony and Thuringia.[16] Following Carolingian practice, Louis organized his armies according to the five main provinces (*regna*) of his kingdom: Bavaria, Franconia, Alemannia, Saxony, and Thuringia. Within each province, the king's *fideles*—not only the counts, but also the bishops and abbots—led local troops.[17] Louis relied heavily on the military contributions of the east Frankish Church, and he expanded considerably the troops owed by his bishops and abbots from the military obligations his father had imposed on them.[18] When the king or one of his sons did not lead a campaign in person, he appointed a powerful magnate the commander (*dux*) of the expedition.

---

[13] *AB*, s.a. 838, 839, pp. 25–26, 33–34.

[14] Nithard, 4.2, p. 42.

[15] Goldberg, "Ludwig der Deutsche und Mähren," 79–86. See further: Halsall, *Warfare and Society*, 77–110; Hartmann, *Ludwig der Deutsche*, 166–72.

[16] The sources report the identity of several of Louis's eastern prefects: Ratpot in the Bavarian Eastland (*Conversio*, chap. 10, p. 120), Ernest in the Bohemian marches (*AF*, s.a. 849, p. 38; *DLG* 72), Thakulf in Thuringia against the Sorbs (*AF*, s.a. 849, 858, 874, pp. 38, 48, 81), and Bernhar in eastern Saxony against the Danes and Obodrites (Rimbert, *Vita Anskarii*, chap. 16, p. 37). For Louis's promotions of Carloman and Louis the Younger, see chap. 8.

[17] For example, see *AF*, s.a. 849, 857, pp. 38, 47; *DLG* 72. In general, see Friedrich Prinz, *Klerus und Krieg im früheren Mittelalter* (Stuttgart, 1971).

[18] For the important role of the east Frankish bishops and abbots in raising royal armies, see Bigott, *Ludwig der Deutsche*, 124–36. Bigott convincingly argues that Louis the German significantly expanded the military service owed by the eastern monasteries (and did not renew their preexisting exemptions from military service), as described in the 817

As under his predecessors, Louis's armies consisted of a combination of troops: the private retinues of vassals belonging to the counts, bishops, abbots, and other great men; the king's own bodyguard of royal vassals; and levies of freemen who owed military service.[19] It seems that Louis envisioned a continuation of the assistance system (*adiutorium*) of military service established by Charlemagne. According to that policy, only freemen who possessed at least four homesteads of land served in the army, while smaller landowners had to club together and send one of their number. Anyone who neglected military service had to pay an extremely heavy fine of sixty *solidi* (roughly fifty cows), known as the *haribann*.[20] The army was held together by a hierarchy of lordship and fidelity among the king, his *fideles*, the lesser nobles and vassals, and the freemen. Louis decreed that every freeman was to choose a lord within his kingdom—either himself or one of his *fideles*.[21] There is evidence that Louis took this system of "universal" military service seriously and made sure that it was enforced by his *fideles*.[22] Nevertheless, Carolingian capitularies indicate that this military service was plagued by abuses. Common freemen tried to get out of serving in the army because it was costly and dangerous and prevented them from working their fields. Moreover, lords could use military service as an institution to enrich themselves. For example, they might allow freemen to avoid military service by handing over their land and becoming dependent serfs. Louis and his brothers knew about these abuses and tried to correct them. They decreed that freemen were not to desert their lords and that royal *fideles* were to act justly and reasonably toward their men.[23]

Chroniclers stressed that Louis often raised large armies for his campaigns against the Slavs.[24] Historians, however, have hotly debated just how many soldiers made up a large Carolingian army. The chief problem in de-

---

Notitia de servitio monasteriorum, in *Corpus Consuetudinum Monasticarum*, ed. Cassius Hallinger (Siegburg, 1963), 1:493–99.

[19] For royal vassals, see Nithard, 3.6, p. 38; *Freising* 661; *AF*, s.a. 880, p. 94.

[20] In times of foreign invasion, however, all free men (regardless of their landholdings) were obliged to defend the homeland, a service known as *lantweri*: MGH *Capitularia* 2:71 (c. 5).

[21] Louis and his brothers jointly issued this command in 847: ibid., chaps. 2, 5.

[22] A missive of Louis's preserved in a Passau formulary book freed an old man from military service and paying the *haribann* and instructed him to send his son instead. The fact that this was preserved in a collection of form letters suggests that royal missives concerning the military service of specific individuals were not unusual: *Collectio Pataviensis*, no. 3, in MGH *Formulae*, 457–58; Hartmann, *Ludwig der Deutsche*, 168.

[23] MGH *Capitularia* 2:71 (cc. 3, 4).

[24] For example, see *AF*, s.a. 849, 864, 869, pp. 38 ("cum exercitu copioso"), 62 ("cum manu valida"), 68 ("collectis copiis"); *AX*, s.a. 845, 872, pp. 14 ("congregato exercitu magno"), 30–31 ("ingens exercitus").

termining the size of Carolingian armies is that chroniclers seldom offered precise numbers, and when they did, it is difficult to ascertain the accuracy of their reports. To put it crudely, the two main schools of opinion concerning the size of Carolingian armies are "big" (multiple tens of thousands) and "small" (low to middle thousands).[25] In fact, there is more common ground between these "maximalist" and "minimalist" schools than is often recognized. In an article on Carolingian and Ottonian military service, Karl Ferdinand Werner (a proponent of the "big" school) argued that Charlemagne's army north of the Alps rivaled that of the western late Roman empire: roughly 100,000 soldiers, about 30,000 of whom went to war on horseback.[26] If Werner is correct, this indicates that Louis's territories of 843 possessed roughly a third of that military strength, or about 30,000 soldiers eligible for service. Werner's rough estimate seems reasonable. Louis's kingdom of 843 included 24 bishoprics, 28 monasteries, and from 100 to 200 counties.[27] Thus his eastern territories could have produced an army of about 30,000 soldiers if every bishopric, monastery, and county contributed 100 to 200 men, a number that is within the realm of believability.

As Werner himself emphasized, however, it is crucial to differentiate between the theoretical maximum number of men a king could call up and the actual number of soldiers he took with him in the field. While Louis in theory perhaps could call up about 30,000 men, there is no evidence that he ever raised such a massive army for a single campaign. Indeed, the sources state explicitly that Louis usually raised armies from only one or two provinces within his kingdom for a given expedition.[28] Moreover, it is likely that Louis sometimes reduced the rates of service required of his subjects when he fought the Slavs. Charlemagne had done likewise, decreeing that only one out of every six eligible Saxons was to serve against the Avars, and one of every three when fighting the Bohemians.[29] This points to the conclusion that which provinces provided soldiers and how many were negoti-

[25] Bachrach, *Early Carolingian Warfare*, 57–59, estimates that a total of 100,000 men were eligible for military service in the Carolingian empire north of the Alps, and he argues that Carolingian armies on campaign often approached that number. In contrast, Halsall, *Warfare and Society*, 119–33, argues that Carolingian armies seldom numbered above 5,000 or 6,000 and never above 10,000. Reuter, "Plunder and Tribute," 75–94, claims that Carolingian armies were even smaller, usually fewer than 2,000 soldiers.

[26] Karl Ferdinand Werner, "Heeresorganisation und Kriegsführung im deutschen Königreich des 10. und 11. Jahrhunderts," *SS Spoleto* 15 (1968): 813–32, at 821.

[27] For bishoprics and monasteries, see Bigott, *Ludwig der Deutsche*, 289–90. Werner ("Heeresorganisation," 819; and "Missus-marchio-comes," 191) estimates that Charlemagne's empire north of the Alps had 500–700 counties, while Ganshof (*Frankish Institutions*, 29) estimates 400 counties, not including Brittany and Pannonia.

[28] For example, see *AF*, s.a. 858, 869, 872, pp. 49, 68, 75–76; *DLG* 72.

[29] MGH *Capitularia* 1:136 (c. 2).

ated between Louis and his magnates on a campaign-by-campaign basis. Factors such as the objective of the expedition, the distance of the march, the availability of food, and the extent of the king's support determined how large an army would be sent. Werner's implied estimate of approximately 30,000 eligible soldiers from Louis's territories suggests that each of the five provinces in his kingdom yielded roughly 6,000 fighting men. But because Louis probably sometimes required military service at reduced rates, east Frankish armies raised from one or two provinces likely ranged from a small force of 2,000 soldiers to a large army of 12,000.[30] The chroniclers' repeated emphasis on the large size of Louis's armies suggests that they often approached 10,000 men. As Louis well knew, however, the effectiveness of his armies hinged on the soldiers' training, organization, equipment, and supplies, not their absolute numbers.[31] A smaller and disciplined force of well-equipped soldiers, like the one Louis led in the Ries and at Fontenoy, was far more effective (and, just as important, far easier to provision) than a large, unwieldy army that included poorly trained and ill-equipped peasant-soldiers.

Louis developed a complex military infrastructure to support his regular campaigns against the Slavs. He usually campaigned in the summer, especially in August.[32] The reason was food: hay for the horses was harvested in July, and wheat for the soldiers in August.[33] Louis's campaigns against the Slavs on average seem to have lasted about a month, which would have required enormous quantities of supplies to provision his army. Before a campaign, Louis mustered his armies near the borders of his kingdom, such as at Paderborn in Saxony or Tulln in Upper Pannonia.[34] For his campaigns in the southeast against the Bohemians and Moravians, Louis used ships and the roads along the Danube to facilitate the movement of troops and sup-

[30] This concurs with my earlier estimate (arrived at through the logistics of siege warfare against large Slavic fortresses) that Louis's armies numbered 5,000–7,000, and perhaps as high as 10,000 soldiers: Goldberg, "Ludwig der Deutsche und Mähren," 80–81.

[31] Nithard, 1.5, p. 7, stressed that a small but disciplined (*unanimes*) group of soldiers could defeat a much larger army that was quarrelsome and disorganized (*discordes et inordinati*).

[32] For example, see *AF*, s.a. 846, 848, 856, pp. 36 ("circa medium mensem Augustum"), 37 ("quasi mediante mense Augusto"), 47 ("mense vero Augusto").

[33] Riché, *Daily Life*, 135. Charlemagne renamed July *Hewimanoth* (Hay Month) and August *Aranmanoth* (Month of Ripening Wheat): Einhard, *VK*, chap. 29, p. 33. Horses require about ten pounds of fodder per day, in addition to the same amount of grain. For the logistics of horses in premodern warfare, see Donald W. Engels, *Alexander the Great and the Logistics of the Macedonian Army* (Berkeley, 1978), 126–27.

[34] *AX*, s.a. 845, p. 14; *AF*, s.a. 845, p. 35; Nicholas I, *Epistolae de rebus Franciae*, no. 26, in MGH *Epistolae* 6:293.

plies.[35] Louis's use of ships may explain the group of Frisian vassals in his entourage: Frisians were well known for their nautical skills, and Charlemagne had used a Frisian fleet during his Avar campaigns.[36] The king and his magnates possessed estates along the Franco–Slavic borders, and their produce would have been essential for supplying armies. In Saxony, two powerful families, the Ecbertiner and Liudolfings, possessed numerous estates and forts between the Weser and Elbe rivers, while Louis's commander of the Sorbian march, Thakulf, held lands near the Bohemian border.[37] Our most detailed picture of frontier landholding comes from the Bavarian Eastland, where Louis and the Bavarian bishops, abbots, and counts possessed numerous estates along the Danube between Regensburg and Tulln, in what today is southeastern Germany and northern Austria.[38] The fact that Regensburg and Tulln were both situated along the network of Roman roads and had ports on the Danube explains their strategic importance for the military organization of the southeast.

Louis's campaigns against the Slavs usually focused on the capture of rebellious fortresses. At the first sign of an invading Frankish army, the Slavs withdrew their forces and supplies to their strongholds and attempted to wear down the Frankish army with devastating surprise attacks.[39] Louis typically did not try to capture fortresses through direct assault (that is, with battering rams and ladders), a strategy that required very large armies and a willingness to sustain heavy casualties.[40] Instead, his armies laid siege to the fortress, cut off its food and water, constructed fortified camps outside, and tried to force the defenders either to give battle or to surrender.[41] Sometimes the Franks attempted to burn the Slavic fortifications, although this

[35] *AF*, s.a. 849, 872, pp. 39, 76; *DLG* 25; *Inquisitio de theloneis Raffelstettensis*, in MGH *Capitularia* 2:249–52; Raymond Chevallier, *Roman Roads*, trans. N. H. Field (Berkeley, 1976), 172–75. Charlemagne likewise had used a Danube fleet during the Avar wars: *ARF*, s.a. 791, p. 88.

[36] *Freising* 661; *AF*, s.a. 791, p. 12. Mitterauer, *Karolingische Markgrafen*, 97–99, 103, suggests that Louis's eastern prefect, Ratpot, also was of partial Frisian ancestry.

[37] Krüger, *Studien zur sächsischen Grafschaftsverfassung*, 65 (map 8); *Fulda* 578.

[38] For Louis's numerous grants and confirmations of lands along the Danube to Bavarian churchmen, see *DLG* 2, 3, 8, 9, 18, 25, 64, 86, 96, 109, 116. Several of Louis's frontier counts held lands on the Danube near Linz: *Regensburg* 26 (William), 37 (Chozil), 52 (Ernest); *DLG* 64 (William). See further Goldberg, "Ludwig der Deutsche und Mähren," 83–84 and nn. 54–55. Wolfram, *Grenzen und Räume*, 252, provides a map of the possessions of the Bavarian monasteries in the Eastland.

[39] A good example is the strategy of the Slavic *dux* Borna in 819: *ARF*, s.a. 819, p. 151.

[40] For example, in 855 Louis declined attacking a Moravian fortress because of the risk of heavy casualties: *AF*, s.a. 855, pp. 45–46.

[41] For example, see *AF*, s.a. 849, 851, 855, 864, 869, 870, 871, pp. 38–39, 41, 46, 62, 68–69, 74, 76; *AX*, s.a. 872, p. 31.

Frankish soldiers lay siege to two fortresses. This illumination of the exploits of Joab from the Golden Psalter of St.-Gall vividly depicts Carolingian siege warfare. The besieging army wears heavy iron armor, shoots arrows at the defenders inside the fortresses, and uses torches to set fire to the fortifications. Note the heavy casualties before the gates. Such difficult siege warfare was common in Louis the German's campaigns against the Slavs in the east. Stiftsbibliothek St. Gallen, Codex 22, p. 141.

was of limited effectiveness against the better-made fortresses with stone walls.[42] The Franks harried the surrounding countryside with fire and sword, thereby depleting the region of food and threatening the rebels with starvation.[43] A good example of this frontier warfare took place in 851, when the Sorbs gathered a large army on the Elbe River, besieged some of the Saxon fortresses, and burned down others.[44] The Sorbs clearly had good intelligence about Carolingian politics and had planned their attack accordingly. At that moment, Louis's kingdom was recovering from a serious famine (a constant danger during the ninth century), and Louis was far to the west at Meersen, where he was meeting with his brothers.[45] Louis was "enraged" when he learned of the Sorbs' rebellion. After returning to his kingdom, he raised an army and invaded the territory of the Sorbs. He besieged one of their fortresses and destroyed their crops, thereby forcing them to surrender "more through hunger than by iron."[46]

One advantage the Franks had over the Slavs was in military equipment and training.[47] Carolingian legislation required that every soldier have a shield, spear, bow, and a quiver of twelve arrows. Moreover, noblemen and their vassals were expected to have additional better, and more socially prestigious, equipment: a long sword, short sword, coat of mail, helmet, and, the badge of noble status, a horse. Frankish swords and armor were superior to those used by the Slavs, and Charlemagne therefore had forbidden their export to Slavic lands by merchants.[48] The Golden Psalter, which seems to have been produced in the scriptorium of St.-Gall in the later ninth century, contains vivid scenes of Hebrew warriors laying siege to fortified cities and carrying the same equipment as that described in Carolingian capitularies.[49] Outfitted like Frankish noblemen on campaign, these Old Testament soldiers are shown wearing ornate helmets and suits of iron armor, carrying round shields, spears, swords, and bows, and riding war horses. Although Frankish troops did not constitute a professional, salaried army, the Carolingians made sure they were sufficiently trained and organized. Nithard

---

[42] For example, see *AF*, s.a. 869, p. 69.

[43] *AF*, s.a. 855, 869, 872, pp. 46, 69, 76; *AX*, s.a. 869, 872, pp. 29, 31.

[44] *AX*, s.a. 851, pp. 17–18.

[45] *AF*, s.a. 850, pp. 40–41; *AB*, s.a. 851, pp. 60–64. For famines, see Riché, *Daily Life*, 249–51.

[46] *AF* 851, p. 41. *Annals of Fulda*, trans. Reuter, 32, omits the siege.

[47] Simon Coupland, "Carolingian Arms and Armour in the Ninth Century," *Viator* 21 (1990): 29–55; Halsall, *Warfare and Society*, 93, 163–76.

[48] *Capitulare missorum in Theodonis villa datum secundum, generale*, chap. 7, in MGH *Capitularia* 1:123.

[49] Christoph Eggenberger, *Psalterium Aureum Sancti Galli: Mittelalterliche Psalterillustration im Kloster St. Gallen* (Sigmaringen, 1987), 13–14.

stressed that Louis and Charles frequently drilled their troops during campaigns to instill them with "nobility and discipline" and teach them difficult military maneuvers like the "feigned retreat."[50]

On the rare occasion that it came to a pitched battle on an open field, as at Fontenoy, Frankish generals adhered to a usual formula of engagement. They would arrange their troops—often a combination of mounted and foot solders—on favorable terrain opposite the enemy army. Then they gave the signal to attack. The soldiers first fired their bows and threw their spears, then advanced to fight at close quarters. The clash of the two armies would continue until one side was overrun or turned in flight, usually resulting in a bloody rout. In the end, the victorious side would despoil the dead of their valuable arms and armor. A ninth- or tenth-century Latin epic known as the *Waltharius* offers a dramatic, and probably more or less accurate, depiction of a "typical" Carolingian military engagement:

Now [the commander] surveyed the battle site and then deployed
His battle-line, arrayed to fight, through fields and plains.
Within a spear's throw of each other stand the two
Assembled armies; from both sides a noise arises
Into the air: the trumpets blare their awful sound;
At once from everywhere dense clouds of weapons fly.

. . . .

At last, when every javelin from both lines
Was thrown, then every hand is reaching for a sword.
They draw their flashing blades and swing their shields around;
At length, the battle lines converge, renew the fray.
Some of the horses charge and shatter breast to breast;
Some of the riders are unhorsed by a hard shield.

. . . .

[The victorious army] cuts down those resisting, slaughters those who run
Until it gains full victory in the lot of war.
Then rushing to the corpses it despoils them all.[51]

Although frontier warfare was an expensive and dangerous business, it nevertheless afforded Louis an important arena for asserting his political leadership, personal charisma, and manliness. Until the mid-860s, Louis often commanded his armies in person, giving him regular opportunities to work face-to-face with the nobles and lead them in battle. Kings typically

[50] Nithard, 3.6, p. 38. For the importance of the feigned retreat in early medieval warfare, see Bachrach, "*Caballus et Caballarius,*" 191–92.
[51] English translation from *Waltharius*, trans. and ed. Kratz, ll. 179–208, pp. 11–13.

addressed their troops before battle to strategize and boost morale, and it therefore was to Louis's advantage that he was a good speaker and possessed a deep booming voice.[52] Louis's personal preferences for simple Frankish clothes, iron armor, and the "equipment of battle" must have impressed the troops with his devotion to the soldier's life.[53] According to Notker, Louis berated soldiers in his army who did not adhere to his strict code of military attire. He wrote:

[Louis] followed Charlemagne's example [of austere attire] not once but throughout his entire life. He held no one worthy of his attention and instruction unless he wore only armor over wool and linen clothes when on campaign against an enemy. And if he happened to run into one of his subjects who was ignorant of his strict discipline and was wearing silk, gold, or silver, the king berated him with the following words and taught him an important lesson: "Just look at you strutting around in gold, silver, and scarlet. You stupid idiot! Isn't it enough that you might die in battle? But you would rather hand over to the enemy your valuables to adorn their heathen idols. It would have been better if you used them to redeem your soul." From his early youth until his seventieth year, the unconquered Louis exulted in iron.

Notker had reliable information about Louis from his abbot, Grimald, who often was at court and went on campaign with the king.[54] It is therefore likely that Notker here captured something of Louis's grim sense of irony, the kind of humor one would expect from a soldier-king who had spent much of his adult life at war.

Louis surrounded his campaigns against the polytheistic Slavs with an aura of Christian warfare against the heathens. As Notker's anecdote illustrates, the Franks saw campaigns against the pagan Slavs as contests against the enemies of the Faith, similar to the wars waged by the Israelites as recounted in the Old Testament. It seems that Louis heightened this sense of Christian warfare by carrying with his army a banner, in the shape of a cross, that contained a relic of the True Cross. Baturich of Regensburg's pontifical

---

[52] Nithard, 3.6, p. 37; Notker, *GK* 2.11, pp. 67–68.

[53] Notker, *GK* 2.17, pp. 87–88; Regino, *Chronicon*, s.a. 876, p. 110.

[54] Ratpert, *Casus sancti Galli*, chap. 9, p. 216, mentioned "omnes labores et itinera, sive ad curtem, sive in expeditionem et ad omnes alias necessitates" of St.-Gall's abbot. Ermanrich, *Epistola ad Grimaldum*, in MGH *Epistolae* 5:536–37, 539, similarly stressed Grimald's numerous duties and journeys for the king.

contains a "Blessing of the Cross" for just such a military standard.[55] This blessing was to be recited over the cross before battle while the entire army bowed and prayed for victory and forgiveness of their sins. Here Louis may have been consciously imitating Byzantine imperial practices. The eastern emperors marched to war behind a golden cross standard containing a relic of the True Cross, and before battle the Byzantine standards were blessed while the soldiers prayed.[56] Louis apparently had an opportunity to meet Byzantine ambassadors during his years at his father's court, and it is therefore possible that he knew of such eastern military rituals.[57]

THE NORTHEAST: THE ELBE SLAVS AND DANES

The year after the Treaty of Verdun, Louis immediately went to war against the Obodrites, a relatively populous Slavic people who lived beyond the lower Elbe.[58] Louis's conflict with the Obodrites illustrates the complex range of diplomatic and military strategies he employed to reestablish Frankish tributary lordship over the Slavs. The Obodrites reportedly were "planning to defect," which could indicate a range of rebellious behavior, such as forming illicit alliances, attacking fortresses along the Frankish borders, and refusing to send tribute.[59] One of the Obodrite rulers, Goztomuizli, had used the civil war to assert himself as an independent king (*rex*). In 844, Louis crossed the Elbe with an army of east Franks, invaded the land of the Obodrites, and defeated them in battle. Goztomuizli died (the details of his end are not reported), and Louis won over the remaining Obodrite princes "through a combination of force and enticements" [aut vi aut gratia]. They came before Louis, submitted to his overlordship, promised him

[55] *Benedictio crucis*, in Baturich of Regensburg's pontifical, Clm 14510, fols. 71v–72v. *DLG* 66 refers to Louis's *sancta ac venerabilis dominica crux sua*. See further Goldberg, "Equipment of Battle," 66–67.

[56] Michael McCormick, *Eternal Victory: Triumphal Rulership in Late Antiquity, Byzantium and the Early Medieval West* (Cambridge, 1986), 246–48.

[57] For example, Louis the Pious received Byzantine ambassadors at Rouen immediately after the 824 Breton campaign: *ARF*, s.a. 824, p. 165. Because Louis the German had participated in that campaign alongside his father, he presumably was at Rouen.

[58] Louis's 844 campaign against the Obodrites is reported in *AF*, s.a. 844, p. 35; *AB*, s.a. 844, p. 48; *AX*, s.a. 844, pp. 13–14; *AH*, s.a. 844, p. 17. On the organization of the Obodrites in the ninth century, see Wolfgang Fritze, "Die Datierung des Geographus Bavarus und die Stammesverfassung der Abodriten," *ZSP* 21 (1952): 326–42.

[59] The Obodrites did all these things under Louis the Pious: *ARF*, s.a. 817, 819, 821, 823, pp. 147, 149–50, 156–57, 160, 162; *AB*, s.a. 838, 839, pp. 25–26, 33–35. The *AF*, s.a. 877, p. 89, equated "defectionem molientes" with "solitum dare censum rennuunt."

fidelity, and theoretically became his client rulers (*duces*). The situation remained unstable, however, and the Obodrites "began plotting to rebel as soon as he departed."

As often was the case in campaigns against the Slavs, Louis faced serious logistical constraints when fighting the Obodrites in 844. Louis presumably attacked the Obodrites in August, his usual month for going to war. In 844 Louis was at Regensburg on July 28, at Thionville in the middle kingdom in early October (for the first post-Verdun meeting with his brothers), and then again at Regensburg on October 28.[60] Thus, between July 28 and October 28, Louis traversed a massive triangle in central Europe, following an itinerary that took him from Regensburg to the Obodrite territory (about 300 miles), then from the Obodrite territory to Thionville (about 375 miles), and finally from Thionville back to Regensburg (about 300 miles). On horseback, Louis and his troops could have traveled rapidly within his kingdom, as fast as thirty miles per day.[61] If one takes into account the time needed to travel these distances, it becomes evident that Louis had only about a month from mid-August to mid-September to defeat the Obodrites, set up the new client rulers, and negotiate treaties with them—hardly enough time for a stable and lasting regime change. Here one sees the logistical constraints that time, geography, food, and rates of travel placed on Louis's campaigns. Warfare against the Slavs usually took place in the midst of other pressing matters, forcing the king to juggle eastern warfare with western politics as best he could.

Another obstacle Louis faced with the Obodrites in 844 was that, as often happened, their local rebellion had larger "international" dimensions. Historically, the chief rival of the Franks for control of the lower Elbe was the king of Denmark. In the first half of the ninth century, the Danish kingdom was the most powerful polity in Scandinavia, covering not only modern Denmark but also southern Sweden and the Vestfold west of modern Oslo.[62] Since the early ninth century, Danish attempts to expand overlordship along the Baltic and Elbe had been a major cause of instability in the region.[63] Like the Slavs, the Danes and other Scandinavians had good intelligence about Carolingian politics, and they had intensified their raids on

---

[60] *AB*, s.a. 844, p. 48; *DLG* 37, 39.

[61] Bachrach, "Animals and Warfare," 716–19 and nn. 46, 50. Horses generally require one full day of rest per week or will break down from injuries.

[62] John Haywood, *The Penguin Historical Atlas of the Vikings* (London, 1995), 34–35. For relations between the Carolingians and the Vikings in general, see Janet L. Nelson, "The Frankish Empire," in *The Oxford Illustrated History of the Vikings*, ed. Peter Sawyer (Oxford, 1997), 19–47.

[63] For the conflict between the Danish king Godfrid and Charlemagne over control of the lower Elbe, see *ARF*, s.a. 808–10, pp. 125–26, 128–33.

the Continent during the civil wars of the 830s and early 840s. Moreover, in 838 the powerful King Horik I of Denmark (813–54) had demanded that Louis the Pious concede to him lordship over the Obodrites, which had precipitated a large-scale rebellion of the Elbe Slavs, including the Obodrites, Wilzes, Linones, Sorbs, and Colodices.[64] The Stellinga rebellion had heightened the instability in the region, since it threatened to result in an alliance among the Danes, Elbe Slavs, and Saxon peasants. In early 845, Horik sought to exploit this ongoing unrest by sending a large fleet up the Elbe.[65] The Saxon nobles rallied stiff resistance and defeated the Danes, however, forcing the Danish survivors to flee to their ships. On the way home, the Danes sacked the Saxon fortress of Hamburg on the lower Elbe, which Louis the Pious had established in 831 as an archbishopric to bring Christianity to the Scandinavians. The Danish pirates plundered the city for two days and burned down the cathedral, monastery, and library, forcing Archbishop Anskar of Hamburg to flee.[66]

Louis sought to resolve this ongoing crisis through a combination of diplomacy and military strength. After the sack of Hamburg in 845, he sent Count Cobbo, the brother of Abbot Warin of Corvey, to demand that Horik submit to Frankish overlordship and pay reparations for the 845 invasion.[67] Cobbo's embassy to Horik was successful: the Danish king sent envoys to Louis asking for a peace treaty and promising to return the captives and treasure from the 845 raid.[68] Louis presumably demanded the same terms that had existed under his father: that Horik pledge friendship and obedience to him, withhold support from Viking raiders, and regularly send ambassadors with gifts to reaffirm their alliance.[69] This peace treaty with Horik provided the key for reasserting Frankish lordship over the lower Elbe. In 845 Louis held an important assembly at Paderborn in Saxony at which he received the submission of the Elbe Slavs and Danes. The Slavs

[64] *AB*, s.a. 838, 839, pp. 25–26, 33–35.

[65] *AB*, s.a. 845, p. 49; *AF*, s.a. 845, p. 35. The *AB* claimed that the Danish fleet numbered 600 ships, although that estimate seems implausibly high: *Annals of St.-Bertin*, trans. Nelson, 61n3. Nevertheless, King Horik's personal organization of the fleet suggests that it was unusually large.

[66] Rimbert, *Vita Anskarii*, chap. 16, pp. 37–38.

[67] *Translatio sancti Germani*, chaps. 14–15, in MGH SS 15:13. When Cobbo arrived at Horik's court, he found a Viking leader named Ragnar showing off the gold and silver he had plundered from Paris. This report suggests how Viking raids on the Continent were part of the struggle for power and status among the Scandinavian nobility back home.

[68] *AB*, s.a. 845, pp. 50–51.

[69] *AB*, s.a. 836, 839, pp. 19–20, 34. Horik had his own reasons for wanting a secure border with Saxony. At this time, he aspired to wrestle parts of what is today southern Sweden from King Olaf of the Svears, and he also faced political challenges at home from his pirate nephews: Rimbert, *Vita Anskarii*, chap. 30, p. 60; *AB*, s.a. 850, p. 59.

sent ambassadors to Louis, rendered tribute and hostages, and requested a peace treaty. Louis granted their request and dismissed them.[70] The mention of hostages is significant. In an effort to force Slavic peoples to remain loyal, Louis demanded that their rulers give him high-ranking hostages, often their own sons and relatives. It seems that these Slavic hostages were treated with honor at Louis's court, thereby establishing social ties between the east Frankish and Slavic dynasties.[71] However, they lived under the constant threat of execution if their rulers rebelled.

After the submission of the Danes and Elbe Slavs in 845, Louis maintained Horik's loyalty through diplomatic pressure. Louis gave refuge to rivals of Horik, thereby signaling that he would back them against the Danish king if he broke the peace treaty and rebelled.[72] Archbishop Anskar of Hamburg (to whom Louis granted the additional bishopric of Bremen after the destruction of his see in 845), also served as Louis's frequent ambassador to King Horik and his successor, Horik II (854–ca. 857).[73] Anskar became influential at the court of the two Horiks, and he worked hard to maintain good relations between the two kingdoms and spread the Christian faith. Louis's diplomatic strategy seems to have been effective, as there were no more rebellions among the Danes and Obodrites until the year after Horik II's death.[74]

Louis may have signaled his reassertion of tributary lordship over the Elbe Slavs and Danes with the compilation of a unique document, the *Catalogue of Fortresses and Regions to the North of the Danube*.[75] The single copy of

---

[70] *AX*, s.a. 845, p. 14; *AF*, s.a. 845, p. 35. At Paderborn Louis also received ambassadors from the Bulgars, presumably to renew their peace treaty.

[71] This is suggested by the fictional account of the Frankish nobleman Walter, who served as a hostage at the court of Attila the Hun in the epic *Waltharius*, ll. 77–340, pp. 6–18. For other examples of Slavic hostages, see *AF*, s.a. 862, 871, pp. 56, 74. In general, see Adam J. Kosto, "Hostages in the Carolingian World (714–840)," *EME* 11 (2002): 123–47.

[72] *AF*, s.a. 852, pp. 41–42.

[73] Rimbert, *Vita Anskarii*, chaps. 22, 24, pp. 47–48, 52–53. For a good overview of Anskar's career and the Frankish mission to Scandinavia, see Bigott, *Ludwig der Deutsche*, 111–18, 170–81. Bigott emphasizes that, in contrast to his generous support of the archbishop of Salzburg's missionary work in Carantania and Lower Pannonia, Louis gave little material assistance to Anskar of Hamburg's missionary work in Scandinavia. Although this is true, it should be remembered that Louis actively supported the missionary work of the Saxon bishops and abbots within Saxony itself. Because of the recent pagan Stellinga uprising, Louis wanted to focus the limited resources of the Saxon Church on the Christianization of his own territories.

[74] In 858, a Danish force attacked Saxony but was repulsed, and Louis sent an army beyond the Elbe against the Obodrites and their southern neighbors, the Linones: *AB*, s.a. 858, p. 78; *AF*, s.a. 858, p. 49.

[75] The *Descriptio civitatum et regionum ad septentrionalem plagam Danubii*, often misleadingly referred to as the Bavarian Geographer, survives in Munich, Clm 560, fols. 149v–150r. For an edition and commentary, see Erwin Herrmann, *Slawisch-germanische*

the *Catalogue of Fortresses* survives in a Reichenau manuscript from the second half of the ninth century, and the original text seems to have been compiled between 844 and 862 at Louis's court. The *Catalogue of Fortresses* reflects the point of view of Louis's regime, since it refers to the Slavic territories as the "regions that border on our frontiers." It lists in north-to-south order the peoples to the east of Louis's kingdom and the number of their major fortresses (*civitates*).[76] This emphasis on fortresses once again highlights the increasing political and military significance of Slavic strongholds in Frankish diplomacy and warfare with the Slavs. The first section reads:

> Catalogue of the Fortresses and Regions to the North of the Danube: Those who live next to the borders of the Danes are called the North Obodrites, in whose region there are 53 fortresses divided among their client rulers. The Wilzes [have] 95 fortresses and four regions. The Linones are a people who have seven fortresses. Next to them live those called Bethenics, Smeldings, and Morizans who have 11 fortresses. Next to them are those called Hevelles who have eight fortresses. Next to them is the region of those called Sorbs in whose region there are many people. They have 50 fortresses. Next to them are those called Dalaminzes who have 14 fortresses. Among the Bohemians are 15 fortresses. The Moravians have 11 fortresses. The region of the Bulgars is immense. That numerous people has [only] five fortresses, since their great multitude does not require [more] fortresses. The people called Merehans have 30 fortresses. Those are the regions that border on our frontiers.

The fact that the *Catalogue of Fortresses* singles out the Obodrites as "divided among their client rulers" [per duces suos partite] points to the conclusion that it was compiled soon after the 844 campaign against the Obodrites, when, in the words of the *Annals of Fulda*, Louis "placed them under client

---

Beziehungen im südostdeutschen Raum von der Spätantike bis zum Ungarnsturm: Ein Quellenbuch mit Erläuterungen (Munich, 1965), 212–22. For the dating of the *Descriptio civitatum* and its connections to Louis's court, see Bernhard Bischoff, *Die südostdeutschen Schreibschulen und Bibliotheken in der Karolingerzeit* (Wiesbaden, 1960–80), 1:262n3; Fritze, "Die Datierung des Geographus Bavarus," 326–42; Wattenbach, Levison, and Löwe, *DGM* 6:790.

[76] The organization of the *Descriptio civitatum* suggests that it was modeled on a late Roman geographical treatise known as the *Roster of Gallic Cities* (*Notitia Galliarum*), a copy of which was at Louis's court in the Grimalt Codex, 48–51; Bischoff, "Bücher am Hofe Ludwigs des Deutschen," 206. Like the *Descriptio civitatum*, the *Roster of Gallic Cities* listed each province of the western Roman empire and its number of *civitates*.

rulers" [per duces ordinavit]. It is possible that Louis ordered the compilation of the *Catalogue of Fortresses* to aid in calculating tribute payments from neighboring peoples. The most likely setting for the codification of this document was the 845 Paderborn assembly when Louis "received, heard, and dismissed" legates from the Danes, Slavs, and Bulgars.

THE SOUTHEAST: BOHEMIA AND MORAVIA

While Louis successfully reestablished tributary lordship over the Elbe Slavs, he had more difficulties with the Bohemians and Moravians in the southeast. The Bohemians were a confederation of several Slavic peoples concentrated along the upper Elbe (Labe), Sazava, and Berounka rivers in what is today the western Czech Republic.[77] They first appeared in the Frankish sources in 805–6, when Charlemagne sent two armies against them.[78] The Moravians were the eastern neighbors of the Bohemians. They lived along the March-Morava River, about sixty miles north of Vienna.[79] The Moravians show up for the first time in 822, alongside the Bohemians and other Slavic peoples bringing tribute to Louis the Pious.[80] Bavarian missionaries from Passau and Salzburg were active in Moravia by the 820s, and Adalram of Salzburg and Raginar of Passau came into conflict over the borders of their dioceses in the Bavarian Eastland. Louis seems to have settled this dispute in the late 820s, ruling that Passau's diocese extend as far east as the Raab River, thereby placing Moravia within Passau's jurisdiction.[81]

[77] On early medieval Bohemia, see Gojda, *Ancient Slavs*, 44–57; Barford, *Early Slavs*, 111–12, 251–56.

[78] *ARF*, s.a. 805, 806, pp. 120, 122.

[79] For ninth-century Moravia, see especially Karl Bosl, "Das Grossmährische Reich in der politischen Welt des 9. Jahrhunderts," *SBAW* 7 (1966): 1–33; Wolfram, *Grenzen und Räume*, 248–67; Barford, *Early Slavs*, 54–58, 108–11. I am not convinced by revisionist arguments that would rather situate ninth-century Moravia farther to the southeast, either at Sirmium (Sremska Mitrovica) on the Sava River or at the confluence of the Theiss and Maros rivers: Imre Boba, *Moravia's History Reconsidered: A Reinterpretation of the Medieval Sources* (The Hague, 1971); Bowlus, *Franks, Moravians, and Magyars*; Martin Eggers, *Das "Grossmährische Reich": Realität oder Fiktion? Eine Neuinterpretation der Quellen zur Geschichte des mittleren Donauraumes im 9. Jahrhundert* (Stuttgart, 1995). For critiques of these revisionist arguments, see Heinz Dopsch, "Passau als Zentrum der Slawenmission: Ein Beitrag zur Frage des 'Grossmährischen Reiches,'" *SA* 28–29 (1985–86): 5–28; Wolfram, *Salzburg*, 87–100.

[80] *ARF*, s.a. 822, p. 159.

[81] This ruling is recorded in a forged diploma, purportedly by Louis, that probably contains reliable information: *DLG* 173; Wolfram, *Grenzen und Räume*, 178, 227. For Pas-

During Louis's reign, the Moravian Slavs emerged as a serious rival of the Franks for control of Slavic Europe. The political power of ninth-century Moravia arose from its increasing wealth and long-distance trade. Moravia was located along the ancient Amber Road that linked Venice and the Adriatic with the Slavic world via the eastern Alpine passes and Carnuntum on the Danube. After Charlemagne's destruction of the Avar empire, trade along the Amber Road revived significantly, as demonstrated by the numerous ninth-century Byzantine and Arab coins found along it.[82] By the early 830s, a Slavic prince named Moimir I (ca. 830–46) had managed to make himself supreme ruler of Moravia—in essence, a king. Throughout Louis's reign, Moimir and his successors, Rastislav (846–70) and Svatopluk (870–94), struggled to free Moravia from Frankish overlordship and build an independent Slavic kingdom.[83] The first suggestion of Moimir's policy of independence vis-à-vis the Franks was in about 833, when he drove into exile Pribina, the Franco-friendly Slavic ruler of Nitra who later became Louis's *dux* of Lower Pannonia.[84] Moimir was a serious threat to Louis. Not only had he united the Moravians under his rule, but the ongoing Christianization of the Moravians meant that he had access to the trappings of Christian kingship: liturgy, relics, church architecture, and writing. Like all Slavic rulers, Moimir had good intelligence about Carolingian politics, and he used the civil war as an opportunity to "plot a rebellion" and try to throw off the yoke of Frankish overlordship.[85]

Louis intended to invade Moravia in 846, and he made extensive preparations for the campaign. He planned to employ the common military strategy of invading from two directions (the "pincer movement") to avoid the logistical difficulties of provisioning a single massive army. This required sending one army from Bavaria along the Danube through Upper Pannonia, and a second from Saxony along the Elbe through Bohemia. Here Louis was following the strategy of his grandfather, who in 791 had

---

sau's jurisdiction and missionary work in Moravia, see Dopsch, "Passau als Zentrum," 7–20.

[82] McCormick, *Origins*, 369–84.

[83] Historians and archeologists have often called this Slavic polity Great Moravia or the Great Moravian Empire, although this lofty phrase (often tainted with overtones of modern nationalism) is based on a mistranslation of the tenth-century treatise *De administrando imperio* by the Byzantine emperor Constantine VII Porphyrogenitus: Constantine, *De administrando*, chap. 13, p. 64. Constantine used the phrase "megale Morabia" in the sense of "Moravia beyond the borders of the empire," not "Great Moravia": Wolfram, *Grenzen und Räume*, 317.

[84] *Conversio*, chap. 11, pp. 122–26.

[85] *AF*, s.a. 846, p. 36.

attacked the Avars with multiple armies, one of which traveled through Bohemia.[86] In the case of Moravia, the pincer strategy was a difficult and dangerous one, since the journey from the Saxon borders through Bohemia to Moravia was some 350 miles. If Louis's Saxon army had to bring its own supplies on wagons and be prepared for Slavic attacks, it could travel only about ten miles each day, making the trip one that lasted about six weeks. However, if the Saxons were on horseback and could depend on safe passage and supplies from the Bohemians, they could make the journey to Moravia in under two weeks.[87] It apparently was to arrange this safe passage that Louis had a highly unusual meeting with the Bohemian rulers in early 845. On January 13, fourteen Bohemian *duces* and their followers came to Louis's palace and received baptism, a sign of their submission to Louis's overlordship.[88] In addition, they apparently pledged to give supplies and support to Louis's Saxon army the following year. Such agreements were not new. The Carantanian Slavs were obliged to render a tax (*coniectum*), which presumably included food, for the archbishop of Salzburg whenever he journeyed through their territory.[89] This strategy of invading Moravia through Bohemia appealed to Louis, and many of his later campaigns against the Bohemians were in part aimed at securing this second invasion route to Moravia.

Louis and his magnates made additional preparations for the 846 campaign. On January 10 at Regensburg, Louis made a generous gift of one hundred homesteads in the Bavarian marches to his *dux* of Lower Pannonia, Pribina.[90] Pribina was the old adversary of Moimir, who had driven him out

---

[86] *ARF*, s.a. 791, p. 89; *AF*, s.a. 791, p. 12. Louis had had the opportunity to inspect this route personally when his father forced him to retreat through Bohemia in 840: *AF*, s.a. 840, pp. 30–31.

[87] The *AF*, s.a. 872, p. 76, confirm that the armies that invaded Moravia through Bohemia traveled on horseback.

[88] *AF*, s.a. 845, p. 35. Historians usually have taken this brief report in the *AF* at face value, seeing it as part of Bavarian missionary work among the Bohemians: Hartmann, *Ludwig der Deutsche*, 113; Bigott, *Ludwig der Deutsche*, 169. Dušan Třeštík, "The Baptism of the Czech Princes in 845 and the Christianization of the Slavs," in *Historica: Historical Sciences in the Czech Republic* (Prague, 1995), 7–59, argues that the Bohemian princes accepted baptism in an effort to prevent Louis from invading their territory.

[89] *DLG* 112.

[90] *DLG* 45. The original diploma does not survive, but an eighteenth-century Eichstätt catalogue records that the lands were located "next to the Valchau River" [iuxta fluvium Valchau]. Some scholars have suggested that this is a reference to the Valpo River near Osijek in modern Croatia. However, this must be rejected because there is no evidence Louis controlled that region: Hans Pirchegger, "Karantanien und Unterpannonien zur Karolingerzeit," *MÖIG* 33 (1912): 283. It is possible that these estates were in the

of Nitra, and Louis presumably made this grant to help supply Pribina's troops in the upcoming campaign. Louis placed his supporter, Bishop Erchanbert of Freising, in charge of salt supplies for his army. Salt was an essential mineral for soldiers and horses (especially during the hot summer months), and kings therefore had to ensure that their armies had sufficient salt rations. Louis had granted Kempten, where Erchanbert was abbot, the right to take six carts and three ships of salt from the salt springs at Reichenhall without having to pay tolls or taxes.[91] Then less than three months before Louis's army set out in 846, Erchanbert acquired an estate at Reichenhall with salt-boiling cauldrons.[92] Louis may also have used troops from the middle Rhine, which would explain a generous grant made by his Upper Pannonian count, Werner, to Samuel, the bishop of Worms and abbot of Lorsch. Only two weeks before Count Werner set out with Louis's armies, he gave Lorsch several estates on the middle Rhine that Louis had granted him ten years earlier.[93] Werner made the grant for the salvation of the "most glorious lord prince, King Louis," suggesting that he saw Lorsch's patron saint, Nazarius, as a special protector of the upcoming expedition.

Louis set out against the Moravians in mid-August, when wheat and hay were plentiful for his army.[94] While the Bavarian army invaded Moravia through Upper Pannonia, Louis personally led the second army from Saxony, across the Elbe, and through Bohemia. Upon reaching Moravia, Louis encountered little resistance. Moimir seems to have fled or been killed, and Louis set up his relative, Rastislav, as the new client ruler (*dux*) of Moravia. The previous career of Rastislav is unknown, but it is conceivable that he had earlier served as a hostage for Moimir at Louis's court. Louis clearly thought that Rastislav would remain loyal, and he presumably extracted from him oaths of fidelity, hostages, and a promise to pay annual tribute. Louis's faith in Rastislav was initially well founded: for the next eight years there is no report of a Moravian rebellion.

At this moment, however, Louis's army fell victim to an ever-present danger of Carolingian warfare: conflicts among the magnates in the army. One of the main risks of going on campaign was not facing enemy troops

---

Wachau (Wahowa) on the Danube near Krems, where Louis gave lands to Herrieden, Salzburg, and Niederalteich: *DLG* 2, 102, 116.

[91] *DLG* 24, 36.
[92] *Freising* 682.
[93] *DLG* 19; *Lorsch* 27.
[94] *AF*, s.a. 846, p. 36; *AB*, s.a. 846, p. 53; *AX*, s.a. 846, p. 15; *AH*, s.a. 846, p. 17. Dümmler, *GOR* 1:298n1, misinterpreted Louis's march through Bohemia as a separate campaign.

but managing the bitter rivalries among the king's generals, who constantly jockeyed with each other for power, status, and *dignitas*. This brings to mind Notker's comment about soldiers wearing fine clothing and jewelry on campaign: even outside the borders of the kingdom, nobles wanted to assert their dignity vis-à-vis their peers. Perhaps it was to lessen such aristocratic rivalries that Louis imposed the requirement of simple military attire on his soldiers. Such division among Louis's troops dangerously exposed them to the surprise attacks in which the Slavs excelled.

This is what happened as Louis led the Saxons home through Bohemia in September 846. Louis's men began to fight among themselves, and at the same time some of the Bohemian rulers broke the treaty and attacked. Because Louis apparently had relied on the Bohemians for supplies, their treachery was grave indeed, threatening his army with starvation. As a result, Louis retreated "through the land of the Bohemians with great difficulty and heavy losses to his army." A diploma that probably should be dated September 15, 846, sheds light on the aristocratic divisions within Louis's army.[95] As soon he returned to his kingdom, Louis issued a diploma at Roding, which was located northeast of Regensburg in the Bavarian Forest near the Frankish–Bohemian border. At the request of Bishop Baturich of Regensburg and Counts Werner and Pabo, Louis made a grant of land in Upper Pannonia to a priest named Dominic, who was Salzburg's representative at Pribina's court at Moosburg.[96] Although Dominic, Baturich, Werner, and Pabo could have returned home from Moravia more safely through Upper Pannonia, they apparently had accompanied the king through Bohemia to support him as he led the Saxons back home. In the

[95] *DLG* 38. This diploma was issued on September 15, but the precise year in the mid-840s has remained uncertain because of errors in the dating clause. BM 1379 and Kehr, *DLG* 38, tentatively suggest 844, while Bigott, *Ludwig der Deutsche*, 171n256, suggests 847–50. However, the diploma probably should be dated September 15, 846, and interpreted in light of Louis's return from Moravia. The king issued the diploma at Roding in the Bavarian Forest, not far from the Frankish–Bohemian border in the Nordgau. The circumstances under which Louis issued this diploma suggest haste, as would be expected after his harrowing retreat from Bohemia. Roding did not have a palace or royal estate (the customary setting for the granting of a royal diploma), and Louis is otherwise not known to have visited there. Also unusual is the fact that the Roding diploma was written by a new unskilled scribe named Reginbert, who produced a diploma that was "extremely inelegant and full of errors," including the bad dating clause (*DLG*, xxi–xxii). The strongest case for dating the Roding diploma to 846 is that it fits exactly with Louis's known itinerary during the Moravian campaign of that year.

[96] *Conversio*, chap. 11, p. 124; Wolfram, *Salzburg*, 323–24. Dominic had earlier served as a notary at Louis's court. The estate Louis granted Dominic was at Lebenbrunn, located halfway between Moosburg and Vienna and thus strategically situated to supply Pribina's forces as they marched to and from Moravia.

face of Bohemian treachery and surprise attacks, it would hardly be surprising if tensions ran high between Louis's Bavarian and Saxon magnates. Louis therefore broke off his march toward Saxony and made a hasty departure from Bohemia by way of Roding. Once safely within the borders of his kingdom, he rewarded his Bavarian supporters to compensate them for their hardships. It was a disastrous conclusion to the campaign, rivaling the calamitous 778 ambush of Charlemagne's army in the Spanish marches as immortalized in the *Song of Roland*. As Prudentius summed up, Louis returned home "badly shaken" [conterritus].

Louis spent the next several years struggling to reassert control over Bohemia. In 847, he waged a successful campaign against the Bohemians, and the following year he sent his son, Louis the Younger, against them.[97] This leadership role taken by the approximately thirteen-year-old Louis the Younger was his first and indicates that his father was preparing him to enter the political arena. If the *Annals of Fulda* are to be believed, the 848 Bohemian campaign was a success (although this is questionable, since the other annals are silent); the king's son "crushed them and compelled them to send legates asking for a peace treaty and give hostages." At an assembly in Mainz at the beginning of October, Louis "received, heard, and dismissed" legates of the Northmen and Slavs, implying that at least some of the Slavic peoples brought him the annual tribute.[98] The king then hurried back to Regensburg, where in mid-October he held another assembly with the leading magnates in charge of the Slavic frontiers.[99] During that assembly, Louis converted all Pribina's Lower Pannonian benefices near Lake Balaton (save those Pribina held from the archbishop of Salzburg) into personal property. Louis made this generous concession to reward the Slavic *dux* for his loyal service, presumably in the recent campaigns against the Bohemians and Moravians. This grant clearly had important ramifications for the administration of the Eastland, since Louis made it in the presence of the assembled bishops of Salzburg, Freising, Regensburg, and Passau, his two elder sons Carloman and Louis the Younger, the frontier counts Ernest, Ratpot, Werner, and Pabo, as well as the count of the palace, Fritilo, and other Bavarian nobles.

The following year, the Bohemians "in their usual fashion renounced their fidelity and planned to rebel against the Franks," forcing Louis to

[97] *AF,* s.a. 848, p. 37; *AB,* s.a. 847, 848, p. 55.
[98] *AF,* s.a. 848, p. 37.
[99] *Conversio,* chap. 12, pp. 128–29 and n. 160; *DLG* 46. I follow Wolfram, *Salzburg,* 325–30, who argues that the *Conversio's* date of 848 should be accepted. Cf. Hartmann, *Ludwig der Deutsche,* 193–94 and n. 361, who follows Kehr, *DLG* 46, and argues for a redating to 847.

launch yet another campaign against them.[100] The 849 campaign again illustrates the problem of disputes among the magnates, which repeatedly endangered Louis's armies. Louis fell ill at the last minute, preventing him from leading his troops in person, so he sent "counts and many abbots with a large army" under Ernest, "commander of those regions and first among the king's friends." In a repetition of the events in 846, Louis's army was initially successful but then suffered a major defeat because of conflicts among the nobles. The Franks constructed a fortified camp outside a Bohemian fortress, and amid heavy fighting and archery attacks they breached the walls and compelled the Bohemians to sue for peace. But at this point a conflict broke out between Ernest and Thakulf, the commander of the Sorbian march, who also was in the Frankish army.[101] Ernest clearly outranked Thakulf: Ernest was the king's designated commander of the expedition, and the witness list of Louis's 848 grant to Pribina ranked Ernest first and Thakulf sixth among the counts.[102] Nevertheless, Thakulf was a nobleman of considerable standing. He was commander of the Thuringian border against the Sorbs, a prominent patron of Fulda, and Abbot Hatto of Fulda's envoy to Rome. Thakulf had his own political ambitions in the Slavic territories: he was "knowledgeable about the laws and customs of the Slavic people," and a later Fulda charter gave him the grand title of count of Bohemia.[103]

The presence of these two ambitious commanders in an army while the king lay sick in bed was a recipe for trouble. The vanquished Bohemians sent envoys suing for peace, not to Ernest, but to Thakulf, ostensibly because of his familiarity with Slavic customs. But in light of Slavic intelligence about Frankish politics, it is likely that the Bohemians knew about the rivalry between Thakulf and Ernest and were trying to exploit it by "subverting" the hierarchy of Louis's army. Since Thakulf had been injured by an arrow, he received the Bohemian envoys sitting on his horse to hide his wound. When the other Frankish magnates learned that the Bohemians had submitted to Thakulf while he proudly sat on his horse, they took it as an insult to their *dignitas*: "They were indignant toward him, as if he desired to surpass the others and take over supreme command for himself." To reassert

---

[100] *AF*, s.a. 849, pp. 38–39; *AX*, s.a. 849, p. 16; *AB*, s.a. 849, p. 58. In February 849, Louis may have been with Abbot Hatto of Fulda at Forchheim in eastern Franconia, not far from the Bohemian border, perhaps preparing for the upcoming campaign: *DLG* 53, 54. These diplomas could also be dated 850.

[101] Concerning Thakulf, see *AF* 849, 858, 873, 874, pp. 38, 49, 81; *Epistolarum Fuldensium fragmenta*, no. 31, in MGH *Epistolae* 5:531. Thakulf appeared as witness to several Fulda grants between 837 and ca. 859: *Fulda* 507, 555, 577.

[102] *DLG* 46.

[103] *AF*, s.a. 849, p. 38; *Fulda* 578.

their "valor and daring," the affronted nobles launched a disorganized second attack on the Bohemians, resulting in a military debacle of the first order. The Bohemians now overcame the Franks, slew many of them, and compelled the survivors to leave behind hostages in return for safe passage home. This defeat was a serious blow to the reputation of Louis's army. Contemporaries described his soldiers as "disgracefully overcome" and "deeply humiliated," while others blamed the barbarians' victory on demonic powers.[104]

The 849 campaign once again illustrates the ever-present danger of conflicts over power, status, and dignity among the magnates and the necessity for the king to manage these rivalries. The personal leadership of the king was essential to Frankish politics and warfare, because he possessed the highest rank and dignity in the kingdom. Only the king could command proud magnates like Ernest and Thakulf without insulting them, and in turn they could obey the king without losing face in the eyes of their peers. Moreover, because the king monopolized diplomatic and military rituals such as receiving the surrender of an enemy, his presence alleviated a chief source of *discordia* among the nobles. But Louis's illness in 849 opened the door to strife among the magnates. As Prudentius once again summed up the situation, "the army learned while being cut down in flight what a loss the absence of their leader was to them."

Following the disastrous 849 campaign, an uneasy truce settled over the Bavarian borders. During the next four years Louis spent a remarkable amount of time at Regensburg, his headquarters for monitoring the southeast.[105] The bishops of Salzburg, Passau, and Regensburg were prominent royal counselors in this period, and the king issued diplomas in which he praised each of them as "our intimate counselor" [familiaris noster].[106] Because of their extensive lands along the Danube in Bavaria and Upper Pannonia, these bishops were stalwart supporters of the king's efforts to subdue the Bohemians and Moravians. While at Regensburg in 851–52, Louis granted Gozbald of Würzburg-Niederaltaich, Liupram of Salzburg, and Hartwig of Passau the right to conduct property transactions with local nobles, presumably to help them consolidate their estates along the Franco–Slavic borders.[107] Louis's frontier counts likewise engaged in land transac-

---

[104] *AB*, s.a. 849, p. 58; *AX*, s.a. 849, p. 16; *AF*, s.a. 849, p. 39.

[105] Louis was at Regensburg during Christmas 850, March and November 851, January, October, and Christmas 852, as well as January–March and July 853: *DLG* 58–60, 62, 64–67; *AF*, s.a. 852, p. 43.

[106] *DLG* 60, 62, 64, 66.

[107] *DLG* 59, 60, 62. Louis also granted this privilege to Bishop Samuel of Worms-Lorsch: *DLG* 47.

tions along the Danube. For example, Count William gave a rich grant of lands in the Traungau and Upper Pannonia to the monastery of St.-Emmeram, and in January 853 Louis confirmed this grant at the request of his *familiaris*, Erchanfrid of Regensburg.[108] At this time Chozil, the son of *dux* Pribina who had risen in Louis's service to the rank of count, also gave properties along the Danube to St.-Emmeram, and from the same region as those William had given.[109] The importance of Chozil's grant for the defense of the Slavic borders is illustrated by the fact that it was witnessed by Prefect Ratpot as well as Counts Gundram and Gundpold.[110]

Overall, Louis's diplomacy and warfare with the Slavs in the decade after Verdun demonstrate his determination to reestablish the traditional Carolingian tributary lordship over the Slavs as well as the considerable obstacles to this policy. Through overlordship, Louis sought to protect his kingdom's eastern borders by a buffer zone of loyal Slavic peoples and to secure a valuable source of income in the form of annual tribute. At the same time, this policy carried with it an important ideological dimension, since it presented Louis as a triumphant Frankish king and quasi-imperial ruler of many peoples in the tradition of Charlemagne.

By the ninth century, however, Slavic rulers posed serious challenges to the Franks. Because the Slavs were divided among numerous princes and lords, Louis was forced to carry out diplomacy with scores of individual local Slavic rulers. These Slavic princes were becoming increasingly wealthy and powerful as the result of rising long-distance trade and their construction of large, well-defended fortresses. Slavic rulers also had good intelligence about Carolingian politics and were ready to exploit episodes of turmoil brought on by civil war, famine, aristocratic rivalries, and the absence of the king. The biggest danger Slavic rulers posed was their willingness to ally with the king's enemies within his own kingdom, as had almost occurred when the Stellinga revolted during the civil war. To secure his rule within his territories, therefore, Louis needed to compel the neighboring Slavs to surrender to him, either through diplomatic negotiations or warfare.

To wage successful wars against such well-fortified foes, Louis developed

---

[108] *DLG* 64. William's properties were located at Rosdorf and Sierning in the Traungau, on the Erlauf River and at Herilungefeld in Upper Pannonia, and north of the Danube between the Aist and Naarn rivers. Louis had already granted Regensburg lands near Herilungefeld on the Erlauf River: *DLG* 8. The following month (February 853), the king made a land grant in western Bavaria to St.-Emmeram: *DLG* 65.

[109] *Regensburg* 37. Chozil's lands were located at Rosdorf, Rennersdorf (between Rosdorf and Linz), and Struming (near Linz). Widemann dates this charter "vor 859," but because Ratpot is listed as the first witness it should be dated before his rebellion in 854.

[110] Gundram may have been the count of Carniola, whereas Gundpold may have been count of the Bavarian Isengau: Mitterauer, *Karolingische Markgrafen*, 88, 90, 107, 162, 169.

a complex military organization that could sustain annual, large-scale siege campaigns beyond his borders. These campaigns were expensive and risky. Siege warfare did not readily yield booty and plunder, since the Slavs moved their valuables inside their fortresses at the first sign of an invading Frankish army. Indeed, throughout this period, not a single chronicler mentions the capture of Slavic treasure by Frankish armies, underscoring the point that Louis did not wage these wars for easy loot. Moreover, Louis's troops suffered defeats alongside victories, especially because of ongoing disputes among his generals that exposed his armies to surprise attacks. The fact that Louis nevertheless pushed ahead with these campaigns indicates the real threat that rebellious Slavic rulers posed to his power. By the early 850s Louis had been at least partially successful in making them submit to his lordship. At the Mainz assembly in 852, he once again "heard and dismissed the legates of the Bulgars and Slavs," which was the *Annals of Fulda*'s shorthand for saying that they brought him tribute and renewed their peace treaties with him.[111]

---

[111] *AF*, s.a. 852, p. 42: "legationes Bulgarorum Sclavorumque audivit et absolvit." Compare the language of the *AF* and the *AX* for Louis's diplomacy with the Slavs in 845: "Nordmannorum, Sclavorum, quoque et Bulgarorum legationes suscepit, audivit, et absolvit" (*AF*, s.a. 845, p. 35); and "gentiles . . . miserunt ei munera et obsides et petierunt pacem. At ille, concessa pace, reversus est de Saxonia" (*AX*, s.a. 845, p. 14).

CHAPTER FIVE
CONSOLIDATION AND REFORM, 844–852

I n the midst of his ongoing warfare and diplomacy with the Slavs, Louis was struggling to consolidate his kingship within his own territories. The Treaty of Verdun did not found a coherent east Frankish kingdom. Instead, Louis inherited an assortment of disunited provinces that had no historical blueprint for an independent polity. The primary tools Louis had at his disposal for building a kingdom beyond the Rhine were active personal rule, cooperation with the nobles, and an alliance with the Church. While consolidating his power, Louis remained deeply involved in Carolingian diplomacy with his brothers to prevent a renewed outbreak of civil war. Louis's political consolidation in the east was a slow, ongoing process that took almost a decade. Nevertheless, by 852 Louis's kingship and political support had become increasingly secure, transforming his rule "in east Francia" from a mere claim into an emerging political reality. Reflecting this growing political stability, Louis's kingdom witnessed an unprecedented flourishing of Church reform and literary production in the decade after Verdun. Through the patronage of scholars and ecclesiastical reform, Louis and the churchmen around his court gave cultural meaning to the emerging east Frankish kingdom.[1]

---

[1] For the politics of this period, see Dümmler, *GOR* 1:216–379; Nelson, *Charles the Bald*, 132–59; Hartmann, *Ludwig der Deutsche*, 44–45.

After 843, two main forces threatened to undermine the truce. The first was the ongoing bitter rivalry among Louis and his brothers. Although the Treaty of Verdun preached peace and brotherly love, in truth the heirs of Louis the Pious remained as suspicious of each other as ever. In the years immediately after Verdun, Carolingian diplomacy was defined by Louis's and Charles's enduring distrust of Lothar. Despite his repeated defeats during the civil war, Lothar emerged in a surprisingly strong position after 843. Lothar continued to support Charles's adversary, Pippin II of Aquitaine, thereby undermining Charles's rule in his own kingdom. Lothar's enduring connections to the eastern nobles such as Bishops Otgar of Mainz and Samuel of Worms meant that he could make trouble for Louis as well. Lothar used his imperial title as a pretext to interfere in his brother's kingdoms. Two months after the Treaty of Verdun, he granted immunity and royal protection to St.-Denis's properties "both on this side of and beyond the Rhine," even though only Louis in theory could grant immunity to ecclesiastical properties within his borders.[2] The following year, Lothar had his uncle and archchaplain, Drogo of Metz, appointed papal vicar of Gaul and Germania in an (unsuccessful) attempt to assert ecclesiastical jurisdiction over his brothers' kingdoms.[3] In response to their brother's predatory meddling in their kingdoms, Louis and Charles clung to the alliance they had struck at Fontenoy and Strasbourg.

The second main concern of the kings after Verdun was the ever-present danger of political conflicts caused by the magnates. The Carolingians always had had to reckon with powerful Frankish nobles and families. But the existence of multiple rival courts now made aristocratic politics even more complex and volatile. Although Verdun in theory created three separate kingdoms, powerful magnates maintained ties throughout the former empire. According to the division of 843, each nobleman was to choose one of the three kings as his lord and hold benefices and offices only from him.[4] However, the nobles' right to keep their private properties wherever they were found meant that they maintained ties to multiple kingdoms. This was

---

[2] *DLoI* 80.

[3] *AB*, s.a. 844, p. 46.

[4] Although no copy of the Treaty of Verdun survives, it almost certainly adopted the provisions concerning the nobility in earlier Carolingian divisions. Cf. *Divisio regnorum*, chaps. 9, 10, in MGH *Capitularia* 1:128; *Ordinatio imperii*, chap. 9, in MGH *Capitularia* 1:272.

King in East Francia

a potential source of instability, since it blurred political loyalties and enabled the subjects of one ruler to cause trouble for another. These enduring "international" ties of leading Frankish nobles shaped political relations among the Carolingians for the remainder of the ninth century. As Janet Nelson summed up, the nobles' " 'amphibious' existence was a constant reminder of the provisional character of the 843 frontiers."[5]

An example of a Frankish magnate who maintained political connections to multiple courts and kingdoms was Louis the Pious's former seneschal Adalhard.[6] During the civil war, Charles made Adalhard lay abbot of Tours, and at Fontenoy Adalhard led the third contingent of Louis and Charles's army. Adalhard's widespread influence is demonstrated by the fact that Charles married his niece in December 842, "because in this way he thought he could win for himself the majority of the people."[7] Adalhard's precise familial connections are unclear, although he reportedly was related to the east Frankish Konradiner count, Gebhard of Lahngau.[8] Although Adalhard selected Charles as his lord in 843, he maintained ties to Louis's kingdom through properties he owned in the east. Only two months after Verdun, Adalhard granted the bulk of his extensive estates in Alemannia and the Wormsgau to St.-Gall.[9] Adalhard's donation was a gesture of friendship to Louis: St.-Gall belonged to Louis's counselor, Grimald, and Adalhard expressly gave the land for the salvation of Louis's soul. But Adalhard maintained control of these eastern lands by stipulating that he, his wife, and his heirs would continue to hold them during their lifetimes (which was the standard precarial arrangement) and that they could purchase them back from St.-Gall if they wished. In this way, Adalhard ensured the safety of his properties in Louis's kingdom while pursuing a political career at the court of Charles the Bald, but he left open the possibility that he might one day return to the east.

Adalhard's manipulation of landholding becomes more complex when one considers that many of his lands were held by his vassals. Like most

---

[5] Nelson, *Charles the Bald*, 149.

[6] Concerning Adalhard, see Ferdinand Lot, "Note sur le sénéchal Alard," in *Recueil des travaux historiques* (Geneva, 1970), 2:591–602; Nelson, *Charles the Bald*, 127–29, 142; Depreux, *Prosopographie*, 80–82.

[7] Nithard, 4.6, pp. 48–49.

[8] *AB*, s.a. 861, p. 85 and n. 4.

[9] *St.-Gall* 386. For an identification of the lands of this grant, see Michael Borgolte, "Kommentar zu Austellungsdaten, Actum- und Güterorten der älteren St.-Galler Urkunden (Wartmann I und II mit Nachträgen in III und IV)," in *Subsidia Sangallensia*, vol. 1: *Materialien und Untersuchungen zu den Verbrüderungsbüchern und zu den älteren Urkunden des Stiftsarchivs St.-Gallen*, ed. Michael Borgolte, Dieter Geuenich, and Karl Schmid (St.-Gall, 1986), 393 and n. 386.

magnates, Adalhard had his own private retinue of soldiers, whom he supported through loans of land, that is, through benefices. Adalhard's grant to St.-Gall included benefices held by his vassals, and he specified that they could continue to hold these lands during their lifetimes. In this way, not only Adalhard but his vassals as well maintained their lands in the east while pursuing careers in Charles's service. Adalhard's charter for St.-Gall lists thirty-five witnesses, many of whom presumably were these vassals. The seventh witness to Adalhard's grant was Nidhart, who presumably was Nithard, the author of the *Four Books of Histories* who had fought among Adalhard's troops at Fontenoy. In the final book of his *Histories*, which he finished in March 843, Nithard had been highly critical of Adalhard's influence at Charles's court, presumably because Adalhard had not helped him secure a benefice or office.[10] Adalhard apparently had rectified that situation by October, however, by granting Nithard one of his own lands in the east. Thus, once again, Nithard was in his entourage of vassals.

Adalhard did not remain in Charles's favor for long. The year after Adalhard made his grant to St.-Gall, Charles revoked Adalhard's western honors and redistributed them to other supporters. Charles apparently did this because he held Adalhard partly responsible for a devastating military debacle at the hands of Pippin II of Aquitaine. In 844, Pippin II of Aquitaine, who resolutely defended his claims to his father's kingdom, ambushed Charles's forces and killed many of Charles's supporters.[11] Among the dead was Nithard, who perished from a grisly sword blow to the head, abruptly ending his career as a Carolingian historian.[12] In the wake of this crushing defeat, Charles revoked Adalhard's *honores*, compelling Adalhard to move to another kingdom: not to Louis's (who still was Charles's ally), but to Lothar's, where Adalhard also had ties. To spite his half brother, Lothar gave Adalhard a county on the Moselle near Trier. This had menacing implications for Charles, since Adalhard was still extremely influential. In this way, Adalhard's far-flung connections enabled him to make a political jump from one kingdom to another, but the move threatened to undermine the fragile truce among the three kings.

The careers of Adalhard and Nithard illustrate the enduring empirewide ties of the Frankish magnates and their vassals after Verdun and the political instability they could cause. In spite of their wealth and power, magnates always were vulnerable, since they held their offices and *honores* at the grace of the king. An unexpected political or military crisis could precipitate a great

---

[10] Nithard, 4.6, p. 49; Nelson, "Public *Histories*," 217–26.
[11] *AB*, s.a. 844, pp. 46–47.
[12] Nelson, "Public *Histories*," 235–37; idem, *Charles the Bald*, 6, 141–42.

man's downfall, compelling him and his retinue to move to another royal court and region of the empire where he still had political ties. In this way, a redistribution of royal favor in the entourage of one king could spark a chain reaction that had repercussions throughout Frankish Europe. For decades to come, Adalhard and powerful magnates like him would continue to shape political relations among Charlemagne's descendants.

In the wake of the ambush of his army, Charles demanded the first post-Verdun assembly with his brothers in October 844 at Thionville. The Treaty of Verdun outlined a kind of congress system, stipulating that Lothar, Louis, and Charles were to meet regularly and address common concerns facing the united Church and kingdom. The brothers exchanged numerous envoys before their first meeting, which underscored the enduring distrust among them. When they finally met, the kings reaffirmed their oaths of "brotherly love" and promised to punish those magnates who fomented *discordia*, such as Adalhard.[13] Louis's main concern was strengthening Charles's tenuous position in his western kingdom in order to counterbalance Lothar. At the urging of Louis and Charles, the three brothers sent ambassadors to Charles's adversaries (especially Pippin II), threatening them with a united campaign if they refused to make peace. Meanwhile, Drogo of Metz presided over an ecclesiastical synod nearby at Yütz, issuing canons that admonished the kings to maintain fraternal peace and correct abuses harming the Church.[14] The Yütz canons were read to the kings and their *fideles*, and the kings promised to uphold them.

Louis remained Charles's ally throughout the 840s, and he increasingly played the role of peacemaker between his two brothers. Louis's motivations were based more on calculation and Realpolitik than brotherly love: he needed Charles as an ally to keep Lothar in check, but at the same time he wanted Lothar's good will so he could consolidate his support among the eastern nobles. In 846, the simmering tensions between Lothar and Charles unexpectedly erupted when Charles's vassal Giselbert abducted Lothar's daughter, carried her off to Aquitaine, and married her.[15] (The name of Lothar's daughter is unknown, as is her opinion of her new husband.) Giselbert's deed was audacious and shocking, since the Carolingians jealously guarded their daughters to prevent the "aristocratic appropriation of legitimate Carolingian blood."[16] But, like Adalhard, Giselbert was struggling to maintain his *honores* and status in the post-843 world. Giselbert had been count of the Maasgau on the lower Meuse, and during the civil war he had

---

[13] *AB*, s.a. 844, p. 48.
[14] MGH *Concilia* 3:27–35.
[15] *AF*, s.a. 846, p. 36.
[16] Nelson, *Charles the Bald*, 148.

defected from Lothar to Charles.[17] Giselbert made the mistake of jumping the wrong way: the Maasgau ended up in the middle kingdom, and Lothar therefore revoked his county and benefices. By abducting Lothar's daughter and making himself Lothar's son-in-law, Giselbert sought to force Lothar to readmit him into his circle of *fideles* and grant him back his county. Giselbert's abduction of Lothar's daughter once again highlights the independence of the Frankish magnates and their readiness to take matters into their own hands if they felt a king had denied them their "rightful" honors and *Königsnähe*. Although the Carolingians did not like to admit it, they were vulnerable to the independent ambitions of the magnates.

Giselbert's scandalous deed had serious ramifications. Because Giselbert had become Charles's vassal, Lothar held Charles responsible for Giselbert's actions, and thus an isolated dispute quickly mushroomed into an interregnal crisis. In 846, to avert a renewed outbreak of civil war, Louis hurried west to Charles's side, and they publicly declared that Giselbert had acted without their knowledge and consent. Louis met with Lothar later that summer, although he was unable to reconcile him with Charles. When the three brothers met again at Meersen in February 847, the most pressing issue was the restoration of good relations between Lothar and Charles to ensure their cooperation "in our common kingdom" [in nostro communi regno].[18] Although bitter rivals, the three kings were united in their desire to clamp down on unpredictable and dangerous aristocratic behavior, like that of Giselbert. Their very first point of discussion was limiting conflicts caused by unruly nobles: "Concerning the peace, concord, and harmony of the three brother-kings: that they should be united by true and not false bonds of love, and that henceforth no one should be able to sow the seeds of scandal among them."[19] The kings went on to formulate a plan to restore good government with the cooperation of the magnates: overcoming the enemies of Church and state, achieving restitution of ecclesiastical property, protecting the rights of their *fideles*, putting an end to banditry and crimes against the poor, and punishing those who abducted women (once again obviously meaning Giselbert).[20]

The brothers also addressed the important issue of royal succession. This was a matter of pressing concern not only for the kings but also for the nobles, who did not want a replay of the succession crisis of the 830s. By 847, Lothar and Louis already had adult sons, while the previous year Charles's wife had given birth to a boy. Charles named his son Louis (known to his-

[17] Nithard, 3.2–3.3, p. 31.
[18] MGH *Capitularia* 2:68–71.
[19] Ibid., 69 (c. 1).
[20] Ibid., 69 (cc. 2–4, 6–8).

tory as Louis the Stammerer because of a speech impediment), presumably in honor of Louis the Pious but perhaps also in recognition of his alliance with Louis the German. At Meersen, the kings decreed that if one of them died, his sons would be allowed to inherit their father's kingdom "according to the clearly defined partitions existing at this time." The kings and nobles therefore prepared for yet another division of the kingdom within a generation. Notably absent from this agreement was Pippin II of Aquitaine, who once again was dealt out of dynastic succession.

At the end of the 847 meeting, each of the three kings read a public statement (*adnuntiatio*) before the assembled nobles.[21] These statements, written in straightforward Latin, give us a glimpse of the basic Latin fluency the kings could expect from their churchmen and better-educated lay supporters.[22] Lothar, who remained at odds with Charles over the Giselbert affair, made a vague and seemingly disingenuous statement about the restoration of brotherly cooperation. Louis and Charles, on the other hand, outlined specific steps for strengthening Charles's kingship in west Francia. Louis announced that they were sending legates to Pippin II of Aquitaine, the Bretons, and King Horik I of Denmark to demand that they stop making trouble in Charles's kingdom. Louis further announced that their "dear brother Lothar" had agreed to order his supporters to stop opposing Charles and his *fideles*, an open admission of Lothar's plotting against the youngest brother. For his part, Charles outlined practical guidelines for improving the relations between lords and vassals within their kingdoms, and he announced another common assembly to take place on June 24 in Paris.

Despite the rhetoric of *pax et concordia*, relations between Lothar and Charles remained tense, and the scheduled Paris assembly was scrapped. Louis nevertheless persisted in his efforts to reconcile his brothers. Later in 847, he invited Lothar to his kingdom and honored him with feasts and gifts, although he failed to end the quarrel between Lothar and Charles.[23] The following February, Louis again met with Lothar at Koblenz on the border of their kingdoms. This time Lothar tried to convince Louis to abandon his alliance with Charles and unite with him "according to the law of brotherhood," thus playing up the fact that Charles was their half brother (and perhaps insinuating that Louis the Pious had not really been Charles's father). But Louis, who still distrusted his elder brother, avoided giving in to Lothar's "skilled persuasions."[24] The following year, Louis finally brokered

[21] Ibid., 70–71.

[22] It is possible that such speeches also were translated into Romance and Frankish for those who could not understand Latin.

[23] *AF*, s.a. 847, p. 36.

[24] *AF*, s.a. 848, p. 37.

a reconciliation between Giselbert and Lothar, thereby paving the way for a rapprochement between Lothar and Charles in January 849.[25] Nevertheless, Louis and Charles remained committed to their alliance. When Louis and Charles met a few months later, "they showed themselves united by such a bond of fraternal love that they publicly exchanged staffs and each thereby commended to the other his kingdom, wife, and books"—an illuminating ranking of Carolingian priorities—"should he outlive him."[26]

Like the events surrounding Adalhard, the Giselbert affair illustrates the complex interconnections of Carolingian diplomacy and aristocratic politics after 843. As magnates such as Adalhard and Giselbert struggled to salvage their careers and settle old scores, their far-flung connections could set off chain reactions that crossed political borders and shaped diplomatic relations among their kings. It was for this reason that the kings repeatedly made decrees against aristocratic *discordia* and placed such emphasis on the participation of the magnates at their diplomatic meetings. It is no coincidence that the chroniclers highlighted the role of public ceremonies such as feasting, gift giving, reading statements, and exchanging staffs. Through such rituals, the kings sought to rebuild a sense of aristocratic community and make magnates such as Adalhard and Giselbert, as well as vassals such as Nithard, partners in maintaining peace and order. As always, political stability was not possible without the help of the nobility.

The reconciliation between Lothar and Charles also opened the door for better relations between Louis and Lothar. During the summer of 850, Louis and Lothar met at Cologne, where they reaffirmed the *pax* between them.[27] At Cologne they dealt with matters that crossed the borders of their kingdoms and thus required cooperation. For example, Lothar confirmed Fulda's rights to free trade within his kingdom on the condition that the Fulda monks pray for him and his brother.[28] Louis and Lothar also took care of matters concerning several Saxon counts who were Lothar's *fideles* but had connections to Louis's kingdom. One case concerned Count Waltbert, Lothar's supporter and a descendant of the famous Saxon rebel Widukind, who had led the Saxon resistance against Charlemagne. Waltbert had founded a monastery at Wildeshausen on his family's lands southwest of Bremen, within Louis's borders. In 850, Waltbert journeyed to Rome to acquire relics for his monastery, a matter that Louis and Lothar probably discussed at Cologne.[29] In a letter of introduction to Pope Leo IV for Walt-

---

[25] *AF*, s.a. 848, pp. 37–38; *AB*, s.a. 849, p. 56.
[26] *AB*, s.a. 849, p. 57.
[27] *AX*, s.a. 850, p. 17.
[28] *DLoI* 111.
[29] *DLoI* 108–10; *Translatio sancti Alexandri*, chap. 4, in MGH *SS* 2:676–78.

bert, Lothar emphasized the persistent problem of the Saxons and Frisians, who clung to their ancestral polytheism under the influence of their pagan neighbors, the Danes and Slavs, and it was on these grounds that Lothar requested relics for Waltbert's monastery.[30] In this way, Lothar made amends for his alliance with the Stellinga rebels a decade earlier. After the Cologne meeting, Lothar and Louis announced their *pax* by hunting together in the Osning Mountains north of Paderborn in Saxony with a small group of nobles. The Osning hunting trip made a considerable impression, and many "marveled" at the new cooperation between the brothers.

This amity among the three brothers culminated at the second Meersen assembly, which took place in 851.[31] At Meersen, the brothers renewed and expanded their resolutions for fraternal accord from the first Meersen summit, and they issued their new decrees "by the common counsel and consent of their leading men."[32] Once again, the central issue was the maintenance of fraternal cooperation and harmony in the face of perennial tensions arising from magnates such as Adalhard and Giselbert. The brothers outlawed discord and rebellion, pledged mutual help and the common prosecution of criminals, and promised to respect the inheritance rights of each other's sons should one of them die. The kings also discussed the reciprocal cooperation between themselves and the nobles that had always been the foundation of Carolingian government. In return for their fidelity, the kings promised their nobles "that henceforth we will not punish anyone, deprive him of *honores*, oppress him, or afflict him with undeserved machinations against law, justice, authority, and just reason."[33] As at the first Meersen assembly, the second concluded with a public statement from each king. Louis's speech reflected the optimism at the conclusion of the meeting:

> There is great need for us and the Christian people, whom God has committed to us, to be in concord and united with each other, as is God's will and befits true fraternity. But since God placed the kingdom in our hands after our father, we have hardly done what was necessary in all matters. Because of this, many hardships contrary to God have af-

[30] *DLoI* 110. It perhaps was also during the Cologne meeting that Lothar confirmed a grant from his Saxon supporter Esich, "an illustrious man and our count," to the monastery of Corvey in Louis's kingdom: *DLoI* 112. (This diploma lacks a dating clause and therefore can only be dated to 844–50.) The estate Esich had granted Corvey was situated within Lothar's borders at Kessenich near Bonn, and Lothar had granted it to him several months before the Treaty of Verdun, "on the condition that he never leave our fidelity, but remain unwaveringly obedient without ever abandoning us": *DLoI* 70.

[31] MGH *Capitularia* 2:72–74.

[32] *AB*, s.a. 851, p. 60.

[33] MGH *Capitularia* 2:73 (c. 6).

flicted both us and you. Since with God's help we have recently been united as we ought, you should know that each of us is prepared to help his brother wherever there is need, both within our homeland and outside our homeland, either in person or through his son or *fideles*, both in counsel and aid, as a brother should rightly behave toward his brother.[34]

For the moment at least, the "regime of confraternity" seemed to have become a reality.

POLITICAL CONSOLIDATION

In the midst of this ongoing diplomacy, Louis was working to expand his political support among the eastern nobles. Not surprisingly, in the decade after Verdun, the magnates of Bavaria retained their royal favor, and the king richly rewarded them for their loyalty. Prominent among Louis's advisers were the Bavarian bishops and the frontier counts Ernest, Ratpot, Werner, Pabo, and William.[35] The nobles from Bavaria also dominated Louis's court administration. Baturich of Regensburg was Louis's archchaplain until his death in 847, while the Bavarian nobleman Fritilo served as count of the palace into the 850s. The son of Prefect Ratpot, also named Ratpot (II), served as the king's steward, and Louis's cupbearer, Wippo, was a relative of the abbot of Metten.[36] Through such officers in the palace, the magnates of Bavaria maintained contact with the king, even when they themselves were absent from court. The prominence of Louis's "old guard" was reflected at his 848 Regensburg assembly. When Louis gave *dux* Pribina all his Lower Pannonian benefices as personal property, the first eleven witnesses, in rank order, were Bishops Liupram of Salzburg, Erchanbert of Freising, Erchanfrid of Regensburg, and Hartwig of Passau; the king's elder sons Carloman and Louis the Younger; and Counts Ernest, Ratpot, Werner, Pabo, and Fritilo.[37]

Louis used this group of longtime supporters to consolidate his eastern kingship. Many of these noblemen had preexisting ties to regions outside Bavaria, and Louis promoted them to bishoprics, monasteries, and counties

[34] Ibid., p. 74.
[35] *DLG* 35–38, 45, 46, 49, 60, 62, 64–66, 72, 85, 99; *AF*, s.a. 849, p. 38.
[36] *DLG* 88, 96; *Freising* 663, 672, 807.
[37] *Conversio*, chap. 12, p. 128; *DLG* 46.

to expand his influence within his enlarged kingdom. For example, Louis gave his Upper Pannonian count, Werner, the additional county of the Lobdengau on the middle Rhine, the region from which Werner's family hailed.[38] Louis consolidated his control of western Alemannia by granting the monastery of Kempten to Bishop Erchanbert of Freising and a number of counties to Count Pabo of Carantania.[39] Although Abbot Grimald of St.-Gall apparently did not hold office in Bavaria (he may have held a Bavarian monastery), he too numbered among Louis's longtime supporters. Louis named Grimald archchaplain in 847 and high chancellor in 854, thereby unifying those two court offices in Grimald's hand (with some interruptions) until his retirement from royal service in 870.[40] In addition to St.-Gall, in 847 Louis gave Grimald the important monastery of Wissembourg in Alsace, thereby making that monastery a western political foothold in a region that otherwise belonged to Lothar. Through such promotions of his longtime *fideles*, Louis transformed them into a nobility that gave coherence to his enlarged eastern kingdom.

Louis also sought to win over magnates who had supported Lothar, or at least had displayed vacillating loyalties, during the civil war. Although Louis did purge a few high-profile former opponents, he prudently preferred the carrot to the stick.[41] For example, in 844–45 Louis made a string of grants and concessions to noblemen and noblewomen in Franconia.[42] Most of the grants involved regional monasteries, and these acts of royal generosity therefore enabled Louis to inject himself into preexisting local networks around such ecclesiastical foundations. In one instance, Louis granted royal lands north of Mainz to the nearby monastery of Kettenbach, which his "venerable and faithful man," Count Gebhard of Lahngau, had founded.[43] Gebhard was a leading member of the powerful Konradiner family and a relative of Ernest and Adalhard, and after Verdun Gebhard's sons, Uto, Berengar, and Waldo, received eastern counties and monasteries, apparently

---

[38] Werner gave estates on the lower Neckar to Lorsch in 825: *Lorsch* 656. Louis had granted Werner estates in the Rhinegau in 836: *DLG* 19. Innes, *State and Society*, 213, emphasizes Werner's family ties to the middle Rhine. Counts Werner and Ernest participated in pious donations to Lorsch and St.-Gall: *Lorsch* 27–28 (Werner), 1618 (Ernest?); *St.-Gall* 389 (Werner), 411 (Ernest), 412 (Ernest), 432 (Ernest).

[39] *DLG* 36; Borgolte, *Grafen*, 189–90.

[40] For Louis's patronage of Grimald, see *DLG* 69–71, 83, 87.

[41] For Louis's purges, see Innes, *State and Society*, 212. The Rupertiner count of the upper Rheingau, Robert the Strong, moved west on his own accord: Karl Ferdinand Werner, "Untersuchungen zur Frühzeit des französichen Fürstentums," *Die Welt als Geschichte* 3–4 (1959): 146–93, at 160–63.

[42] *DLG* 34, 39, 40, 43b.

[43] *DLG* 40.

with Louis's approval.[44] Kettenbach was not a "royal" monastery controlled by the king but rather a private aristocratic foundation in the hands of a prominent local family (a so-called Eigenkloster). Thus, by making a donation to Kettenbach, Louis built up his friendship with a powerful eastern family and inserted himself into the local circle of the monastery's patrons. The preamble of Louis's diploma for Gebhard expressed the hoped-for effect of this royal largesse: "If we incline the ears of our Serenity justly and reasonably to the petitions of our faithful men, we fittingly carry out the custom of kings and make those faithful men even more faithful and devoted to our service." Louis issued his diploma for Gebhard not while he was on the middle Rhine but when he was far to the southeast at Regensburg. Gebhard had traveled far to seek an audience with the king, and Louis presumably honored and entertained his guest with banquets, gifts, hunting excursions, conversations about Scripture, and other aristocratic pastimes. Like most diplomas, therefore, Gebhard's is a fragmentary remnant of a more general context of courtly meetings through which the king established social ties and political allegiances—in the language of the time, friendship (*amicitia*)—with powerful regional elites.

In contrast to Louis's influence in Bavaria and the middle Rhine, his influence in Saxony remained less secure. The two main reasons were that the Stellinga uprising of the Saxon peasants had been a serious blow to Frankish landlordship and the Church in the region, and a general dearth of royal estates in Saxony prevented Louis from making prolonged visits to the region. Indeed, between 843 and 851, Louis made only one significant sojourn into Saxony—for the 845 Paderborn assembly. Louis's long absence from Saxony enabled the regional nobles to expand their power at the expense of the king and royal government. "Corrupt and crafty judges" oppressed the people by subverting justice, while others usurped estates belonging to the king.[45] Nevertheless, during the 840s and 850s, the bishops of Osnabrück and Verden, the abbot of Corvey, and the abbess of Herford traveled to the middle Rhine and Bavaria for grants of land and rights, indicating that at least some of the Saxon magnates pursued ties with the king in return for royal patronage.[46]

Louis faced a major obstacle in consolidating his power in his eastern territories: Archbishop Otgar of Mainz. During the civil war, Otgar had been Lothar's ardent supporter and Louis's sworn enemy. As archbishop of

---

[44] Jackman, *Konradiner,* 70–73 and table 1; *Annals of Fulda,* trans. Reuter, 47n4. Another Gebhard became bishop of Speyer before 847, and his name suggests that he too was related to the Konradiner: MGH *Concilia* 3:160 and n. 26; *DLG* 92.

[45] *AF,* s.a. 852, p. 42.

[46] *DLG* 51, 57, 61, 73, 93.

Mainz, Otgar commanded tremendous power and influence among the bishops and abbots of his massive eastern archdiocese, in effect blocking Louis from winning their support. Indeed, with the exception of his long-time *familiaris* Gozbald of Würzburg, Louis did not issue a single diploma for an east Frankish bishop during the period 840–47, which points to the conclusion that they remained loyal to Otgar—and thus, by extension, to Lothar.[47] Louis lacked the strength to depose Otgar outright: Otgar's family, the Otachars, was deeply entrenched in the Mainz region, and the uncanonical removal of an archbishop would have drawn heavy censure from the bishops and the pope.[48] Nevertheless, after 843 Louis took steps to limit Otgar's power. Immediately after the Verdun meeting, Louis journeyed to the important Franconian monastery of Hersfeld, where he ruled that tithes in Thuringia belonged to that monastery rather than to Mainz, thereby delivering an economic blow to Otgar.[49] Moreover, Louis forbade Otgar from holding a synod of the bishops and abbots of his archdiocese, thereby removing one of the most important expressions of his archiepiscopal power.[50]

Louis's standoff with the east Frankish bishops ended when Otgar died on April 21, 847.[51] The death gave Louis the opportunity to make a grand gesture of reconciliation with the east Frankish Church. Two months later, the approximately sixty-year-old Raban became the next archbishop, almost certainly through Louis's appointment.[52] Although Louis had compelled Raban to resign as abbot of Fulda during the civil war, he had reestablished good relations with the churchman after the Treaty of Verdun. Sometime before 847, Louis had met with Raban at the Fulda estate of Rasdorf. There the king and former abbot had a friendly conversation about Scripture, and

---

[47] A point emphasized by Bigott, *Ludwig der Deutsche*, 95–104.

[48] Louis is not known to have deposed a single bishop during his reign: Bigott, *Ludwig der Deutsche*, 243–45, 247. On the Otachars, see Innes, *State and Society*, 60–65.

[49] *DLG* 32, 33; Lampert, *Annales*, s.a. 845, p. 25. Louis confirmed the monastery's royal protection, immunity, and freedom of abbatial elections, and he stipulated that "neither the bishop of the city of Mainz [nor his archdeacon] usurp any power for himself in the aforementioned monastery, unless according to what is established in the holy canons, that is, to preach, ordain, and confirm, or to carry out those things that legally pertain to his office." Abbot Brunward of Hersfeld was a supporter of Louis's: Bigott, *Ludwig der Deutsche*, 42, 96–97.

[50] For Otgar's few known activities after 843, see Böhmer and Will, *RGME* 1:61–63.

[51] *AF*, s.a. 847, p. 36. In the epitaph for his longtime friend, Raban tactfully downplayed Otgar's tumultuous political career ("Victorious patience ruled his breast, in turmoils it was his firm anchor. Without anger, calm and sweet, he happily carried out the office of bishop"): Raban, *Carmina*, no. 87, in MGH *Poetae Latini* 2:238–39.

[52] The importance of Raban's appointment for Louis's reconciliation with the east Frankish Church is stressed by Bigott, *Ludwig der Deutsche*, 104–23; idem, "Die Versöhnung von 847: Ludwig der Deutsche und die Reichskirche," in *LDZ*, ed. Hartmann, 121–40.

it is likely that they also discussed the possibility of Raban succeeding Otgar.[53] Raban had considerable prestige for his family, piety, and learning, and he maintained connections to Lothar and leading bishops, abbots, and nobles throughout the former empire by sending them letters and religious works.[54] In this way, Raban's promotion to archbishop helped heal the remaining rifts between Louis, Lothar, and the eastern clergy and nobles. As Abbot Hatto of Fulda summed up in a letter to Pope Leo, Raban became archbishop of Mainz "with the overwhelming support of the Frankish princes."[55] This paved the way for Louis's reconciliation with the east Frankish clergy. In the two years following Raban's promotion, Louis made an impressive string of grants to east Frankish prelates who previously had not received royal patronage: Bishops Samuel of Worms-Lorsch, Esso of Chur, Gozbert of Osnabrück, and Waltgar of Verden; Abbots Hatto of Fulda and Spatto of Amorbach; as well as Archbishop Raban himself.[56]

In the same year as Raban's appointment to archbishop, Louis commanded him to hold his kingdom's first ecclesiastical synod at Mainz.[57] The 847 Mainz synod formally marked Louis's reconciliation with the east Frankish Church, and it was attended by most of the bishops from Mainz's large archdiocese. In the cover letter of the synod's canons addressed to Louis, Raban announced that the political and spiritual might of the east Frankish Church now stood firmly behind Louis's kingship and family. The archbishop ordained that all the eastern bishops, abbots, monks, and priests perform 3,500 Masses and sing 1,700 Psalters for their king, his wife, and their children, "asking with deep devotion that omnipotent God grant you lasting health and prosperity, strengthen your kingdom from every enemy on this earth, and after the end of this life grant you eternal glory with His saints."[58] Although the Carolingians had overseen a far-reaching program of ecclesiastical, monastic, and spiritual reform in the empire, the east Frankish Church had suffered from negligence and abuses during the turmoil of the 830s and 840s. Raban and his fellow bishops now sought to revive the Carolingian Church reforms in his archdiocese. Raban expressly looked to the "good old days under Emperor Charlemagne" as the model of reform,

[53] Raban, *Epistolae*, no. 33, in MGH *Epistolae* 5:465–67; Mayke De Jong, "The Empire as *Ecclesia*: Hrabanus Maurus and Biblical *Historia* for Rulers," in Hen and Innes, *Uses of the Past*, 208–10.

[54] Raban, *Epistolae*, in MGH *Epistolae* 5:381–516. Raban wrote over half of his surviving letters after Louis the Pious's death.

[55] *Epistolarum Fuldensium fragmenta*, no. 31, in MGH *Epistolae* 5:531.

[56] DLG 47, 51–57.

[57] MGH *Concilia* 3:150–77; Wilfried Hartmann, *Die Synoden der Karolingerzeit in Frankenreich und Italien* (Paderborn, 1989),222–26.

[58] MGH *Concilia* 3:159–62.

A portrait of the monk and scholar Raban kneeling before the cross. During the period between his appointment to the archbishopric of Mainz in 847 and his death in 856, Raban presided over the reform of the east Frankish Church and deeply influenced the cultural life of Louis's kingdom. From a copy of Raban's *In Praise of the Holy Cross* (ca. 840). © Bibliotheca Apostolica Vaticana (Vatican), Reg. lat. 124, fol. 35v.

and he took many of his decrees directly from the last Mainz synod of Charlemagne's reign in 813. In this way, the 847 Mainz synod heralded Louis as the defender of the Church in the tradition of his grandfather.

Now that Raban had delivered the support of the east Frankish clergy, he sought the king's help in defending the Church against the nobles. One matter in particular concerned Raban: the seizure of Church property. During the 830s and 840s, many nobles apparently had taken possession of estates belonging to the Church, either through outright usurpations or through the permission of bishops and abbots, who had been forced to build up their military retinues during the civil war by distributing benefices and precarial grants to their vassals. Now that the civil war was over, Raban wanted to reclaim estates belonging to Mainz and other bishoprics and monasteries within his archdiocese. Most bishoprics and monasteries enjoyed royal immunity and protection, and thus any infringement on their properties demanded that the king come to their defense. But some eastern nobles were urging Louis to turn a blind eye to aristocratic possession of Church property. This deeply worried Raban, and he told the king as much.[59] Raban decreed that anyone who usurped Church property that was under royal protection and immunity was to be excommunicated and exiled, and he boldly admonished the king not to back down from this stance under pressure from the nobles.[60]

Thus, even in this moment of reconciliation, there were enduring conflicts, and these conflicts not surprisingly focused on the bedrock of aristocratic power—land. Although Louis had intended Raban's appointment to be a gesture of reconciliation between himself and the eastern Church and nobles, the new archbishop threatened to undermine this moment of consensus by demanding the return of usurped Church lands. It probably was in connection with Raban's decree that Louis now granted Bishop Samuel of Worms-Lorsch, who was a close friend of the archbishop, the right to trade lands and slaves freely with nobles.[61] Through swaps of estates, the king, bishops, and nobles could begin to untangle the messy arrangements of ecclesiastical landholding that had developed over the course of the tumultuous two previous decades. Nevertheless, it appears that Raban met stiff resistance when he tried to reclaim lands belonging to his archbishopric. Soon after the 847 synod, the vassals of the archbishopric conspired against Raban, compelling Louis to come to Mainz the following year and broker a

---

[59] Ibid., 161–62.
[60] Ibid., 166 (c. 6).
[61] *DLG* 47. This diploma can be dated either January 11, 847 or 848.

reconciliation.[62] Louis was caught between a rock and a hard place: he wanted to support his new archbishop, but he did not want to alienate the east Frankish nobles who held ecclesiastical property. Like most Carolingian kings, Louis sometimes had to turn a blind eye to nobles who held Church lands. Thus, several years later, Raban repeated verbatim the 847 decree concerning the restitution of Church properties.[63]

Louis's political consolidation in the east culminated with an unprecedented kingdomwide progress in 852.[64] Although Louis had visited the individual provinces of his kingdom before, this marked the first time he traveled through all his territories in a single continuous journey. Through this ceremonial progress, Louis asserted his kingship in the localities and reinforced ties with the regional elite. He commenced his kingdomwide itinerary with an important event on September 1, 852: Raban's dedication of the new royal chapel Louis had built at Frankfurt. The Frankfurt church was a monument to Louis's Christian kingship beyond the Rhine, since Frankfurt was the most important royal palace in Franconia. Louis dedicated his new church to Saint Mary, the patron saint of Aachen, thereby transforming Frankfurt into the Aachen of the east. The Frankfurt chapel symbolized the king's reconciliation with the east Frankish Church, and the dedicatory inscription on it read "This temple was rebuilt by the most noble King Louis and dedicated by Raban, the archbishop of the church of Mainz."[65] Following the dedication of the new church, Raban held another synod at Mainz in October.[66] The 852 Mainz synod was truly kingdomwide because it was attended by the bishops of east Francia, Bavaria, and Saxony. (The Bavarian bishops had been conspicuously absent at Mainz in 847.) While the bishops and abbots met together, Louis held an assembly with his counts and royal officials. The king dealt with royal business, settled outstanding legal disputes, and received ambassadors from the Bulgars and Slavs. Louis also gave the bishops' decrees the imprimatur of royal law by formally approving the canons of the synod.

---

[62] *AF,* s.a. 848, p. 37. It also was during this synod that Louis and the eastern bishops condemned the heretic Gottschalk for his preaching of the doctrine of predestination: MGH *Concilia* 3:179–84.

[63] MGH *Concilia* 3:242–43 (c. 4).

[64] *AF,* s.a. 852, pp. 42–43. This was the first kingdomwide itinerary of an east Frankish king, a practice that later became customary under the Ottonians and Salians: Roderich Schmidt, *Königsumritt und Huldigung in ottonisch-salischer Zeit* (Constance, 1961); John W. Bernhardt, *Itinerant Kingship and Royal Monasteries in Early Medieval Germany, c. 936–1075* (Cambridge, 1993), 45–70.

[65] Böhmer and Will, *RGME* 1:67 (no. 18).

[66] MGH *Concilia* 3:235–52; Hartmann, *Synoden,* 228–33.

After the conclusion of the 852 Mainz synod, Louis traveled back to Bavaria, then returned west, sailed down the Rhine to Cologne, and set out for Saxony. The king's long absence from Saxony had led to serious abuses by local nobles, a fact that highlights the importance of the king's continual personal intervention for effective royal government. Earlier that year, the Saxon counts had murdered Louis's supporter, the Danish exile Harold, apparently without consulting the king. Moreover, other Saxon nobles had been subverting justice and usurping royal estates to expand their wealth and power. Louis therefore held an assembly at the bishopric of Minden, where he corrected perversions of justice and reasserted control over royal lands.[67] After the assembly, Louis journeyed rapidly through eastern Saxony and halted to judge legal disputes "as far as opportunity permitted," an indication of the general dearth of royal estates in that region.[68] Louis continued south to Thuringia, where he held yet another local assembly at Erfurt and issued decrees concerning the enforcement of justice. He then returned to Bavaria in time to celebrate Christmas at Regensburg.

Louis's 852 kingdomwide progress heralded the establishment of his rule "in east Francia." In three months, Louis had traveled over nine hundred miles, held several assemblies, and visited every territory within his kingdom. Louis's activities in 852 expressed his kingship in profoundly traditional Carolingian terms. The joint ecclesiastical synod and secular assembly at Mainz, the reception of "barbarian" ambassadors, the proclamation of laws, the reclaiming of fiscal lands, and the enforcement of justice all embodied the essence of good Carolingian government. By holding assemblies and Church synods, meeting with the nobles of his territories, and intervening directly in local politics, Louis asserted that his territories were part of a coherent eastern realm united under his rule. Moreover, his new royal chapel of St.-Mary at Frankfurt served as a permanent symbol of his Christian kingship. The 852 royal itinerary signaled that, almost a decade after the Treaty of Verdun, Louis's territories had begun to coalesce into an east Frankish kingdom.

[67] On December 8, the king apparently stopped at the Saxon convent of Herford to which he made a rich grant of lands in Westphalia, including an estate "from the benefice that Count Hrodrad held," perhaps one of "wicked usurpers" from whom Louis had reclaimed crown lands: *DLG* 61. I am inclined to date this diploma to 852, although some scholars prefer 851: BM 1403; Kehr's introduction to *DLG* 61; *Annals of Fulda*, trans. Reuter, 34n11; Hartmann, *Ludwig der Deutsche*, 124.

[68] Of Louis's seven recorded grants of Saxon estates (a relatively low number), all were located in western Saxony (Westphalia) and central Saxony (Angria), suggesting that royal lands, such as they were, fell thickest on the ground in those regions: *DLG* 28, 29, 61, 73, 93, 95, 143.

The return to peace after Verdun precipitated a decade of unprecedented ecclesiastical reform and literary output in the east Frankish Church. "The teachers' harvest now bears fruit," wrote Louis's chaplain, Ermanrich, "so that everywhere those learned in grammar and philosophy chant measured hymns in the holy Church."[69] The period between 843 and the mid-850s represented a high point of Church reform and cultural production east of the Rhine, reinforcing the picture of this decade as one of political stability and consolidation under Louis's kingship. At the heart of this flowering of east Frankish letters was the central theme of the Carolingian Renaissance: the renewal (*renovatio*) of the Christian religion and learning that took its inspiration from the late antique Church of Augustine, Jerome, and Gregory the Great. The Carolingian Renaissance emphasized the Frankish king's duty to protect the Church, defend orthodoxy, and foster the spread of Christianity, and Louis embraced this ideal. "It is hardly necessary," Raban told Louis, "to give you examples of the kings and emperors of correct faith and true belief. Since the time of Emperor Constantine [the Great, 306–37], the first emperor to defend the Christian religion and honor God's churches, until your own day, they have labored so that God's Church has peace, His religion is pure, and His servants freely serve Him without hindrance."[70] Ultimately, Louis saw his support of the Church and Christian learning as a matter of political survival, since Scripture taught that God would abandon a ruler who neglected to defend the true faith.

In the process of importing the Carolingian Renaissance east of the Rhine, Louis and the eastern churchmen adapted Christian learning and literature to fit the unique history and culture of Germania. The east Frankish Church had its own distinctive ecclesiastical history, monastic centers, saint cults, and vernacular languages that were reflected in the work of its scholars. Perhaps most significant was the fact that, compared with the churches of Gaul and Italy, the east Frankish Church was relatively young and economically underdeveloped. Much of Germania had not been part of the Christian Roman empire, and it was not fully Christianized until the eighth century, especially through the work of Anglo-Saxon missionaries like Saint Boniface (d. 754),

---

[69] Ermanrich, *Vita Sualonis*, 196. For east Frankish letters and learning under Louis the German, see Wattenbach, Levison, and Löwe, *DGM* 6; Wallace-Hadrill, *Frankish Church*, 329–45; Hartmann, *Ludwig der Deutsche*, 212–41.

[70] MGH *Concilia* 3:162.

the founder of Fulda.[71] As a result, the wealth and infrastructure of the east Frankish Church, especially in frontier regions like Saxony, Thuringia, and the Bavarian Eastland, were not equal to that west of the Rhine or south of the Alps.[72] Louis encouraged the production of scholarship after 843, but it largely took place in eastern monastic centers such as Fulda, St.-Gall, Lorsch, St.-Emmeram, Reichenau, and Corvey rather than at court. The primary objective of this cultural movement was to build up the basic foundations of the east Frankish Church: improving monastic schools, building churches, collecting relics, and increasing the holdings of monastic libraries.

Louis was a highly educated Carolingian prince, and he created a court environment that prized piety, learning, and scholarship. "No cleric," Notker wrote, "dared to remain in his service or even come into his sight unless he knew how to read and sing. He despised monks who broke their vows and loved those who kept them with deep affection."[73] Notker apparently was not exaggerating. On one occasion, Louis dismissed from court a cleric named Elefans and replaced him with a slave named Gundpert "because he was more skilled and intelligent at writing and reading."[74] Raban praised Louis as an avid and thoughtful reader (*lector diligens, prudens lector*) who was deeply interested in Scripture, and he urged the king to discuss the theological treatises he sent him with the keen readers (*sagacissimi lectores*) in his entourage.[75] Even while conducting diplomacy, Louis found time for theology. During one Carolingian summit, Louis discussed the books of Genesis and Psalms with Bishops Hincmar of Reims and Altfrid of Hildesheim. When pressing business cut their conversation short, Louis requested that Hincmar send him a treatise explaining the obscure seventeenth verse of Psalm 104.[76] Louis even tried his hand at composing poetry, a true sign of his Latin learning. He wrote some verses to a Salzburg priest named Baldo, asking him to clarify ambiguities in a treatise Baldo had sent him:

We thank you, Baldo

. . . .

For the pious writings you sent us filled our spirit with joy.

. . . .

---

71 Wallace-Hadrill, *Frankish Church*, 143–61.

72 Thus, when Louis received a request from the Bulgar khan to send missionaries to Christianize his kingdom, he was compelled to ask his brother Charles for sacred vessels, vestments, and books to help equip his priests: *AB*, s.a. 866, pp. 133–34.

73 Notker, *GK* 2.11, p. 69.

74 *DLG* 152.

75 Raban, *Epistolae*, nos. 18, 37, in MGH *Epistolae* 5:423, 473–74.

76 Hincmar, *De verbis psalmi: Herodii domus dux est eorum, ad Ludowicum Germaniae regem*, in *PL*, ed. J.-P. Migne, vol. 125 (Paris, 1852), cols. 957–62.

Recently you sent us a work
That our mind could not fully understand,
Because a deep riddle ran throughout the text.
Do you know what needs to be added to your words here?
We ask that you explain this to us clearly.[77]

    Louis's palace was well stocked with books. A surviving treasure catalogue from the royal chapel at Frankfurt reflects the predominance of religious books at the east Frankish court. It lists eighteen codices, including books from the Old and New Testament, liturgical manuscripts, one monastic rule book, and two martyrologies (that is, books recording the feast days of saints).[78] Louis reportedly bound some of the books in his library with gold covers as thick as a man's finger.[79] Louis's court also valued classical literature. The private library of Louis's archchaplain, Grimald of St.-Gall, contained the works of Caesar, Virgil, Vegetius, and Boethius.[80] But, in agreement with the Church Fathers, those at court tended to value classical literature not for its own sake but rather for its usefulness in furthering their understanding of Scripture. As Ermanrich wrote to Grimald, studying Virgil was like looking for gold in a pile of excrement: "As dung gets the fields ready to bring forth better crops, so the works of pagan poets are like stinking manure. Although they are not true, they greatly aid in understanding divine eloquence."[81]

    Louis's court also was a center of music.[82] The liturgy was chanted in the early medieval Church, so the study of music was essential for the performance of the Mass. As part of the Carolingian *renovatio*, Louis's predecessors had tried to standardize the different kinds of ecclesiastical music throughout the empire by importing the supposedly "authentic" Roman chant believed (incorrectly) to have been created by Gregory the Great. (This style of chant, which in the end became a hybrid of Roman and Frankish texts and melodies, therefore became known as Gregorian chant.) Metz in particular had become a center of Roman song north of the Alps, and Roman chant therefore became known as the Metz chant or, in Frankish, *Mette*.[83] Louis reportedly employed only clerics who were skilled in chanting, and his court library was stocked with antiphonaries (that is, books for

<hr/>

[77] Louis, *Ad Baldonem*, in MGH *Poetae Latini* 2:643–44.
[78] Lorsch Rotulus, verso.
[79] Notker, *GK* 2.11, p. 69.
[80] Bischoff, "Bücher am Hofe Ludwigs des Deutschen," 196–97, 199–200, 210–11.
[81] Ermanrich, *Epistola ad Grimaldum abbatem*, in MGH *Epistolae* 5:563.
[82] For the role of music in Carolingian reform, see Contreni, "Carolingian Renaissance," 742–46.
[83] Notker, *GK* 1.10, p. 15.

the chanting of the Mass).[84] During Louis's lifetime, someone added neums (musical notations for chant) into his book of private prayer, the Ludwig Psalter.[85] From time to time Louis probably visited the bishopric of Freising, only a day's ride from Regensburg, where musicians were famous for their skill at playing the organ.[86] Louis enjoyed listening to chant in church and wanted to understand its deeper meanings. When he met with Raban at Rasdorf, the king requested that Raban compose a treatise explaining the mystical significance of ecclesiastical song.[87] In his short work for Louis, Raban interpreted the chant of the different services as symbolizing mankind's sin, salvation, and final judgment. In this way, music helped lift the king's mind from his daily political struggles to what really mattered: the salvation of his soul.

From the beginning of his reign, Louis surrounded himself with a group of monastic leaders who were learned, pious, and committed to improving the basic standards of the east Frankish Church. Louis succinctly outlined his vision of a well-qualified abbot: he had to be "acceptable according to the *Rule* of Saint Benedict, both in morals as well as learning, and adorned with other good qualities for the service of omnipotent God."[88] Louis's close ecclesiastical advisers in the decade after Verdun were just such abbots and bishop-abbots: Gozbald of Würzburg-Niederaltaich, Baturich of Regensburg–St.-Emmeram, Ratleig of Seligenstadt, Grimald of St.-Gall, Liupram of Salzburg–St.-Peter, Erchanbert of Freising-Kempten, and Raban of Mainz-Klingenmünster. These Church prelates around Louis shared common traits: they all were monks (with the exception of Grimald, who was a member of the secular clergy), established scholars and teachers, devoted to relic collecting and the cult of saints, and committed to building churches and collecting books. Most of all, they were active in the king's service. For example, Louis's first archchaplain and *familiaris*, Gozbald, acquired the relics of saints Cyprian and Sebastian for his church at Kleinochsenfurt on the Main River, and he also wrote a *Translation of the Holy Martyrs Agapitus and Felicissimus*, recounting how Louis sent him to Rome to acquire relics for the Bavarian church of Isarhofen.[89] During Gozbald's tenure as bishop,

[84] Ibid., 2.11, p. 69; Lorsch Rotulus, verso.
[85] Ludwig Psalter, fol. 1r.
[86] *Fragmenta registri Iohannis VIII papae*, no. 24, in MGH *Epistolae* 7:287.
[87] Raban, *Epistolae*, no. 33, in MGH *Epistolae* 5:465–67.
[88] *DLG* 48, 58.
[89] Concerning Gozbald, see Dümmler, *GOR* 2:428–30; Fleckenstein, *Hofkapelle* 1:167–68; Alfred Wendehorst, *Das Bistum Würzburg*, Germania Sacra, n. s. (Berlin, 1962), 1:42–46; Heinz Löwe, "Gozbald von Niederaltaich und Papst Gregor IV," in *Festschrift für Bernhard Bischoff*, ed. J. Autenrieth and F. Brunhölzl (Stuttgart, 1971), 164–77; Hansjörg Wellmer, *Persöhnliches Memento im deutschen Mittelalter* (Stuttgart, 1973), 19–20; Watten-

Würzburg's scriptorium reached a high point in manuscript production.[90] Baturich of Regensburg had been a student of Raban's at Fulda, and as Louis's archchaplain he exchanged poems, books, relics, students, and prayers with Raban and acted as Fulda's patron at court.[91] Under Baturich's supervision, the libraries of Regensburg and St.-Emmeram grew significantly, and the scribes' writing became standardized.[92] With Louis's help, Liupram of Salzburg and Hitto of Freising also journeyed to Rome and obtained new relics for their churches.[93]

The best example of an abbot in royal service was Grimald of St.-Gall and Wissembourg, who served intermittently as Louis's chancellor and archchaplain between 833 and his retirement from public life in 870.[94] Grimald had studied and taught at the Alemannian monastery of Reichenau, and he had a reputation as a teacher, poet, builder, and book collector. Because he had spent time at Charlemagne's palace and served as chaplain under Louis the Pious, he embodied the political and ideological continuity between Louis the German and his predecessors.[95] Under Grimald's abbacy, the St.-Gall and Wissembourg scriptoria excelled in manuscript output and artistic quality, and with the help of royal builders he constructed magnificent new churches decorated with gold, silver, marble columns, and frescos for his two monasteries.[96] Grimald was also devoted to the cult of saints. He owned a copy of the *Passion of Saint Emmeram* (the pa-

---

bach, Levison, and Löwe, *DGM* 6:669, 731, 810. For Gozbald's learning and relics, see Ermanrich, *Epistola ad Grimaldum abbatem*, in MGH *Epistolae* 5:568; *Ad epistolas variorum supplementum*, no. 3, in MGH *Epistolae* 5:618.

[90] Bernhard Bischoff and Josef Hofmann, *Libri Sancti Kyliani: Die Würzburger Schreibschule und die Dombibliothek im VIII. und IX. Jahrhundert* (Würzburg, 1952), 18–23, 170–72.

[91] Raban, *Ad Baturicum episcopum*, in MGH *Poetae Latini* 2:173–74; *Epistolae variorum*, no. 35, in MGH *Epistolae* 5:359–60; *Epistolarum Fuldensium fragmenta*, in MGH *Epistolae* 5:517–18. See further, Dümmler, *GOR* 2:433–34; Georg Swarzenski, *Die Regensburger Buchmalerei des X. und XI. Jahrhunderts* (Leipzig, 1901), 20–21; Bernhard Bischoff, "Literarisches und künstlerisches Leben in St. Emmeram (Regensburg) während des frühen und hohen Mittelalters," *SMGB* 51 (1933): 103–4; Fleckenstein, *Hofkapelle* 1:168–70; Wattenbach, Levison, and Löwe, *DGM* 6:798–802.

[92] Bischoff, *Schreibschulen*, 1:177–79, 200–203, 205–8, 214, 226–27, 231–32, 236.

[93] *Translatio sanctorum Alexandri papae et Iustini presbyteri*, chap. 1, in MGH *SS* 15.1:286–88; *Translatio sancti Hermetis*, in MGH *SS* 15.1:410.

[94] Concerning Grimald, see Dümmler, *GOR* 2:430–31, 434–38; Fleckenstein, *Hofkapelle* 1:89, 168–76; Geuenich, "Beobachtungen zu Grimald," 55–68. Grimald also was abbot of an unidentifiable third monastery: Bigott, *Ludwig der Deutsche*, 34–35.

[95] Ermanrich, *Epistola ad Grimaldum abbatem*, in MGH *Epistolae* 5:534.

[96] Books: Paul Lehmann, *Mittelalterliche Bibliothekskataloge Deutschlands und der Schweiz*, vol. 1: *Die Bistümer Konstanz und Chur* (Munich, 1918), 82–89; Bischoff, "Bücher am Hofe Ludwigs des Deutschen," 187–212; Hannes Steiner, "Buchproduktion und Bibliothekszuwachs im Kloster St. Gallen unter den Äbten Grimald und Hartmut," in *LDZ*, ed. Hartmann, 161–83. Building projects: Ratpert, *Casus sancti Galli*, chap. 8, pp. 192–94;

tron saint of Louis's Bavarian capital), and his Grimalt Codex recorded the feast days of other east Frankish saints: Saint Hermes (Salzburg), Saint Regula (Zurich), Saints Sergius and Bachus (Wissembourg), and Saint Gall.[97] In 864, Grimald presided over the translation of the relics of Saint Otmar into St.-Gall's basilica, and soon thereafter he moved them to a new basilica he had built and deposited them in a reliquary made of gold and silver.[98] Throughout his long public career, Grimald was constantly busy in royal service, and Ermanrich therefore referred to him as Louis's "faithful Iolaus," the companion of mythological Hercules.[99]

In this milieu of learned churchmen around Louis's court, the composition and dedication of works of literature became profoundly political. Books, literary works, and poetry served to reinforce ties of patronage and *amicitia* between churchmen and the palace and to heal political rifts caused by the civil war. In 842, for example, the influential Grimald helped his friend and former student Walahfrid Strabo regain his abbacy at Reichenau from which Louis had exiled him two years earlier.[100] It may have been as a veiled plea for help during his exile that Walahfrid dedicated to Grimald his beautiful pastoral poem "Hortulus" (The little garden). In that work, Walahfrid compared Grimald's monastery of Wissembourg to a well-ordered garden where Grimald taught students in peace while Walahfrid stood outside and enviously peeked over the high walls.[101] After regaining Reichenau through Grimald's help, Walahfrid sent Louis gifts and verses congratulating him for his victories over Lothar:

Pious king, merciful king, and lover of true virtue:
Receive with a warm heart what Paldman [Walahfrid's messenger] brings you.
I give great thanks for your piety
To the eternal Father, Who makes you reign with power,
Gives you pious habits,
And grants you all good things through your many triumphs.
Most holy father, take care
To give the Lord thanks for the many rewards
Through which He protected you in your hour of need
And gave you lasting peace.[102]

Ermanrich, *Epistola ad Grimaldum abbatem*, in MGH *Epistolae* 5:565; *In Wizunburg*, in MGH *Poetae Latini* 2:393; Grimalt Codex, 52.

97 Bischoff, "Bücher am Hofe Ludwigs des Deutschen," 196, 207.
98 Ratpert, *Casus sancti Galli*, chap. 9, pp. 214–16.
99 Ermanrich, *Epistola ad Grimaldum abbatem*, in MGH *Epistolae* 5:536, 539.
100 Ibid., 566.
101 Walahfrid, *De cultura hortorum*, in MGH *Poetae Latini* 2:335–50.
102 Walahfrid, *Carmina*, no. 71, in MGH *Poetae Latini* 2:410–11.

Like Grimald, Walahfrid devoted himself to royal service, which was costly and time-consuming.[103] It also was dangerous. In 849 Walahfrid drowned in a boating accident while on a diplomatic mission from Louis to Charles.[104]

Another east Frankish churchman who used literature to cultivate ties to the court was the monk Ermanrich.[105] Ermanrich was a member of the new generation of east Frankish scholars who came of age during Louis's reign. He had studied at the best east Frankish schools: at Fulda under Raban, then at court under Gozbald and Grimald while he served as a royal chaplain, and later at Reichenau and St.-Gall. In the early 840s, Ermanrich wrote the *Life of Saint Sualo*, an Anglo-Saxon companion of Saint Boniface, who became a hermit at remote Solnhofen on the Altmühl River in southeastern Franconia.[106] Ermanrich wrote the *Life* at the request of Raban's nephew, Gundram, who had recently elevated Sualo's relics at Solnhofen, and he sent a copy of his work to their former teacher at Fulda, Rudolf. A few years later, Ermanrich composed the *Life of Saint Hariolf,* the eighth-century founder of the monastery of Ellwangen (west of Solnhofen).[107] Ermanrich dedicated this work to his former teacher and the king's *familiaris,* Gozbald of Würzburg-Niederalteich, who was a relative of Hariolf.

Ermanrich also dedicated several works to Grimald. While Ermanrich was living at St.-Gall in the early 850s, he sent to Grimald at court a copy of his *Life of Saint Hariolf* as well as a long didactic treatise, his *Letter to Abbot Grimald.*[108] Ermanrich's *Letter* was an assortment of theological, grammatical, philosophical, hagiographic, and classical material to assist Grimald in teaching his young students at court. But, as Ermanrich admitted, his real reason for composing the *Letter* was to win Grimald's *amicitia.* At the beginning of his *Letter,* Ermanrich praised the king's archchaplain for his learning, virtue, courtliness, and royal service, and he extolled Louis as a second Solomon and Charlemagne. Ermenrich used the image of a river to convey Louis's illustrious lineage and free-flowing generosity, although he be-

---

[103] Ermanrich, *Epistola ad Grimaldum abbatem,* in MGH *Epistolae* 5:539, stressed the high financial burdens of royal service.

[104] Ibid., 564, 566.

[105] Concerning Ermanrich, see Ernst Dümmler, "Über Ermanrich von Ellwangen und seine Schriften," *FDG* 13 (1873):473–85; Wilhelm Schwarz, "Die Schriften Ermanrichs von Ellwangen," *ZWL* 12 (1953): 181–89; idem, "Ermanrich von Ellwangen," *ZWL* 15 (1956): 279–81; Wilhelm Forke, "Studien zu Ermanrich von Ellwangen," *ZWL* 28 (1969): 1–104; Fleckenstein, *Hofkapelle* 1:179–80; Wattenbach, Levison, and Löwe, *DGM* 6:762–66; Heinz Löwe, "Ermanrich von Passau, Gegner des Methodius: Versuch eines Persönlichkeitsbildes," *MGSL* 126 (1986): 221–41; Bigott, *Ludwig der Deutsche,* 25.

[106] Ermanrich, *Vita Sualonis,* 189–246.

[107] Ermanrich, *Vita Hariolfi,* 9–49.

[108] Ermanrich, *Epistola ad Grimaldum abbatem,* in MGH *Epistolae* 5:534–79.

moaned the limitations imposed on the king's beneficence by civil wars, Slavic rebellions, and the constraints of his borders. He wrote to Grimald:

> You still abide by that delightful river and shining branch of virtue flowing from the foremost spring in all Europe: Louis our most beloved king. Although he is constricted by the borders of his lands, he still surpasses Hercules the centaur-slayer in valor and Odysseus in agility. Ask the nearby Slavs and you will not doubt what I say! In that poor yet nourishing river we have more abundance than the Scythian Don and more beauty than the Nile. We give thanks to the king, since he provides a clear and healthy spring from which we drink up all things good and beneficial. Inexhaustible, he offers a drink to all who come to him, as he so desires. But alas! That convenient spring has not always flowed freely. It was often obstructed, first by the machinations of certain men not belonging to the royal family, and then by pagans and foreigners. As a result, a desert was created where wild beasts roamed free. At last, overflowing in himself and not without personal danger, his great patience became exhausted and, with God protecting him, he defended the state with arms. In his household you live like faithful Iolaus and stand at his right hand. You know that his piety, valor, and character are far superior to those of other kings. His power comes from God alone, and his greatest treasure is wisdom. It is said that he excels all others in wisdom, and in your estimation his only equal is his grandfather. In his presence you keep your old mind sharp and, as if having Charlemagne before your very eyes, there is nothing that you suffer or fear.[109]

In the end, Ermanrich's efforts to build up *amicitia* with Gozbald, Grimald, and Louis paid off: in 866 Louis appointed him bishop of Passau.

The best example of literature and scholarship advancing a political career is the case of Raban, who was the most prolific Carolingian scholar of the ninth century.[110] Raban had been raised and educated as a monk at Fulda, and he had also studied at Tours with the preeminent Carolingian scholar Alcuin. (Alcuin gave Raban the nickname "Maur," after the disciple of the early monastic leader Saint Benedict.) Like many Carolingian scholars, Raban was not a daring, original thinker but one whose mind was firmly rooted in the monastic curriculum of the Bible and Church fathers. Raban's gift lay in selecting, excerpting, and organizing quotations from early Chris-

---

[109] Ibid., 536–37.
[110] Wattenbach, Levison, and Löwe, *DGM* 6:687–88, 698–705; Raymund Kottje and Harald Zimmermann, eds., *Hrabanus Maurus: Lehrer, Abt und Bischof* (Wiesbaden, 1982).

tian thinkers such as Augustine, Jerome, Ambrose, and Gregory the Great and incorporating them into his own numerous biblical commentaries and religious treatises. This was exactly the kind of scholarship the young east Frankish Church needed to compensate for its general dearth of books, schools, and educated churchmen.

Raban's support of Lothar during the civil war forced Louis to depose him as abbot of Fulda in 841. Between 841 and 847, Raban withdrew in voluntary exile to Fulda's monastic cell at Petersberg, and while there he undertook a significant writing campaign to regain Louis's favor. Like Walahfrid and Ermanrich, Raban turned to the king's faithful Iolaus, Grimald, for help. He composed for him a martyrology, and in his dedication he thanked Christ for giving him Grimald as his *amicus* and "safe harbor" in the midst of his "shipwreck."[111] During these years of exile, Raban also composed his great work, a massive illustrated encyclopedia of ancient and Christian knowledge, *On the Nature of Things and the Etymologies of Names and Words*, and he sent a copy to the king upon request.[112] In addition, Raban sent Louis commentaries on Daniel, Maccabees, and ecclesiastical chant.[113] Although Raban's exile kept him out of the circle of service and patronage at court, he expressed the hope that his theological works would remind Louis of his loyalty and desire to serve him.[114] As in the case of Walahfrid and Ermanrich, this strategy ultimately worked: in 847 Louis promoted Raban to archbishop of Mainz, thus securing his position as Louis's counselor and the leader of the east Frankish Church.

Another scholar who wrote in Raban's defense during his exile was the Fulda monk and scholar Rudolf (d. 865), whom the *Annals of Fulda* praised as an "excellent teacher, notable historian and poet, and a most noble practitioner of all the arts."[115] Rudolf's career was intimately bound up with Raban's. He had been Raban's student, he worked in the Fulda chancery as a scribe, and he succeeded Raban as head of the Fulda monastic school. Around 838, at Raban's request, Rudolf wrote the *Life of Saint Leoba*, a kinsman and helper of Saint Boniface, whose relics Raban had translated to

---

[111] Raban, *Ad Grimoldum*, in MGH *Poetae Latini* 2:169–70; Raban, *Martyrologium*, ed. John McCulloh, in CCCM 44 (Turnhout, 1979). Raban also dedicated the same martyrology to Louis's high chancellor Ratleig after becoming archbishop: Raban, *Epistolae*, no. 48, in MGH *Epistolae* 5:502–3.

[112] Raban, *De universo*, in PL, ed. J.-P. Migne, 111:9–614.

[113] Raban, *Epistolae*, nos. 33–35, 37, in MGH *Epistolae* 5:465–70, 472–74. On the ideological significance of Raban's theological treatises for Carolingian rulers, see De Jong, "Empire as *Ecclesia*," 191–226.

[114] Raban, *Epistolae*, no. 35, in MGH *Epistolae* 5:469.

[115] *AF*, s.a. 865, p. 63. Concerning Rudolf, see Wattenbach, Levison, and Löwe, *DGM* 6:709–13.

Fulda's church at Petersberg—the site of Raban's later exile.[116] Sometime during Raban's exile, Rudolf wrote his *Miracles of the Saints Translated to Fulda's Churches*, which he intended as a defense of Raban by depicting his former abbot as a second Saint Boniface.[117] In fascinating detail, Rudolf described the great contributions Raban had made to the Christianization of Germania as abbot of Fulda: building thirty churches on Fulda's scattered estates, adorning them with gold, silver, tapestries, and Latin inscriptions, and depositing in them miracle-working relics from Rome. Rudolf emphasized that Raban was not a power-hungry prelate involved in the tumultuous arena of high politics but rather a humble pastor devoted to studying, writing, teaching, building, and relic collecting.[118] Rudolf poignantly concluded his history of Raban's work as abbot with his exile during the civil war.[119] In this way, Rudolf pointed to the injustice of Raban's exile and urged a reconciliation with the king. Only by restoring good relations with Raban, Rudolf implied, could Louis continue the Christianization of his kingdom.

During the civil war, Rudolf also apparently began writing (or perhaps supervising the compilation of) the so-called *Annals of Fulda*, the most important ninth-century east Frankish chronicle. Rudolf wrote the *Annals of Fulda* between 838 and 863 as a continuation of an earlier eastern annal, perhaps written by Einhard.[120] Like many eastern nobles, Rudolf had displayed divided loyalties during the civil war, oscillating between his support of Lothar and Louis. He blamed Louis's fall from grace in 838 on the "enviousness of the emperor's advisers," and in 841 he singled out Adalbert of Metz as the "instigator of the disputes" against Louis. Nevertheless, following Raban's lead, Rudolf initially supported Lothar, and he fled west with Raban and his brother, Count Guntram, after Louis's victory in the Ries in 841.[121] Rudolf stressed the legitimacy of Lothar's emperorship, reporting that Louis the Pious had given Lothar the imperial title and capital and that the Franks accepted Lothar as his father's successor. The real turning point in Rudolf's attitude toward Louis was Raban's promotion to archbishop of Mainz in 847. Only at that point did Rudolf bestow on Louis the title "king" and "king of the east Franks" in the *Annals of Fulda*, thereby acknowledging

---

[116] Rudolf, *Vita Leobae abbatissae Biscofesheimensis*, in MGH SS 15.1: 118–31.

[117] Rudolf, *Miracula sanctorum in Fuldenses ecclesias translatorum*, in MGH SS 15:328–41; Wattenbach, Levison, and Löwe, *DGM* 6:709 and n. 176. In the preface, Rudolf explained that he modeled his work on Einhard's *Translation and Miracles of Saints Marcellinus and Peter.*

[118] Rudolf, *Miracula sanctorum in Fuldenses ecclesias translatorum*, chaps. 1, 15, pp. 330, 341.

[119] Ibid., chap. 15, p. 340.

[120] See introduction.

[121] *Fulda* 534.

the legitimacy of his kingship. Rudolf seems to have accompanied Raban to Mainz in 847, since beginning in that year he regularly described Raban's activities as archbishop and made frequent mention of events in and around Mainz. Rudolf may have hoped to succeed Raban as archbishop, since the *Annals of Fulda* voiced unusual criticism of Louis and his counselors when they appointed other candidates in 856 and again in 863.[122] One of these royal counselors undoubtedly was Grimald, whom the *Annals of Fulda* never mentioned by name, in spite of his tremendous political influence. It may be that Rudolf had cool relations with Grimald, which would explain why Rudolf, unlike Walahfrid, Ermanrich, and Raban, never achieved high office. Rudolf's apparent distance from court also explains the *Annals of Fulda*'s fragmentary reports of Louis's activities and the fact that these seem based on hearsay rather than firsthand information.[123] At the end of the day, Raban, not Louis, was the center of Rudolf's world.

Once promoted to archbishop of Mainz, Raban breathed new life into the Carolingian Church reforms in the east. He described the 847 Mainz synod as an effort to restore the "Golden Age" of Church reform under Charlemagne that had culminated in the reform councils of 813 but had been seriously undermined by the turmoil of the civil war.[124] At the synods of 847 and 852, Raban and the east Frankish bishops and abbots legislated on the major topics addressed by earlier Carolingian synods: the Catholic faith, baptism and penance, the public peace, the power of bishops, ecclesiastical rights and properties, payment of tithes, the priesthood, clerical celibacy, monasticism, and the care of the poor.[125] But both synods also issued new canons that focused on topics dealing with the laity that earlier synods had not addressed in such detail.[126] These new canons dealt with the serious crimes of laymen and laywomen, such as taking bribes in court, murder, abortion, adultery, and illicit forms of marriage. Raban believed that there had been a notable increase of wandering bands of laymen who were guilty of bloodshed, vice, and gluttony (perhaps as a result of the political and social disruptions caused by the civil war), and he decreed that laymen guilty of murder were to perform penance by giving up their swordbelts, wives, and aristocratic foods (especially meat, wine, mead, and beer).[127] In

---

[122] *AF*, s.a. 856, 863, pp. 46–47, 57, and the corresponding textual notes; *Annals of Fulda*, trans. Reuter, 38n2, 50n9. Rudolf's criticisms are preserved in manuscript group 3 (the oldest manuscript group that apparently preserves Rudolf's original text), although they were later rewritten in manuscript groups 1 and 2.

[123] For examples of rumors, see *AF*, s.a. 848, 855, pp. 37, 45.

[124] MGH *Concilia* 3:160–61.

[125] Ibid., 150–77, 235–52; Hartmann, *Synoden*, 222–33.

[126] MGH *Concilia* 3:171–76 (cc. 19–31), 243–50 (cc. 6–13).

[127] Ibid., 171 (c. 20), 248–49 (c. 11).

this way, Raban recognized the secular aristocracy and its preoccupation with weapons, warfare, sex, and feasting (what Karl Leyser saw as the emerging culture of knighthood), but he asserted that membership in that class was an honor that demanded at least minimum standards of Christian conduct.[128] Taken together, the synods of 847 and 852 articulated the agenda for Raban's pontificate: to revive Charlemagne's Church reforms and to improve the mores of the eastern lay aristocracy.

Two particular obstacles confronted the east Frankish bishops and abbots: the underdevelopment of the Church in Saxony, and the general problem of spreading the faith among populations that spoke Germanic languages. Although Saxony had several rich monasteries, including Corvey and Herford, the ninth-century Saxon Church suffered from a general dearth of wealth, land, and infrastructure.[129] This posed a serious problem to the spread of Christianity, since the nuts and bolts of missionary work—building parish churches, stocking them with relics, educating priests and monks, and providing them with liturgical books, chalices, and clothing—were extremely expensive. The already weak structure of the Saxon Church received an additional blow when the Danes destroyed the archbishopric of Hamburg in 845, forcing Louis to rectify the situation by creating the "double" bishopric of Hamburg-Bremen.[130] Another obstacle facing the Saxon Church was that, until 870, its bishops were administratively divided between those subject to the archbishopric of Mainz in Louis's kingdom (Paderborn, Halberstadt, Hildesheim) and those under the archbishopric of Cologne in the middle kingdom (Münster, Bremen, Minden, Osnabrück, Verden). For this reason, Raban's synods of 847 and 852 were significant milestones in the integration of Saxony into the east Frankish Church. The bishops of Paderborn, Halberstadt, Hildesheim, Hamburg-Bremen, Osnabrück, and Verden went to Mainz in 847, and five years later the bishop of Münster attended as well.[131]

The greatest obstacle facing the Saxon Church was the persistence of polytheism among the hostile Saxon peasants, who had openly rejected Christianity and attempted to destroy the Church during the Stellinga rebellion of 841–42. "I know all too well," Raban wrote Bishop Hemmo of Halberstadt, "that you face serious opposition, not only from the pagans who are your neighbors, but also from the common people who through

[128] Leyser, "Early Medieval Canon Law," 51–71.
[129] Christopher Carrol, "The Bishoprics in Saxony in the First Century after Christianization," *EME* 8 (1999): 219–46.
[130] Rimbert, *Vita Anskarii*, chap. 22, pp. 47–48; Bigott, *Ludwig der Deutsche*, 111.
[131] MGH *Concilia* 3:160, 241.

their insolence and uncouth customs cause your paternity serious hardship and leave you no time for frequent prayer and serious study."[132] At the 845 Paderborn assembly, Louis made an important ecclesiastical appointment to address this very problem: he named Ebbo, the former archbishop of Reims, the new bishop of Hildesheim.[133] Louis's appointment of Ebbo underscored the king's concern about enduring polytheism among the Saxon peasants. Ebbo had been born to a family of servile status on one of Charlemagne's Saxon estates. Because he demonstrated unusual talent and intelligence, Louis the Pious had appointed Ebbo archbishop of Reims, although Ebbo was deposed for his role in the 833 rebellion. This highly unusual rise of a former slave drew considerable protest from Frankish nobles such as the blue-blooded Thegan in his *Deeds of Emperor Louis*.[134] But as a former Saxon slave, Ebbo had the social background to win over the embittered Saxon peasants to the Christian faith.[135] Just as important, Ebbo had the linguistic skills to communicate fluently with the Saxon peasants, since Old Saxon was a Germanic dialect distinct from Frankish, much more closely akin to Anglo-Saxon spoken in Britain. It was presumably for these reasons that in 845 Louis decided, against canon law, to appoint the deposed archbishop of Reims the new bishop of Hildesheim.[136] Presumably for these same considerations, Louis also appointed Ebbo's relative Gozbert to the vacant Saxon bishopric of Osnabrück, and the Anglo-Saxon monk Hemmo as bishop of Halberstadt. Throughout his reign, Louis remained concerned about enduring paganism in Saxony. As late as 870, Louis bemoaned the "rude people of the Saxons" who only recently had come to the new faith— "or at least are urged to come."[137]

Like Louis and Raban, Rudolf was deeply concerned about the Christianization of Saxony. In the *Annals of Fulda*, Rudolf noted with abhorrence the Stellinga rebellion of the Saxon peasants against their lawful lords, and

[132] Raban, *Epistolae*, no. 36, in MGH *Epistolae* 5:471.

[133] Concerning Ebbo, see H. Goetting, "Ebo," *LMA* 3.2, cols. 1527–29; Bigott, *Ludwig der Deutsche*, 98–101.

[134] Thegan, *GH*, chap. 44, pp. 232–38; Stuart Airlie, "Bonds of Power and Bonds of Association in the Court Circle of Louis the Pious," in *CH*, ed. Godman and Collins, 200–204.

[135] The social significance of Ebbo's Saxon background should not be minimized. Radbert stressed that Wala had earlier won the respect of the hostile Saxons because he himself was half Saxon, fluent in their tongue, and often attired in their distinctive clothing and shoes: Radbert, *Epitaphium Arsenii*, bk. 1.

[136] Cf. Bigott, *Ludwig der Deutsche*, 101, who argues that Louis appointed Ebbo bishop of Hildesheim against canon law to counter political opposition among the Saxon nobles. The two explanations are not mutually exclusive.

[137] *Epistolae Colonienses*, no. 6, in MGH *Epistolae* 6:248–49.

he dedicated his *Life of Saint Leoba* to Hathumod (d. 875), the young daugh-ter of the prominent Saxon count Liudolf.[138] Rudolf devoted an entire trea-tise to Saxony—his *History of the Saxons*.[139] In that work, Rudolf drew upon oral traditions, classical works, Bede, and Einhard's *Life of Charlemagne* to tell the history of the Saxons, from their semimythical arrival on the Conti-nent until the present. Rudolf also used the famous Roman ethnography of the early Germanic peoples, the *Germania* of Tacitus, a rare copy of which was in the Fulda library.[140] At its heart, Rudolf's *History of the Saxons* was a defense of the Saxon nobles—their ancestry, character, and conversion to Christianity—written with the intent of freeing them from blame for the Stellinga rebellion. He argued for the alleged "biological" purity of the Saxon nobility vis-à-vis the peasants: he described the Saxon nobles as a dis-tinct "race" [genus] and emphasized their strict segregation from the other social "castes" [differentiae] in Saxony. Rudolf asserted that the Saxon no-bles were the descendants of the conquerors of the region, whereas those of lower birth were the offspring of the original indigenous peoples whom the Saxon conquerors had made into tribute-paying serfs.[141] In this way, Rudolf implied that the only "real" Saxons were the nobles. He wrote:

The Saxons were careful to preserve their race and nobility. *They did not taint themselves through marriages with other peoples or with those inferior to them, and they strove to make their own people pure and distinct. Almost every man among their large number has the same clothing, body size, and hair color.* [From Tacitus, *Germania*, chap. 4] That people consists of four castes: nobles, freemen, freedmen, and slaves. Their laws stipulate that no group transgress the boundaries of its own lot through carnal marriages. Rather, a nobleman should take a noble wife, a free man a free woman, a freed man should be joined to a freed woman, and a male

[138] *AF*, s.a. 842, p. 33; Rudolf, *Vita Leobae abbatissae Biscofesheimensis*, prologue, in MGH *SS* 15:121. On Hathumod, see Agius, *Vita Hathumodae*, in MGH *SS* 4:165–89; Krüger, *Studien*, 66–67; Matthias Becher, *Rex, Dux und Gens: Untersuchungen zur Entste-hung des sächsischen Herzogtums im 9. und 10. Jahrhundert* (Husum, 1996), 73.

[139] Although a Fulda monk named Meginhard later incorporated this work into his *Translation of St. Alexander*, it seems that Rudolf originally wrote it as an independent work about the Saxon people and that it had nothing to do with Saint Alexander's relics. For a facsimile edition, see *Translatio S. Alexandri auctoribus Ruodolfo et Meginharto Fulden-sibus: Landesbibliothek Hannover MS I 186*, ed. Helmar Härtel, Facsimilia Textuum Manu-scriptorum, Texthandschriften des Mittelalters in Faksimile 5 (Hildesheim, 1979). See further Wattenbach, Levison, and Löwe, *DGM* 6:711–14.

[140] Anglo-Saxon missionaries presumably brought copies of Tacitus's *Germania* and *Annales* to Fulda in the eighth century: L. D. Reynolds, ed., *Texts and Transmission: A Sur-vey of the Latin Classics* (Oxford, 1983), 406–11.

[141] *Translatio sancti Alexandri*, ed. Härtel, fol. IV.

slave to a female slave. If anyone takes a wife who is not his equal and more distinguished in lineage, he is to pay with the loss of his life.[142]

After describing in detail the former polytheism of the Saxons (again borrowing from Tacitus) and Charlemagne's conquest of the region, Rudolf ended on a triumphant note—the conversion of the Saxon nobles to Christianity. "They renounced the worship of demons and the rest of their native ceremonies and accepted the sacraments of the Christian faith and religion. Thus united with the Franks they were made one people with them. They were initiated into the sacraments of the true faith and were baptized in the name of the Father, Son, and Holy Spirit. With a growing faith and true religion they were united to God's people up to the present day."[143] In this way, Rudolf's *History of the Saxons* defended the lineage, valor, and Christian faith of the Saxon nobility and attempted to free them from any association with the Stellinga rebellion. It is testimony to how deeply the Saxon peasant uprising had horrified the Franks that Rudolf deemed such a treatise necessary.

The second major obstacle Louis and Raban faced in their efforts to reform the east Frankish Church was language.[144] In Carolingian Europe, Latin was the language of the Church, Bible, liturgy, and Christian learning. This posed a particular linguistic problem for Louis's kingdom, which lay east of the rough Romance–Germanic linguistic border west of the Rhine. As a result, the vast majority of Louis's subjects spoke the Germanic vernacular as their first language, and Notker therefore instinctively spoke of "we who speak the Germanic or Teutonic language."[145] Louis's subjects did not speak a single "German" language, however, but rather Germanic dialects that varied from province to province. The chief linguistic division in his kingdom was between speakers of "high" (that is, southern) Germanic dialects (Frankish, Alemannian, Bavarian, and Thuringian) and "low" (that is, northern) Germanic dialects (Saxon and Frisian). Frankish literally was the *lingua Franca* of Louis's court, which would have been easily understandable to all east Franks, Bavarians, Alemans, and Thuringians but somewhat less so to the Saxons.[146] While Romance speakers could learn Latin relatively easily, Germanic speakers would have had a more difficult time, since Latin

---

[142] Ibid., fol. 2r.

[143] Ibid., fol. 4r. Here Rudolf borrowed from Einhard, *VK*, chap. 7, p. 10.

[144] For an overview of the complexities of language in the Carolingian period, see McKitterick, *Carolingians and the Written Word*, 6–13.

[145] Notker, *GK* 1.10, p. 15.

[146] Louis's chancery therefore distinguished between the *lingua Theodisca*, i.e., Frankish, and *lingua eorum*, the "tongue of [the Saxons]": *DLG* 24, 25, 36, 93, 95. The *AF*, s.a. 852, p. 42, referred to the Saxons as a distinct *gens*.

was an entirely different language.[147] As a result, only east Frankish church-men, nuns, and well-educated lay noblemen and noblewomen—probably no more than the top 5 percent of Louis's subjects—would have been able to understand, speak, and/or read Latin and therefore have had direct access to Christian learning and the Bible.

To foster the Christian faith among their subjects, Louis and Raban initi-ated a kingdomwide effort to translate Scripture and other religious texts into the Germanic vernacular.[148] The east Frankish king and archbishop were building upon and modifying Charlemagne's interest in vernacular languages and literature. According to Einhard, Charlemagne had ordered the writing down of heroic oral Frankish poetry, composed a Frankish grammar, and given Frankish names to the twelve months and twelve winds.[149] Moreover, in 794 Charlemagne clarified that God could be prayed to in any language (not just the three official languages of the Church—Latin, Greek, and Hebrew), and the 813 synod of Tours called for preaching "in the rustic Romance or Germanic languages."[150] However, Charle-magne's initiative seems to have had only a limited impact. His collection of Frankish poetry and his grammar book do not survive, and from his reign there are only a few short and practical Germanic translations of Christian texts. In addition, Charlemagne's successor apparently had little interest in vernacular literature because of its close associations with non-Christian oral poetry. According to Thegan, Louis the Pious "rejected the pagan songs that he had learned as a youth," perhaps a reference to classical Roman poetry such as Virgil as well as to Frankish poetry.[151] During Louis the Pious's reign, moreover, not one of the numerous Church councils re-newed the earlier call for preaching in the vernacular.

Louis the German and Raban sought to strike a balance between Charle-magne and Louis the Pious's divergent attitudes toward vernacular litera-ture and preaching. They urged the production of vernacular Germanic lit-

[147] McKitterick, *Carolingians and the Written Word*, 21–22; Nelson, "Literacy in Car-olingian Government," 9–12.

[148] For vernacular literature under the Carolingians, see esp. Wallace-Hadrill, *Frank-ish Church*, 377–89; Edwards, "German Vernacular Literature," 141–70. For the notable increase of the vernacular under Louis the German, see Wolfgang Haubrichs, "Die Prae-fatio des Heliand: Ein Zeugnis der Religion- und Bildungspolitik Ludwigs des Deutschen," *JVNS* 89 (1966): 7–32; idem, "Ludwig der Deutsche und die volkssprachige Literatur," in *LDZ*, ed. Hartmann, 214–25; Geuenich, "Die volkssprachige Überliefer-ung," 104–30, esp. 121–30; Patrick J. Geary, "Germanic Tradition and Royal Ideology in the Ninth Century: The *Visio Karoli Magni*," reprinted in Geary, *Living with the Dead*, 49–76.

[149] Einhard, *VK*, chap. 29, pp. 33–34.

[150] MGH *Concilia* 1:171 (c. 52), 255 (c. 15), 268 (c. 25), 271–72 (c. 45), 296 (c. 14).

[151] Thegan, *GH*, chap. 19, p. 200 and n. 101.

erature, but only for Christian ends. In a panegyric for Louis the German, the poet Sedulius praised the east Frankish king for transforming the *barbara lingua* into a medium to praise God. He wrote:

Let the barbarian tongue, resounding alleluias,
Learn to sing and offer harmonious praises,
So that great Louis's strong right hand and mighty
Wrath be forever appeased.
Now every rank and all the babbling people
Hasten from their northern lands.
Pious Solomon, with prayers they long to honor
You and choose you for their king.[152]

Louis's personal interest in Christian vernacular poetry is also suggested by the poem *Muspilli*, which combined the form of secular heroic poetry with overtly Christian content and survives only in the margins of Louis's copy of *On the Creed against the Jews, Pagans, and Arians*.[153] At the 847 Mainz synod, moreover, Raban revived the 813 canon that called for preaching in the Romance and Germanic vernaculars so that everyone could understand the basic tenets of the Catholic faith: the salvation of the good and damnation of the wicked, the resurrection and final judgment, and the kinds of behavior through which one could obtain salvation.[154]

The eastern churchmen around Louis, who all were native Germanic speakers, shared this interest in the vernacular to further the Christian faith. Many of these men would have been deeply influenced by the legacy of eighth-century Anglo-Saxon missionaries who had imported to Germania the insular tradition of vernacular translations of Christian texts. Raban had studied with the Anglo-Saxon Alcuin, and under him Fulda became a center of Frankish vernacular poetry and translations. During Raban's abbacy, the Fulda monks produced several minor Frankish translations of basic Christian texts (such as baptismal vows) as well as the lone-surviving piece of Frankish heroic secular poetry, the "Lay of Hildebrand."[155] Moreover, during the early 830s, the Fulda monks composed the earliest surviving translation of Scripture into Frankish, the so-called Tatian translation.[156] This was a translation of a Gospel harmony (that is, a synthesis of the four Gospels in

---

[152] Sedulius, *Carmina*, no. 30, in MGH *Poetae Latini* 3:195–97.
[153] Concerning the *Muspilli*, see chap. 1.
[154] MGH *Concilia* 3:164 (c. 2).
[155] Wattenbach, Levison, and Löwe, *DGM* 6:707–9.
[156] J. Knight Bostock, *A Handbook on Old High German Literature*, 2nd ed. (Oxford, 1976), 155–68; Karen Konyk Purdy, "Tatian," in *DLB* 148:283–86.

a single book) by the second-century Roman author Tatian. The Fulda translation of Tatian's harmony displayed the original Latin text on the right-hand page and a literal Frankish translation on the left. The production of the Tatian translation was a major scholarly achievement that could not have happened without Raban's consent and encouragement. Grimald likewise had a personal interest in Frankish, since he copied the vernacular names of the months and winds from Einhard's *Life of Charlemagne* into his Grimalt Codex.[157] There also was interest in Christian vernacular poetry at Freising under Louis's supporter, Bishop Erchanbert. About 850, a Freising churchman composed a short vernacular poem, the *Lay of Saint Peter,* perhaps on the occasion of Erchanbert's dedication of Freising's new church of St.-Peter.[158]

In producing these vernacular translations, east Frankish churchmen faced deeply rooted cultural biases. Frankish churchmen tended to view Latin, Greek, and Hebrew as the only "proper" languages of the Church, and they therefore often dismissed Germanic as a *lingua barbara.* To refute these prejudices, several east Frankish churchmen appealed to the historical precedent of the fourth-century translation of the Bible into Gothic by the missionary bishop Ulfila (ca. 311–83).[159] During the reign of Constantine the Great's son, Constantius II, Ulfila had performed missionary work among the Goths living beyond the Danube, and to that end he translated the Bible into Gothic. Louis's kingdom possessed several copies of Ulfila's Gothic translation, including the Codex Carolinus at Grimald's monastery of Wissembourg.[160] In a short ecclesiastical history composed in the early 840s, Walahfrid noted that the Goths "spoke our—that is, the Germanic—language [nostrum, id est Theotiscum, sermonem], and, as chroniclers show, late scholars of that people translated the holy Scripture into their own language, of which today a few traces are found."[161] Another scholar interested in Ulfila's Gothic translation was the Salzburg teacher Baldo. Baldo wrote a commentary on Gothic letters, copied excerpts from Ulfila's Gothic Bible, tried to translate these excerpts into Frankish, and included phonetic marks for pronunciation. The east Frankish court had close ties with Baldo: Louis

[157] Grimalt Codex, 16.

[158] The *Lay of Saint Peter* survives in a copy of Raban's commentary on Genesis (Munich, Clm 6260, fol. 158v), copied at Freising ca. 850: Anatoly Liberman, "Petruslied," in *DLB* 148: 252–54.

[159] Haubrichs, *Anfänge,* 327–38; Peter Heather and John Matthews, trans., *The Goths in the Fourth Century* (Liverpool, 1991), 133–41.

[160] Heather and Matthews, *Goths,* 155–58.

[161] Walahfrid Strabo, *Libellus de exordiis et incrementis quarundam in observationibus ecclesiasticis rerum,* chap. 7, ed. and trans. Alice L. Harting-Correa (Leiden, 1996), 72.

composed his poem thanking Baldo for his religious writings, and Baldo later became the chancellor of Louis's eldest son, Carloman.[162]

Louis and Raban seem to have been behind the single greatest Carolingian translation of Scripture into the vernacular, the Old Saxon *Heliand* (Savior).[163] The *Heliand* is a moving version of the Gospel story, rendered in six thousand lines of Old Saxon verse in the grand epic style of *Beowulf*. Christ becomes a "mighty chieftain" and "lord of earls," Herod a "renowned giver of rings," and the twelve apostles Christ's "loyal thegns." The author intended the *Heliand* to be recited before Saxon aristocratic audiences, since its heroic style reflected the nobles' taste for oral vernacular poetry. The Old Saxon *Heliand* was based on the Fulda copy of Tatian's Gospel harmony, which indicates that the Fulda scriptorium was involved in the *Heliand* translation project. A surviving Latin preface to the *Heliand* reported that, before 840, the "most pious Augustus Louis" urged translations of the Scriptures into Frankish (*Theudisca lingua*) and Saxon (*Germanica lingua*), so that the uneducated (*illiterati*) might have access to divine knowledge alongside literate people.[164] On the basis of this remark, scholars have long debated whether the *Heliand*'s Latin preface referred to Louis the Pious or Louis the German. However, internal evidence in the poem itself suggests that it was the latter. When recounting how the Jews urged Pilate to crucify Jesus, the *Heliand* author added as an aside: "The leaders of the Jews had incited all the poor people [thia aramun man alla] to ask . . . for Christ to be killed on the cross."[165] This identification of the poor as the betrayers of Christ has no scriptural basis whatsoever, so it must have come out of the mind of the *Heliand* author. Such pronounced hatred of the poor makes sense only after the Stellinga revolt of 841–42, when there would have been widespread mistrust of the peasants by the Saxon nobles. This conjecture in turn points to the conclusion that Louis the German was the "Augustus Louis" who urged translations of Scripture into Frankish and Saxon for the benefit of the unlettered eastern nobles. This project of vernacular Christian translations complemented Raban's ecclesiastical legislation, since both aimed at Christianizing the secular nobles and transforming them into "soldiers of Christ." The surviving manuscripts of the *Heliand* demonstrate its rapid dissemination through the monasteries of Saxony,

---

[162] Louis, *Ad Baldonem*, in MGH *Poetae Latini* 2:643–44; *DCarloman* 1–2.

[163] On the *Heliand*, see Edwards, "German Vernacular Literature," 152–53; Haubrichs, *Anfänge*, 331–41; idem, "Ludwig der Deutsche," 214–25; Anatoly Liberman, "Heliand," in *DLB* 148:189–95.

[164] Haubrichs, "Ludwig der Deutsche," 217–25.

[165] *Heliand*, chap. 64, ll. 5413–18, p. 191.

which seems to corroborate that it was commissioned by the king.[166] The earliest surviving manuscript of the *Heliand* was copied around 850 at the monastery of Corvey, which may indicate that it was composed there under the supervision of Louis's Saxon supporter, Abbot Warin.

The last major ninth-century translation of Scripture into the vernacular was Otfrid of Wissembourg's *Book of the Evangelists*.[167] Unlike the other literary works considered thus far, this Frankish translation of the Gospel story was composed by Otfrid after 852, sometime between 863 and 871. Nevertheless, Otfrid had ties to Raban, Grimald, and Louis, so I consider his work here. Otfrid had studied at Fulda under Raban in the 830s, when the Fulda scriptorium composed the Tatian translation, and he later became a monk in Grimald's Alsatian monastery of Wissembourg. Otfrid's *Book of the Evangelists* consists of more than seven thousand lines of rhyming Frankish verse, and he dedicated his vernacular translation of the Gospel story to several leading east Frankish figures: Archbishop Liutbert of Mainz, Bishop Salomon II of Constance, and the St.-Gall monks Hartmut (Grimald's deputy abbot) and Werinbert. Otfrid also dedicated a copy of this work to Louis. There are close artistic similarities between the illuminations in a copy of Otfrid's manuscript in Vienna (Codex Vindobonensis 2687) and the portrait of Louis in his Ludwig Psalter, which suggests that the east Frankish court and the Wissembourg scriptorium cooperated in the production of Otfrid's Frankish translation.[168] In his vernacular dedication to Louis, Otfrid praised him as a traditional Frankish king: noble, pious, wise, just, bold, and strong. Otfrid compared Louis to David, who likewise had enjoyed God's protection during his struggles to expand his kingdom. He concluded his dedication to Louis with the words:

Themo dihton ih thiz buah; oba er habet iro ruah,
Odo er thaz giweizit, thaz er sa lesan heizit,
Er hiar in thesen redion mag horen evangelion,
Waz Krist in then gibiete Frankono thiete.

For [Louis] I compose this book. If he is interested in these things,
Or if he commands it to be read aloud,

---

[166] Bernhard Bischoff, "Paläographische Fragen deutscher Denkmäler der Karolingerzeit," *FS* 5 (1971): 104–5.

[167] On Otfrid's *Liber evangeliorum*, see Edwards, "German Vernacular Literature," 154–57; Haubrichs, *Anfänge*, 354–83; idem, "Ludwig der Deutsche," 227–32; Albert L. Lloyd, "Otfrid von Weissenburg," in *DLB* 148:110–20; Chiara Staiti, "Das Evangelienbuch Otfrids von Weissenburg und Ludwig der Deutsche," in *LDZ*, ed. Hartmann, 233–54.

[168] Goldberg, "Equipment of Battle," 67–68 and n. 108.

He will hear the Gospels in these words,
What Christ commanded in them to the Frankish people.[169]

In his dedication to Liutbert of Mainz and in the introductory chapter (titled "Why the Author Dictated This Book in Germanic"), Otfrid gave voice to the growing linguistic confidence among the churchmen around Louis's court.[170] Otfrid argued that the Franks had as much right to create a body of Christian literature in their own tongue as did the Hebrews, Greeks, and Romans, asking, "Why should the Franks alone hesitate to begin to sing the praise of God in Frankish?" Otfrid lamented that Germanic speakers had produced no poets to rival Virgil, Lucan, or Ovid, although he admitted that Frankish was "uncouth and undisciplined and also unaccustomed to being held back by the regulating bridle of the grammatical art." Frankish used irregular spellings, difficult pronunciation and poetic meters, awkward non-Latin letters (z, k, and w), and noun genders that differed from Latin. Echoing the *Heliand* preface, Otfrid explained that his chief motivation was to make the Bible available to the Frankish-speaking *illiterati* and create an alternative to heroic vernacular poetry (*ludus secularium*): "I composed part of the Gospels in Germanic so that a reading of this poetry might drown out the voice of the songs of laymen, and, swept away in the sweetness of the Gospels in their own language, they might learn to reject the song of frivolous histories."

Between 843 and the early 850s, Louis transformed his disunited eastern territories into a nascent kingdom "in east Francia." As this chapter and the previous one demonstrate, Louis built the east Frankish kingdom through the traditional strategies of Carolingian kingship: active personal rule, an alliance with the nobility and the Church, tributary lordship over the Slavs, and frequent military campaigns across his kingdom's borders. This political consolidation led to a decade of general peace and stability east of the Rhine, enabling Louis and his churchmen to preside over a period of ecclesiastical reform and literary production. Before continuing with the political narrative, I turn to another major achievement of Louis's after Verdun: the creation of a coherent system of kingship and government.

---

[169] Otfrid, *Ad Ludowicum*, ll. 87–90, in *Liber evangeliorum*, 14.
[170] Otfrid, *Ad Liutbertum*, in *Liber evangeliorum*, 16–26, 34–44.

CHAPTER SIX
KINGSHIP AND GOVERNMENT

By the early 850s, Louis not only had won the support of the eastern Church and nobility. He also had established a system of kingship and government throughout his realm. Historically, the eastern territories of the Carolingian empire had been peripheral to direct royal government. Previous Frankish kings only occasionally had ventured beyond the Rhine, usually to wage periodic military campaigns against the "barbarian" Saxons and Slavs. During his twenty-six-year reign, for example, Louis the Pious crossed the Rhine only eight times, and three of those crossings were during campaigns against Louis the German.[1] All told, Louis the Pious spent less than two years in the east—only about 7 percent of his reign as emperor. As a result, the Merovingians and Carolingians had tended to rule indirectly in Germania through powerful magnates—dukes, prefects, counts, bishops, and abbots—who, in theory at least, were royal representatives loyal to the crown.

It was Louis the German who transformed the eastern territories of the empire from a "distant zone" of Frankish kingship to one of direct royal rule. Some historians have assumed that Louis the German presided over a decline of Carolingian royal power east of the Rhine as a way to account for the relative weakness of Ottonian kingship in the tenth century.[2] In fact, just

---

[1] BM 587a–92 (815: Paderborn and Frankfurt), 766a–78a (822–23: Frankfurt), 832a–b (826: Salz and Frankfurt), 872 (829: Tribur and Frankfurt), 899c–904 (832: campaign against Louis the German), 963b–c (836: Frankfurt and Seligenstadt), 984f–93 (839: campaign against Louis the German), 1003c–14c (840: campaign against Louis the German).

[2] Timothy Reuter, "The Medieval German *Sonderweg*? The Empire and Its Rulers in the High Middle Ages," in *Kings and Kingship in Medieval Europe*, ed. Anne Duggan (Lon-

the opposite is true. In the decade after Verdun, Louis imported and intensified beyond the Rhine the traditional institutions of Carolingian kingship and government. As always, Louis remained dependent on the cooperation of the nobles. But he had a deep belief in the supremacy of royal power, and he made the eastern nobles conform to the more rigid framework of Carolingian royal government. He asserted his authority as a divinely appointed king, tightened control of the crown's economic resources, and insisted that the eastern bishoprics, monasteries, and counties were public offices belonging to the state (*res publica*), which he could grant and revoke at will. The creation of an effective system of kingship and government east of the Rhine was the most significant and lasting achievement of Louis's long reign.[3]

STAGING MAJESTY

As Timothy Reuter observed, "to be a king is . . . not simply a matter of status or action, but also of style."[4] Like all Carolingian kings, Louis actively worked to create an aura of royal majesty, a phenomenon historians have labeled "sacral kingship."[5] Royal majesty was a central element of Carolingian kingship, since it helped the ruler convince the nobles to obey his commands and cooperate in royal government. It was natural for nobles to take royal majesty seriously. By coming to court, attending royal assemblies, and participating in royal government, the nobles shared in the king's majesty as his allies and faithful men. Noblemen and noblewomen likewise cultivated their own aura of majesty—what contemporaries called nobility (*nobilitas*)— through pride in their ancestors, elaborate clothing, conspicuous consump-

don, 1993), 179–211, esp. 196–97 and nn. 45, 48; Althoff, "Königsherrschaft und Konfliktbewältigung," 37–38 and n. 43; Fried, "Frankish Kingdoms, 817–911," 155; Roper Pearson, *Conflicting Loyalties*, 128–29, 138, 140.

    [3] For Carolingian government, see Ganshof, *Frankish Institutions*; McKitterick, *Frankish Kingdoms*, 77–105; Nelson, "Kingship and Royal Government," 383–430; Hartmann, *Ludwig der Deutsche*, 123–72.

    [4] Timothy Reuter, "*Regemque, quem in Francia pene perdidit, in patria magnifice recepit*: Ottonian Ruler Representation in Synchronic and Diachronic Comparison," in *Herrschaftsrepräsentation im Ottonischen Sachsen*, ed. Gerd Althoff and Ernst Schubert (Sigmaringen, 1998), 363–80, at 364. For the best discussion of Carolingian ceremony and ritual, see Nelson, "Lord's Anointed," 127–31. However, I heed the cautionary warnings of Philippe Buc, *The Dangers of Ritual: Between Early Medieval Texts and Social Scientific Theory* (Princeton, 2001), about accepting uncritically chroniclers' reports of political rituals.

    [5] For sacral kingship, see Leyser, *Rule and Conflict*, 75–107.

tion, and pious donations to monasteries. The king and nobles therefore spoke the same ceremonial language. Royal majesty simply was *nobilitas* on a much grander scale.

Louis surrounded himself with the royal pomp and symbolism of a traditional Carolingian king.[6] After 833, he consistently used the royal title "king by the favor of Divine Grace" (*divina favente gratia rex*). This "absolute" royal title stressed the divine right of Louis's kingship and rejected the limitation of his rule to a single people or province. Louis's royal seal containing the image of the Roman emperor Hadrian visually equated him with his father and grandfather, since they too had used similar seals with bearded Roman emperors. The private library of Louis's archchaplain, Grimald, stressed the Frankish and Carolingian foundations of Louis's kingship in that it contained copies of the *Book of the History of the Franks*, Einhard's *Life of Charlemagne*, and Thegan's *Deeds of Emperor Louis*.[7] The *Annals of Fulda* likewise rooted Louis's eastern kingship in Carolingian royal tradition, since they prefaced his reign with an account of the triumphant rise of his dynasty under Pippin II, Charles Martel, Pippin III, and Charlemagne.[8] The chanting of royal acclamations at the east Frankish court expressed the Christian sacrality of Louis's power and authority. The royal acclamations on the first pages of the Grimalt Codex, which were modeled on those used by his father and grandfather, hailed Louis as the "great and pacific king crowned by God." These acclamations offered prayers to Christ and the saints for the health and salvation of Louis, Emma, their children, and the army of the Franks.[9] In Ermanrich's eyes, Louis was "our unconquered king, our head after God Himself."[10]

Throughout his life, Louis was satisfied with the royal title *rex* and never called himself "emperor" in official documents. One explanation for this titular restraint is that since the reign of his father, the imperial title increasingly was tied to rule in Italy and a papal coronation in Rome. Thus, during Louis's lifetime, Lothar I and Lothar's eldest son, Louis II of Italy, monopolized the imperial title. This association of the imperial title with the Italian kingdom was a devaluation of its universalist connotations, and the *Annals of Fulda* therefore gave Lothar I's son the oxymoronic designation "emperor of

---

[6] For an exploration of Louis's royal representation, see Goldberg, "Equipment of Battle," 41–78.

[7] Bischoff, "Bücher am Hofe Ludwigs des Deutschen," 210–11; Tremp, *Studien zu den "Gesta Hludowici imperatoris,"* 64.

[8] *AF*, s.a. 714–838, pp. 1–28.

[9] Grimalt Codex, 1–3. These acclamations date to the 850s or 860s.

[10] Ermanrich, *Epistola ad Grimaldum abbatem*, in MGH *Epistolae* 5:539.

Italy."[11] Louis the German clearly favored a more traditional concept of Frankish royal power, like the one championed by the east Frank Einhard. In the *Life of Charlemagne*, Einhard consistently called Charlemagne *rex*, and he notably downplayed the importance of Charlemagne's imperial coronation for his greatness. The civil war had reinforced this idea that royal power proceeded from aristocratic support and military might, not from the imperial title. Nevertheless, Louis's kingship over multiple peoples and provinces embodied the Frankish idea of imperial power. The *Annals of Fulda* defined an emperor and augustus as a king of multiple kingdoms, and Notker described an emperor and caesar as a ruler of many peoples.[12] A scribe in the entourage of the bishop of Freising therefore instinctively referred to Louis as the "most serene emperor" during an assembly of east Franks, Bavarians, and Alemans.[13] Thus, although Louis presented himself as a traditional king of the Franks in the mold of Charlemagne, his kingship carried with it overtones of imperial power.

Like his father and grandfather, Louis donned elaborate clothing and regalia during important ceremonial events to make visible his royal majesty.[14] Louis apparently wore a crown during special occasions at court. Louis's first royal seal depicted him with a jeweled diadem, and the east Frankish royal acclamations heralded Louis as *a Deo coronatus*, "crowned by God." Although Louis the Pious excluded his namesake from a share of the Carolingian regalia, Louis the German apparently won a share when he and Charles captured Lothar's treasury at Fontenoy.[15] During assemblies and diplomatic meetings, Louis sat on a raised throne and carried a royal staff, and he and his sons wore silk vestments with gold hems, golden spurs, and swordbelts.[16] Also like Charlemagne and Louis the Pious, Louis the German preferred

[11] *AF*, s.a. 859, 865, 871, 875, pp. 53, 63, 74, 84. The *AF*, s.a. 872, 873, pp. 75, 81, similarly called the Byzantine ruler "emperor of the Greeks."

[12] *AF*, s.a. 869, pp. 69–70; Notker, *GK* 1.26, p. 35.

[13] *DLG* 66. This genuine report survives in a forged diploma of Otto II. Kehr believed Louis's imperial title was a later interpolation, although there is no evidence for this, since the rest of the document seems genuine. For other examples of imperial references to Louis, see Heinz Zatschek, "Die Erwähnungen Ludwigs des Deutschen als Imperator," *DA* 6 (1943): 374–78.

[14] For the ceremonial attire of Charlemagne and Louis the Pious, see Einhard, *VK*, chap. 23, pp. 27–28; Thegan, *GH*, chap. 19, pp. 202–4.

[15] Astronomer, *VH*, chap. 63, p. 548; Adelerius of Fleury, *Miracula*, chap. 41, pp. 498–99.

[16] Notker, *GK* 2.18, p. 88 (throne); *DLG* 66 (dais); *AB*, s.a. 849, 873, pp. 57 (staff), 191 (royal vestments and swordbelts). Louis seems to have been buried in a plaid silk tunic with gold hems and gold spurs, presumably attire he wore while alive: Friedrich Behn, *Die karolingische Klosterkirche von Lorsch an der Bergstrasse* (Berlin, 1934), 4–5; Schramm and Mütherich, *Denkmale*, pp. 128, 242 (no. 37).

the traditional "dress and equipment of the old Franks," thereby underscoring the continuity of his regime with those of his father and grandfather. Notker gave a detailed eyewitness description of Louis's clothing and regalia during one of his visits to St.-Gall:

> Shoes gilded on the outside decorated with shoelaces three cubits long, leg wrappings with intricate patterns, and under them linen garments for the leg and hip of the same color yet varied by the most ingenious work. Long laces were bound over the leg wrappings in a crisscross pattern, inside and out, front and back. Then came a white linen tunic and a belt girded with a sword. The sword was encased in a sheath, leather holder, and white canvas cover hardened by wax to stiffen the scabbard against the thigh when the sword was drawn to slaughter pagans. The last item of dress was a gray or blue cloak in the shape of a double square, so that when it was worn about the shoulders it hung down to the feet in the front and back but on the sides hardly came to the knees. In the right hand was carried a staff of apple wood, wonderful for its regular knots, both hard and threatening, with a handle of gold and silver with engraved patterns.[17]

Louis's traditional Frankish attire was a statement of royal legitimacy. When Charles the Bald donned Byzantine regalia in 876, the *Annals of Fulda* (which at that point were being written in the circle of Louis's archchaplain, Liutbert of Mainz) scoffed that Charles "scorned the entire tradition of the Frankish kings and held the glories of the Greeks to be the best."[18] The implication was that Louis the German was the true upholder of Frankish royal tradition. A portrait of Louis in a martyrology from Reichenau similarly showed him in Frankish attire like that described by Notker.[19] The Reichenau artist painted Louis wearing a crown, tunic, leggings, and blue cloak while sitting on a raised throne and holding a staff. Like the surviving portraits of other Carolingians, the Reichenau artist portrayed Louis with the distinctive features of his dynasty: short hair, large eyes, a long aquiline

---

[17] Notker, *GK* 1.34, pp. 46–47; Dümmler, *GOR* 2:414 and n. 2; Schramm and Mütherich, *Denkmale*, 95.

[18] *AF*, s.a. 876, p. 86.

[19] Biblioteca Apostolica Vaticana, Reg. lat. 438, fol. 1v; Schramm and Mütherich, *Denkmale*, 127–28 (no. 36). This portrait is found in a copy of Wandalbert of Prüm's *Martyrology*, which was originally dedicated to Lothar I. However, this copy was made at Reichenau during the third quarter of the ninth century and refers to the unnamed ruler as *rex* instead of *imperator*, pointing to the conclusion that it was made for Louis the German.

nose, droopy moustache, and powerful upper body. Although it is impossible to know if this is an accurate physical depiction of Louis, the artist's message was clear: Louis was a traditional Carolingian king.

Courtly splendor magnified the king's majesty. The main stages for royal display were Regensburg and Frankfurt, where Louis built magnificent new royal chapels dedicated to Saint Mary in imitation of Aachen.[20] Louis had builders (*palatini magistri*) in his entourage, which suggests that he oversaw ongoing building projects around his kingdom.[21] Although Louis's palaces and chapels have not survived, Notker reported that they were large and stately and incorporated Roman stonework.[22] One gets a sense of east Frankish royal architecture from the surviving gate-hall at Lorsch, which Louis's son, Louis the Younger, constructed between 876 and 882.[23] The Lorsch gate-hall is decorated with vibrant red-and-white geometric stonework, windows, vaulted arches, classical columns, and carved stone reliefs, some of which were appropriated from old Roman buildings. In this way, royal architecture suggested the king's quasi-imperial power. Royal architecture also shaped political ceremonies. At Regensburg, for example, Louis walked barefoot behind the cross from his palace to the monastery of St.-Emmeram outside the city's walls.[24] The fact that the Lorsch gate-hall is raised on arches suggests that it was constructed for triumphal entries into the monastery when the king visited.

At court, Louis surrounded himself with treasures to dazzle his nobles and foreign ambassadors.[25] Louis's royal chapels housed gold, silver, and jeweled reliquaries, crowns, crosses, chalices, candelabras, liturgical garments, tapestries, and numerous Bibles and liturgical codices.[26] According to Notker, Louis decorated his palace with gold found in old burials at Regensburg, which were discovered when he ordered part of the Roman walls dismantled to acquire stones for his new royal chapel.[27] Baturich of Regensburg's pontifical in fact contains a "prayer for vessels uncovered in old places" to purify objects "artfully made by heathens," suggesting that the

---

[20] *DLG* 155, 161; *DLY* 18. See further: Dümmler, *GOR* 1:359–60, and *GOR* 2:422; Ing. Leonhardt, "Die Alte Kapelle in Regensburg und die karolingische Pfalzanlage," *Zeitschrift für Bauwesen* 75 (1925): 83–110.

[21] Grimalt Codex, 52.

[22] Notker, *GK* 2.11, p. 69.

[23] Werner Jacobsen, "Die Lorscher Torhalle: Zum Probleme ihrer Datierung und Deutung," *Jahrbuch des Zentralinstituts für Kunstgeschichte* 1 (1985):9–41.

[24] Notker, *GK* 2.11, pp. 68–69.

[25] *AF*, s.a. 869, p. 69; Notker, *GK* 2.11, p. 69.

[26] Lorsch Rotulus, verso.

[27] Archeologists have in fact uncovered burials from the Agilolfing period within the Roman walls at Regensburg: Brühl, *Palatium und Civitas* 2:250.

The king in majesty. This portrait of Louis the German is found on the first page of his copy of Wandalbert of Prüm's *Martyrology*, made at Reichenau in the third quarter of the ninth century. Louis sits on an elevated throne, wears Frankish royal attire and a crown, holds a staff, and receives a codex from a bowing monk. The dedication above the portrait reads "Rex rerum, rector clemens, seniorque, benigne suscipe dignatus que fert munuscula servus" (King of all things, merciful ruler, and lord: kindly receive the little gifts your worthy servant brings). © Bibliotheca Apostolica Vaticana (Vatican), Reg. lat. 438, fol. 1v.

A rare surviving example of Carolingian royal architecture. This picture shows the gate-hall that marked the entrance to the Rhineland monastery of Lorsch. Louis the German's son, Louis the Younger, seems to have constructed this gate-hall to mark the royal procession route to the "many-colored church" (*ecclesia varia*) that housed his father's tomb. The building is decorated with classical motifs, Roman stonework, and vibrant red-and-white geometric patters, hinting at the architectural style of other royal buildings that have not survived. (Note that the tall roof and bell tower are later additions.) Photograph by author.

king and bishop used excavated Roman artifacts to decorate the palace and churches.[28] Here Louis was following the example of Charlemagne, who appropriated columns, marble, and statues from Italy to adorn his palace at Aachen.[29] Louis's court also boasted luxury items, exotic foods, and wonders from distant lands. On one occasion, Bishop Solomon I of Constance sent him "a small cloak of remarkable color and another one of woven material, large palm branches with their fruits, a small bundle of cinnamon, galingale, clove, mastic, and Indian pepper, dried Carian figs, pomegranates, an ivory comb, scarlet oak berries, cicadas, parrots, a white fish, and an extremely long bone of a marine fish."[30] The greatest royal treasures were relics, which

28 *Oratio super vasa reperta in locis antiquis*, Clm 14510, fols. 74v–75r.
29 Einhard, *VK*, chap. 26, pp. 30–31.
30 *Collectio Sangallensis*, no. 29, in MGH *Formulae*, 415. For gifts from Byzantium, see *AF*, s.a. 872, 873, pp. 75, 81.

made the king's court the meeting place of terrestrial and heavenly power.[31] During one assembly, Louis debated with his Bavarian magnates about whether the relics being offered for sale by a relic dealer named Felix were genuine.[32] Unable to decide, they decreed a three-day fast from wine, meat, mead, beer, milk, and eggs so that God would send them a sign concerning the relics' authenticity. The presence of relics at court sanctified royal power. Louis had his magnates swear loyalty to him on the relics of Saint Emmeram and other saints, thereby equating their political loyalty to him with their faith in God.[33]

Behavior was closely monitored at Louis's palace, revealing that the "courtization of warriors" (to use a phrase from Norbert Elias) had its origins at the Carolingian (and probably the Merovingian) palace.[34] Courtly behavior glorified the king and made manifest the hierarchy of the nobles around him. Those who came to court did not simply approach the king on their own but rather were formally led before him and his intimate counselors.[35] As depicted in the portrait of Louis from Reichenau, people who received an audience apparently bowed before him, rendered gifts, and addressed him in exalted terms such as "Your Excellency" and "Your Highness."[36] During assemblies the great magnates stood or sat around Louis's throne in rank order, thereby transforming the royal hall into a visual representation of the kingdom's political hierarchy, with the king at its apex.[37] Courtly behavior expressed political continuity with Louis's predecessors. Grimald brought the "most elegant courtly customs" he had imbibed at the courts of Charlemagne and Louis the Pious to the east Frankish palace.[38] Louis paid close attention to the conduct of those in his entourage and corrected any crass or uncouth behavior with a glance of his piercing eyes.[39] Louis's court was a center of hunting, feasting, gift exchange, and discussions of Scripture, activities that helped cement the social bonds between the king and his nobles.[40] The deeply pious Louis also

[31] For relics of martyrs in the Frankfurt chapel, see *AB*, s.a. 873, pp. 191–92.

[32] *Epistolae variorum*, no. 23, in MGH *Epistolae* 5:338; Patrick J. Geary, *Furta Sacra: Thefts of Relics in the Central Middle Ages*, rev. ed. (Princeton, 1990), 48.

[33] *AF*, s.a. 869, p. 68.

[34] Norbert Elias, *The Civilizing Process*, trans. Edmund Jephcott (Oxford, 1994), 465–75; Innes, "'A Place of Discipline,'" 59–76.

[35] *DLG* 26.

[36] For one bishop's exalted forms of address to Louis (and self-deprecating references to himself), see *Collectio Sangallensis, no. 29*, in MGH *Formulae*, 415.

[37] *DLG* 66; MGH *Concilia* 3:443–44.

[38] Ermanrich, *Epistola ad Grimoldum abbatem*, in MGH *Epistolae* 5:536.

[39] Notker, *GK* 2.11, pp. 69–70.

[40] Einhard and Thegan remarked on the role of hunting and banquets at the courts of Charlemagne and Louis the Pious: Einhard, *VK*, chap. 22, p. 27; Thegan, *GH*, chap. 19,

performed frequent acts of devotion—praying, going to Mass, studying Scripture, fasting, making pilgrimages, and walking barefoot behind the cross—thereby underscoring his identity as God's terrestrial representative.[41]

The most distinctive aspect of Louis's royal persona was his close association with martial symbolism to project his image as a victorious military leader. Indeed, at Louis's court, iron weapons and military rituals rivaled gold regalia and courtly splendor as emblems of his kingship. "He was more devoted to the equipment of battle than the splendor of banquets," Regino wrote. "For him iron was the greatest treasure, and he valued the hardness of iron more than the glitter of gold."[42] Notker concurred: "From his youth to his seventieth year, the unconquered Louis exulted in iron" in imitation of his grandfather, "that man of iron Charlemagne."[43] Louis was the first medieval king to place the emblems of the spear and shield on his royal seal, and he commanded that all royal monasteries render two spears, two shields, and two warhorses to him annually.[44] The militarism of Louis's court reflected the politics of his reign, since he had won his kingdom on the battlefields of the Ries and Fontenoy. The Grimalt Codex contained historical entries recording how Louis had triumphed in the battles of the Ries and Fontenoy "with the Lord's help," indicating that the east Frankish court commemorated those victories as judgments of God in favor of Louis's kingship.[45] It probably was no coincidence that Louis first allowed his sons to co-subscribe a royal diploma on the anniversary of the battle of the Ries in 857: they were his heirs, and they therefore shared in his God-given military victories.[46] In the militarized political culture of the Frankish nobility, Louis's reputation for valor mattered. In contrast, contemporaries criticized Charles the Bald for being "more timid than a hare,"

---

p. 204. For hunting, feasting, and gift giving under Louis the German, see *AB*, s.a. 841, 864, pp. 37–38 (feasting), 114 (hunting trips and hunting preserves); *AF*, s.a. 847, p. 36 (feasting and gift exchange); *AX*, s.a. 850, p. 17 (hunting); *DLG* 152 (a court official in charge of royal forests); *Regensburg* 31 (a hunting official); Raban, *Epistolae*, no. 37, in MGH *Epistolae* 5:473–74 (discussion of Scripture). In general, see Nelson, "Lord's Anointed," 120–24.

41 Raban, *Epistolae*, no. 33, in MGH *Epistolae* 5:465–67; *AF*, s.a. 874, p. 82; Notker, *GK* 2.11, pp. 68–69; *AI*, s.a. 861, p. 741. On this topic, see Raymund Kottje, "König Ludwig der Deutsche und die Fastenzeit," in *Mysterium der Gnade: Festschrift für Johann Auer*, ed. Heribert Rossmann and Joseph Ratzinger (Regensburg, 1975), 307–11.

42 Regino, *Chronicon*, s.a. 876, p. 110.

43 Notker, *GK* 2.17, p. 88.

44 Schramm, *Die deutschen Kaiser*, p. 322 (no. 49); *DLG* 70; Ratpert, *Casus sancti Galli*, chap. 8, p. 202.

45 Grimalt Codex, 27.

46 *DLG* 82.

frequently paying off Viking raiders, and "never emerging as the victor in battle."[47]

Louis's ongoing warfare with the Slavs and policy of tributary lordship over them provided frequent occasion for dramatic militaristic ceremonies. After successful campaigns, Louis's court celebrated with processions, bell ringing, and cheering, "as is the custom."[48] Louis's frequent "receiving, hearing, and dismissing" of foreign ambassadors—the *Annals of Fulda's* shorthand for receiving tribute and renewing peace treaties—served as a ritualized barometer of his military might and made visible his quasi-imperial rule over neighboring "barbarians."[49] In a panegyric for Louis, Sedulius asserted that his lordship over the Danes and Slavs surpassed the might of Julius Caesar, Augustus, and Louis the Pious and implied that his only equal was his famous grandfather.[50] Notker brought alive the drama of Louis's martial image in a memorable anecdote about a legation of Danish envoys to the east Frankish court. He wrote:

> When the kings of the Northmen each sent him gold and silver as a sign of loyalty and their swords as tokens of their lifelong subjection and surrender, King Louis ordered that the coins be thrown to the pavement, scorned, and trampled under foot like dirt. The swords, however, he ordered to be passed to where he was presiding on his lofty throne so that he could test their strength. Fearing that some suspicion of treachery might be leveled against them, the legates handed the swords to the emperor at their own risk, that is, in the manner that servants hand knives to their masters with the points toward themselves. He grasped one by the hilt and attempted to bend it from its tip to its handle, but it snapped between his hands stronger than iron. One of the envoys then drew his own sword from its sheath and offered it to Louis in the manner of servants so that he might test it. "My lord," he said, "I believe that this sword will be found as strong and flexible as your most victorious right hand could desire." Caesar accepted the sword and, gripping its hilt, bent it like a twig from its tip and then slowly allowed it to straighten. He was a Caesar indeed!. . . . For out of

[47] *AX*, s.a. 869, p. 27; *AF*, s.a. 875, p. 85.

[48] *DLG* 72; *AF*, s.a. 869, 870, pp. 68, 72.

[49] *AF*, s.a. 845, 848, 852, 856, 866, 870, 873, 874, 877, pp. 35, 37, 42, 47, 65, 72, 78–79, 83, 89 (referring to the renewal of their "customary" tribute payments); *AX*, s.a. 845, p. 14. For an insightful discussion of Carolingian rituals of overlordship, see Smith, "*Fines imperii*," 169–89.

[50] Sedulius, *Carmina*, no. 30, in MGH *Poetae Latini* 3:195–97.

the entire population of Germania, he alone with God's help rose to the ancient strength and courage of men. The legates were impressed and said to each other, "Would that our rulers held gold so cheap and iron so precious!"[51]

While Louis's public persona was decidedly militaristic, his wife and daughters endowed the palace with a more refined, feminine sanctity.[52] In the 850s, Louis gave his three daughters, Hildegard, Ermengard, and Bertha, to the monastic life and gave them a string of east Frankish convents: Münsterschwarzach in Franconia; Chiemsee in Bavaria; and Sts.-Felix-and-Regula (Zurich), Säckingen, and Buchau in Alemannia.[53] By making his daughters nuns and giving them convents to hold as proprietors and quasi-abbesses (a common Carolingian practice in the ninth century), Louis surrounded his family with an aura of female sanctity and placed these royal women in positions of power and authority throughout his territories.[54] In this way, Louis's daughters became local representatives of the crown. For example, in 853 Louis founded the convent of Sts.-Felix-and-Regula on the royal estate in Zurich and bestowed it upon his eldest daughter, Hildegard.[55] A "powerful and most distinguished virgin of Christ," Hildegard oversaw the construction of the church of Sts.-Felix-and-Regula, where she was buried in 856. Her epitaph, perhaps composed at court, stressed her virginity, piety, and royal blood:

In this tomb lies the most worthy virgin of Christ,
Hildegard, shining in her excellent morals.
She was the daughter of the distinguished King Louis.
On her own accord she dedicated her mind to God.

---

[51] Notker, *GK* 2.17–18, pp. 87–89. It seems that Notker based his story on the Danish embassy to Louis's court in 873, when King Halbden sent Louis a sword with a gold hilt: *AF*, s.a. 873, pp. 78–79.

[52] On Louis's wife and daughters, see Dümmler, *GOR* 2:425–28; Hartmann, *Ludwig der Deutsche*, 64–66, 77–79; Deutinger, "Königsherrschaft im Ostfränkischen Reich," part 1, pp. 122–25.

[53] Louis made Hildegard and, following her death in 856, Bertha proprietor (*rectrix*) of Münsterchwarzach near Würzburg, Sts.-Felix-and-Regula in Zurich, and Säckingen on the upper Rhine. Louis also made his third daughter, Ermengard, *rectrix* of Buchau in eastern Alemannia and Chiemsee in Bavaria: *DLG* 67, 79, 81, 82, 91, 110; *DCIII* 7; Bigott, *Ludwig der Deutsche*, 29, 36.

[54] For the increasing association of Carolingian women with the monastic life during the ninth century, see Le Jan, *Famille et pouvoir*, 298–302; Simon MacLean, "Queenship, Nunneries and Royal Widowhood in Carolingian Europe," *Past and Present* 178 (2003): 3–38.

[55] *DLG* 67.

The blessed virgin completed twice eighteen years of her life
And then departed for her Bridegroom.
She died on December 23.[56]

Louis's daughters also served as local mediators of patronage between the palace and the provinces. Lothar I's son, Lothar II, for example, entreated Bertha to be a "tireless spokeswoman for strengthening the friendship with our dearest uncle, her father, and with her beloved mother."[57] By making his daughters nuns, Louis jealously placed them beyond the reach of his magnates, since a nobleman like Giselbert might dare to abduct a king's unmarried daughter but not an abbess betrothed to Christ Himself. Louis already had three sons, and he did not want to contend with ambitious sons-in-law.

Queen Emma also contributed to the royal majesty and feminine sanctity of her husband's palace. The royal acclamations for Louis in the Grimalt Codex heralded Emma as "our queen," and they beseeched six female saints (Felicity, Perpetua, Petronela, Lucy, Agnes, and Cecilia) to protect her.[58] Early in his reign, Louis apparently made Emma the lay proprietor of the convent of Obermünster in Regensburg, an office she held until her death in 876.[59] As queen, Emma had the important responsibility of managing the royal household.[60] Sometimes Emma was at Frankfurt when Louis was at Regensburg (and vice versa), suggesting that she served as Louis's representative at one royal capital when he was at the other.[61] However, the patriarchal Louis carefully circumscribed his wife's independent power of patronage, perhaps to avoid the kind of scandals that hounded her sister Judith. During their forty-nine years of marriage, Emma "intervened" in her husband's diplomas (that is, asked the king to make a grant to a third party) only three times.[62] This is a remarkably low number of interventions for a Carolingian queen, indicating that Louis discouraged her involvement in politics.

---

[56] Grimalt Codex, 28, 33.

[57] DLoII 34.

[58] Grimalt Codex, 1.

[59] This report is based on two forged diplomas of the eleventh century, although they seem to contain reliable information: DLG 174; DCIII 157; Bigott, *Ludwig der Deutsche*, 28–29, 273.

[60] Hincmar, *De ordine palatii*, chap. 5, pp. 72–74; Pauline Stafford, *Queens, Concubines, and Dowagers: The King's Wife in the Early Middle Ages* (Athens, GA, 1983), 93–114; Nelson, "Kingship and Royal Government," 400–401.

[61] *AB*, s.a. 864, 875, pp. 114–15, 199; *AF*, s.a. 874, 875, p. 83.

[62] Emma's three interventions occurred during the last thirteen years of her life—for her daughter's convent of Sts.-Felix-and-Regula, for the Saxon nuns of Herford (where her Ecbertiner relative, Hadwig, was abbess), and for the Lotharingian monastery of Prüm: DLG 110, 128, 141.

Emma, however, had access to another important avenue of patronage—gift giving. As part of her duties supervising the royal household, a queen dispensed annual gifts to the king's vassals and servants.[63] Indeed, the Augsburg episcopal museum preserves an elegant liturgical belt that Emma gave Witgar, Louis's chancellor between 858 and 860 and later abbott of Ottobeuren and bishop of Augsburg.[64] The Witgar belt is a rare artifact of east Frankish courtly splendor and a testament to Emma's generosity. It is made of red silk woven with gold thread, and its ends are decorated with eagles, tassels, and pearls. The inscription sewn along its length reads, "The shining and most holy Queen Emma gave this belt to Witgar, a man full of sacred breath."[65] The belt originally contained a piece of Saint Mary's belt, although that relic was subsequently removed.

It is likely that Emma wove this belt herself (or at least supervised its construction), since Carolingian queens prided themselves on their skills as seamstresses and distributed belts and other gifts to officials at court.[66] The Witgar belt therefore provides a unique window onto Emma's self-representation. Most striking is her bold claim to be *sanctissima*, "most holy." The other term she used to describe herself, *nitens*, "shining," also carried powerful connotations of female sanctity and virginity. The epitaph for Emma's daughter, Hildegard, similarly described her as the "most worthy virgin of Christ, shining in her excellent morals," while Raban used the same term to describe the Virgin Mary.[67] Emma emphasized this message of sexual purity by giving her husband's chancellor what essentially was a double chastity belt: a liturgical girdle—the badge of a churchman's virginity[68]—that contained a relic of the Virgin Mary's belt.

[63] Hincmar, *De ordine palatii*, chap. 5, pp. 72–74.

[64] Concerning Witgar's belt, see Schramm and Mütherich, *Denkmale*, pp. 126, 238, no. 32. On Witgar, see Dümmler, *GOR* 2:436–37; Fleckenstein, *Hofkapelle* 1:174–75; Bigott, *Ludwig der Deutsche*, 31–32, 140, 145, 151, 284. See also my forthcoming article on Emma, Witgar, and the Witgar-Belt: "*Regina nitens sanctissima Hemma*: Queen Emma (827–876), Bishop Witgar of Augsburg, and the Witgar-Belt," forthcoming in *Representations of Power in Medieval Germany, 800–1500*, ed. Simon MacLean and Björn Weiler (Turnhout, 2005).

[65] "Hanc zonam regina nitens sanctissima Hemma Witgario tribuit sacro spiramine plenum"(!). The fact that Emma did not refer to Witgar as *abbas* or *episcopus* suggests that she gave the belt to him while serving as chaplain after 858 but before his promotion to abbot of Ottobeuren and bishop of Augsburg in the summer of 860.

[66] Notker, *GK* 2.21, p. 92; Dümmler, *GOR* 3:672; Jane Hyam, "Ermentrude and Richildis," in *Charles the Bald*, ed. Gibson and Nelson, 161–62.

[67] Grimalt Codex, 33; Raban, *Carmina*, no. 16, in MGH *Poetae Latini* 2:181: "casta virago nitet."

[68] Raban, *De institutione clericorum libri tres*, ed. Detlev Zimpel, Freiburger Beiträge zur mittelalterlichen Geschichte: Studien und Texte 7 (Frankfurt, 1996), 1.16–17, pp. 310–11.

Given the highly ascetic standards of Carolingian Christianity, it is unlikely that Emma could claim to be *sanctissima* without implying that she had taken a vow of chastity. Emma was at least in her mid-forties, and thus well beyond reproductive age, when Witgar first appeared as chancellor in 858. Carolingian women who survived infancy had a life expectancy of only about thirty-four to forty-one years, thus making the long-lived Emma somewhat unusual among queens.[69] According to the Carolingian Church, men and women were to have sex only within the bounds of marriage and only to produce children, "not just when feeling frisky" [non sit causa luxuriae].[70] In theory, therefore, a wife who lived beyond the age of fertility was to stop having sex with her husband, who in turn was not to have sex with anyone else. Of course, many aging couples must have ignored the Church's decrees in the privacy of their own bedchambers. Nevertheless, the fact that Emma publicly claimed to be "most holy" and closely associated herself with the Virgin Mary implies that she took a vow of chastity after she could no longer conceive. Such a vow would have complemented her position as lay proprietor of Obermünster, a convent that was dedicated to the Virgin Mary. The highly pious Louis also may have accepted this age-imposed sexual abstinence, since, unlike most Carolingian men, he is not known to have fathered any illegitimate children. The Witgar belt therefore points to the conclusion that Emma, and perhaps Louis as well, was living a quasi-monastic life of celibacy by the 850s, a situation that would have heightened the aura of Christian sanctity around the royal family.

[69] Dutton, "Beyond the Topos," 81–83, 93–94.

[70] *Episcoporum ad Hludowicum imperatorem relatio*, in MGH *Capitularia* 2:45–46; Georges Duby, *The Knight, the Lady, and the Priest: The Making of Modern Marriage in Medieval France*, trans. Barbara Bray (Chicago, 1993), 30–31.

A queenly gift. Queens often gave ornate belts as gifts to prominent figures at court, and Emma gave this liturgical belt to her husband's chancellor, Witgar. The inscription woven into it reads "Hanc zonam regina nitens sanctissima Hemma Witgario tribuit sacro spiramine plenum" (The shining and most holy Queen Emma gave this belt to Witgar, a man full of sacred breath). The belt, which Emma herself may have woven, is made of red silk embroidered with gold thread. Witgar served as Louis's chancellor during 858–60, and Louis appointed him abbott of Ottobeuren and bishop of Augsburg as a reward for his service. Diözesanmuseum St. Afra, Augsburg.

Louis had the good fortune to rule during a period of economic expansion in Europe. Although the late antique economy reached a nadir in the sixth century, beginning in the seventh there commenced a "long slow rise of the western European economies" that continued beyond the year 1000.[71] The economic resources of the Carolingians never came close to the lucrative taxation system of the Roman emperors. Nevertheless, a rising population, efficient estate management, active local markets, and growing long-distance trade provided the Carolingians with increasing sources of income.[72] Although they did not create it, Louis's predecessors had fostered this economic growth by introducing a new royal silver penny, the *denarius*, standardizing weights and measures, protecting merchants, and founding new markets.

Like all Frankish rulers, Louis's kingship depended on the accumulation and distribution of wealth from a wide range of sources: royal estates, tariffs on trade, taxes, and tribute. The general impression one gets from the evidence is that Louis's kingdom was not quantitatively poorer than the western and middle kingdoms.[73] Indeed, this was the whole point of the Treaty of Verdun—that the brothers make a "really fair division of the kingdom" that took into account all the royal economic resources.[74] The intensity of east Frankish economic activity varied significantly from region to region, however, and it is therefore more accurate to think of regional econom*ies* rather than a single, interconnected economy.

The king's chief source of income was his royal estates. Louis's lands were most dense in the two royal heartlands of his kingdom: Bavaria and the middle Rhine. A typical royal estate yielded a wide range of agricultural products and livestock (wheat, spelt, oats, pigs, hay, wood, and the like), while others generated more specialized goods, such as wine, fish, salt, and textiles.[75] The king could use these products in different ways. They could

[71] Georges Duby, *The Early Growth of the European Economy*, trans. Howard B. Clarke (Ithaca, 1974); Jean-Pierre Devroey, "The Economy," in *The Early Middle Ages: Europe, 400–1000*, ed. Rosamond McKitterick (Oxford, 2001), 97–129; McCormick, *Origins*.

[72] Riché, *Carolingians*, 312–24; Verhulst, "Economic Organization," 481–509; idem, *Carolingian Economy*.

[73] Reuter, *Germany*, 94–102; Verhulst, *Carolingian Economy*, 55–56, 77–79, 98–100, 105–7, 111–12.

[74] *AB*, s.a. 842, p. 43.

[75] A "typical" royal estate: *DLG* 155; vineyards: *DLG* 112, 123, and Regino, *Chronicon*, s.a. 842, p. 75; fisheries: *DLG* 117, 136; textile workshops (*gynaecea*): *DLG* 30; salt works: *DLG* 24, 36, 116.

be sent to the court to feed the royal entourage, kept at that estate to await the king's arrival, or sold at a local market on the king's behalf. There was considerable variation in the organization of labor on the king's estates. East of the Rhine, slaves traditionally worked aristocratic estates, while semi-free serfs rendered dues (but not services) to the lord's manor.[76] However, by the ninth century, the king, Church, and nobles increasingly imported the more oppressive Frankish bipartite demesne organization, in which serfs owed both dues and services. (It was largely in an effort to ward off Frankish land-lordship that the Saxon Stellinga had rebelled.) On the eastern frontiers, moreover, ethnic Slavs (perhaps captives from warfare) often made up the slave labor on royal and Church lands, and Louis's diplomas therefore sometimes substituted the ethnic term for Slav, *Sclavus*, for the classical term for slave, *mancipium*.[77] Three court officials—the seneschal, the wine stew-ard, and the constable—were responsible for ensuring that the court always had sufficient food, a job that must have been extremely complex.[78] Local officials known as judges managed the king's estates, and they had a reputa-tion for abusing their powers. Hincmar of Reims warned Louis to avoid the temptation of amassing "piles of gold and silver" by appointing greedy es-tate managers who oppressed the serfs, forced them into unaccustomed labor services, and imposed on them unjust exactions and fines.[79] Hincmar argued that Louis's court should be able to live off the produce of his own estates, so he did not have to exact food and supplies from his bishops, ab-bots, abbesses, counts, and nobles and thereby force them to oppress their own laborers. Whether the king could always do this is doubtful.

Louis's kingdom benefited from long-distance trade within and across its borders. Different regions of Louis's kingdom produced different local products. For example, at Reichenhall near Salzburg (literally, the "Salt Fortress") were valuable salt springs, while eastern Franconia produced pine trees, tree pitch, freshwater crabs, and fish.[80] Slavic traders traveled the mer-chant road through Thuringia and Franconia to the city of Mainz, where other merchants came by ship and land to sell grain.[81] Merchants who sailed

---

[76] Reuter, *Germany*, 98; Verhulst, "Economic Organization," 492–93; idem, *Carolin-gian Economy*, 55–56.

[77] *DLG* 8, 64, 80. These are the earliest recorded uses of the word *Slav* to mean "slave."

[78] Hincmar, *De ordine palatii*, chap. 5, pp. 74–76.

[79] MGH *Concilia* 3:422–23 (c. 14).

[80] Ermanrich, *Vita Sualonis*, chap. 4, pp. 214–17; Wolfram, *Grenzen und Räume*, 364–65.

[81] Egil, *Vita sancti Sturmi*, chap. 7, in MGH *SS* 2:369; Einhard, *Translatio et miracula sanctorum Marcellini et Petri*, 3.6, in MGH *SS* 15.1: 250.

the North and Baltic seas gathered in Hamburg on the lower Elbe to trade goods from Dorestad in Frisia, Hedeby in Denmark, and Birka in the Svear kingdom.[82] Imports into Louis's kingdom included brightly dyed Frisian cloaks and exotic luxury goods from the East, such as silks, ermine skins, cinnamon, and pepper.[83] Louis established trade agreements with neighboring "barbarian" rulers, and he collected the traditional royal tariff on salt from Reichenhall, ships coming to port at Worms, and merchants traveling along the Rhine between Strasbourg and the North Sea.[84] The *Inquiry on the Raffelstetten Tolls* reported the lucrative tolls (paid in salt) that Louis exacted on goods traded at royal markets along the Danube by Jews and other merchants. These goods included slaves, foodstuffs, horses, cows, wax, and, of course, salt.[85]

Another valuable source of royal income was tribute. The Danes and various Slavic peoples frequently brought Louis tribute (*censum, tributum, munera, annua dona*), according to the standard practice of Carolingian overlordship.[86] Unfortunately, no source reports the amount of ninth-century Slavic tribute payments, but it is possible to get a rough estimate by applying other known tribute amounts to the neighboring peoples listed in the *Catalogue of Fortresses and Regions to the North of the Danube*. This calculation suggests that Louis could demand some 335 pounds of silver annually from the Slavs and Danes.[87] The estimate seems reasonable since it is about the same tribute that the wealthy Lombard duchy of Benevento paid the

---

[82] Rimbert, *Vita Anskarii*, chap. 24, pp. 52–53.

[83] Notker, *GK* 1.34, 2.9, 2.17, 2.21, pp. 47, 63, 86–87, 92; *Collectio Sangallensis*, no. 29, in MGH *Formulae*, 415.

[84] *AF*, s.a. 873, pp. 78–79; *DLG* 24, 36, 89, 148. In general, see Ganshof, *Frankish Institutions*, 43–45.

[85] *Inquisitio de theloneis Raffelstettensis*, in MGH *Capitularia* 2:249–52.

[86] *AF*, s.a. 845, 848, 852, 856, 866, 870, 873, 874, 877, pp. 35, 37, 42, 47, 65, 72, 78–79, 83, 89; *AX*, s.a. 845, p. 14; Notker, *GK* 2.18, pp. 88–89.

[87] The *AB*, s.a. 865, p. 113, stated that the traditional annual tribute of the Bretons (a relatively large and powerful people) was fifty pounds of silver. Widukind, 3.68, p. 170, reported that the Saxons fined a rebel *dux* of the Wagres (a small Slavic people) fifteen pounds of silver—perhaps as much as an annual tribute payment. According to the *Fourth Book of the Chronicle of Fredegar with Its Continuations*, ed. J. M. Wallace-Hadrill (London, 1960), chap. 74, p. 63, the Saxons paid the Merovingian kings five hundred cows (worth about 7,000 *denarii* or 30 pounds of silver). These reports suggest a range of 15–50 pounds of silver for annual tribute payments. On the basis of these amounts, one can tentatively assign probable tribute payments to Louis's neighbors as reported in the *Descriptio civitatum*: 50 pounds of silver from the most powerful peoples (the Danes, Bohemians, and Moravians), 15 from the smaller peoples (Wilzes, Linones, Bethenics, Smeldings, Morizans, Hevelles, Siusles, Dalaminzes, and Merehans), and 25 from those somewhere in between (Obodrites and Sorbs). This suggests that Louis could demand approximately 335 pounds of silver annually.

Franks.[88] Of course, frequent rebellions made it likely that Louis often received only half the owed tribute in a given year. Nevertheless, the estimate still suggests an annual income of some 170 pounds of silver. To put the sum in perspective, this amount was enough wealth for the king to reward sixty-eight young noblemen with a complete set of military equipment—a horse, coat of armor, helmet, sword, shield, and spear—every year.[89] While the calculation is only an approximation, it gives a sense of the important contribution of foreign tribute to Louis's economic resources. Louis therefore had economic as well as political and ideological motives for pursuing his policy of tributary overlordship in the east.

In one category—coinage—the east Frankish economy was significantly less developed than that in the west. Although Gaul and Italy had maintained active money economies since antiquity, the use of coinage in Germania was limited mainly to the territories along the Rhine and Danube, which served as arteries of waterborne trade.[90] Elsewhere in the less Romanized regions of Saxony, Thuringia, and eastern Franconia, the economy seems to have been essentially nonmonetary and based on barter. According to the evidence of single coin finds, the circulation of Carolingian silver pennies along the Rhine and Danube peaked in the second quarter of the ninth century, slowly declined in the third quarter, and then significantly fell off after Louis's death during the last quarter.[91] The pattern of minting in the east likewise suggests a slowing monetary economy during the ninth century. Although Louis the Pious had mints at Mainz, Strasbourg, Regensburg, and three additional, unidentified locations, Louis the German minted silver pennies only at Mainz and two unidentified places.[92]

Several concurrent factors probably caused this decline in coin minting and circulation in Germania during Louis's reign. The increased Viking activity around the North Sea and on the Continent in general hindered long-distance trade and the peaceful circulation of coinage. Moreover, the 843 division may have discouraged the movement of merchants and coins from coin-rich Gaul to the coin-poor Germania. Perhaps most significant, the previously thriving market (*emporium*) of Dorestad at the mouth of the Rhine declined dramatically during the 840s and 850s, the long-term con-

[88] The Beneventans paid 7,000 gold *solidi* annually, equivalent to 350 pounds of silver: *ARF*, s.a. 814, p. 141.
[89] For the values of military equipment, see Riché, *Daily Life*, 119.
[90] Blackburn, "Money and Coinage," 551–55.
[91] Mark Blackburn, "Coin Circulation in Germany during the Early Middle Ages: The Evidence of Single-Finds," in *Fernhandel und Geldwirtschaft*, ed. Bernd Kluge (Sigmaringen, 1993), 37–54.
[92] Karl F. Morrison, *Carolingian Coinage* (New York, 1967), 172 (nos. 594–96).

sequence of the gradual silting of the Rhine, which made access to Dorestad by ship impossible.[93] As a result, trade in northern Francia and the North Sea after about 850 shifted farther west to the *emporium* of Quentovic on the English Channel, a development that resulted in fewer coins traveling up the Rhine into Germania. None of these factors was within Louis's control, but together they had an adverse impact on his kingdom's monetary economy.

Nevertheless, the apparent backwardness of the east Frankish monetary economy as suggested by coin finds is probably exaggerated. Although many hoards of Charles the Bald's coins have been found in modern times, not a single one has been unearthed from Louis's kingdom. The reason for this discrepancy is that Charles's kingdom suffered from disruptive Viking raids, forcing Charles's subjects to bury their wealth in times of invasion. In contrast, Louis's kingdom was largely free from foreign invasions, enabling his subjects to keep their wealth above ground. Also, because Louis's successors periodically recalled old coinage, melted it down, and reminted it, over time most of Louis's coins would have been destroyed. Yet the handful of Louis's silver pennies that have been found show that he maintained the style and weight of his predecessors. Louis's *denarii* from Mainz, which have his monogram on one side and the city's name on the other, weigh 1.67 grams—the weight set by Charlemagne.[94]

Whether Louis taxed his subjects directly is a crucial question, since taxation is a good barometer of the extent and intrusiveness of medieval government. By the ninth century, there were few if any remnants of Roman taxation in western Europe, yet the Carolingians were able to create new forms of taxation.[95] Charles the Bald, for example, raised huge levies on his kingdom to pay off Viking raiders on numerous occasions. Although Louis luckily was never forced to do this, he had other forms of taxation at his disposal. By the ninth century, the Carolingians imposed a general annual tax in the eastern territories of the empire—a tax known as the *osterstufa*, "eastern levy."[96] It appears that all freemen in Germania paid the annual *osterstufa* to the king, either in local goods, such as honey or fur pelts, or in coin, and that the counts were responsible for raising this annual tax and turning it

[93] Simon Coupland, "Trading Places: Quentovic and Dorestad Reassessed," *EME* 22 (2002): 209–32.

[94] Morrison, *Carolingian Coinage*, 88–89, 124–25, 172 (nos. 90–93, 321, 594–596).

[95] Chris Wickham, "The Fall of Rome Will Not Take Place," in *Debating the Middle Ages: Issues and Readings*, ed. Lester K. Little and Barbara H. Rosenwein (Oxford, 1998), 45–57. Wickham critiques Jean Durliat's argument for continuity in taxation between the late Roman and Carolingian empires: Jean Durliat, *Les finances publiques de Dioclétien aux Carolingiens (284–888)*, Beihefte der Francia 21 (Sigmaringen, 1990).

[96] Innes, *State and Society*, 156–59.

over to the king.[97] Although the origin of the tax is unclear, it may have evolved out of tribute payments the Merovingians had imposed on the eastern peoples during the sixth and seventh centuries. By the Carolingian period, this eastern tribute had become a new form of royal taxation. The historically peripheral nature of Louis's territories therefore placed a unique form of general taxation at his disposal.

The *osterstufa* was not the only tax Louis raised. On at least one occasion, he exacted a tax of one *denarius* from every homestead belonging to the royal fisc (*regales possessiones*)—that is, lands used directly by the king as well as benefices held by the king's men—to help Christians in the Holy Land.[98] Some reports state that Louis imposed this tax not only on royal properties but also on every homestead in his kingdom.[99] Although it is uncertain which report is accurate, either way the tax must have fallen on hundreds, if not thousands, of homesteads. Such an undertaking would have required considerable organization and record keeping on the part of royal officials. Moreover, because the tax was to be sent to the Holy Land, it must have been raised in coin rather than goods, thereby stimulating the eastern monetary economy by forcing those who owed the tax to obtain coins to pay it. Louis's Holy Land tax suggests his emulation of his grandfather, since Charlemagne had sent gifts to Christians in the Holy Land before his imperial coronation in 800.[100] Taken together, the *osterstufa* and Holy Land tax demonstrate that Louis had forms of taxation at his disposal and was able to create new forms as well. Although this system of taxation did not rival that of the Roman emperors, it undoubtedly made a significant contribution to Louis's coffers.

ROYAL GOVERNMENT

Carolingian Europe was a dangerous place. Even when there was no civil war, local violence was common: aristocratic feuds, lordly abuse of peasants,

---

[97] Thus in a diploma dated 839, Louis the Pious referred to the "portion of the tax or tribute paid to us annually from Alemannia from the Eritgau hundred under the supervision of Count Conrad": *WUB* 1, no. 102.

[98] Notker, *GK* 2.9, p. 65. Concerning this report, see Michael Borgolte, *Der Gesandtenaustausch der Karolinger mit den Abbasiden und mit den Patriarchen von Jerusalem* (Munich, 1976), 136–37.

[99] Notker, *GK* 2.9, p. 65, textual n. u: "de singulis hobis vel mansis possessionum legalium."

[100] *ARF*, s.a. 800, p. 110.

the abduction of women, banditry, border raids, and the like.[101] In the sobering words of Chris Wickham, "it is an abiding impression left by all early medieval documentation that people behaved, or could behave, dreadfully to each other." Louis's kingdom was no exception. Raban complained of bands of violent laymen who wandered throughout the eastern cities and provinces and spent their time carousing and causing trouble.[102] Private feuds left men blind, maimed, and crippled, forcing them to turn to the shrines of saints in the desperate hope of miraculous healing.[103] Churchmen too were sometimes guilty of homicide and manslaughter.[104] In addition to violence, one had to fear aristocratic corruption. Nobles took bribes, perverted justice, forced poor freemen into servitude, usurped estates belonging to the crown and Church, and skimmed the profits of royal government. The Carolingians frequently legislated against such abuses, although it is doubtful that these decrees had any real impact. And no legislation could protect travelers from the ravenous wolves that prowled the dark forests of Germania.[105]

Like all of Carolingian Europe, Louis's kingdom was dramatically undergoverned. Carolingian kingship was not autocratic but rather "supervisory." The king depended on the support and cooperation of the nobles to govern his far-flung territories, and he intervened in local politics only sporadically. Except in rare cases like that of the Saxon Ebbo, nobles had a virtual monopoly on the most powerful political and ecclesiastical offices. For most of Louis's non-noble subjects, the ruler they knew was the local lord: the bishop, abbot, count, or nobleman whose lands they worked, in whose military contingent they served, and in whose church they worshiped. From a modern perspective, the institutions of Carolingian government at the king's disposal were limited. The king had only a rudimentary court administration and literate bureaucracy, and the annual assembly provided the chief institution of royal government. Ultimately, the king's power depended on his constant leadership in politics, diplomacy, and warfare. If he fell ill or died, his kingdom could quickly fall apart.

Despite these daunting obstacles, the Carolingians did not abandon the Roman concept of a *res publica* or "state."[106] Although the Frankish kingdoms were fragile polities, the Carolingian kings used the ideology of the

---

[101] Wickham, "Rural Society," 533–35; Halsall, *Violence and Society.*
[102] MGH *Concilia* 3:171–73 (cc. 20, 22, 23).
[103] Meginhard, *Translatio sancti Alexandri*, chaps. 6, 11, 14, in MGH SS 2:679–81.
[104] Wolfram, *Grenzen und Räume*, 228.
[105] *AF*, s.a. 850, p. 41.
[106] Janet L. Nelson, "Kingship and Empire," in Burns, *Cambridge History of Political Thought*, 225; Susan Reynolds, "The Historiography of the Medieval State," in *Companion to Historiography*, ed. Michael Bentley (London, 1997), 117–38.

state to bolster their power. Having grown up during the heyday of the Carolingian empire, Louis had a strong belief in the public authority of the king and royal government. Although the noble families of his territories had dominated the bishoprics, monasteries, and counties for centuries, Louis insisted that all these offices were "public," belonging to the state, and that he had the royal prerogative to distribute and revoke them as he wished.[107] Looking back over the ninth century, Regino was especially impressed with Louis's "sober discretion in the giving and revoking of public offices."[108] In moments of political crisis and rebellion, Louis repeatedly punished his opponents by revoking their "public honors," benefices, and even personal property—that is, lands that had never belonged to the crown.[109] Louis's diplomas equated his kingdom with the *res publica* and spoke of the state's agents and public roads.[110] The east Frankish bishops and abbots, who understood Roman concepts of public power from reading authors such as Caesar, Virgil, Tacitus, Sallust, and Vegetius, threw their weight behind this classical concept of the state. The 847 Mainz synod decreed that anyone who formed a sworn association or conspiracy "against the king, ecclesiastical authorities, or the powers of the state established in any way by legitimate arrangement" was to be excommunicated and, if he failed to perform penance, exiled.[111] A Church council at Worms two decades later similarly ordained that any layman who broke faith with the king or "defected to foreign lands in opposition to his own people, the homeland, or the royal power" was to be stripped of all his personal property and excommunicated.[112] In the 860 Treaty of Koblenz, Louis and his brother instinctively equated royal power with the power of the state (*regia vel rei publicae potestas*).[113] Thus, while Louis's government in practice often fell short of a centralized state, he and his ecclesiastical advisers asserted that a state existed nevertheless.

To strengthen his kingship, Louis imported and intensified the entire range of Carolingian government east of the Rhine. The heart of Louis's government was the royal court, a dynamic institution that included the royal family, its servants, the officials and counselors in the royal entourage, and the various nobles who constantly visited his palace. The most impor-

---

[107] Notker, *Continuatio*, 329; *Adonis Continuatio*, 324–25.
[108] Regino, *Chronicon*, s.a. 876, p. 110.
[109] Notker, *GK* 2.11, p. 68.
[110] For example, see *DLG* 13, 22, 25, 70, 148.
[111] MGH *Concilia* 3:165 (c. 5).
[112] Ibid., 4:278 (c. 36).
[113] *Conventus apud Confluentes*, chap. 6, in MGH *Capitularia* 2:155–56.

tant secular official at court was the count of the palace, who, "among his other innumerable duties," heard all judicial appeals to the king.[114] Whereas Louis's early counts of the palace, Timo (ca. 830–37), Morhard (ca. 833), and Fritilo (ca. 837–53), were Bavarians, Rodolt (ca. 854–57) was an Alemannian count, and Erlwin (ca. 865–76) hailed from the middle Rhine—a progression that reflects the transition of Louis's kingship from Bavarian to east Frankish.[115] Numerous other officials and servants around Louis's court included cupbearers, stewards, foresters, deputies, vassals, servants, messengers, and doctors.[116]

An important part of the king's administration was the court chapel, which consisted of the churchmen—known as chaplains—in the king's entourage.[117] The chaplains performed Mass for the king, cared for the relics, books, and liturgical equipment at court, and in general served the king and his family. While at the beginning of his reign Louis's chaplains were mostly Bavarians, over time they came from noble families in Alemannia, Franconia, and, during the last years of his reign, Saxony.[118] An influential archchaplain supervised the court chapel and its chaplains, headed the court school for young noblemen, and in general acted as one of the king's chief counselors.[119] The succession of Louis's archchaplains once again reflected the expansion of his eastern kingship: Gozbald of Niederalteich (served 830–33), Baturich of Regensburg (833–48), Grimald of St.-Gall (848–70), and Liutbert of Mainz (870–76). Baturich's pontifical and the Grimalt Codex contain acclamations and blessings for Louis, underscoring the important role played by the archchaplain in orchestrating royal ceremonies.[120] For some chaplains, service at court was the stepping stone to a career in the Church. Baturich of Regensburg's nephew Erchanfrid, for ex-

---

[114] Hincmar, De ordine palatii, chap. 5, pp. 70–72.

[115] Timo and his son Fritilo II were related to the Bavarian Huosi dynasty, and they appeared repeatedly at court between about 830 and about 853: Carmen de Timone comite, in MGH Poetae Latini 2:120–24; Freising 603, 661; Regensburg 29; DLG 46, 66; Mitterauer, Karolingische Markgrafen, 169–75; Brunner, Oppositionelle Gruppen, 121–22. Morhard appeared as Louis's count of the palace and missus in 833: Thegan, GH, chap. 45, p. 238. Ruadolt was the count of Alaholfsbaar: Borgolte, Grafen, 225; DLG 69; AF, s.a. 857, p. 47. Erlwin was Louis's missus dominicus at Lorsch in 865 and count of the palace at Ingelheim in 876: DLG 117, 170; Innes, State and Society, 226 and n. 20.

[116] DLG 30, 88, 96, 152; Freising 661, 913; Regensburg 45; AF, s.a. 869, p. 69.

[117] For the origins of the Carolingian royal chapel and its organization under Louis, see Fleckenstein, Hofkapelle 1:1–42, 165–85; Bigott, Ludwig der Deutsche, 162–67.

[118] Fleckenstein, Hofkapelle 1:178–85.

[119] Thegan, GH, chap. 47, p. 240; Ermanrich, Epistola ad Grimaldum abbatem, in MGH Epistolae 5:553, 561; St.-Gall, suppl. 21.

[120] Clm 14510, fols. 1–75; Grimalt Codex.

ample, served as a chaplain in the early 830s, succeeded his uncle as bishop (848–64), and became Louis's close counselor.[121] At least seven other bishops served previously in Louis's chapel: Liupram of Salzburg (836–59), Gozbald of Würzburg (842–55), Witgar of Augsburg (860–87), Ermanrich of Passau (866–ca. 874), Adelhelm of Worms (ca. 872), Theotmar of Salzburg (874–907), and Wigbert of Verden (ca. 874).[122] In this way the royal chapel acted as a pool for future bishops and a testing ground for their talent and loyalty to the king.

The court was a center of literacy, record keeping, and written administration. Under Charlemagne, the role of writing in royal government increased dramatically.[123] The nature of Latin literacy in Frankish society was complex: it complemented the spoken word, served as a memory aid, and had an important symbolic value as a badge of education and status.[124] Louis's subjects had lower levels of Latin literacy than did their contemporaries in Italy and Gaul, since it was more difficult for Germanic than for Romance speakers to learn Latin. This helps explain the notable absence of surviving royal legislation (capitularies) from Louis's reign: since counts and other secular officials were less literate than their counterparts in Gaul and Italy, capitularies were of less use as memory aids. (It was the king's spoken word, not the written record of it, that carried the force of law.) Thus an east Frankish scribe instinctively juxtaposed laymen with "priests and other literate people" [presbiteri atque alii litterati].[125] It was for this reason that Louis and Raban urged translations of Scripture and other Christian texts into the vernacular: so the *illitterati* could understand them. The references to vernacular oaths like those at Strasbourg, as well as the occasional slippage from Latin into Frankish in Louis's diplomas, indicate that Frankish was the chief language spoken at the east Frankish court.[126]

Yet the vernacular and oral nature of east Frankish government should not be pushed too far. Louis himself was highly literate, and he made sure that his sons (and presumably his daughters) received an education and learned how to read and even write.[127] Queen Emma apparently prided her-

---

[121] *DLG* 6, 46, 64, 66, 101. For other chaplains to whom Louis made lesser grants, see *DLG* 49, 82, 83, 87, 165.

[122] Fleckenstein, *Hofkapelle* 1:184–85 and n. 133. Three other chaplains received small benefices: *DLG* 49, 81, 165.

[123] Ganshof, *Frankish Institutions*, 53–55.

[124] In general, see McKitterick, *Carolingians and the Written Word*; Nelson, "Literacy in Carolingian Government," 2–36.

[125] *DLG* 66.

[126] *DLG* 24, 25, 36, 122.

[127] Regino, *Chronicon*, s.a. 880, p. 116, described Carloman as "litteris eruditus," while the *AF*, s.a. 879, p. 93, indicate that Carloman was able to write when he lost the use of his voice.

self on her Latin literacy—so much so that no one dared point out a minor grammatical error embroidered into the belt she gave Witgar![128] Some lay officials undoubtedly could read Latin, or at least they had clerics at their disposal who could read, translate, and write for them. For example, Louis's royal envoy Iring owned a copy of Isidore of Seville's commentary on Genesis, while the Bavarian count Rodold had his own chancellor.[129] The numerous east Frankish charter collections recording pious grants to monasteries like St.-Emmeram, St.-Gall, Freising, Lorsch, and Fulda clearly demonstrate that bishops and abbots—themselves royal officials—placed a high premium on administrative record keeping. Thus, when fires destroyed the "arsenal of charters" belonging to the monastery of Klingenmünster and bishopric of Strasbourg, Louis issued diplomas confirming their properties.[130] Although many laymen and laywomen technically may have been illiterate, attending Mass and making pious donations to monasteries enabled them to participate in the Church's culture of literacy.[131]

Like his predecessors, Louis had a court chancery staffed by notaries to produce the written documents he regularly required. The chancery did not constitute a formal institution but rather a loose group of notaries within the royal chapel. An official called the high chancellor (*chancellarius summus*) supervised the royal notaries. Louis's high chancellors were Grimald of St.-Gall (served 833–ca. 840, 854–ca. 857, 861–70), Ratleig of Seligenstadt (ca. 840–54), Witgar (858–60), and Liutbert of Mainz (870–76). Although subordinate to the archchaplain (the two offices were united under Grimald and Liutbert), the high chancellor was an important figure at court, assisted in the court school, and taught scribes to draw up official documents.[132] Unfortunately, fewer governmental documents survive from Louis's court than from those of his brothers, father, and grandfather, in part probably because the early medieval archives do not survive for many east Frankish bishoprics, such as Augsburg, Cologne, Mainz, Worms, and Freising. Nevertheless, the documents that do survive (or those that are mentioned in other sources) reveal that Louis's administration produced written records for the standard range of governmental purposes: diplomatic missives, let-

[128] The dedication reads "Witgario . . . sacro spirimine plenum" instead of "Witgario . . . sacro spirimine pleno."

[129] Iring's Isidore manuscript: Clm 14288. A notice on folio 1r reports: "volumen expositionis in genesis Isidori quod hiringus baturico epo. dedit." Although this manuscript clearly had symbolic prestige value for Iring, this does not preclude the possibility that he could read it (or have it read to him). For Rodold's *cancellarius comitis*, see *Regensburg* 74, 75.

[130] *DLG* 55, 149.

[131] McKitterick, *Carolingians and the Written Word*, 77–134.

[132] Raban, *Epitaphium Ratlaici presbyteri*, in MGH *Poetae Latini* 2:240–41.

ters concerning military service, writs to regional counts, reports from his generals on campaign, records of judicial proceedings, lists of neighboring Slavic peoples, a succession plan for his sons, a detailed inventory of royal resources, and some 170 surviving royal diplomas.[133]

Ratpert's *Misfortunes of St.-Gall* illustrates the complex uses of writing in east Frankish government and society. Ratpert's work was a partisan account of how his monastery won independence from the nearby bishopric of Constance, the kind of local power struggle that was common throughout the Carolingian world. Although Pippin III and Charlemagne had granted St.-Gall immunity and royal protection, the bishops of Constance treated the monastery as a dependency of their bishopric.[134] Finally, Grimald of St.-Gall and Solomon of Constance worked out a compromise: the bishop would abandon all claims over St.-Gall, and in return Grimald would give Constance several of St.-Gall's estates. When Louis held an assembly at Ulm in 854, Grimald and Solomon presented their prearranged settlement to the king and nobles. Louis agreed with the terms, ended the dispute, and ordered diplomas to be drawn up:

> The clement king settled these matters with full consensus. The king then ordered that an official diploma be drawn up immediately in his presence for each party for the perpetual confirmation of this agreement. So that this binding written document would remain unchallenged, he first ordered that only the text containing the specific details [dictata] be written on a scratch piece of parchment [in aliqua scaeda] and presented to him. After he had approved it, he ordered the chancellor [i.e., Grimald] to write out the confirmation of the above agreement on official diplomas [in legitimis cartis]. When they had been written out, he confirmed them with the authentication sign of his own hand and gave one to the bishop and his followers and the other to the abbot and the monks, to be preserved as evidence of perpetual surety, never to be overturned.[135]

[133] *Formulae Augienses*, no. 7, in MGH *Formulae*, 367–68 (diplomatic missives); *Collectio Pataviensis*, no. 3, in MGH *Formulae*, 457–58 (royal letter concerning military service); *DLG* 66 (records of judicial proceedings), 71 (writ to counts), 170 (records of judicial proceedings); *St.-Gall*, suppl. 21 (report of judicial proceedings); *AF*, s.a. 869, p. 67 (letter to king from son on campaign); *Descriptio civitatum* (catalogue of Slavic peoples); *AB*, s.a. 842, p. 43 (*descriptio* of royal resources); *Adonis Continuatio*, 324–25 (*testamentum*); Nithard, 4.5, p. 47 (*descriptio* of royal resources).

[134] Ratpert, *Casus sancti Galli*, chaps. 3–6, pp. 160–84; Theodor Mayer, "Konstanz und St.-Gallen in der Frühzeit," *Schweizerische Zeitschrift für Geschichte* 2.4 (1952): 473–524.

[135] Ratpert, *Casus sancti Galli*, chap. 8, pp. 198–202. The St.-Gall diploma survives, but not that of Constance: *DLG* 69.

Louis then issued another diploma confirming St.-Gall's immunity, royal protection, and free abbatial elections.[136]

As Ratpert's report illustrates, the drawing up of a diploma was a highly ritualized act.[137] Louis first officially settled the dispute by discussing it with his magnates, building a consensus, and making a formal proclamation accompanied by symbolic hand gestures: "He lawfully gave with his own hand the above-mentioned possessions to the bishopric, and likewise he lawfully divided and fully separated with his own hand the monastery from the bishopric."[138] Only then did he order a written record as future proof of his decision. In the process, he publicly displayed his literacy by reading through a preliminary draft, and he then authenticated the diploma by signing his royal monogram.[139] The resulting diploma was a sacred symbol of royal power, an "emblem of majesty." Like those drawn up under his predecessors, Louis's diplomas were written on large pieces of parchment in a dignified, half-cursive chancery script with elongated letters and flourishes, and they were authenticated by the king's monogram and seal. Several years after the Ulm assembly, moreover, Louis's chancellor, Eberhard, modified the traditional Carolingian diploma format to heighten the visual, symbolic, and theocratic elements of Louis's diplomas.[140] Eberhard abandoned the half-cursive chancery script for a new "diplomatic minuscule"; he made more decorative the *chi-rho* monogram at the beginning and the authentication symbols (the king's monogram, the notary's countersign, and the royal seal), dating clause, and "amen" at the end; and he clarified the overall layout of the text. In this way, diplomas functioned as solemn statements about the king's munificence, literacy, and God-given royal authority.

At the same time, Ratpert's account reveals the important practical functions of writing in the conduct of royal government, record keeping, and law. Ratpert reported that the bishops of Constance had earlier seized St.-Gall's diplomas, burned one of them, and tried to replace the other with a forgery, indicating that royal diplomas had real legal force.[141] Louis's proofreading of the draft was not merely a public display of royal literacy: the diploma, which still survives today in the archive at St.-Gall, contains a de-

---

[136] *DLG* 70.

[137] Hagen Keller, "Zu den Siegeln der Karolinger und Ottonen: Urkunden als 'Hoheitszeichen' in der Kommunikation des Königs mit seinen Getreuen," *FS* 32 (1998): 400–441, esp. pp. 431, 435.

[138] Ratpert, *Casus sancti Galli*, chap. 8, p. 198.

[139] Louis seems to have been in the habit of reading preliminary drafts before ordering his scribes to draw up a formal diploma: *DLG* 88.

[140] Kehr's introduction to Louis's diplomas, *DLG* xxiv–xxvii; Keller, "Zu den Siegeln," 413–15; Brousseau, "Urkunden Ludwigs des Deutschen," 116–19.

[141] Ratpert, *Casus sancti Galli*, chaps. 2–6, pp. 156–84.

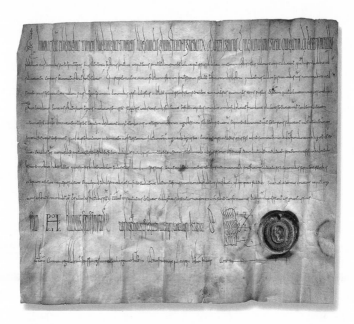

A diploma of Louis the German. This photograph shows the modified diploma style introduced by Louis's chancellor, Eberhard (859–74). Eberhard clarified the overall layout of Louis's diplomas and heightened their visual and symbolic elements, such as the *chi-rho* at the beginning and the king's monogram and seal at the end. This diploma, dated May 1, 859, records Louis's grant of the fiscal lands at Tulln, which he had revoked from Prefect Ratpot for his infidelity, to the monastery of St.-Emmeram. Munich, Bayerisches Hauptstaatsarchiv, Regensburg–St. Emmeram Urk. 10. Photograph courtesy of the Lichtbildarchiv, Marburg.

tailed description of the estates given to Constance (their names, buildings, appurtenances, serfs, and locations), and Louis wanted to get all the specifics right. Moreover, Ratpert failed to mention that Louis sent another, different kind of written document to the Alemannian counts, informing them of St.-Gall's newly confirmed legal immunity and royal protection. Unlike a long diploma, this was a short royal writ, drawn up on a small piece of parchment in a simple minuscule script without a cumbersome seal. It read:

> In the name of the holy and indivisible Trinity. Louis, king by the favor of Divine Grace, sends greetings in the lord Savior to Hatto, Odalrich, and our other counts living in Alemannia. Your industry should know that Grimald and our other faithful men informed us that the monastery of Saint Gall, the confessor of Christ, does not now have the legal privileges [i.e., immunity and royal protection] in certain cases in your courts that our other monasteries and benefices have. We want this

King in East Francia

henceforth to be corrected and for that monastery to have the legal privileges that our other monasteries and benefices have. This is to say that, when necessary, its matters should be investigated with an oath, because we want to have the same power and lordship over that monastery that we have over our other monasteries and benefices. If someone should presume to contradict our decree and command, send him to our presence so he can explain to us why he opposes our commands. Carry out our command if you want to have our grace.[142]

Such businesslike royal writs probably were commonplace in Louis's administration. Indeed, it is likely that writs significantly outnumbered the formal diplomas issued by the king's court. However, very few Carolingian writs survive today, since, unlike diplomas, they did not convey legal rights or privileges, and thus there was little reason to preserve them after the king's command had been carried out.[143] Taken together, the writ and diploma embody the complementary uses of literacy and the written word—the administrative and the ceremonial, the practical and the symbolic—in east Frankish government.

While the court was the heart and brain of royal government, the provinces made up the body. Louis organized the administration of his kingdom according to the five main eastern *regna*: Bavaria, Alemannia, Franconia, Thuringia, and Saxony. Louis divided his armies by *regnum*, and he addressed royal commands to the counts of a given province.[144] There were ethnic components to the eastern provinces, since their inhabitants spoke different Germanic dialects and had their own written law codes and distinctive social and legal customs. But it was Carolingian administrative and military organization more than any archaic "tribal" consciousness that gave coherence to the eastern provinces. By the ninth century, most of the leading families of the eastern *regna* considered themselves Franks, either because they were Frankish transplants to the east or because their ancestors had married into Frankish families.[145] Thus, while the provinces of Germania had emerged as ethnic communities in late antiquity, it was Carolingian government and administration that transformed them into coherent and enduring political units.

Within the east Frankish *regna*, the holders of public offices—counties,

---

[142] *DLG* 71.

[143] The only other surviving example is *DLG* 146, which likewise was preserved at St.-Gall.

[144] For example, see *AF*, s.a. 849, 857, pp. 38, 47; *DLG* 71, 72.

[145] For this pan-Frankish identity of all the nobles north of the Alps, see Notker, *GK* 1.10, p. 13.

A royal writ. In this writ, which probably dates to 854, Louis the German informed the counts in Alemannia of St.-Gall's immunity and royal protection. Its humble appearance provides a stark contrast to the grand style of royal diplomas. It is written on a small piece of parchment in a minuscule script, and it does not contain the formal elements of a diploma, such as the *chi-rho* at the beginning or the monogram, seal, and dating clause at the end. Such writs to local officials were probably common in Louis the German's administration. However, very few survive, since, unlike diplomas, they did not convey legal rights or privileges. Stiftsarchiv St. Gallen, Urk. A4 A5a.

bishoprics, monasteries, and royal benefices—acted as the king's local representatives. Of these, the most important lay official was the count (*comes*), literally, the king's "companion."[146] There seems to have been more than a hundred counts in the east Frankish kingdom, each supervising one or several counties. West of the Rhine, counties typically corresponded to the late Roman *pagus* (a city and its surrounding district). In contrast, the county system was far more messy in the less urbanized east. Eastern counties tended to be uneven, less systematized, sometimes scattered over several districts (*gaus*), and/or found only around royal estates.[147] Within his county, the count was responsible for keeping the peace, supervising royal estates, collecting taxes, enforcing justice in the local court of law (the *mal-*

[146] Concerning counts, see Ganshof, *Frankish Institutions*, 26–34; and the important reconsideration of Innes, *State and Society*, 118–24. Ganshof, *Frankish Institutions*, 28, estimates that there were approximately 400 Carolingian counts north of the Alps.

[147] Michael Borgolte, *Geschichte der Grafschaften Alamanniens in fränkischer Zeit* (Sigmaringen, 1984), esp. 245–58, makes this point for the case of Alemannia. He distinguished between two main types of Alemannian countships: "office-counties" (*Amtsgrafschaften*), which were independent of royal estates and thus more coherent and regular, found especially west of the Black Forest and south of Lake Constance; and "fiscal-counties" (*Königsgutgrafschaften*), which were found only around royal estates and thus more scattered, found especially north and east of Lake Constance.

lus), maintaining public roads and bridges, and mustering the local troops for the army. In frontier regions like the Bavarian marches, Thuringia, and eastern Saxony, moreover, there were the "super counts," known as dukes and prefects, who acted as standing military commanders for the defense of the kingdom and exercised authority over subordinate counts. The king did not pay these counts for their duties but rather gave them benefices in their counties and allowed them to keep one-third of all the fines and tolls they collected. The frequent admonitions in capitularies that counts not oppress the poor and accept bribes in court indicate that they often used the authority bestowed on them by the crown to further their own local power.

Throughout his reign, Louis vigorously defended his right to appoint and revoke counties, thereby motivating his counts to serve him loyally. Louis often promoted laymen with local ties to vacant counties, thereby harnessing their preexisting power and prestige for the benefit of the crown. However, Louis sometimes played off local rivalries by transferring counties from one regional family to another or by imposing outsiders, thereby periodically reinforcing his control of those offices. A good example of both happening simultaneously was the rise of the Udalrichings of Alemannia in the 850s and early 860s. During those years, Louis revoked the Alemannian counties of the Welfs and bestowed them on Count Udalrich, a member of the Udalrichings.[148] At the same time, several other Udalrichs appeared as counts in western Bavaria and Upper Pannonia, presumably through Louis's promotion.[149] Thus, while a Carolingian king like Louis had to rely on powerful noblemen to act as his counts, he had considerable leverage in his ability to select which nobles in particular would receive (or lose) counties. The king's ability to exploit local aristocratic rivalries in granting and revoking counties was one of his chief tools for keeping counts loyal.

The Church was a central pillar of east Frankish government. After Louis's reconciliation with the Church in 847, the east Frankish bishops and abbots acted as royal officials and local representatives of the crown alongside the counts. Louis jealously controlled the appointment of ecclesiastical prelates within his kingdom. He usually permitted technically "free" elections of bishops and abbots by the local clergy or monks, according to canon law, but it appears that he often influenced those elections by making known his royal will to the local clergy and giving them little choice in whom they elected.[150] On some occasions he ran roughshod over canon law and simply

[148] Borgolte, *Grafen*, 255–66. Borgolte designates this count as "Udalrich IV," while another Udalrich (designated as "III") appeared as count in the Alemannian Thurgau and Alaholfsbaar.

[149] *Freising* 745; *DLG* 101, 102.

[150] Bigott, *Ludwig der Deutsche*, 202–42.

installed his own candidates. For example, when Raban of Mainz died in 856, Louis designated his nephew, Charles of Aquitaine, as the next archbishop, "more by the wish of the king and his counselors than by the consent and election of the clergy and people."[151] To ensure that Church offices remained in his control, Louis took a firm line against noble families that tried to "privatize" their control of bishoprics and monasteries. He broke up "episcopal dynasties" that had monopolized bishoprics (such as Otgar's family, the Otachars, at Mainz), and in contrast to Charles the Bald, he refused to bestow monasteries on laymen.[152] On several occasions, moreover, Louis deposed abbots for disloyalty, as happened to Raban during the civil war.[153] However, he apparently never dethroned a bishop, perhaps because he wanted to avoid clashes with Rome, since the pope would have come to the bishop's defense.

Louis demanded that all newly elected bishops and abbots come to his court so he could approve (or reject) their election and formally bestow on them their new offices and lordships (that is, their benefices and jurisdictional rights). For example, when Rimbert was elected archbishop of Hamburg-Bremen in 865, he made the long journey to Louis's palace, with Bishop Theoderich of Minden and Abbot Adalgar of Corvey as his escort. Upon arrival, Rimbert "was received honorably by the king and given his episcopal lordship through the commendation of the bishop's staff according to custom."[154] Here one sees the Carolingian origins of lay investiture, the king's bestowing of ecclesiastical offices and lordships through the symbolic handing over of a staff. Although popes and emperors were to clash bitterly over lay investiture in the eleventh century, in the ninth it was taken as a given, since the Carolingians claimed to be the divinely appointed defenders of the Church. While bishops and abbots sometimes may have had

---

[151] *AF*, s.a. 856, pp. 46–47. Other examples of Louis installing his own candidates include Bishops Hemmo of Halberstadt, Ebbo of Hildesheim, Witgar of Augsburg, Liutbert of Mainz, Ermenrich of Passau, and Willibert of Cologne; Abbots Grimald of St.-Gall and Wissembourg, Brunward of Hersfeld, Erchanbert of Kempten, Hatto of Fulda, and Otgar of Niederalteich; and Louis's wife and daughters who received convents: Emma of Obermünster, Hildegard and Bertha of Münsterschwarzach, Säckingen, and Zurich, and Irmengard of Buchau and Frauenchiemsee.

[152] Nelson, *Charles the Bald*, 61–62; Bigott, *Ludwig der Deutsche*, 213–23, 275–76, 282–83.

[153] Bigott, *Ludwig der Deutsche*, 245–48.

[154] *Vita Rimberti*, chap. 11, p. 90. For other examples of Louis's right of inspection and approval, see *AF*, s.a. 856, p. 47 (Thioto of Fulda); *DLG* 32 (the abbot of Hersfeld), 72 (Anno of Freising), 90 (the abbot of Rheinau); Ratpert, *Casus sancti Galli*, chap. 8, p. 192 (Hartmut of St.-Gall); *Auctarium Garstense*, s.a. 873 (Theotmar of Salzburg). A St.-Gall form letter, apparently dating to Louis's reign, outlined the king's right to inspect newly elected bishops: *Collectio Sangallensis*, no. 1, in MGH *Formulae*, 395–96; Geneviève Bührer-Thierry, *Évêques et pouvoir dans le royaume de Germanie: Les Églises de Bavière et de Souabe, 876–973* (Paris, 1997), 153–54.

second thoughts about the tight grip of the Carolingians on the Church, they put up with it since the alternative—a Church without royal protection and therefore at the mercy of noble predators—was far worse.

Bishops and abbots had extensive governmental duties. They frequently participated in military campaigns alongside the counts, which reveals that they too were responsible for raising and leading local contingents of the army.[155] Prominent bishops and abbots also served as Louis's ambassadors to fellow Carolingians and to the papacy.[156] East Frankish bishops had a heightened role in courts of law as defenders of justice and counterweights to the corruption of the counts and judges.[157] The 847 Mainz synod demanded that "bishops be in agreement with the counts and judges when enforcing justice so that just law might not in any way be undermined by anyone's lies, false testimony, perjury, or bribes."[158] But Raban worried about the toll of judicial responsibilities on pastoral duties. He confided in one east Frankish bishop, "Alas! These days many churchmen neglect preaching and spiritual obligations. They think themselves great if they are placed in charge of secular duties and frequently take part in the quarrels of laymen. They preside in their assemblies like judges and act like the arbiters of their conflicts."[159]

The institution of immunity and royal protection heightened the role of bishops and abbots as royal officials.[160] When the king granted, or confirmed, immunity and protection to a bishopric or monastery, all properties belonging to it were withdrawn from jurisdiction of the local counts and placed directly under the bishop or abbot. In addition, the grant of immunity and protection created a direct relationship and series of reciprocal obligations between the king and the bishop or abbot, thereby enabling the king to involve himself more directly in the business of that bishopric or monastery. Such pockets of ecclesiastical immunity and royal protection could be massive. The monastery of St.-Gall, for example, to which Louis granted immunity and protection in 833 and 854, was the single largest landholder in Alemannia, making its abbot, Grimald, the most powerful royal

---

[155] Bigott, *Ludwig der Deutsche*, 124–35.

[156] Ibid., 136–56.

[157] Hartmann, *Synoden*, 462–67; idem, *Ludwig der Deutsche*, 160.

[158] MGH *Concilia* 3:166 (c. 7).

[159] Raban, *Epistolae*, no. 36, in MGH *Epistolae* 5:471–72.

[160] Ganshof, *Frankish Institutions*, 45–50; Barbara H. Rosenwein, *Negotiating Space: Power, Restraint, and Privileges of Immunity in Early Medieval Europe* (Ithaca, 1999), esp. 97–134. For Louis's grants of immunity, see *DLG* 13, 15, 20, 22, 27, 32, 33, 44, 50, 51, 57, 61, 63, 64, 67, 68, 70, 73, 75, 80, 90, 93, 97, 110, 128, 134, 140, 142, 144, 147, 149, 150, 153, 164; *DArnulf* 66. Bishops and abbots who received immunity and royal protection were expected to pray for the king, his family, and the stability of his kingdom.

representative in the region.[161] The practice of granting immunity and protection belies the argument that grants of royal properties to the Church depleted the landed wealth of the monarchy, one of the traditional explanations for the alleged decline of the Carolingians during the ninth century.[162] On the contrary, it strengthened the crown because it removed royal lands from the reach of lay nobles and transferred them into the hands of bishops and abbots, whose election required the king's approval. The heavy reliance of east Frankish government on the Church, which historians have seen as a hallmark of the Ottonian and Salian rulers in the tenth and eleventh century, was well under way by Louis's reign.[163]

The Church also played an important role as the mouthpiece for royal legislation. According to Carolingian tradition, east Frankish synods legislated on secular as well as ecclesiastical matters. At the 847 and 852 Mainz synods, the bishops and abbots outlined the traditional Carolingian model of good government for Louis's kingdom. They called for *pax et concordia* among the bishops, abbots, counts, and all royal *fideles*, instructing them to assist the king and each other in ruling God's people and carrying out their office.[164] Laymen were to obey bishops in ecclesiastical matters and defend the widows and the orphans, while bishops were to aid counts and judges in enforcing justice.[165] All the powerful men (*potentiores*) were ordered not to oppress the poor, seize their property, force them into servitude, or subvert justice by taking bribes.[166] The east Frankish Church also legislated against criminals and outlaws. At the 852 Mainz synod, for example, the bishops and abbots announced Louis's decisions against two breakers of the peace. They decreed that a certain Albgis, who had carried off another man's wife to Moravia, was to be exiled "by the king's command," while one Batto, who had killed five men, was to separate from his wife and perform penance for the rest of his life.[167]

Like his predecessors, Louis bound his subjects to him through the oath of fidelity.[168] All adult freemen in the kingdom swore a general oath of loy-

---

[161] *DLG* 13, 70.

[162] Nelson, "Kingship and Royal Government," 389–92.

[163] It is doubtful, however, that this amounted to a coherent "imperial Church system," as earlier scholarship suggested: Timothy Reuter, "The 'Imperial Church System' of the Ottonian and Salian Rulers: A Reconsideration," *JEH* 32 (1982): 347–74.

[164] MGH *Concilia* 3:165 (c. 4), 241 (c. 1).

[165] Ibid., 166 (c. 7).

[166] Ibid., 170–71 (cc. 17–19).

[167] Ibid., 248–49 (c. 11).

[168] Ganshof viewed this Carolingian system of fidelity, vassalage, and beneficeholding as the birth of "feudalism": Ganshof, *Frankish Institutions*, 50–53; idem, *Feudalism*, 3rd ed., trans. Philip Grierson (New York, 1964), 20–61. However, Ganshof's model is problematic for the Carolingian period and elsewhere, since it obscures the complexity of

alty, introduced by Charlemagne, in which they promised not to conspire against the king.[169] Moreover, lesser royal officials and members of the king's bodyguard swore an oath of vassalage to the king, thereby becoming the king's "men." But the great magnates—bishops, abbots, counts, estate managers, and important benefice holders—bound themselves to Louis through a more intense personal bond. They commended themselves to the king through the ritual of "joining hands," and they swore a solemn oath of fidelity while placing their hands on a holy object, such as the relics of Saint Emmeram or the king's royal cross.[170] In this way, the leading nobles became Louis's *fideles* and recognized him as their lord. The oath of fidelity was an oath of service to work faithfully for the king and give him counsel and aid.[171] In return for their loyalty, Louis promised that "we will not condemn, dishonor, oppress, or afflict with undeserved schemes anyone against the law, justice, authority, and just reason." Louis and his brothers saw fidelity and lordship as the glue that held their kingdoms together. They decreed that every freeman was to choose a lord, either the king himself or one of his *fideles*.[172]

The oath of fidelity was a powerful tool of Carolingian kingship, since it gave the king the moral right to depose and punish holders of public offices for infidelity and treason. Throughout his reign, Louis vigorously defended his right to bestow and revoke public offices on the grounds of fidelity. "With remarkable speed," Notker wrote, "he was able to anticipate and crush all the plots of his enemies, settle the disputes of his subjects, and arrange every beneficial reward for his faithful men. . . . He punished those

---

political relations and landholding: Susan Reynolds, *Fiefs and Vassals: The Medieval Evidence Reinterpreted* (Oxford, 1994), esp. 75–114. I therefore do not use the term *feudalism*.

[169] In general, see Ganshof, *Frankish Institutions*, 13–15. On several occasions we hear of Louis and his *missi* receiving the oath of fidelity from witnesses who were about to testify in courts of law: *DLG* 66; *St.-Gall*, suppl. 21. In these cases the oath swearers were not the king's vassals or benefice holders but simply his subjects. For a contemporary text of this general oath, see MGH *Capitularia* 2:278.

[170] For example, the *AF*, s.a. 840, p. 31, reported that "Louis bound the east Franks, Alemans, Saxons, and Thuringians to him with the oath of fidelity" [sibi fidelitatis iure confirmant]. For oaths on the relics of Saint Emmeram and the king's cross, see *DLG* 66; *AF*, s.a. 869, p. 68. For references to the ritual of "joining hands," see Einhard, *Epistolae*, . no. 25, in MGH *Epistolae* 5:122; Ratpert, *Casus sancti Galli*, chap. 8, p. 192. Louis also tried to incorporate neighboring Slavic *duces* into this system of fidelity, although this obviously had only limited success: *AF*, s.a. 857, 858, 864, 870, 871, 874, pp. 47, 51, 62, 70, 73, 83.

[171] MGH *Capitularia* 2:73 (c. 6). For the text of the oath of fidelity performed by Charles the Bald's *fideles*, see MGH *Capitularia* 2:296 and n. 1. See further: Charles E. Odegaard, "Carolingian Oaths of Fidelity," *Speculum* 16 (1941):284–96; idem, "The Concept of Royal Power in Carolingian Oaths of Fidelity," *Speculum* 20 (1945): 279–89.

[172] *Conventus apud Marsnam primum, adnuntiatio Karoli*, chaps. 2, 5, in MGH *Capitularia* 2:71.

convicted of infidelity and conspiracy in the following way: he would deprive them of their offices, and under no circumstances or lapse of time would he soften and allow them to return to their previous rank."[173] Regino likewise stressed that Louis demanded "devoted service and sincere fidelity" from his *fideles* and would revoke their "public dignities" if they betrayed him.[174] On numerous occasions, Louis punished nobles guilty of infidelity by revoking their "public honors," benefices, and personal property. For example, when Lothar's supporter, Rato, opposed Louis in the early 830s, Louis seized his properties in Bavaria. As Louis summed up, Rato "forfeited them because of his treachery, and they came into the jurisdiction of our power according to the law."[175] Louis was able to get away with such confiscations because he often regranted the offices and properties to other, more trustworthy, supporters, thereby making the new recipients complicit in his vigorous defense of the inviolability of fidelity. In this way, the oath of fidelity strengthened Louis's control of public offices, pressured nobles to remain loyal, and legitimated his use of coercive force when confronted with rebellion.

Although his kingdom was vast, Louis used three institutions to intensify his direct influence in local politics: royal envoys, itinerant kingship, and annual assemblies. Like his predecessors, Louis sent out powerful officials as royal envoys (*missi dominici*) to ensure the king's rights, enforce justice, supervise the counts, and carry out other important matters of royal business. The *missus dominicus* possessed authority even greater than counts, since he commanded in the king's name (*verbo regis pannavit*) and thus acted as if he were the king himself.[176] In 802, Charlemagne had created a system of envoy-districts known as *missatica*, each supervised by a pair of *missi dominici*, usually a local archbishop and count.[177] However, this *missatica* system (which continued through the reign of Charles the Bald) was limited to

---

[173] Notker, *GK* 2.11, p. 68. For a similar comment on Louis's character, see Regino, *Chronicon*, s.a. 876, p. 110.

[174] Regino, *Chronicon*, s.a. 876, p. 110.

[175] *DLG* 5. For other examples of Louis revoking offices and personal property, see *DLG* 29 (the benefice of Count Banzleib), 96 (the property and office of Prefect Ratpot), 113 (the property of Charles the Bald's vassal Liuthard); *AF*, s.a. 852, 861, 863, 865, 866, pp. 42–43 (reasserting control of royal lands in Saxony), 55 (the public honors of Counts Ernest, Uto, Berengar, Sigihard, and Gerold and Abbot Waldo), 56 (the public honors of his son Carloman), 63 (the public honors of Count Werner), 65 (the properties of the unfaithful vassals of Liutbert of Mainz). Ganshof, *Feudalism*, 20–61, noted that Louis and his successors maintained control over their *fideles*, public offices, and royal lands.

[176] *DLG* 66; Werner, "Missus-marchio-comes," 195. For the king's right of command (*bannum*), see Ganshof, *Frankish Institutions*, 11–12.

[177] Wilhelm August Eckhardt, "Die Capitularia missorum specialia von 802," *DA* 12 (1956): 498–516; Werner, "Missus-marchio-comes," 204–5.

the Frankish heartlands between the Loire and Meuse rivers. In Germania, there had never been a coherent system of *missatica;* instead, *missi ad hoc* simply were appointed to deal with specific matters of royal business. Louis continued and intensified this eastern tradition of *missi ad hoc.* He generally employed high-ranking bishops, abbots, and counts, either in pairs or alone.[178] Louis's *missi* carried out a wide range of royal business: they acted as ambassadors, received oaths of loyalty, punished criminals, investigated property disputes, invested recipients with royal lands, supervised land transactions, and brought judicial appeals before the king. In this way, the institution of royal envoys multiplied the person of the king, enabling him to be in two places at once.

Like most medieval rulers, Louis frequently moved his court around his kingdom.[179] Itinerancy enabled the king periodically to meet with the local nobles, supervise his estates, and in general keep his finger on the pulse of local politics. Yet Louis did not simply rule from the saddle: long periods of stability interspersed his iterations. Louis spent much of his reign in his royal heartlands—Bavaria and the middle Rhine. During the thirty-three years of his reign between the Treaty of Verdun and his death, Louis is reported to have sojourned in Bavaria some forty-seven times and in the middle Rhine some forty times, thus on average visiting each region at least once a year.[180] (Often the annual number was higher.) Within these regions,

---

[178] Thegan, *GH*, chap. 47, p. 240 (Abbot Grimald and Count Gebhard); *Carmen de Timone comite,* in MGH *Poetae Latini* 2:120–24 (Count Timo); *DLG* 1 (unnamed), 66 (Iring), 92 (Bishop Gunzo of Worms), 102 (Count Odolrich of Szombathely), 113 (Louis's vassal, Buobo), 117 (Count Erlwin), 124 (Count Hildebold), 133 (unnamed), 158 (unnamed); *Freising 579* (Count Anzo), 626a (Anternaro); *St.-Gall* 388 (Count Gerold), 405 (Ruatpert), 417 (Bishop Solomon of Constance and Reginolf), suppl. 21 (Abbot Grimald and Count Hatto).

[179] One can get a detailed picture of Louis's itinerary from the reports of his whereabouts in annals and the dating clauses of his diplomas. This methodology comes from the pioneering work of Eckhard Müller-Mertens, *Die Reichsstruktur im Spiegel der Herrschaftspraxis Ottos des Grossen* (Berlin, 1980). The following discussion of Louis's itinerary is based on Eric J. Goldberg, "Creating a Medieval Kingdom: Carolingian Kingship, Court Culture, and Aristocratic Society under Louis of East Francia (840–876)" (Ph.D. diss., University of Virginia, 1998), chap. 6 and tables 1–7. See further: Carlrichard Brühl, *Foedrum, Gistum, Servitium Regis* (Cologne, 1968), 1:33–34 and n. 113, and *Itinerarkarte* II appended to vol. 2; Thomas Zotz, "Ludwig der Deutsche und seine Pfalzen: Königliche Herrschaftspraxis in der Formierungsphase des Ostfränkischen Reichs," in *LDZ,* ed. Hartmann, 27–46; Boris Bigott, "*Per Alemanniam iter:* Überlegungen zur Eingliederung der Alemannia ins Ostfränkische Reich Ludwigs des Deutschen," in *In frumento et vino opima: Festschrift für Thomas Zotz zu seinem 60. Geburtstag,* ed. Heinz Krieg and Alfons Zettler (Ostfildern, 2004), 29–37. For the tenth and eleventh centuries, see Bernhardt, *Itinerant Kingship.*

[180] These numbers are rough approximations because of the numerous lacunae in our knowledge of Louis's whereabouts. If the dates are within about a month of each other, I

Louis frequently stayed at the palaces in Regensburg and Frankfurt. He is reported to have stayed at Regensburg some thirty-six times and at Frankfurt some thirty-one times, again averaging about one visit per year at each palace.[181] These stays often lasted several months, especially during the last years of his reign, when he was an old man.[182] Louis frequently celebrated Christmas at Regensburg and Easter at Frankfurt, and he held a number of assemblies at those palaces.[183] Regensburg and Frankfurt were also centers of royal patronage. Of Louis's 162 surviving diplomas whose place of issuance is known, 39 (24 percent) were granted at Regensburg and 44 (27 percent) at Frankfurt.[184] Yet there was an important distinction in the nature of this patronage: while the recipients of Louis's diplomas at Frankfurt came from all over his kingdom, the majority of Louis's grants at Regensburg went to Bavarian magnates. Thus, although Regensburg maintained its Bavarian character, Louis transformed Frankfurt into the "chief seat of the eastern kingdom."[185]

By medieval standards, the east Frankish kingdom was large. From

---

count two consecutive reports of Louis's presence in Bavaria and the middle Rhine as a single sojourn. Of course, it is possible that Louis in fact left the region and then came back during that period.

[181] Again, this is from the period 844–76. I count two consecutive reports of Louis's presence at Regensburg and Frankfurt as a single stay if the dates are within about a month of each other. The actual number of Louis's stays at Regensburg and Frankfurt is undoubtedly higher because of the numerous vague references to his presence in Bavaria and Francia.

[182] Frankfurt: 855–56 (autumn–March 30), 865 (April–June 19), 872–73 (October 14–January 6), 874–75 (December 25–April 3), 876 (January–April 15); Regensburg: 850–51 (December 26–March 22), 851–52 (November 15–January 16), 852–53 (December 25–March 11), 860 (February 20–May 8), 863–64 (October 29–January 6), 871–72 (autumn–January 6), and 873–74? (September 1–January?). Because of the frequent lacunae in the sources, it is possible that Louis made unrecorded trips between reports of his presence at these two residences. On the other hand, Louis's stays at Frankfurt and Regensburg sometimes must have been longer than recorded.

[183] Although the sources frequently do not specify where Louis celebrated Christmas and Easter, an examination of his known itinerary suggests the following pattern: Christmas at Regensburg: 844, 845, 850, 851, 852, 857, 859, 863, 867, 869, 870, 871, 873; Easter at Regensburg: 844, 845, 848, 853, 860, 871; Christmas at Frankfurt: 846 (or 847), 855, 864, 872, 874; Easter at Frankfurt: 854, 856, 858, 859, 861, 865, 870, 873, 875, 876. Louis is reported to have held assemblies at Regensburg in 848, 853, 861, and 870 and at Frankfurt in 858, 865, 866, 870, 871, 873, 874, and 876. Louis also held a number of assemblies near Frankfurt at Mainz (848, 852, 862), Worms (857, 858?, 859?, 862, 866), Tribur (871, 874, 875 × 2), Bürstadt (873), and Ingelheim (876).

[184] Frankfurt: DLG 13–15, 34, 41–43, 47, 50, 68, 74–76, 89–93, 95–97, 103, 105, 106, 108, 117, 118, 122, 123, 130, 134, 136, 140–42, 144–46, 153, 157–60, 162; Regensburg: DLG 2, 6, 8, 10–12, 20, 35–37, 39, 40, 44–46, 48, 58–60, 62, 64, 65, 67, 86–88, 100, 101, 110–13, 119, 121, 124, 125, 129, 161, 165.

[185] Regino, *Chronicon*, s.a. 876, p. 111.

Frankfurt to Regensburg is roughly two hundred miles, about the distance from Washington, D.C., to New York City or from London to York. Louis overcame these distances with an efficient system of transportation and communication. Royal officials maintained the old Roman roads (*viae publicae*) and bridges along the Rhine and Danube, and Louis frequently traveled by ship along these rivers as well.[186] It is therefore no coincidence that both Frankfurt and Regensburg had ports on major waterways. Louis usually made the journey between Bavaria and the middle Rhine through Alemannia, making that region the most important royal "transit zone" in the kingdom.[187] On average, this journey seems to have taken Louis between two and three weeks, suggesting that he traveled at a leisurely pace through Alemannia and stopped at royal palaces, such as Ulm and Bodman, and at his daughters' convents at Buchau and Säckingen.[188] However, if need be, he could make the journey much more quickly. For example, when a serious rebellion broke out in January 874, Louis made the journey from Bavaria to Frankfurt by way of Augsburg in about a week.[189] Like his predecessors, Louis sometimes required bishoprics and monasteries to provide housing (*gistum*) and food (*fodrum*) for his entourage when it passed through a region. When on the middle Rhine, Louis often stayed at the episcopal cities of Mainz and Worms, and at Regensburg he may have exacted supplies from the bishop.[190] Royal messengers (*sintmanni*) were stationed along the royal itinerary, presumably to deliver urgent messages to and from the king.[191] In an emergency, a messenger could cover the distance from Frankfurt to Regensburg in under five days if fresh horses were available en route.

[186] *Viae publicae*: DLG 25, 90; *AF*, s.a. 849, p. 39. Travel by ship on the Rhine, Main, and Danube: *AF*, s.a. 839, 840, 852, 859, 872, 873, pp. 29, 31, 42, 76, 78. In general, see Wolfram, *Grenzen und Räume*, 365–66.

[187] Every time we can check Louis's itinerary between Bavaria and the middle Rhine, we find him passing through Alemannia (for example, in 832, 840, 857, 858, 861, 873, 874, 875). There is no reference to Louis traveling from Bavaria to the middle Rhine via eastern Franconia, which contrasts with the itinerary of his grandson Arnulf: Elfie-Marie Eibl, "Zur Stellung Bayerns und Rheinfrankens im Reiche Arnulfs von Kärnten," *Jahrbuch für Geschichte des Feudalismus* 8 (1984): 73–113.

[188] This calculation is based on specific references to Louis's itinerary in the *AF* and his diplomas. 831: Altötting (March 27)–Worms (mid-April), about 19 days; 853: Thionville (July 3)–Regensburg (July 21), about 19 days; 860: Regensburg (May 8)–Koblenz (June 1), about 24 days; 861: Frankfurt (April 1)–Regensburg (April 20), about 19 days; 861: Frankfurt (October 26)–Salzburg (November 11), about 16 days; 868: Ingelheim (July 1)–Regensburg (July 23), about 22 days; 874: Augsburg (February 2)–Frankfurt (February 26), about 24 days.

[189] Louis departed Bavaria, was at Augsburg on February 2, but still arrived at Frankfurt in early February: *AF*, s.a. 874, pp. 81–82; DLG 151.

[190] Bigott, *Ludwig der Deutsche*, 189–91.

[191] DLG 30.

In contrast, Louis seldom visited Saxony, Thuringia, eastern Franconia, and the Bavarian marches. When he did, it was usually in the course of a military campaign against the Slavs. These frontier regions were "distant zones" of kingship, where power was firmly in the hands of the local nobility. The long absences of the king from these regions could lead to abuses by counts and other public officials and the usurpation of royal lands, forcing the king to make occasional drastic interventions in those regions.[192] As Janet Nelson summed up, "as power radiated out from palaces and heartlands, it inevitably became less regular, and less intense, nearer the periphery."[193]

The most important institution for holding the kingdom together was the royal assembly.[194] More than any other piece of Carolingian government, the assembly gave concrete social and political meaning to the abstract concept of "kingdom." The assembly turned the king's itinerary on its head: while the itinerary brought the court to the nobles, the assembly brought the nobles to court. Louis's ability to compel the nobles to come to his assemblies was an important barometer of his power. For example, when a group of Alemans ignored the judgment of Iring, Louis's *missus dominicus*, and refused to return lands to the monastery of Kempten, Iring commanded them in the name of the king to travel to Louis's upcoming assembly at Regenunto (near Regensburg) so that the king himself could review the case.[195] This was a significant hardship for the unruly Alemans: it was a journey of about 125 miles in late winter (it was early March), which would have taken them at least five days on horseback as they rode through the chilly Bavarian countryside. In this way, Louis's assemblies provided a regular forum to remind the nobles of his royal power and, when necessary, to intervene directly in the local politics of his far-flung territories.

Louis held two main kinds of assemblies. The majority were traditional general assemblies attended by the bishops, abbots, counts, and other important nobles from the different provinces. Louis almost exclusively held these kingdomwide assemblies on the middle Rhine. Of his some twenty-one reported general assemblies after 843, over three-quarters of them (fif-

[192] *AF,* s.a. 852, pp. 42–43.
[193] Nelson, "Kingship and Royal Government," 387.
[194] Concerning assemblies, see Heinrich Weber, "Die Reichsversammlungen im ostfränkischen Reich" (Ph.D. diss., University of Würzburg, 1962); Timothy Reuter, "Assembly Politics in Western Europe from the Eighth Century to the Twelfth," in *The Medieval World,* ed. Peter Linehan and Janet L. Nelson (London, 2001), 432–50; and especially Stuart Airlie, "Talking Heads: Assemblies in Early Medieval Germany," in *Political Assemblies in the Earlier Middle Ages,* ed. P. S. Barnwell and Marco Mostert (Turnhout, 2003), 29–46.
[195] *DLG* 66. Concerning this document, see Bigott, *Ludwig der Deutsche,* 186–89.

teen) took place on the middle Rhine, especially at Frankfurt, Mainz, Tribur, and Worms.[196] Louis usually held only one general assembly a year, although during the last five years of his reign he notably increased the number to two or three a year to deal with inheritance disputes with his sons and Charles the Bald. Louis announced the date of upcoming assemblies in advance, and he specified which royal officials were to attend.[197] Although Louis did not favor any particular months for general assemblies, he avoided the period between November and February, when snow and bad weather made travel difficult.[198] In addition to these larger assemblies, Louis held smaller regional meetings (*colloquia*) with certain picked counselors.[199] He tended to hold these smaller meetings during the fall and winter months (from October to March), in contrast to the general assemblies, and often he used them to resolve specific, pressing matters that had arisen over the previous year.[200]

The general assembly was the great political and social event of the year. The king, queen, and their children wore their most resplendent royal attire and regalia, and the palace would have been decorated with tapestries and ornaments to convey the king's wealth and majesty. Assemblies must have been extremely costly, since they required the king to provide housing, food, drink, entertainment, and probably gifts for hundreds of attending nobles and dignitaries. The nobles would have come to court in their finest clothes and riding their best horses, eager to ingratiate themselves with the king, reunite with their allies, and keep an eye on their rivals. At the assembly, the king and his nobles reaffirmed their social ties and shared aristocratic culture: they exchanged gifts, hunted, attended Mass, formed mar-

---

[196] Louis is known to have held general assemblies at the following locations: Paderborn (September 845), Mainz (October 848; October 852; 862), Minden (December 852), Ulm (July 854), Worms (March 857; 862), Frankfurt (June 858; June 865; August? 866; January 873; February 874), Regensburg (April 861), Tribur (May 871; April 874; June 875), Forchheim (March 872), Bürstadt (April 873), Metz (August 873), and Ingelheim (May 876). Sometimes Louis's meetings with his brothers and nephews took the place of a general assembly in a given year, such as in 860, 865, and 867.

[197] *AF,* s.a. 858, p. 48 ; *DLG* 170.

[198] Of Louis's nineteen general assemblies for which the month is known, most of them (sixteen) took place between March and October: January, 1; February, 1; March, 2; April, 3; May, 2; June, 3; July, 1; August, 2; September, 1; October, 2; November, 0; December, 1.

[199] Louis is reported to have held regional assemblies and smaller meetings at Regensburg (October 848), Erfurt (December 852), Regenunto (March 853?), Forchheim (February 858), Worms? (June? 858; November 866), Frankfurt (February 870; October 871; February 876), Regensburg? (November 870), Aachen (June 873), and Tribur (August 875).

[200] The increased frequency of smaller *colloquia* during the last years of Louis's reign seems to have been due to his difficulties with his sons over the issue of inheritance.

riage alliances, and the like. Most of all, they feasted. During banquets Louis's table would have flowed with good Riesling wine from his vineyards in the Rhineland, and at Regensburg his guests seem to have been entertained by a jester named Hadaric.[201] The *Waltharius* paints a wonderful picture of what a Carolingian feast must have been like:

At length extravagance reigned among the tables.
The king steps in the hall adorned with tapestries.
. . . .
[And goes to his] throne, which purple and fine cloth
Adorned. He sits and bids two lords to sit down there
On either side; the seneschal then seats the rest.
The guests together occupied a hundred seats.
Each guest, from eating different dishes, breaks out sweating.
When these were taken off, still other foods were brought,
And choicest wine was gleaming in a golden bowl;
For on the linen cloth stand only golden vessels.
. . . .
All vie, with exhortations from their host and king,
And glowing Drunkenness rules the entire hall.[202]

The royal assembly was the truest manifestation of the kingdom, since it instilled the nobles with the sense that they were members of a community of the realm with the king at their head.[203]

At the same time, the assembly was a central institution of government. The king and magnates discussed all pressing issues confronting the kingdom: treaties, alliances, military campaigns, local politics, aristocratic conflicts, and the like. The king distributed patronage to his supporters, admonished public officials to carry out their duties, received foreign ambassadors and tribute, and planned future treaties and military campaigns. Assemblies were important occasions for royal justice. At assemblies Louis, like his predecessors, issued legal decrees on a wide range of topics, from clarifying the servile status of a social class known as *barscalci* to making specific rulings about judicial procedure in courts of law.[204] The king's spoken word had the force of law, so the fact that Louis does not seem to

---

[201] Regino, *Chronicon*, s.a. 842, p. 75; *Regensburg* 64.

[202] *Waltharius*, ll. 290–300, 314–15, translation from *"Waltharius" and "Ruodlieb,"* trans. Kratz, 16–18.

[203] For the role of assemblies in fostering "kingdoms as communities," see Susan Reynolds, *Kingdoms and Communities in Western Europe, 900–1300*, 2nd ed. (Oxford, 1997), 302–19.

[204] *AI*, s.a. 848, p. 741; *AF*, s.a. 852, p. 43.

have issued capitularies does not mean that he was an inactive legislator. He also decreed that his predecessors' capitularies still carried the force of law and thus "were to be upheld at all times and by everyone."[205]

The royal assembly also functioned as the highest court of law in the kingdom. Not surprisingly, disputes were common among the competitive nobles, and these conflicts threatened to undermine the fragile peace with private feuds. Louis therefore spent considerable time at assemblies settling disputes.[206] The assembled nobles helped the king judge these disputes, and it was this broad participation that gave the king's ruling enduring force. Thus the archbishop of Mainz and the abbot of Fulda brought a dispute over tithes before the royal assembly, "because such a matter could not be settled permanently without royal judgment and the counsel of many prudent men."[207] Scattered evidence suggests that Louis settled disputes through standard Carolingian judicial procedure: a combination of taking sworn testimony from local notables knowledgeable about a case, consulting legal experts (*scabini*), taking counsel with his magnates, and, when all else failed, resorting to ordeal by boiling water or trial by combat.[208] In some cases, Louis punished the guilty through ritualized humiliations that dramatically reinforced the finality of his judgment. For example, when Louis convicted the group of Alemans mentioned earlier for usurping Kempten's lands and disregarding the ruling of his *missus dominicus*, the king not only forced them to return the properties but he ordered the laymen among them to carry their saddles on their backs.[209] (He mercifully spared the guilty churchmen this humiliation.) In more serious cases of treason, infidelity, or other grave crimes, Louis's royal justice was ruthless. On numerous occasions Louis ordered traitors and outlaws to be decapitated, hung, blinded, and maimed. Although he never executed his magnates for infidelity, Louis often exiled them and stripped them of their offices and properties.[210] Gallows were so common in Louis's kingdom that Archbishop

---

[205] *Conventus apud Confluentes*, in MGH *Capitularia* 2:156 (cc. 8–9); *DLG* 147.

[206] *AF*, s.a. 848, 852, 872, 873, 875, pp. 37, 42, 75, 78, 83; Ratpert, *Casus sancti Galli*, chap. 8, pp. 198–202; *DLG* 66, 170.

[207] *DLG* 170.

[208] *DLG* 66, 170; Ratpert, *Casus sancti Galli*, chap. 8, pp. 198–202. Louis's archchaplains, Baturich and Grimald, both had blessings for trial by boiling water: Clm 14510, fol. 74r; Grimalt Codex, 18. One churchman from Freising criticized the use of ordeals and trial by combat in royal justice: *Carmen de Timone comite*, in MGH *Poetae Latini* 2:120–24.

[209] *DLG* 66.

[210] *Carmen de Timone comite*, in MGH *Poetae Latini* 2:120–24 (hanging, blinding, and mutilation); *DLG* 5 (revoking property), 29 (revoking a benefice and county), 96 (revoking property and prefecture), 113 (revoking property); *AF* 842, 861, 863, 865, 866, 870, 871, pp. 33–34 (executions), 55 (revoking offices as well as exile), 56 (revoking properties and prefecture), 63 (revoking counties), 65 (hanging, maiming, blinding, revoking properties,

Raban was forced to make decrees about what to do with the criminals' bodies left hanging on them.[211] Gallows were a grim reminder of the king's peace, public order, and the coercive force of royal power.

During the decade after Verdun, Louis transformed his disunited eastern territories into a coherent kingdom. He accomplished this through the traditional strategies of Carolingian government: cultivation of royal majesty, efficient management of economic resources, building up of the rudimentary institutions of Carolingian government, and defense of the public nature of political and ecclesiastical office. Louis's importation of Carolingian government to the regions east of the Rhine was a major achievement, since they had previously been peripheral to direct royal control. Louis was not an innovator in the arena of kingship and government, but instead he relied on the traditional institutions used by his predecessors. This was not because he lacked creativity or initiative but rather because he saw no need to innovate: the governmental strategies of his predecessors served him well in the east.[212] But although, in retrospect, modern historians can see Louis laying the foundations for an independent eastern kingdom, Louis himself continued to think in terms of a larger Carolingian empire. He was not intentionally creating an enduring east Frankish kingdom. Instead, he was raising up his eastern territories to the standards of Carolingian kingship and government in the west. With his kingship secure by the early 850s, Louis could resume his attempts to expand his kingdom westward.

and exile), 72 (blinding and imprisonment), 73 (blinding); *AB*, s.a. 842, pp. 42–43 (beheading, hanging, and maiming).

[211] MGH *Concilia* 3:174 (c. 27).

[212] Here my conclusions echo those of Fleckenstein, *Hofkapelle* 1:184, and Bigott, *Ludwig der Deutsche*, 283–84.

PART III

VISIONS OF EMPIRE

CHAPTER SEVEN
DRANG NACH WESTEN, 853-860

During the nineteenth and early twentieth century, nationalist historians often assumed that the political objective of medieval German rulers was, or at least should have been, the expansion of their borders into Slavic eastern Europe, a historical process they labeled the *Drang nach Osten* or "drive to the east."[1] But, as we have seen, Louis had little interest in eastern expansion. Instead, he preferred Charlemagne's policy of indirect rule over his Slavic neighbors through tributary lordship and client rulers. In truth, Louis's ambitions for imperialist expansion lay in the Frankish west, not the Slavic east. West of the Rhine were the royal heartlands of Francia where Louis had spent his childhood, a region rich with royal palaces, manors, estates, episcopal cities, and monasteries. Louis had won a foothold in these territories by compelling Lothar to cede to him the west Rhenish cities of Mainz, Worms, and Speyer in the Treaty of Verdun. But this did not satisfy Louis, since it only amounted to the eastern half of the kingdom of Austrasia. Throughout his reign, he aspired to continue the expansion of his borders westward.

Louis's ambitions for western expansion again came to the fore beginning

---

[1] During the 1940s, the strongly nationalistic scholarship of Heinz Zatschek argued for Louis's alleged policy of expanding "German racial land" [deutscher Volksboden] into Slavic eastern Europe: *Wie das erste Reich der Deutschen entstand: Staatsführung, Reichsgut und Ostsiedlung im Zeitalter der Karolinger* (Prag, 1940), 166–73; idem, "Ludwig der Deutsche," in Mayer, *Vertrag von Verdun*, 6, 64. For the historiographical assumptions of the German scholarship on *Drang nach Osten*, see Althoff, "Saxony and the Elbe Slavs," 278–80.

in the 850s. Several interrelated factors drove Louis's increasingly imperialistic policies. By the early 850s, Louis had consolidated his rule beyond the Rhine, and he therefore could refocus his energies beyond his western borders. Louis had three adult sons for whom future kingdoms were needed, and these territories might be found in Gaul. Moreover, Lothar I died in 855, bequeathing his middle kingdom to his three sons. Lothar's demise left Louis as the senior Carolingian in Europe and in a position to exploit the political weakness of Lothar's heirs. Louis's plans to expand westward also were defensive. Charles the Bald was in an increasingly strong position in west Francia and likewise aspired to conquests in the middle kingdom. If Louis failed to expand, Charles might do so and become a serious threat.

Adding to the complexity of this renewed Carolingian competition was the ongoing unrest along the Slavic frontiers. During the 850s, Louis faced renewed rebellions in the east. Once again, several interrelated political developments were at play. Louis wanted to place his eldest son, Carloman, in charge of the Bavarian Eastland, which precipitated rebellions among some of Louis's longtime supporters. These rebellions in turn gave Rastislav of Moravia a window of opportunity to create an independent Slavic kingdom, since he could exploit the Frankish aristocratic opposition to Louis. Louis's competition with Charles was another factor, since Charles cleverly courted Slavic rulers in an effort to keep his brother occupied in the east. This growing tension among Louis's imperialist ambitions in Francia, competition with Charles the Bald, and campaigns against rebel Slavs were to define the last two decades of his reign.[2]

THE INVASION OF AQUITAINE

Although ruling a kingdom beyond the Rhine, Louis's court continued to think in terms of a united Frankish Europe. Louis's unlimited royal title, "king by the favor of Divine Grace," implied the ongoing expansion of his rule over peoples and territories, and the imagery of his Hadrian seal suggested his desire to emulate the imperial rule of Louis the Pious and Charlemagne. The Grimalt Codex likewise reflected this pan-European political ideology. Grimald's court handbook contained a copy of the late Roman geographic treatise, the *Notitia Galliarum* (Roster of Gallic cities), which listed all the late Roman metropolitan provinces of western Europe and their sub-

---

[2] For the politics of this period, see Dümmler, *GOR* 1:380–463; Nelson, *Charles the Bald*, 160–96; Hartmann, *Ludwig der Deutsche*, 47–54.

ordinate cities.[3] Grimald's copy of the *Notitia Galliarum* contained entries for Louis's territories of Germania and Bavaria, but it listed them within the larger Roman provincial framework of all western Europe: Italy, Gaul, the Belgic provinces, and Aquitaine. This enduring concept of a united Europe suggests that Louis's court viewed his realm "in east Francia" as part of a larger Frankish kingdom and empire that awaited reunification.

The fraternal accord established at the second Meersen conference in 851 did not last. That peace was based on only a momentary political equilibrium among the three brothers. In 852 that temporary balance of power ended when Charles the Bald captured his nephew and longtime rival, Pippin II of Aquitaine. With Pippin II in custody, Charles became significantly more secure in his kingdom. No longer needing to fear Lothar (who had long supported Pippin II), Charles now pressured Lothar to form an alliance with him. During the summer of 852, Charles "received him with fraternal affection, treated him honorably, negotiated with him in a brotherly fashion, gave him regal gifts, and kindly escorted him home."[4] A motivating force behind this new alliance was Charles and Lothar's common enemy, the Vikings, who had been raiding their kingdoms since the civil war. During the winter of 852–53, the two led a joint campaign against the Vikings on the Seine, the first such cooperative Carolingian expedition since the Treaty of Verdun. To seal their alliance, Lothar and Charles celebrated Christmas and Epiphany together, and Lothar became godfather to Charles's daughter.[5] Not surprisingly, Louis viewed Charles's pact with Lothar as a betrayal of their alliance, which went back to Fontenoy and the Strasbourg Oaths. This was a momentous diplomatic shift. Louis and Charles had been allies for over a decade; for the next quarter century they would be bitter rivals.

The real issue behind this realignment in Carolingian diplomacy was Lothar's old age. Lothar was now almost sixty and thus approaching the age at which Charlemagne and Louis the Pious had died (sixty-seven and sixty-two, respectively). With Lothar's death on the horizon, Louis and Charles both hoped to expand their power over the rich royal heartlands of central Francia. The elderly Lothar had three male heirs among whom he planned to divide the middle kingdom: his eldest son, Louis II, would get the imperial title and Italy; his second son, Lothar II, would inherit Frisia, middle Francia, Alsace, and northern Burgundy, forming a kingdom that became known as Lothar II's *regnum*, or Lotharingia; and his youngest son, Charles the Child, would get Provence and southern Burgundy. To guarantee this

[3] Grimalt Codex, 48–51.
[4] *AB*, s.a. 852, p. 64. See also Nelson, *Charles the Bald*, 169–71, although our interpretations differ slightly.
[5] *AB*, s.a. 853, p. 66.

succession plan, Lothar I needed the support of at least one of his brothers, and in 852 he had settled on Charles the Bald. Soon after striking his alliance with Charles, Lothar made further preparations for his death: he granted his imperial regalia, relics, and library to the monastery of Prüm, where he intended to be buried.[6]

Although left out of the new alliance between Lothar I and Charles, Louis was determined to play a role in the succession politics of the middle kingdom. During his kingdomwide progress in 852, Louis made a highly unusual stop at the city of Cologne.[7] It was unusual because Cologne was in the middle kingdom, and at that moment Lothar I was off fighting the Vikings with Charles. At Cologne Louis held talks with some of the leading Lotharingian magnates, presumably including the powerful archbishop, Gunther (850–63/70), with whom Louis had good relations. Louis and the Lotharingian magnates undoubtedly discussed the succession to the middle kingdom after Lothar's death. Mindful of the ever-shifting nature of political alliances and royal borders, Lothar's magnates were keeping their options open. Although Lothar hoped his sons would inherit his kingdom with Charles the Bald's support, the Lotharingian nobles knew Louis the German would also play a role in this transfer of power from one Carolingian generation to another. Whether Lothar liked it or not, Louis intended to be involved in Lotharingian politics.

As always, some magnates exploited these growing tensions between Louis and his brothers. During the summer of 853, most of the Aquitanian nobles withdrew their allegiance from Charles the Bald and sent envoys and hostages to Louis, requesting that he become king of Aquitaine or that he send one of his sons to become their king.[8] After imprisoning Pippin II, Charles had moved to secure his rule in Aquitaine: in March 853, Charles had ordered the beheading of a certain Aquitanian nobleman named Gauzbert (a punishment reserved for treason), and in April Charles foiled a plot to free Pippin II from prison and restore him to the Aquitanian throne.[9] The Aquitanian nobles resented Charles's intervention in "their" kingdom. Their goal in inviting Louis or one of his sons to rule over them was to force

---

[6] *DLoI* 122.

[7] *AF*, s.a. 852, p. 42.

[8] *AB*, s.a. 853, p. 67; *AF*, s.a. 853, pp. 43–44.

[9] For the execution of Gauzbert and the failed plot to free Pippin II, see *AF*, s.a. 854, p. 44; *Annales Engolismenses*, s.a. 852, in MGH *SS* 16:486; Regino, *Chronicon*, s.a. 860, p. 78; *AB*, s.a. 853, p. 66; *Annals of St.-Bertin*, trans. Nelson, 78n4. Concerning the Aquitanians' support of Louis and the role of the Rorgonides, see Otto Gerhard Oexle, "Bischof Ebroin von Poitiers und seine Verwandten," *FS* 3 (1969): 138–210. In 853, in response to the defection of the Aquitanians, Charles issued a string of capitularies concerning the maintenance of public order: MGH *Capitularia* 2:75–76, 266–76.

Charles out of the region and to secure their accustomed power by acting as kingmaker.

Fearing that this conflict would undermine his succession plans, Lothar I tried to reestablish peace between his brothers. He met with Louis in July 853 at Thionville, although they accomplished little. The powerful Count Adalhard, who had made the large grant to St.-Gall in 843, seems to have played a prominent role in the negotiations between Louis and Lothar. About 844, after a brief stint in Charles's kingdom, Adalhard had moved to Lothar's realm, where he became a count on the Moselle. As one of the preeminent Lotharingian magnates with lands on both sides of the Rhine, Adalhard naturally was concerned about the succession of Lothar's sons and the maintenance of good relations among the kings. During the 853 Thionville meeting, Lothar made a grant to one of Adalhard's vassals at the request of "our dearest brother, the glorious King Louis."[10] The following month, Adalhard was at Charles's court, again presumably working to restore good relations among the brothers.[11]

Recognizing the serious threat that Louis posed, his brothers renewed their alliance. In November 853, they met at Valence, where they issued a joint capitulary concerning the maintenance of public order, and they urged a three-way meeting with Louis at Liège the following February.[12] When Louis failed to show up, Lothar and Charles formed a pact against him, making each other the guardians of their sons, magnates, and kingdoms.[13] The oaths they swore clearly echoed the Strasbourg Oaths, although Louis was now identified as the absent aggressor:

> From the present day and henceforth, if our brother Louis breaks the oath he swore to us, or if he or his sons attack any part of the kingdom that you possess, if you request it, I will give you defensive aid against him, his sons, and all who want to take it from you without just and reasonable cause, as far as the Lord grants me power to do so. And if I outlive you, I will not take that part of the kingdom that you possess but give my consent for your sons to have it. And if they or their *fideles* ask for defensive aid against our brother, his sons, and all who can take it, I will give them aid as far as I am able, as long as you and your sons give us the same aid and do not abandon us.

[10] *DLoI* 128. Adalhard's vassal Heriric later had close ties to Louis the German and Louis the Younger: *DLG* 131; *DLY* 18. For the influence of Adalhard and his probable brother, Gerhard, at Lothar's court, see also *DLoI* 124, 126, 127.

[11] *DCB* 157.

[12] MGH *Capitularia* 2:75–76.

[13] *AB*, s.a. 854, p. 68; MGH *Capitularia* 2:76–78.

Louis failed to appear at Liège in February 854 because he had decided to accept the invitation of the Aquitanian nobles. With Lothar's death on the horizon, possession of Aquitaine would enable Louis to keep Charles the Bald distracted in the southwest, thereby giving Louis a freer hand in the regions where his real territorial ambitions lay: central Francia. The *Annals of Fulda* justified the Aquitanian invasion on the grounds that Charles had become a "tyrant." According to Carolingian political thought, a tyrant did not exercise legitimate power and therefore rightfully could be deposed.[14] The *Annals of Fulda* reported that the Aquitanians asked that Louis "take up the kingship over them himself or send his son to liberate them from the tyranny of king Charles. If he did not, they would be forced to ask for help from foreigners and enemies of the faith [i.e., the Vikings] with danger to the Christian religion, since they could not get it from their orthodox and legitimate lords."[15] This charge of tyranny obviously was part of Louis's efforts to justify an Aquitanian invasion. Nevertheless, in 854 Louis could make the charge stick. Charles had ordered the execution of the Aquitanian Gauzbert without a trial, thus breaking the 847 and 851 Meersen agreements not to punish *fideles* "contrary to law, justice, authority, and fair reason."[16]

Louis made extensive preparations for the 854 invasion. He planned to launch his campaign in February 854, when he knew his brothers would be meeting at Liège near Aachen. He did not intend to lead the army in person but instead to send it under the command of his second son, the nineteen-year-old Louis the Younger, who already had proved his mettle and leadership abilities fighting the Slavs.[17] Louis intended to raise a large army from Franconia, Thuringia, Alemannia, and Bavaria.[18] Since Louis knew his brothers would be meeting in northern Francia, he undoubtedly planned to have his army invade Aquitaine via the southern route, following the Roman road from Bavaria and Alemannia, through Burgundy by way of Besançon and Autun, and across the Loire into Aquitaine.[19] This was an extremely long journey of roughly 350 miles, and Louis therefore arranged for provisions along the line of march. Soon after receiving the invitation from the Aquitanian nobles, on July 21, 853, he founded the convent of Sts.-Felix-and-

14 Nelson, "Kingship and Empire," 229.
15 *AF,* s.a. 853, pp. 43–44.
16 MGH *Capitularia* 2:73, chap. 6.
17 *AF,* s.a. 848, p. 37.
18 *Miracula sancti Martialis,* chap. 7, ed. Oswald Holder-Egger, in MGH *SS* (Hanover, 1887), 15:283.
19 Chevallier, *Roman Roads,* 160–64 and ill. 34.

Regula at Zurich in Alemannia.[20] Louis established Sts.-Felix-and-Regula as a major royal administrative and economic center on his kingdom's southwestern border. He granted the convent the royal manor at Zurich with its considerable surrounding properties, placed it under his immunity and royal protection, and gave it to his eldest daughter, the twenty-five-year-old Hildegard. Zurich had important strategic and military significance. It was located on the main Roman road leading from Alemannia through Burgundy, and at the heart of the village was a late Roman fortress (*castrum, castellum*).[21] Moreover, the lands with which Louis endowed Sts.-Felix-and-Regula included estates that the king had received from his Alemannian military commander (*dux militum regis Luodewici*), Rupert.[22] Rupert's name suggests he was related to the powerful Udalriching family, whom Louis now began to promote to a number of Alemannian counties at the expense of the Welfs.[23] The founding of Sts.-Felix-and-Regula therefore seems to have been part of Louis's logistical preparations to stockpile supplies that his son's large army would need for its westward march into Aquitaine. Sts.-Felix-and-Regula, Louis's only known monastic foundation, was a monument to his western imperialist policies.

Louis's magnates made further preparations for the invasion. A Freising charter that probably should be dated August 13, 853, indicates that Louis's

[20] *DLG* 67. The *AB*, s.a. 853, p. 67, implied that the Aquitanians appealed to Louis in May or soon thereafter. For the foundation of Zurich, see Hans Conrad Peyer, "Zürich im Früh- und Hochmittelalter," in *Zürich von der Urzeit zum Mittelalter*, ed. Emil Vogt, Ernst Meyer, and Hans Conrad Peyer (Zurich, 1971), 172; Judith Steinmann, "Zürich," in *Helvetia Sacra*, pt. 3, vol. 1.3, ed. Elsanne Gilomen-Schenkel (Bern, 1986), 1977–78; Bigott, *Ludwig der Deutsche*, 271.

[21] Reinhold Kaiser, "Castrum und Pfalz in Zürich: Ein Widerstreit des archäologischen Befundes und der schriftlichen Überlieferung?" in *Deutsche Königspfalzen: Beiträge zu ihrer historischen und archäologischen Erforschung*, vol. 4: *Pfalzen-Reichsgut-Königshöfe*, ed. Lutz Fenske, Veröffentlichungen des Max-Plank-Instituts für Geschichte 11.4 (Göttingen, 1996), 93–100.

[22] *Zürich* 67.

[23] Borgolte, *Grafen*, 224. Between about 854 and 861, Louis began to revoke the counties of Conrad the Elder and his son Welf II (Queen Emma's brother and nephew) and bestow them on Udalrich, a member of the powerful Udalriching family, which was the main rival of the Welfs in the region: Borgolte, *Grafen*, 255–66. Alongside the Udalrichings appeared other new counts, including Adalbert in Alpgau and Thurgau and Gerold in Zurichgau and Thurgau: Borgolte, *Grafen*, 21–28, 130. (Adalbert apparently was related to Wolven, the founder of Rheinau: *DLG* 91, 130. Gerold's name suggests that he was a member of the Udalrichings.) The names of these new Alemannian counts—Udalrich, Adalbert, and Gerold—all appeared in the witness list from the 848 Regensburg assembly after the Bavarian magnates: *DLG* 46. It therefore seems that these Alemannian nobles had been "second-tier" supporters of Louis since the 840s, and that in the 850s the king began to promote them at the expense of the Welfs.

fideles, Bishop Erchanbert of Freising and Counts William and Hatto, were active in Alemannia just three weeks after Louis founded Sts.-Felix-and-Regula.[24] On that date, Bishop Erchanbert, who also was abbot of Kempten in eastern Alemannia, made a property transaction with a local nobleman near Ulm, and Counts William and Hatto stood as witnesses to the exchange. The palace of Ulm was Louis's most important royal residence in Alemannia, serving as a crucial stopping point in his regular journeys between Bavaria and the Rhine.[25] The Freising charter emphasized that the lands in question, which were located near Ulm, produced a considerable amount of hay (120 cartloads per year), and it therefore seems that Erchanbert, William, and Hatto were securing supplies for the horses in Louis's army before the upcoming invasion. Erchanbert already was responsible for the salt supplies of Louis's army, since as abbot of Kempten he had the unique privilege of obtaining six wagons and three ships of salt from the salt springs at Reichenhall annually, free from tolls.[26]

Louis the Younger departed from his father's kingdom at the head of a large army in early 854.[27] By early March, he had arrived in Aquitaine. The *Annals of Fulda* painted a bleak picture of Louis the Younger's Aquitanian invasion that makes it seem destined to fail. They reported that only the kinsmen of the late Gauzbert welcomed him and that Louis the Younger therefore judged the undertaking pointless and returned to his father's kingdom in the autumn. However, the fact that Louis the Younger was able to remain in Aquitaine for six months suggests that he in fact found significant support there. Moreover, at first Charles the Bald was unable to muster an effective response to his nephew's invasion. Charles led a counteroffensive into Aquitaine in March, but when his army turned to looting, he was forced to depart the region in late April, "having achieved nothing."

The elderly Lothar now had to reevaluate his plans. Fearing that Charles might be too weak to protect his sons' interests after his death, he met with Louis the German on the Rhine. This tense meeting, which would be the brothers' last, began with a shouting match: "At first they yelled fiercely at each other, but at length they restored concord and allied with each other in

[24] *Freising* 730. Bitterauf dated the charter August 13, ca. 851, since the year is not given in the charter. However, the involvement of Bishop Erchanbert and Counts William and Hatto suggests a connection to Louis's preparations in 853 for the Aquitanian invasion the following February. (Erchanbert died on August 1, 854.) William was Louis's count of the Traungau, while Hatto was count of Bertoldsbaar, Hegau, Affa, and Zurichgau: Mitterauer, *Karolingische Markgrafen*, 104–77; Borgolte, *Grafen*, 60–62.

[25] Schmitt, *Villa Regalis Ulm*, 23–31.

[26] *DLG* 24, 36.

[27] *AB*, s.a. 854, pp. 68–69. See further *AF*, s.a. 854, p. 44; *AX*, s.a. 854, p. 18; BM 1407b.

the name of peace." There is evidence that Lothar made territorial concessions to Louis to guarantee Louis's support for his sons' succession to the
middle kingdom. Soon after their meeting, Bishop Hunger of Utrecht appeared at Louis's court to request confirmation of Utrecht's immunity and
royal protection "within the lordship of our [i.e., Louis's] kingdom."[28] Since
Utrecht was in Frisia and thus beyond Louis's 843 borders, this diploma
suggests that in 854 Lothar momentarily ceded Frisia to Louis in return for
Louis's promise to support his sons' succession.[29] From Lothar's point of
view, this concession did not cost him much, since four years earlier he had
been forced to grant Dorestad and other Frisian counties to the Viking
leader Roric, and Lothar therefore no longer controlled Frisia directly.[30]
Roric had good relations with Louis, since he had earlier spent a period of
exile in the east Frankish kingdom and had become Louis's vassal before returning to his life of piracy.[31] Thus, by the summer of 854, Louis seems to
have had Frisia as well as Aquitaine within his grasp.

Seizing on Charles the Bald's momentary weakness and his new alliance
with Lothar, Louis now apparently planned to take the Aquitanian throne
for himself. After making the grant to Hunger of Utrecht at Frankfurt,
Louis made an unusual trip to Alemannia. In late July, Louis held an assembly at Ulm on the Danube. This was an important event, as it was Louis's
first reported assembly in Alemannia, and it was attended by his sons, Carloman and Charles III, "as well as the other princes of his kingdom."[32] The
fact that Louis decided to hold the Ulm assembly as the Aquitanian invasion
hung in the balance points to the conclusion that he was raising an army. At
Ulm Louis settled the long-standing dispute between Grimald of St.-Gall
and Bishop Solomon of Constance, two local prelates who would have
played a critical part in mustering Alemannian troops.[33]

In the end, however, unforeseen events forced Louis the German to call
off the campaign. When Charles the Bald learned of the alliance between
his brothers, he was greatly alarmed and departed for Attigny, where he met
with Lothar. Charles convinced Lothar to renounce his recent pact with
Louis and reaffirm their earlier alliance. They sent envoys to Louis the German, demanding that he end the "Aquitanian crisis" [adflictio Aquitanica]

[28] *DLG* 68. Louis issued this diploma on May 18, 854, at Frankfurt.
[29] In his introduction to *DLG* 68, Paul Kehr assumed this referred only to Utrecht's
lands east of the Rhine. However, Louis's diploma was an exact copy of Lothar's 845 grant
of the same rights (*DLoI* 89), suggesting that Louis was granting immunity to *all* Utrecht's
properties, not just those within his kingdom.
[30] Coupland, "From Poachers to Gamekeepers," 95–101.
[31] *AF*, s.a. 850, p. 39.
[32] Ratpert, *Casus sancti Galli*, chap. 8, p. 198.
[33] *DLG* 69–71.

and recall his son.[34] Charles then returned to Aquitaine a second time, around the beginning of July.[35] At this moment, the daring Pippin II of Aquitaine managed to escape from his monastic prison in Soissons (or perhaps Charles the Bald intentionally released him),[36] and he returned to his homeland. With their familiar ruler back, the Aquitanians deserted Louis the Younger and rallied behind Pippin II. Deprived of his local support, Louis the Younger was forced to abandon the invasion and returned to his father's kingdom. For the moment, Louis's western ambitions had come to a screeching halt.

REBELLION IN THE SOUTHEAST

The invasion of Aquitaine precipitated renewed instability in the Slavic marches. When the Aquitanians appealed to Louis in 853, Charles the Bald cleverly bribed the Bulgars to ally with the Slavs (apparently the Moravians) and together attack Louis's kingdom.[37] Charles's objective was to keep his brother occupied in the east and thereby prevent him from invading Aquitaine, and it probably was for this reason that Louis did not lead the army himself. This Bulgar–Moravian coalition attacked Louis's borders, although Louis's forces drove it off. The alliance between the Bulgars and the Moravians was a serious threat, since it undermined the two cornerstones of the stability in the east: Louis's 845 *pax* with the Bulgar khan (which they renewed in 852) and the loyalty of Rastislav, whom Louis had installed as *dux* in Moravia in 846.

The real danger of these frontier rebellions was that Slavic rulers quickly allied with the king's enemies within his own borders. This was the case in 853–54. In the course of the Bulgar-Moravian attack, Louis deposed his longtime *fidelis* and prefect of the Eastland, Ratpot, who formed a rebel alliance (*carmula*) with Rastislav of Moravia.[38] Years later, Louis ranted about how Ratpot "withdrew himself from us with all his might and betrayed his faith and oaths with utter infidelity."[39] But in truth Ratpot seems to have

[34] MGH *Capitularia* 2:277–78.
[35] *DCB* 164. See further *DCB* 165–68 for Charles's itinerary in Aquitaine and patronage of the local nobles.
[36] *Annals of St.-Bertin*, trans. Nelson, 79n8.
[37] *AB*, s.a. 853, p. 68. The Bulgars seem to have attacked Lower Pannonia south of the Drava River: Wolfram, *Salzburg*, 314.
[38] *AI*, s.a. 854, p. 744.
[39] *DLG* 96. *Regensburg* 37 seems to allude to this same rebellion. The charter records a grant of frontier estates from Count Chozil, the son of *dux* Pribina of Lower Pannonia,

been more of a victim than a traitor. Louis appears to have deposed Ratpot to make way for his eldest son, Carloman, whom he intended to make prefect of the Bavarian Eastland. Faced with political ruin, Ratpot had little choice but to ally with Rastislav in a desperate attempt to defend his long-held position in the southeast. There is a striking parallel here with the downfall of Count Baldric of Friuli in 828, whom Louis the Pious had deposed on trumped-up charges of cowardice to make way for the young Louis the German.[40] In the *Annals of Fulda*, Rudolf passed over Ratpot's downfall in silence, suggesting that some were uncomfortable with his treatment by the king. Ratpot's family had been patrons of Fulda, and Rudolf may have felt that the king had acted unfairly.[41]

Rastislav's 854 alliance with Ratpot marked a new phase of Moravian hostility toward the east Frankish king. Although Louis had installed Rastislav as his client *dux* in 846, by the early 850s Rastislav felt secure enough to challenge Frankish overlordship. For the rest of his reign, Rastislav pursued an effective policy of allying with Louis's adversaries, such as Ratpot. Another example of Rastislav's strategy took place two years earlier. In 852, Louis had exiled a certain Albgis for abducting the wife of one of his subjects, and Albgis "took her across the farthest borders of the kingdom into the still rude Christian land of the Moravians."[42] But far from being a "rude" Christian, Rastislav was a civilized and cunning Slavic prince who had all the trappings of Christian kingship at his disposal. Through the nascent Moravian Church founded by Bavarian missionaries, Rastislav could legitimize his rule, make himself king, and form far-flung alliances with other Christian rulers against the east Frankish king. Louis could not afford to allow an independent Slavic Christian kingdom to emerge in his back yard. Rastislav had to be brought to heel.

In 855 Louis therefore launched his second invasion of Moravia. At the royal estate at Aibling in southern Bavaria during Lent, Louis oversaw preparations for the upcoming campaign.[43] The evidence suggests that, like the strategy he had devised in 846, this plan involved invading Moravia with two armies, one of which would come from Saxony and march through Bohemia. An unusual guest at Aibling was Louis's Saxon supporter, Abbot Warin of Corvey, who apparently was involved in the precampaign prepara-

---

and Ratpot stood as the first witness. The Regensburg scribe ominously addressed the charter "to all faithful and unfaithful Christians." Widemann dated this charter "vor 859," but Ratpot's title of *comes* indicates that it took place before Ratpot's downfall in 854.

[40] *ARF*, s.a. 828, p. 174.

[41] Mitterauer, *Karolingische Markgrafen*, 100–103.

[42] MGH *Concilia* 3:248–49 (c. 11).

[43] At Aibling Louis carried out diplomacy with his nephew, Louis II of Italy: *DLG* 72.

tions.[44] Louis now granted Warin properties near Bremen, probably in return for his upcoming military support. Also while at Aibling, the king sent Count Ernest at the head of the Bavarian army against the Bohemians as a preemptive strike to secure the second invasion route to Moravia. Ernest's Bohemian expedition was successful, and he returned to Bavaria in triumph.

Despite these preparations, the 855 Moravian campaign was a failure. The reason was Moravia's unusually developed system of fortresses, what the *Annals of Fulda* referred to as the Moravian "civitates et castella."[45] Modern archeological excavations reveal that ninth-century Moravia had more than thirty fortified centers, ranging from smaller fortresses guarding Moravia's borders to large, centrally located fortified towns.[46] The largest and most sophisticated Moravian fortress that has been excavated was at Mikulčice on the Morava River, located seventy-five miles north of the Danube, a site that one archeologist has dubbed the "capital of the lords of Great Moravia."[47] Expanded several times during the late eighth and ninth centuries, the fortress at Mikulčice had two chief components: a main stronghold (the "acropolis") of about fifteen acres, which contained a stone palace, five stone churches, and numerous aristocratic graves; and a lower, tongue-shaped forecastle of about seven acres containing numerous houses along narrow streets. Massive stone-faced walls, twenty-six feet high and ten feet thick, defended the entire stronghold, and a main fortified gate was located at the end of the forecastle. The circumference of Mikulčice's walls measured roughly 5,200 feet, delineating an area only slightly smaller than Louis's Bavarian capital of Regensburg. In addition, an arm of the Morava River eighty feet wide surrounded the entire fortress, serving as a formidable moat that was bridged at the main gate. Ninth-century chroniclers referred to Mikulčice (or another massive Moravian fortress like it) on several occasions, describing it as an "extremely well defended fortress" [civitas munitissima] and "Rastislav's indescribable fortress, unlike all the much older ones" [illa ineffabilis Rastizi munitio et omnibus antiquissimis dissimilis].[48] The latter description implies that Rastislav had rebuilt one of his large fortresses (perhaps at Mikulčice itself) as the seat of his power, thereby setting it apart from all the other Moravian strongholds. Rastislav's mighty fortresses would occupy a central position in the Franco-Moravian conflict for the next two decades.

Indeed, Louis's 855 campaign foundered before the walls of one of

<hr />

44 *DLG* 73.
45 *AF,* s.a. 870, p. 71.
46 Staňa, "Mährische Burgwälle," 157–208.
47 Ibid., 186–87; Poulík, "Mikulčice," 1–32.
48 *AX,* s.a. 872, p. 31; *AF,* s.a. 869, p. 69.

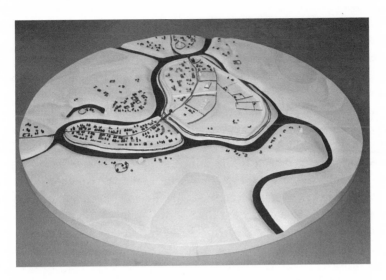

A well-fortified opponent. This model showing the ninth-century Moravian fortress at Mikulčice is based on archeological excavations. The large twenty-four-acre fortress was defended by massive stone-faced walls that were twenty-six feet high and ten feet thick, and were crowned by a wooden palisade. An eighty-foot-wide arm of the Morava River surrounded the fortress and served as a moat. The fortress consisted of two parts: the main upper fortress (the "acropolis"), which contained a palace, several churches, rich aristocratic cemeteries, and artisan workshops; and the lower, tongue-shaped forecastle with numerous houses lined along narrow streets—presumably quarters for soldiers. In the region around the fortress were numerous churches, workshops, farms, and cemeteries. Reproduced by permission of the Brno Archaeological Institute.

Rastislav's strongholds. The *Annals of Fulda* reported: "King Louis led an army with little success into the land of the Moravian Slavs against their ruler Rastislav who was rebelling against him. He returned without victory, for the time being preferring to leave an enemy protected (as it was reported) by an extremely strong wall than to sustain heavy losses to his soldiers in risky fighting."[49] The evident surprise of the chronicler when he learned of the size of Rastislav's fortifications ("firmissimum, ut feritur, vallum") suggests that Rastislav had rebuilt one of his strongholds (again, perhaps at Mikulčice) since Louis had installed him as *dux* nine years earlier. Unprepared for a prolonged siege that would have dangerously exposed his army to food shortages, disease, and surprise attacks, Louis was forced to withdraw from the region. As Louis retreated, his army resorted to the standard strategy of ravaging the countryside, and it defeated a large Moravian force that attacked the king's camp. Nevertheless, sensing triumph,

[49] *AF*, s.a. 855, pp. 45–46.

Rastislav's army shadowed the retreating Franks and pillaged many of their estates across the Danube after they had departed from Moravia.

Rastislav's rebellion had broader geopolitical implications for the entire Franco-Slavic frontier. Louis needed a larger and better equipped army to lay siege to Rastislav's mighty fortress, which in turn demanded that Louis secure the contested second invasion route through Bohemia. For the next two years, Louis devoted his efforts to that end. In August 856, Louis led an expedition along the second invasion route. He crossed the Elbe, subjected the Sorbs and the Dalaminzes, and then invaded Bohemia from the north and forced the submission of several *duces*.[50] Louis paid a high price for this campaign. He lost a large part of his army in battle, including his longtime Saxon supporter, Count Bardo, a close ally of Abbot Warin of Corvey. Nevertheless, Louis grimly persevered. The following year he launched yet another campaign against the Bohemians under the joint command of Bishop Otgar of Eichstätt, his count of the palace, Rudolt, and Count Ernest's son, Ernest II.[51] This is the first reference to Louis's placing an army under the command of a bishop (as opposed to bishops simply serving in the army), marking his increasing reliance on Church prelates as generals to defuse the ever-present danger of conflicts among the magnates. (Louis could not lead the campaign in person because he met with his nephew, Emperor Louis II of Italy, at Trent in midsummer to reassert his control of the Brenner Pass.)[52] In this campaign, the Frankish army captured the fortress of a Bohemian ruler named Sclavitag, who had been rebelling "tyrannically" against the Franks for many years.[53] Sclavitag fled and sought refuge with Rastislav, again highlighting Rastislav's strategy of aiding Louis's enemies. Louis installed Sclavitag's brother as the new ruler of the Bohemian fortress after he had rendered oaths of fidelity and presumably hostages as well.

In the midst of these campaigns, in 856 Louis promoted the twenty-six-year-old Carloman to prefect of the Bavarian marches.[54] By now, the king's eldest son seems to have emerged as a charismatic prince and gifted general. Regino described Carloman as the paragon of Carolingian manhood:

[50] *AF*, s.a. 856, p. 47; *AB*, s.a. 856, p. 72.

[51] *AF*, s.a. 857, p. 47.

[52] This trip to Trent seems to have taken place between June 2, when the king was at Bodman on Lake Constance, and August 18, when he was at Regensburg: *DLG* 83–85; Dümmler, *GOR* 1:418–19.

[53] Sclavitag was the son of Wiztrach, who likewise had rebelled against Louis. The location of the *civitas Wiztrachi ducis* is uncertain. Jiří Slàma, "Civitas Wiztrachi ducis," *Historische Geographie: Beiträge zur Problematik der mittelalterlichen Siedlung und der Wege* 11 (1973): 3–30, suggests Zabusany (near Brüx-Duchcar) in northwestern Bohemia.

[54] *Al*, s.a. 857, p. 744; *Auctarium Garstense*, s.a. 856, p. 565.

That most excellent king was learned in letters, devoted to the Christian religion, just, peaceful, and morally upright. The beauty of his body was exceptional, and his physical strength was a wonder to behold. He possessed a very warlike spirit. He waged numerous wars against the Slavic kingdoms with his father, and even more without him. He always returned the victor in triumph and expanded the borders of his empire with glorious iron. He was mild to his own men and a living terror to his enemies. He was charming in speech, humble, and endowed with great cleverness for managing business of the realm. He was so skilled that he was the very embodiment of royal majesty.[55]

Echoing Regino, Notker described Carloman as a "real ass-kicker" [bellicosissimus], which was high praise from the St.-Gall monk.[56]

While promoting his eldest son, however, Louis also took measures to limit Carloman's powers. With three adult sons, Louis wanted to keep a grip on royal power and avoid a repetition of the rebellions against Louis the Pious during the 830s.[57] Unlike his father and grandfather, Louis refused to grant his sons the royal title during his lifetime, thereby severely limiting their ability to wrest power from him. Moreover, although Louis appointed Carloman as eastern prefect, he denied him the prefect's seat at Tulln in Upper Pannonia. Instead, Louis appointed Carloman prefect of the Carantanians (*praelatus Carantanis*), indicating that Carloman's benefices were in the more peripheral region of Carantania.[58] Carloman had the title, but not the actual power, of prefect of the southeast.

Louis took additional steps to counterbalance Carloman's power. Although the king had revoked Ratpot's properties at Tulln, he allowed his royal steward, Ratpot II, who was the son (or relative) of the former prefect, to hold these estates.[59] Here one sees that the downfall of a prominent magnate did not always mean the ruin of his close relatives. In this case, Louis's concern about his eldest son convinced him to permit Ratpot II to keep his father's lands at Tulln as a check to Carloman. At this time Louis also pro-

---

[55] Regino, *Chronicon*, s.a. 880, p. 116.

[56] Notker, *Continuatio*, 329.

[57] *Adonis Continuatio*, 324–25.

[58] *AF*, s.a. 863, p. 56. Bowlus, *Franks, Moravians, and Magyars*, p. 119 and n. 11, offers a different interpretation of Carloman's promotion to prefect of Carantania.

[59] *DLG* 96. Prefect Ratpot had bequeathed his properties at Tulln to St.-Emmeram in 837 with the option of buying them back if he had a son. This points to the conclusion that Ratpot II had not been born yet in 837 and therefore at most he was nineteen at the time of Carloman's promotion: *Regensburg* 29. Ratpot II seems to have remained an influential figure at court and in the southeast: MGH *Capitularia* 2:154; *AF*, s.a. 871, p. 74.

moted another magnate to power in the southeast: Bishop Otgar of Eichstätt.[60] When the wealthy Bavarian abbacy of Niederalteich fell vacant in 855, Louis bestowed it on Otgar. Louis clearly viewed Otgar's appointment as an important one, since he overrode his earlier promise to the Niederalteich monks of free abbatial elections.[61] The monastery of Niederalteich, which was dedicated to the soldier-saint Maurice, played a key role in Louis's control of the Bavarian marches: it had strategic properties in Upper Pannonia, and the abbot enjoyed the jurisdictional rights traditionally reserved for a monastery's advocate (that is, lay representative), in effect making him a count.[62] Louis's unusual decision to place Otgar in command of the 857 Bohemian campaign demonstrates the bishop-abbot's importance to the king's administration of the southeast. Upon Otgar's return to Regensburg after the campaign, the king rewarded him with properties north of the Danube near the Bohemian border.[63] In this way, Otgar of Eichstätt and Ratpot II both served as powerful counterweights to Carloman. Having learned from his father's hardships, Louis was determined to keep his sons on short leashes.

THE INVASION OF GAUL

In early 855, Lothar's declining health momentarily placed the growing hostilities between Louis and Charles on the back burner. Prudentius reported that "Lothar fell ill, and this gave the brothers Louis and Charles reason to restore concord."[64] Lothar immediately complained that Charles had abandoned their alliance. However, Lothar sensed that his end was near, and he became a monk at the monastery of Prüm to prepare his soul for judgment. (Lothar in his old age reportedly had a ménage à trois with two serving girls, so he may have had much to repent for!)[65] Lothar lived as a monk for only six days before dying on September 29, 855.

Upon his brother's death, the approximately forty-five-year-old Louis

---

[60] Bigott, *Ludwig der Deutsche*, 134–35, rightly suggests that Louis's increased use of bishops and abbots as military commanders was a response to his sons' rebelliousness, although he overlooks Otgar's key role in Louis's efforts to maintain control of the Eastland (p. 130).

[61] *DLG* 48, 80.

[62] *DLG* 2, 48, 59, 80.

[63] *DLG* 86. Louis made this second grant to Otgar at the request of his *fidelis* Eginulf, concerning whom see *DLG* 46; *Regensburg* 31; *DCarloman* 25.

[64] *AB*, s.a. 855, p. 70.

[65] *AB*, s.a. 853, p. 67.

became the senior Carolingian in Europe. Revealing the growing influence he wielded beyond his borders, the Lotharingian magnates now brought the twenty-year-old Lothar II before Louis at Frankfurt to be made king.[66] Louis agreed to his nephew's elevation to king of Lotharingia, but he demanded territorial concessions in return. When Lothar II came to Frankfurt, he had in his custody his ten-year-old brother, Charles the Child. Charles was a sickly boy (he apparently suffered from epilepsy), and Lothar II began to put pressure on him to become a monk.[67] With Charles the Child out of the way, Louis the German and Lothar II might divide Alsace, Provence, and Burgundy between them. Indeed, there is evidence that Lothar II briefly conceded Alsace to his eastern uncle in 855. Early the following year, the Alsatian bishop of Strasbourg, Ratold, came to Frankfurt and asked Louis to confirm Louis the Pious's grant of immunity and royal protection to his see, an indication that Ratold now recognized Louis the German as his king.[68] With Lothar I dead and Alsace within his grasp, Louis began thinking of his power in heightened imperial terms. The east Frankish chancery adopted the imperial rhetoric of Louis the Pious's diploma: it described Strasbourg as situated "within the lordship of our empire," and he commanded the bishop "faithfully to obey our imperial command" and to pray "for the safety of ourselves, our wife, children, and the entire empire granted to us by God." In the end, however, Louis could not make his claim to Alsace stick. During the summer of 856, Lothar I's three sons met in Burgundy and accepted their father's planned division of the middle kingdom: Emperor Louis II got Italy, Lothar II received Lotharingia (that is, middle Francia, Frisia, Alsace, and northern Burgundy), and Charles the Child got Provence and southern Burgundy.[69] Once again, Louis the German was forced to suspend his western imperialist ambitions.

[66] *AF*, s.a. 855, p. 46. These Lotharingian magnates presumably included Gunther of Cologne and Count Adalhard, the latter of whom had visited Lorsch soon before Lothar's death and exchanged lands with Abbot Samuel: *Lorsch* 1922. Adalhard remained an influential magnate under Lothar II: *DLoII* 5, 14.

[67] *AB*, s.a. 856, p. 73; Nelson, *Charles the Bald*, 180–81.

[68] *DLG* 75. Louis's chancery based his diploma on a lost diploma of his father's granting immunity and royal protection to Strasbourg. Louis also made his first recorded grant to Grimald's Alsatian monastery of Wissembourg on May 18, 854 or 856: *DLG* 76. Concerning the geopolitical significance of Alsace in the ninth century, see Thomas Zotz, "Das Elsass—Ein Teil des Zwischenreichs?" in *Lotharingia—Eine europäische Kernlandschaft um as Jahr 1000*, ed. Hans-Walter Herrmann and Reinhard Schneider (Saarbrücken, 1995), 49–70, esp. 58–62. However, Zotz (p. 59), argues that Louis's 856 confirmation of Strasbourg's immunity and royal protection only concerned the bishopric's territories east of the Rhine and therefore did not reflect Louis's claims over all Alsace. See further Bigott, *Ludwig der Deutsche*, 183n312.

[69] *AB*, s.a. 856, p. 73.

Louis spent the next several years biding his time until another opportunity arrived to invade Gaul.[70] He got an unexpected opportunity to consolidate his power in Franconia with the deaths of the four leading prelates, Gozbald of Würzburg, Samuel of Worms-Lorsch, Raban of Mainz, and Hatto of Fulda, enabling him to influence the appointment of their successors.[71] His most strategic appointment was at Mainz. In 855 Charles the Bald had recaptured Pippin II of Aquitaine, and Charles then appointed his own son king of the region.[72] At this time, Pippin II of Aquitaine's younger brother, Charles of Aquitaine, escaped monastic imprisonment and fled to Louis the German. When Raban of Mainz died in 856, Louis and his advisers decided to appoint his fugitive Aquitanian nephew the new archbishop, even though this went against the will of the Mainz clergy and people.[73] Louis's appointment was bound up with his imperialist aspirations in the west. By making Charles of Aquitaine his new archbishop, Louis promoted a Carolingian prince with extensive ties to the western nobility and open enmity to Charles the Bald to his inner circle of counselors. At the same time, Charles of Aquitaine's appointment disqualified him for the Aquitanian throne, thereby removing one of Louis's rivals for royal power in the west. Charles the Bald was in fact extremely vulnerable in 856: he had fallen ill, and he faced serious Viking invasions. Moreover, in 856 the Neustrian and Aquitanian nobles formed a conspiracy against him and invited Louis the German to become their king.[74] However, Louis the German was campaigning in the east against the Slavs, and the Neustrians and Aquitanians therefore were forced to reconcile themselves to Charles the Bald.[75]

Louis resolved to seize Charles the Bald's kingdom in 858. The *Annals of Fulda* presented Louis's invasion of Gaul as unplanned and a reluctant response to Charles the Bald's growing tyranny. This is hardly convincing. Louis had been scheming such an undertaking since Lothar I's death, and the Neustrians and Aquitanians had repeatedly invited him to become their king since 856.[76] This faction of western magnates resented Charles the Bald's recent imposition of his two sons over them (Louis the Stammerer in

---

[70] Louis often resided at Frankfurt and Worms in these years, and he held an assembly at Worms in March 857: *AF*, s.a. 855–58, pp. 45–49; *DLG* 74–76, 78, 79, 89–93. During these years Louis patronized Worms, Fulda, Würzburg, Lorsch, and Speyer: *DLG* 74, 78, 79, 89, 92.

[71] *AF*, s.a. 855, 856, pp. 45–47.

[72] *AB*, s.a. 855, p. 70. Charles the Bald's second son was named Charles. He was born in 847–48 and died in 866.

[73] *AF*, s.a. 856, pp. 46–47; Bigott, *Ludwig der Deutsche*, 197–98.

[74] *AB*, s.a. 856, p. 72; MGH *Capitularia* 2:293 (chap. 2).

[75] Charles pardoned the conspirators: MGH *Capitularia* 2:279–85.

[76] *AB*, s.a. 856, p. 72; *AF*, s.a. 858, pp. 49–50.

Neustria and Charles in Aquitaine), and these princely promotions sparked a rebellion similar to Ratpot's uprising in the Bavarian marches against Carloman.[77] Among these disaffected nobles was Robert the Strong, the powerful Rupertiner count of Angers who could claim kinship to Louis through the eastern king's mother. Charles's court increasingly feared another invasion by his brother. In the summer of 858, Charles's powerful adviser, Archbishop Hincmar of Reims, wrote to the east Frankish king urging him not to invade his brother's kingdom at the peril of his soul.[78] Because of his increasing mistrust of his brother, Charles the Bald made a defensive alliance with Lothar II in 857. In response, Louis the German journeyed across the Alps to Trent, where he struck a counteralliance with his nephew, Louis II of Italy.[79] In truth, the moment for a western invasion was favorable: Charles the Bald was facing Viking pirates on the Seine, and in early 858 he was forced to raise an enormous tribute from his bishops, abbots, counts, and nobles—686 pounds of gold and 3,250 pounds of silver—to ransom the abbot of St.-Denis from a group of Vikings. As a result, a group of Neustrian counts led by Robert the Strong allied with the Bretons and drove Louis the Stammerer out of the region.[80]

Louis spent the first half of 858 making preparations for the upcoming invasion.[81] He was busy meeting with regional magnates, whose military support would be crucial for the success of the upcoming campaign. From Regensburg, which he visited in early February, he made a quick trip to Forchheim in eastern Franconia to speak with certain counselors, and in early March he held an assembly at Ulm with the Alemannian counts. At this time, Louis promoted several Alemans in his administration. Count Rudolt of Alaholfsbaar became count of the palace, and Adalhelm (a relative of Count Adalhelm of Thurgau and Zurichgau) became a chaplain under Archchaplain Grimald of St.-Gall.[82] Thus, by 858, two of Louis's highest court officials—his archchaplain and count of the palace—as well as at least one chaplain were all prominent noblemen from Alemannia, suggesting the growing importance of the nobles of that region for Louis's military plans to

[77] Nelson, *Charles the Bald*, 181–89; *Annals of St.-Bertin*, trans. Nelson, 82n6.

[78] Flodoard, *Historia*, 3.20, p. 263 and n. 5.

[79] *AB*, s.a. 857, p. 74; *DLG* 85. At his meeting with Lothar II, Charles expressed his hope for future peace and harmony with his half brother: MGH *Capitularia* 2:293–95 (c. 1). Louis had met with Lothar II at Koblenz in February 857, although no alliance came of this: *AF*, s.a. 857, p. 47. The following year Lothar II also allied with Charles the Child of Provence: *AB*, s.a. 858, p. 77.

[80] *AB*, s.a. 858, pp. 76–79; *Annals of St.-Bertin*, trans. Nelson, pp. 86–87 and nn. 7, 8.

[81] *AF*, s.a. 858, pp. 48–49; *DLG* 88.

[82] Ruadolt and Adalhelm: *DLG* 69, 83, 87; *AF*, s.a. 857, p. 47; Borgolte, *Grafen*, 38–39, 225. Witgar: *DLG* 88; Fleckenstein, *Hofkapelle* 1:175.

expand westward. Previously dominated by Bavarians, Louis's court by 858 had a decidedly Alemannian stamp. Also while at Ulm, Louis received a high-ranking embassy from his recent ally, Louis II of Italy. During that meeting, Louis presumably sought to win the Italian emperor's support, or at least an assurance of neutrality, for his invasion of Gaul.

In the early spring, Louis then went to Frankfurt to celebrate Easter and continue his preparations with his leading men. Once again, Louis took steps to ensure that there were sufficient supplies for his army's upcoming march into Gaul. In March and April, Louis issued a string of diplomas involving supporters who held lands along the western borders of his kingdom: Abbot Eigilbert of Lorsch, his Alemannian vassal Wolven, his daughter Hildegard of Zurich, Bishop Gebhard of Speyer, a number of Gebhard of Speyer's vassals, and Bishop Gunzo of Worms.[83] Although Louis's chancery presented these transactions as acts of royal piety and munificence, they clearly involved estates along his kingdom's western borders that were to provision his troops as they moved west. For example, on March 18, Louis granted Abbot Eigilbert of Lorsch an exemption from tolls for his monastery's ship on the Rhine and at the port of Worms.[84] Louis planned to launch his invasion of Gaul from Worms, and this grant therefore enabled the abbot of Lorsch to help stockpile supplies at Worms from his monastery's extensive estates along the Rhine. The following month, Bishop Gunzo of Worms, acting as Louis's *missus dominicus*, supervised a huge transfer of estates located west of the Rhine.[85] In this transaction, Bishop Gebhard of Speyer received a large number of estates for his personal use from his vassals. These estates were located west of Speyer, some as far west as the Saar region in Lotharingia itself, directly on the road to Metz. It seems that Louis's promotion of a nobleman named Witgar to chancellor at this time likewise was tied up with his efforts to secure supplies. Witgar possessed a number of estates in Lothar II's kingdom near Langres (a city that marked the intersection of several major roads) that produced a massive amount of provisions: two thousand *modii* (roughly four thousand gallons) of wheat and five hundred wagons of hay annually.[86] In the midst of these preparations at Frankfurt, Louis received messengers from Lothar II re-

[83] *DLG* 89–92.

[84] *DLG* 89. It may have been at this time that Louis's chief lay supporter, Count Ernest, made a grant in the Wormsgau to Lorsch: *Lorsch* 1618 (which should be dated 856–61).

[85] *DLG* 92.

[86] Witgar's contested possession of these lands is recorded in *DLoII* 15 (dated 860). I discuss the significance of this diploma in my forthcoming article "*Regina nitens sanctissima Hemma.*"

questing a meeting at Koblenz in May to dissuade him from invading Gaul. However, it must have been obvious to Lothar's messengers that the wheels of war already were grinding ahead. Lothar II therefore did not show up at the Koblenz meeting and instead formed a defensive alliance with Charles the Bald against the eastern king.

Louis's war of conquest faced serious obstacles. As was the case during the early 840s, the lesser nobles and freemen—whom the *Annals of Fulda* described as the "common multitude" [vulgus]—had little desire to wage another dangerous, costly, and morally questionable civil war against fellow Christians. Louis therefore needed to convince his rank-and-file soldiers of the justice of his invasion of Gaul. At the same time, Louis needed to make it seem that his invasion of Gaul was not imminent so that he could catch Charles the Bald off guard. To those ends, Louis devised a clever ruse. He ordered three armies to gather in July—not to invade Gaul but ostensibly to fight various rebel Slavs.[87] Believing that his brother's troops were committed to wars in the east, in July Charles the Bald led an army against the Vikings on the Seine.[88] However, it seems that Louis had secretly arranged for a highly choreographed embassy to arrive from Gaul just as he was assembling his troops. "Suddenly and unexpectedly" on July 16, Abbot Adalhard of St.-Bertin and Count Odo of Troyes arrived at Louis's court. Before the assembled eastern troops, they beseeched Louis to "liberate" them from Charles the Bald's "tyranny," threatening that they would be forced to ally with the pagan Vikings if he did not come to their aid. The *Annals of Fulda* echoed the official spin of the east Frankish court:

> The king was deeply troubled when he heard these things, for he was now in a double bind. If he acquiesced to the pleas of the people, he would have to move against his brother, which was wicked. However, if he spared his brother, he would be forced to abandon liberating a people in distress, which would be equally wicked. On top of all this was a serious additional concern: the common multitude suspected that everything he did in this matter came out of a desire not to help the people but merely to expand his kingdom. But the truth was far different from this opinion of the common multitude, as all those knowing the counsels of the king can truly testify. Placed under such a burden of cares, at length he acquiesced to the counsel of his wise men and relied on his clear conscience, for he preferred to act for the good of many than to consent to the obstinacy of a single man [i.e., Charles the Bald].

---

[87] *AF*, s.a. 858, p. 49. Louis was at Frankfurt on June 13: *DLG* 93.
[88] *AB*, s.a. 858, p. 78.

Thus he gave in to the legates' requests and promised that with God's help he would come according to the wishes of the people desiring his presence.[89]

Despite this court propaganda, the opinion of the multitude was correct: Louis was driven by the desire for territorial expansion. Regino, who otherwise had a high opinion of Louis, saw this clearly half a century later. He wrote that the western magnates "approached King Louis across the Rhine and enticed his heart to win his brother's kingdom, promising to give themselves and their kingdom over to his lordship. The hearts of kings are greedy and never satisfied, and with this argument they easily won him over to their scheme."[90]

Louis's plan was as brazen as it was straightforward: to depose his half brother and seize the western throne for himself.[91] In the middle of August, he regathered his army at Worms and from there led them south to Strasbourg, turned west along the Roman road to Metz, and then entered the heart of Charles's kingdom.[92] On September 1, Louis arrived in Ponthion, where he received the submission of the magnates of the region. Louis had timed his campaign brilliantly. At that moment Charles the Bald was off fighting the Vikings near Rouen, and with him were his two sons as well as Lothar II. Louis and his army pushed on to Sens, where he was welcomed by the powerful Archbishop Wenilo, and then continued to Orléans. After receiving the submission of the Aquitanians, Neustrians, and Bretons, Louis set out to hunt down Charles. When Charles learned of his brother's invasion, he broke off his siege of the Vikings and hurried to Brienne on the Aube River, where he received reinforcements from Burgundy. Louis rejected Charles's pleas for peace, and on November 12 the two brothers prepared their armies for battle.[93] A replay of the battle of Fontenoy seemed imminent, with Louis now playing the role of Lothar. But when Charles saw the size of Louis's eastern army and witnessed the number of his own supporters who had gone over to his brother, he realized he could not win by

[89] *AF*, s.a. 858, pp. 49–50.

[90] Regino, *Chronicon*, s.a. 866, p. 90.

[91] For Louis's invasion of Charles's kingdom, see *AB*, s.a. 858, pp. 78–79; *AF*, s.a. 858, pp. 50–51; BM 1435b–n, 1436a–f; Dümmler, *GOR* 1:426–46; Nelson, *Charles the Bald*, 188–92.

[92] Louis made grants to the Ecbertiner convent of Herford just before setting out for Gaul and soon after returning, which would seem to indicate that his army included Saxon troops: *DLG* 93, 95. Louis sent Carloman and Louis the Younger to guard the eastern borders of the kingdom, the latter of whom led a large army against the Obodrites: *AH*, s.a. 858, p. 18; *AI*, s.a. 858, p. 744.

[93] During the negotiations, Hincmar of Reims excommunicated the west Frankish magnates who had gone over to Louis: BM 1435k.

force and so chose the prudent course of fleeing from certain defeat to Burgundy. Bereft of their leader, the remainder of Charles's supporters had no choice but to submit to Louis.

At this moment, Louis made a critical decision. He chose not to pursue Charles and instead allowed his eastern army to return home. The author of the *Annals of Fulda* saw this decision as a serious mistake: "He was led by an incautious sense of security and sent back home the whole of his army that he had led from the east, vainly placing his trust and hope in those who had deserted and betrayed their own lord." In truth, Louis had little choice. It was already mid-November, and Charles was sure to take refuge in a fortified Burgundian city such as Auxerre or Autun. A protracted siege in the middle of the winter would have placed considerable strain on Louis's army, whose common soldiers already had little enthusiasm for the renewed civil war. Moreover, despite Louis's extensive logistical preparations, by now his army had been on the march for three months and was running out of food, and his soldiers therefore had begun to plunder the countryside.[94] But requisitioning supplies was a time-consuming and difficult strategy that dangerously exposed one's troops to surprise attacks. Facing the onset of winter, low morale among the common soldiers, and a general lack of supplies, Louis had no choice but to send his army home.

As a veteran of several civil wars, Louis knew that the key to gaining the western throne was winning the support of the magnates and Church, not threatening them with an occupying army. Thus, after Charles's flight, Louis quickly journeyed west to Troyes, the seat of his supporter Odo. At Troyes Louis solidified the backing of the western magnates by granting them counties, monasteries, benefices, and royal lands, thereby making them complicit in his seizure of power. Louis then hurried north to the important royal palace of Attigny in the west Frankish heartlands. By now, he had proclaimed himself king of west Francia. At Attigny he issued a diploma dated "with Christ's favor in the twenty-sixth year of the lord and most pious King Louis ruling in east Francia, the first year ruling in west Francia."[95] Archbishop Wenilo of Sens now emerged as one of Louis's chief western supporters: he publicly performed the Mass for Louis, urged him to force Charles's *fideles* to swear the oath of fidelity to him, and offered to use his influence to win the support of the west Frankish bishops.[96] Lothar II also ap-

[94] BM 1435i.

[95] *DLG* 95 (December 7, 858). Louis issued this diploma for his royal *fidelis*, Tuto, with whom he exchanged lands in the Kraichgau and Lobdengau. For speculation about Tuto's identity, see Innes, *State and Society*, p. 216 and n. 94.

[96] In June 859 Charles the Bald drew up a list of specific charges against Wenilo: MGH *Concilia* 3:464–67.

peared at Attigny, and Wenilo helped persuade him to renounce his alliance with Charles and come over to Louis. Louis rewarded Wenilo for his support, granting him the monastery of St.-Colombe in Sens and bestowing the bishopric of Bayeaux on one of his relatives. Wenilo was to earn lasting infamy for his betrayal of Charles the Bald. The eleventh-century epic, the *Song of Roland*, transformed him into the archtraitor Ganelon, the faithless vassal of Charlemagne. But in 858, Wenilo believed he was throwing his support behind the king who was about to become the new Charlemagne.

The *Annals of Fulda* also blamed the failure of Louis's invasion on the treachery of Queen Emma's Welf nephews, Conrad the Younger and Hugh the Abbot.[97] According to that chronicler, Louis sent Conrad and Hugh to spy out Charles's position in Burgundy. However, to avenge injuries Louis had done to them, Conrad and Hugh betrayed Louis and reported to Charles that he had only a small force with him and thus could be overcome with a large army. But, once again, we cannot take the *Annals of Fulda* at face value. The idea that Charles learned of the departure of the east Frankish army through Conrad and Hugh makes little sense: Charles would have had scouts reporting Louis's activities, and Charles himself made a reconnaissance trip north in late November.[98] Moreover, it is highly unlikely that Louis placed much trust in these Welf brothers, since Conrad the Younger and Hugh had gone over to Charles the Bald five years earlier. In return for their switch of loyalty, Charles had granted them the Burgundian county of Auxerre and the wealthy monastery of St.-Germain (also in Auxerre).[99] After Conrad and Hugh's departure west in 853, Louis had begun to revoke the Alemannian counties of their father and brother, Conrad the Elder and Welf II, and to bestow them on the rival Udalriching family.[100] Apparently it was this injury—the loss of the family counties in Alemannia—that the younger Conrad and Hugh wanted to avenge in 858.[101] Given this preexist-

[97] For a good discussion of these events, see Nelson, *Charles the Bald*, 177–80, although I do not follower her redating of Conrad and Hugh's embassy to Charles to 853.

[98] Charles made a quick trip from Burgundy to Francia and was at Avenay (south of Reims) in late November: *DCB* 199.

[99] *DCB* 156. During the 858 invasion, Charles never lost the support of the Burgundian nobility, and the Welfs were prominent among them. On January 6, 859, Charles had participated in the translation of Saint Germain's relics at Auxerre into a new crypt built by Conrad the Elder. Three days later Charles made a rich grant to Hugh's monastery: Heiric, *Miracula sancti Germani episcopi Autissiodorensis*, 2.101, in *PL*, ed. J.-P. Migne, vol. 124 (Paris, 1852), cols. 1254–55; *DCB* 200.

[100] Borgolte, *Geschichte*, 255; idem, *Grafen*, 165–70, 259, 290–91.

[101] *AF* 858: "cuius animum ad ultionem iniuriarum suarum erexerant filii Cuonrati comitis." *Annals of Fulda*, trans. Reuter, 43, translates "ad ultionem iniuriarum suarum" as "to avenge himself for the injuries done him [i.e., Charles]," although it makes more sense if the word *suarum* is taken as a reference to the injuries done to the Welfs.

ing hostility toward the Welfs, Louis hardly could have been surprised that they betrayed him and went over to Charles in 858. In other words, the Welf brothers did not jump ship; Louis pushed them overboard. The *Annals of Fulda* were scapegoating a group of nobles who already had fallen from Louis's favor.

The real reason the 858 invasion failed was Louis's inability to win the support of the western bishops beyond Wenilo of Sens. Only the blessing of the bishops—especially the influential Archbishop Hincmar of Reims, whose archdiocese encompassed the west Frankish royal heartlands—could grant an aura of legitimacy to Louis's ruthless coup. Louis sent a letter requesting that Hincmar and the western bishops meet with him on November 25 at Reims to discuss the "restoration of the holy Church and the state and safety of the Christian people." At this crucial juncture, the west Frankish bishops "saved Charles the Bald's bacon."[102] Instead of appearing at Reims, they hastily arranged a synod at Quierzy, where Hincmar composed a long letter to Louis in their name.[103] Politely addressing Louis as the "glorious king" (although not "most glorious"), they lamely excused themselves from the Reims assembly on account of the short notice. Although they did not reject Louis outright, for the moment they declined to become his *fideles*. They urged Louis to prove his desire to defend the west Frankish Church and people by respecting ecclesiastical immunities, restoring monasteries granted to laymen, appointing upstanding royal ministers, and driving out the Vikings. The bishops emphasized their desire to proceed slowly and cautiously in initiating any regime change, pointing out that such a measure would require a synod of all the bishops north of the Alps—especially those who had anointed Charles king. In the meantime, they suggested that Louis reread the book of Kings and ponder the lesson of David's refusal to raise his hand against King Saul because he was the Lord's anointed.

Hincmar's decision to remain loyal to Charles was, at least in part, a political calculation. It is possible that Louis had been courting Hincmar's support before the 858 invasion. At unknown dates, Louis and Hincmar exchanged numerous letters, and Louis once sent the archbishop the valuable iron for a bell for one of Reims's churches. Moreover, on another occasion, Louis restored to Reims lands in the Wormsgau, Vosges, and Thuringia that had been usurped.[104] But as the most powerful archbishop in west Francia, Hincmar had tremendous influence at Charles the Bald's court. Hincmar

---

[102] Innes, *State and Society*, 216.
[103] MGH *Capitularia* 3:403–27.
[104] Flodoard, *Historia*, 3.20: 262–67.

could not be certain that he would attain the same status if Louis seized the west Frankish throne, since Louis already had his own coterie of ecclesiastical advisers, including Grimald of St.-Gall, Charles of Mainz, and, most recently, Wenilo of Sens. In the end, Hincmar decided to play it cautiously in 858: he did not reject Louis's bid for the western throne outright, but he also did not swear loyalty to him either. Like most Frankish magnates, Hincmar was skilled at sitting on a fence.

Louis's failure to win the support of the western bishops shattered his plans. Without their backing, he could not legitimate his seizure of power. Louis's desperation to win over Hincmar led him to visit Reims in mid-December, in spite of the archbishop's repeated objections to such a visit.[105] During their meeting, Hincmar apparently refused to budge from the position he had outlined at Quierzy and declined to invite the eastern king to celebrate Christmas with him. Frustrated once again, Louis was forced to turn north and celebrate Christmas at St.-Quentin, near the border of Lotharingia. In effect, his retreat eastward had begun. Soon after Christmas, Charles the Bald moved north with an army, forcing Louis to depart from his kingdom. Charles celebrated January 15, 859, as the day he recovered his throne.[106]

Louis spent the next two years picking up the pieces from his failed invasion. During the spring and summer of 859, Louis sent repeated embassies to Charles and Lothar II seeking reconciliation.[107] Charles the Bald and Lothar II immediately renewed their defensive alliance, and they ordered that a joint west Frankish–Lotharingian synod under Archbishops Hincmar of Reims and Gunther of Cologne be convened at Metz to draft a list of demands for the eastern king. The demands were as follows: that Louis admit wrongdoing for his invasion and the plundering by his army, perform public penance, renounce his ties to his western supporters, and agree to a meeting at which the kings would restore *pax et concordia*.[108] Although the bishops considered Louis "unofficially" excommunicated for associating with the western nobles who had betrayed Charles, they emphasized that, for the sake of rebuilding goodwill, the east Frankish king should not "officially" be excommunicated if he agreed to Charles and Lothar's demands.

Louis used his usual diplomatic skill to wiggle out of this humiliating situation. Hincmar of Reims was charged with bringing the list of demands to Louis. However, Gunther of Cologne, with whom Louis had good rela-

105 Ibid., 3.20, 3.21, pp. 263, 285.
106 *DCB* 246, 247.
107 *AF*, s.a. 859, p. 53.
108 MGH *Concilia* 3:435–43.

tions, secretly came to the east Frankish court in advance and advised Louis of the Metz resolutions before Hincmar's arrival. At this moment, Louis was at Frankfurt with a group of supporters from Saxony, Alemannia, and Bavaria.[109] When Louis learned of Hincmar's imminent arrival, he quickly set out westward to intercept the delegation, bringing only three supporters with him: Grimald of St.-Gall and Bishops Theoderich of Minden and Solomon of Constance. Louis apparently did this to buy time: with only three advisers in tow, he could claim that he was unable to respond immediately to Hincmar's demands, since he would need to consult with a larger body of advisers.[110] This ploy was one of Louis's tried-and-true diplomatic strategies: delay through ongoing negotiation.

Louis gave an audience to Hincmar on Sunday, June 4, 859, at Worms. The king carefully orchestrated the meeting to reassert his God-given royal authority and to make clear that Hincmar, who was largely responsible for his failed invasion of Gaul, could not push him around. Louis received Hincmar while he stood before the altar in the Worms cathedral, and he had Hincmar stand on his left, saving the more honored right-hand position for his (technically lower-ranking) three advisers, Grimald, Theoderich, and Solomon. Their meeting, held in Latin, was brief and tense.[111] Louis began with disarming directness. He said to the archbishop of Reims, "I ask that you pardon me if I have offended you in any way, so that from the outset I can speak freely with you." Taken aback, Hincmar at first responded vaguely: "This matter can be quickly settled, since we offer what you ask of us." Not satisfied, Grimald, Theoderich, and Solomon demanded that Hincmar "do as our lord asks: pardon him." Hincmar answered, "I forgive and pardon those offenses he committed against me, that is, against my own person. But concerning those evils done against the Church and people committed to me, I freely give you counsel and offer help according to God's will, so that you may be saved, if that is what you want." At this point, Louis abruptly brought the meeting to an end. He said to Hincmar: "You sent me your letter with the chapter headings [from the Metz synod] and came here with this case already decided. But I have only two or three supporters with me, since I hurried here without others. I cannot enter into any

[109] In addition to Theoderich of Minden, Solomon of Constance, and Grimald of St.-Gall, Louis's supporters also included Abbess Hadwig of Herford, representatives of the bishop of Regensburg, Bishop Badurad of Paderborn, Witgar, and apparently several Saxon laymen: *DLG* 95–97.

[110] Bigott, *Ludwig der Deutsche*, 139.

[111] Hincmar's minutes from the Worms meeting survive: *Relatio legatorum*, in MGH *Concilia* 3:443–44.

formal discussion of these charges before considering them with our bishops, because—thanks be to God!—I did nothing without their counsel. Only then can I respond to them." Having accomplished little, a frustrated Hincmar returned home and reported to Charles that his embassy had accomplished nothing. Louis had won the upper hand in the diplomatic exchange. But it was a petty victory that probably left a bitter aftertaste in Louis's mouth. After all, Hincmar had single-handedly thwarted his scheme to reunite the empire.

The negotiations dragged on for another year, frequently mediated by Lothar II, who acted as the peace broker between the two brothers. The three kings met during the summer of 859. But because of their enduring mistrust, they held their talks on an island in the Rhine near Andernach while their supporters waited on the shore.[112] After lengthy discussions, they were unable to reach an agreement. The sticking point was that Louis wanted Charles to restore the offices and honors to the western magnates who had supported him, revealing Louis's continued efforts to maintain political backers in Charles's kingdom. Charles understandably refused—Robert the Strong and Odo of Troyes were still rebelling against him—and the three kings therefore put off the matter until a later conference. In the meantime, Louis sent Abbot Thioto of Fulda to the new pope, Nicholas I (858–67), to give an acceptable explanation for his invasion. With the aid of Louis's ally, Emperor Louis II of Italy, the abbot of Fulda returned with a letter of pardon from Nicholas. Louis planned to present this papal pardon to Charles and Lothar II at a meeting at Basel in October 859, although, in the end, the meeting never took place.[113]

The three kings finally restored concord at Koblenz in June 860.[114] The venue, apparently selected by Louis, emphasized his regained political and military strength: Koblenz was on the western border of his kingdom (thus compelling the two kings to travel to him), and the town was situated within an old Roman fortress. Louis came to Koblenz with an especially broad group of supporters from all his territories: Bishops Altfrid of Hildesheim, Solomon of Constance, Theoderich of Minden, Liutbert of Münster, Geb-

---

[112] *AF*, s.a. 859, p. 53. Charles the Bald, Lothar II, Charles of Provence, and a large body of west Frankish, Lotharingian, and Burgundian bishops had met at Savonnières near Toul in June 859 to deal with the numerous problems brought about by Louis's invasion. The bishops urged Louis the German and Charles the Bald to restore "caritas fraterna et concordia pacis," and Charles the Bald made a series of formal charges against Louis's west Frankish supporter, Wenilo of Sens: MGH *Concilia* 3:447–89.

[113] *AF*, s.a. 859, pp. 53–54; *AB*, s.a. 859, p. 81; BM 1289c.

[114] *AB*, s.a. 860, p. 83; *AF*, s.a. 860, pp. 54–55; MGH *Capitularia* 2:152–58.

hard of Speyer, Abbot Witgar of Ottobeuren, Counts Ernest, Werner, Liuthar, Beringar, Adalbert, Christian, and Liudolf, as well as the royal steward Ratpot II.[115] Louis also brought with him his young grandsons, Arnulf and Hugh, the illegitimate sons of Carloman and Louis the Younger, perhaps to underscore that his eastern branch of the Carolingian dynasty was there to stay. Louis achieved a significant victory at the Koblenz meeting. No longer were there discussions of penance or excommunication, as Hincmar had demanded the previous year. The only issue now on the table was reestablishing an equal peace among the kings. Each king publicly swore an oath of mutual counsel and aid and promised not to plot to usurp each other's kingdom. The bishops and laymen presented a list of capitularies for royal approval that reiterated the decrees from the 851 Treaty of Meersen: peace and concord among the kings; defense of the Church and people; punishment for outlaws and sowers of discord; and law and justice for the kings' subjects. The kings also read a series of public statements in the vernacular to ensure the understanding of the nobles: Louis and Lothar II read in Frankish, and Charles in both Romance and Frankish.[116] Louis's chief concern was negotiating pardon for the western magnates who had come over to him during his invasion, a concern that revealed his determination to remain involved in the aristocratic politics of his brother's kingdom. After Charles had read his statement, Louis turned to his brother and said in Romance, "Now, if you please, I want to have your word concerning those men who pledged fidelity to me." Charles responded in a raised voice in Romance that he would give full amnesty to all those who had supported the east Frankish king during his invasion. He promised to return their family lands as well as property given to them by Louis the Pious (but not those bestowed by himself) if they swore to be loyal in the future, on the condition that Louis do the same for those who had supported Charles with properties in the east.[117]

---

[115] MGH *Capitularia* 2:154.

[116] Charles's preliminary *adnuntiatio* emphasized the important role Lothar II had played in restoring peace between him and Louis the German. Charles had rejected Lothar's first proposal of terms for the agreement between him and Louis the German, but he accepted his second proposal. Lothar's statement expressed his commitment to adhere to the assembly's resolutions.

[117] Louis did restore some of the Welf lands to Conrad the Elder, since the following year he confirmed an exchange of properties in Alemannia between Grimald and the "illustrious Count Conrad": *DLG* 103. Despite his title, however, Louis did not reinvest Conrad or his son Welf II with their former Alemannian counties: Borgolte, *Grafen*, 168. Charles also expressed his potential willingness to restore properties and honors he gave the rebels, on the condition that those magnates return to his fidelity. (For an English

Thus, between 853 and 860, Louis failed twice in attempts to expand his kingdom westward. In both cases, he invested considerable time, energy, and resources in planning the invasions, and it was only by the slimmest of margins that he failed. Had Pippin II not escaped from his monastic prison during the summer of 854, or had Hincmar of Reims decided to back the eastern king in 858, Louis would have reunified much, if not all, of the Carolingian empire. Although failures, Louis's attempts to annex Aquitaine and Gaul demonstrate that he continued to see his world through the lenses of a unified Frankish kingdom. For the remainder of his reign, Louis would continue his policy of *Drang nach Westen*.

---

translation, see Nelson, *Charles the Bald*, 195–96.) Charles had in fact already pardoned Wenilo of Sens the previous year without an episcopal hearing: *AB*, s.a. 859, p. 82.

CHAPTER EIGHT
TRIALS AND TRIUMPHS, 861-870

After the 860 Treaty of Koblenz, Louis continued his policy of western expansion. During the next decade, however, the king faced a series of interrelated crises and challenges to his rule. Much of this political turmoil arose from the fact that, now in his fifties, Louis was approaching old age. Throughout the Middle Ages, aging kings often encountered challenges from their heirs, and Louis was no exception. Echoing conflicts that had occurred during the last decade of his father's reign, Louis confronted repeated rebellions from his adult sons, who felt chafed by their domineering father and yearned to rule in their own right. As always, these royal heirs became the focal point of aristocratic ambition and unrest, as magnates rallied around the next generation of Carolingian kings in the hope of defending and expanding their wealth and power. During the 860s, Louis also fell victim to other perennial threats to aging medieval rulers: illness and injury. Louis almost died twice during this decade, and these life-threatening crises precipitated dramatic political reactions throughout his kingdom, and indeed across Europe.

The crises Louis faced during the 860s had important international dimensions. In the course of rebelling against their father, Louis's sons allied with the increasingly powerful Rastislav of Moravia. By now, Rastislav had become a significant political figure in Europe, and he pursued his own farsighted diplomacy on the world stage. Seeking to free himself from Louis's overlordship, Rastislav formed a defensive alliance with Constantinople. This Byzantine–Moravian entente was a new diplomatic axis in eastern Europe and caused a series of counteralliances among Louis, Rome, the Bavarian Eastland, and the Bulgar court. Carolingian dynastic politics compounded the complexity of these diplomatic webs. Louis and Charles the Bald now focused their energies on territorial conquest in the middle kingdoms of their three nephews, forcing Lothar I's sons to form defensive alliances against their grasping uncles. Despite these considerable political and diplomatic challenges, Louis's policies during this period ended in success: by 870, he had managed to defend his power both within and beyond his borders and annex the eastern half of Lotharingia. The 860s therefore provide a case study of an aging ruler's effective response to conflict and crisis.[1]

CONSPIRACIES AND REBELLIONS

As Louis had feared, his ambitious son Carloman began pursuing his own independent politics soon after becoming prefect of the Eastland in 856. Carloman had good reason to feel that his father unfairly limited his power. Louis had become king of Bavaria at around the age of fifteen, and the following year he had married Carloman's mother, Queen Emma. In contrast, Louis forced Carloman to wait until he was twenty-six before appointing him prefect (not king). Even then, Louis did not allow Carloman to marry, thereby preventing him from forming his own independent household. Adding insult to injury, Louis had denied Carloman the prefect's seat in the Eastland—Tulln in Upper Pannonia—and instead confined him to the peripheral region of Carantania. Louis took these measures to prevent a repeat of the rebellions of the 830s, but Carloman was struggling under his own pressures. As a Carolingian approaching middle age, he needed to start a family and build his own political base. Otherwise he risked being swept into the historical dustbin already filled with could-have-been Frankish princes.

Carloman's first known act of independence was an affair with a woman named Liutswind in the 840s. Political ambition as well as princely testosterone seem to have driven this relationship. Liutswind was a well-connected noblewoman: she apparently was the daughter of the Bavarian count Ratolt, and her sister was married to the east Frankish count Sigihard

---

[1] The most thorough discussion of the politics of the 860s still is Dümmler, *GOR* 2:1–302. Kasten, *Königssöhne*, 498–541, offers a good account of Louis's relations with his sons during the last two decades of his reign. See further: Nelson, *Charles the Bald*, 190–220; Hartmann, *Ludwig der Deutsche*, 54–60; Bigott, *Ludwig der Deutsche*, 140–50.

of the Kraichgau.[2] Through this liaison, therefore, Carloman forged alliances with powerful magnates in Bavaria and on the middle Rhine. When Liutswind bore Carloman a son around 850, he named the boy Arnulf. Although not a royal name like Charles, Louis, or Pippin, Arnulf nevertheless carried strong Carolingian connotations. It had been the name of the revered Carolingian ancestor Bishop Arnulf of Metz (ca. 614–47), whom the ninth-century Carolingians honored as a saint and descendant of the first Merovingian king, Clovis (highly dubious on both counts).[3] Thus, although Carloman did not give his illegitimate son a royal name, he bestowed on him a very Carolingian name. Carloman was keeping his options open. If need be, he could later "activate" his illegitimate son's Carolingian blood and make him a royal heir. (As it turned out, Carloman's son would later attain the purple and became the east Frankish king, Arnulf of Carantania, ruling from 887 to 899.) In 860 Arnulf was in Louis the German's entourage alongside the illegitimate son of Louis the Younger, Hugh. This suggests that the king was supervising the military training of his grandsons and, at the same time, keeping them at his court in the hope of ensuring his sons' loyalty.[4]

Carloman rebelled against his father in 857, with the intention of creating an independent principality in the Eastland. His immediate objective was to annex Upper Pannonia from his seat in Carantania, so he began by plundering along the Schwarza River northeast of the Semmering Pass, the strategic gateway that linked Carantania to Upper Pannonia.[5] He then turned against his father's supporters in the Eastland, many of whom belonged to the powerful Wilhelminer family. Carloman drove into exile the Wilhelminer Count Rihheri of Szombathely, forcing Rihheri's relative, Count Pabo of Carantania, to lead a revolt with his fellow counts (*cum sociis comitibus*) against the king's son.[6] Pabo's fellow counts presumably included

---

[2] On Sigihard and Liutswind, see *DLG* 53, 94; *DArnulf* 87, 136; Mitterauer, *Markgrafen*, 212–27, 226.

[3] Riché, *Carolingians*, 15–17; *Annals of St.-Bertin*, trans. Nelson, 161n20. Louis the Pious had named his first son, born to him by a concubine, Arnulf: Werner, "Nachkommen," 446 (III.9); Boshof, *Ludwig der Fromme*, 59. The fact that Carloman likewise gave his son this name suggests that he did not consider Liutswind his legal wife.

[4] The witness list from the 860 Koblenz summit contains the name-pair "Arnulfus, Hugo": MGH *Capitularia* 2:154.

[5] *AI*, s.a. 857, p. 744.

[6] Concerning Pabo, see Wolfram, *Salzburg*, 304–5, 317. Mitterauer, *Karolingische Markgrafen*, 160–62, believed that Pabo's *seditio* was a rebellion against King Louis. However, it is far more likely that Pabo's *seditio* was a reaction against Carloman's effort to seize control of the Eastland. Mitterauer argued that the 857 entry in the *AI* should be redated to late 859 or early 860, since he otherwise could not explain why Louis referred to

other members of the Wilhelminer family loyal to the king: Counts William of the Traungau and Witagowo of Carantania, *dux* Pribina of Lower Pannonia (who seems to have been married to a Wilhelminerin), and Pribina's son, Count Chozil.[7] In this way, Carloman's seizure of Lower Pannonia forced Louis's *fideles* to unite against his rebel son.

Carloman had timed his rebellion well; it coincided with his father's 858 invasion of Gaul, which momentarily gave Carloman a free hand in the southeast. Although his father ordered him to lead a campaign against Rastislav in 858, Carloman instead struck an alliance with him. The *Old Salzburg Annals* reported that "Rastislav swore a pact with Carloman. They once again set in order the wastelands of the Bavarians, and they lived in peace without war."[8] In the ninth century, the phrase *deserta Boiorum*, "wastelands of the Bavarians," designated Upper Pannonia and Lower Pannonia, where the Avars had formerly had their empire.[9] Yet what the chroniclers saw as a second-rate frontier wasteland had become a political fulcrum in the balance of power east of the Rhine. Having seized Upper Pannonia the previous year, Carloman in 858 seems to have conceded neighboring Lower Pannonia to Rastislav in return for his support. The king's son knew how to play one enemy against another. Lower Pannonia was in the hands of King Louis's staunch supporter, *dux* Pribina, who governed the region from his massive swamp fortress at Moosburg. By granting Pribina's principality to Rastislav, Carloman therefore instigated a war between those two Slavic princes and was able to stand on the sidelines to watch them fight it out. In early 860, Pribina appeared at Louis's court in Regensburg, pointing to the conclusion that Rastislav had successfully driven him out of his duchy.[10] Pribina asked the king to confirm his recent grant of lands in Lower Pannonia to Niederalteich, which seems to have been his desperate

---

Pabo as "fidelis comes noster" in a diploma dated October 1, 859: *DLG* 99. However, if one sees Pabo leading a rebellion against Carloman and remaining loyal to Louis, then there is no contradiction in the sources, and the date of 857 in the Salzburg annals can be accepted.

[7] Mitterauer, *Karolingische Markgrafen*, 104–17, 144. For Pabo's relations with Witagowo, see *DLG* 99.

[8] *AI*, s.a. 858, p. 744; *AF*, s.a. 858, p. 49.

[9] Einhard reported that Upper and Lower Pannonia became a "wasteland" [vacua, desertus] after Charlemagne's conquest of the Avar empire, and in the early tenth century Regino still referred to the region as the "wastelands of the Pannonians and Avars" [Pannoniorum et Avarum solitudines]: Einhard, *VK*, chap. 13, p. 16; Regino, *Chronicon*, s.a. 889, p. 132 and n. 3. The Anglo-Saxon translation of *Orosius* from the court of Alfred the Great similarly described Upper and Lower Pannonia as a wasteland (*westenne*) bounded by Moravia, Carantania, and Bulgaria: *The Old English Orosius*, vol. 1.1, ed. Janet Bately, Early English Text Society, suppl. series 6 (London, 1980), 13.

[10] *DLG* 100.

attempt to prevent his properties from falling into Rastislav's hands. Pribina's efforts were in vain, however. He died fighting the Moravians soon thereafter.[11]

Frustrated in his effort to conquer the west, Louis now had to prevent a disaster in the east. When Louis returned from Gaul in early 859, he responded to the alliance between Carloman and Rastislav by building up the power of his loyal Bavarian *fideles* in the Eastland. In this way, the king sought to solidify his support in the southeastern marches and tip the balance of power back in his favor. His first act was to grant Prefect Ratpot's former seat at Tulln with its rich fiscal lands to Bishop Erchanfrid of Regensburg.[12] In his diploma, Louis threw down the gauntlet to his rebel son, asserting that "no prefect whosoever"—that is, Carloman—should dare take possession of Tulln. For the time being, Louis permitted Ratpot's presumable son, the royal steward Ratpot II, to hold the Tulln estates in precarial arrangement from St.-Emmeram as a bulwark against Carloman. Louis spent the winter of 859–60 in Bavaria, where he issued an impressive series of grants throughout the Eastland to his supporters.[13] On November 20, 860, at Mattighofen, Louis made a truly spectacular gift to Archbishop Adalwin of Salzburg. He confirmed Salzburg's possession of Szombathely and Postrum-Szentpéterfa, and in addition he gave to Salzburg its twenty-four benefices strewn throughout Upper and Lower Pannonia and Carantania.[14] Louis's diplomas emphasized that he made these grants at the request of his leading Bavarian supporters in the Eastland: Bishops Adalwin of Salzburg, Erchanfrid of Regensburg, Hartwig of Passau, and Otgar of Eichstätt, *dux* Pribina, and the Carantanian Count Pabo. These longtime supporters had much to lose if the rebellion of Carloman and Rastislav succeeded.

Despite Louis's flood of grants to supporters in the Eastland, Carloman's rebellion had gained momentum.[15] By early 861, the king's son had won over a number of his father's chief supporters, headed by Count Ernest. Winning the support of Ernest was a major coup for Carloman, since Ernest was the "greatest among all the king's great men." Hincmar of Reims, who at this point became the author of the *Annals of St.-Bertin*, indicated that Carloman had enticed away his father's chief supporter by marrying Ernest's daughter. Through this marriage alliance, Ernest sought to hitch his wagon to Carloman's rising star and guarantee his place (and the

[11] *Conversio*, chap. 13, p. 132; Wolfram, *Salzburg*, 315n633.

[12] DLG 96. Louis issued this grant on May 1, 859, at Frankfurt.

[13] DLG 98–102. Bowlus, *Franks, Moravians, and Magyars*, 133–40, offers a different interpretation of these grants.

[14] DLG 102; Wolfram, *Grenzen und Räume*, 252–53.

[15] *AF*, s.a. 861, p. 55; *AB*, s.a. 861, p. 85.

place of his son, Ernest II) among Carloman's inner circle of advisers when the aging Louis died. Carloman won over other leading eastern nobles as well: Ernest's three Konradiner nephews, Counts Uto and Berengar and Abbot Waldo; the brother-in-law of Carloman's mistress, Count Sigihard of the Kraichgau; and a certain Count Gerold. Ernest, Berengar, and Sigihard had all attended the Treaty of Koblenz with King Louis in June 860, indicating that they turned coat sometime between the late summer of 860 and early 861.[16]

With the backing of these Frankish magnates and Rastislav's military support, Carloman annexed the Eastland and eastern Bavaria up to the Inn River. This was a stunning seizure of territory, encompassing all the royal estates and benefices in Upper Pannonia, the important royal manors of Altötting, Ranshofen, and Mattighofen in eastern Bavaria, as well as the archbishopric of Salzburg itself. Even the *Annals of Fulda*, whose author showed striking sympathy toward the king's eldest son and heretofore had passed over his rebellion in silence, had to admit that Carloman was a rebel: "He drove out the commanders to whom had been entrusted the defense of the Pannonian and Carantanian frontier and placed the march under his own men. This greatly angered the king who suspected rebellion." With Carloman and Rastislav in control of the Eastland, Louis's *fideles*, Count Pabo of Carantania and the late Pribina's son, Count Chozil, took refuge in Bavaria, the former at Salzburg and the latter at Regensburg.[17] Like his father, Chozil granted his lands near Lake Balaton to the Bavarian Church in a desperate attempt to place them beyond the reach of the rebels.[18]

Louis knew that if he did not respond decisively he risked a replay of the 833 Field of Lies, with himself cast in the role of Louis the Pious. Thus, in April 861, he held an assembly in Regensburg at which he accused Ernest, Uto, Berengar, Waldo, Sigihard, and Gerold of infidelity and stripped them and their accomplices of their public honors.[19] Louis's actions demonstrate both the strengths as well as the limitations of his power vis-à-vis the eastern nobles. In the face of the most serious challenge to his rule since the civil war, Louis was able to use the charge of infidelity to strip a powerful rebel faction of magnates (who probably were not present at the assembly) of their *publici honores*, thereby defending his control of the east Frankish "state." Yet Louis's power was not absolute. He could do this only within the context of an assembly, underscoring that he needed the nobles' consent to convict rebels of treason. Moreover, on this occasion, Louis was not strong

16 MGH *Capitularia* 2:154.
17 *Auctarium Garstense*, s.a. 861, p. 565; Wolfram, *Salzburg*, 305n590.
18 *Freising* 887 (March 21, 861).
19 *AF*, s.a. 861, p. 55; *AH*, s.a. 861, p. 18.

enough to seize the rebels' private lands, and he instead allowed them to "remain within their homeland on their property." The downfall of this powerful faction had repercussions throughout the Carolingian kingdoms that were, at least in part, beyond Louis's control. Uto, Berengar, and Waldo packed up and moved to the court of Charles the Bald, along with their relative, Count Adalhard (whom Lothar II now drove out of the middle kingdom at Louis's urging because of Adalhard's ties to the eastern rebels). Charles was only too happy to spite his brother by giving these refugee magnates new *honores*.

Louis moved to overcome his rebel son through his usual combination of diplomacy, trickery, threats, and warfare. When Carloman refused to submit, an enraged Louis proclaimed before a crowd of courtiers that "his son Carloman, from that moment and henceforth, as long as he lived and reigned, would never possess public *honores* with his consent."[20] At this moment, a group of Hungarians attacked the eastern borders of Louis's kingdom.[21] The Hungarians were a nomadic steppe people from central Asia, and this was their first appearance on the stage of European history. Although the *Annals of St.-Bertin* give no details about the causes or consequences of the raid, it seems likely that Carloman and Rastislav had hired the group of Hungarians to attack Louis's borders.[22] In response to Carloman's and Rastislav's ongoing rebellion, Louis negotiated a counteralliance (*foedus pacis*) with Khan Boris of Bulgaria.[23] Rastislav's recent annexation of Lower Pannonia must have concerned Boris, giving him common cause with the Frankish king. In the summer of 863, Louis launched a well-executed surprise campaign against Carloman, while Boris sent a Bulgar army from the east. Louis made his preparations for the 863 campaign during Easter at Salzburg, over which he had reasserted his control.[24] Louis cleverly made it seem that he was leading this campaign against Rastislav, but at the last minute he moved against his son, who was holed up in Carantania. Carloman's supporter, Count Gundachar, who commanded Carloman's army, was guarding the Semmering Pass to Carantania, but the king bribed him to betray his son and submit to him instead. Gundachar's defection left Carloman no choice but to surrender, and the king took his rebel

---

[20] *AF*, s.a. 863, p. 56. Again the *AF* show sympathy toward Carloman.

[21] *AB*, s.a. 862, p. 93. For the early history of the Hungarians, see Szabolcs de Vajay, *Der Eintritt des ungarischen Stämmebundes in die europäische Geschichte (862–933)* (Mainz, 1968), 11–15.

[22] By analogy, in the Hungarians' next appearance in European sources, King Arnulf in 892 hired them as mercenaries to help fight the Moravians: *AF(B)*, s.a. 892, p. 121.

[23] *AF*, s.a. 863, p. 56; *AB*, s.a. 864, 866, pp. 113, 133; Wolfram, *Salzburg*, 314.

[24] *AI*, s.a. 863, p. 741.

son into custody. In return for his support, Louis bestowed the prefecture of Carantania on the turncoat Gundachar. Bishops Adalwin of Salzburg and Otgar of Eichstätt apparently played important roles in the 863 campaign, since Louis at this time made several substantial land grants in Upper Pannonia and Carantania to them.[25]

Rastislav of Moravia heightened the international dimensions of this crisis in the Eastland by turning to Constantinople. In 862, Rastislav sent an embassy to the Byzantine emperor, Michael III (842–67), requesting that Constantinople send him a bishop and teacher to explain the Christian faith to the Moravians in their own language (Slavic).[26] In theory, Rome and Constantinople were part of a united Catholic Church, and it therefore would be anachronistic to speak of a Roman Catholic–eastern Orthodox split in the ninth century. In practice, however, Rome and Constantinople were increasingly estranged because of cultural, linguistic, theological, and political differences. Before 862, Rastislav considered himself loyal to the Roman Church: Moravia had been Christianized by Catholic missionaries from Bavaria, and Rastislav had unsuccessfully appealed to the papacy for a bishop to free the Moravian Church from east Frankish ecclesiastical control.[27] But by requesting a bishop from Constantinople in 862, Rastislav indicated that he wanted to align Moravia with the Byzantine Church. The political implications were profound. By asking Constantinople for a bishop, Rastislav sought to place Moravia under the protection of the Byzantine emperor and thereby free himself from Louis's overlordship.

Emperor Michael and his gifted patriarch of Constantinople, Photius, saw the Moravian appeal as an opportunity to expand Byzantine political and cultural influence over Moravia.[28] A Byzantine–Moravian alliance was the natural response to the recent Franco–Bulgar entente, which threatened to make the Bulgar kingdom loyal to Rome—an abhorrent prospect for Constantinople. Emperor Michael sent two envoys of exceptional caliber (although not of episcopal rank) to Moravia: the brothers Constantine

[25] The king also oversaw a major reorganization of Otgar's properties in Bavaria and the Eastland, again highlighting his importance for the king's control of the Eastland: *DLG* 109, 111, 112, 115, 116; *Regensburg* 39.

[26] *VC*, chap. 14, pp. 66–67; *VM*, chap. 5, p. 88; Wolfram, *Grenzen und Räume*, 259–67.

[27] Michael Richter, "Die politische Orientierung Mährens zur Zeit von Konstantin und Methodius," in *Die Bayern und ihre Nachbarn*, ed. H. Wolfram and A. Schwarcz (Vienna, 1985), 1:281–92.

[28] George Ostrogorsky, *History of the Byzantine State*, 2nd English ed., trans. Joan Hussey (New Brunswick, NJ, 1969), 210–60. For a good discussion of Byzantine diplomacy in the ninth century, see Jonathan Shepard, "Byzantine Relations with the Outside World in the Ninth Century: An Overview," in *Byzantium in the Ninth Century: Dead or Alive?* ed. Leslie Brubaker (Aldershot, 1998), 167–80.

(Cyril) and Methodius of Thessalonica.[29] Constantine was an extremely gifted scholar and linguist and a professor of philosophy at the imperial university in Constantinople, earning him the cognomen "the Philosopher."[30] His brother Methodius had been the Byzantine governor of a Slavic principality, and he later became abbot of the monastery of Mount Olympus in Asia Minor.[31] Several years earlier, Michael had included Constantine and Methodius in an embassy to renew the Byzantine alliance of "love and friendship" with the Khazars north of the Black Sea.[32] Now the Byzantine emperor sent the brothers with gifts and letters to solidify a similar alliance with Rastislav and to dazzle him with the cultural sophistication of Constantinople.

In 863 Rastislav welcomed Constantine and Methodius and gave them permission to teach in his kingdom. The Byzantine churchmen spent the next forty months in Moravia, during which time they introduced a Church liturgy in the Slavic tongue.[33] Both men knew Slavic from Thessalonica, and before arriving in Moravia they had developed the first Slavic script, known as Glagolica, based on the Greek alphabet. Constantine and Methodius also translated into Slavic several lengthy biblical texts, including the Gospels, Acts of the Apostles, and Psalms. The use of Slavic gave Constantine and Methodius a considerable advantage over churchmen from Bavaria, who celebrated the Mass in Latin and had only limited knowledge of Slavic. Not surprisingly, the Bavarian episcopate strongly opposed the presence of Byzantine churchmen in Moravia, and they condemned their use of Slavic for the liturgy as heretical. But there was little the Bavarian churchmen could do as long as the Greek missionaries enjoyed Rastislav's protection. Another obstacle facing the Bavarian Church was that Bishop Hartwig of Passau, in whose diocese Moravia lay, had suffered a stroke that left him paralyzed and unable to speak. The Bavarian churchmen in Moravia therefore were deprived of leadership just when they needed it most.

As usual, Louis responded to this new challenge with a combination of diplomacy and warfare. In 864, he planned to launch a major campaign against Rastislav with the support of his new ally, Khan Boris. Louis arranged to meet Boris with his Bulgar army in August at Tulln and then jointly invade Moravia, "making Rastislav obey him whether he wanted to or not." Boris had even hinted that he might receive baptism at Tulln as part

[29] For the early careers of Constantine and Methodius, see Dvornik, *Byzantine Missions*, 53–72.
[30] *VC*, chaps. 3–4, pp. 28–34.
[31] *VM*, chaps. 2–3, pp. 86–87.
[32] *VC*, chaps. 8–11, pp. 42–63.
[33] *VC*, chaps. 14, 15, pp. 66–70.

of his alliance with Louis.[34] Before the campaign, Louis dispatched Bishop Solomon of Constance to Rome to win Pope Nicholas I's blessing for the impending showdown with Moravia.[35] Solomon discussed with the pope a number of pressing issues facing the east Frankish Church, including how the diocese of Passau had been "fragmented and brought to ruin" by the defection of the Moravians. At first Pope Nicholas was somewhat cool toward Louis's envoy, reproaching the east Frankish king for not taking a stronger stand vis-à-vis the recent marital troubles of King Lothar II. (Lothar II had divorced his barren wife and remarried, actions that Rome adamantly opposed.) But, in the end, Pope Nicholas saw Louis as a useful ally in his ongoing struggle with Constantinople over papal supremacy, a conflict known as the Photian Schism.[36] Moreover, the pope was overjoyed with the suggestion that Khan Boris might convert to Catholicism, a development that would be a major coup for the Roman Church. In early 864, therefore, Nicholas and Louis affirmed a common front against Constantinople and Moravia: the east Frankish king promised the pope obedience "as a son to his father and a student to his teacher," while Nicholas performed fasts and prayers for the success of Louis's upcoming campaign against Rastislav.

Louis's 864 campaign against Rastislav was a success, although it did not proceed without impediment.[37] At the last minute Boris pulled out of the 864 campaign (perhaps because of the serious famine that ravaged his kingdom that year), and soon thereafter he accepted baptism from Constantinople and Byzantine Christianity for his kingdom.[38] Although deprived of

[34] *AB*, s.a. 864, p. 113.

[35] Nicholas I, *Epistolae*, no. 26, in MGH *Epistolae* 6:290–93. Solomon discussed with the pope other issues concerning the east Frankish Church as well: the unification of the bishoprics of Hamburg and Bremen under Anskar; the need for the pope to send the pallium to the new archbishop of Mainz, Liutbert; the problem of two incapacitated Bavarian bishops, one of whom was Hartwig of Passau; and the possibility that King Horik II of Denmark and Khan Boris of Bulgaria might be willing to receive baptism. For a discussion of this letter, see Bigott, *Ludwig der Deutsche*, 153–55.

[36] The Photian Schism centered on Emperor Michael's uncanonical deposition of Patriarch Ignatius of Constantinople in 858 and appointment of Photius, something that Nicholas adamantly opposed. Concerning the Photian Schism, see Nicholas I, *Epistolae*, nos. 84–86, 98, in MGH *Epistolae* 6:440–51, 553–65; Francis Dvornik, *The Photian Schism: History and Legend* (Cambridge, 1970), 1–158; idem, "Photius, Nicholas I and Hadrian II," *Byzantinoslavica* 34 (1973): 33–50. On Pope Nicholas I, see *Liber Pontificalis* (*The Lives of the Ninth-Century Popes*), trans. Raymond Davis (Liverpool, 1995), 189–203.

[37] *AF*, s.a. 864, p. 62; *AH*, s.a. 864, p. 18. Louis was at Regensburg on August 20 and Mattighofen on October 2, so we know that he waged the campaign in less than forty-four days: *DLG* 113, 115.

[38] For the date and circumstances of Boris's baptism, see Shepard, "Slavs and Bulgars," 239–41. Shepard now favors a date of 865 for Boris's baptism (personal correspondence).

The steep mountain at Devín where Louis trapped Rastislav within a Moravian fortress in August 864. Louis compelled Rastislav and his magnates to surrender, turn over hostages, and swear new oaths of loyalty. The mountain at Devín overlooks the confluence of the Morava (March) and Danube rivers, and therefore it was ideally situated for a stronghold on the Moravian–Frankish border. The remains of a ninth-century fortress have been excavated on top of the mountain, although the castle ruins visible in this picture date to a later period. Photograph courtesy of Mestské Muzeum Bratislava.

Boris's military support at the last minute, Louis nevertheless managed to pull off a significant victory against Rastislav. The king led a large army beyond the Danube, apparently took Rastislav by surprise, and trapped him within the Moravian fortress of Devín. As archeologists have shown, the stronghold at Devín was a smaller, border-defense fortress at the top of a steep, rocky mountain overlooking the confluence of the Danube and Morava rivers.[39] Unable to escape the Frankish siege, the Moravian ruler surrendered. Louis compelled Rastislav to turn over numerous high-ranking hostages and swear a new oath of fidelity in concert with all the Moravian magnates.

Through this victory, Louis also reasserted control over Lower Pannonia, which Rastislav apparently had annexed in 858 as the result of his

[39] For the identification of Dowina as Devín, see *AF*, s.a. 864, p. 62n1; Staňa, "Mährische Burgwälle," 196 and map 7.8; Shepard, "Slavs and Bulgars," 242. Cf. Dümmler, *GOR* 2:86–87n4; Bowlus, *Franks, Moravians, and Magyars*, 140–41 and n. 78.

agreement with Carloman. The king now installed Chozil, son of the late Pribina, as the ruler of Lower Pannonia with his seat at Moosburg. But whereas Pribina had ruled Lower Pannonia as a semi-independent Slavic *dux*, Louis attempted to bind his son to him more closely by making Chozil a count.[40] Chozil's comital title indicates Louis's desire to integrate the Slavic principality of Lower Pannonia more directly into the east Frankish hierarchy of the state, thereby making Chozil's lordship a "public honor" and thus dependent on faithful service. With Lower Pannonia again under Frankish control, Archbishop Adalwin of Salzburg traveled there in late 864 to reassert Salzburg's ecclesiastical jurisdiction in the contested region.[41] The Bavarian archbishop celebrated Christmas with Chozil at Moosburg, and in January 865 he consecrated numerous churches in Lower Pannonia and installed a priest loyal to Salzburg at each. Later in 865, Adalwin returned a second time to preach and consecrate additional churches, some thirty in all.

In spite of these successes, the political situation remained unstable as long as Louis obstinately refused to come to terms with his eldest son. Carloman had legitimate grievances against his father, since previous Carolingian rulers traditionally granted more political independence to their sons at much earlier ages. Later in 864 the daring Carloman managed to escape from his father's custody by pretending to go hunting, whereupon he fled back to Carantania and, with the help of his supporters, regained power.[42] Louis had to face the fact that these rebellions would continue until he assuaged his son's resentment by granting him more power and independence. In 865, therefore, the king made extensive concessions to Carloman in return for his loyalty. He reestablished good relations with his son, reappointed him prefect, restored all his former frontier regions (Upper Pannonia and Carantania), and granted him extensive *honores*.[43] Moreover, as an acknowledgment of Carloman's authority, Louis renounced his own right to make further grants of lands in the Eastland.[44] These were considerable concessions, indicating the king's desire to reach a lasting peace with his eldest son. The strategy worked: Carloman remained loyal for the rest of his

[40] For Chozil's *comes* title, see *Regensburg* 37; *Freising* 887; *AI*, s.a. 874, p. 742; Wolfram, *Salzburg*, 333–34.

[41] *Conversio*, chap. 13, pp. 130–34; Wolfram, *Salzburg*, 330–32.

[42] *AB*, s.a. 864, p. 114. The *AF* pass over Carloman's imprisonment and escape in silence.

[43] *AB*, s.a. 865, p. 117.

[44] Louis's last diploma for a recipient in the southeast is *DLG* 116 for Otgar of Eichstätt-Niederalteich, dated December 18, 863–64. Carloman co-subscribed this diploma.

father's reign, and he immediately took the lead in the offensive against Moravia.

Louis's concessions to Carloman, however, upset the balance of power throughout the kingdom. One magnate who felt squeezed was Werner, Louis's longtime *fidelis* and count in Upper Pannonia and the Lobdengau. Werner allied with Rastislav, apparently in a desperate attempt to defend his power in the Eastland against the king's rapacious son. According to the *Annals of Fulda*, "Count Werner, one of the leading men of the Franks, was accused before King Louis of inciting and urging Rastislav against him. He was therefore deprived of his public honors."[45] There is a notable parallel here with the rebellion a decade earlier of Prefect Ratpot, who likewise lost his *honores* to make way for Carloman, forcing him into an alliance with Rastislav. Once again, the sacrifice of a longtime supporter was the price Louis had to pay for peace with his eldest son. It probably is no coincidence that Louis's seizure of Werner's *honores* took place just months after the death of the still-powerful former count, the *vir magnificus* Ernest.[46] Werner and Ernest were closely related, perhaps through Werner's mother.[47] Werner does not seem to have had a son, whereas Ernest's son, Ernest II, apparently went into exile in 861 as punishment for his part in his father's rebellion.[48] Thus, as Ernest's son-in-law and the eastern prefect, Carloman had a claim to some, if not all, of Ernest's and Werner's *honores* and lands. Between 854 and 865, the three magnates who had assisted in Louis's rise to power—Ratpot, Ernest, and Werner—had all fallen in the southeast. Carloman had become their political heir.

Soon after his settlement with Carloman, Louis decreed a succession plan for his three sons after Easter at Frankfurt.[49] Louis made the 865 division plan in an effort to mollify any resentment his younger sons felt about his recent concessions to Carloman. In the division of Frankfurt, Louis's chief concern was to avoid the mistakes of the *Ordinatio imperii* by making a (more or less) equal division of his kingdom among his three sons. Begin-

[45] *AF,* s.a. 865, p. 63.
[46] *AX,* s.a. 865, p. 23; *AF,* s.a. 864, 865, p. 63; *Regensburg* 52.
[47] Mitterauer, *Karolingische Markgrafen,* 130, 136–37.
[48] Ernest II had participated in the 857 campaign against the Bohemians: *AF,* s.a. 857, p. 47. Hincmar mentions an Arnostus among Lothar II's vassals in 865: *AB,* s.a. 865, p. 120. After Louis the German's death, Carloman made Ernest II a count in Pannonia (Mitterauer, *Karolingische Markgrafen,* 132–37, 205), but this does not preclude the possibility that Carloman seized Ernest's lands in 865.
[49] For the 865 division, see Notker, *Continuatio,* 329; *Adonis Continuatio,* 324–25; Dümmler, *GOR* 2:119–20; BM 1459a; Hartmann, *Ludwig der Deutsche,* 70–71. Cf. Kasten, *Königssöhne,* 524–25, who suggests a date of 866–69 for Louis's division.

ning in the 850s, Louis had associated his sons with strategic frontier regions and granted them prefectures there: Carloman in the Bavarian Eastland, Louis the Younger on the Elbe frontier in eastern Saxony and
Thuringia, and Charles III in the Alemannian Breisgau.[50] In the 865 division, Louis assigned his sons their frontier commands and then extended
their future territories into the adjacent regions. The result was a blueprint
for three future kingdoms: Bavaria, the southeastern marches, and lordship
over the Bohemians and Moravians for Carloman; Franconia, Thuringia,
Saxony, and the tributary Slavs along the Elbe and Saale for Louis the
Younger; and Alemannia and Chur-Rhaetia for Charles III. In truth, however, the 865 division favored Louis's eldest two sons, Carloman and Louis
the Younger, who, unlike Charles III, already had proved their leadership
abilities in battle against the Slavs. Carloman and Louis the Younger each
received one of the two east Frankish royal heartlands (Bavaria and the
middle Rhine) as well as tribute-paying "barbarians," while Charles III did
not. Following standard Carolingian practice, Louis recorded the 865 inheritance plan in a (now lost) written decree (*testamentum*) that presumably
outlined the details of royal succession: the preservation of his sons' cooperation after his death, the necessity of defending the Church, and his plan for
their kingdoms after the death of any one of them.

Although a concession to his sons, the 865 Division of Frankfurt also
highlighted Louis's determination to "keep a firm grip on supreme royal
power over them."[51] The king did not allow his sons to take possession of
their future kingdoms before his death, nor did he grant them the royal title
of *rex* during his lifetime. In this way, Louis made his sons' continued loyalty a precondition of their eventual inheritance. Moreover, Louis was careful to maintain control of the reins of government. He made the 865 division "on the condition that, as long as he was living, his sons would have
certain named royal estates and be able to settle lesser legal cases, while all
the bishoprics, monasteries, counties, public fiscs, and all major judgments
were reserved for him."[52] In this way, Louis used the Division of Frankfurt
as an opportunity to reassert his control of the "public" institutions of royal
government.

Within months of the 865 division, however, the thirty-year-old Louis

---

[50] For Louis the Younger's command on the Elbe frontier, see *AF,* s.a. 858, 866, 869,
pp. 49, 64, 68; *AH,* s.a. 858, p. 18; Rimbert, *Vita Anskarii,* chap. 41, p. 75. In about 859,
Louis appointed Charles III the royal governor (*princeps, rector*) of the Breisgau: *St.-Gall*
534, 551, 553, 555, 574, 575, 579, 585; Michael Borgolte, "Karl III und Neudingen: Zum
Problem der Nachfolgeregelung Ludwigs des Deutschen," *ZGO* 125 (1977): 21–55.

[51] *Adonis Continuatio,* 324–25.

[52] Notker, *Continuatio,* 329.

the Younger made a bold move to expand his power. Louis the Younger was cut from the same muscular cloth as his father and elder brother. He had distinguished himself on several occasions as a military leader against the Slavs, and he boasted that "we delight in strength and no-nonsense practicality, not luxury and vanity."[53] Louis the Younger was in a position similar to that of Carloman a few years earlier: he had an illegitimate son, Hugh, but remained unmarried, and he now desired more political independence.[54] In 865, Louis the Younger betrothed himself—against his father's wishes—to the daughter of the powerful Count Adalhard.[55] This marriage alliance threatened to undermine the balance of power in the Frankish kingdoms. It seems that Adalhard did not have a son, so Louis the Younger's betrothal to his daughter made Louis a potential heir to Adalhard's extensive lands in Lotharingia, the Wormsgau, and Alemannia.[56] Although Louis the German and Charles the Bald were bitter rivals, they were united in their desire to keep their sons out of Lotharingian politics. During a meeting at Cologne in 865, therefore, Charles the Bald helped reconcile Louis the Younger to his father, but only on the condition that he abandon Adalhard's daughter.

This settlement did not assuage the younger Louis. The following year, he organized a full-blown conspiracy against his father. According to the *Annals of Fulda*, Louis the Younger "took it badly that the king had taken away certain benefices from him and given them to his brother Carloman and [so he] rebelled against the king."[57] The king's second son rallied his

---

[53] For Louis the Younger's boast, see *Collectio Sangallensis*, no. 27, in MGH *Formulae*, 412.

[54] Louis the Younger's illegitimate son Hugh was in his grandfather's entourage in 860 along with his cousin Arnulf: MGH *Capitularia* 2:154. According to Notker, Hugh grew up to be a "most dashing and warlike young man," although, unlike Arnulf, he never attained the purple. To Louis the Younger's profound grief, Hugh later died while fighting the Vikings: Notker, *Continuatio*, 330; *AF(M)*, s.a. 880, p. 94; Regino, *Chronicon*, s.a. 879, pp. 115–16.

[55] *AB*, s.a. 865, pp. 123–24.

[56] *Annals of St.-Bertin*, trans. Nelson, 128n17, 177n3. For Adalhard's lands in the Wormsgau and Alemannia, see *St.-Gall* 386. In 861, Adalhard moved back to Charles the Bald's kingdom and became the guardian of Louis the Stammerer: *AB*, s.a. 861, pp. 85, 87.

[57] *AF*, s.a. 866, pp. 64–65; *AB*, s.a. 866, pp. 131–32. Although the *AF* do not identify these benefices, it is possible that they included the *honores* of Ernest and Werner that Carloman apparently seized the previous year. Ernest and Werner's *honores* had spanned from the Eastland to the middle Rhine. Ernest had estates in Franconia, while Werner had also been count of the Lobdengau: *Ex vita Reginswindis*, chaps. 1–5, in MGH *SS* 15:359–60; *Lorsch* 1618; *DLG* 94. If Louis the German had allowed Carloman to seize Ernest and Werner's Franconian benefices, then Louis the Younger's anger is understandable, since the 865 division earmarked Franconia and the middle Rhine for him. Perhaps it was to strengthen his contested claims to Ernest and Werner's lands that Louis the

supporters in Saxony and Thuringia and, in addition, all the nobles with grievances against Louis the German. Louis the Younger won over the recently dishonored Werner, Uto, and Berengar, promising to return them to their former rank in exchange for their support. Another figure who enlisted in Louis the Younger's rebellion was the commander of his bodyguard, Henry, who was another Frank with a grudge. His father had been Count Poppo of Thuringia, the leader of the east Frankish Babenberg family who lost his offices during the civil war. Louis the Younger now sent Henry to Rastislav to persuade the Moravian ruler to "plunder all the way to Bavaria, so that with his father and faithful men occupied in that region he would have a free hand to carry out what he had begun." Louis the Younger's supporters probably also included the two prominent brothers Counts Bruno and Otto (known to History as Otto the Illustrious), who held benefices in eastern Saxony and Thuringia. Bruno and Otto were leaders of the Franco-Saxon Liudolfing (Ottonian) dynasty, and Louis the Younger married their sister, Liutgard, some time between 865 and 874.[58]

Louis the German demonstrated extraordinary vigor in responding to his middle son's 865 rebellion. Between early September and late October, the king traveled with remarkable speed back and forth between Bavaria and the middle Rhine, helping Carloman drive out Rastislav while negotiating a truce with his rebel middle son. On October 28 at Worms, Louis finalized a peace with Louis the Younger through the mediation of Archbishop Liutbert of Mainz (863–89), who had succeeded Charles of Aquitaine as the head of the east Frankish Church.[59] Liutbert was an Alemannian nobleman and former monk and teacher at Reichenau, and he played a prominent role as

---

Younger had betrothed himself to Adalhard's daughter, since Adalhard was related to Ernest's Konradiner nephews: *AB*, s.a. 861, p. 85.

[58] Bruno and Otto were the sons of Count Liudolf, who had been in Louis the German's entourage at Koblenz in 860: MGH *Capitularia* 2:154. On the Liudolfings, see Eduard Hlawitschka, "Zur Herkunft der Liudolfinger und zu einigen Corveyer Geschichtsquellen," *RV* 38 (1974): 92–165, esp. 162; Becher, *Rex, Dux und Gens*, 66–109. Otto the Illustrious married the daughter of Louis the Younger's supporter, Henry. Otto's son, named after his father-in-law, became the first Ottonian king, Henry I (919–36). For Louis the Younger's marriage to Liutgard, see Dümmler, *GOR* 2:279 and n. 2; Becher, *Rex, Dux und Gens*, p. 141 and n. 823. Soon after becoming king, Louis the Younger made rich grants to "our faithful counts, Bruno and Otto": *DLY* 3, 4.

[59] Although Archbishop Charles died on June 4, Liutbert was not installed until November 30, which was an unusually long delay (as noted in the *AF*, s.a. 863, p. 57). The delay apparently was due to Louis's campaign against the rebellious Carloman in the southeast that summer. Louis was at Regensburg in the late autumn and winter of 863–864: *DLG* 110–12. Concerning Liutbert, see Rudolf Schieffer, "Liutbert," *NDB* 14, 722–23; Bigott, *Ludwig der Deutsche*, 142–44, 199–201. For Liutbert's extensive connections east of the Rhine, see Althoff, "Über die von Erzbischof Liutbert auf die Reichenau übersandten Namen," 219–42.

Louis's adviser and envoy during the last decade of Louis's reign. Louis also reasserted his power through a gruesome demonstration of royal justice. In the course of Louis the Younger's rebellion, there had been a serious uprising at Mainz in which several of Archbishop Liutbert's vassals were killed. In response, "some were hung from gallows, others lost their fingers and toes and were blinded, and not a few abandoned all their possessions and became exiles to escape death."[60] In this way, the king made clear the penalty for participation in future rebellions.

THE CONTEST FOR EASTERN EUROPE

For the remainder of the 860s, Louis and Carloman waged a campaign to reassert Frankish control over Moravia. The Moravian issue was increasingly bound up in the larger contest between Rome and Constantinople for ecclesiastical jurisdiction in eastern Europe. Although Khan Boris had submitted to Byzantium in 864, his objective remained the creation of an independent Bulgar Church to bolster his power.[61] Not wanting to become the puppet of Constantinople, Boris defected to the Catholic Church in 866. He sent envoys to Pope Nicholas and Louis the German, asking them for a bishop and priests.[62] Boris's decision to turn to the Catholic Church was political. Given the great distance between his capital at Pliska and the west, a Catholic bishop, in practice, would be subject to him. At this moment, Pope Nicholas and King Louis saw their objectives in eastern Europe as complementary. Louis wanted a military alliance with Boris against Moravia, Nicholas hoped to win the Bulgars for the Catholic Church, and both pursued strongly anti-Byzantine policies.

Louis used the Bulgar appeal as an opportunity to reaffirm his alliance with Khan Boris against Moravia and Byzantium. In late 866 Nicholas sent an embassy of bishops to Boris's court to transform the Bulgar kingdom into a Catholic realm, and Louis sent his own delegation of priests and deacons the following year.[63] The high priority Louis placed on the 867 embassy to the Bulgarian kingdom is demonstrated by the fact that he appointed as its

[60] *AF,* s.a. 866, p. 65. Pope Nicholas sent to Louis the German's sons a letter concerning the "honor due to parents": *AF,* s.a. 867, p. 66.

[61] Shepard, "Slavs and Bulgars," 243–48. In 865 Boris faced a serious pagan uprising in his kingdom, and he used it as an opportunity to centralize his power by executing fifty-two of the leading Bulgar nobles: *AB,* s.a. 866, p. 133.

[62] *AF,* s.a. 866, p. 65; *AB,* s.a. 866, pp. 133–34.

[63] Nicholas I, *Epistolae,* no. 99, in MGH *Epistolae* 6:568–600.

head his former chaplain, Ermanrich, whom he had just appointed bishop of Passau. As the new bishop of Passau, Ermanrich was responsible for the Frankish counteroffensive against the Byzantine missionaries in Moravia. Boris "received [Ermanrich and the east Frankish priests] with due veneration" and apparently renewed his alliance with the east Frankish king.[64]

At the time of Boris's appeal to the west, Louis faced renewed diplomatic intrigue in eastern Europe. In late 866, Constantine and Methodius departed from Moravia for Venice to find passage on a ship to Constantinople.[65] On their way, the Greek missionaries were welcomed in Lower Pannonia by Count Chozil, who received them with honor, showed interest in their Slavic writing and liturgy, and entrusted to them fifty students for instruction in Slavic letters. Chozil's hosting of Constantine and Methodius cannot be explained simply as a Slavic ruler's enthusiasm for his "native" language and culture. Chozil's ethnopolitical identity reflected the complexity of frontier politics: he was half Slav and half Bavarian, a Catholic, a Frankish count, Louis's *fidelis*, and probably fluent in Frankish and Latin as well as Slavic. It is difficult to believe that Louis looked favorably on Chozil's welcoming of the Byzantine churchmen, and the king may have considered Chozil's actions outright treason. But Chozil was pursuing his own self-interest amid the complex webs of diplomacy in eastern Europe. Although loyal to Louis, Chozil had no love for Carloman, who had helped the Moravians to kill his father. Carloman's recent reappointment as eastern prefect put Chozil's position in jeopardy, since the king's son undoubtedly wanted to put Lower Pannonia in the hands of his own supporters. By welcoming Constantine and Methodius in 866, Chozil may have been gesturing his willingness to join the Byzantine–Moravian alliance as protection

---

[64] *AB*, s.a. 866, p. 133. Concerning Ermanrich's embassy, the *AF*, s.a. 867, pp. 65–66, reported: "King Louis agreed to the petitions of the Bulgars and sent Bishop Ermanrich with priests and deacons to preach the Catholic faith to that people. But when they had arrived there, the bishops sent by the Roman pontiff had already filled all that land with preaching and baptizing. Thus, after receiving permission from the [Bulgar] king, they returned home." On the basis of this passage, historians have viewed Ermanrich's mission to the Bulgars as a failure thwarted by Rome: Dümmler, *GOR* 2:191; *Annals of St.-Bertin*, trans. Nelson, 137n35. This interpretation is doubtful. Louis cannot realistically have hoped to incorporate Bulgaria into the Bavarian Church, since Boris's capital at Pliska was over six hundred miles away. Moreover, the east Frankish Church lacked the wealth and material resources for sustained missionary work among the Bulgars. Thus Louis had been forced to ask Charles the Bald for liturgical vessels, vestments, and books to send along with Ermanrich: *AB*, s.a. 866, pp. 133–34. As the new bishop of Passau, Ermanrich's chief concern was confronting the Byzantine missionaries in Moravia, not the distant Bulgar Church.

[65] *VC*, chaps. 15–16, pp. 70–75.

against the rapacious Carloman. Once again, Frankish control of Lower Pannonia was becoming tenuous.

As part of his effort to expand Rome's jurisdiction in eastern Europe, Pope Nicholas now sought to win over Constantine and Methodius. Throughout his pontificate, Nicholas pursued an overarching agenda of re-asserting Roman universalism vis-à-vis Constantinople. An important element of this plan was Nicholas's desire to reclaim the eastern ecclesiastical archdioceses of Illyricum, Dacia, and Macedonia (roughly encompassing modern Slovenia, Croatia, western Hungary, Serbia, Bosnia and Herzegovina, Albania, Macedonia, and Greece) that had been lost to Byzantium in the eighth century.[66] With his recent success in the Bulgarian kingdom, Nicholas had taken a large step toward that goal. Much of the population of Illyricum, Dacia, and Macedonia were Slavic speakers, and Nicholas had realized that Constantine and Methodius's Slavic writing and liturgy would greatly help him reassert Rome's authority over those regions. When the Byzantine churchmen arrived in Venice in early 867, Nicholas sent messengers who persuaded them to come to Rome.[67] Constantine and Methodius arrived in Rome several months later, and they were greeted by Nicholas's successor, Pope Hadrian II (867–72). Hadrian was determined to continue Nicholas's policies, and he received Constantine and Methodius with honor. The new pope accepted Constantine and Methodius's Slavic translations of the Scriptures, consecrated their Slavic disciples as priests, and even allowed them to sing the Slavic liturgy in Rome's churches. Pope Hadrian's acceptance of the Slavic liturgy was an unprecedented break with Catholic tradition (heretofore the Catholic Church allowed the liturgy to be sung only in Latin, Greek, and Hebrew), and it highlights his goal of reclaiming the Slavic-speaking eastern ecclesiastical provinces for Rome.

In the end, political events convinced the Byzantine churchmen to accept papal supremacy and continue the mission to the Slavs in Rome's name. While staying in Rome between late 867 and early 869, Constantine and Methodius learned of stunning developments in Constantinople.[68] During the summer of 867, Emperor Michael and Patriarch Photius, angered over Pope Nicholas's interference in the Bulgar Church, held a synod in Constantinople at which they excommunicated the pope, declared

---

[66] In 860 Nicholas had requested that Emperor Michael return to Rome its three former archdioceses of Macedonia, Dacia, and Illyricum: Nicholas I, *Epistolae*, no. 82, in MGH *Epistolae* 6:438. For the historical origins of papal authority in this region, see A. H. M. Jones, *The Later Roman Empire, 284–602* (Baltimore, 1992), 2:888–89 and map 2.

[67] *VC*, chap. 17, pp. 75–77; *VM*, chap. 6, p. 89.

[68] Ostrogorsky, *History of the Byzantine State*, 232–35.

heretical the Roman doctrine on the Holy Spirit, and asserted that Roman interference in the Byzantine Church was unlawful. But on the night of September 23, the co-emperor, Basil, murdered Michael in his sleep and seized the imperial throne. To shore up support for his regime, the new emperor, Basil I (867–86), ended the Photian Schism with Rome and established good relations with Hadrian.[69] This unexpected rapprochement between Constantinople and Rome eliminated any conflict of interest that might have prevented Constantine and Methodius from serving the papacy.[70] With the help of the Byzantine churchmen, Pope Hadrian decided to revive the Roman archdiocese of Illyricum. In 869, he consecrated Methodius the papal envoy to the Slavs and archbishop of Sirmium, the metropolitan seat of Illyricum.[71] (Constantine had died on February 14, 869, in Rome.) Hadrian intended the revived archdiocese of Illyricum under Methodius's leadership to serve as the ecclesiastical framework within which Lower Pannonia and Moravia would come directly under Roman jurisdiction. In turn, Rastislav and Chozil won ecclesiastical independence for their provinces from the Bavarian Church.

After almost a decade of rebellions, King Louis resumed the offensive against Moravia.[72] In May 868 at an east Frankish synod in Worms, Louis reaffirmed his opposition to the Byzantine–Moravian alliance.[73] Louis had

[69] Hadrian II, *Epistolae ad res orientales pertinentes*, nos. 37, 38, in MGH *Epistolae* 6:747–50.

[70] At the same time, the continued presence of Arab pirates in the Mediterranean and Adriatic made return to Constantinople nearly impossible: Hadrian II, *Epistolae ad res orientales pertinentes*, nos. 39, 40, in MGH *Epistolae* 6:753, 758.

[71] According to a letter of questionable authenticity preserved in the *VM*, Hadrian recommended Methodius to Chozil, Rastislav, and Svatopluk, asserted that their lands belonged to Rome, and endorsed the use of Slavic for the liturgy: *VM*, chap. 8, pp. 90–92, 181–82n48; Hadrian II, *Epistolae ad res orientales pertinentes*, no. 43, in MGH *Epistolae* 6:763–64. In the words of the *VM*, Hadrian consecrated Methodius "to the bishopric of Pannonia, to the seat of Saint Andronicus, an apostle of the seventy"—a reference to the Illyrican metropolitan see of Sirmium within the late Roman province of Pannonia II.

[72] Louis's new confidence is suggested by a new royal seal he introduced during the summer of 866. Like his first Bavarian seal, the new seal depicted Louis in the style of a triumphant Roman emperor. He is shown in profile, clean shaven, and wearing a Roman cloak and laurel wreath, and next to him are the martial emblems of the spear and shield. Louis used this third seal intermittently during the last decade of his reign alongside his Hadrian seal: Schramm, *Die deutschen Kaiser*, p. 322, no. 51; *DLG*, xxxii–xxxiii.

[73] MGH *Concilia* 4:246–311; *AF*, s.a. 868, pp. 66–67; Nicholas I, *Epistolae*, no. 102, in MGH *Epistolae* 6:610. On this synod, see Wilfried Hartmann, *Das Konzil von Worms 868: Überlieferung und Bedeutung* (Göttingen, 1977); idem, *Synoden der Karolingerzeit*, 301–9. Nicholas had requested that Charles the Bald and the west Frankish bishops also hold a synod, so that the Western Church could present a united front against Byzantium: Nicholas I, *Epistolae*, nos. 100–101, in MGH *Epistolae* 6:600–609; *AB*, s.a. 867, pp. 137–140.

held this synod at the request of the pope to address the Roman conflict with Constantinople, and it was presided over by Archbishop Liutbert of Mainz. The 868 Worms synod, which also was attended by Archbishop Adalwin of Salzburg and twenty bishops, issued a *Response against the Heresy of the Greeks* that refuted the 867 synod of Constantinople.[74] The Worms synod also addressed the recent rebellions in Moravia and the Eastland, proclaiming that any layman who broke faith with the king or "defected to foreign lands in opposition to his own people, homeland, or the royal power" was to be stripped of all his personal property and excommunicated.[75] In addition, the east Frankish bishops decreed that any churchmen involved in sworn associations or conspiracies against the Church (here they probably were thinking of Constantine, Methodius, and their disciples) were to be deposed.[76]

Although Louis attempted to maintain good relations with Pope Hadrian, he broke with Rome over the creation of an independent archdiocese in Illyricum that encompassed Lower Pannonia and Moravia.[77] Not only would an Illyrican Church have forced Louis to surrender ecclesiastical jurisdiction in the southeast, but it effectively would have compelled him to recognize the political independence of the Moravian and Lower Pannonian Slavs. At the heart of this conflict were two rival geopolitical conceptions of Slavic eastern Europe, one rooted in late Roman and the other in Carolingian history. Hadrian based his claims to that region on late Roman ecclesiastical organization, while Louis justified Frankish lordship in the southeast by right of Charlemagne's conquest over the Avars.[78] These two rival claims of jurisdiction in eastern Europe put Hadrian and Louis on a crash course. At least one east Frankish churchman apparently opposed Louis's adversarial stance to Rome: Abbot Thioto of Fulda. In 869, Louis took the unusual step of deposing Thioto for disobeying him, presumably over the Moravian issue, and replaced him with a Fulda monk named Sigihard, who became one of Louis's leading supporters in the war with Moravia.[79]

[74] MGH *Concilia* 4:291–307.

[75] Ibid., 278 (c. 36).

[76] Ibid., 289 (c. 74).

[77] Louis frequently sent Hadrian letters and envoys, and as late as June 870 the pope still praised Louis for his *constantia* toward Rome: Hadrian II, *Epistolae ad res orientales pertinentes*, nos. 25–27, in MGH *Epistolae* 6:730–33, at 730.

[78] As Louis summed up in a diploma for Otgar of Eichstätt, "Our grandfather the lord Charlemagne gave his faithful men permission to seize and take possession of hereditary lands for the growth of God's churches in Pannonia": *DLG* 109.

[79] *AH*, s.a. 869, p. 18; *Annalista Saxo*, s.a. 869, p. 580. Although Thioto's offense against the king is not reported, it is likely that the abbot of Fulda opposed Louis's efforts

In 869, Louis and Carloman launched their counteroffensive against Rastislav.[80] Early that year, Carloman fought two successful engagements against Rastislav and returned with plunder. This is the first mention of the Franks' capture of plunder from the Moravians. Paradoxically, it seems to reflect Rastislav's growing military confidence against the Franks. Because open battles offered the best opportunity for a victorious army to capture booty (through the looting of corpses), the plunder taken by Carloman's troops suggests that Rastislav now felt confident enough to meet the Franks on the battlefield outside the walls of his fortresses.[81] Louis planned to invade Moravia again, later in August, with two armies. He intended to lead one himself against Rastislav, while Carloman would lead the other against Rastislav's nephew, Svatopluk. Svatopluk had risen to power in Moravia in the early 860s, and Rastislav and Svatopluk had jointly appealed to Constantinople in 862. According to the *Annals of Fulda*, Rastislav had granted his nephew a quasi-independent principality (*regnum, patria*) within Moravia. Rastislav ruled from his "indescribable fortress," perhaps Mikulčice in central Moravia, while Svatopluk held "Rastislav's old city" [urbs antiqua Rastizi].[82] This "old city" that served as the seat of Svatopluk's principality most likely was the large Moravian fortress excavated twenty miles upstream from Mikulčice at Staré Město, which literally means "old city" in Czech.[83]

Just as Louis gathered his forces in August, however, he suddenly fell ill.

---

to reimpose political and ecclesiastical control over Moravia, since Thioto had close relations with Rome. Fulda was unique among east Frankish monasteries in being directly under the authority of the pope, and Thioto had served as Louis's envoy to Pope Nicholas: *AF*, s.a. 859, p. 53. His successor, Sigihard, was more amenable to Louis's hard line vis-à-vis Moravia. While Louis was making preparations for his 869 Moravian campaign at Regensburg, on May 9 the abbot-elect Sigihard came before him and received from him the monastery of Fulda. Several years later, Louis placed Sigihard in command of an army against the Moravians: *AF*, s.a. 872, p. 76. Cf. Bigott, *Ludwig der Deutsche*, 245–47.

[80] *AF*, s.a. 869, pp. 68–70; *AB*, s.a. 869, p. 157. In this year, Louis the Younger also led an army of Thuringians and Saxons against a rebellious confederation of Sorbs and Bohemians and defeated them, although with considerable losses to his soldiers.

[81] The *AF*, s.a. 869, pp. 67–68, reported that there was a battle between Frankish and Moravian armies in which Carloman's former vassal, Count Gundachar, who had defected to Rastislav, was killed.

[82] *AF*, s.a. 869–71, pp. 69, 70, 73–74.

[83] *AF*, s.a. 871, p. 74; Bosl, "Das Grossmährische Reich," 5; Staňa, "Mährische Burgwälle," 188–89. The German name for Staré Město is Altstadt. Cf. *Annals of Fulda*, trans. Reuter, 60n9. Although the *AF* equate Svatopluk's *regnum* and *patria* with the *urbs antiqua Rastizi*, historians often assume that it was at Nitra: Dvornik, *Byzantine Missions*, 91; Karl Bosl, "Probleme der Missionierung des böhmisch-mährischen Herrschaftsraumes," in *Siedlung und Verfassung Böhmens*, ed. František Graus and Herbert Ludat (Wiesbaden, 1967), 108.

Illness was a constant danger for Carolingian rulers, since personal leadership was the cornerstone of effective kingship and warfare. For most of his reign, Louis seems to have enjoyed a strong constitution and good health. Several years earlier, for example, Louis had made a speedy recovery ("in brevi convalescens") when he took a serious fall from his horse while hunting.[84] But by 869 Louis was an old man according to Carolingian standards, and his sudden illness forced him to remain in bed and relegate command of his army to his youngest son, Charles III. The 869 campaign met with modest success. Carloman and Charles III put Rastislav's army to flight, harried the Moravian countryside, burned some smaller fortresses, seized significant plunder, and returned home in triumph. However, they were unable to capture Rastislav's massive fortress, meaning that the Moravian ruler—who according to one chronicler now ruled as an independent king (*rex*)—remained in power.[85]

When Carloman and Charles III returned in triumph to Regensburg, they received disheartening news. Their father's illness had become so serious that his doctors had given up hope of recovery. But, characteristically, Louis was not willing to relinquish power. When his doctors despaired of his life, the king gathered all the gold and silver he could find in his coffers and gave it to monasteries and the poor "so that he might deserve to be cured by the Heavenly Doctor to Whom he had commended himself and all his possessions." Against all odds Louis did recover, and by early 870 he was well enough to depart for Frankfurt.[86] The king arrived on the Feast of the Purification of the Virgin Mary (February 2), a date that seemed to herald his own miraculous purification and recovery to health.

It may have been during Louis's illness in 869 that a "Prayer to Be Recited before the Cross" was added on the final blank pages of Louis's private

[84] *AB*, s.a. 864, pp. 114–15. For an earlier illness of Louis, see *AB*, s.a. 849, p. 58.

[85] *AF*, s.a. 869, pp. 68–69; *AX*, s.a. 869, p. 28. The 869 campaign also provided an opportunity to consolidate the landholding of Louis's supporters in Upper Pannonia near the Moravian-Pannonian border. A Freising charter reported that the "most pious Carloman" and his army stopped at the palace at Baden, about twenty miles south of Vienna: *Freising* 898c; Mitterauer, *Karolingische Markgrafen*, 91–97, 103. At Baden, Carloman presided over an important dispute settlement in favor of Freising concerning properties at Pitten (located about twenty miles south of Baden) that had belonged to Prefect Ratpot: *Freising* 899.

[86] *AF*, s.a. 870, p. 70; *DLG* 130. Moreover, from his sickbed the king had managed to negotiate a peace treaty with the Bohemians, and the king sent Carloman and Charles III to Bohemia to confirm it: *AB*, s.a. 869, p. 164. (*Annals of St.-Bertin*, trans. Nelson, p. 162 and n. 22, mistakenly states that only Charles III went to Bohemia.) The *AF*, s.a. 869, p. 70, reported that the Bohemians "asked for and received the handshake from Carloman"—a common ritual of submission along the Franco-Slavic frontiers: Karl J. Leyser, "Ritual, Ceremony and Gesture: Ottonian Germany," in Leyser, *Communications* 1:191–92.

book of prayer, the Ludwig Psalter.[87] Echoing the *Annals of Fulda*'s reference to the infirm king turning to the "Heavenly Doctor," the "Prayer to Be Recited before the Cross" in the Ludwig Psalter repeatedly invoked the language of illness and medicine: it described God as the Highest Doctor, the cross as medicine, and God's forgiveness as a medium of healing. Adjacent to this prayer, an artist added a portrait of Louis bowing before Christ on the cross surrounded by Saint Mary, Saint John, and the personifications of the sun and moon.[88] The artist depicted Louis in an attitude of fitting humility before Christ the True King, since he kneels and wears no crown or regalia. Louis's humble appearance is a striking contrast to the picture presented by Christ, who is decidedly muscular, hairy, and the very embodiment of vigorous manhood. The central message conveyed by the portrait and prayer therefore was that Christ, the Highest Doctor, was Louis's special protector. It is possible that the prayer and portrait were added to the Ludwig Psalter in response to the king's life-threatening illness in 869. Thus, we may actually be looking at the words and images the ailing Louis had before his eyes as he besought Christ to forgive his sins and spare his life.

The following year, Carloman achieved a stunning victory over Rastislav, although not through warfare but rather through secret diplomacy and trickery. Carloman had entered into clandestine negotiations with Svatopluk, who in 870 agreed to commend himself and his Moravian principality to Carloman.[89] Svatopluk's position vis-à-vis Rastislav was analogous to that of Carloman toward King Louis a decade earlier: by allying with the enemy, he could expand his own independent power. Rastislav was "beside himself with rage" when he learned of his nephew's betrayal, and he plotted for assassins to strangle him at a banquet. But Svatopluk caught wind of his uncle's plot and evaded death by pretending to go hawking. When Rastislav set out with his soldiers to hunt down his nephew, Svatopluk turned the tables and

---

[87] *Oratio ante crucem dicenda*, in Ludwig Psalter, fols. 119r–v.

[88] Ludwig Psalter, fol. 120r. This portrait was painted by one of the artists who illuminated Otfrid's *Book of the Evangelists* (or a fellow Wissembourg monk with a very similar style), which places its date at the same time as Otfrid's work: 863–71. For the close connections between the portrait in the Ludwig Psalter and the Vienna copy of Otfrid's *Liber evangeliorum*, see Goldberg, "Equipment of Battle," 67–70 and n. 108. In a forthcoming article, "Ritual, Misunderstanding, and the Contest for Meaning: The Example of the Disrupted Royal Assembly at Frankfurt (873)," in MacLean and Weiler, *Representations of Power*, Simon MacLean suggests that the portrait in the Ludwig Psalter is of Charles III and was added in response to his outburst during the 873 Frankfurt assembly. (For that event, see chap. 9 in this volume.) However, the close connections between the Ludwig Psalter portrait and the Vienna Otfrid manuscript make it highly unlikely that the portrait was added after 871, the *terminus post quem non* for the composition of Otfrid's *Liber evangeliorum*.

[89] *AF*, s.a. 870, pp. 70–71.

The king turns to Christ, the Highest Doctor. A portrait of Louis the German kneeling before Christ on the cross, surrounded by Saint Mary, Saint John, and the personifications of the sun and moon. This portrait was added to the last page of the Ludwig Psalter some time between 863 and 871 at the monastery of Wissembourg, perhaps in response to the king's life-threatening illness in 869. Along with the portrait, a "Prayer to Be Recited before the Cross" was also added, which uses the language of illness and healing to describe the king's penance. Staatsbibliothek zu Berlin—Preussischer Kulturbesitz, MS theol. lat. fol. 58, fol. 120r.

captured his uncle. Svatopluk then sent Rastislav in bonds to Carloman, who in turn dispatched the Moravian rebel under guard to Regensburg.

With Rastislav behind bars, Carloman took the unprecedented step of annexing Moravia outright. "With no one resisting, Carloman invaded Rastislav's kingdom, received the surrender of all the fortresses and castles, and set the kingdom in order and placed it under the rule of his own men." As a reward for capturing his uncle, Carloman allowed Svatopluk to retain his Moravian principality at Staré Město. But Carloman placed the rest of Moravia under the control of Counts William II and Engilschalk, the sons of Count William I of the Traungau.[90] As longtime colonists in the Eastland, the Wilhelminer family possessed rich estates north of the Danube between the Aist River and the Vienna basin, making them bitter rivals of the Moravians. (William II and Engelschalk reportedly were brutal governors who inflicted great hardships on the Moravian people.)[91] By capturing the Moravian *civitates et castella*, moreover, Carloman succeeded in seizing Rastislav's royal treasure (*gaza regia*). The extensive ninth-century burial goods excavated at Moravian sites such as Mikulčice, which include rings, necklaces, bracelets, chalices, spurs, swords, daggers, and axes, reveal the breathtaking beauty and tremendous value of such treasure.[92] With Carloman's acquisition of such astonishing wealth, his political prospects took a tremendous leap forward. The annexation of Moravia also was a serious blow to the inchoate Roman-Slavic Church, since Carloman's forces captured Archbishop Methodius. Carloman's conquest of Moravia sent shock waves throughout Europe. Hincmar bitterly reported that Louis's envoys were overjoyed and haughty because of Louis's recovery of health and Rastislav's imprisonment.[93] The author of the *Annals of Xanten* (who actually was writing at Cologne) commenced his report of Rastislav's capture with the dramatic rubric, "NOW FOR CARLOMAN'S VICTORY. . . ."[94]

TRIUMPH IN EAST AND WEST

As these dramatic events unfolded in the east, Louis continued his policy of *Drang nach Westen*. The east Frankish court legitimized Louis's ongoing

---

[90] *AF*, s.a. 871, p. 73; Mitterauer, *Karolingische Markgrafen*, 178–87.

[91] *AF(B)*, s.a. 884, p. 111.

[92] *Grossmähren und die christliche Mission bei den Slawen: Ausstellung der Tschechoslowakischen Akademie der Wissenschaften, 8 März bis 8 Mai 1966*, ed. Institut für Österreichkunde (Vienna, 1966).

[93] *AB*, s.a. 870, pp. 169–70.

[94] *AX*, s.a. 871 [*sic*], p. 130.

Visions of Empire

western imperialism by portraying him as an imperial ruler and the second Charlemagne. In his *Letter to Abbot Grimald* written in the early 850s, Ermanrich had depicted Louis as a new Charlemagne, "Karolus optimus," unjustly constrained by the narrowness of his territories.[95] In the later 860s, east Frankish churchmen intensified this royal ideology. In 867, Archchaplain Grimald (or one of his scribes) entered a prominent historical notice into the Grimalt Codex that recounted the transfer of Carolingian imperial power (*imperium*) from Charlemagne, to Louis the Pious, and then to Louis the German. It read:

> 815 [actually, 814]: In the year of the incarnation of our lord Jesus Christ 815, Charles, the greatest of all augustuses, departed from this world on January 28 at Aachen during the third hour of the day. He ruled for forty-seven years and died in the seventy-second year of his life.

> 840: That same year, his son Louis took up the imperial power and ruled for twenty-six years, until the year of the incarnation of our lord Jesus Christ 840. He departed from this world on June 29 on an island in the Rhine near the palace of Ingelheim.

> 867: After him, his son and namesake Louis took up the imperial power in east Francia. Thus far, that is up to the year of the incarnation of our lord Jesus Christ 867, he has ruled twenty-seven years.[96]

That same year, Grimald commissioned an elegant copy of Einhard's *Life of Charlemagne* by a court scribe, further indicating that the east Frankish court looked to Louis's grandfather as the model Frankish king.[97] Indeed, Louis and Grimald may have been responsible for disseminating manuscripts containing the *Royal Frankish Annals* and Einhard's *Life of Charlemagne*, thereby anchoring the east Frankish regime in Carolingian royal and imperial tradition.[98] Also during the 860s, an author with ties to Louis's court composed a

---

[95] Ermanrich, *Epistola ad Grimaldum abbatem*, in MGH *Epistolae* 5:536–37.

[96] Grimalt Codex, 18. This is the latest datable entry in the Grimalt Codex: Bischoff, "Bücher am Hofe Ludwigs des Deutschen," 204.

[97] Concerning this manuscript, see Bischoff, "Bücher am Hofe Ludwigs des Deutschen," 199–200; Matthias M. Tischler, *Einharts "Vita Karoli": Studien zur Entstehung, Überlieferung und Rezeption* (Hanover, 2001), 1:41, 102–51. Bischoff, "Bücher am Hofe Ludwigs des Deutschen," 203, argues that the scribe who copied Grimald's *Vita Karoli* had also made some of the entries in the Grimalt Codex.

[98] McKitterick, "Political Ideology in Carolingian Historiography," p. 172 and nn. 31–32. McKitterick cites the work of Lenka Kolarova, "The Transmission and Dissemination of Carolingian Annals" (M.Phil. diss., Cambridge University, 1995); I was unable to obtain a copy in the United States.

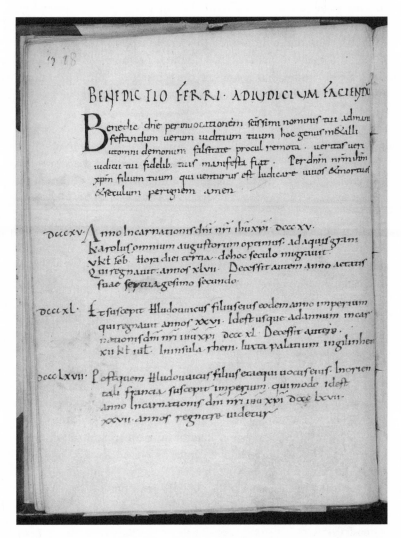

Louis the German as heir to the empire. A historical entry in the Grimalt Codex of Louis's archchaplain, Grimald of St.-Gall. This entry, dated 867, records the obituaries of Charlemagne and Louis the Pious and the passing of their imperial power (*imperium*) to Louis the German. Stiftsbibliothek St. Gallen, Codex 397, p. 18.

short literary work titled the *Vision of Charlemagne*, which purported to record a prophetic dream of Louis's grandfather. In reality, the *Vision of Charlemagne* was written to glorify Louis himself as the defender of the Church and the only worthy ruler among Charlemagne's grandsons.[99] At the 868 Worms synod, the presiding archbishop, Liutbert of Mainz, described Louis's kingship in explicitly imperial terms. He dated a charter witnessed by all the assembled bishops and abbots "in the twenty-eighth year of the imperial rule [imperium] of the most glorious King Louis."[100] Of course, Louis did not have a monopoly on imitating his grandfather, and Charles the Bald likewise fashioned himself as a second Charlemagne.[101] In this way, the struggle for the Carolingian empire between Louis the German and Charles the Bald was becoming a contest for Charlemagne's legacy.

This growing imperial conception of Louis's kingship also found expression in the liturgy of his palace. During the 860s, the monastery of Lorsch composed an unusual liturgical manuscript for Louis's court—the so-called Lorsch Rotulus.[102] The Lorsch Rotulus is a beautiful eight-foot-long parchment scroll that contains the longest surviving Carolingian litany of the saints (534 names), and it concludes with acclamations for Louis, Emma, and their children. The long list of saints on the Lorsch Rotulus is highly distinctive, since it was closely modeled on the litanies of the Roman Mass that had been imported north of the Alps during the reign of Charlemagne as part of the Carolingian liturgical reforms. In this way, the Lorsch Rotulus established an "imperial" Roman and Carolingian litany at the east Frankish court that invoked on the behalf of Louis and his family the saints whose cults flourished throughout the empire. It is possible that Abbot Theoderich of Lorsch presented Louis with the Lorsch Rotulus during the 868 Worms synod. Rogation Sunday—a solemn day reserved for chanting penitential litanies like those in the Lorsch Rotulus—fell during the Worms synod on May 23, and on that day Louis made an advantageous exchange of lands with Abbot Theoderich for the benefit of his monks.[103] In his diploma, Louis specified that the Lorsch monks should "pray for the Lord's

[99] Geary, "Germanic Tradition," 49–76.

[100] In Liutbert's charter for the Saxon convent of Neuenheerse: MGH *Concilia* 4:309–11. Breaking with the tradition of Louis's chancery, Liutbert dated Louis's reign from 840 (instead of 833), thereby emphasizing that Louis was his father's direct successor.

[101] William W. Diebold, "*Nos quoque morem illius imitari cupientes*: Charles the Bald's Evocation and Imitation of Charlemagne," *AK* 75 (1993): 271–300.

[102] Stadt- und Universitätsbibliothek Frankfurt, MS Barth. 179; Krüger, "*Sancte Nazari ora pro nobis*," 184–202, convincingly argues that the Lorsch Rotulus was made at Lorsch for Louis's court.

[103] *DLG* 126.

mercy for the salvation of ourselves, our wife, and our dearest children, as well as for the redemption of our predecessors' souls." It therefore is possible that the Lorsch monks presented the Lorsch Rotulus to Louis during the 868 Worms synod to invoke the army of heaven to the defense of his kingship and dynasty as he had requested.

During the 860s, the middle kingdom became the proving ground for Louis's imperial ambitions. After the Treaty of Koblenz, Louis and Charles focused their efforts on winning the middle kingdom from their nephews, Louis II of Italy, Lothar II, and Charles the Child. At the heart of this struggle was one of the most infamous scandals of the Middle Ages: Lothar II's divorce.[104] Throughout the 860s, Lothar II sought to divorce his barren queen, Theutberga, and marry Waldrada, a noblewoman who earlier had borne him a son named Hugh. The stakes were political as well as personal. Lothar II wanted to make Waldrada his queen to legitimize Hugh as his royal heir, and at the same time he seems truly to have loved Waldrada and disliked Theutberga.[105] With the support of Archbishops Gunther of Cologne and Thietgaud of Trier, Lothar II divorced Theutberga in early 860 at a synod in Aachen. Lothar turned to the traditional weapon deployed against royal women—sexual scandal—to justify the divorce. He and his bishops ruthlessly pressured Queen Theutberga into admitting a series of horrendous, and obviously fabricated, sexual crimes: that she had had anal sex with her brother before her wedding, thereby conceived a child through witchcraft, and then aborted the fetus.[106] Two years later, Gunther and Thietgaud crowned Waldrada at Aachen and proclaimed her Lothar II's queen.[107]

The divorce quickly erupted into a pan-European conflict. Lothar II had seriously underestimated Pope Nicholas, who saw the Lotharingian king's divorce as a test case for papal authority north of the Alps. The pope rallied to Theutberga's defense and excommunicated Waldrada and Archbishops Gunther and Thietgaud.[108] For their part, Louis the German and Charles the Bald both sought to use Lothar II's vulnerability to expand their borders into Lotharingia. After the Treaty of Koblenz, Louis, Charles, and Lothar II met together on numerous occasions and formed various combinations of diplomatic alliances. Despite its rhetoric of *pax et caritas*, this diplomacy was driven by Realpolitik. What made a particular alliance desirable at a given moment depended on a range of constantly shifting factors: rebellions of

[104] Concerning Lothar II's infamous divorce, see Stuart Airlie, "Private Bodies and the Body Politic in the Divorce Case of Lothar II," *Past and Present* 161 (1998): 3–38.

[105] Nelson, *Charles the Bald*, 198–99.

[106] *AB*, s.a. 860, p. 82.

[107] *AB*, s.a. 862, pp. 93–94.

[108] *AB*, s.a. 863, 864, pp. 98–103, 105–12, 115; *AF*, s.a. 863, pp. 57–61.

sons and magnates, Slavic and Viking attacks, diplomacy with foreign rulers, and the interventions of Pope Nicholas. Charles the Bald and Hincmar of Reims generally remained hostile toward Lothar II, defended Queen Theutberga, and meanwhile made several unsuccessful attempts to annex Lotharingia and Provence.[109] Because the rebellions of his sons and Rastislav kept him occupied in the east, Louis the German sought to exploit Lothar II's vulnerability more through diplomacy than aggression.[110] Louis offered his support to Lothar II, but only in exchange for grants of territories and estates in the middle kingdom either to himself or to the east Frankish Church.[111] For example, in the very year Lothar had resumed his relationship with Waldrada (857), Waldrada courted Louis's favor by granting her family's estates along the Brenner Pass at Merano to the east Frankish bishopric of Chur.[112] Because Waldrada hailed from Alsace, Louis strengthened his growing ties to the nobility of that region by supporting (or at least not openly opposing) his nephew's divorce.[113] Then, in return for an alliance in 860 against Charles the Bald, Lothar II momentarily promised to give Alsace to Louis.[114] In 862 Louis furthered his connections to the

[109] Charles the Bald welcomed the refugees Theutberga and her brother Hubert at his court, appointing the one abbess of Avenay and the other abbot of St.-Martin: *AB*, s.a. 864, p. 116; *Annals of St.-Bertin*, trans. Nelson, p. 93 and n. 7. In late 861, Charles the Bald made an abortive attempt to seize Provence from the sickly Charles the Child: *AB*, s.a. 861, p. 87; Karl Schmid, "Ein karolingischer Königseintrag im Gedenkbuch von Remiremont," *FS* 2 (1968): 115–23; *Annals of St.-Bertin*, trans. Nelson, 96n14. In 866 Charles made an unsuccessful attempt to seize Lotharingia: *AB*, s.a. 866, p. 132.

[110] Personal considerations probably also played a role, since Lothar II's chief supporter, Archbishop Thietgaud of Trier, was the brother of Louis's archchaplain, Grimald. Thietgaud and Gunther of Cologne urged their fellow Lotharingian bishops "above all else frequently to invite King Louis [to Lothar's court] and diligently seek with him the common good, since our peace will be in the peace between those kings": *AB*, s.a. 864, p. 107.

[111] In 866, Lothar II and his count of the palace, Ansfrid, granted territories in Lotharingia to Lorsch: *Lorsch* 33–35. In return for Louis's promise not to invade his kingdom while he went to Rome in 869, Lothar II granted properties in Alsace to Louis's daughter, Bertha of Sts.-Felix-and-Regula, "so that she might be a steadfast advocate [cooperatrix] for strengthening the friendship with our dearest uncle, her father, and with her dearest mother": *DLoII* 34. Lothar II made other political concessions to Louis. For example, at a meeting in 862 at Mainz, Lothar II persuaded the reluctant Archbishop Gunther of Cologne to agree to Louis's plan to transform Anskar's see of Hamburg-Bremen into an archbishopric: *AB*, s.a. 862, p. 93; Rimbert, *Vita Anskarii*, chap. 23, pp. 48–51; Nicholas I, *Epistolae*, no. 26, in MGH *Epistolae* 6:291–92.

[112] *DLG* 84. Louis briefly conceded the convent of Sts.-Felix-and-Regula to Waldrada after the death of his eldest daughter, Hildegard, who had been *rectrix* of that convent, in 856: MacLean, "Queenship," 21.

[113] For Waldrada's Alsatian ties, see Schmid, "Ein karolingischer Königseintrag," 128–34.

[114] *AB*, s.a. 860, pp. 83–84.

Alsatian nobility by arranging the marriage of his youngest son, Charles III, to Richgard, a relative of the powerful Alsatian count, Erchanger.[115] When Lothar II was forced to go to Rome to negotiate with the pope in 867, Louis forced his nephew to commend to him his son Hugh, Alsace, and the entire middle kingdom.[116]

After 865, Louis the German and Charles the Bald formed an alliance, spurred by the hope that Lothar II and Louis II of Italy would both die without male heirs.[117] (Their sickly nephew, Charles the Child, had died in 863, and Louis II of Italy and Lothar II had divided his kingdom between them.) Immediately after the Synod of Worms in 868, Louis met with Charles the Bald at Metz in Lotharingia, without Lothar II himself being present.[118] In the church of St.-Arnulf where their father was buried, the two kings swore to make an equal division of Lotharingia and Italy should the opportunity present itself, "according to God's will, for the restoration, honor, and defense of the holy Church, for our shared honor, security, and benefit, and for the salvation and peace of the Christian people." Louis and Charles held this meeting in the presence of a small gathering of bishops, which suggests that the 868 Metz assembly had the air of a secret negotiation.[119] At Louis's side stood Liutbert of Mainz, Altfrid of Hildesheim, and Witgar of Augsburg, which indicates that at least some of the eastern bishops actively supported the expansion of Louis's kingdom.

Lothar II resolved to go to Rome and try to win the support of the new pope, Hadrian, for his marriage to Waldrada. In 868 and 869 he sent messengers to his uncles and met with them individually, requesting that they refrain from invading his kingdom while he went to Rome.[120] Although Charles flatly refused, Louis agreed—but, as usual, at the price of lands in Alsace.[121] Lothar II met with Hadrian and courted his favor through numerous gifts and the personal intervention of his sister-in-law, the influential Empress Engelberga of Italy. Hadrian's response was positive: he re-

---

[115] *AB*, s.a. 862, p. 93; Borgolte, "Karl III und Neudingen," 36–39.

[116] *AB*, s.a. 867, pp. 136–37.

[117] Louis the German and Charles the Bald met together in 865 and 867. The fact that their meetings took place in Lotharingia (at Tusey, Cologne, and Metz) in Lothar II's absence underscores their ongoing exploitation of their nephew's weakness.

[118] MGH *Capitularia* 2:167–68; *Annals of St.-Bertin*, trans. Nelson, p. 115 and n. 15.

[119] Hincmar of Reims neglected to mention the 868 Metz assembly in the *AB*, which further suggests the meeting's secret nature.

[120] In 868 Pope Hadrian also sent letters to Louis the German and Charles the Bald, warning them not to invade the kingdoms of their nephews: *AB*, s.a. 868, p. 143; Hadrian II, *Epistolae de rebus Franciae*, no. 6, in MGH *Epistolae* 6:702–4.

[121] *AB*, s.a. 868, 869, pp. 150, 153; *DLoII* 34.

ceived the Lotharingian king honorably, lifted his ban of excommunication, and agreed to a council to reexamine the marriage. During Lothar's journey home, however, a disastrous epidemic struck his army in Tuscany. At the early age of thirty-four, the ill-fated Lothar II died at Piacenza on Sunday, August 8, 869.

Charles the Bald must have had spies in Lothar II's entourage who rode like the wind, because only fifteen days later he received word of his nephew's death while he was at Senlis, northeast of Paris.[122] This was a tremendous stroke of luck, since Louis the German lay ill at that moment in Regensburg. The Lotharingian magnates sent envoys to Charles, urging him not to try to seize Lotharingia until Louis the German could come to discuss a division of the middle kingdom. Ignoring the recent oaths at Metz, Charles decided to invade Lotharingia, a course of action urged by Hincmar.[123] Charles was crowned king of Lotharingia on September 9 in the basilica of St.-Stephen in Metz in an elaborate ceremony that Hincmar himself choreographed.[124] Over the next several months, Charles won over the magnates of Lothar II's former kingdom, and when his wife, Ermentrude, suddenly died, he quickly married Richildis, the sister of the powerful Lotharingian Count Boso.[125] The *Annals of Fulda*, which by now were being written in the circle of the influential Archbishop Liutbert of Mainz, echoed the outrage of Louis's court: "Following the counsel of wicked men [i.e., Hincmar of Reims], Charles ordered a diadem to be placed on his head in the city of Metz by the bishop of that city and that he be called emperor and augustus, as one who possesses two kingdoms."[126] From his sickbed Louis sent messengers to Charles demanding an equal division of the middle kingdom according to their recent oaths at Metz. But Charles was resolute, and he likewise ignored demands from Emperor Louis II of Italy and Pope Hadrian that he depart from Lotharingia. Like Charlemagne reincarnate, Charles the Bald celebrated Christmas in 869 at Aachen.

---

[122] The distance from Piacenza to Senlis was almost 450 miles, indicating that the messengers raced north at an extraordinarily fast pace—about thirty miles per day. For the date of the messenger's arrival, see *Annals of St.-Bertin*, trans. Nelson, 157n11.

[123] *AB*, s.a. 869, p. 157.

[124] *Ordines coronationis Franciae*, ed. Jackson, 1:87–109; Nelson, "Lord's Anointed," 118–19; idem, "Hincmar of Reims on King-Making: The Evidence of the *Annals of St.-Bertin*, 861–882," in *Coronations: Medieval and Early Modern Monarchic Ritual*, ed. János Bak (Berkeley, 1990), 16–34.

[125] Boso was the nephew of Theutberga and Hubert. Charles granted Boso the strategic monastery of St.-Maurice, guarding the Mons Iovis Pass to Italy: *Annals of St.-Bertin*, trans. Nelson, 93n7, 164n31.

[126] *AF*, s.a. 869, pp. 69–70.

To Charles's dismay, however, his brother recuperated and arrived at Frankfurt in early February.[127] Louis the German immediately began to turn the tide in Lotharingia through the usual combination of patronage, diplomacy, and the threat of military force. At Frankfurt Louis received the submission of many Lotharingian magnates, restored their benefices seized by Charles, and won over some nobles who initially had submitted to Charles. Louis's most important move was appointing a supporter to the vacant Lotharingian archbishopric of Cologne.[128] In early January, Charles attempted to install his own candidate, Abbot Hilduin of St.-Bertin, against the will of Cologne's clergy. In response, Louis secretly sent Liutbert of Mainz with a group of bishops to Cologne, where they installed a member of the local clergy, Willibert, as the new archbishop. As a result, Charles was unable to appoint his own candidate. Louis also consolidated his support in Lotharingia by mediating disputes among prominent local nobles. On April 12 at Tribur, Louis judged an important case in favor of the wealthy Lotharingian monastery of Prüm, whose new abbot, Ansbald, thereby became one of his chief supporters in the middle kingdom. Louis returned to Prüm lands on the east Frankish–Lotharingian border near Bingen, thereby fostering the political and territorial cohesion of those two realms.[129] As Louis's diploma explained, the lands he restored to Prüm had been usurped by the recent rebel Werner. Nevertheless, Louis described Werner as "our count," indicating that he also had restored Werner's county in the Lobdengau.[130] Louis's judgment at Tribur therefore benefited both parties: both Ansbald of Prüm and the recently dishonored Count Werner. Notker later praised Louis for "never under any circumstances or after any passage of time" restoring public offices to those found guilty of infidelity.[131] Werner's case shows that this was not always true. In early 870, Louis was desperate to shore up his support along the east Frankish–Lotharingia border, and under these circumstances he was willing to forgive old grievances.

Meanwhile, Louis sent Charles an ultimatum: unless his brother departed from Lotharingia, "he would wage war against him without any hes-

---

[127] *AF*, s.a. 870, p. 70.

[128] For these events, see *AF*, s.a. 870, p. 70; *AX*, s.a. 871, p. 29; Regino, *Chronicon*, s.a. 869, pp. 98–100; *Epistolae Colonienses*, nos. 2–10, in MGH *Epistolae* 6:242–55; Bigott, *Ludwig der Deutsche*, 146–47, 203–5.

[129] *DLG* 131. Louis's vassal Heiric had granted these lands to Prüm in 853: *DLoI* 128. For the background to this diploma, see Innes, *State and Society*, 218–20.

[130] A diploma of Louis the Younger confirms the restoration of Werner's Lobdengau county: *DLY* 2.

[131] Notker, *GK* 2.11, p. 68.

itation."[132] After further negotiation, Louis and Charles finally agreed to meet in August on the Meuse near Meersen and work out an equal division of the middle kingdom.[133] But at this moment, an accident almost ruined Louis's reversal of fortunes. On the way to his meeting with Charles, Louis stopped at the royal estate of Flamersheim between Koblenz and Aachen. Regino reported:

> When Louis had gone up to the balcony of the building amid a multitude of attendants, the balcony, which was weakened and decayed with age, suddenly collapsed with a great snapping of beams. The king was gravely injured amid the ruins and broke two ribs. Everyone rushed over and thought him dead. However, Louis stood up where he had fallen and showed himself to his men, assuring them that he had suffered no harm. Moreover, if it can be believed, he concealed his injury and the following day set out to meet his brother at Meersen. Such was that prince's hardihood and courageous spirit that, while some of his companions heard the crack of his broken ribs grinding together, no one heard him draw a deep breath or utter a groan.[134]

An important counselor also seems to have been hurt in the collapse: Louis's old archchaplain, Grimald. It was precisely at this moment that the elderly Grimald withdrew from royal service and retired to St.-Gall, presumably because of an injury he sustained at Flamersheim.[135] The Flamersheim disaster therefore seems to have deprived Louis of his longtime counselor and archchaplain on the eve of the most important diplomatic meeting since Verdun.

Despite these setbacks, Louis won a major victory over Charles at the Meersen meeting in August 870.[136] Given the high stakes, Louis did not want to reveal the extent of his injuries, and he did a remarkable job hiding them from Charles. (Hincmar, who was at the meeting, believed Louis had only been somewhat shaken and had recovered quickly.)[137] As in 843, the kings had undertaken an extensive survey of Lotharingia, recording the

---

[132] *AB*, s.a. 870, p. 169.

[133] MGH *Capitularia* 2:191–92.

[134] Regino, *Chronicon*, s.a. 870, pp. 100–101; *AF*, s.a. 870, p. 71.

[135] Grimald's last appearance as archchaplain was at Tribur on April 12, 870: *DLG* 131. By the time Louis issued his next surviving diploma at Aachen on September 25, he had appointed Liutbert of Mainz his new archchaplain: *DLG* 132. For Grimald's retirement, see Ratpert, *Casus sancti Galli*, chap. 9, pp. 216–18.

[136] For the date of the meeting, see Dümmler, *GOR* 2:297n2; BM 1478h.

[137] *AB*, s.a. 870, p. 171: "aliquantulum naufragatus in breve convaluit."

royal resources—the bishoprics, monasteries, counties, royal estates, and benefices—upon which the division was based.[138] They made the division on the general premise that Louis would get the eastern regions, Charles the western regions, and the border would run roughly north to south. The 870 Meersen division essentially revived the short-lived partition of Frankish Europe north of the Alps that Louis and Charles had made at Aachen in 842, with Charles receiving Neustria and the west and Louis Austrasia and the east. Louis received the royal capital at Aachen, both Lotharingian archbishoprics (Cologne and Trier), the important palaces of Nijmegen and Thionville, thirty-nine monasteries, and some thirty counties. In addition, Louis exploited his strong position by extorting two further concessions from his brother. "For the preservation of peace and affection," Charles added to Louis's share the important episcopal city of Metz and the Moselle county around it, and the swathe of territory between Liège and Trier that included the wealthy monasteries of Prüm, Stablo, and Echternach.[139] Overall, Louis had extended his borders over roughly half of Lotharingia, two-thirds of Frisia, all of Alsace, and the eastern portion of Burgundy, greatly enriching his resources "with all the royal estates, either in the hands of the king or his vassals." Thirty years after his father's death, Louis finally ruled from his grandfather's capital.

Louis was in no condition to sit on his grandfather's throne, however. In his determination to meet with Charles, Louis had not given his doctors time to treat his injuries sustained at Flamersheim, which included a wound that had become infected. In another display of his grim determination to maintain power, Louis ordered his doctors to perform an operation to remove the infected tissue when he returned to Aachen.[140] In an age without anesthetics, the pain must have been excruciating. Louis almost did not survive, and he was confined to bed at Aachen for two months. Many portents seemed to predict his death (strange lights in the night sky, earthquakes, excessive heat, floods, and cattle pestilence), and "all prayed that these monstrous things might be turned to good."[141] Indeed, Louis himself apparently

---

[138] MGH *Capitularia* 2:193–94; *AB*, s.a. 870, pp. 172–74. See further BM 1480. The division did not recognize Louis II of Italy's claims to Lotharingia, even though Lothar II apparently had named him his heir. The brothers also swore henceforth to maintain fraternal peace: Regino, *Chronicon*, s.a. 876, p. 111.

[139] Charles's additional concessions also suggest the influence of the elderly Count Adalhard, whose lands were situated in the region around Metz and who had become one of Louis's chief Lotharingian supporters: *AB*, s.a. 872, 873, pp. 185, 192–93; *Annals of St.-Bertin*, trans. Nelson, 177n3, 183n11.

[140] *AB*, s.a. 870, p. 175: "Hludowicus . . . conputrescentem carnem ab eisdem medicis secari fecit."

[141] *AF*, s.a. 870, p. 71.

believed he was going to die, and he therefore made preparations to be buried in the Aachen crypt built by his parents. He gave the Aachen burial church to his supporter, Abbot Ansbald of Prüm, so that Prüm's monks would care for it and "invoke the Lord's mercy for our salvation, the salvation of our wife and dear children, and for the redemption of the souls of our predecessors."[142] If he could not rule from Charlemagne's capital, then Louis at least wanted to be buried near his grandfather's side.[143]

Yet even while at death's door, Louis moved to consolidate his power in Lotharingia. He ordered that a synod be held at Cologne on September 26, presided over by Archbishops Liutbert of Mainz, Bertulf of Trier, and Willibert of Cologne, thus symbolizing the unification of the east Frankish, Lotharingian, and Saxon churches.[144] At this time, Louis appointed Liutbert of Mainz his new archchaplain and high chancellor as Grimald's successor, thereby making the Mainz archbishop his chief counselor.[145] Louis also received envoys from Louis II of Italy and Pope Hadrian II, who insisted that Lotharingia was the rightful inheritance of the Italian emperor.[146] Nevertheless, Hadrian took a conciliatory tone toward the east Frankish king. The pope praised Louis's loyalty to Rome and urged that he cooperate with Emperor Louis II.[147] Louis the German responded with his tried-and-true tactic of delay through negotiation. He sent an embassy to Louis II and Hadrian, assuring them of his *constantia* to the Roman Church, and he urged Hadrian personally to come to Francia. Louis the German declared that he had acted in the common interests of himself and Emperor Louis II, a claim that was dubious but not overtly hostile.

Against all odds, Louis once again recovered by late October, and he set out for Bavaria to deal with Carloman's momentous recent conquest of Moravia.[148] At Regensburg, Louis held a triumphal assembly to proclaim his victory over the Moravians and assuage doubts about his health. With an eye to public spectacle that recalled Roman military triumphs, Louis commanded the Slavs to send ambassadors with gifts, and he had Rastislav pre-

---

[142] *DLG* 133 (October 17, 870).

[143] Cf. Nelson, "Carolingian Royal Funerals," 166–67 and n. 153.

[144] At the 870 Cologne synod the three archbishops sought to rectify the abuses that had crept into the Church during the long vacancies at Cologne and Trier: MGH *Concilia* 4:396–401.

[145] *DLG* 132.

[146] *AF*, s.a. 870, p. 72; *AB*, s.a. 870, 175; Hadrian II, *Epistolae de rebus Franciae*, nos. 21–26, in MGH *Epistolae* 6:724–32.

[147] Hadrian II, *Epistolae de rebus Franciae*, no. 25, in MGH *Epistolae* 6:730–32.

[148] *AF*, s.a. 870, p. 72; *AB*, s.a. 870, pp. 175–76. Louis celebrated the Feast of All Saints (November 1) at Frankfurt, where he confirmed Prüm's immunity and royal protection: *DLG* 134.

sented to him bound with a heavy chain. While the assembled Franks, Bavarians, and Slavs condemned Rastislav to death for treason, Louis "mercifully" commuted his punishment to blinding and imprisonment.[149] Also at Regensburg, Louis (whom the *Life of Saint Methodius* described as a czar or emperor) and the Bavarian bishops tried Methodius, who had been captured during Carloman's annexation of Moravia, for usurping ecclesiastical authority within the jurisdiction of the Bavarian Church.[150] During the trial, the Bavarian bishops treated Methodius roughly, and Ermanrich of Passau even threatened him with a horsewhip.[151] But, like the binding and blinding of Rastislav and the Slavic rendering of tribute, the abuse of Methodius apparently was part of the triumphal ceremonies Louis orchestrated at the Regensburg assembly to reassert his kingship. In the end, the king and his bishops sentenced Methodius to imprisonment in an unidentified monastery, where he stayed for the next three years.[152]

The Regensburg assembly also served as an opportunity for Louis and his bishops to legitimize their claims of jurisdiction over Moravia and Lower Pannonia. In 870, a Salzburg churchman—perhaps Archbishop Adalwin himself—composed one of the most important east Frankish historical works, the *Conversion of the Bavarians and the Carantanians*.[153] The *Conversion* was written to rehearse Salzburg's contested claims to the ecclesiastical province of Lower Pannonia. By tracing in vivid detail the history of Salzburg's missionary work in Bavaria and its eastern marches from the time of Saint Rupert (d. 710), the *Conversion* sought to refute Pope Hadrian's creation of the archbishopric of Illyricum under Methodius the Philosopher. The *Conversion* glorified "our lord King Louis" as a second Charlemagne for upholding Frankish political and ecclesiastical control of the Eastland, and it is likely that a copy was presented to Louis himself. The most likely occasion for the circulation of this work at court was the 870 Regensburg as-

---

[149] For the ideological dimensions of the punishment of blinding, see Geneviève Bührer-Thierry, "'Just Anger' or 'Vengeful Anger'? The Punishment of Blinding in the Early Medieval West," in Rosenwein, *Anger's Past*, 75–91.

[150] *VM*, chap. 9, pp. 93–94; MGH *Concilia* 4:402–5. Concerning Methodius's trial at Regensburg, see Joseph Schütz, "Die Reichssynode zu Regensburg (870) und Methods Verbannung nach Schwaben," *Südost-Forschungen* 33 (1974): 1–14; Hartmann, *Synoden*, 309–10; Klaus Gamber, "Erzbischof Methodios vor der Reichsversammlung in Regensburg des Jahres 870," in *Symposium Methodianum: Beiträge der Internationalen Tagung in Regensburg (17. bis 24. April 1985) zum Gedenken an den 1100. Todestag des hl. Method*, ed. Klaus Trost, Ekkehard Vökl, and Erwin Wedel (Neuried, 1988), 111–15.

[151] *Fragmenta registri Iohannis VIII papae*, nos. 20–24, in MGH *Epistolae* 7:283–87.

[152] Bigott, *Ludwig der Deutsche*, 176n278, reviews the various scholarly arguments for Methodius's possible place of incarceration (perhaps Ellwangen, Reichenau, or near Freising).

[153] For the author of the *Conversio*, see Wolfram, *Salzburg*, 193–97.

sembly, when Louis and the Bavarian bishops condemned Methodius for in-fringing on their ecclesiastical jurisdiction in Lower Pannonia and Moravia.

It is possible that another major literary work was presented to Louis at the 870 Regensburg assembly as well: Otfrid's vernacular *Book of the Evangelists*. Otfrid's multiple dedications enable us to date his Frankish translation of the Gospels' story to 863–71. However, Otfrid's dedicatory verses to Louis suggest that he presented his work to the king in late 870 after the Treaty of Meersen and Louis's recovery to health.[154] With the first and last letters of his dedicatory verses to Louis, Otfrid spelled out the acclamation: "Eternal salvation to Louis, king of the eastern kingdoms."[155] This intitula-tion, "king of the eastern kingdoms" [orientalium regnorum rex], suggests Louis's newly acquired territories in late 870, which included not only the east Frankish kingdom but eastern Lotharingia and Moravia as well. In ef-fect, this royal title appears to have been Otfrid's refutation of Charles's seizure of Lotharingia in 869, when, in the words of the *Annals of Fulda*, Charles "ordered himself to be called emperor and augustus as one who possesses two kingdoms."[156] In his first verses to the king, Otfrid stressed Louis's military might and rule over the "land of the Franks" [ubar Frankono lant]. Otfrid's dedication began:

Louis the mighty, filled with wisdom,
He rules the entire eastern kingdom as befits a king of the Franks.
All his power extends over the land of the Franks.
Let me tell you this: his power rules it all.[157]

Otfrid went on to address lingering concerns about Louis's recent frail health. He asserted that "in his chest is a very strong heart," and he offered a prayer for Louis's health and long life.[158] Otfrid's claim that "now we live in happy, peaceful times" may allude to Rastislav's capture and imprison-ment, which seemed to mark the end of the long-standing war with Moravia.[159] Otfrid compared Louis to King David, who likewise had long endured hardships but expanded his kingdom with God's help. He wrote:

---

[154] Otfrid, *Ad Ludowicum*, in his *Liber evangeliorum*, 8–15. For an analysis of the the-matic sections of Otfrid's dedication to Louis, see Staiti, "Das Evangelienbuch Otfrids," 233–54. My interpretation for the dating of 870 follows the arguments of Wilhelm Luft, "Die Abfassungszeit von Otfrids Evangelienbuch," *ZDA* 40 (1896): 246–53; and Horst Dieter Schlosser, "Zu Datierung von Otfrieds 'Evangelienbuch,'" *ZDA* 125 (1996): 386–91.

[155] Otfrid, *Ad Ludowicum*, in his *Liber evangeliorum*, 8.

[156] *AF*, s.a. 869, p. 70.

[157] Otfrid, *Ad Ludowicum*, ll. 1–4, in his *Liber evangeliorum*, 8.

[158] Ibid., l. 15, p. 8.

[159] Ibid., l. 29, p. 10.

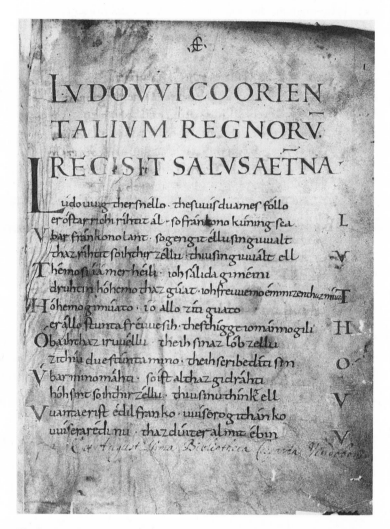

The king receives a Frankish translation of the Gospels. This photograph shows the dedication of Otfrid of Wissembourg's *Book of the Evangelists*, which he completed between 863 and 871, to Louis the German. While the verses are in Frankish, Otfrid's salutation to Louis is in Latin. It reads "Ludowico orientalium regnorum regi sit salus aeterna" (Eternal salvation to Louis, king of the eastern kingdoms!). The title "king of the eastern kingdoms" suggests that Otfrid gave the copy of his *Book of the Evangelists* to Louis after the Treaty of Meersen in 870, when Louis acquired the second "kingdom" of eastern Lotharingia. Bildarchiv der Österreichischen Nationalbibliothek, Codex Vindobonensis 2687, fol. 1r.

If someone undertook a fight against David,
The merciful Lord immediately protected him
And always helped him when in need and great danger.
The Lord lightened all the years of his life (which were very hard for him),
Until he succeeded in expanding his kingdom.
For this reason Louis can be compared to David.[160]

As in the case of the *Conversion of the Bavarians and the Carantanians*, the most likely setting for the presentation of Otfrid's *Book of the Evangelists* to Louis would have been the 870 Regensburg assembly, at which Louis asserted his recovery to health and proclaimed his expanded rule as "king of the eastern kingdoms."

As Louis celebrated Christmas at Regensburg in 870, he must have felt very pleased. After half a century of struggle that went back to the *Ordinatio imperii*, he had secured the entire kingdom of Austrasia and the imperial capital of Aachen. Moreover, he had weathered a decade of rebellions, imprisoned Rastislav and Methodius, reasserted control over Lower Pannonia, and annexed Moravia. On top of all that, he had survived two near brushes with death in as many years, a fact that must have convinced him that he still enjoyed God's favor. Although Louis could not know it, this moment represented the political high point of his long reign.

---

[160] Ibid., ll. 51–56, p. 12.

CHAPTER NINE
THE CALL OF ROME, 871-876

B y the 870s, Louis was in his sixties and, according to Carolingian standards, an old man. But the elderly king's recent successes in Moravia and Lotharingia filled his mind
with visions of further territorial conquests. During the
last years of his reign, Louis focused all his energies on a final crowning
achievement: Italy and Rome. With Emperor Louis II of Italy still without an
heir, the old king sought to win the Italian kingdom and western imperial
crown—either for himself or for his eldest son, Carloman. Not surprisingly,
this plan sparked a new series of rebellions from the king's younger two sons,
who feared an uneven succession plan like the *Ordinatio imperii* half a century
earlier. Given his own vigorous opposition to the 817 division, Louis's fa-
voritism toward Carloman suggests the extent to which he had become preoccupied—one might even say obsessed—with dreams of reviving the Carolingian empire. Louis's pursuit of imperial ambitions and his younger sons'
challenges to these policies were to define the last years of his long reign.[1]

CARLOMAN, ITALY, AND LOTHARINGIA

The choice of the forty-year-old Carloman as the future emperor and
ruler of Italy made sense for several reasons. Carloman was Louis's eldest

---

[1] For the politics of these years, see Dümmler, *GOR* 2:303–411; Nelson, *Charles the
Bald*, 221–53; Hartmann, *Ludwig der Deutsche*, 56–60.

son, and in 870 his political star was on the rise from his recent triumphs in Moravia. Geopolitics likewise made Carloman the obvious choice as the next ruler of Italy, since his future Bavarian kingdom was accessible to Italy via the Brenner Pass. Family politics also played a role. According to Hincmar, in the 870s Queen Emma was urging her husband to favor their eldest son, a situation that led Ernst Dümmler to brand Carloman a "mamma's boy" [Muttersönchen]![2] The queen's role in her husband's imperial schemes is striking, since the sources do not mention any previous participation by her in politics. Perhaps the king's frail health in 869–70 compelled him to rely more on her counsel in his old age. Another hint of Carloman's growing imperial ambitions is that around this time he rebuilt the monastery at the palace of Altötting in eastern Bavaria and dedicated it to the patron saint of Aachen, Frankfurt, and Regensburg—the Virgin Mary—as well as to "numerous other saints whose relics we were able to collect with God's help."[3]

Louis's imperial plans for Carloman involved newly acquired eastern Lotharingia as well as Italy. The king's 865 division of Frankfurt does not seem to have addressed his sons' inheritance of the Lotharingian territories, which Louis did not acquire until five years later. Along with planning to place Carloman on the imperial throne, Louis considered bequeathing to his eldest son an expanded kingdom consisting of Bavaria, Italy, and eastern Lotharingia, thereby reuniting the two imperial capitals of Aachen and Rome. This plan was a return to an *Ordinatio imperii*–type division, but with Carloman playing the role of Lothar I. By the mid-860s, Carloman had already begun to involve himself in the politics of the middle kingdom and solicit the support of prominent Lotharingian magnates. In 864, Carloman helped the powerful Lotharingian magnate Abbot Hubert of St.-Maurice

---

[2] *AB*, s.a. 870, p. 176: "Qui [Louis the Younger and Charles III] sentientes, satagente matre, inclinatiorem esse voluntatem patris erga Karlomannum quam erga se." I concur with the translation of Dümmler, *GOR* 2:317, 337; Johannes Fried, *König Ludwig der Jüngere in seiner Zeit: Zum 1100 Todestag des Königs* (Lorsch, 1984), 8; and Kasten, *Königssöhne*, 524. In contrast, *Annals of St.-Bertin*, trans. Nelson, 170, interprets "satagente matre" to refer to Emma's egging on of her younger two sons. Several pieces of evidence support the interpretation that Emma was favoring Carloman in the 870s. First, in a diploma dated October 20, 871, Emma and Carloman jointly intervened before King Louis on behalf of the monastery of Prüm: *DLG* 141. Second, when Louis in 875 paid a visit to Emma at Regensburg after she had suffered a stroke, Carloman was at her side. On that occasion, the king made a pious grant for Emma's health and salvation, and Carloman cosubscribed the diploma: *DLG* 161. There is no corroborating evidence for the interpretation that Emma was supporting her younger two sons against Carloman. Hartmann, *Ludwig der Deutsche*, 256, argues that Louis in his last years sought to make Carloman heir to the entire east Frankish kingdom, although the evidence does not support this interpretation.

[3] *DCarloman* 2.

(Agaune) acquire the additional monastery of Lobbes.[4] Since the monastery of St.-Maurice guarded the strategic Mons Iovis (Great Saint Bernard) Pass that connected Italy with southern Burgundy, Hubert's support was crucial for Carloman's hope to inherit a composite "empire" that united Bavaria, Italy, and eastern Lotharingia.

As one would expect, Louis the Younger and Charles III deeply resented their elder brother's preferential treatment and expanded inheritance. The king's younger sons wanted the wealthy territories of eastern Lotharingia, since those rich Frankish heartlands bordered on their future kingdoms in Franconia and Alemannia. Moreover, they took it badly that their father was giving lands on the middle Rhine to Lotharingian recipients, thereby depleting the fund of fiscal estates within their inheritance portions and placing them at Carloman's disposal as the heir apparent to eastern Lotharingia.[5] As the *Annals of Fulda* summed up, the king "revoked from [his younger two sons] a certain part of the kingdom of the Franks, which the king had set aside for them to have after his death, and gave it to their brother Carloman."[6] When Louis the Younger and Charles III learned this, they rebelled. In early 871 they gathered a large army and occupied the Speyergau on the east Frankish–Lotharingian border, thereby asserting their claims to the middle Rhine and the adjacent Lotharingian territories. Following their customary strategy, the rebel princes sought alliances with their father's enemies: they turned to Charles the Bald for help, and they apparently also appealed to Svatopluk of Moravia.[7] After much negotiation, however, Louis the German managed to placate his younger two sons somewhat "with flattering

[4] *DArnulf* 64; cited in MacLean, "Carolingian Response," 40n62. See further *Annals of St.-Bertin*, trans. Nelson, 93n7. It may not be coincidence that Carloman's first-documented involvement in Lotharingian politics occurred in the same year that he and his father reached a peaceful settlement that ended the son's rebellion (864). As one of the terms of their reconciliation, Carloman may have demanded that his father favor him as the heir to Lotharingia.

[5] For example, in February 871, Louis confirmed Abbot Ansbald of Prüm's lands on the east bank of the Rhine near Worms and Speyer: *DLG* 136. Because the king could call on the abbot of Prüm for political and military support, this confirmation guaranteed that important estates on the middle Rhine would indirectly be at the disposal of the future ruler of eastern Lotharingia, namely, Carloman.

[6] *AF*, s.a. 871, pp. 72–73; *AB*, s.a. 871, pp. 181–82.

[7] Although the *AF*, s.a. 871, pp. 72–73, do not state explicitly that Louis the Younger and Charles III sought an alliance with Svatopluk, the details they provide strongly point to that conclusion. At this time, Carloman imprisoned Svatopluk (who was still ruling a Moravian principality as a client *dux* alongside Carloman's supporters) on unspecified charges of infidelity. Moreover, during an assembly at Tribur, the king inflicted the punishment for treason—blinding—on a certain Saxon vassal of Count Henry. Henry was Louis the Younger's chief supporter, and he had served as Louis the Younger's liaison to Rastislav during the 866 rebellion: *AF*, s.a. 866, p. 65.

words and promises of benefices." The king then made a formal progress through eastern Lotharingia to consolidate his power there.

Pressing political events ultimately forced King Louis to reach a more lasting settlement with his unhappy younger sons. In September 871 while still at Aachen, Louis the German received the news that Louis II of Italy had been murdered. The report of the Italian emperor's death is a good example of the role of rumor and misinformation in Carolingian politics: although the news turned out to be false, for several weeks the east and west Frankish kings believed it was true.[8] Because Louis the German immediately wanted to launch an invasion of Italy and seize the imperial throne, he had no choice but to come to terms with his younger sons. On his way to Frankfurt, he met with Louis the Younger and Charles III and brokered a reconciliation "without any difficulty" by granting them "certain benefices." The king gave Charles III the strategic Alpine province of Chur-Rhaetia and dispatched him with all speed to defend the Mons Iovis Pass to Italy against Charles the Bald, who was hastening there through Burgundy.[9]

Meanwhile, Louis the German prepared for the Italian invasion with his men at Frankfurt. The king planned to use Saxon and Lotharingian forces in the campaign across the Alps, and at Frankfurt he made grants for Bishop Theoderich of Minden, Count Waltbert of Westphalia, the monastery of Prüm, and a large number of Lotharingian benefice holders.[10] Also at Frankfurt were Queen Emma and Carloman, who apparently intended to accompany Louis to Italy and take part in a joint imperial coronation in Rome. Emma and Carloman intervened before the king on the behalf of the monastery of Prüm and the Lotharingian magnate Otbert, illustrating Carloman's position as the heir apparent to eastern Lotharingia with the queen's support.[11] In his grant to Prüm, Louis emphasized the sacrality of his dynasty. He made the unusual provision that twenty clerics were to be established at the churches of St.-Justina and St.-Mary in Bachem (southwest of

---

[8] For the account of how this rumor arose, see *AB*, s.a. 871, pp. 182–84.

[9] *AA*, s.a. 871, p. 180; *AB*, s.a. 871, p. 183. Charles III's mission was to win control of the region south of the Jura Mountains around Lake Geneva (which belonged to Louis II of Italy, now presumed dead), bind the local nobles to him with oaths of fidelity, and guard the Mons Iovis Pass. A diploma and several Lorsch charters from late 871 suggest that, as part of his concessions to Louis the Younger and Charles III, Louis confirmed the east Frankish–Lotharingian borders from 843, thereby guaranteeing that they (and not Carloman) would inherit the royal lands on the middle Rhine: *DLG* 141; *Lorsch* 1196, 2259, 2267, 2534.

[10] *DLG* 140–42.

[11] *DLG* 141. Otbert had been one of the chief supporters of Lothar I: Dümmler, *GOR* 2:335 and n. 5.

Cologne) and devote themselves to prayer and feeding of the poor "for our salvation and the salvation of our beloved wife Emma and dearest children."

It is also possible that an unusual coronation blessing (*ordo*) was composed for Louis and Emma on the eve of their departure for Italy. This coronation blessing for a royal couple, which survives in a Vatican manuscript, was written in the western region of Louis's kingdom during the third quarter of the ninth century, perhaps during the mustering of Louis's forces at Frankfurt in October 871.[12] The *ordo* is not related to the other surviving Carolingian coronation blessings, and its "high" style freely mixes the language of kingship and empire. In light of the political and ideological context in 871, it is possible that this coronation blessing was composed to articulate Louis and Emma's claims to the Italian throne and imperial title on the eve of their departure from Frankfurt for Rome. The *ordo*, which consists of four sections, reads:

> God, supreme Rewarder and Sympathizer of all, defend the kingdoms of those whom You joined in chastity that is pleasing to You. Suppress the rebellious heathens, establish their peoples in Your peace. Let them obey Your command. May You be the protector of their empire.

> Give profitable counsel to those to whom You gave such praiseworthy wisdom. Let them exist in Your power, not the power of the world. May these rulers wearing diadems observe the divine commandments at all times. Let them fear You so that they might not fear mortals, let them take confidence in Your fortitude rather than their own power. Look after them closely and take care of them.

> [Addressing the king and queen:] Consider carefully, venerable ones of the Lord, according to what kind of love you would rule. We would not dare to say those things publicly to the Lord unless He knew us to hope for them privately.

> Holy Divinity, extend the Roman empire to the furthest borders, may its boundaries be girded by the lapping ocean. Let our princes command the world so that the world does not command them. Let them

---

[12] Biblioteca Apostolica Vaticana Reg. lat. 421, fol. 25v. For a detailed discussion and edition of this little-studied Carolingian *ordo*, see Reinhard Elze, "Ein karolingischer Ordo für die Krönung eines Herrscherpaares," *Bullettino dell'Instituto Storico Italiano per il Medio Evo e Archivio Muratoriano* 98 (1992): 417–23. Elze dated the *ordo* ca. 850–75 and identified its provenance as somewhere in western Germany, although he declined to suggest a specific context for its use.

fear You so that they might not fear anything else. Let them come to Your diadem from this earthly crown. May You Who created the humble purple in them give them the nuptial stole [i.e., eternal life]. Grant them the kingdom where neither life ends nor joy fades.

Ultimately, we cannot know whether this blessing was ever used to crown Louis and Emma. Nevertheless, it suggests that east Frankish churchmen were experimenting with coronation blessings that reflected Louis and Emma's heightened imperial policies during the final decades of their reign. In any event, the Italian campaign never materialized. Around the beginning of November Louis learned that Emperor Louis II of Italy was still alive, which forced Louis the German to put his imperial schemes on hold.

PRINCE SVATOPLUK, VALIANT AND TERRIBLE

When Carloman arrived at Frankfurt in October 871, he brought grim news of recent events in the east. In 870, Carloman had annexed Moravia and placed its *civitates et castella* under the rule of his Bavarian supporters, Counts William II and Engelschalk. However, in return for handing over Rastislav, Carloman had allowed Svatopluk to retain his Moravian principality (*regnum, patria*) centered on "Rastislav's old fortress" at Staré Město. But Carloman imprisoned Svatopluk in early 871, presumably because he suspected the Moravian prince of joining the rebellion of Louis the Younger and Charles III. Believing that Svatopluk was dead, the Moravians at Staré Město selected a surviving member of the Moravian royal family named Sclagamar and made him their ruler.[13] Sclagamar had been a priest, which likely indicates that the Moravian ruling dynasty was beginning to run out of male heirs—presumably because so many had been given to the Franks as hostages.[14] In 871 Sclagamar made war on William II and Engelschalk and attempted to drive them from Moravia. But Carloman's men defeated Sclagamar and his large army and compelled him to retreat to his stronghold at Staré Město.

[13] *AF*, s.a. 871, pp. 73–74.

[14] Indeed, it is possible that Sclagamar himself had earlier been a hostage. Just months after Louis had compelled Rastislav to turn over "as many high-ranking hostages as he commanded" in 864, Otgar of Eichstätt granted an estate near the Frankish–Moravian border to a certain Slav named Sleimar, perhaps a variant spelling of Sclagamar: *DLG* 165. It is conceivable that Louis had placed Sclagamar-Sleimar under Bishop Otgar's supervision and granted him an estate as a prebend while he served as a pledge for Rastislav's loyalty.

With Sclagamar in rebellion, Carloman decided to employ the common strategy of using one "barbarian" leader to wage war against another. Carloman had already come to the conclusion that the accusations of infidelity against Svatopluk were unfounded, and he therefore released the Moravian prince from prison. Carloman sent Svatopluk back to Moravia with a large Bavarian army and numerous "royal gifts" to depose Sclagamar and reassume control of Staré Město. To strengthen his alliance with Svatopluk, Carloman bound him to his family through bonds of spiritual kinship (*familiaritas*).[15] Around this time Carloman's son, the approximately twenty-year-old Arnulf, had a son out of wedlock by an unnamed mistress. Carloman and Arnulf had Svatopluk stand as the boy's godfather at his baptism, and they gave him the decidedly un-Carolingian—indeed Moravian—name of Svatopluk after the godfather. (The boy grew up to become King Zwentibald of Lotharingia, 895–900.) The motivation behind Carloman and Arnulf's unusual alliance with Svatopluk becomes clear when viewed in its larger political context. Carloman hoped to become ruler of Italy, and he therefore needed to be ready to launch an invasion across the Alps at any moment. Carloman and Arnulf therefore needed a firm alliance with the head of the Moravian royal family to secure their eastern borders during the imminent Italian campaign.

The cunning Svatopluk had his own plans, however. He secretly plotted to avenge Carloman's "insult" (the annexation of Moravia), drive the Franks from the region, and seize the entire Moravian kingdom for himself. When Svatopluk and the Bavarian army arrived at Staré Město, Svatopluk quickly captured the fortress according to Carloman's plan. Once inside its walls, however, Svatopluk "in typical Slavic fashion" renounced his loyalty to Carloman, rallied a large Moravian force, and launched a devastating surprise attack on the unsuspecting Bavarian army encamped outside. The Moravians took a great number of soldiers hostage, killed the rest (including Carloman's governors, William II and Engelschalk), and rid Moravia of the Frankish occupation.[16] The booty seized by the Moravians must have been tremendous: wagons, supplies, horses, shields, spears, helmets, and espe-

[15] Regino, *Chronicon*, s.a. 890, p. 134; Dümmler, *GOR* 2:317 and n. 4. Gerd Althoff, "Zu Bedeutung der Bündnisse Svatopluks von Mähren mit Franken," in Trost, Völkl, and Wedel, *Symposium Methodianum*, 13–21, argues that the diplomacy between Svatopluk and the Frankish rulers in 870–94 was shaped by alliances of "friendship" [amicitia], which brought with them enduring reciprocal political obligations among the parties involved. Although this was true at certain moments, much of the time the driving force in Franco–Moravian relations was the competing self-interests of the individual political figures involved.

[16] *AF*, s.a. 871, pp. 73–74; *AB*, s.a. 871, p. 182; *AX*, s.a. 872, pp. 30–31; Mitterauer, *Karolingische Markgrafen*, p. 180.

cially the highly prized Frankish coats of mail and swords. Because of this victory, the Moravians could henceforth face the Franks on an equal footing on the battlefield. Svatopluk immediately capitalized on this triumph by forming an alliance through marriage with the neighboring Bohemians, thus uniting the two Slavic peoples against the Franks.[17] The *Annals of Fulda* echoed the dismay of the east Frankish court at this shocking reversal of fortune: "All the joy of the Noricans [i.e., Bavarians] from their many previous victories was changed into mourning and lamentation. Carloman was horrified when he learned of his army's annihilation, and, compelled by necessity, he ordered that all the hostages in his kingdom be collected and returned to Svatopluk." This brilliant surprise attack established Svatopluk's reputation as a skilled ruler and mighty general. The *Annals of Fulda* branded him a "mind full of trickery and cunning" and the "womb of all treachery," while Regino described him as "King Svatopluk of the Moravian Slavs, a man who was most prudent among his people and"—like Louis the German himself—"extremely cunning by nature."[18] The Byzantine court remembered Svatopluk as "valiant and terrible to the nations that were his neighbors."[19] The elderly King Louis faced a new rising star in Moravia.

Louis realized the grave threat posed by Svatopluk. The following year, 872, the elderly king mustered a "massive army" to crush the new lord of Moravia. As usual, Louis wanted to invade Moravia from two directions: Carloman would lead the Bavarians from the south, while a second army would invade through Bohemia. But this campaign conflicted with Louis's imperial schemes. He had arranged to meet Empress Engelberga, the influential wife of Louis II of Italy, in May at Trent to negotiate Carloman's succession to Italy.[20] For this reason, Louis could not lead the second army on its dangerous march through Bohemia to Moravia. But if the king did not go in person, he risked the possibility of crippling conflicts among his generals, as had happened in 846 and 849. Louis therefore wanted one of his younger sons to command the second army to mitigate disputes among his troops.

Not surprisingly, Louis the Younger and Charles III had little desire to help their elder brother, whom they thought the king and queen unfairly favored. In this way, filial tensions over inheritance threatened to undermine

---

[17] The *AF*, s.a. 871, pp. 74–75, report that an unnamed Moravian magnate (perhaps Svatopluk himself) married the daughter of a Bohemian *dux*. See further Dümmler, *GOR* 2:336 and n. 2.

[18] *AF(B)*, s.a. 884, 894, pp. 111, 125; Regino, *Chronicon*, s.a. 894, p. 143.

[19] Constantine, *De administrando*, chap. 41, pp. 180–81.

[20] For the career of Louis II of Italy's wife, see Charles E. Odegaard, "The Empress Engelberga," *Speculum* 26 (1951): 77–103.

Louis's imperial plans and the stability of his eastern borders with the Slavs. In an effort to resolve this impasse, the king held an unusual assembly with his army and younger two sons in March at Forchheim, not far from the Bohemian border. At that meeting, Louis once again sought to settle the inheritance disputes among his sons. Louis "made peace with his sons, who were disputing the partition of the kingdom among themselves, and he indicated clearly who was to have which part after his death. There in the sight of the entire army his sons, Louis [the Younger] and Charles [III], confirmed with an oath their faith to him and that they would serve him all the days of their life."[21] The presence of the army was critical. Louis wanted to convince his rank-and-file soldiers that his sons would cooperate during the upcoming Moravian campaign and thereby would not endanger them more than was necessary. Indeed, the king also made the vassals (*homines*) of Louis the Younger and Charles III swear oaths of loyalty.[22] The participation of the princes' vassals was important, since these nobles had been stoking—and therefore could also help curb—the filial rivalries among the king's sons. In return for their oaths, the king apparently made a major concession to his younger two sons: he agreed to divide eastern Lotharingia between them rather than leaving it to Carloman.[23] In spite of these efforts, however, the king's plans failed miserably. Many nobles believed that his sons and their vassals gave their oaths insincerely, and in the end Louis the Younger and Charles III flatly refused to aid Carloman in the upcoming invasion of Moravia.

In spite of these setbacks, Louis pushed ahead with the 872 campaign against Svatopluk. In May Carloman invaded Moravia with a large Bavarian army, while a force of Saxons and Thuringians marched through Bohemia. As the king feared, the absence of a royal leader opened the door to disputes among the Saxon and Thuringian troops: "Because they did not have the king with them and did not want to cooperate with each other, they turned their backs and fled before the enemy. Having lost many of their number they returned in disgrace." In response, two additional armies were sent: one, under the command of Archbishop Liutbert of Mainz, defeated six rebel Bohemian rulers near the Vltava (Muldau) River, while Bishop Arn of

---

[21] *AF,* s.a. 872, p. 75. Cf. *Annals of Fulda,* trans. Reuter, 67n3; Reuter interpreted this passage as evidence for the archaic Frankish notion that an assembly was a mustering of the troops (*Heerschau*).

[22] *AB,* s.a. 872, p. 186.

[23] Upon his father's death in 876, Louis the Younger laid claim to the "portion of the kingdom that his father left him, specifically the part that [Louis the German] received from his brother Charles with his consent and oath" in 870: *AB,* s.a. 876, p. 207; Dümmler, *GOR* 2:337n2. Regino, *Chronicon,* s.a. 876, p. 112, reported that Louis the German left Charles III "certain cities in Lotharingia."

Würzburg and Abbot Sigihard of Fulda brought reinforcements to Carloman in Moravia.[24] The Franks put Svatopluk's army to flight and forced it to take refuge in an "extremely well-fortified stronghold," perhaps the massive fortress at Mikulčice.[25] The Franks besieged the fortress for a long time and inflicted serious losses on the Moravians, although they failed to capture it. Meanwhile, Carloman laid waste to the Moravian countryside. But, once again, Svatopluk executed a masterful surprise counterattack: he secretly led a force to the Danube and devastated the troops of Bishop Embricho of Regensburg that were guarding the Bavarian fleet. The army under Arn of Würzburg and Sigihard of Fulda fared little better. After fighting the Moravians and suffering significant losses, they returned home through Bohemia "with great difficulty."

LAST YEARS

Louis knew his absence from the 872 Moravian campaign was a serious risk. The fact that he took this gamble reveals the high priority he now gave to the issue of the Italian succession and the imperial crown. In May Louis journeyed across the Brenner Pass to Trent, where he met with Empress Engelberga and several Italian bishops, who were acting as the representatives of Emperor Louis II and Pope Hadrian.[26] During the 872 Trent meeting, Louis the German secretly conceded eastern Lotharingia to Louis II of Italy and swore oaths with Engelberga. In return, Engelberga seems to have accepted Carloman as her husband's heir. While at first it seems puzzling that Louis the German would grant his Lotharingian territories to his Italian nephew, this scheme makes sense in terms of his imperial plans for Carloman. As Louis II of Italy's heir, Carloman once again would inherit both Italy and eastern Lotharingia. Louis the German was playing fast and loose

[24] The *AF*, s.a. 872, p. 76, textual n. l, and n. 2, name the six Bohemian *duces* defeated by Liutbert of Mainz: Zwentislan, Witislan, Heriman, Spoitimar, Moyslan, and Goriwei. (Note that the third name, Heriman, was Germanic rather than Slavic, which suggests that at least one Bohemian *dux* was of partial Frankish ancestry.) The last name, Goriwei, is probably a variant spelling of Boriwoi-Bořivoj. Bořivoj I (d. ca. 899) was lord of the fortress at Levý Hradec north of Prague and a member of the Přemyslid dynasty that ruled the Czechs, a people within the Bohemian confederation who lived near the confluence of the Elbe and Vltava rivers. A decade later he received baptism at Svatopluk's court and began the unification of Bohemia with the Moravian ruler's help: Barford, *Early Slavs*, 252–53.

[25] *AX*, s.a. 872, p. 31; *AI*, s.a. 872, p. 744.

[26] *AB*, s.a. 872, p. 185; MGH *Capitularia* 2:341–42.

with the rules of inheritance, going back on his recent promises at Forchheim to leave his Lotharingian territories to Louis the Younger and Charles III. Moreover, Louis the German knew that he would remain the de facto ruler of eastern Lotharingia, since at the moment his nephew Louis II was facing a serious rebellion by the Beneventans in southern Italy.[27] Charles the Bald was deeply disturbed when he learned the details of the Trent meeting. Charles held an assembly at Gondreville to have his magnates renew their oaths of fidelity and promise to help him defend his kingdom—both what he now held and what God might grant him in the future.[28] Once again, the brothers were preparing for civil war.

In the short term, Louis the German's Trent negotiations eroded his political support at home. The Moravian campaign had been a failure, and the king's younger sons resented their father's duplicitous scheme to reestablish Carloman as the heir to eastern Lotharingia. In the words of Hincmar, Charles III (and presumably Louis the Younger as well) felt his father was "plotting to ruin him for the benefit of his brother Carloman."[29] Moreover, when Louis's Lotharingian supporters learned the details of the Trent agreement, they were angry that they had not been consulted. To settle these ongoing tensions over his succession plans for Carloman, Louis announced a general assembly in January 873 at Frankfurt "to discuss the state and prosperity of his kingdom" with his bishops and nobles, and he specified that his younger two sons and the Lotharingians were to attend.[30] It was unusual for Louis to hold a large assembly in January because inclement weather made travel difficult, so the date highlights the urgency with which Louis wanted to settle the various conflicts among his sons and nobles. Moreover, it probably was not a coincidence that the anniversary of Charlemagne's death (January 28) fell during the 873 assembly. We know that Louis's court observed the anniversary of Charlemagne's death because the historical entry in the Grimalt Codex that recorded Louis the German's inheritance of the Carolingian *imperium* began with Charlemagne's obituary. Thus, by scheduling the 873 assembly during the observance of Charlemagne's death, Louis suggested that his inheritance plans for Carloman were part of a larger design to revive Charlemagne's empire.

The widespread grievances against the elderly king had, however, mush-

---

[27] *AB*, s.a. 871, 873, pp. 182–84, 192.

[28] MGH *Capitularia* 2:341–42. Pope Hadrian had intimated to Charles the Bald that he, not Carloman, would succeed Emperor Louis II of Italy: Dümmler, *GOR* 2:344–52; Nelson, *Charles the Bald*, 238.

[29] *AB*, s.a. 873, p. 190.

[30] Nelson's translation of *Annals of St.-Bertin*, 182, mistakenly implies that Carloman was present.

roomed into conspiracy. Louis the Younger and Charles III secretly planned to depose their father at the Frankfurt assembly. As one contemporary summed up, "they forgot their oaths of the previous year and plotted tyrannously to deprive their father of his kingdom and throw him in prison."[31] In this way, the king's younger sons sought to reenact the infamous Field of Lies that had occurred four decades earlier, this time featuring their elderly father in the role of the hapless Louis the Pious. At the last minute, however, Charles III found that he could not go through with the rebellion.[32] According to Hincmar (who was well informed about these events), on January 26 Charles III unexpectedly jumped up in the midst of the assembled bishops and counts and announced his desire to "abandon the world" and never have sex with his wife, the Alsatian noblewoman Richgard, whom he had married in 862.[33] He then dropped his sword belt and began to take off his princely clothes, although he was shaking so violently that he was unable to disrobe. Everyone at the assembly was thunderstruck, and they immediately attributed the prince's outburst to demonic possession. The king therefore commanded that his son (who was moaning "Woe! Woe!" in Frankish) be taken into the Frankfurt chapel, where Archbishop Liutbert chanted the Mass to exorcise the evil spirit. The bishops then led Charles III around the Frankfurt chapel to the shrines of various saints, "so that their merits and prayers might free him from the demon and he might be able by God's mercy to recover his sanity."

Although ninth-century people accepted diabolical influence as an explanation for Charles III's shocking behavior, the modern historian would like a more nuanced interpretation. The need for a more careful examination is especially important because, partly owing to his 873 outburst, historians traditionally have dismissed Charles III as an incompetent, weak, and even epileptic prince who represented the alleged decline of the Carolingian monarchy.[34] This image has been compounded by Charles III's modern cognomen, "the Fat," even though there is no contemporary evidence that

[31] *AX*, s.a. 873, p. 31.

[32] For reports of the following events, see *AF*, s.a. 873, pp. 77–78; *AB*, s.a. 873, pp. 190–92; *AX*, s.a. 873, pp. 31–32; *Vita Rimberti*, chap. 20, pp. 96–97. For analysis, see Janet L. Nelson, "A Tale of Two Princes: Politics, Text, and Ideology in a Carolingian Annal," *SMRH* 10 (1988): 105–41; Paul Edward Dutton, *The Politics of Dreaming in the Carolingian Empire* (Lincoln, NE, 1994), 211–16; MacLean, "Ritual, Misunderstanding, and the Contest for Meaning."

[33] *AB*, s.a. 862, p. 93; Borgolte, "Karl III und Neudingen," 36–39.

[34] For example, Dümmler, *GOR* 2:353, attributed Charles III's outburst to a weakness of political resolve, describing him as "more timid and good natured than his heartless brother Louis." MacLean, *Kingship and Politics*, 23–24 and *passim*, reviews the negative image of Charles III in the historiography and offers a convincing favorable reassessment of his abilities as a ruler.

he was unusually corpulent. In fact, the historical evidence suggests that Charles III cut a dashing figure: he reportedly was tall, blond, and extraordinarily strong.[35] To explain his outburst, we must first recognize that Charles III, like many Carolingian princes, was under intense political and psychological pressures. Over the previous two years, Charles III had rebelled repeatedly against his father at the urging of Louis the Younger and his own vassals. At the same time, the stakes of rebellion had become horrifically high. Only weeks earlier, Charles the Bald had taken the radical step of blinding his own son for conspiring against him.[36] Moreover, like many ninth-century laymen, Charles III seems to have been genuinely pious. In the words of Regino, he "feared God, kept God's commandments with his whole heart, and devotedly obeyed the ecclesiastical laws. He was generous in alms, unceasingly given to prayer and the melodies of psalms, and unflaggingly devoted to the praises of God."[37] As a layman with deeply pious Christian beliefs, Charles III apparently felt deeply conflicted about the demands secular politics forced on him: sex, violence, pride, and rebellion.[38]

What is clear is that, on January 26, Charles III resolved not to go through with his impious conspiracy against his father. Hincmar's report that the king's son "desired to abandon the world" implies that Charles III made a vow to give up secular politics and become a monk. However, Simon MacLean has recently suggested that Charles III's outburst may not have been a monastic vow but rather a spontaneous act of public penance to make amends for his part in the impending conspiracy.[39] In any case, what made Charles III's outburst so disturbing was its complete spontaneity, since the king and nobles usually worked out details of public rituals in private and in advance before they were enacted publicly. Charles III's unexpected outburst therefore was a shocking break with the unwritten conventions of courtly behavior.

Whether monastic vow or penance, Charles's surprising eruption alerted the king to his sons' plot to depose him. It was a moment of real danger for the king, since some of the magnates must have been involved in the conspiracy as well. In the ensuing turmoil, King Louis managed to retain control of the situation and defuse the rebellion before it began. When Louis the Younger unexpectedly found himself abandoned by Charles III, he threw himself at his father's feet, confessed their plot, and begged forgive-

---

[35] Notker, *GK* 1.34, p. 47 and n. 3; Dümmler, *GOR* 3:291 and n. 1; *AF,* s.a. 873, p. 77.

[36] *AB,* s.a. 873, p. 190.

[37] Regino, *Chronicon,* s.a. 888, pp. 128–29.

[38] Nelson, "Monks," 132–38.

[39] MacLean, "Ritual, Misunderstanding, and the Contest for Meaning."

ness.[40] Louis the German accepted his namesake's submission. According to the *Annals of Fulda*, the king rebuked him with the following words: "Do you not see, my son, to whose lordship [i.e., Satan's] you and your brother gave yourselves when you tried to plot this evil scheme against me? If you did not before, you understand now that, according to the true saying, *Nothing is hidden that will not be revealed* [Matthew 10:26]. Therefore confess your sins and do penance and humbly ask God that they may be forgiven of you. I for my part pardon you as far as I can."[41]

Louis the German spent the spring and summer mending relations with his sons and shoring up political support in the wake of the failed coup. Only four days after Charles III's outburst, the king confirmed St.-Gall's immunity, royal protection, and judicial rights.[42] In this way, Louis asserted his enduring control of Alemannia, in spite of the recent conspiracy and unusual behavior of the heir apparent to that region. By April, the king had dissuaded Charles III from becoming a monk (if that indeed had been his intention) and reinstated him as the royal governor of Alemannia.[43] To pacify Louis the Younger, the king again pledged that his namesake, not Carloman, would inherit eastern Lotharingia as well as the middle Rhine. Thus on March 9, the king confirmed Prüm's possession of a church on the middle Rhine, and he allowed his namesake to subscribe his diploma for the first time with the royal title *rex*.[44] After Easter, the king held an assembly at Bürstadt (near Worms), where he staged a highly choreographed scene of father–son harmony that was the opposite of the incidents at the Frankfurt assembly earlier that year. At Bürstadt the king allowed Louis the Younger and Charles III to judge the nobles' disputes, settling by himself only those cases his sons could not. "Thus it came to pass that everyone coming from

---

[40] *AX*, s.a. 873, p. 32. Hartmann, *Ludwig der Deutsche*, 72–73, 255–56, interprets Louis the Younger's unconditional surrender (*deditio*) as evidence for a heightened reliance on ritualized submissions to resolve disputes under Louis. In this way, Hartmann presents Louis as foreshadowing the Ottonian, Salian, and Hohenstaufen emperors, who, as Gerd Althoff has shown, frequently used choreographed rituals of submission (like groveling at the ruler's feet) to humiliate rebels while leaving their power intact: Gerd Althoff, "Das Privileg der *deditio*," reprinted in Althoff, *Spielregeln*, 99–125. However, Louis the Younger's groveling at the 873 Frankfurt assembly is the only reported ritualized surrender during his father's long reign. As Althoff recognized, the Carolingians were able to punish criminals and rebels more aggressively than did their Ottonian successors: Althoff, "Königsherrschaft und Konfliktbewältigung," 37–38.

[41] *AF*, s.a. 873, pp. 77–78.

[42] *DLG* 144.

[43] Louis resumed addressing royal writs to that region "to our dear son Charles and all our counts and other faithful men in Alemannia": *DLG* 146.

[44] *DLG* 145.

all around had their disputes properly settled and returned joyfully home."[45]
The king then departed for Aachen, where he held a secret meeting to shore
up the wavering support of the Lotharingian magnates. The king capped his
visit to the region with his first Lotharingian general assembly in August at
Metz.[46]

Once again, however, crisis in the east intervened. While at Metz, Louis
received an urgent message that Carloman required his immediate help
against the Slavs.[47] Hincmar implied that Carloman had suffered a serious
defeat, perhaps during a campaign against Svatopluk of Moravia.[48] The
messengers reported to King Louis that "unless he go as fast as possible to
Carloman in the Wendish march, he would never see him again."[49] Adding
to this new crisis was the fact that Archbishop Adalwin of Salzburg had died
on May 14, leaving the Bavarian Church without political leadership. Despite his advanced years, the king responded with alacrity. He immediately
departed from Metz, crossed the Rhine at Strasbourg on August 26, and
reached Regensburg by the second week of September. En route, Louis appointed a Salzburg priest named Theotmar the new archbishop of Bavaria
and had him consecrated as soon as he himself arrived at Regensburg.[50]
Louis dispatched messengers to the neighboring Slavic rulers and reestablished peace with them by whatever terms he could negotiate. He also received legates from the Bohemians, but suspecting them of treachery, he
threw them into his dungeon.

Another dimension of this crisis with the Slavs involved Louis's relations
with the new pope, John VIII (872–82). An old but active Roman nobleman,
John VIII worked unceasingly to uphold papal leadership in the Church,
form alliances advantageous to Rome, and protect Italy from Muslim pirates. As pope he also vigorously defended Rome's ecclesiastical jurisdiction
over the newly revived archdiocese of Illyricum.[51] In the summer of 873,
John VIII sent a number of letters to Louis's court. Basing his arguments on

[45] *AF,* s.a. 873, p. 78.

[46] At Aachen Louis made grants to Abbot Hildebold of Stavelot-Malmédy and Bishop
Ratald of Strasbourg: *DLG* 147–49. Louis also granted extensive counties in northern
Frisia to the Viking pirate Roric in return for his oaths of fidelity and hostages. For
Roric's adventurous career, see Janet L. Nelson, "Vikings and Others," *TRHS,* 6th ser., 13
(2003): 1–28, at 13–15. At this time, Louis called for a synod to be held in September at
Cologne under the joint auspices of Archbishops Willibert of Cologne, Liutbert of
Mainz, and Bertolf of Metz: Dümmler, *GOR* 2:368–69.

[47] *AB,* s.a. 873, pp. 193–94.

[48] Earlier that year Louis had received an embassy from Svatopluk of Moravia, although the details are not reported: *AF,* s.a. 873, p. 78.

[49] *AB,* s.a. 873, pp. 193–94.

[50] *AI,* s.a. 873, p. 744.

[51] Wolfram, *Grenzen und Räume,* 263–64.

held this synod at the request of the pope to address the Roman conflict with Constantinople, and it was presided over by Archbishop Liutbert of Mainz. The 868 Worms synod, which also was attended by Archbishop Adalwin of Salzburg and twenty bishops, issued a *Response against the Heresy of the Greeks* that refuted the 867 synod of Constantinople.[74] The Worms synod also addressed the recent rebellions in Moravia and the Eastland, proclaiming that any layman who broke faith with the king or "defected to foreign lands in opposition to his own people, homeland, or the royal power" was to be stripped of all his personal property and excommunicated.[75] In addition, the east Frankish bishops decreed that any churchmen involved in sworn associations or conspiracies against the Church (here they probably were thinking of Constantine, Methodius, and their disciples) were to be deposed.[76]

Although Louis attempted to maintain good relations with Pope Hadrian, he broke with Rome over the creation of an independent archdiocese in Illyricum that encompassed Lower Pannonia and Moravia.[77] Not only would an Illyrican Church have forced Louis to surrender ecclesiastical jurisdiction in the southeast, but it effectively would have compelled him to recognize the political independence of the Moravian and Lower Pannonian Slavs. At the heart of this conflict were two rival geopolitical conceptions of Slavic eastern Europe, one rooted in late Roman and the other in Carolingian history. Hadrian based his claims to that region on late Roman ecclesiastical organization, while Louis justified Frankish lordship in the southeast by right of Charlemagne's conquest over the Avars.[78] These two rival claims of jurisdiction in eastern Europe put Hadrian and Louis on a crash course. At least one east Frankish churchman apparently opposed Louis's adversarial stance to Rome: Abbot Thioto of Fulda. In 869, Louis took the unusual step of deposing Thioto for disobeying him, presumably over the Moravian issue, and replaced him with a Fulda monk named Sigihard, who became one of Louis's leading supporters in the war with Moravia.[79]

---

[74] MGH *Concilia* 4:291–307.

[75] Ibid., 278 (c. 36).

[76] Ibid., 289 (c. 74).

[77] Louis frequently sent Hadrian letters and envoys, and as late as June 870 the pope still praised Louis for his *constantia* toward Rome: Hadrian II, *Epistolae ad res orientales pertinentes*, nos. 25–27, in MGH *Epistolae* 6:730–33, at 730.

[78] As Louis summed up in a diploma for Otgar of Eichstätt, "Our grandfather the lord Charlemagne gave his faithful men permission to seize and take possession of hereditary lands for the growth of God's churches in Pannonia": DLG 109.

[79] *AH*, s.a. 869, p. 18; *Annalista Saxo*, s.a. 869, p. 580. Although Thioto's offense against the king is not reported, it is likely that the abbot of Fulda opposed Louis's efforts

Louis that Pan since Late An ting the sixth astical property rs.[52] Here John ion over Lower on since Charle

nally learned of nd incarceration pt his fate secret Anno of Freising thodius's where been duped. He alzburg, Anno of Methodius's trial em for their un bade the Bavarian om prison. In ad ome to the papal nno, and Ermen is's biographer in

ad little choice but corted Methodius ructing Carloman, atia, Montemir, to Illyricum.[56] How d forbade Method tongue" (although

Epistolae 7:280–81, 283–

Epistolae 7:283–86. Anno ring him of his loyalty: 287.

MGH *Epistolae* 7:282–83, l jurisdiction in Lower arg consecrated Chozil's he Bavarian Church still hodius's release: *AI*, s.a.

preaching in it was still permitted), ordering him to use Latin or Greek instead.[57] Although John VIII's predecessor had established Methodius's archiepiscopal seat at Sirmium (the late Roman capital of Illyricum), geopolitical realities in 873 made it necessary for Methodius to move the center of his activities farther to the northeast. (Sirmium was located in, or at least near the border of, the Bulgar kingdom, which in 870 had again become part of the Byzantine Church.) At first Methodius stayed at Moosburg with *dux* Chozil of Lower Pannonia.[58] But Chozil's death around 875 forced Methodius to return to Moravia, where he was welcomed by Svatopluk and his Slavic disciples. Within several years, the Moravian court became the center of Methodius's archbishopric.[59]

Louis the Younger sought to exploit his father's and elder brother's setbacks in the Slavic marches. In January 874 he led a final rebellion against the king, although this time Charles III declined to participate.[60] Louis the Younger held secret talks with some of the king's counselors in the church of Sts.-Marcellinus-and-Peter at Seligenstadt, apparently with the objective of making himself king. The location of Louis the Younger's secret meeting was ideologically significant, since Seligenstadt had served as the focal point for criticism of Louis the Pious during the late 820s. In his *Translations and Miracles of Saints Marcellinus and Peter*, Einhard reported how the Archangel Gabriel had appeared at Seligenstadt in 828 and had dictated a list of complaints against Louis the Pious. Moreover, Einhard narrated how, because of the emperor's sins, a demon named Wiggo (a play on the emperor's name Ludwig) also appeared at Seligenstadt and claimed responsibility for the natural catastrophes of famine, plague, and cattle disease that struck the Frankish kingdom in the 820s.[61] Louis the Younger undoubtedly knew these stories. During his childhood, his father's high chancellor had been Ratleig, the abbot of Seligenstadt. Ratleig had been Einhard's notary during the 820s and had personally delivered the warnings from the Archangel Gabriel to Louis the Pious.

Einhard's report of the supernatural revelations at Seligenstadt half a century earlier struck an ominous chord in 874. Throughout the early 870s, a host of devastating natural disasters ravaged the east Frankish kingdom

---

ccessful engagements
he first mention of the
adoxically, it seems to
st the Franks. Because
orious army to capture
r taken by Carloman's
ugh to meet the Franks
.[81] Louis planned to in-
es. He intended to lead
d lead the other against
n to power in Moravia
had jointly appealed to
of Fulda, Rastislav had
ty (*regnum, patria*) within
ortress," perhaps Mikul-
tislav's old city" [urbs an-
seat of Svatopluk's princi-
s excavated twenty miles
terally means "old city" in

wever, he suddenly fell ill.

ia, since Thioto had close rela-
n monasteries in being directly
ved as Louis's envoy to Pope
more amenable to Louis's hard
ions for his 869 Moravian cam-
l came before him and received
uis placed Sigihard in command
Bigott, *Ludwig der Deutsche*, 245–

year, Louis the Younger also led
confederation of Sorbs and Bo-
losses to his soldiers.
vas a battle between Frankish and
Count Gundachar, who had de-

eich," 5; Staňa, "Mährische Burg-
Altstadt. Cf. *Annals of Fulda*, trans.
um and *patria* with the *urbs antiqua*
vornik, *Byzantine Missions*, 91; Karl
ährischen Herrschaftsraumes," in
s and Herbert Ludat (Wiesbaden,

---

[57] John VIII, *Epistolae*, no. 201, in MGH *Epistolae* 7:161 and n. 2.

[58] *VM*, chap. 10, pp. 93–94.

[59] The last reference to Chozil is in *AI*, s.a. 874, p. 742; Wolfram, *Salzburg*, 311n633. In a letter dated 880, John VIII referred to Methodius as the "archbishop of the holy Moravian Church": John VIII, *Epistolae*, no. 255, in MGH *Epistolae* 7:222.

[60] *AF*, s.a. 874, pp. 81–82.

[61] Einhard, *Translatio et miracula sanctorum Marcellini et Petri* 3.13–14, in MGH *SS* 15:252–53; Dutton, *Politics of Dreaming*, 91–100, 219–24.

and much of Europe. In 870 there were excessive heat spells, floods, earthquakes, cattle pestilence, and heavenly portents, and two years later hail, lightning storms, and earthquakes ruined crops, killed men and animals, and burned down the cathedral at Worms.[62] In 873, a horrifying plague of locusts arrived from the east, devouring a hundred plowlands of wheat near Mainz in a single hour and causing great famine throughout Europe. The author of the *Annals of Fulda* saw the plague as an expression of divine wrath for the sins of Louis the German's subjects, while others compared it to God's punishment of the Egyptian pharaoh.[63] A final calamity struck during the winter of 873–74: excessive cold and snow that caused famine and death throughout Europe.[64] According to the *Annals of Fulda*, nearly one-third of the population in western Europe died from the cold. It is impossible to know if this is accurate, but if it is, it suggests a calamity of the magnitude of the Justinianic Plague in the sixth century or the Black Death in the fourteenth. What is certain is that Louis the German was surrounded by horrific scenes of human suffering and death during the last years of his life.

Amid these natural disasters, Louis the Younger's latest rebellion at Seligenstadt implied that God had forsaken his father, just as had happened to Louis the Pious a half century earlier. In this way, Louis the Younger's 874 conspiracy challenged the divine sanction of his elderly father's kingship and paved the way for his overthrow. Louis the German traveled quickly from Regensburg to Frankfurt when he learned of his son's secret conference with his counselors. Upon his arrival in early February, the king immediately took steps to defuse the rebellion and reassert his faltering rule.[65] He held talks with his faithful men to discuss the "concord and state of the kingdom," and in late April he held a general assembly at Tribur.

The old king took seriously the charge that his sinfulness had caused the recent natural disasters in his kingdom. To assuage God's wrath, the king undertook a striking campaign of prayer and penance. During the penitential season of Lent (the forty days between Ash Wednesday and Easter), Louis "put aside the business of secular matters and made time for prayer." His middle son's latest conspiracy caused the king to ponder the Archangel Gabriel's criticism of his father—and, by extension, his own chances of salvation. This spiritual anxiety led to one of the most memorable events in Louis's long reign. One night during Lent at Frankfurt, the king had a terri-

---

[62] *AF*, s.a. 870–73, pp. 71–72, 76–77, 79–80.

[63] *AB*, s.a. 873, p. 193; *AX*, s.a. 873, p. 33.

[64] *AF*, s.a. 874, pp. 81, 83.

[65] Although the *AF*, s.a. 874, p. 82, claimed that the king arrived in Frankfurt at the beginning of February, a diploma reveals that he was still en route in Augsburg on February 2: *DLG* 151.

fying dream of his father suffering in purgatory. The *Annals of Fulda* reported:

> In Lent when he put aside the business of worldly matters for the sake of prayer, one night he saw in a dream his father, Emperor Louis, suffering in great pain. He spoke to him in the Latin speech thus: "I beseech you in the name of our lord Jesus Christ and the Triune Majesty that you save me from these torments in which I am trapped so that at last I can have eternal life." Horrified by this vision, he sent letters to all the monasteries in his kingdom, urgently beseeching that they intervene with their prayers before the Lord for a soul in torment.[66]

The author of the *Annals of Fulda* immediately connected the king's dream with Einhard's report of the supernatural revelations at Seligenstadt in 828. He continued:

> From this it should be understood that, although the above-mentioned emperor did many praiseworthy things pleasing to God, he permitted many things contrary to God's law in his kingdom. For if . . . he had heeded the admonitions of the Archangel Gabriel arranged in twelve chapters, which Einhard gave him to read and carry out, perhaps he would not have suffered such things.

Louis the German also voiced his concern about the safety of his kingdom and the salvation of his and his relatives' souls in his diplomas. On March 4, in his first grant after the disturbing dream, the king gave property to the Lotharingian monastery of Stablo in the Ardennes. Louis the Pious had been fond of hunting in that region, and Louis the German made the donation "for the salvation of our father, mother, wife, and sons in the hereafter." Louis's chancery inserted a highly unusual preamble into the diploma that seems to record the king's own words at this moment of spiritual crisis.[67] Suggesting the king's lifelong study of warfare and the Bible, the preamble freely mixed the language of fortifications and Scripture. The diploma began as follows:

> In the name of the holy and indivisible Trinity. Louis, king by the favor of Divine Grace, to all those living within the ramparts of our king-

---

[66] *AF*, s.a. 874, p. 82. Flodoard confirmed that Louis sent Hincmar a letter describing his nocturnal vision and asking him to pray for his father: Flodoard, *Historia*, 3.18, 3.20, pp. 259, 266–67.

[67] *DLG* 154. Kehr overlooked the context of this diploma and interpreted the "unkanzleimässiger Stil" as evidence that the diploma was "stark überarbeitet."

dom, both now and in the future. We believe it builds a mighty fortification around our kingdom if we grant with a cheerful heart suitable rewards to God and His servants for the love of God and the remission of our sins. We are confident that such grants increase our power in this present age and that our earthly goods will be compensated with heavenly rewards in the future kingdom. Thus it is written: *Honor the Lord with your substance and with the first fruits of all your produce* [Proverbs 3:9] and *Almsgiving delivers from death and keeps you from going into the fire* [Tobit 4:10].

It is significant that this unusual preamble quoted from the book of Tobit. That apocryphal Old Testament text told the story of Tobit, a Jewish official in Assyria, who was cursed for eight years as divine punishment for burying an executed Jewish criminal. However, Tobit's faithful son, Tobias, managed to free his father from his curse through the help of the archangel Raphael. The story ends with Tobit dying after a long life and Tobias giving his father a proper burial. On his deathbed, Tobit admonished his son about the importance of giving alms. This biblical story about a son who helped cure his cursed father obviously struck a chord with the elderly Louis the German after the vision of his father suffering in purgatory. Heeding the advice of Tobit, Louis turned to almsgiving in an effort to prevent his father's soul, and his own, "from going into the fire."

Louis remained preoccupied with prayer, penance, sin, and salvation throughout the spring and summer of 874. During Easter week (April 11–18) he made a rare pilgrimage to Fulda "for the sake of prayer," and on May 4 he made a grant to the monastery of Lorsch "for the increase of our eternal reward and for the redemption of the souls of our lord grandfather and father."[68] By coincidence, the series of natural disasters largely abated by the spring of 874 and did not return until after Louis's death.[69] By the summer of 874, therefore, Louis the German may have believed that his campaign of prayer and penance had successfully assuaged God's wrath and truly built a "mighty fortification" around his kingdom.

Louis devoted the remainder of his reign to securing Carloman's inheritance in Italy. At first glance, Pope John VIII's anger over the imprisonment of Methodius would seem to represent a serious blow to Louis's Italian schemes, since the east Frankish king needed Rome's support if Carloman

[68] *DLG* 156.
[69] See the table of natural disasters in Riché, *Daily Life*, 250–51. The sole exception was a comet and an isolated flood at Eschborn in the Niddagau in 875: *AF*, s.a. 875, p. 84.

were to succeed the heirless Louis II of Italy.[70] This was particularly true because Pope John VIII and Emperor Louis II were allies in the defense of Italy against Muslim pirates. But in recent years, Louis the German had gained significant leverage in Italy through a treaty with the eastern emperor, Basil I. Although Basil initially took a conciliatory stance vis-à-vis the pope, in the early 870s the Byzantine emperor reversed these policies. In 870 Constantinople enraged Rome by ruling that the Bulgar kingdom fell under the jurisdiction of the Byzantine Church, thereby ending Roman ecclesiastical control there. That same year, Basil abandoned his alliance with Emperor Louis II of Italy against the Muslims, resulting in a fiery exchange of insults between the eastern and western emperors.[71] In the midst of this diplomatic realignment, Basil and Louis the German became allies. In January 872, the Byzantine emperor sent ambassadors with gifts and letters to King Louis and established a pact of friendship (*amicitia*) between them.[72] The diplomatic language of *amicitia* suggests an alliance between equals, pointing to the conclusion that Basil pledged to support Louis the German's plans to make Carloman the emperor of Italy.[73] This theory is supported by one of the Byzantine emperor's gifts to Louis: a "crystal of marvelous size decorated with gold and precious gems with a large part of the salvation-bringing cross." The Byzantine emperors traditionally associated their rule with the True Cross, and in imperial processions in Constantinople Basil used a golden cross-banner that contained relics of the True Cross.[74] Basil's gift of this imperial relic therefore points to his recognition of Louis's imperial claims in Italy. In November 873, Basil sent a second embassy to Louis the German to renew their alliance of *amicitia*.[75] By now, their alliance was overtly hostile toward Emperor Louis II. Earlier that year, Basil had allied with Duke Adalgis of Benevento against Louis II, sending a fleet to support Adalgis's rebellion against the Italian emperor. In return, Adalgis promised to pay tribute to Constantinople.[76]

The alliance with Constantinople gave Louis the German the leverage he needed to bring Louis II and John VIII to the bargaining table. In the early summer of 874, the east Frankish king made a trip across the Alps and

---

[70] Dümmler, *GOR* 2:381–83, interpreted Methodius's release in 873 as a major victory for Rome over Regensburg, and he criticized John VIII's handling of the Church in Illyricum as "arbitrary and ruthless" and a "base injustice."

[71] Steven Fanning, "Imperial Diplomacy between Francia and Byzantium: The Letter of Louis II to Basil I in 871," *Cithara* 34 (1994): 3–15.

[72] *AF*, s.a. 872, p. 75.

[73] Dümmler, *GOR* 2:337.

[74] McCormick, *Eternal Victory*, 152–59.

[75] *AF*, s.a. 873, p. 81.

[76] *AB*, s.a. 873, p. 192; Regino, *Chronicon*, s.a. 871, pp. 104–5; Dümmler, *GOR* 2:371–72.

met with the western emperor and the pope near Verona.[77] At Verona, Louis the German won a major diplomatic victory: Emperor Louis II officially recognized Carloman as his heir to Italy and the imperial throne.[78] To solidify this agreement, Louis II commended himself to Louis the German (that is, he literally became "his man") and granted him a number of properties in northern Italy. Moreover, Empress Engelberga became Louis the German's "spiritual daughter," and the two Louises jointly committed Engelberga to Pope John's protection. In return, Louis the German made a number of concessions: he apparently abandoned his alliance with Emperor Basil, and he finally agreed to the creation of an independent archbishopric of Illyricum over the Slavs.[79] With these matters settled, Pope John VIII brokered a lasting peace between Louis the German and Svatopluk.[80] After the Verona meeting, Louis the German traveled back across the Alps to Forchheim, where

> he received the legates of Svatopluk asking for a peace treaty and promising fidelity. The head of this legation was the Venetian priest John [presumably Pope John VIII's legate]. So that the king would believe him beyond the shadow of a doubt, John confirmed everything he said with an oath: that is, that Svatopluk would remain faithful to the king all the days of his life and pay each year the tribute stipulated by the king, if in return it were only granted him to go about his business quietly and live peacefully.[81]

Louis the German had played a skilled game of diplomatic chess and won far more than he had lost. He had conceded the Slavic Church to Rome, but in return the emperor and the pope recognized Carloman as the heir to Italy. In addition, Svatopluk had finally submitted to Frankish overlordship

[77] *AF*, s.a. 874, p. 82; Odegaard, "Empress Engelberga," 86. This was Louis's only known visit to Italy itself. His previous meetings with Italian rulers and envoys had taken place in his kingdom or at Trent in the Alps.

[78] Although the *AF* are silent about the details of the 874 Verona meeting, the outlines of this agreement are recorded in a number of scattered sources: John VIII, *Epistolae*, no. 293, in MGH *Epistolae* 7:256; *DLG* 157, 171; *DCarloman* 4; *De imperatoria potestate in urbe Roma libellus*, ed. Georg Heinrich Pertz, in MGH *SS* 3 (Hanover, 1839), 721–22. The 874 Verona agreement was similar to the deal Louis the German struck with Lothar II in 867, when the Lotharingian king commended his son Hugh and his entire kingdom to his uncle: *AB*, s.a. 867, pp. 136–37. Cf. Dümmler, *GOR* 2:374–75.

[79] After 873, there are no more reports of Louis the German's alliance of *amicitia* with Emperor Basil.

[80] In addition, Louis the German and Louis II of Italy convinced John VIII to recognize Willibert as archbishop of Cologne and to send him the pallium: John VIII, *Epistolae passim collectae*, nos. 1–2, in MGH *Epistolae* 7:313–15.

[81] *AF*, s.a. 874, pp. 82–83.

and agreed to pay the annual tribute. In the end, Louis was willing to sacrifice the Bavarian Church's jurisdiction over the Slavs for Carloman's inheritance of Italy and the imperial crown.

The 874 Peace of Forchheim also marked the final resolution for Louis's long-standing inheritance disputes with his sons. At Forchheim he held talks with Carloman and Louis the Younger and presumably confirmed his modified succession plan. In addition to the *regna* granted to them in the 865 Division of Frankfurt, Carloman would inherit Italy and the imperial throne, while Louis the Younger and Charles III would divide the Rhineland and eastern Lotharingia between them. By now, Louis had granted extensive estates to his sons in their future kingdoms. Louis's recent grant to the monastery of Lorsch, for example, involved properties in the Rheingau that already were in the hands of Charles III.[82]

Louis the German's plan to place Carloman on the Italian throne necessitated negotiations with Charles the Bald. The absence of Charles III at Forchheim is explained by the fact that his father had sent him to Gaul to arrange a meeting with the west Frankish king.[83] When Louis the German arrived at Aachen in July en route to the meeting with Charles the Bald, he received an encouraging report: his fifty-one-year-old brother had come down with dysentery, an illness that often proved fatal. Louis therefore waited at Aachen "quite a long time," undoubtedly contemplating an invasion of western Lotharingia and Gaul if his brother died. Charles recovered, however, and in early December the two kings finally met, but the venue was changed to Liège to accommodate Charles's frail health.[84] Their discussions presumably focused on the Italian succession, although they apparently did not come to any resolution. Armed conflict over Italy now became likely. After decades of alliances, rivalries, and broken promises, this was to be the last time Louis the German and Charles the Bald would meet face-to-face.

When Louis returned to Frankfurt to celebrate Christmas, he received disheartening news: the elderly Queen Emma, whom he had left behind in Bavaria, had suffered a stroke and lost the use of her voice.[85] After Easter in 875, Louis traveled to Regensburg to visit her, and on May 18 he made a gift to his royal chapel in Regensburg "for the health and salvation of our beloved wife Emma."[86] Also at the queen's sickbed was her favorite son,

---

[82] *DLG* 156.

[83] *AB*, s.a. 874, pp. 196–97.

[84] *AF*, s.a. 874, p. 83; *AB*, s.a. 874, pp. 196–97. Hincmar reported that the kings met at Herstal near Liège.

[85] *AF*, s.a. 874, p. 83.

[86] *DLG* 161.

Carloman, who subscribed the king's diploma. This was the last time Louis would see his wife. She died the following year on January 31, 876, and was buried in the monastic church of St.-Emmeram.[87] Emma had been married to Louis for forty-nine years, making her the longest-reigning Carolingian queen on record.

Bereft of his lifelong companion, the old king grimly prepared for war in Italy. He made preparations with his sons and magnates at Tribur on the middle Rhine, where he held assemblies in May and August.[88] Around this time Louis sent a Fulda monk named Hagano to Pope John VIII and Emperor Louis II, presumably to carry on further negotiations concerning the Italian succession.[89] Throughout the spring and summer, Louis the German made an unusual burst of grants for Alemannian recipients, including Abbot Hartmut of St.-Gall and the prominent Count Adalbert, suggesting that he planned to mobilize Alemannian troops in the looming war across the Alps.[90]

But the issue of military service for the impending Italian campaign exacerbated tensions among the king's sons and magnates. Indeed, a shocking outbreak of violence occurred at the Tribur assembly in May: "There a serious quarrel broke out between the Franks and Saxons. They would have cut each other down in mutual slaughter had Louis the Younger not quickly intervened with his men."[91] While the *Annals of Fulda* shed no light on the cause of this conflict, several charters from Freising do. Several months earlier, a "certain count of the most serene lord King Louis" named Waldperht made an exchange of lands with Bishop Anno of Freising.[92] This Waldperht was Louis's leading Saxon supporter, Count Waltbert of Westphalia.[93] On March 24, 875, Count Waltbert gave Anno of Freising properties at Reutberg in southern Bavaria between Freising and the Brenner Pass. This clearly was an important exchange, since it was made at Freising "in the presence of the venerable bishop and others of the king's leading men." Indeed, around this time several other prominent nobles made grants of lands

[87] For Emma's burial in Regensburg, see Franz Fuchs, "Das Grab der Königin Hemma (d. 876) zu St. Emmeram in Regensburg," in *Regensburg und Ostbayern: Max Piendl zum Gedächtnis*, ed. F. Karg (Kallmünz, 1992), 1–12.

[88] *AF*, s.a. 875, pp. 83–84; *AB*, s.a. 875, pp. 197–98; *DLG* 163–64.

[89] Hagano was received warmly by the pope, although he died at Verona during his trip home: Bigott, *Ludwig der Deutsche*, 155 and n. 169.

[90] *DLG* 158–61, 163–65. The king also confirmed Abbot Sigihar of Fulda's tithes from his properties: *DLG* 162.

[91] *AF*, s.a. 875, p. 83.

[92] *Freising* 913.

[93] *DLG* 95, 142.

just north of the Brenner Pass to Freising, further contributing to the bishopric's extensive estates along that strategic Alpine route to Italy.[94] One of these grantors was the Frankish nobleman Egino, who also numbered among Louis's *fideles.*[95]

The best explanation for these grants to Freising is that the king and his magnates were making preparations for Carloman to invade Italy when Louis II died, an undertaking that required control of lands along the Brenner route to provision his army. Waltbert's and Egino's gifts to Freising indicate that the king planned to use Saxon and Frankish troops alongside Bavarians for the Italian invasion. Indeed, Count Waltbert had been prominent among Louis's generals in 871 when the king mustered his troops at Frankfurt in response to the false rumor of the Italian emperor's death.[96] It is therefore likely that the conflict between the Franks and Saxons at the 875 Tribur assembly involved the issue of military service in the upcoming Italian invasion. Louis the German wanted his supporters, including Waltbert and Egino, to lead Saxon and Frankish troops alongside Carloman's Bavarian forces, and for that reason they were involved in transactions of land near the Brenner Pass. However, Louis the Younger naturally opposed sending troops from his future territories to support the Italian conquests of his rival brother. Once again, discord among the king's sons and their supporters threatened Louis the German's imperial schemes.

In the midst of these preparations, the fifty-year-old Louis II of Italy died on August 12, 875. Although Empress Engelberga backed the 874 Verona accord with Louis the German, many Italian magnates argued that Charles the Bald should become the next Italian emperor. As a result, two embassies were sent north of the Alps, one requesting that Louis and the other that Charles come to Italy and claim the throne.[97] The two kings learned of their nephew's death at about the same time: Louis the German heard the news while he still was at Tribur, and Charles the Bald found out about it while he was at Douzy on the Moselle.[98] Charles the Bald reacted more quickly. He gathered an army in Burgundy, crossed the Mons Iovis Pass in early Sep-

---

[94] *Freising* 907 (dated 870–75), 909 (870–75), 914 (May 20, 875). The new Freising bishop, Arnold, was in the king's company in 875–76: *Freising* 915.

[95] *DLG* 121, 125; *Freising* 898, 909. Egino's brother, Count Managold, had been a supporter of Louis the German throughout his reign: *DLG* 46, 170; Mitterauer, *Karolingische Markgrafen*, 91–103. It is possible that Egino (or one of his relatives) was the Frankish count by that name who waged a bloody feud involving Saxons and Thuringians in the early 880s: *AF(M)*, s.a. 883, p. 100; *AF(B)*, s.a. 882, p. 109; Becher, *Rex, Dux und Gens*, 93–95.

[96] *DLG* 142.

[97] Andrew of Bergamo, *Historia*, chap. 19, p. 229.

[98] *AF*, s.a. 875, p. 84; *AB*, s.a. 875, p. 198.

tember, and went to Pavia (the capital of northern Italy), where he was welcomed by a large number of Italian nobles.

Louis the German was enraged when he learned that his brother, the "tyrant of Gaul," had arrived in the region south of the Alps ahead of him. In response, the east Frankish king launched his own invasion of Italy.[99] However, the disorganization of Louis's campaign indicates that he had not yet solved the disputes among his sons. The king planned to have Carloman and Charles III lead two separate armies over the Alps, one from Bavaria and the other from Alemannia. However, Charles III arrived in Italy before Carloman had even set out from Bavaria, thereby undermining the effectiveness of a coordinated attack. Charles III (whom the Italians nicknamed Carlito, or "Charlie," to distinguish him from his uncle) arrived in Milan in August, where he was welcomed by Count Berengar of Friuli and the other Italian magnates who supported Louis the German. But Charles III's supporters soon turned to looting, giving Charles the Bald the opportunity to drive his nephew out of Italy via the Brenner Pass to Bavaria. Only after Charles III's ignominious retreat across the Alps did Carloman set out for Italy with a Bavarian army. At that moment, Louis the German and his younger two sons were at Regensburg, which suggests that the king was trying to convince them to participate in Carloman's Italian expedition.[100] Louis the Younger and Charles III apparently refused, and Carloman therefore marched to Italy alone "with as many men as he could muster."

The forty-five-year-old Carloman conducted his invasion of Italy with a combination of strategic skill and political pragmatism. Charles the Bald tried to prevent Carloman from reaching Italy by marshaling his forces to block the Brenner route north of Verona. However, Carloman cleverly outmaneuvered his uncle by leading his troops along the difficult valley of the Brenta River, which flows from Trent to the southeast and gains the Italian plain north of Padua. Having arrived in northeastern Italy, Carloman opted for negotiation over battle. Several factors recommended this decision. Without Charles III's support, Carloman's Bavarian army was outnumbered by Charles the Bald's west Frankish and Italian forces. Moreover, at this moment Carloman must have been concerned about his father's old age. Louis the German might die at any moment, and Carloman therefore needed to keep his Bavarian army intact for the likely ensuing power struggle against his younger brothers. A risky battle south of the Alps against Charles the

[99] For the 875 Italian campaigns, see Andrew of Bergamo, *Historia*, chap. 19, pp. 229–30; *AB*, s.a. 875, p. 198; *AF*, s.a. 875, pp. 84–85; *AV*, s.a. 875, p. 40.

[100] On October 3 at Regensburg, Louis the German issued a diploma for his cleric Balding, and he allowed Louis the Younger and the recently returned Charles III to subscribe: *DLG* 165.

Bald's superior forces therefore was foolhardy. Furthermore, Charles the Bald offered Carloman "gold, silver, and an infinite multitude of precious gems" if he became his ally, and the west Frankish king promised that he would immediately depart from Italy if Carloman did likewise. Carloman prudently accepted these terms. He met with his uncle on the Brenta River, and they established a truce until the following May. In addition, Charles the Bald pledged to support Carloman after Louis the German died.[101] With these terms agreed to, Carloman returned to Bavaria. While he had postponed his bid for the Italian throne, Carloman arrived home in a strong position: his army was intact, he now possessed a considerable amount of treasure to buy political support, and he had won his uncle as a future ally against his brothers.

Meanwhile, Louis the German and Louis the Younger had invaded west Francia with a large army. According to the *Annals of Fulda*, Louis the German invaded Gaul "to compel [Charles the Bald] to leave Italy." Although undoubtedly true, Louis also saw Charles's absence as an opportunity to seize some, if not all, of Charles's territories. En route, Louis stopped at the important city of Metz in late November to rally his Lotharingian forces.[102] At Metz, Louis laid claim to all of Lotharingia. His chancery began dating his diplomas "in the thirty-eighth year of the reign of the most serene King Louis in east Francia, and in the sixth after attaining Lothar [II]'s kingdom."[103] Louis then marched to Attigny in Charles's kingdom and celebrated Christmas there, the same west Frankish palace where he had wintered during his failed 858 invasion of Gaul.[104]

As before, Louis's 875 invasion of Gaul played off rival factions around the west Frankish court. One of Louis's western supporters was Charles the Bald's former chamberlain, Engelram, who had fallen from favor in 871–72 through the influence of Charles the Bald's queen, Richildis.[105] Engelram therefore had urged the east Frankish king to invade Gaul and seize the throne. In response, Richildis ordered the western magnates to reaffirm

[101] Upon Louis the German's death in 876, Hincmar stated that Carloman did not come to Charles the Bald as Charles earlier had told him to, which seems to be a reference to their 875 alliance on the Brenta River: *AB*, s.a. 876, p. 210.

[102] *DLG* 166–69. At Metz Louis assumed control of the vacant archbishopric with its rich estates and dependent monasteries. (Adventius of Metz had died earlier that year.) Bigott, *Ludwig der Deutsche*, 234–35.

[103] *DLG* 167–68. Louis's new dating clause echoed that of Charles the Bald immediately after his annexation of Lotharingia in 869: *DCB* 328, 330, 333, 334.

[104] Louis's hasty invasion of Gaul in 875 did not enable him to prepare sufficient supplies for his troops, and the east Frankish army turned to plundering and looting along its line of march: *AF*, s.a. 875, pp. 84–85; *AB*, s.a. 875, pp. 198–99; MGH *Capitularia* 2:350–51.

[105] Concerning Engelram, see *Annals of St.-Bertin*, trans. Nelson, 173n4.

with an oath their commitment to resist the eastern king. Ironically, another western supporter of Louis's was Hincmar of Reims, who had thwarted Louis's invasion of Gaul eighteen years earlier. But in 875 Hincmar was angry that Charles the Bald intended to make Ansegis of Sens, rather than himself, papal vicar north of the Alps. Hincmar circulated a letter to the bishops and nobles in his archdiocese, ostensibly urging them to remain loyal to Charles the Bald but in fact voicing harsh criticism of him, thus effectively sanctioning capitulation to Louis.[106] Indeed, Louis seems to have won significant support among his brother's magnates, this time including a number of west Frankish bishops.[107]

In the end, however, Charles the Bald brilliantly outmaneuvered his older brother. Disregarding the safety of his kingdom and his recent promises to Carloman, Charles pushed ahead with his goal of winning Italy and the imperial crown.[108] The sources agree on the strategy Charles used to convince Pope John VIII to abandon the 874 Verona agreement with Louis the German: offers of extensive gifts and bribes (*dona, pecunia, multa et pretiosa munera*).[109] John VIII therefore welcomed the west Frankish king to Rome, and the pope grandly reenacted Charlemagne's imperial coronation seventy-five years earlier by crowning Charles the Bald emperor on Christmas day.[110] Charles soon departed Rome, and in February at Pavia he arranged for the government of Italy.[111] He then hurried back over the Mons Iovis Pass and returned to Gaul. Charles's triumphant return forced Louis the German to retreat to the east in January 876. At a large assembly in June at Ponthion, Charles proclaimed his newly won imperial dignity.[112] He introduced a new imperial bull with the inscription "Revival of the Roman and Frankish empire," and he wore a Frankish costume with a gilded robe and carried a golden staff given to him by the pope.[113] More-

---

[106] Ibid., 188n9.

[107] John VIII, *Epistolae passim collectae*, no. 6, in MGH *Epistolae* 7:318–20.

[108] At Pavia in late September he won over many Italian magnates, and his chancery began dating his diplomas "in the thirty-sixth year of the reign of King Charles, the sixth in succession to Lothar [II], and the first in succession to Louis [II]": *DCB* 383, 384.

[109] *AF*, s.a. 875, p. 85; *AB*, s.a. 876, p. 200; *AV*, s.a. 875, p. 40.

[110] Charles assumed the lofty title "by the grace of omnipotent God Himself emperor augustus" and immediately began issuing diplomas for Italian recipients: *DCB* 400, 401.

[111] MGH *Capitularia* 2:98–104. To defend his newly won kingdom from Carloman, Charles appointed Boso, Queen Richildis's brother, as the duke and imperial *missus* in Italy and arranged for him to marry Louis II of Italy's only daughter, Ermengard: *DCB* 402, 403; *AB*, s.a. 876, pp. 200–201; Regino, *Chronicon*, s.a. 877, p. 113.

[112] *AB*, s.a. 876, pp. 201–6; MGH *Capitularia* 2:347–53.

[113] For Charles's imperial seal, see Schramm, *Die deutschen Kaiser*, 165, 305 (no. 34). Charles the Bald also commissioned a silver chest known as the Ellwangen Chest, which depicted him in Byzantine regalia and clothing: Percy Ernst Schramm, "Neuentdeckte

over, on the last day of the assembly, Charles appeared in Byzantine imperial dress with a diadem, and John VIII's legates heralded him and Richildis as emperor and empress.

Charles the Bald's smashing success caused great disappointment at the court of Louis the German, whose policies had focused on winning Italy and the imperial crown for the last half decade. The *Annals of Fulda* bitterly compared Charles the Bald to the African tyrant Jugurtha, who had lavishly bribed the Roman senate in 112 BC.[114] Moreover, because Charles appeared in Byzantine imperial regalia at the Ponthion assembly, the *Annals of Fulda* criticized him for "scorning the entire tradition of the Frankish kings and holding the glories of the Greeks to be the best."[115] In spite of recent setbacks, Louis refused to give up his claims to Italy. He held assemblies with his magnates on the middle Rhine in February, March, and May, and he rejected out of hand John VIII's threats of excommunication for him and his supporters.[116] Louis sent Charles an embassy headed by Archbishop Willibert of Cologne and Counts Adalhard and Megingoz and demanded a portion of the Italian kingdom "in accord with hereditary right and as had been confirmed to him with an oath"—a reference to the 874 Verona agreement.[117]

In response, the papal legates read out two letters from John VIII addressed to Louis the German's bishops and counts.[118] The pope harshly criticized the eastern magnates for participating in Louis's invasion of Gaul, and he threatened them with excommunication if they did not urge their king to seek peace with the new emperor. John VIII saved his harshest criticism for Louis himself. Revealing his subtle grasp of Carolingian history, the pope gave Louis the insulting title of king of Bavaria, thereby implying that Charles the Bald's imperial coronation had revived the *Ordinatio imperii*. The pope wrote of the east Frankish king:

> He resents his brother who has been raised above him by the apostolic see, just as Cain resented his brother's sacrifice, that is to say, his obedience. Filled with wrath and gnashing his teeth, he attacked his brother, infected his faithful men with numerous lies, impelled them to commit

---

Bildnisse Karls des Kahlen, seiner Gemahlin und seines Sohnes (876/7)," in Schramm, *Kaiser, Könige und Päpste*, 2:116–18, 338–40.

[114] *AF,* s.a. 875, p. 85.

[115] *AF,* s.a. 876, p. 86.

[116] *AF,* s.a. 876, pp. 85–86; *DLG* 170; MGH *Capitularia* 2:351 (cc. 2, 4).

[117] *AB,* s.a. 876, p. 203.

[118] John VIII, *Epistolae passim collectae*, nos. 7–8, in MGH *Epistolae* 7:320–26.

perjury against the name of the terrible God, and exulted in ripping out by the roots the peace of his brother's longtime kingdom. Stirred up by his sinful men and accomplices, he acquiesced and hastened into evil— to the still-damp fields of Fontenoy that he soaked with human blood in his youth. Now in decrepit old age he still lives for battles and slaughter and hastens to shed the blood of Christians for his own ambition.

Was this true? Had Louis's reign been little more than one long civil war in the pursuit of personal glory? Louis and his counselors did not see it that way. The *Annals of Fulda*'s critique of Charles for wearing Byzantine imperial regalia and "scorning the entire custom of the Frankish kings" implied that Louis was the true upholder of Carolingian royal tradition and thus the rightful ruler of Frankish Europe. Louis therefore refused to renounce his claims south of the Alps, in spite of papal excommunication of himself and his supporters. While at Ingelheim in July, he received an embassy from Empress Engelberga requesting that he confirm all her lands in Italy, a clear indication that he still had significant support there.[119]

Charles boasted that he would conquer Louis's kingdom, and in response Louis raised an army and threatened to invade Charles's territories. But Louis and Charles were both old men, and illness now became a significant factor in this final round of their struggle for empire. In August Charles fell ill for several weeks at Châlons and so was forced to send ambassadors to his brother asking for a peaceful settlement of the Italian issue.[120] But soon thereafter, Louis likewise fell seriously ill at Frankfurt. When Charles recovered and learned this news, he immediately invaded eastern Lotharingia and arrived at Cologne by mid-September.[121] Charles proclaimed himself ruler of his ailing brother's kingdom. He issued a diploma dated "in the thirty-seventh year of the reign of Emperor Charles in Francia, the seventh in succession to Lothar [II], the second of his imperial rule, and the first in succession to King Louis."[122] Two weeks later, Charles received a joyous report: his brother Louis had died at Frankfurt on August 28, 876.

Louis had died on the feast of Saint Augustine, the most revered authority in the Catholic Church and a theologian deeply studied by Frankish

---

[119] *DLG* 171. This is Louis the German's last surviving diploma.
[120] *AB*, s.a. 876, p. 206.
[121] Josef Prinz, "Der Feldzug Karls des Kahlen an dem Rhein im September 876," *DA* 33 (1977): 543–45.
[122] *DCB* 413.

churchmen like Raban and Hincmar. According to Einhard, Augustine's great work, the *City of God*, had been Charlemagne's favorite book.[123] In that work, Augustine had argued that all humanity was divided into two groups: the citizens of the city of God who would be saved, and the citizens of the earthly city who were doomed to eternal damnation. Because of his pessimism about man's sinful nature, Augustine believed that the Roman emperors would never be able to create a Christian empire that truly united the city of God with the earthly city. But the Carolingians had been more optimistic. Alongside their numerous power struggles, broken oaths, and ruthless Realpolitik, Charlemagne's descendants clung to the ideal of a Frankish Europe that united all its inhabitants into a single Christian people. Louis the German had spent much of his life struggling to rebuild his grandfather's and father's Christian empire from his kingdom in the east. As Louis lay on his deathbed at Frankfurt, with his brother threatening invasion at nearby Cologne, it must have occurred to him that he had failed. But Louis may also have taken solace in the fact that he left behind three able sons, one of whom might one day reunite the empire. The dying king could be certain of one thing: the struggle would go on.

---

[123] Einhard, *VK*, chap. 24, p. 29.

EPILOGUE

A nd the struggle did go on.[1] Louis the German's burial
was immediately swept up by the conflict with Charles
the Bald. Louis had hoped to be laid to rest in the Carolingian burial church at Aachen near Charlemagne's
tomb. But when he died on August 28, 876, at Frankfurt, Charles the Bald's
occupation of eastern Lotharingia made that impossible. Fearing his uncle's
imminent invasion from across the Rhine, Louis the Younger (the only son
present at the time of his father's death) was compelled to bury his father
"with honor" at Lorsch, the royal monastery nearest to Frankfurt.[2]

Louis the Younger sought to use his father's burial to legitimate his nascent regime in the face of his uncle's plans for imperial conquest. A royal
sarcophagus excavated at Lorsch in 1800 that is believed to have contained
Louis the German's remains suggests that Louis the Younger buried his father in proud Frankish military attire: a brown tunic made of silk with gold
hems, boots, and golden spurs.[3] The sarcophagus was decorated with classical ionic columns, and it also contained a piece of parchment "written upon
in a foreign language" and a slate tablet "with an unknown script"—both
presumably Frankish. To house his father's sarcophagus, Louis the Younger

---

[1] For the politics of the late ninth century, see Dümmler, *GOR* 3; Fried, *Ludwig der
Jüngere*; Reuter, *Germany*, 73–137; MacLean, "Carolingian Response," 21–48; idem, *Kingship and Politics*.

[2] *AF*, s.a. 876, p. 86.

[3] Although the skeleton and burial goods disappeared during the Napoleonic Wars, a
written record of the contents of the sarcophagus survives: Behn, *Karolingische
Klosterkirche*, 4–5; Schramm, *Denkmale*, 128, 242 (no. 37).

began construction of a new burial church at Lorsch as well as the gate-hall that marked the procession route to the royal tomb.[4] This new royal crypt became known as the many-colored church (*ecclesia varia*), apparently because it was decorated with vibrant colors and classical motifs like those of the surviving gate-hall. It seems that Louis the Younger intended these Frankish royal elements surrounding his father's burial as a challenge to the imperial claims of Charles the Bald. The epitaph above Louis the German's tomb expressed the dynastic solidarity Louis the Younger hoped to receive from his two brothers in confronting their western imperial uncle:

May this king now reign happily throughout the ages with the saints
And enjoy God's love as he did in this world.
His people does not drift apart as if left without heirs,
Nor does his race weaken internally on this side and that.
For three heirs now shine in the kingdom like their father:
Who can break this triple-stranded rope?
He who left behind such heirs does not die himself
But lives in his offspring under the Lord's protection.
May He Who arranged the stars protect these three heirs for our sake,
And may there be a place in Heaven for him who is now deceased.[5]

A month after his father's death on October 8, Louis the Younger managed to lead the east Franks, Saxons, and Thuringians to a smashing victory over Charles the Bald in the battle of Andernach (between Cologne and Koblenz), forcing the emperor to retreat from eastern Lotharingia. Charles the Bald died the following year on October 6, 877, after ruling as emperor for less than two years. The last of Charlemagne's grandsons was dead.

Not surprisingly, the hoped-for fraternal cooperation and "triple-stranded rope" voiced in Louis the German's epitaph did not come to pass. In November 876, Louis the German's three sons met in the Ries, where their father had won his important victory over Lothar's forces thirty-five years earlier.[6] There they divided their father's kingdom among them according to the inheritance plans worked out over the previous decade: Carloman got Bavaria, the Eastland, and a claim to Italy; Louis the Younger received Franconia, eastern Lotharingia, Saxony, and Thuringia; and Charles

---

    [4] Jacobsen, "Lorscher Torhalle," 9–41.
    [5] *Epitaphium Ludovici Germanici (?)*, in MGH *Poetae Latini* 4.3: 1034. Although the surviving copy of the fragmentary epitaph does not name the east Frankish king, the fact that it refers to the ruler's three royal heirs makes it all but certain that it was Louis the German.
    [6] *AF*, s.a. 876, p. 89.

The king is dead. A sarcophagus excavated at Lorsch in 1800 that is believed to have contained the remains of Louis the German. Although the contents of the sarcophagus disappeared, a written report states that it contained a skeleton dressed in a brown silk tunic with gold hems and boots with golden spurs. It also contained a piece of parchment and a tablet written in a "foreign language" and "unknown script," presumably Frankish. The sandstone sarcophagus itself is decorated with classical ionic columns. Louis the Younger, the only son at Frankfurt when Louis the German died on August 28, 876, presided over his father's burial at nearby Lorsch. Photograph courtesy of the Verwaltung der Staatlichen Schlösser und Gärten Hessen.

III took Alemannia, Chur-Rhaetia, Alsace, and several Lotharingian cities. Although the brothers swore oaths of fidelity to each other in Frankish (the texts of which were written down and preserved in archives), there was to be little cooperation among Louis the German's sons. During the last quarter of the ninth century, Carolingian politics became even more complex as the multiple heirs of Louis the German and Charles the Bald competed with each other while pursuing their own agendas of conquest. In 877 Carloman belatedly made good on the 874 Verona agreement and became king of Italy. However, Carloman soon fell ill and died in early 880, leaving Bavaria to Louis the Younger and Italy to Charles III. In 880 Louis the Younger annexed western Lotharingia, and in 881 Charles III marched to Rome and was crowned emperor. When Louis the Younger died in January 882, he named Charles III his heir. Then, in 885, the west Frankish magnates invited Charles III to become their king after the deaths of Charles the Bald's heirs. In this way, Charles III attained his father's dream of reuniting the empire.

Although the heirs of Louis the German and Charles the Bald were all capable rulers, by the mid-880s the Carolingian family suddenly found itself teetering on the brink of dynastic ruin. Beginning in the late 870s, the royal dynasty witnessed a horrific and unprecedented epidemic of premature royal deaths: Charles the Bald's son and heir, Louis the Stammerer (d. 879); Louis the Younger's two sons, Louis (d. 879) and Hugh (d. 880); Carloman of Bavaria (d. 880); Louis the Younger (d. 882); and Louis the Stammerer's two sons, Louis III of Neustria (d. 882) and Carloman of Aquitaine (d. 884). Moreover, Carloman of Bavaria and Louis the Younger died without leaving legitimate male heirs, as did Charles the Bald's two grandsons. When Charles III reunited the empire in 885, he likewise had no legitimate heir but only an illegitimate young son named Bernard. At that moment, the only other legitimate male Carolingian was the six-year-old son of Louis the Stammerer, Charles the Straightforward.

Some historians have suggested that the short reigns of Louis the German's descendants were caused by a sickness inherited from Queen Emma, perhaps epilepsy, arteriosclerosis, or a propensity for stroke.[7] These medical explanations are not fully convincing, since, as we have seen, both Emma and Louis the German were healthy, long-lived rulers. Indeed, this was the very problem. Because Louis the German had lived so long, his three sons were unusually old when they became kings—46, about 41, and 37. In contrast, during the previous five generations, the average age of a Carolingian ruler at the time of his father's death had been only about twenty-six.[8] This was a serious setback for Louis the German's heirs, since the average life expectancy of Carolingian men was only around forty years.[9] It is true that several members of the east Frankish royal family seem to have suffered strokes, but these illnesses afflicted them relatively late in life.[10] Louis the German's descendants therefore did not die prematurely. Indeed, by Carolingian standards, Carloman, Louis the Younger, Charles III, and Arnulf were relatively healthy men who all surpassed the average Carolingian male life expectancy and reached ages of 50, about 47, 49, and about 49, respec-

---

[7] Zatschek, *Wie das erste Reich der Deutschen entstand*, 296–303; Hans J. Oesterle, "Die sogenannte Kopfoperation Karls III, 887," *AK* 61 (1979): 445–51. MacLean, *Kingship and Politics*, 39–41.

[8] At the time of their own father's death, Charles Martel was 27, Pippin III about 26, Charlemagne 26, Carloman 17, Louis the Pious 36, Bernard of Italy 13, Lothar I 45, Louis the German about 30, and Charles the Bald 17.

[9] Dutton, "Beyond the Topos of Senescence," 91–92.

[10] Emma had a stroke in 874 when she was in her sixties; Carloman had one in 879 at age forty-nine. The illnesses of the approximately forty-six-year-old Louis the Younger in 881, of the forty-seven-year-old Charles III in 886, and of the approximately forty-seven-year-old Arnulf in 897 also may have been due to strokes, although this is not certain.

tively. The real problem was Louis the German's longevity, which forced his heirs to begin their royal careers unusually late in life. This was a serious problem, since, as in the case of Louis the German during the 830s and 840s, a new Carolingian king usually needed at least a decade to overcome political opposition and military threats and thereby consolidate his rule.

This mounting dynastic crisis after the deaths of Louis the German and Charles the Bald highlights a cornerstone of Carolingian success over the previous two centuries: the family's remarkable ability to produce able, long-reigning male kings generation after generation, most of whom left behind adult male heirs. As Louis the German's reign demonstrates, effective Carolingian kingship depended on active personal rule and effective response to ongoing conflict and crisis. The Carolingians held power for so long by managing rivalries among the nobles, controlling royal resources and the distribution of public offices, leading armies, and overcoming constant political opposition. However, in the midst of the dynastic crisis of the late ninth century, Frankish magnates outside the Carolingian male line could realistically contemplate, for the first time since 751, making a bid for the throne. The first sign of cracks in the Carolingian monarchy was the short-lived coup of Boso of Vienne, who had risen to prominence under Charles the Bald and was married to Louis II of Italy's daughter.[11] In 879, Boso took advantage of the sudden power vacuum caused by the unexpected death of Louis the Stammerer and had himself crowned king of Provence, thereby becoming the first non-Carolingian king in 128 years. The remaining four Carolingians—Louis the Younger, Charles III, Louis III of Neustria, and Carloman of Aquitaine—immediately recognized the threat Boso posed to their family's long-standing monopoly on Frankish kingship. In a rare moment of Carolingian cooperation, the four kings quickly united and, through a series of coordinated military campaigns in 879–80, largely snuffed out Boso's rebel regime. Thus, while Boso's grab for the purple reflected the mounting dynastic crisis within the Carolingian family, it did not mark a decline of Carolingian political and military power. On the contrary, the Carolingian response to Boso's rebellion demonstrates that in 880 the Carolingians could still respond effectively to political crises and challenges to their power.

Within several years, however, the ongoing epidemic of Carolingian deaths, coupled with Charles III's continued lack of a legitimate male heir, created the real possibility that the male line of the Carolingian regime

---

[11] For Boso's career and the Carolingian response to his rebellion, see Stuart Airlie, "The Nearly Men: Boso of Vienne and Arnulf of Bavaria," in Duggan, *Nobles and Nobility*, 25–41; MacLean, "Carolingian Response," 21–48.

might actually die out. During the mid-880s, Charles III focused his efforts on establishing his young illegitimate son, Bernard, as his heir through a series of complex diplomatic maneuvers and negotiations.[12] But Charles III, who was forty-six when he reunited the empire, was losing a race against the clock. He had fallen seriously ill in 886 (perhaps from a stroke), and in early 887 he had his blood let to relieve a pain in his head. The ailing emperor announced an assembly in November 887 at Tribur, probably to have the magnates recognize Bernard as his heir. At that moment, Carloman of Bavaria's illegitimate son, Arnulf, who had been ruling the Eastland as prefect, staged a coup. The approximately thirty-seven-year-old Arnulf had serious grievances against his uncle. Charles III had blocked Arnulf from succeeding his father, Carloman, in 880, and he had sided against Arnulf in a bloody war along the Pannonian–Moravian frontier in the early 880s known as the Wilhelminer Feud. Moreover, Charles III refused either to grant Arnulf more power and territories or to recognize him as a potential successor. The emperor's plan to make Bernard his heir at the Tribur assembly in November 887 therefore backed Arnulf into a corner and forced him to stage a coup. As Louis the German had done many times during the 830s and early 840s, Arnulf gathered an army of Bavarians and Slavs and marched to the middle Rhine to make a bid for the throne. Once again, the eastern nobles were forced to size up competing bids for kingship. When they saw Charles III's declining health and Arnulf's strong military backing, they not surprisingly defected to the latter. By late November, Arnulf had proclaimed himself king at Frankfurt.[13] Charles died soon thereafter on January 13, 888, having ruled a reunited empire for less than three years.

It was the death of the heirless Charles III in 888, not of Charlemagne in 814, that marked the great turning point for the Carolingian dynasty. It is not clear if Arnulf intended to seize the entire empire in 887, but initially only the eastern magnates recognized his kingship. In the words of the Bavarian continuator of the *Annals of Fulda*, "while celebrating Christmas and Easter with fanfare at Regensburg, King Arnulf received the leading men of the Bavarians, east Franks, Saxons, Thuringians, Alemans, and a great part of the Slavs."[14] Thus, when Charles III died in early 888, the territories of Italy and Gaul were left without a Carolingian king for the first time in over a century. As a result, a number of Frankish magnates from outside the Carolingian male line set themselves up as kings, thereby

[12] MacLean, *Kingship and Politics*, 123–98.
[13] *DArnulf* 1.
[14] *AF(B)*, s.a. 888, p. 116.

spelling an end to a united Frankish empire and the Carolingians' monopoly on kingship.

Historians have rightly identified Arnulf's 887 coup as a decisive moment for the "foundation"—or, more accurately, "re-foundation"—of the east Frankish kingdom, since it reunited the realm of his grandfather.[15] There is no evidence that Arnulf's coup represented an incipient "German" national consciousness among the eastern peoples and their desire for their own king.[16] Instead, Arnulf exploited the long-standing political alliances of the leading eastern families to Louis the German's dynasty. Between 843 and 887, several generations of eastern nobles had grown up in the service of Louis the German and his sons, regularly attended their royal assemblies, served in their armies, and held offices and benefices with their approval. In 887, these east Frankish aristocrats sought to preserve their long-held power and *Königsnähe* by supporting Louis the German's only surviving grandson. Thus, within a decade of Louis the German's death, the eastern nobles began to congeal into a political community that could give fragile cohesion to the east Frankish kingdom.

One sees this eastern aristocratic allegiance to Louis the German's family in the historical works of Notker. Notker had grown up at the important royal monastery of St.-Gall, where Louis's archchaplain, Grimald, had been abbot, and he wrote during the last years of Charles III's rule. In a short genealogical treatise composed on the occasion of Charles III's imperial coronation in 881, Notker showed a striking loyalty to Louis the German's dynasty.[17] Notker praised Louis the German as the "most glorious king," and he expressed his fervent hope that Charles III and Arnulf would thrive, "so that the lamp of Louis the Great might not be extinguished from the house of the Lord."

Notker continued to voice his allegiance to the east Frankish Carolingians in his *Deeds of Charlemagne*, which he wrote for Charles III between 884 and 886.[18] Throughout that work, Notker gave a strongly east Frankish view of Carolingian history, and he placed particular emphasis on the memory of Louis the German. Notker drove home this point through his apoc-

---

[15] Concerning Arnulf's 887 coup, see esp. Hagen Keller, "Zum Sturtz Karls III," *DA* 22 (1966): 333–84; Reuter, *Germany*, 119–24; MacLean, *Kingship and Politics*, 191–98. On Arnulf's reign, now see Franz Fuchs and Peter Schmid, eds., *Kaiser Arnolf: Das ostfränkische Reich am Ende des 9. Jahrhundert* (Munich, 2002).

[16] As argued by Walter Schlesinger, "Kaiser Arnulf und die Enstehung des deutschen Staates und Volkes," reprinted in Kämpf, *Entstehung des deutschen Reiches*, 94–109.

[17] Notker, *Continuatio*, 329–30.

[18] MacLean, *Kingship and Politics*, 199–229.

ryphal story of Louis the Pious's presentation of the young Louis the German to the elderly Charlemagne.[19] Notker based this anecdote on the biblical story of Joseph's presentation of his sons, Manasseh and Ephraim, to the elderly Jacob (Genesis 48). Although Manasseh was Joseph's firstborn son, Jacob gave his blessing to Ephraim and predicted that his offspring would be greater than the children of his elder brother. Notker's implication was clear—Louis the German and his descendants represented the chief line of the Carolingian dynasty—and he wove this biblical allusion throughout the *Deeds of Charlemagne*. Appropriating the image of Joseph and his offspring as a fruitful tree, he described Louis the German's sons as leafy branches growing out of their father's thighs.[20] But Notker worried that the epidemic of royal deaths would cut short Louis the German's "most fertile root" and prevent the Carolingians from driving out the Vikings, whose raids on the Continent had intensified in recent years. In an aside that is the crux of the entire work, Notker addressed Charles III directly:

> May your own sword hardened in the blood of the Northmen resist [the Vikings], joining to it the sword of your brother Carloman, stained with the blood of the same people. But that sword, which now belongs to your faithful man, Arnulf, is rusting away—not because of cowardice, but because of his poverty and limited territories. But by your order and command that sword could once again be made sharp and bright. Under the protection of your lofty bough, only that lone branch [i.e., Arnulf], along with the most fragile twig Bernard, sprouts from Louis [the German]'s most fertile root.[21]

After his coup, Arnulf consciously modeled himself on Louis the German and thereby presented himself as the continuator of the east Frankish royal tree. He held assemblies at his grandfather's eastern capitals of Frankfurt and Regensburg, used his grandfather's title "king by the favor of Divine Grace," and frequently made donations to eastern churches for the salvation of Louis the German's soul.[22] Indeed, when in 893 the first and only son of Arnulf and his queen, Uota, was baptized, Bishops Hatto of Mainz and Adalbero of Augsburg "named him Hludawic in honor of [Arnulf's] grandfather."[23] By choosing his grandfather's name, Arnulf and his bishops ex-

---

[19] Notker, *GK* 2.10, p. 66.

[20] Ibid., 1.34, p. 47. Cf. Genesis 49:22.

[21] Ibid., 2.14, p. 78.

[22] For Arnulf's emulation of his grandfather, see Eduard Hlawitschka, *Lotharingien und das Reich an der Schwelle der deutschen Geschichte* (Stuttgart, 1968), 68–73.

[23] *AF(B)*, s.a. 893, p. 122: "nomine avi sui Hludawicum appellaverunt." For the increased power and influence of bishops such as Hatto of Mainz and Adalbero of Augsburg

pressed their hope that his son would grow up to be a second Louis the German and continue the east Frankish Carolingian dynasty under his leadership. The boy did in fact grow up to become King Louis the Child (900–911), the last east Frankish king from Louis the German's dynasty.

While Arnulf reforged his grandfather's east Frankish kingdom during the winter of 887–88, however, the rest of the empire fragmented under a series of kings from outside the Carolingian male line: Odo in west Francia, Berengar in Italy, Rudolf in Burgundy, Boso's son Louis in Provence, and Wido II in west Francia and then Italy. These powerful nobles came from families that were longtime supporters of the Carolingians, and most of them were related to the Carolingians through marriage. In this sense, the new kings who rose to power in 888 were not upstarts but rather the Carolingians' natural heirs.[24] These magnates had been thrust onto the throne in the regional power vacuums created by the Carolingian dynastic crisis and Charles III's death. Having risen so high in Carolingian service, they either had to make a bid for the purple themselves or risk being crushed by rivals.[25]

Writing with the benefit of hindsight, Regino emphasized the role of aristocratic competition among the magnates in propelling the rise of non-Carolingian kings in 888 and beyond. In what is perhaps the most revealing passage about Carolingian politics penned by any chronicler, Regino described the cutthroat struggles for power and *dignitas* among the nobles—struggles that always had been present in Frankish Europe. For over a century, the Carolingians had successfully managed just such aristocratic rivalries and overcome the political crises they engendered. But in the sudden absence of effective Carolingian kingship, all that was left was aristocratic conflict. Regino wrote:

> After [Charles III's] death, the kingdoms under his authority, being deprived of their legitimate heir, broke apart. Instead of waiting for their natural lord [Arnulf], each chose a king for itself from its innards. This caused great turmoils and wars: not because the Frankish princes lacked men of nobility, courage, and wisdom who could rule the kingdoms, but because their equality of nobility, dignity, and power encouraged discord among them. No one clearly outranked the others so that the rest would deign to submit to his lordship. Francia produced many

---

in east Frankish politics during the late ninth century, see Bührer-Thierry, *Évêques et pouvoir*, esp. 37–43, 53–70.

[24] Airlie, "Aristocracy," 448–50.
[25] Airlie, "Nearly Men," 35.

princes worthy to rule the kingdom, but fortune armed them for mutual destruction in their striving for valor.[26]

In a profound sense, the sudden and unexpected collapse of the Carolingian empire in 888 is the exception that proves the rule about Carolingian success. Up to that moment, there had been no real decline in the effectiveness of Carolingian kingship. Between 751 and 888, Carolingian rulers like Charlemagne, Louis the German, and Charles the Bald had managed, responded to, and overcome the kind of ever-present aristocratic rivalries and political conflicts Regino described. But when Arnulf seized the east Frankish throne in late 887, for the first time in Gaul and Italy there was no legitimate adult Carolingian king to step into the aristocratic vortex and bring the magnates to heel. The aristocratic dynamic in 888 was the same as it had been for centuries. What was new was the lack of a legitimate Carolingian king who could rise above the fray and keep the magnates from tearing the empire apart. The illegitimate Arnulf understood this. Thus, when a faction of western magnates (including Hincmar's successor, Fulco of Reims) offered him the west Frankish crown in the summer of 888, Arnulf prudently declined because he apparently realized he could not easily win the support of the entire western nobility. Instead of opting for another civil war, Arnulf supplied Odo with a crown for his coronation and formed an alliance with him. (Arnulf also recognized several of the other new Frankish kings.) At the same time, like his predecessors, Arnulf pursued imperial ambitions in Lotharingia and Italy. He appointed his illegitimate son, Svatopluk (Zwentibald), king of Lotharingia in 895, and the following year Arnulf was crowned emperor of Italy by Pope Formosus. The struggle for the empire was not over, but after 887 the Carolingians would be only one of the several competing royal families in Europe.

The eastern nobles' political alliances with Louis the German's dynasty again came into play when Arnulf died in 899. The following year, the eastern magnates brought Arnulf's only legitimate heir, Louis the Child, to Forchheim and "made him king over them, crowned him, dressed him in royal ornaments, and raised him to the throne of the kingdom."[27] Like Arnulf's coup in 887, the elevation of Louis the Child in 900 was another decisive moment for the foundation of an enduring east Frankish kingdom.[28] Arnulf's son was only seven years old, and the eastern magnates could have

[26] Regino, *Chronicon*, s.a. 888, p. 129.
[27] Ibid., s.a. 900, p. 148.
[28] Reuter, *Germany*, 126–27.

either allowed the east Frankish kingdom to break apart or chosen Charles the Bald's grandson, Charles the Straightforward (who had succeeded Odo as king of west Francia in 898), as their ruler. But the eastern nobles sought to preserve their long-standing influence and *Königsnähe* at the east Frankish palace by rallying to Louis the German's young great-grandson. By now, the east Frankish kingdom had begun to take on a loose political cohesion that transcended the rule of any individual king. Hatto of Mainz explained to Pope John IX that "although [Louis the Child] is very young . . . , we prefer to follow old custom rather than novelties . . . lest the united kingdom fall into pieces."[29] Bishops Hatto of Mainz and Adalbero of Augsburg became the guardians of the young king, and they stressed the continuity of the east Frankish monarchy by authenticating Louis the Child's diplomas with Louis the German's Hadrian seal, which had become one of the "royal ornaments" of the east Frankish monarchy.[30]

While Hatto of Mainz and Adalbero of Augsburg rallied to the defense of the east Frankish dynasty, however, it was during Louis the Child's minority that powerful regional magnates emerged in control of the eastern *regna*— the so-called stem-dukes. In the absence of strong royal leadership and in the face of new invaders from the east, the Magyars, these powerful nobles stepped into the local power vacuums and assumed quasi-royal leadership on the provincial level: raising and commanding regional armies, residing in royal palaces and manors, issuing diplomas and coinage, and exercising at least some control over the Church. In this way, the eastern magnates forged the so-called younger stem duchies—namely, Bavaria, Alemannia, Franconia, Thuringia, Saxony, and Lotharingia—which became a cornerstone of the political constitution of the east Frankish kingdom in the tenth century.[31] These eastern duchies were much like the principalities that had emerged in Gaul in the power vacuum after Charles III's death.[32] The east

---

[29] Harry Bresslau, "Der angebliche Brief des Erzbischofs Hatto von Mainz an Papst Johann IX," in *Historische Aufsätze Karl Zeumer zum 60. Geburtstag als Festgabe dargebracht* (Weimar, 1910), 9–30, at 27, cited in Airlie, "Nearly Men," 28. See further Helmut Beumann, "Die Einheit des ostfränkischen Reichs und der Kaisergedanke bei der Königserhebung Ludwigs des Kinds," *Archiv für Diplomatik* 23 (1977): 142–63.

[30] Louis the Younger likewise had used his father's Hadrian seal. See Kehr's introduction to *DLY*, il.

[31] Reuter, *Germany*, 127–34; and more generally Hans-Werner Goetz, *"Dux" und "Ducatus": Begriffs- und verfassungsgeschichtliche Untersuchungen zur Entstehung des sogenannten "jüngeren" Stammesherzogtums an der Wende vom neunten zum zehnten Jahrhundert* (Bochum, 1977).

[32] For the emergence of the west Frankish principalities in the later ninth and tenth centuries, see Jean Dunbabin, *France in the Making, 843–1180* (Oxford, 1985), 27–37, 44–92.

Frankish kingdom therefore endured into the tenth century, but in a far more decentralized shape than when Louis the German first created it.

When the eighteen-year-old Louis the Child died without an heir in 911, Louis the German's dynasty came to an end. Nevertheless, the first two non-Carolingian kings the nobles raised to the east Frankish throne were magnates with close historical ties to the east Frankish royal family: Conrad I (911–18), who was related to Louis the Child through Arnulf's Konradiner wife, Uota; and Henry I (919–36), whose Liudolfing aunt, Liutgard, had been married to Louis the Younger. Beginning with Henry I, the Liudolfing-Ottonian dynasty ruled the east Frankish kingdom for a century. Under the Ottonians, the struggle for empire continued, but, like Arnulf, the new east Frankish kings focused their imperialist ambitions on Italy and Lotharingia, not all of Europe. Imperial horizons had shrunk since Louis the German's day. Nevertheless, like Louis the German himself, the Ottonians saw Charlemagne as the ideal Frankish king and emperor.[33] Thus, while ruling a kingdom first created by Charlemagne's grandson, the Ottonians looked back to Charlemagne as the font of royal authority. In this way, the memory of Louis the German's reign slowly faded into the long shadow of his famous grandfather.

[33] Hagen Keller, "Die Ottonen und Karl der Grosse," *FS* 43 (2000): 112–31.

APPENDIX I
MAPS

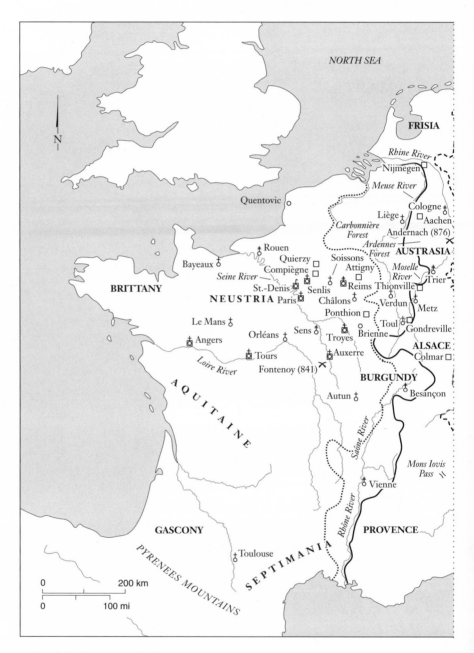

NORTH SEA

FRISIA

Rhine River
Nijmegen

Meuse River

Cologne
Liège
Aachen
Andernach (876)

Quentovic

Carbonnière Forest
Ardennes Forest

AUSTRASIA

Rouen
Quierzy
Soissons
Attigny
Moselle River
Trier

Bayeaux
Compiègne
Seine River
St.-Denis
Senlis
Reims
Thionville

BRITTANY

NEUSTRIA Paris
Châlons
Verdun
Metz

Ponthion
Toul
Gondreville

Le Mans

Orléans
Sens
Troyes
Brienne

Angers

ALSACE
Colmar

Tours
Auxerre

Fontenoy (841)

BURGUNDY

Loire River

A Q U I T A I N E

Autun
Besançon

Saône River

Mons Iovis Pass

Vienne

GASCONY

PROVENCE

Rhône River

Toulouse

S E P T I M A N I A

P Y R E N E E S   M O U N T A I N S

N

0   200 km
0   100 mi

Carolingian Europe in the ninth century

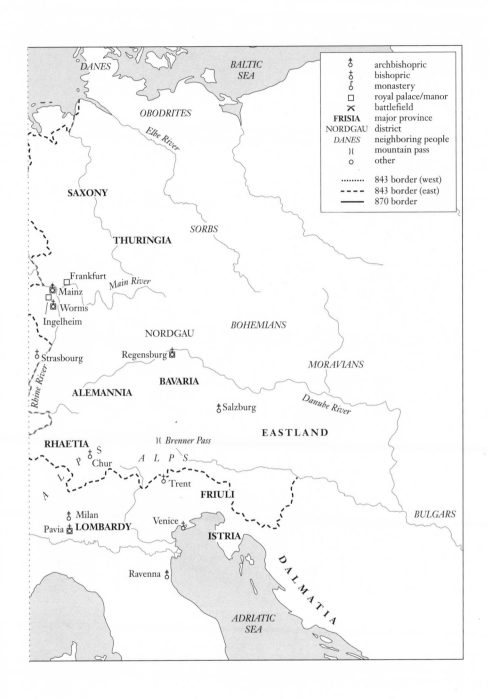

DANES

BALTIC
SEA

OBODRITES

Elbe River

SAXONY

SORBS

THURINGIA

Frankfurt

Mainz

Worms

Main River

Ingelheim

BOHEMIANS

NORDGAU

Strasbourg

Regensburg

MORAVIANS

BAVARIA

ALEMANNIA

Salzburg

Danube River

RHAETIA

Brenner Pass

EASTLAND

A L P S

A L P S

Chur

Trent

FRIULI

BULGARS

Milan

Venice

Pavia LOMBARDY

ISTRIA

D A L M A T I A

Ravenna

ADRIATIC
SEA

archbishopric
bishopric
monastery
royal palace/manor
battlefield
FRISIA   major province
NORDGAU district
DANES   neighboring people
        mountain pass
o   other

········ 843 border (west)
- - - -   843 border (east)
——————   870 border

The eastern regions of Carolingian Europe

BALTIC
SEA

WILZES

LINONES

Oder River

H E V E L L E S

Elbe River

S O R B S

D A L A M I N Z E S

B O H E M I A N S

M O R A V I A N S

NORDGAU
Regensburg
Niederalteich

Passau

BAVARIA
Altötting

Tulln

Chiemsee   Salzburg

UPPER PANNONIA

Danube River

Raab River

LOWER

L. Balaton

CARANTANIA

Moosburg ○

PANNONIA

Trent

Drava River

CARNIOLA

Verona

Sava River

**BULGAR
EMPIRE**

	archbishopric
	bishopric
	monastery
□	royal palace/manor
✕	battlefield
FRISIA	major province
NORDGAU	district
DANES	neighboring people
)(	mountain pass
○	other

....	843 border (west)
- - - - -	843 border (east)
————	870 border

0   100   200 km

0   50   100 mi

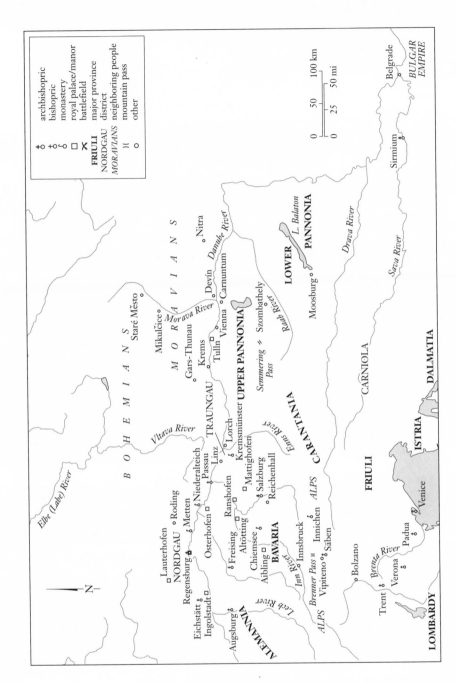

Bavaria and its frontiers

Legend:
- ⊕ archbishopric
- ✚ bishopric
- ○ monastery
- □ royal palace/manor
- ✕ battlefield
- FRIULI major province
- NORDGAU district
- *MORAVIANS* neighboring people
- ‖ mountain pass
- ○ other

Scale: 0 — 50 — 100 km / 0 — 25 — 50 mi

BULGAR EMPIRE
Belgrade
Sirmium
DALMATIA
ISTRIA
Venice
Padua
Verona
Trent
Bolzano
LOMBARDY
ALPS
Brenner Pass
Vipiteno • Säben
Innichen
Innsbruck
Inn River
FRIULI
CARNIOLA
Drava River
Sava River
LOWER PANNONIA
L. Balaton
Moosburg
Raab River
Szombathely
Semmering Pass
CARANTANIA
ALPS
Enns River
UPPER PANNONIA
Carnuntum
Vienna
Tulln
Devin
Danube River
Nitra
M O R A V I A N S
Morava River
Staré Město
Mikulčice
Krems
Gars-Thunau
TRAUNGAU
Lorch
Kremsmünster
Reichenhall
Salzburg
Mattighofen
Chiemsee
Aibling
BAVARIA
Altötting
Freising
Ranshofen
Osterhofen
Passau
Niederaltreich
Metten
Roding
NORDGAU
Lauterhofen
Regensburg
Eichstätt
Ingolstadt
Augsburg
ALEMANNIA
Lech River
B O H E M I A N S
Vltava River
Elbe (Labe) River
—N—

APPENDIX 2
GENEALOGIES

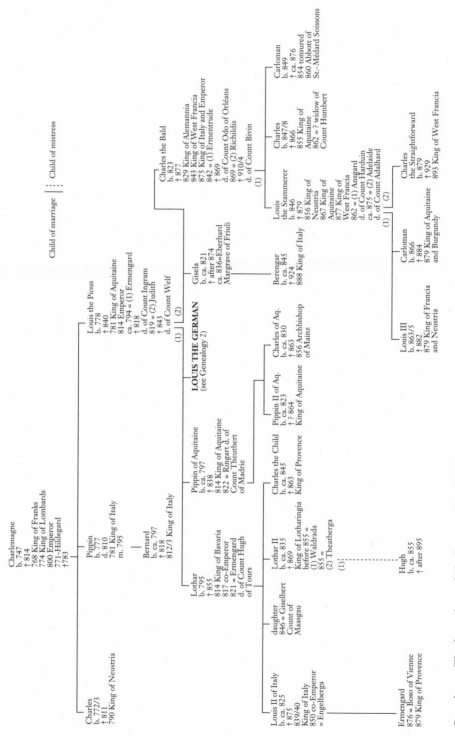

Genealogy 1. The descendants of Charlemagne (simplified)

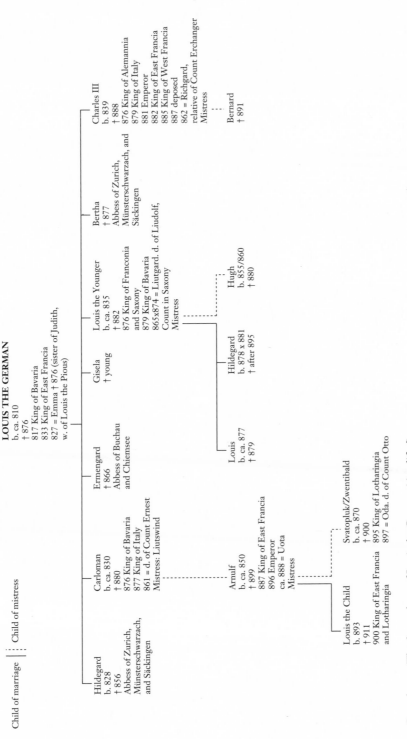

Genealogy 2. The descendants of Louis the German (simplified)

SELECTED BIBLIOGRAPHY

MANUSCRIPT SOURCES

Baturich of Regensburg's pontifical. Munich, Clm 14510, fols. 1–75.
Grimalt Codex. Stiftsbibliothek St. Gallen 397.
Lorsch Rotulus. Stadt- und Universitätsbibliothek Frankfurt, MS Barth. 179.
Louis's copy of Wandalbert of Prüm's *Martyrology*. Biblioteca Apostolica Vaticana, Reg. lat. 438.
Ludwig Psalter. Staatsbibliothek zu Berlin—Preussischer Kulturbesitz, MS theol. lat. fol. 58.

PRINTED PRIMARY SOURCES

Adelerius of Fleury. *Miracula sancti Benedicti*. Ed. Oswald Holder-Egger. In MGH *SS* 15:474–97. Hanover, 1887.
Ado of Vienne. *Chronicon*. Ed. Georg Heinrich Pertz. In MGH *SS* 2:315–23. Hanover, 1829.
Adonis Continuatio prima. Ed. Georg Heinrich Pertz. In MGH *SS* 2:324–25. Hanover, 1829.
Agnellus of Ravenna. *The Book of the Pontiffs of the Church of Ravenna*. Trans. Deborah Mauskopf Deliyannis. Washington, DC, 2004.
———. *Liber pontificalis ecclesiae Ravennatis*. Ed. Oswald Holder-Egger. In MGH *SRL*, 265–391. Hanover, 1878.
Die alten Mönchslisten und die Traditionen von Corvey. Vol. 1. Ed. Klemens Honselmann. Paderborn, 1982.
Andrew of Bergamo. *Historia*. Ed. Georg Waitz. In MGH *SRL*, 220–30. Hanover, 1878.
Annales Alamannici. In *Untersuchungen zur frühalemannischen Annalistik: Die Murbacher Annalen, mit Edition*, ed. Walter Lendi. Freiburg, 1971.
Annales Altahenses maiores. Ed. Wilhelm von Giesebrecht. In MGH *SS* 20:772–824. Hanover, 1868.
Annales de Saint-Bertin. Ed. Félix Grat, Jeanne Vielliard, and Suzanne Clémencet. Paris, 1964.

Annales ex annalibus Iuvavensibus antiquis excerpti. Ed. Harry Bresslau. In MGH *SS* 30.2: 727–47. Hanover, 1934.

Annales Fuldenses sive annales regni Francorum orientalis. Ed. Friedrich Kurze. MGH *SRG* 7. Hanover, 1891.

Annales Hildesheimenses. Ed. Georg Waitz. MGH *SRG.* Hanover, 1878.

Annales Mettenses Priores. Ed. Bernhard von Simson. MGH *SRG.* Hanover, 1905.

Annales Vedastini. Ed. Bernhard von Simson. MGH *SRG* 12. Hanover, 1909.

Annales Xantenses. Ed. Bernhard von Simson. MGH *SRG* 12. Hanover, 1909.

Annalista Saxo. Ed. Georg Waitz. In MGH *SS* 6:542–777. Hanover, 1844.

The Annals of Fulda. Trans. Timothy Reuter. Manchester, 1992.

The Annals of St.-Bertin. Trans. Janet L. Nelson. Manchester, 1991.

Annales regni Francorum. Ed. Friedrich Kurze. MGH *SRG* 6. Hanover, 1895.

Astronomer. *Vita Hludowici imperatoris.* Ed. and trans. Ernst Tremp. MGH *SRG* 64. Hanover, 1995.

Auctarium Garstense. Ed. Wilhelm Wattenbach. In MGH *SS* 9:561–69. Hanover, 1851.

Braune, Wilhelm, ed. *Althochdeutsches Lesebuch.* 16th ed. Tübingen, 1979.

Capitularia regum Francorum. Ed. Alfred Boretius and Viktor Krause. In MGH *Capitularia* 1, 2.1, and 2.2. Hanover, 1890–1897.

Carolingian Chronicles. Trans. Bernard Scholz. Ann Arbor, 1970.

Codex Diplomaticus Fuldensis. Ed. Ernst Friedrich Johann Dronke. Kassel, 1850.

Codex Laureshamensis. 3 vols. Ed. Karl Glöckner. Darmstadt, 1929–36.

Constantine Porphyrogenitus. *De administrando imperio.* Ed. and trans. Gy. Moravcsik and R. J. H. Jenkins. Washington, DC, 1967.

Conversio Bagoariorum et Carantanorum: Das Weissbuch der Salzburger Kirche über die erfolgreiche Mission in Karantanien und Pannonien. Ed. and trans. Herwig Wolfram. Vienna, 1979.

Die "Conversio Bagoariorum et Carantanorum" und der Brief des Erzbischofs Theotmar von Salzburg. Ed. and trans. Fritz Lošek. MGH *Studien und Texte* 15. Hanover, 1997.

Corpus Christianorum: Continuatio Mediaevalis. Turnhout, 1966–2004.

Descriptio civitatum et regionum ad septentrionalem plagam Danubii. Ed. Erwin Herrmann. In *Slawisch-germanische Beziehungen im südostdeutschen Raum von der Spätantike bis zum Ungarnsturm: Ein Quellenbuch mit Erläuterungen,* 212–22. Munich, 1965.

Dutton, Paul Edward, trans. *Charlemagne's Courtier: The Complete Einhard.* Peterborough, 1998.

Einhard. *Vita Karoli Magni.* Ed. Georg Pertz. MGH *SRG.* Hanover, 1911.

Elze, Reinhard. "Ein karolingischer Ordo für die Krönung eines Herrscherpaares." *Bullettino dell'Instituto Storico Italiano per il Medio Evo e Archivio Muratoriano* 98 (1992): 417–23.

Epistolae Karolini aevi 3. MGH *Epistolae* 5. Berlin, 1899.

Epistolae Karolini aevi 4. MGH *Epistolae* 6. Berlin, 1902–25.

Epistolae Karolini aevi 5. MGH *Epistolae* 7. Berlin, 1912–28.

Ermanrich of Ellwangen. *Vita Hariolfi.* In *Ellwangen 764–1964,* ed. Viktor Burr, 1:9–49. Ellwangen, 1964.

——. *Vita Sualonis.* In *Quellen zur Geschichte der Diözese Eichstätt,* vol. 1: *Biographien der Gründungszeit,* ed. Andreas Bauch. Regensburg, 1984.

Ermold the Black. *In Honorem Hludowici Pii.* In *Ermold le Noir: Poème sur Louis le Pieux et Épîtres au roi Pépin,* ed. and trans. Edmond Faral. Paris, 1932.

Flodoard. *Historia Remensis Ecclesiae.* Ed. Martina Stratmann. MGH *SS* 36. Hanover, 1998.

Formulae Merowingici et Karolini Aevi. Legum Sectio V. Ed. Karl Zeumer. MGH *Formulae.* Hanover, 1886.

Fouracre, Paul, and Richard A. Gerberding, trans. *Late Merovingian France: History and Historiography, 640–720.* Manchester, 1996.

Selected Bibliography

The Fourth Book of the Chronicle of Fredegar with Its Continuations. Ed. and trans. J. M. Wallace-Hadrill. London, 1960.

Heather, Peter, and John Matthews, trans. *The Goths in the Fourth Century.* Liverpool, 1991.

Heliand. In *Heliand und Genesis*, 10th ed., ed. Otto Behaghel. Tübingen, 1996.

Hincmar. *De ordine palatii.* Ed. Thomas Gross and Rudolf Schieffer. MGH *Fontes* 3. Hanover, 1980.

———. *De verbis psalmi: Herodii domus dux est eorum, ad Ludowicum Germaniae regem.* Ed. J.-P. Migne. In *PL* 125, cols. 957–62. Paris, 1852.

Jacob, Georg, trans. *Arabische Berichte von Gesandten an germanische Fürstenhöfe aus dem 9. und 10. Jahrhundert.* Berlin, 1927.

Die Konzilien der karolingischen Teilreiche, 843–859. Ed. Wilfried Hartmann. MGH *Concilia* 3. Hanover, 1984.

Die Konzilien der karolingischen Teilreiche, 860–874. Ed. Wilfried Hartmann. MGH *Concilia* 4. Hanover, 1998.

Lampert of Hersfeld. *Annales.* In *Lamperti Monachi Hersfeldensis Opera*, ed. Oswald Holder-Egger. MGH *SRG* 38. Hanover, 1894.

Liber Pontificalis (The Lives of the Ninth-Century Popes). Trans. Raymond Davis. Liverpool, 1995.

Liber Possessionum Wizenburgensis. Ed. Christoph Dette. Mainz, 1987.

Necrologia Germaniae. Ed. Paul Piper. MGH *Necrologia* 6. Berlin, 1884.

Nithard. *Historiarum libri IV.* Ed. Ernest Müller. MGH *SRG* 44. Hanover, 1907.

Notitia de servitio monasteriorum. In *Corpus Consuetudinum Monasticarum*, ed. Cassius Hallinger, 1:493–99. Siegburg, 1963.

Notker the Stammerer. *Breviarium regum Francorum: Continuatio.* Ed. Georg Heinrich Pertz. In MGH *SS* 2:329–30. Hanover, 1829.

———. *Gesta Karoli magni imperatoris.* Ed. Hans F. Haefele. MGH *SRG*, n. s. 12. Berlin, 1959.

Ordines coronationis Franciae: Texts and Ordines for the Coronation of Frankish and French Kings and Queens in the Middle Ages. Vol. 1. Ed. Richard A. Jackson. Philadelphia, 1995.

Otfrid of Wissembourg. *Evangelienbuch.* Ed. and trans. Gisela Vollmann-Profe. Stuttgart, 1987.

Poetae Latini aevi Carolini 1. Ed. Ernst Dümmler. MGH *Poetae Latini* 1. Berlin, 1881.

Poetae Latini aevi Carolini 2. Ed. Ernst Dümmler. MGH *Poetae Latini* 2. Berlin, 1884.

Poetae Latini aevi Carolini 3.1–3. Ed. Ludwig Traube. MGH *Poetae Latini* 3. Berlin, 1886–96.

Poetae Latini aevi Carolini 4.1–3. Ed. Karl Strecker. MGH *Poetae Latini* 4. Berlin, 1881–99.

Raban. *De institutione clericorum libri tres.* Ed. Detlev Zimpel. Freiburger Beiträge zur mittelalterlichen Geschichte: Studien und Texte 7. Frankfurt, 1996.

———. *De procinctu Romanae miliciae.* Ed. Ernst Dümmler. *ZDA* 15 (1872): 443–51.

———. *De universo.* Ed. J.-P. Migne. In *PL* 111, cols. 9–614. Paris, 1852.

———. *Martyrologium.* Ed. John McCulloh. In *CCCM* 44. Turnhout, 1979.

Radbert. *Epitaphium Arsenii.* Ed. Ernst Dümmler. *Abhandlungen der Königlichen Akademie der Wissenschaften zu Berlin, Phil.—Historische Abhandlungen* 2 (1900): 1–98.

Ratpert. *Casus sancti Galli.* Ed. and trans. Hannes Steiner. MGH *SRG* 75. Hanover, 2002.

Receuil des Actes de Charles II le Chauve, roi de France. 3 vols. Ed. Georges Tessier. Paris, 1943–55.

Receuil des Actes de Pépin I et Pépin II, rois d'Aquitaine. Ed. L. Levillain. Paris, 1926.

Regino of Prüm. *Chronicon.* Ed. Friedrich Kurze. MGH *SRG* 50. Hanover, 1890.

Rimbert. *Vita Anskarii.* Ed. Georg Waitz. MGH *SRG* 55. Hanover, 1884.

Rudolf of Fulda. *Miracula sanctorum in Fuldenses ecclesias translatorum.* Ed. Georg Waitz. In MGH *SS* 15.1: 328–41. Hanover, 1829.

———. *Translatio sancti Alexandri.* Ed. Georg Heinrich Pertz. In MGH *SS* 2: 673–76.

Hanover, 1829. Facsimile edition: *Translatio S. Alexandri auctoribus Ruodolfo et Meginharto Fuldensibus: Landesbibliothek Hannover MS I 186.* Ed. H. Härtel and W. Milde. Facsimilia Textuum Manuscriptorum. Texthandschriften des Mittelalters in Faksimile 5. Hildesheim, 1979.

——. *Vita Leobae abbatissae Biscofesheimensis.* Ed. Georg Waitz. In MGH *SS* 15.1: 118–31. Hanover, 1887.

Scriptores. 30 vols. MGH *SS.* Hanover, 1824–1924.

Thegan. *Gesta Hludowici imperatoris.* Ed. and trans. Ernst Tremp. MGH *SRG* 64. Hanover, 1995.

Die Traditionen des Hochstifts Freising, vol. 1: *744–926.* Ed. Theodor Bitterauf. Quellen und Erörterungen zur bayerischen und deutschen Geschichte, n. s. 4. Munich, 1905.

Die Traditionen des Hochstifts Passau. Ed. Max Heuwieser. Quellen und Erörterungen zur bayerischen Geschichte, n. s. 6. Munich, 1930.

Die Traditionen des Hochstifts Regensburg und des Klosters S. Emmeram. Ed. Josef Widemann. Quellen und Erörterungen zur bayerischen Geschichte, n. s. 8. Munich, 1943.

Traditiones Wizenburgenses: Die Urkunden des Klosters Weissenburg, 661–864. Ed. Karl Glöckner and Anton Doll. Darmstadt, 1979.

Die Urkunden Arnolfs. Ed. Paul Kehr. MGH *Diplomata regum Germaniae ex stirpe Karolinorum* 3. Berlin, 1940.

Die Urkunden Karls III. Ed. Paul Kehr. MGH *Diplomata regum Germaniae ex stirpe Karolinorum* 2. Berlin, 1936–37.

Die Urkunden Lothars I und Lothars II. Ed. Theodor Schieffer. MGH *Diplomata Karolinorum* 3. Berlin, 1966.

Die Urkunden Ludwigs II. Ed. Konrad Wanner. MGH *Diplomata Karolinorum* 4. Munich, 1994.

Die Urkunden Ludwigs des Deutschen, Karlomanns und Ludwigs des Jüngeren. Ed. Paul Kehr. MGH *Diplomata regum Germaniae ex stirpe Karolinorum* 1. Berlin, 1932–34.

Die Urkunden Pippins, Karlmanns und Karls des Grossen. Ed. Engelbert Mühlbacher. MGH *Diplomata Karolinorum* 1. Berlin, 1956.

Die Urkunden Zwentibolds und Ludwigs des Kindes. Ed. Theodor Schieffer. MGH *Diplomata regum Germaniae ex stirpe Karolinorum* 4. Berlin, 1960.

Urkundenbuch der Abtei Sanct Gallen. 2 vols. Ed. Hermann Wartmann. Zurich, 1863–66.

Urkundenbuch der Stadt und Landschaft Zürich. Vol. 1. Ed. Jakob Escher and Paul Schweizer. Zurich, 1888.

Vegetius. *Epitome of Military Science.* Trans. N. P. Milner. 2nd ed. Liverpool, 1996.

Visio Karoli Magni. Ed. in Patrick J. Geary, "Germanic Tradition and Royal Ideology in the Ninth Century: The *Visio Karoli Magni.*" In Geary, *Living with the Dead,* 74–76.

Vita Constantini. In *Zwischen Rom und Byzanz: Leben und Wirken der Slavenapostel Kyrillos und Methodios nach den Pannonischen Legenden und der Klemensvita: Bericht von der Taufe Russlands nach der Laurentiuschronik.* Trans. Josef Bujnoch. Slavische Geschichtsschreiber 1. Graz, 1958.

Vita Methodii. In *Zwischen Rom und Byzanz: Leben und Wirken der Slavenapostel Kyrillos und Methodios nach den Pannonischen Legenden und der Klemensvita: Bericht von der Taufe Russlands nach der Laurentiuschronik.* Trans. Josef Bujnoch. Slavische Geschichtsschreiber 1. Graz, 1958.

The "Vita" of Constantine and the "Vita" of Methodius. Trans. Marvin Kantor and Richard S. White. Michigan Slavic Materials 13. Ann Arbor, 1976.

Vita Rimberti. Ed. Georg Waitz. MGH *SRG* 55. Hanover, 1884.

Walahfrid Strabo. *De imagine Tetrici.* In Herren, "*De imagine Tetrici* of Walahfrid Strabo," 118–39.

——. *Libellus de exordiis et incrementis quarundam in observationibus ecclesiasticis rerum.* Ed. and trans. Alice L. Harting-Correa. Leiden, 1996.

Waltharius. In *"Waltharius" and "Ruodlieb."* Ed. and trans. Denis M. Kratz. New York, 1984.

Widukind. *Rerum gestarum Saxonicarum libri III.* In *Quellen zur Geschichte der sächsischen Kaiserzeit,* ed. and trans. Paul Hirsch, Max Büdinger, Wilhelm Wattenbach, Albert Bauer, and Reinhold Rau. Darmstadt, 1977.

Wirtembergisches Urkundenbuch. Ed. by the Königliches Staatsarchiv in Stuttgart. Stuttgart, 1849.

SECONDARY SOURCES

Airlie, Stuart. "The Aristocracy." In McKitterick, *New Cambridge Medieval History,* 2:431–50.

———. "Bonds of Power and Bonds of Association in the Court Circle of Louis the Pious." In Godman and Collins, *Charlemagne's Heir,* 191–204.

———. "Narratives of Triumph and Rituals of Submission: Charlemagne's Mastering of Bavaria." *TRHS,* 6th ser., 9 (1999): 93–119.

———. "The Nearly Men: Boso of Vienne and Arnulf of Bavaria." In Duggan, *Nobles and Nobility,* 25–41.

———. "The Political Behavior of Secular Magnates in Francia, 829–79." D. Phil. thesis, Oxford University, 1985.

———. "Private Bodies and the Body Politic in the Divorce Case of Lothar II." *Past and Present* 161 (1998): 3–38.

———. "Review Article: After Empire—Recent Work on the Emergence of Post-Carolingian Kingdoms." *EME* 2 (1993): 153–61.

———. "*Semper fideles?* Loyauté envers les Carolingiens comme constituant de l'identité aristocratique." In Le Jan, *La Royauté,* 129–43.

———. "Talking Heads: Assemblies in Early Medieval Germany." In *Political Assemblies in the Earlier Middle Ages,* ed. P. S. Barnwell and Marco Mostert, 29–46. Turnhout, 2003.

———. "True Teachers and Pious Kings: Salzburg, Louis the German, and Christian Order." In *Belief and Culture in the Middle Ages: Studies Presented to Henry Mayr-Harting,* ed. Richard Gameson and Henrietta Leyser, 89–105. Oxford, 2001.

Althoff, Gerd. "Königsherrschaft und Konfliktbewältigung im 10. und 11. Jahrhundert." Reprinted in Althoff, *Spielregeln,* 21–56.

———. "Das Privileg der *deditio.*" Reprinted in Althoff, *Spielregeln,* 99–125.

———. "Saxony and the Elbe Slavs." In Reuter, *New Cambridge Medieval History,* 3:267–92.

———. *Spielregeln der Politik im Mittelalter.* Darmstadt, 1997.

———. "Über die von Erzbischof Liutbert auf die Reichenau übersandten Namen." *FS* 14 (1980): 219–42.

———. *Verwandte, Freunde und Getreue: Zum politischen Stellenwert der Gruppenbindungen im früheren Mittelalter.* Darmstadt, 1990.

———. "Zu Bedeutung der Bündnisse Svatopluks von Mähren mit Franken." In *Symposium Methodianum: Beiträge der Internationalen Tagung in Regensburg (17. bis 24. April 1985) zum Gedenken an den 1100. Todestag des hl. Method,* ed. K. Trost, E. Völkl, E. Wedel, 13–21. Neuried, 1988.

Althoff, Gerd, Johannes Fried, and Patrick J. Geary, eds. *Medieval Concepts of the Past: Ritual, Memory, Historiography.* Cambridge, 2002.

Arnold, Benjamin. *Medieval Germany, 500–1300: A Political Interpretation.* Toronto, 1997.

Bachrach, Bernard S. "Animals and Warfare in Early Medieval Europe." *SS Spoleto* 30 (1985): 707–64.

———. "*Caballus et Caballarius* in Medieval Warfare." In *The Study of Chivalry,* ed. Howell Chickering and Thomas H. Seiler, 173–211. Kalamazoo, MI, 1988.

———. "Charles Martel, Mounted Shock Combat, the Stirrup, and Feudalism." *SMRH* 7 (1970): 49–75.

——. *Early Carolingian Warfare: Prelude to Empire*. Philadelphia, 2001.

——. "Medieval Military Historiography." In Bentley, *Companion to Historiography*, 203–20.

Barford, P. M. *The Early Slavs*. Ithaca, 2001.

Barraclough, Geoffrey. *The Crucible of Europe: The Ninth and Tenth Centuries in European History*. Berkeley, 1976.

Barthélemey, Dominique. "La chevalerie carolingienne: Prélude au XIe siècle." In Le Jan, *La Royauté*, 159–75.

Becher, Matthias. *Rex, Dux und Gens: Untersuchungen zur Entstehung des sächsischen Herzogtums im 9. und 10. Jahrhundert*. Husum, 1996.

Beeby, Susan, David Buckton, and Zdeněk Klanica, eds. *Great Moravia: The Archaeology of Ninth Century Czechoslovakia*. London, 1982.

Behn, Friedrich. *Die karolingische Klosterkirche von Lorsch an der Bergstrasse nach den Ausgrabungen von 1927–1928 und 1932–1933*. Berlin, 1934.

Bentley, Michael, ed. *Companion to Historiography*. London, 1997.

Bernhardt, John W. *Itinerant Kingship and Royal Monasteries in Early Medieval Germany, c. 936–1075*. Cambridge, 1993.

Beumann, Helmut. "Die Einheit des ostfränkischen Reichs und der Kaisergedanke bei der Königserhebung Ludwigs des Kinds." *Archiv für Diplomatik* 23 (1977): 142–63.

Beyerle, Konrad. "Von der Gründung bis zum Ende des freiherrlichen Klosters (724–1427)." In *Die Kultur der Abtei Reichenau*, ed. Konrad Beyerle, 55–212. Munich, 1925.

Bigott, Boris. *Ludwig der Deutsche und die Reichskirche im Ostfränkischen Reich (826–876)*. Husum, 2002.

——. "*Per Alemanniam iter*: Überlegungen zur Eingliederung der Alemannia ins Ostfränkische Reich Ludwigs des Deutschen." In *In frumento et vino opima: Festschrift für Thomas Zotz zu seinem 60. Geburtstag*, ed. Heinz Krieg and Alfons Zettler, 29–37. Ostfildern, 2004.

——. "Die Versöhnung von 847: Ludwig der Deutsche und die Reichskirche." In Hartmann, *Ludwig der Deutsche und seine Zeit*, 121–40.

Bischoff, Bernhard. "Bücher am Hofe Ludwigs des Deutschen." Reprinted in *Mittelalterliche Studien*, by B. Bischoff, 3:187–212. Stuttgart, 1981.

——. "The Court Library of Louis the Pious." In *Manuscripts and Libraries in the Age of Charlemagne*, by B. Bischoff, trans. Michael M. Gorman, 76–92. Cambridge, 1994.

——. "Literarisches und künstlerisches Leben in St. Emmeram (Regensburg) während des frühen und hohen Mittelalters." *SMGB* 51 (1933): 102–42.

——. "Paläographische Fragen deutscher Denkmäler der Karolingerzeit." *FS* 5 (1971): 101–30.

——. *Die südostdeutschen Schreibschulen und Bibliotheken in der Karolingerzeit*. 2 vols. Wiesbaden, 1960–80.

Bischoff, Bernhard, and Josef Hofmann. *Libri Sancti Kyliani: Die Würzburger Schreibschule und die Dombibliothek im VIII und IX Jahrhundert*. Würzburg, 1952.

Blackburn, Mark. "Coin Circulation in Germany during the Early Middle Ages: The Evidence of Single-Finds." In *Fernhandel und Geldwirtschaft*, ed. Bernd Kluge, 37–54. Sigmaringen, 1993.

——. "Money and Coinage." In McKitterick, *New Cambridge Medieval History*, 2:538–59.

Boba, Imre. *Moravia's History Reconsidered: A Reinterpretation of the Medieval Sources*. The Hague, 1971.

Böhmer, Johann Friedrich, and Engelbert Mühlbacher. *Regesta Imperii*, vol. 1: *Die Regesten des Kaiserreichs unter den Karolingern, 751–918*. 2nd ed. Innsbruck, 1908.

Böhmer, Johann Friedrich, and Cornelius Will. *Regesten zur Geschichte der Mainzer Erzbischöfe*. Vol. 1. Innsbruck, 1887.

Borgolte, Michael. *Der Gesandtenaustausch der Karolinger mit den Abbasiden und mit den Patriarchen von Jerusalem*. Munich, 1976.

——. *Geschichte der Grafschaften Alamanniens in fränkischer Zeit*. Sigmaringen, 1984.

——. *Die Grafen Alemanniens in merowingischer und karolingischer Zeit: Eine Prosopographie*. Sigmaringen, 1986.

——. "Karl III und Neudingen: Zum Problem der Nachfolgeregelung Ludwigs des Deutschen." *ZGO* 125 (1977): 21–55.

——. "Kommentar zu Austellungsdaten, Actum- und Güterorten der älteren St.-Galler Urkunden (Wartmann I und II mit Nachträgen in III und IV)." In *Subsidia Sangallensia*, vol. 1: *Materialien und Untersuchungen zu den Verbrüderungsbüchern und zu den älteren Urkunden des Stiftsarchivs St.-Gallen*, ed. Michael Borgolte, Dieter Geuenich, and Karl Schmid, 323–476. St.-Gall, 1986.

Boshof, Egon. "Einheitsidee und Teilungsprinzip in der Regierungszeit Ludwigs des Frommen." In Godman and Collins, *Charlemagne's Heir*, 161–89.

——. *Ludwig der Fromme*. Darmstadt, 1996.

——. "Das ostfränkische Reich und die Slavenmission im 9. Jahrhundert: Die Rolle Passaus." In *Mönchtum-Kirche-Herrschaft 750–1000*, ed. Dieter R. Bauer, Rudolf Hiestand, Brigitte Kasten, and Sönke Lorenz, 51–76. Sigmaringen, 1998.

Bosl, Karl. *Franken um 800: Strukturanalyse einer fränkischen Königsprovinz*. 2nd ed. Munich, 1969.

——. "Das Grossmährische Reich in der politischen Welt des 9. Jahrhunderts." *SBAW* 7 (1966): 1–33.

Bostock, J. Knight. *A Handbook on Old High German Literature*. 2nd ed. Oxford, 1976.

Bouchard, Constance. "Family Structure and Family Consciousness among the Aristocracy in the Ninth to Eleventh Centuries." *Francia* 14 (1986): 639–58.

Bowlus, Charles R. *Franks, Moravians, and Magyars: The Struggle for the Middle Danube, 788–907*. Philadelphia, 1995.

Braunfels, Wolfgang, ed. *Karl der Grosse: Lebenswerk und Nachleben*. 5 vols. Düsseldorf, 1965–67.

Bresslau, Harry. "Der angebliche Brief des Erzbischofs Hatto von Mainz an Papst Johann IX." In *Historische Aufsätze Karl Zeumer zum 60. Geburtstag als Festgabe dargebracht*, 9–30. Weimar, 1910.

Brousseau, Nicholas. "Die Urkunden Ludwigs des Deutschen und Karls des Kahlen—ein Vergleich." In Hartmann, *Ludwig der Deutsche und seine Zeit*, 95–119.

Brown, Warren. *Unjust Seizure: Conflict, Interest, and Authority in an Early Medieval Society*. Ithaca, 2001.

Brühl, Carlrichard. *Deutschland-Frankreich: Die Geburt zweier Völker*. Cologne, 1990.

——. *Fodrum, Gistum, Servitium Regis: Studien zu den wirtschaftlichen Grundlagen des Königtums im Frankenreich und in der fränkischen Nachfolgestaaten Deutschland, Frankreich und Italien vom 6. bis zur Mitte des 14. Jahrhunderts*. Cologne, 1968.

——. "Fränkischer Krönungsbrauch und das Problem der 'Festkrönungen.'" *HZ* 194 (1962): 265–326.

——. *Palatium und Civitas: Studien zur Profantopographie spätantiker Civitates vom 3. bis zum 13. Jahrhundert*, vol. 2: *Belgica I, beide Germanien und Raetia II*. Cologne, 1990.

Brunner, Karl. *Oppositionelle Gruppen im Karolingerreich*. Vienna, 1979.

Buc, Philippe. *The Dangers of Ritual: Between Early Medieval Texts and Social Scientific Theory*. Princeton, 2001.

Bührer-Thierry, Geneviève. *Évêques et pouvoir dans le royaume de Germanie: Les Églises de Bavière et de Souabe, 876–973*. Paris, 1997.

——. "'Just Anger' or 'Vengeful Anger'? The Punishment of Blinding in the Early Medieval West." In Rosenwein, *Anger's Past*, 75–91.

Burns, J. H., ed. *The Cambridge History of Political Thought, c. 350–c. 1450*. Cambridge, 1988.

Carrol, Christopher. "The Bishoprics in Saxony in the First Century after Christianization." *EME* 8 (1999): 219–46.

Chevallier, Raymond. *Roman Roads.* Trans. N. H. Field. Berkeley, 1976.

Chropovský, Bohuslav. "The Situation of Nitra in the Light of Archaeological Finds." *Historica* 8 (1964): 5–33.

Classen, Peter. "Karl der Grosse und die Thronfolge im Frankenreich." In *Festschrift für Hermann Heimpel*, 3:109–34. Göttingen, 1972.

Collins, Roger. *Charlemagne.* Toronto, 1998.

——. "Pippin I and the Kingdom of Aquitaine." In Godman and Collins, *Charlemagne's Heir*, 363–89.

——. "The 'Reviser' Revisited: Another Look at the Alternative Version of the *Annales Regni Francorum*." In Murray, *After Rome's Fall*, 191–213.

Contreni, John J. "The Carolingian Renaissance: Education and Literary Culture." In McKitterick, *New Cambridge Medieval History*, 2:709–57.

Corradini, Richard. *Die Wiener Handschrift Cvp 430: Ein Beitrag zur Historiographie in Fulda im frühen 9. Jahrhundert.* Frankfurt, 2000.

Coupland, Simon. "Carolingian Arms and Armour in the Ninth Century." *Viator* 21 (1990): 29–55.

——. "From Poachers to Gamekeepers: Scandinavian Warlords and Carolingian Kings." *EME* 7 (1998): 85–114.

——. "Trading Places: Quentovic and Dorestad Reassessed." *EME* 22 (2002): 209–32.

Cubitt, Catharine, ed. *Court Culture in the Early Middle Ages.* Turnhout, 2003.

Davies, Wendy, and Paul Fouracre, eds. *The Settlement of Disputes in Early Medieval Europe.* Cambridge, 1986.

De Jong, Mayke. "Carolingian Monasticism: The Power of Prayer." In McKitterick, *New Cambridge Medieval History*, 2:622–53.

——. "The Empire as *Ecclesia*: Hrabanus Maurus and Biblical *Historia* for Rulers." In Hen and Innes, *Uses of the Past*, 191–226.

——. "Power and Humility in Carolingian Society: The Public Penance of Louis the Pious." *EME* 1 (1992): 29–52.

Dekan, Ján. *Moravia Magna: The Great Moravian Empire: Its Art and Times.* Bratislava, 1980.

Depreux, Philippe. *Prosopographie de l'entourage de Louis le Pieux (781–840).* Sigmaringen, 1997.

Deutinger, Roman. "Königsherrschaft im Ostfränksichen Reich. Ein pragmatische Verfassungsgeschichte der späten Karolingerzeit." Habilitationsschrift. Munich, 2004.

Diebold, William. "*Nos quoque morem illius imitari cupientes*: Charles the Bald's Evocation and Imitation of Charlemagne." *AK* 75 (1993): 271–300.

Dopsch, Heinz. *Geschichte Salzburgs.* Vol. 1. Salzburg, 1983–84.

——. "Passau als Zentrum der Slawenmission: Ein Beitrag zur Frage des 'Grossmährischen Reiches.'" *SA* 28–29 (1985–86): 5–28.

——. "Slawenmission und päpstliche Politik zu den Hintergründen des Methodius-Konfliktes." *MGSL* 126 (1986): 303–40.

Duggan, Anne J., ed. *Nobles and Nobility in Medieval Europe.* Woodbridge, U.K., 2000.

Dümmler, Ernst. *Geschichte des ostfränkischen Reichs.* 2nd ed. 3 vols. Leipzig, 1887–88.

——. "Über Ermanrich von Ellwangen und seine Schriften." *FDG* 13 (1873): 473–85.

Dunbabin, Jean. *France in the Making, 843–1180.* Oxford, 1985.

Durliat, Jean. *Les finances publiques de Dioclétian aux Carolingiens (284–888).* Beihefte der Francia 21. Sigmaringen, 1990.

Dutton, Paul Edward. "Beyond the Topos of Senescence: The Political Problems of Aged Carolingian Rulers." In *Aging and the Aged in Medieval Europe*, ed. Michael M. Sheehan, 75–94. Toronto, 1990.

——. *The Politics of Dreaming in the Carolingian Empire.* Lincoln, NE, 1994.

Dvornik, Francis. *Byzantine Missions among the Slavs: Saints Constantine-Cyril and Methodius.* New Brunswick, NJ, 1970.

———. *The Photian Schism: History and Legend.* Cambridge, 1970.

———. "Photius, Nicholas I and Hadrian II." *Byzantinoslavica* 34 (1973): 33–50.

Eckhardt, Wilhelm August. "Die Capitularia missorum specialia von 802." *DA* 12 (1956): 498–516.

Edwards, Cyril. "German Vernacular Literature: A Survey." In McKitterick, *Carolingian Culture*, 141–70.

Eggenberger, Christoph. *Psalterium Aureum Sancti Galli: Mittelalterliche Psalterillustration im Kloster St. Gallen.* Sigmaringen, 1987.

Eggers, Martin. *Das "Grossmährische Reich": Realität oder Fiktion? Eine Neuinterpretation der Quellen zur Geschichte des mittleren Donauraumes im 9. Jahrhundert.* Stuttgart, 1995.

Eggert, Wolfgang. *Das ostfränkisch-deutsche Reich in der Auffassung seiner Zeitgenossen.* Berlin, 1973.

Eibl, Elfie-Marie. "Zur Stellung Bayerns und Rheinfrankens im Reiche Arnulfs von Kärnten." *Jahrbuch für Geschichte des Feudalismus* 8 (1984): 73–113.

Eiten, Gustav. *Das Unterkönigtum im Reiche der Merovinger und Karolinger.* Heidelberg, 1907.

Elias, Norbert. *The Civilizing Process.* Trans. Edmund Jephcott. Oxford, 1994.

Engels, Donald W. *Alexander the Great and the Logistics of the Macedonian Army.* Berkeley, 1978.

Erkens, Franz-Reiner. "*Divisio legitima* und *unitas imperii*: Teilungspraxis und Einheitsstreben bei der Thronfolge im Frankenreich." *DA* 52 (1996): 423–85.

Ernst, Raimund. "Karolingische Nordostpolitik zur Zeit Ludwigs des Frommen." In *Östliches Europa: Spiegel der Geschichte. Festschrift für Manfred Hellmann zum 65. Geburtstag,* ed. Carsten Goehrke, Erwin Oberländer, and Dieter Wojtecki, 81–107. Wiesbaden, 1977.

———. *Die Nordwestslaven und das fränkische Reich.* Berlin, 1974.

Fanning, Steven. "Imperial Diplomacy between Francia and Byzantium: The Letter of Louis II to Basil I in 871." *Cithara* 34 (1994): 3–15.

Fichtenau, Heinrich. *Living in the Tenth Century.* Trans. Patrick J. Geary. Chicago, 1991.

Fleckenstein, Josef. *Die Hofkapelle der deutschen Könige,* vol. 1: *Grundlegung: Die karolingische Hofkapelle.* Stuttgart, 1959.

———. "Über die Herkunft der Welfen und ihre Anfänge in Süddeutschland." In Gerd Tellenbach, *Studien und Vorarbeiten,* 71–136.

Forke, Wilhelm. "Studien zu Ermanrich von Ellwangen." *ZWL* 28 (1969): 1–104.

Fouracre, Paul. *The Age of Charles Martel.* Harlow, U.K., 2000.

———. "Frankish Gaul to 814." In McKitterick, *New Cambridge Medieval History,* 2:85–109.

———. "The Origins of the Nobility in Francia." In Duggan, *Nobles and Nobility,* 17–24.

Fried, Johannes. "The Frankish Kingdoms, 817–911: The East and Middle Kingdoms." In McKitterick, *New Cambridge Medieval History,* 2:142–68.

———. *König Ludwig der Jüngere in seiner Zeit: Zum 1100 Todestag des Königs.* Lorsch, 1984.

———. "Ludwig der Fromme, das Papstum und die fränkische Kirche." In Godman and Collins, *Charlemagne's Heir,* 231–74.

———. *Der Weg in die Geschichte: Die Ursprünge Deutschlands bis 1024.* Berlin, 1994.

Friedmann, Bernhard. *Untersuchungen zur Geschichte des abodritischen Fürstentums bis zum Ende des 10. Jahrhundert.* Berlin, 1986.

Friesinger, Herwig. *Die Slawen in Niederösterreich.* St. Pölten, 1976.

Friesinger, Herwig, and Falko Daim, eds. *Die Bayern und Ihre Nachbarn.* Vol. 2. Vienna, 1985.

Fritze, Wolfgang. "Die Datierung des Geographus Bavarus und die Stammesverfassung der Abodriten." *ZSP* 21 (1952): 326–42.

———. "Probleme der abodritischen Stammes- und Reichsverfassung und ihrer Entwicklung von Stammesstaat zum Herrschaftsstaat." In *Siedlung und Verfassung der Slaven zwischen Elbe, Saale und Oder,* ed. H. Ludat, 141–219. Giessen, 1960.

Fuchs, Franz. "Das Grab der Königin Hemma (d. 876) zu St. Emmeram in Regensburg."
In *Regensburg und Ostbayern: Max Piendl zum Gedächtnis*, ed. F. Karg, 1–12. Kallmünz, 1992.

Fuchs, Franz, and Peter Schmid, eds. *Kaiser Arnolf: Das ostfränkische Reich am Ende des 9. Jahrhundert*. Munich, 2002.

Gamber, Klaus. "Erzbischof Methodios vor der Reichsversammlung in Regensburg des Jahres 870." In *Symposium Methodianum: Beiträge der Internationalen Tagung in Regensburg (17. bis 24. April 1985) zum Gedenken an den 1100. Todestag des hl. Method*, ed. Klaus Trost, Ekkehard Vökl, and Erwin Wedel, 111–15. Neuried, 1988.

Ganshof, François Louis. "Am Vorabend der ersten Krise der Regierung Ludwigs des Frommen: Die Jahre 828 und 829." *FS* 6 (1972): 39–54.

——. *The Carolingians and the Frankish Monarchy*. Trans. Janet Sondheimer. London, 1971.

——. *Feudalism*. Trans. Philip Grierson. 3rd ed. New York, 1964.

——. *Frankish Institutions under Charlemagne*. Trans. Bryce Lyon and Mary Lyon. Providence, 1968.

——. "Louis the Pious Reconsidered." In Ganshof, *Carolingians*, 261–72.

——. "On the Genesis and Significance of the Treaty of Verdun (843)." In Ganshof, *Carolingians*, 289–302.

——. "Some Observations on the *Ordinatio imperii* of 817." In Ganshof, *Carolingians*, 273–88.

Ganz, David. "The *Epitaphium Arsenii* and Opposition to Louis the Pious." In Godman and Collins, *Charlemagne's Heir*, 537–50.

Garipzanov, Ildar H. "The Image of Authority in Carolingian Coinage: The *Image* of a Ruler and Roman Imperial Tradition." *EME* 8 (1999): 197–218.

Geary, Patrick J. *Furta Sacra: Thefts of Relics in the Central Middle Ages*. Rev. ed. Princeton, 1990.

——. "Germanic Tradition and Royal Ideology in the Ninth Century: The *Visio Karoli Magni*." Reprinted in Geary, *Living with the Dead*, 49–76.

——. *Living with the Dead in the Middle Ages*. Ithaca, 1994.

——. *Phantoms of Remembrance: Memory and Oblivion at the End of the First Millennium*. Princeton, 1994.

Geuenich, Dieter. "Beobachtungen zu Grimald von St. Gallen, Erzkapellan und Oberkanzler Ludwigs des Deutschen." In *Litterae Medii Aevi: Festschrift für Johanne Autenrieth*, ed. Michael Borgolte and Herrad Spilling, 55–61. Sigmaringen, 1988.

——. "Ludwig der Deutsche und die Entstehung des ostfränkischen Reichs." In *Theodisca: Beiträge zur althochdeutschen und altniederdeutschen Sprache und Literatur in der Kultur des frühen Mittelalters*, ed. Wolfgang Haubrichs, Ernst Hellgart, Reiner Hildebrandt, Stephan Müller, and Klaus Ridder, 313–29. Berlin, 2000.

——. "Die volkssprachliche Überlieferung der Karolingerzeit aus der Sicht des Historikers." *DA* 39 (1983): 104–30.

Gibson, Margaret T., and Janet L. Nelson, eds. *Charles the Bald: Court and Kingdom*. 2nd ed. Aldershot, 1990.

Gockel, Michael. *Karolingische Königshöfe am Mittelrhein*. Göttingen, 1970.

Godman, Peter, and Roger Collins, eds. *Charlemagne's Heir: New Perspectives on the Reign of Louis the Pious*. Oxford, 1990.

Goetting, H. "Ebo." *LMA* 3.2, cols. 1527–29.

Goetz, Hans-Werner. *"Dux" und "Ducatus": Begriffs- und verfassungsgeschichtliche Untersuchungen zur Entstehung des sogenannten "jüngeren" Stammesherzogtums an der Wende vom neunten zum zehnten Jahrhundert*. Bochum, 1977.

——. "Regnum: Zum politischen Denken der Karolingerzeit." *Zeitschrift der Savigny-Stiftung für Rechtsgeschichte, germanische Abteilung* 104 (1987): 110–90.

Gojda, Martin. *The Ancient Slavs: Settlement and Society*. Edinburgh, 1991.

Goldberg, Eric J. "Creating a Medieval Kingdom: Carolingian Kingship, Court Culture, and Aristocratic Society under Louis of East Francia (840–876)." Ph.D. diss., University of Virginia, 1998.

——. "Ludwig der Deutsche und Mähren: Eine Studie zu karolingischen Grenzkriegen im Osten." In Hartmann, *Ludwig der Deutsche und seine Zeit*, 67–94.

——. "'More Devoted to the Equipment of Battle Than the Splendor of Banquets': Frontier Kingship, Martial Ritual, and Early Knighthood at the Court of Louis the German." *Viator* 30 (1999): 41–78.

——. "Popular Revolt, Dynastic Politics, and Aristocratic Factionalism in the Early Middle Ages: The Saxon *Stellinga* Reconsidered." *Speculum* 70 (1995): 467–501.

——. "*Regina nitens sanctissima Hemma*: Queen Emma (827–876), Bishop Witgar of Augsburg, and the Witgar-Belt." In *Representations of Power in Medieval Germany, 800–1500*, ed. Simon MacLean and Björn Weiler. Turnhout, 2005.

Graus, František, and Herbert Ludat, eds. *Siedlung und Verfassung Böhmens in der Frühzeit.* Wiesbaden, 1967.

Grossmähren und die christliche Mission bei den Slawen: Ausstellung der Tschechoslowakischen Akademie der Wissenschaften, 8 März bis 8 Mai 1966. Ed. Institut für Österreichkunde. Vienna, 1966).

Halsall, Guy, ed. *Violence and Society in the Early Medieval West.* Woodbridge, U.K., 1998.

——. *Warfare and Society in the Barbarian West, 450–900.* London, 2003.

Hartmann, Wilfried. *Das Konzil von Worms 868: Überlieferung und Bedeutung.* Göttingen, 1977.

——. *Ludwig der Deutsche.* Darmstadt, 2002.

——. "Ludwig der Deutsche—Portrait eines wenig bekannten Königs." In Hartmann, *Ludwig der Deutsche und seine Zeit*, 1–26.

——, ed. *Ludwig der Deutsche und seine Zeit.* Darmstadt, 2004.

——. *Die Synoden der Karolingerzeit in Frankenreich und Italien.* Paderborn, 1989.

Hasty, Will, and James Hardin, eds. *Dictionary of Literary Biography*, vol. 148: *German Writers and Works of the Early Middle Ages: 800–1170.* Detroit, 1995.

Haubrichs, Wolfgang. *Geschichte der deutschen Literatur von den Anfängen bis zum Beginn der Neuzeit*, vol. 1: *Von den Anfängen zum hohen Mittelalter*, pt. 1: *Die Anfänge: Versuche volksspachiger Schriftlichkeit im frühen Mittelalter (ca. 700–1050/60).* Frankfurt, 1988.

——. "Ludwig der Deutsche und die volkssprachige Literatur." In Hartmann, *Ludwig der Deutsche und seine Zeit*, 214–25.

——. "Die Praefatio des Heliand: Ein Zeugnis der Religions- und Bildungspolitik Ludwigs des Deutschen." *JVNS* 89 (1966): 7–32.

Haywood, John. *The Penguin Historical Atlas of the Vikings.* London, 1995.

Heather, Peter G. "Frankish Imperialism and Slavic Society." In *The Origins of Central Europe*, ed. Przemyslaw Urbańczyk, 171–90. Warsaw, 1997.

Hen, Yitzhak. "The Annals of Metz and the Merovingian Past." In Hen and Innes, *Uses of the Past*, 175–90.

Hen, Yitzhak, and Matthew Innes, eds. *The Uses of the Past in the Early Middle Ages.* Cambridge, 2000.

Herren, Michael W. The *De imagine Tetrici* of Walahfrid Strabo: Edition and Translation." *JML* 1 (1991): 118–39.

Herrmann, Erwin. *Slawisch-germanische Beziehungen im südostdeutschen Raum von der Spätantike bis zum Ungarnsturm. Ein Quellenbuch mit Erläuterungen.* Munich, 1965.

Herrmann, Joachim. "Herausbildung und Dynamik der germanisch-slawischen Siedlungsgrenze im Mitteleuropa." In Wolfram and Schwarcz, *Bayern und ihre Nachbarn*, 1:269–80.

Hlawitschka, Eduard. *Lotharingien und das Reich an der Schwelle der deutschen Geschichte.* Stuttgart, 1968.

——. "Zur Herkunft der Liudolfinger und zu einigen Corveyer Geschichtsquellen." *RV* 38 (1974): 92–165.

Hyam, Jane. "Ermentrude and Richildis." In Gibson and Nelson, *Charles the Bald*, 161–62.

Innes, Matthew. "Kings, Monks and Patrons: Political Identities and the Abbey of Lorsch." In Le Jan, *La Royauté*, 301–24.

——. "'A Place of Discipline': Carolingian Courts and Aristocratic Youth." In Cubitt, *Court Culture in the Early Middle Ages*, 59–76.

——. *State and Society in the Early Middle Ages: The Middle Rhine Valley, 400–1000*. Cambridge, 2000.

Jackman, Donald C. *The Konradiner: A Study in Genealogical Methodology*. Veröffentlichungen des Max-Planck-Instituts für Europäische Rechtsgeschichte, Sonderhefte 47. Frankfurt, 1990.

Jacobsen, Werner. "Die Lorscher Torhalle: Zum Probleme ihrer Datierung und Deutung." *Jahrbuch des Zentralinstituts für Kunstgeschichte* 1 (1985): 9–41.

Jarnut, Jörg. "Die frühmittelalterliche Jagd unter rechts- und sozialgeschichtlichen Aspekten." *SS Spoleto* 31 (1985): 765–808.

Jones, A. H. M. *The Later Roman Empire, 284–602*. 2 vols. Baltimore, 1992.

Kämpf, Hellmut, ed. *Die Entstehung des deutschen Reichs*. Darmstadt, 1976.

Kantorowicz, Ernst. *Laudes Regiae: A Study in Liturgical Acclamations and Medieval Ruler Worship*. Berkeley, 1946.

Kasten, Brigitte. *Königssöhne und Königsherrschaft: Untersuchungen zur Teilhabe am Reich in der Merowinger- und Karolingerzeit*. MGH *Schriften* 44. Hanover, 1997.

Kehr, Paul. "Die Kanzlei Ludwigs des Deutschen." *APAW* (1932): 1–32.

——. "Die Schreiber und Diktatoren der Diplome Ludwigs des Deutschen." *NA* 50 (1935): 1–105.

Keller, Hagen. "Die Ottonen und Karl der Grosse." *FS* 43 (2000): 112–31.

——. "Zu den Siegeln der Karolinger und Ottonen: Urkunden als 'Hoheitszeichen' in der Kommunikation des Königs mit seinen Getreuen." *FS* 32 (1998): 400–441.

——. "Zum Sturz Karls III." *DA* 22 (1966): 333–84.

King, P. D. "The Barbarian Kingdoms." In Burns, *Cambridge History of Political Thought*, 145–46.

Koller, Heinrich. "König Ludwig der Deutsche und die Slawenmission." In *Historia docet: Sborník prací k poctě šedesátých narozenin prof. PhDr. Ivana Hlaváčka*, ed. Miloslav Polívka and Michal Svatoš, 167–92. Prague, 1992.

Konecny, Silvia. "Die Frauen des karolingischen Königshauses." Ph.D. diss., University of Vienna, 1976.

Kornbluth, Genevra. *Engraved Gems of the Carolingian Empire*. University Park, PA, 1995.

Kosto, Adam J. "Hostages in the Carolingian World (714–840)." *EME* 11 (2002): 123–47.

Kottje, Raymund. "König Ludwig der Deutsche und die Fastenzeit." In *Mysterium der Gnade: Festschrift für Johann Auer*, ed. Heribert Rossmann and Joseph Ratzinger, 307–11. Regensburg, 1975.

Kottje, Raymund, and Harald Zimmermann, eds. *Hrabanus Maurus: Lehrer, Abt und Bischof*. Wiesbaden, 1982.

Krüger, Astrid. "*Sancte Nazari ora pro nobis*—Ludwig der Deutsche und der Lorscher Rotulus." In Hartmann, *Ludwig der Deutsche und seine Zeit*, 184–202.

Krüger, Karl Heinrich. "Herrschaftsnachfolge als Vater-Sohn-Konflikt." *FS* 36 (2002): 225–40.

Krüger, Sabine. *Studien zur sächsischen Grafschaftsverfassung im 9. Jahrhundert*. Göttingen, 1950.

Lehmann, Paul. *Mittelalterliche Bibliothekskataloge Deutschlands und der Schweiz*. Vol. 1: *Die Bistümer Konstanz und Chur*. Munich, 1918.

Le Jan, Régine. *Famille et pouvoir dans le mond Franc, VIIIe–Xe siècles*. Paris, 1995.

——. "Frankish Giving of Arms and Rituals of Power: Continuity and Change in the Carolingian Period." In Theuws and Nelson, *Rituals of Power*, 281–309.

——, ed. *La Royauté et les élites dans l'Europe carolingienne*. Lille, 1998.

Selected Bibliography

Leonhardt, Ing. "Die Alte Kapelle in Regensburg und die karolingische Pfalzanlage." *Zeitschrift für Bauwesen* 75 (1925): 83–110.

Leyser, Karl J. *Communications and Power in Medieval Europe*, vol. 1: *The Carolingian and Ottonian Centuries*. Ed. Timothy Reuter. London, 1994.

——. "Early Medieval Canon Law and the Beginnings of Knighthood." Reprinted in Leyser, *Communications*, 1: 51–71.

——. "Early Medieval Warfare." Reprinted in Leyser, *Communications*, 1:29–50.

——. "The German Aristocracy from the Ninth Century to the Early Twelfth Century." *Past and Present* 41 (1968): 25–53.

——. "Henry I and the Beginning of the Saxon Empire." Reprinted in *Medieval Germany and Its Neighbours, 900–1250*, by K. Leyser, 11–42. London, 1982.

——. "Ritual, Ceremony and Gesture: Ottonian Germany." Reprinted in Leyser, *Communications*, 1:189–214.

——. *Rule and Conflict in an Early Medieval Society: Ottonian Saxony*. London, 1979.

——. "*Theophanu Divina Gratia Imperatrix Augusta*: Western and Eastern Emperorship in the Later Tenth Century." Reprinted in Leyser, *Communications*, 1:143–64.

——. "Three Historians." Reprinted in Leyser, *Communications*, 1:19–28.

Lot, Ferdinand. "Note sur le sénéchal Alard." In Lot, *Recueil des travaux historiques*, 2:591–602.

——. *Recueil des travaux historiques*. 3 vols. Geneva, 1968–73.

Löwe, Heinz. "Ermanrich von Passau, Gegner des Methodius: Versuch eines Persönlichkeitsbildes." *MGSL* 126 (1986): 221–41.

——. "Gozbald von Niederaltaich und Papst Gregor IV." In *Festschrift für Bernhard Bischoff*, ed. J. Autenrieth and F. Brunhölzl, 164–77. Stuttgart, 1971.

Luft, Wilhelm. "Die Abfassungszeit von Otfrids Evangelienbuch." *ZDA* 40 (1896): 246–53.

MacLean, Simon. "The Carolingian Response to the Revolt of Boso, 879–887." *EME* 10 (2001): 21–48.

——. *Kingship and Politics in the Late Ninth Century: Charles the Fat and the End of the Carolingian Empire*. Cambridge, 2003.

——. "Queenship, Nunneries and Royal Widowhood in Carolingian Europe." *Past and Present* 178 (2003): 3–38.

——. "Ritual, Misunderstanding, and the Contest for Meaning: The Example of the Disrupted Royal Assembly at Frankfurt (873)." In *Representations of Power in Medieval Germany, 800–1500*, ed. S. MacLean and Björn Weiler. Turnhout, 2005.

Mayer, Theodor. "Konstanz und St.-Gallen in der Frühzeit." *Schweizerische Zeitschrift für Geschichte* 2.4 (1952): 473–524.

——, ed. *Der Vertrag von Verdun, 843*. Leipzig, 1943.

McCormick, Michael. *Eternal Victory: Triumphal Rulership in Late Antiquity, Byzantium and the Early Medieval West*. Cambridge, 1986.

——. "The Liturgy of War in the Early Middle Ages: Crises, Litanies, and Carolingian Monarchy," *Viator* 15 (1984): 1–23.

——. *Origins of the European Economy: Communications and Commerce, AD 300–900*. Cambridge, 2001.

McKitterick, Rosamond, ed. *Carolingian Culture: Emulation and Innovation*. Cambridge, 1994.

——. *The Carolingians and the Written Word*. Cambridge, 1989.

——, ed. *The Early Middle Ages: Europe 400–1000*. Oxford, 2001.

——. *The Frankish Church and the Carolingian Reforms*. London, 1977.

——. *The Frankish Kingdoms under the Carolingians, 751–987*. London, 1983.

——. *History and Memory in the Carolingian World*. Cambridge, 2003.

——, ed. *New Cambridge Medieval History*, vol. 2: *C. 700–c. 900*. Cambridge, 1995.

——. "Political Ideology in Carolingian Historiography." In Hen and Innes, *Uses of the Past*, 162–74.

——, ed. *The Uses of Literacy in Early Medieval Europe*. Cambridge, 1990.

Mitterauer, Michael. *Karolingische Markgrafen im Südosten: Fränkische Reichsaristokratie und bayerischer Stammesadel im österreichischen Raum*. Vienna, 1963.

Morrison, Karl F. *Carolingian Coinage*. New York, 1967.

Müller-Mertens, Eckhard. *Die Reichsstruktur im Spiegel der Herrschaftspraxis Ottos des Grossen*. Berlin, 1980.

Murray, Alexander Callander, ed. *After Rome's Fall: Narrators and Sources of Early Medieval History*. Toronto, 1998.

Nelson, Janet L. "The *Annals of St.-Bertin*." In Gibson and Nelson, *Charles the Bald*, 23–40.

——. "Carolingian Royal Funerals." In Theuws and Nelson, *Rituals of Power*, 131–84.

——. *Charles the Bald*. London, 1992.

——. "The Frankish Empire." In *The Oxford Illustrated History of the Vikings*, ed. Peter Sawyer, 19–47. Oxford, 1997.

——. *The Frankish World, 750–900*. London, 1996.

——. "Hincmar of Reims on King-Making: The Evidence of the *Annals of St.-Bertin*, 861–882." In *Coronations: Medieval and Early Modern Monarchic Ritual*, ed. János Bak, 16–34. Berkeley, 1990.

——. "Kingship and Empire." In Burns, *Cambridge History of Political Thought*, 211–51.

——. "Kingship and Empire in the Carolingian World." In McKitterick, *Carolingian Culture*, 52–87.

——. "Kingship and Royal Government." In McKitterick, *New Cambridge Medieval History*, 2:383–430.

——. "The Last Years of Louis the Pious." In Godman and Collins, *Charlemagne's Heir*, 147–59.

——. "Literacy in Carolingian Government." Reprinted in Nelson, *Frankish World*, 2–36.

——. "The Lord's Anointed and the People's Choice: Carolingian Royal Ritual." Reprinted in Nelson, *Frankish World*, 99–131.

——. "Making a Difference in Eighth-Century Politics: The Daughters of Desiderius," In Murray, *After Rome's Fall*, 171–90.

——. "Monks, Secular Men and Masculinity, c. 900." In *Masculinity in Medieval Europe*, ed. D. M. Hadley, 121–42. London, 1999.

——. "Ninth-Century Knighthood: The Evidence of Nithard." Reprinted in Nelson, *Frankish World*, 75–87.

——. *Politics and Ritual in Early Medieval Europe*. London, 1986.

——. "Public *Histories* and Private History in the Work of Nithard." Reprinted in Nelson, *Politics and Ritual*, 195–237.

——. "A Tale of Two Princes: Politics, Text, and Ideology in a Carolingian Annal." *SMRH* 10 (1988): 105–41.

——. "Vikings and Others." *TRHS*, 6th ser., 13 (2003): 1–28.

——. "Violence in the Carolingian World and the Ritualization of Ninth-Century Warfare." In Halsall, *Violence and Society*, 90–107.

Noble, Thomas F. X. "Louis the Pious and His Piety Reconsidered." *Revue Belge* 58 (1980): 297–316.

——. "The Monastic Ideal as a Model for Empire: The Case of Louis the Pious." *Revue Bénédictine* 86 (1976): 235–50.

——. "The Revolt of King Bernard of Italy in 817: Its Causes and Consequences." *Studi Medievali* 15 (1974): 315–26.

Odegaard, Charles E. "Carolingian Oaths of Fidelity." *Speculum* 16 (1941): 284–96.

——. "The Concept of Royal Power in Carolingian Oaths of Fidelity." *Speculum* 20 (1945): 279–89.

——. "The Empress Engelberga." *Speculum* 26 (1951): 77–103.

Oesterle, Hans J. "Die sogenannte Kopfoperation Karls III, 887." *AK* 61 (1979): 445–51.

Oexle, Otto Gerhard. "Bischof Ebroin von Poitiers und seine Verwandten." *FS* 3 (1969): 138–210.

Ostrogorsky, George. *History of the Byzantine State*. Trans. Joan Hussey. 2nd English ed. New Brunswick, NJ, 1969.

Pirchegger, Hans. "Karantanien und Unterpannonien zur Karolingerzeit." *MÖIG* 33 (1912): 272–319.

Pohl, Walter. *Die Awarenkriege Karls des Grossen, 788–803*. Vienna, 1988.

Postan, M. M., and Edward Miller, eds. *The Cambridge Economic History of Europe*. 2nd ed. Vol. 2. Cambridge, 1987.

Poulík, Josef. "The Latest Archaeological Discoveries from the Period of the Great Moravian Empire." *Historica* 1 (1959): 5–70.

——. "Mikulčice: Capital of the Lords of Great Moravia." In *Recent Archaeological Excavations in Europe*, ed. Rupert Bruce-Mitford, 1–31. London, 1975.

Prinz, Friedrich. *Klerus und Krieg im früheren Mittelalter*. Stuttgart, 1971.

Prinz, Josef. "Der Feldzug Karls des Kahlen an dem Rhein im September 876." *DA* 33 (1977): 543–45.

Reuter, Timothy. "Assembly Politics in Western Europe from the Eighth Century to the Twelfth." In *The Medieval World*, ed. Peter Linehan and Janet L. Nelson, 432–50. London, 2001.

——. "The End of Carolingian Military Expansion." In Godman and Collins, *Charlemagne's Heir*, 391–405.

——. *Germany in the Early Middle Ages, c. 800–1056*. London, 1991.

——. "The 'Imperial Church System' of the Ottonian and Salian Rulers: A Reconsideration." *JEH* 32 (1982): 347–74.

——. "The Medieval German *Sonderweg*? The Empire and Its Rulers in the High Middle Ages." In *Kings and Kingship in Medieval Europe*, ed. Anne Duggan, 179–211. London, 1993.

——, ed. and trans. *The Medieval Nobility: Studies on the Ruling Classes of France and Germany from the Sixth to the Twelfth Century*. Amsterdam, 1978.

——, ed. *New Cambridge Medieval History*, vol. 3: *C. 900–c. 1024*. Cambridge, 1999.

——. "Plunder and Tribute in the Carolingian Empire." *TRHS*, 5th ser. (1985): 75–94.

——. "*Regemque, quem in Francia pene perdidit, in patria magnifice recepit*: Ottonian Ruler Representation in Synchronic and Diachronic Comparison." In *Herrschaftsrepräsentation im Ottonischen Sachsen*, ed. Gerd Althoff and Ernst Schubert, 363–80. Sigmaringen, 1998.

Reynolds, L. D., ed. *Texts and Transmission: A Survey of the Latin Classics*. Oxford, 1983.

Reynolds, Susan. *Fiefs and Vassals: The Medieval Evidence Reinterpreted*. Oxford, 1994.

——. "The Historiography of the Medieval State." In Bentley, *Companion to Historiography*, 117–38.

——. *Kingdoms and Communities in Western Europe, 900–1300*. 2nd ed. Oxford, 1997.

Riché, Pierre. *The Carolingians: A Family Who Forged Europe*. Trans. Michael Idomir Allen. Philadelphia, 1983.

——. *Daily Life in the World of Charlemagne*. Trans. Jo Ann McNamara. Philadelphia, 1988.

Richter, Michael. "Die politische Orientierung Mährens zur Zeit von Konstantin und Methodius." In Wolfram and Schwarcz, *Die Bayern und ihre Nachbarn*, 1:281–92.

Roper Pearson, Kathy Lynne. *Conflicting Loyalties in Early Medieval Bavaria: A View of Socio-Political Interaction, 680–900*. Aldershot, 1999.

Rosenwein, Barbara H., ed. *Anger's Past: The Social Uses of an Emotion in the Middle Ages*. Ithaca, 1998.

——. *Negotiating Space: Power, Restraint, and Privileges of Immunity in Early Medieval Europe*. Ithaca, 1999.

Schieffer, Rudolf. *Die Karolinger*. 2nd ed. Stuttgart, 1997.

——. "Liutbert." *NDB* 14, 722–23.

——. "Väter und Söhne im Karolingerhause." In *Beiträge zur Geschichte des Regnum Francorum*, 149–64. Beihefte der Francia 22. Paris, 1990.

Schlosser, Horst Dieter. "Zu Datierung von Otfrieds 'Evangelienbuch.'" *ZDA* 125 (1996): 386–91.

Schmid, Karl. "Ein karolingischer Königseintrag im Gedenkbuch von Remiremont." *FS* 2 (1968): 96–134.

——. "Königtum, Adel und Klöster zwischen Bodensee und Schwarzwald." In Tellenbach, *Studien und Vorarbeiten*, 225–334.

Schmid, Peter. *Regensburg: Stadt der Könige und Herzöge im Mittelalter*. Kallmünz, 1977.

Schmidt, Roderich. *Königsumritt und Huldigung in ottonisch-salischer Zeit*. Constance, 1961.

Schmitt, Ursula. *Villa Regalis Ulm und Kloster Reichenau: Untersuchungen zur Pfalzfunktion des Reichsklostergutes in Alemannien (9.–12. Jahrhundert)*. Veröffentlichungen des Max-Planck-Instituts für Geschichte 42. Göttingen, 1974.

Schneidmüller, Bernd. *Die Welfen: Herrschaft und Erinnerung (819–1252)*. Stuttgart, 2000.

Schramm, Percy Ernst. *Die deutschen Kaiser und Könige in Bildern ihrer Zeit, 751–1190*. Munich, 1983.

——. *Kaiser, Könige und Päpste: Gesammelte Aufsätze zur Geschichte des Mittelalters*. 4 vols. Stuttgart, 1968–71.

Schramm, Percy Ernst, and Florentine Mütherich. *Denkmale der deutschen Könige und Kaiser*. Vol. 1. Munich, 1981.

Schreibmüller, Hermann. "Audulf: Der frühest bezeugte Graf im Taubergau." *MJGK* 3 (1951): 53–69.

Schütz, Joseph. "Die Reichssynode zu Regensburg (870) und Methods Verbannung nach Schwaben." *Südost-Forschungen* 33 (1974): 1–14.

Schwarz, Wilhelm. "Ermanrich von Ellwangen." *ZWL* 15 (1956): 279–81.

——. "Die Schriften Ermanrichs von Ellwangen." *ZWL* 12 (1953): 181–89.

Schwarzmaier, Hansmartin. "Die Reginswindis-Tradition von Lauffen: Königliche Politik und adelige Herrschaft am mittleren Neckar." *ZGO* 131 (1983): 163–98.

Screen, Elina. "The Importance of Being Emperor: Lothar I and the Frankish Civil War, 840–843." *EME* 12 (2003): 25–51.

Semmler, Josef. "*Renovatio Regni Francorum*: Die Herrschaft Ludwigs des Frommen im Frankenreich 814–829/830." In Godman and Collins, *Charlemagne's Heir*, 125–45.

Shepard, Jonathan. "Byzantine Relations with the Outside World in the Ninth Century: An Overview." In *Byzantium in the Ninth Century: Dead or Alive?* ed. Leslie Brubaker, 167–80. Aldershot, 1998.

——. "Slavs and Bulgars." In McKitterick, *New Cambridge Medieval History*, 2:228–48.

Sickel, Theodor. "Beiträge zur Diplomatik, I: Die Urkunden Ludwig's des Deutschen bis zum Jahre 859." *SKAW* 36.3 (1861): 329–402.

——. "Beiträge zur Diplomatik, II: Die Urkunden Ludwig's des Deutschen in den Jahren 859–876." *SKAW* 39.1 (1862): 105–77.

Slàma, Jiří. "Civitas Wiztrachi ducis." *Historische Geographie: Beiträge zur Problematik der mittelalterlichen Siedlung und der Wege* 11 (1973): 3–30.

Smith, Julia M. H. "*Fines imperii*: The Marches." In McKitterick, *New Cambridge Medieval History*, 2:169–89.

——. *Province and Empire*. Cambridge, 1992.

——. "Religion and Lay Society." In McKitterick, *New Cambridge Medieval History*, 2:654–78.

Sós, Agnes. *Die slawische Bevölkerung Westungarns im 9. Jahrhundert*. Münchener Beiträge zur Vor- und Frühgeschichte 22. Munich, 1973.

Spindler, Max, ed. *Handbuch der bayerischen Geschichte*. 2nd ed. Munich, 1981.

Stafford, Pauline. *Queens, Concubines, and Dowagers: The King's Wife in the Early Middle Ages*. Athens, GA, 1983.

Staiti, Chiara. "Das Evangelienbuch Otfrids von Weissenburg und Ludwig der Deutsche." In Hartmann, *Ludwig der Deutsche und seine Zeit*, 233–54.

Staňa, Čeněk. "Mährische Burgwälle im 9. Jahrhundert." In Friesinger and Daim, *Bayern und Ihre Nachbarn*, 2:158–208.

Steiner, Hannes. "Buchproduktion und Bibliothekszuwachs im Kloster St. Gallen unter den Äbten Grimald und Hartmut." In Hartmann, *Ludwig der Deutsche*, 161–83.

Štěpánek, Miroslav. "Die Entwicklung der Burgwälle in Böhmen vom 8. bis 12. Jahrhundert." In Graus and Ludat, *Siedlung und Verfassung Böhmens*, 49–69.

Stepanov, Tsvetelin. "The Bulgar Title ΚΑΝΑΣΥΒΙΓΙ: Reconstructing the Notions of Divine Kingship in Bulgaria, AD 822–836." *EME* 10 (2001): 1–19.

Štih, Peter. "Pribina: Slawischer Fürst oder fränkischer Graf?" In *Ethnogenese und Überlieferung: Angewandte Methoden der Frühmittelalterforschung*, ed. Karl Brunner and Brigitte Merta, 209–22. Vienna, 1994.

Störmer, Wilhelm. *Früher Adel: Studien zur politischen Führungsschicht im fränkisch-deutschen Reich vom 8. bis 11. Jahrhundert.* 2 vols. Stuttgart, 1975.

———. "Zum Problem der Slawenmission des Bistums Freising im 9. Jahrhundert." *MGSL* 126 (1986): 207–20.

Swarzenski, Georg. *Die Regensburger Buchmalerei des X und XI Jahrhunderts.* Leipzig, 1901.

Tellenbach, Gerd. *Königtum und Stämme in der Werdezeit des Deutschen Reiches.* Weimar, 1939.

———. *Studien und Vorarbeiten zur Geschichte des grossfränkischen und frühdeutschen Adels.* Forschungen zur oberrheinischen Landesgeschichte 6. Freiburg, 1957.

Theuws, Frans, and Janet L. Nelson, eds. *Rituals of Power from Late Antiquity to the Early Middle Ages.* Leiden, 2000.

Tischler, Matthias M. *Einharts "Vita Karoli": Studien zur Entstehung, Überlieferung und Rezeption.* 2 vols. Hanover, 2001.

Tremp, Ernst. "Ludwig der Deutsche und das Kloster St. Gallen." In Hartmann, *Ludwig der Deutsche und seine Zeit*, 142–45.

———. *Studien zu den "Gesta Hludowici imperatoris" des Trierer Chorbischofs Thegan.* MGH Schriften 32. Hanover, 1988.

Třeštík, Dušan. "The Baptism of the Czech Princes in 845 and the Christianization of the Slavs." In *Historica: Historical Sciences in the Czech Republic*, 7–59. Prague, 1995.

Vajay, Szabolcs de. *Der Eintritt des ungarischen Stämmebundes in die europäische Geschichte (862–933).* Mainz, 1968.

Verhulst, Adriaan. *The Carolingian Economy.* Cambridge, 2002.

———. "Economic Organization." In McKitterick, *New Cambridge Medieval History*, 2:481–509.

Waitz, Georg. *Ueber die Gründung des deutschen Reichs durch den Vertrag von Verdun.* Kiel, 1843.

Wallace-Hadrill, J. M. Michael. *The Frankish Church.* Oxford, 1983.

Ward, Elizabeth. "Agobard of Lyons and Paschasius Radbertus as Critics of the Empress Judith." In *Women in the Church*, ed. W. J. Sheils and Diana Woods, 15–25. Oxford, 1990.

———. "Caesar's Wife: The Career of Empress Judith, 819–829." In Godman and Collins, *Charlemagne's Heir*, 205–27.

Wattenbach, Wilhelm, Wilhelm Levison, and Heinz Löwe, eds. *Deutschlands Geschichtsquellen im Mittelalter*, vol. 6: *Die Karolinger vom Vertrag von Verdun bis zum Herrschaftsantritt der Herrscher aus dem sächsischen Hause: Das ostfränkische Reich.* Weimar, 1990.

Weber, Heinrich. "Die Reichsversammlungen im ostfränkischen Reich." Ph.D. diss., University of Würzburg, 1962.

Wellmer, Hansjörg. *Persöhnliches Memento im deutschen Mittelalter.* Stuttgart, 1973.

Wendehorst, Alfred. *Das Bistum Würzburg.* Germania Sacra, n. s. Berlin, 1962.

Werner, Karl Ferdinand. "Heeresorganisation und Kriegsführung im deutschen Königreich des 10. und 11. Jahrhunderts." *SS Spoleto* 15 (1968): 813–32.

——. "*Hludovicus Augustus*: Gouverner l'empire chrétien—Idées et réalités." In Godman and Collins, *Charlemagne's Heir*, 3–123.

——. "Important Noble Families in the Kingdom of Charlemagne—A Prosopographical Study of the Relationship between King and Nobility in the Early Middle Ages." In Reuter, *Medieval Nobility*, 137–202.

——. "Missus-marchio-comes: Entre l'administration centrale et l'administration locale de l'empire carolingien." In *Histoire comparée de l'administration (IVe–XVIIIe siècle)*, ed. Werner Paravicini and Karl Ferdinand Werner, 191–239. Beihefte der Francia 9. Munich, 1980.

——. "Die Nachkommen Karls des Grossen bis um das Jahr 1000 (1–8 Generation)." In *Karl der Grosse*, vol. 4: *Das Nachleben*, ed. Wolfgang Braunfels and Percy Ernst Schramm, 403–84. Düsseldorf, 1967.

——. "Untersuchungen zur Frühzeit des französischen Fürstentums." *Die Welt als Geschichte* 3–4 (1959): 146–93.

Wickham, Chris. "The Fall of Rome Will Not Take Place." In *Debating the Middle Ages: Issues and Readings*, ed. Lester K. Little and Barbara H. Rosenwein, 45–57. Oxford, 1998.

——. "Rural Society in Carolingian Europe." In McKitterick, *New Cambridge Medieval History*, 2:510–37.

Wolfram, Herwig. *Die Geburt Mitteleuropas*. Vienna, 1987.

——. *Grenzen und Räume: Geschichte Österreichs vor seiner Entstehung*. Vienna, 1995.

——. "Lateinische Herrschertitel im neunten und zehnten Jahrhundert." In *Intitulatio II: Lateinische Herrscher- und Fürstentitel im neunten und zehnten Jahrhundert*, ed. Herwig Wolfram, 19–178. *MIÖG* Ergänzungsband 24. Vienna, 1973.

——. *Salzburg, Bayern, Österreich: Die "Conversio Bagoariorum et Carantanorum" und die Quellen ihrer Zeit*. Vienna, 1995.

Wolfram, Herwig, and Andreas Schwarcz, eds. *Die Bayern und ihre Nachbarn*. Vol. 1. Vienna, 1985.

Wood, Ian. *The Merovingian Kingdoms, 450–751*. London, 1994.

Zatschek, Heinz. "Die Erwähnungen Ludwigs des Deutschen als Imperator," *DA* 6 (1943): 374–78.

——. "Ludwig der Deutsche." In Mayer, *Vertrag von Verdun*, 31–65.

——. "Die Reichsteilungen unter Kaiser Ludwig dem Frommen." *MIÖG* 49 (1935): 186–224.

——. *Wie das erste Reich der Deutschen entstand: Staatsführung, Reichsgut und Ostsiedlung im Zeitalter der Karolinger*. Prague, 1940.

Zotz, Thomas. *Der Breisgau und das alemannische Herzogtum*. Sigmaringen, 1974.

——. "Das Elsass—Ein Teil des Zwischenreichs?" In *Lotharingia—Eine europäische Kernlandschaft um as Jahr 1000*, ed. Hans-Walter Herrmann and Reinhard Schneider, 49–70. Saarbrücken, 1995.

——. "Ludwig der Deutsche und seine Pfalzen: Königliche Herrschaftspraxis in der Formierungsphase des Ostfränkischen Reichs." In Hartmann, *Ludwig der Deutsche und seine Zeit*, 27–46.

INDEX

Note: Page numbers in italics refer to illustrations. *LG* refers to Louis the German, *LP* refers to Louis the Pious, and *CB* refers to Charles the Bald.

Cobbo, Count, 97–98, 134, 134n67
Codex Vindobonensis 2687, 184
coinage, 201, 204–6
colloquia, 227, 227nn199–200
Cologne, 115n125, 296, 299, 299n144, 318n46
confraternity books (*libri memoriales*), 66
coniurationes (sworn associations), 65, 105–6, 208
Conrad I, king of east Francia (r. 911–18), 346
Conrad the Elder, 91, 92n27, 239n23, 256, 256n99, 261n117
Conrad the Younger, 256–57, 256n101
conspiracies/rebellions (861–70), 264–79; Byzantine-Moravian alliance, 263–64, 270–72, 280–83; Carloman's independence/alliances, 264–65, 274; Carloman's rebellion (857), 265–66n6, 265–70; Carolingians, 266–67; Hungarian attack on eastern borders, 269; LG's and Boris's campaign against Rastislav (864), 271–74, 272n37, 273; LG's campaign against Carloman, 269–70; LG's division/inheritance plan of 865, 275–77; and LG's grants to eastern supporters, 267–68; Louis the Younger's rebellion (866), 277–78n37, 277–79, 279n60; punishment for rebellion, 208, 279
Constantine, Saint (Byzantine missionary), 15n40, 270–71, 280–82
Constantinople, 271, 283. *See also* Byzantium
Conversion of the Bavarians and the Carantanians, 16, 84–85, 142n99, 300–301, 303
coronations/coronation blessings (*ordines*), 52–54, *53*, 308–9, 308n12
Corvey monastery, 97–98, 98n59, 155n30, 166
counties/counts, 215–17, 216nn146–47
counts of the palace, 208–9, 209n114
courtly behavior, 194

Deeds of Charlemagne (Notker), 1–2, 16, 26, 26nn6–7, 341–42
Deeds of Emperor Louis (Thegan), 15, 55, 76–77, 82, 177, 188
Denmark, 133–37, 134n65, 134n67, 134n69, 135n74
Devín, 273, *273*
dignity: of nobles, 45–46, 141, 143–44; and piety, 46–47; political importance of, 45–46
diplomas/grants, 17–18, 17nn48–49, 62; format of, 108–9, 108n107, 213, 213n139, *214*, *216*; at Frankfurt, 224; legal force of, 213–14, *216*; by LG, 17, 62–63, 62n23, 72,

76–78, 97–98, 98n59, 213, 213n139, *214*; from LG, 62–63, 62n23; to LG's eastern supporters, 267–68; from Lothar I, 17n49, 50–51, 51n103, 155n30; precarial, 101, 101n74; at Regensburg, 224; Roding diploma, 141, 141n95; regarding St.-Gall, 212–13; for Strasbourg, 249, 249n68
dispute settlement, 229, 229n208
Division of Kingdoms plan (806), 28–29
Division of the Kingdom (831), 61–63, 69–70
Dominic, 141, 141n96
Dorestad, 204–5
Drang nach Osten (drive to the east), 233
Drogo, bishop of Metz, 71, 93–94, 107, 148, 151
dukes, administrative role of, 217
Dümmler, Ernst, 8, 13, 60n12, 315n34, 324n70

Earlier Annals of Metz, 39
eastern Europe, contest for, 279–303; LG's and Boris's alliance against Moravia/Byzantium, 279–80; LG's and Carloman's Moravian campaigns (860s), 279–85, 284n79, 285n85; Roman vs. Carolingian claims, 283, 283n78, 318–19
east Frankish Church: abbots, deposing of, 218; bishops/abbots, elections/appointments/inspection of, 217–19, 218n154; bishops/abbots, elections/appointments of, 218n151; bishops/abbots, governmental duties of, 219–20, 219n160; and ecclesiastical music, 167–68; episcopal dynasties, 218; and government, 217–20, 218n151, 218n154, 219n60, 220n163; immunity/protection of bishoprics/monasteries, 219–20, 219n160 (*see also under* St.-Gall monastery); Latin vs. vernacular used by, 179–81; lay investiture, 218; LG's reconciliation with, 159–63; literary output in (*see* scholarship/literary production); negligence/abuses of, 160; on predestination, 163n162; reforms in, 160, *161*, 162, 175–76, 185; restitution of properties of, 162–63; role in raising armies, 123–124n18; and Scripture translated into the vernacular, 179–85, 210; in the west vs. the east, 165–66, 166n72. *See also* Saxon Church
Ebbo, bishop of Hildesheim, 177, 177nn135–36, 218n151
Eberhard, count of Friuli, 92n27, 213, 213n139, *214*
Ecbertiners, 54, 59, 97–98, 127, 254n92
economy/royal resources, 201–6, 230

offices/honors, 4, 10–11, 87, 208, 221–22, 222n175, 268–69. *See also under* Frankish nobility
Old Saxon, 177
On the Military Sciences (Vegetius), 40, 42
On the Nature of Things and the Etymologies of Names and Words (Raban), 173
"On the Statue of Theoderich" (Walahfrid), 57–58
ordeals/trials, 229, 229n208
Ordinatio imperii, 29, 29n15, 31–32, 46, 50, 52, 54, 58–59, 61–62, 69–70, 85, 304. *See also* Louis the Pious, and his sons' rebellions
orientalis Francia, 73
Ormurtag, Khan, 48–49
osterstufa (an annual tax), 205–6, 206n97
Otachars, 159, 218
Otfrid of Wissembourg: *Book of the Evangelists*, 184, 301, 301n154, *302*, 303
Otgar, archbishop of Mainz, 83n126, 88–91, 89n12, 92, 98–99, 105, 158–59, 159n51, 218n151, 246–48, 248n60, 248n63
Otgar, bishop of Eichstätt, 267, 270, 274n44, 309n14
Ottonians. *See* Liudolfing-Ottonian dynasty
Otto the Illustrious, Count, 278, 278n58

Pabo, count of Carantania, 79, 141, 156–57, 265–68
Paderborn assembly (840), 97–98
Paderborn assembly (845), 134–35, 135n70, 137, 158, 177
paganism. *See* polytheism
partible inheritance, 10–11, 27–28
Paschal, pope, 50
Passau diocese, 272
peasant population/conditions, 109–10, *111*, 112
Photian Schism, 272, 272n36, 281–82
Pippin, king of Aquitaine (son of LP), 26, 28, 31, 51, 51n104, 72n68, 91. *See also* Louis the Pious, and his sons' rebellions
Pippin II of Aquitaine (grandson of LP), 51, 91–92, 101–2, 104n90, 148, 150, 153, 235, 242, 250, 262
Pippin III (r. 741–68), 3, 23, 52–53, 338n8
poetry, vernacular, 36–37, 180–82, 185
polytheism, 110, 112, 154–55, 176–79
Poppo, count of Grabfeld, 71n59, 92, 93n35, 278
precarial grants, 101, 101n74
prefects, 217
Pribina, 83–85n135, 138–40, 142, 265–67
provinces (*regna*), 215–17, 216nn146–47
Prudentius, bishop of Troyes, 142, 144, 248;

Annals of St.-Bertin, 6n13, 15–16, 59–60, 64, 87
Prüm monastery, 296, 296n129, 299n148, 307

Quartinus, 50, 50n99
Quierzy synod (858), 257

Raban, abbot of Fulda (and archbishop of Mainz), 15n39, 18, 33, 36, 40, 40n54, 42, 61n16, 71, 71n59, 76–77, 89, 93n35, 96–97n51, 100–101, 104n91, 159–65, 159n49, *161*, 168, 172–77, 180–81, 183–84, 207–8, 210, 218–20, 229–30, 250
Raginar of Passau, 137
Rastislav, king of Moravia, 138, 140, 234, 242–46, 263, 266–67, 269, 273–75, 284–86, 288, 299–301
Ratimar, 83–85n135
Ratleig, abbot of Seligenstadt, 96–97, 97n52, 211, 320
Rato, 78, 222
Ratolt, Count, 92–93, 249, 264–65
Ratpert, 103n86; *Misfortunes of St.-Gall*, 16, 212–14
Ratpot, Prefect, 15n40, 67, 67n40, 79–81, 79n105, 80n113, 81nn115–16, 84–85, 84–85n135, 116, 123n16, 127n36, 145, 156, 242–43, 242–43n39, 247n59, 267–68
Ratpot II, 156, 247, 247n59, 248, 260–61, 267
record keeping/writing, 210–15, *214*, *216*
Regensburg, 51, 127, 142, 156, 168–69, 191, 191n27, 224, 299–301, 303
Regino of Prüm, 16, 32, 39–40, 44–46, 195, 208, 222, 246–47, 253, 266n9, 311, 343–44
regna (provinces), 215–17, 216nn146–47
Reichenau monastery, 96, 96n50, 166
Reichenhall, 202–3
relics, 168–71, 193–94
res publica/state, 207–8, 230
Rhine/Rhineland, 114–15, 115n125, 204–5
Richgard, 293–94, 315
Richildis, Queen, 295, 330–32
Ries, 99–101, 195
Rihheri, count of Szombathely, 79, 265
Rimbert, archbishop of Hamburg-Bremen, 218
rivers, transportation along, 225
roads, 225
Robert the Strong, 251, 260
Roding diploma (846), 141, 141n95
Romance language, 105, 179–80
royal benefices, administrative role of, 215–17

The Consumption of Justice
Emotions, Publicity, and Legal Culture in Marseille, 1264–1423
by Daniel Lord Smail

Weaving Sacred Stories
French Choir Tapestries and the Performance of Clerical Identity
by Laura Weigert